ADAPTATIONS

FROM SHORT STORY

TO BIG SCREEN:

ADAPT

THREE RIVERS PRESS
NEW YORK

ATIONS

Edited by Stephanie Harrison

35 Great Stories
That Have Inspired
Great Films

A complete list of permissions appears on pages 617–619.

Published in the United States by Three Rivers Press, an imprint of the Crown Publishing Group, a division of Random House, Inc., New York.

www.crownpublishing.com

Three Rivers Press and the Tugboat design are registered trademarks of Random House, Inc.

Library of Congress Cataloging-in-Publication Data

Adaptations : from short story to big screen : 35 great stories that have inspired great films / edited by Stephanie Harrison.—1st ed.
p. cm.
1. Short stories—Translations into English. 2. Short stories, American. 3. Short stories, English. 4. Film adaptations—History and criticism. I. Harrison, Stephanie, 1961–
PN6120.2.A33 2005
791.43'6—dc22 2005003441

ISBN 1-4000-5314-5

Printed in the United States of America

DESIGN BY ELINA D. NUDELMAN

10 9 8 7 6 5 4 3 2 1

First Edition

For my parents

CONTENTS

PART V Graphic Stories: Flying Under the Radar

PART VI Five All-But-Lost Stories

PART VII The Good, the Bad, and the Unadaptable

PART XI The Independents: Money Changes Everything

ACKNOWLEDGMENTS

First of all, I'd like to thank professors Sid Dobrin, Robert Ray, and David Leavitt for their early encouragement. Thanks also to the librarians at the University of Florida and at the Cleveland Public Library for their help when needed. (The latter institution is a public treasure.) I'm particularly grateful to Deb Oestreicher, Steve Korpieski, Donna Jarrell, and Ruth and David Swartz for their encouragement and comments. This could never have been done without the professionals, Farley Chase and Carrie Thornton, who knew what needed to be done and when. And finally, particular and heartfelt thanks to Margaret Barnes for reading each section promptly, carefully, and enthusiastically; her comments, quibbles, and kudos were invaluable. I'm so, so grateful for our friendship.

INTRODUCTION

Short Story to Big Screen

And because the stories were held here in fluid form, they retained the ability to change, to become new versions of themselves, to join up with other stories and so become yet other stories; so that unlike a library of books, the Ocean of the Streams of Story was much more than a storeroom of yarns. It was not dead, but alive.

—Salman Rushdie, *Haroun and the Sea of Stories*

Reading the story that inspired a beloved movie is a little like meeting your mother-in-law for the first time: It's never less than a revelation. Included here are several movies with strong—you might even say overwhelming—parental personalities. *The Killers*, inspired by the classic Hemingway story of the same name. *Dark Eyes*, drawn from Chekhov's masterpiece "The Lady with the Pet Dog." *The Swimmer*, adapted from the well-loved Cheever story. Conventional movie wisdom has it that adaptations of such pedigree are doomed to failure. Béla Balázs, one of the first film theorists to address adaptations, even went so far as to state it in absolute terms: "One may perhaps make a good film out of a bad novel, but never out of a good one."

As it turns out, conventional wisdom holds true in this case about as often as it usually does, which is to say, sometimes. All three of the abovementioned films are successful on their own terms, even if they have not achieved the acclaim of their august parents. Admittedly, as predicted, there have been many failures—and the occasional bad seed. With the exception of *The Killers*, Hemingway's stories have spawned a slew of mediocre films. F. Scott Fitzgerald's work has never been captured well on screen, even though he attempted a screenplay himself, based on his story "Babylon Revisited." (It was never filmed.) Great stories are rule breakers, almost by definition. They contain something indefinable that makes them more than the sum of their parts. It's this X factor that makes their transition to film so difficult. Screenwriter Ben Hecht may have put it best when he complained about adapting Hemingway's *Farewell to Arms*: "The son-of-bitch writes on water."

The perils of adapting a tour de force are not always under the filmmaker's control. When stories (or authors) have entered into popular mythology, both critics and public alike resist their being tampered with. (Remember the beating director Roland Joffé and star Demi Moore took for their "free" adaptation of Nathaniel Hawthorne's *The Scarlet Letter*?—"The script takes more liberties with the text than Elizabeth Berkley did with that pole in *Showgirls*," complained *USA Today*). For this reason, films adapted from excellent but lesser-known tales have often been better received. Here, the short story has a distinct advantage over the novel: few short stories are embedded in the public's consciousness in the way that popular novels often are. Raymond Carver's influence on the generation of writers following him is indisputable, yet his name is not immediately recognized by the average reader. Nor, despite his international reputation, is Julio Cortázar's. This made Robert Altman's task of adapting Carver's stories *(Short Cuts)*, and Michelangelo Antonioni's task of adapting Cortázar's story *(Blow-Up)*, much easier. In both cases the director had a sensibility and artistic control that complimented the work and, while they both teased out some themes and dropped others, their films were rarely disparaged as unfaithful.

Hollywood, though, has always felt more comfortable with pulp fiction (the kind that used to appear in *Black Mask* and *Dime Western*) and popular fiction *(The Saturday Evening Post, McCall's, Collier's)*. Stories from these sources have given rise to many classic films, including *All About Eve*, *Bringing Up Baby*, *Stagecoach*, and *Meet John Doe*, to name but a few. Tearsheets from popular magazines were routinely circulated around studios, on the off chance that a story might make a good film. And sometimes it did. Paradoxically, "potboilers" have often been the springboard for high cinema art.

For the most part, these source stories—particularly those considered popular fiction—have either been dismissed outright or benignly overlooked. (Pulp fiction has fared better, with strong champions and the cachet of cult.) Nearly a dozen of the stories included here are either long out of print or have never before been printed in book form. It's a rare story, regardless of quality, that isn't savaged by time, so this loss is not at all surprising. But these stories are worth another look, if only because there was something that propelled them across the boundaries of form. (Sometimes multiple times: "Mr. Blandings Builds His Castle" gave rise to a novel and its sequel, a movie, and a radio show; "The Wisdom of Eve" has been the basis for a play, a film, and a musical.) These stories offer us a glimpse into the creative process, and not just of filmmaking.

There is a tendency to treat a finished work as if it has been dictated whole by a highly literate muse, rather than pieced together, improved and expanded, woven and welded. Reading Fitzgerald, it's easy to accept Hemingway's statement that he had "talent as natural as the pattern on a butterfly's wing." But Fitzgerald himself didn't describe his work as effortless. In his *Notebooks* he wrote: "I have asked a lot of my emotions—one hundred and twenty stories. The price was high, right up with Kipling, because there was one little drop of something not blood, not a tear, not my seed, but me more intimately than these in every story, it was the extra I had." Like many writers, he worked and tested his themes in short stories, then later pilfered parts of them for his novels. When "Babylon Revisited" was revised for his collection *Taps at Reveille*, he marked a section for deletion because it had been reused in *Tender Is the Night.*

Fitzgerald's use of the short story as germination ground is not unique. Raymond Chandler considered his stories "cannibalized" when he used their material to create his novels. The two short stories that provide the basis for *The Big Sleep*, "Killer in the Rain" and "The Curtain," were not published in book form in his lifetime. Not every writer, though, has felt the need to bury his early published source material. Carver, a prodigious rewriter, published as many as four versions of some stories. The story included here, "Jerry and Molly and Sam," is one of the few used for *Short Cuts* that he did not rewrite and republish. Unlike Fitzgerald and Chandler, Carver was unbothered by this—he considered each version a different story.

While Fitzgerald used his stories to further his novels, both aesthetically and financially—in his lifetime, all of his novels combined earned him total royalties of $31.77—the demise of many of the mass-market magazines and their discontinued use of short stories has made this a more difficult scenario for contemporary writers. Still, while paying venues for short stories began drying up in the late '50s, surprisingly, writers have never stopped writing them. Part of this has to do with the challenges and felicities of the form. But the story has always been, and continues to be, a place to test material. W. P. Kinsella expanded "Shoeless Joe Jackson Comes to Iowa" into *Shoeless Joe*, and Mary O'Hara expanded her prize-winning story, "My Friend Flicka," into a novel, when their stories were well received. It has also, particularly recently, become common practice for authors to publish self-contained novel chapters as short stories, as Jean Shepherd did with "Red Ryder Nails the Hammond Kid," published in *Playboy.* It is the second chapter of his novel *In God We Trust: All Others Pay Cash.*

The art of storytelling has never really been as static as we like to think. Publishing a work may provide artificial closure, but stories that resonate tend to find new forms. The process becomes even more fluid when films are thrown into the mix. When Stanley Kubrick purchased the rights to

Arthur C. Clarke's "The Sentinel," the two took a highly unusual approach. Rather than immediately tackling a screenplay—"about the least ideal way of communicating information," Kubrick said, "especially if it's visual or emotional"—they decided to expand the story into a novel. Instead of a novel, though, they ended up with what Kubrick later called a "fifty-thousand word prose 'thing.' " At this point, work on the novel and screenplay became concurrent, with Clarke taking ownership of the novel and Kubrick the screenplay, but with each giving feedback on the other's work. Clarke, who was occasionally frustrated by this process—he had hoped the novel would precede the movie—ended up making his final revisions to the novel "after we had seen the rushes based on the screenplay based on earlier versions of the novel . . . and so on."

Almost every story here is representative of a larger creative process, one that crosses all kinds of form boundaries. A few of these stories are occasionally clunky—for example, Hagar Wilde's "Bringing Up Baby" or Mary Orr's "The Wisdom of Eve"—and yet there is something about them that has transcended not only form, but craft. (It's also worth noting that in both cases the author wasn't finished; Wilde cowrote the screenplay for *Bringing Up Baby* and Orr expanded her story into the stage play of the same name.) So, rather than viewing a film adaptation as a cultural replacement for a story or novel, it seems closer to the truth to view each work as a variation on a theme.

When Twentieth Century–Fox released its 1966 remake of *Stagecoach*, starring Bing Crosby and Ann-Margret, it threatened, in a full-page notice in *Variety*, to "vigorously" prosecute the exhibition of the 1939 original. In response, Pauline Kael railed: "Surely the public should have the right to see the old as well as the new? And not just for its own sake but because that's how we learn about an art. How else do we develop a critical sense about new novels, new paintings, new music, new poetry? If the old is legally retired, we become barbarians (movie barbarians, at least) without a past." Surely, it stands to reason, this same argument should extend to Ernest Haycox's story "Stage to Lordsburg," upon which John Ford's 1939 *Stagecoach* was based.

Somehow we need to teach ourselves how to approach adaptations fairly, as neither movie barbarians nor literary purists. A film shouldn't need to spring fully formed from a writer/director's loins in order to be deemed good. Nor should an adaptation be tethered too tightly to its source. (*The Scarlet Letter* didn't fail because it was unfaithful; it failed because it wasn't a very good film.) For artistic, financial, and practical reasons—(there will always be a large percentage of people who never read the literary source)—films must succeed on their own terms. At the same time, though, they shouldn't replace the stories they're based on—though we, the reading public, have let this happen all too often. In the best cases, adaptations extend, enhance, and elaborate on their sources. And when the pairing of director and author is complimentary, as with Cortázar and Antonioni, or Altman and Carver, they do even more. Then the works and themes of each artist gain synergy and resonance when taken in concert, and even the differences are instructive. It may, in fact, be Altman who has come closest to pointing the way for us, when he said, with admirable simplicity, "In the end the film is there and the stories are there and one hopes there is a fruitful interaction."

The stories are here.

PART I

THE DIRECTORS:

TRANSLATORS, MAGICIANS, COLLABORATORS, AND THIEVES

"Jerry and Molly and Sam"
by Raymond Carver

Short Cuts, directed by Robert Altman, 1993

"Blow-Up"
by Julio Cortázar

Blow-Up, directed by Michelangelo Antonioni, 1966

"Your Arkansas Traveler"
by Budd Schulberg

A Face in the Crowd, directed by Elia Kazan, 1957

"Rear Window" ("It Had to Be Murder")
by Cornell Woolrich

Rear Window, directed by Alfred Hitchcock, 1954

Movies have to be *about* something. They can dazzle us with special effects, wow us with an eight-minute tracking shot, or intrigue us with a cartoonlike color palette. But we still expect a story. A story visually told, perhaps—but a *story* nonetheless.

And that's why "film feeds off literature like sharks off a marlin," as film theorist George Bluestone once said. Director Stanley Kubrick was a compulsive reader, sometimes tearing through a book a day in his constant search for new material. Alfred Hitchcock told of imagining the shape of a film, then having to search for a story to fit his visualization. Howard Hawks claimed that the hardest part of making a movie was finding a good story, then figuring out how to tell it. Steven Spielberg agrees. Even Michelangelo Antonioni was a reader, although he claimed the best way to approach a book was to read it, then forget it. Directors, especially those of the auteur ilk, get a lot of credit for their successes and a lot of blame for their failures. But, like prominent CEOs, they depend a great deal on others. Unless directors write their own material, they will have to go to the source: writers. And there are as many approaches to this as there are directorial personalities.

The Translator: Altman and *Short Cuts*

In 1990, while flying home from Italy, Robert Altman read a book of short stories by Raymond Carver. "I was so moved by the way he told stories," he later said, "what he told and what he didn't tell and how he made a story out of the slightest little incident. I was just amazed by it and I thought this is what we should do in film."

For just over a decade, from the early 1970s through the mid-'80s, Carver led the return to realistic fiction that revels in the quotidian. His stories feature hard-drinking, unhappily married, working-class folk who live, as Tess Gallagher, Carver's second wife, puts it, "with no safety net and no imagination of a safety net." The residents of "Carver Country" drift through life—often in an alcoholic haze—and end in a place very close to where they started. The epiphanies, if you can call them that, are small and internal. As his friend Tobias Wolff has said, Carver "is not a particularly quotable writer. That's one of his virtues, that he never tried to achieve a beautiful line. It's the steadiness and quietness of the prose that creates his sense of reality." And it's reality Carver was after: "As far as I'm concerned," he told an interviewer, "the best art has its reference points in real life."

There is an autobiographical element to his work. Like many of his characters, Carver grew up working class and was, for most of his adult life, a dedicated alcoholic. Throughout his first marriage he was plagued by financial concerns that kept him from his writing. Of his work, he said, "I'm just bearing witness to something I know something about. Most things in the world I don't know anything at all about. . . . I'm bearing witness to what I can." Because of his concern with small moments in the lives of ordinary people, Carver is often compared to Chekhov, and his declarative prose style invites comparison to Hemingway. Yet his sensibility is unquestionably reflective of his own generation. His pared-down realism, tinged with a dash of hopelessness, suited the period following Watergate, and by the time of his death from lung cancer in 1988, Carver was arguably the most influential literary writer in the country.

Enter Altman. If ever a director was poised to exploit the contemporary short story—now so firmly associated with Carver—Altman was that director. By the time he discovered Carver's stories, Altman had already directed twenty-five feature films (including *M*A*S*H*, *McCabe and Mrs. Miller*, *The Long Goodbye*, and *Thieves Like Us*), not to mention countless television episodes. He'd honed a signature directorial style consisting of overlapping dialogue, improbably large casts, mock-documentary realism, improvisation, and the use of nonprofessional actors. Most important, though, he'd already made *Nashville*, a rambling narrative that loosely weaves the story lines of twenty-four characters, without, as Pauline Kael put it, the "clanking of plot." Arguably one of the best films ever made—it appears on countless top-100 lists—*Nashville*'s lack of narrative thrust baffled many. When asked about his reputation as a "problem director," Altman stated, "I'm not difficult. My work may be difficult, but if in fact it is difficult, it just further enforces what I have to say: that all I make films about is what I see and the way things appear to me."

So why wouldn't Altman admire Carver's stories? There's an obvious link between a writer who is "just bearing witness" and a filmmaker who is making films about "the way things appear to me." Between a writer who eschews quotable lines and a director who uses untrained actors. Between a writer who strives for realistic-sounding dialogue through the use of stammers, pauses, and repeated lines and a director who strives for the same through the use of overlapping sound. Between a writer who resists neatly tied-up endings and a director who has said, "Many people, I guess, want to know exactly what it is they're supposed to think.... Well, my message is that I am not going to do their work for them." Beyond all this, though, there are deeper affinities. They both look upon their characters with an unflinching but surprisingly nonjudgmental eye. They are both interested in the hyperreality of small moments. And they both balance intuitiveness with painstaking craftsmanship. And yet, it's one thing for Altman to have admired Carver's stories; it's quite another that he knew how to translate them well for film. Only someone with Altman's résumé could have seen the possibilities in a random selection of nine unconnected, unplotted stories. And, of course, one poem.

In the case of *Short Cuts*, the role of translator is one Altman wears gracefully, but not naturally. His relationship with writers has often been rocky, the writers forced to watch as their words are reduced to rubble. Brian McKay, who wrote the screenplays for several of Altman's films, including *McCabe and Mrs. Miller*, says, "If you want me to get in line with the rest of the angry writers, I will. But it's more complicated than that. I think what Bob really wants is the European credit: 'A Film by Robert Altman.' And, often, he deserves it." Yet when he is impressed with a work, Altman has been known to gush. He loved Edward Anderson's novel *Thieves Like Us*, and wanted to make as few changes as possible. And then there's Carver. Still, Altman lets it be known that *Short Cuts* is *his*.* "I read all of Ray's writings, filtering him through my own process. The film is made of little pieces of his work that form sections of scenes and characters out of the most basic elements of Ray's creations—new and *not* new."

And that, according to Tess Gallagher, would have been okay with Carver. "Risking trespass, I will say I believe Ray's attitude toward Altman's use of his work would have been one of permission to an artist of equal stature.... He was a straight-on admirer of Altman's films." Gallagher admires *Short Cuts*—and believes Carver would have, too—for both its fidelity and its infidelity. "The failure of so many scripts of Carver stories by others I'd seen prior ... had been to stay so close to the original that a robotic pandering to the text resulted. They were like someone ice skating with an osprey's egg on which the bird is still nesting."

* He did, however, work with screenwriter Frank Barhydt.

The problems of fidelity can be illustrated by "Jerry and Molly and Sam," one of the nine stories chosen by Altman for the film. The title refers to three very minor characters—one of them a briefly mentioned childhood dog—who are not central to the story. Or are they? It's this importance placed on absence that gives Carver's stories much of their power and that attracted Altman in the first place. But it's an untranslatable element, as is Carver's heavy use of introspection. The challenge for Altman was to find cinematic equivalents, which, he admitted, "manifest themselves in unexpected ways." Yet for all the things that Altman was forced to change, or chose to change, he kept a great deal too: a pervasive dark humor, an emphasis on fate or luck, a bubbling violence under the surface. The movie was hailed by critics, with Michael Wilmington of the *Chicago Tribune* raving, "Some movies can lay claim to being the best thing around in a week, a month, a year. Robert Altman's *Short Cuts* is closer to being one of the all-time bests, among the finest American films since the advent of sound."

It also serves as one of the best examples of an artist grappling to translate the work of another artist—and ending up with something that looks very much like a handshake.

The Magician: Antonioni and *Blow-Up*

If you read Italian director Michelangelo Antonioni's interviews (he gave quite a few), or his essays (he wrote thirty or so), it's hard to avoid noticing that he rarely mentions Julio Cortázar, the author of the story upon which his masterpiece, *Blow-Up,* is based. Only when directly asked about the South American author does he acknowledge the movie's origins, as in a 1979 interview: "I read Cortázar's story, I liked it, and I wrote a subject, adapting it to myself."

Well. If this sounds like faint praise, remember it comes from the same man who said, "As the director, I am God. I can allow myself any kind of liberty." Antonioni put the "A" in auteur; on his sets, he was the indisputable alpha personality. By the time he directed *Blow-Up* in 1966 he had almost a dozen films under his belt and had distinguished himself as a director primarily concerned with images. To Antonioni, words and images are in opposition—and words are propaganda or, worse yet, lies. "Someone once said that words, more than anything else, serve to hide our thoughts," he told an audience of Italian film students. He distrusted screenplays, saying, "This is the limit of the script: to give words to events that reject words." And he used dialogue only when an image would not suffice.

telling was more than his tendency; it was a philosophical f this I am firmly convinced—" he said, "that cinema today ed to the truth rather than to logic. And the truth of our daily her mechanical, conventional, nor artificial, as stories gener- l if films are made that way, they will show it."

aps this distrust of words, this sense that stories are artificial, his disdain for literary sources. For Antonioni, a story or a just one of any number of items that he—the magician— his hat before pulling out a rabbit: "I prefer [to say]: In that ain events happened in the world, I saw certain people, I was tain books, I was looking at certain paintings, I loved X, I idn't have any money, I wasn't sleeping much." (Yet, despite all of this protestation, Antonioni began writing at a young age and continued to write throughout his life. He adapted portions of his story collection, *That Bowling Alley on the Tiber* [1987], into *Beyond the Clouds*, starring John Malkovich as the "director.") Reinventing cinema was his aim, and new techniques were all in service of finding answers to fundamental questions: "What is it that torments and motivates modern man? Of all that has happened and is now happening in the world, what are the repercussions inside a man, what are the consequences in his most intimate relationships and dealings with others? Today, more than ever, these are the questions we should keep in mind when we prepare ourselves to make a film."

So it's no wonder Antonioni was attracted to Cortázar's story: Cortázar was trying to do in words what Antonioni was trying to do with images. Cortázar was seeking a way to explode the narrative mechanism, to find a way to tell a story that was in tune with his times ("Blow-Up" was first published in 1958) and the troubled politics of Latin America. "The truth is, each day . . . I write worse and worse, from an aesthetic point of view," he said in an interview. "It may be absurd for a writer to insist on discarding his work instruments. But I think those instruments are false. I want to wipe my slate clean, start from scratch." "Blow-Up," with its shifting points of view and absolutely unreliable narrator, does just that. It's a conceptual story, an idea with words wrapped around it, a halting, backstepping, existential Jabberwocky. "It'll never be known how this has to be told," the first paragraph begins, "in the first person or in the second, using the third person plural or continually inventing modes that will serve for nothing. If one might say: I will see the moon rose, or: we hurt me at the back of my eyes, and especially: you the blond woman was the clouds that race before my your his our yours their faces. What the hell."

Both Cortázar and Antonioni are interested in art as exploration, as provocation. Each in his chosen form has worked to strip the expository from story, forcing the reader/viewer to fill in missing pieces. Both concern themselves with the interplay of form and content. But Cortázar is more playful than Antonioni, less aware (maybe self-consciously so) of his stature as an artist. "The truth is that I don't care a straw for Literature with a capital L; the only thing that interests me is searching for (and sometimes finding) myself in a contest with words that eventually produces something called a book." Throughout his career, play (and gamesmanship) was at the center of his work. *Hopscotch*, probably his most famous novel, is constructed for two possible readings. First, in the normal sequential fashion, and second, using a hopscotch sequence (chapters 73, 1, 2, 116, 3, 84 . . .). Now considered the first hypertext novel, it anticipates the possibilities of the World Wide Web's nonsequential structure. But for Cortázar, it was about the game. "It would be absolutely impossible for me to live if I couldn't play," he claimed.

And play he did, always. Near the end of his life, he embarked on a road trip with his companion Carol Dunlop, even though both men were suffering from leukemia. The rules were: Take a full thirty days to complete the 800-kilometer drive from Marseille to Paris, without ever leaving the Southern Turnpike. Confine stops to exactly two per day, but the second must be an overnight stay, regardless of whether or not there is a hotel or just a narrow turnoff. Food and water to be replenished by friends at designated intervals. The resulting chronicle, "The Autonauts of the Cosmopike," is a strange and touching record of two dying men. Perhaps it's his sense of play that has harmed Cortázar's legacy; he has not become a lion of Latin American letters in the way that his contemporaries Jorge Luis Borges and Gabriel García Márquez have. But it takes courage to canonize someone who never took himself seriously. "I shall consider myself until my death an amateur," Cortázar said, "one who writes because he feels like it, but I have no notion of literary professionalism."

On the face of it, "Blow-Up" appears to be an unadaptable story. The narrator is anonymous and unreliable; the narrative is elliptical and contradictory. Critics still don't agree on the story's interpretation, or even on the events within it. And that, of course, is precisely the point: For Cortázar, form equals content. Antonioni's film, considered by many to be one of the best ever made, has generated even more discussion—the scholarly articles alone would fill up several stadiums. In the end, though, Antonioni himself likens this to theoretical tail-chasing: "*Blow-Up* is a film that lends itself to many interpretations because the issue behind it is precisely the appearance of reality. Therefore, everyone can think what he wants."

It would probably rankle Antonioni no end to discover that as a magician, he turned out to be a very good translator.

The Collaborator: Kazan and *A Face in the Crowd*

Elia Kazan had many detractors—just ask the people in the audience who sat on their hands when he was presented with an Honorary Award at the 1998 Oscars ceremony—but he was always quick to give credit to the writers he worked with. And he worked with many of the best: Tennessee Williams, John Steinbeck, William Inge, Clifford Odets, Harold Pinter, Thornton Wilder, and of course, Budd Schulberg, with whom he collaborated on two films, *On the Waterfront* and *A Face in the Crowd.* "That's Budd," Kazan was quick to say in interviews when asked to take credit for things that were present in Schulberg's screenplays. Or "I think what Budd did there . . ."

The two men enjoyed an unusually close collaboration and friendship. According to Kazan, they began working together "on the theory that misery loves company." Both were in professional and personal slumps, due in large part to their "friendly" testimonies before the House Un-American Activities Committee. (Both men had been members of the Communist party, but had severed their ties when the party began to exert artistic pressure. In his statement to the press, Schulberg told of his refusal to surrender to the party's request that he submit the outline and galley proofs for his novel *What Makes Sammy Run?* Kazan's story was similar: "I was tired of regimentation, being told what to think and say and do.") Schulberg and Kazan had more than political woes in common, though; they had an interest in the same type of material. During their first working session they discovered that they had both recently been involved with aborted screenplays about the New York waterfront—Kazan's with playwright Arthur Miller, Schulberg's based on a newspaper series about the longshoreman's union. Not surprisingly, their first project together became *On the Waterfront,* winner of eight Academy Awards, including Best Director for Kazan and Best Screenplay for Schulberg. Three years later they collaborated on another social commentary, *A Face in the Crowd:* "Budd and I had such a good time doing *On the Waterfront* I said, 'Let's do another picture together.' He knew the kind of thing I was thinking about so he suggested a short story he had written called 'Your Arkansas Traveler.' I read it and liked it and that was it."

Social criticism has always been a strong aspect of Schulberg's work, and "Your Arkansas Traveler" is no exception. Lonesome Rhodes, the story's protagonist, comes down with "a severe case of American success," television-style. "I believe the novelist should be an artist cum sociologist," Schulberg has said. "I think he should see his characters in social perspective. I think that is one of his obligations." Much of his work, like "Arkansas Traveler," uses the microcosm of the entertainment industry to explore the American success ethic. (He is perhaps the only writer to ever use the phrase "You success!" as an epithet.) As the son of B. P. Schulberg, one of the earliest movie moguls, he is uniquely qualified to exploit that setting. With his first novel, *What Makes Sammy Run?* (1941), Schulberg created an iconic antihero in his copyboy-to-studio-head, anything-to-succeed Sammy Glick. Since then, people as varied as Sammy Davis Jr. and David Geffen have declared, "I'm *not* Sammy Glick!"

With *A Face in the Crowd* Schulberg and Kazan explored a number of difficult topics. Success: "One of the points we wanted to make with the picture," Kazan said, "was the fantastic upward mobility in this country, the speed with which a man goes up and goes down. That we both knew well, because we'd both been up and down a few times." Politics: "It was about a phenomenon that was happening in America at that time. We were always talking about and looking out for native, grass-roots fascism." Television: "We were both aware that television could be what it has, in fact, turned out to be, an almost hypnotic terrible force."

To write the screenplay, Schulberg rented a house close to Kazan's in Connecticut where they did research and decided on a general outline. Then they separated and Schulberg wrote the first draft of the screenplay. When he finished, Kazan read it and suggested rewrites. Then they cast it together, going around to clubs and picking up entertainers. Andy Griffith, who played Lonesome Rhodes, was, at the time, a stand-up comic with no training or experience as an actor. They had heard his record ("something about football," Kazan said) and liked it. When shooting began, Kazan urged Schulberg to be there. Afterward, Kazan edited the film, then called Schulberg back in to discuss. "It was a totally collaborative effort," Kazan said, "even down to the book, for which I wrote the preface. Theoretically, I think one man should make a picture. But in the case where an author and a director have had the same kinds of experience, have the same kind of taste, the same historical and social point of view, and are as compatible as Budd and I are, it works out perfectly."

Kazan's career—with and without Schulberg—is impressive and can be summed up by the question he's asked himself at every critical juncture: "Where's the next hill?" With the Group Theatre in New York City he was an actor, stage manager, and director. There, he directed the premiers of Tennessee Williams's *A Streetcar Named Desire* and Arthur Miller's *Death of a Salesman.* With Cheryl Crawford and others, he cofounded the Actors Studio. On the other coast, he directed *East of Eden,*

A Streetcar Named Desire, and *Splendor in the Grass* (besides his work with Schulberg). He was instrumental in launching the careers of Marlon Brando (giving him $20 for bus fare to meet with Williams about the role of Stanley Kowalski in *A Streetcar Named Desire*), James Dean, Julie Harris, Eva Marie Saint, Warren Beatty, and Lee Remick. In the 1960s he began writing novels, and two of his final films are based on his own works, *America, America* and *The Arrangement* (from his bestseller). Kazan's final film was *The Last Tycoon,* based on F. Scott Fitzgerald's unfinished novel, which, by a strange twist of fate, is based in part on Schulberg's reminiscences of his Hollywood childhood. (Schulberg and Fitzgerald had become friends while working on a screenplay. When Fitzgerald showed Schulberg a rough draft of the first few chapters of *Tycoon,* he said, according to Schulberg, "There'll be quite a few lines you'll recognize. I hope you won't mind.")

Often called a "social realist"—a term he wasn't altogether happy with—Kazan was always concerned with inward struggle set within a social context. In this regard he was a good balance for Schulberg's predominately outward focus. (Andy Griffith lent a humanizing touch to *A Face* as well, although Kazan said he had to get him drunk to film the difficult final scene.) "I was particularly proud of *A Face in the Crowd,* and still am," Kazan wrote in his autobiography. Still, the film wasn't well received when it came out, although now it's hard to avoid using the word "prescient" to describe it. In the 1970s the *New York Times* said it anticipated the Watergate hearings; a decade or so later, people said it anticipated Ronald Reagan. It paved the way for films with similar themes, like *Network* and *Bob Roberts.* "Finally," Kazan said, summing up his thoughts on the film, "what I think was that it was ahead of its time."

A Face in the Crowd is perhaps the best example of a director and writer completely in sync. Call it the "we" factor: "I don't know why it didn't go," Kazan mused in an interview. "We said: 'Oh, they're not ready for it,' and in a way they weren't. We said: 'Oh, they don't want us to criticize America,' and in a way they didn't. And we said: 'Oh, they think we are communists, and putting America down, trying to destroy America,' and we were attacked some for that. But I think a picture that tries to do something as difficult as this picture has to be perfect, and I don't think we were, not quite."

The Thief: Hitchcock and *Rear Window*

Alfred Hitchcock was a tireless self-promoter from the very beginning. He directed his first silent feature in 1925, and by 1927 he had already developed the now-famous caricature of his profile. His Christmas gift to friends and colleagues that year was a small linen bag containing a wooden puzzle, which, when assembled, revealed the eight-stroke drawing. That same year, he began his campaign to be taken seriously as an artist. In an open letter to the *London Evening News*, he wrote: "Film directors live with their pictures while they are being made. They are their babies just as much as an author's novel is the offspring of his imagination. And that seems to make it all the more certain that when moving pictures are really artistic they will be created entirely by one man."* It's no wonder that many who worked with him, including writers, received short shrift.

Cornell Woolrich, the author of "Rear Window" (originally titled "It Had to Be Murder"), is one of those people. By the mid-1940s, Woolrich was one of the most successful suspense writers in the country, but his personal life was almost Norman Bates-ish. For twenty-five years, until his mother's death in 1957, he lived with his mother in the Hotel Marseilles, "trapped in a love-hate relationship which dominated his external world," according to his biographer, Francis Nevins. He may have hinted at his feelings about this situation in his dedication to *Phantom Lady*, one of his most successful novels, published in 1942, the same year as "Rear Window":

To Apartment 605
in unmitigated thankfulness
(at not being in it anymore)

Later, he explained that this referred to his attempts to move away from his mother, although that move proved short. (He took another room in the same hotel.) By his own admission, Woolrich led "a completely uneventful life, as far as outward incident is concerned . . . I have traveled now and then, but I suspect it was wasted effort. A hotel room is a hotel room."

It is therefore fitting that Woolrich's autobiography begins with a love letter to his typewriter: "We first met, you and I, a long time ago. This was a mating if ever there was one. A life-long partnership, a fellowship, a combine, of flesh and of thin steel casing, of fingertips and of keys. . . ." Although he aspired to literary works like those of F. Scott Fitzgerald, he began with pulp fiction and screenplays before graduating to the hard-boiled crime stories that mark the best of his work. (While in Hollywood he met and married the daughter of a studio executive, but they separated

* Hitchcock often contradicted himself. Later he wrote, "The old saying, 'No one man ever made a picture,' is entirely true."

after three months. She is not even mentioned in his autobiography.) By the late 1960s more of his fiction—he also published under the pseudonyms "William Irish" and "George Hopley"—had been adapted into film noir than any other writer's, prompting the title "Father of Film Noir." In 1968, diabetic and alcoholic, he ignored a badly infected foot, which then required amputation. He died soon afterward and was buried beside his mother.

Woolrich and Hitchcock seem a match made in heaven, but "Rear Window" kicked around Hollywood for almost a decade before the deal was done. Some speculate that it was the lack of romance in the story that caused Hitchcock to overlook it. Content was not of great interest to him—"I don't bother about plot"—but instead he looked for a work that he could stamp with his style. That's where screenwriter John Michael Hayes comes in.

The screenplay for *Rear Window* began a felicitous collaboration between Hitchcock and Hayes that would span four films over a period of two years. (The other films are *To Catch a Thief*, *The Trouble with Harry*, and *The Man Who Knew Too Much*.) Hayes's forte was snappy, occasionally suggestive dialogue and richly drawn, sympathetic characters, and with him, Hitchcock's films achieved a light touch that they lacked both before and after. The main ingredient Hayes had to add to the Woolrich story was a compelling romance, a requirement for a film with the Hitchcock label. Of Hitchcock's sixty or so films, over two-thirds are adaptations, usually of relatively unknown novels, plays, or short stories. As Steven DeRosa, Hayes's biographer, puts it, "Hitchcock learned a valuable lesson from his first Hollywood production, *Rebecca*, which was billed as 'David O. Selznick's production of Daphne du Maurier's celebrated novel . . . directed by Alfred Hitchcock.' Thenceforth, whatever the source material, Hitchcock would make it his own. After all, it was 'Alfred Hitchcock's *Rear Window*,' not 'Alfred Hitchcock's film of Cornell Woolrich's classic suspense story. . . .' "

In fairness to Hitchcock, it should be noted that he did occasionally give credit to writers, although almost never by name. In an interview with *Cinema*, he continued to make a distinction between content (the writer) and style (the director):

HITCHCOCK: Well, look, I make a film—*Dial M for Murder*—and what have I really had to do with that? Nothing. It was a stage play, written for the stage, written by an author. All I had to do there was to go in and photograph it.

INTERVIEWER: But the success or the failure on the screen is going to be dependent upon you—not upon the writer. But . . .

HITCHCOCK: No.

INTERVIEWER: . . . You don't believe that?

HITCHCOCK: No, because if that original material hadn't been there, I might . . . I could have done all kinds of things with it. It wouldn't have helped.

And again: "I do not let the writer go off on his own and just write a script that I will interpret. I stay involved with him and get him involved in the direction of the picture. So he becomes more than a writer; he becomes part maker of the picture."

Still, Hayes's memory is a little different: "The best part was that he essentially left me alone to do my work." The worst part? "His distinct stinginess in offering credit where credit was due." Their collaboration ended when Hitchcock awarded Angus MacPhail, an earlier collaborator and friend, coscreenwriting credit for their fourth film, *The Man Who Knew Too Much.* Although Hayes won by arbitration and was given sole credit, he and Hitchcock never worked together again. DeRosa observes, "While Hitchcock's quest for a suitable replacement for Grace Kelly has become part of Hollywood lore, it should also be noted that Hitchcock never found another John Michael Hayes. Following his collaboration with Hayes, Hitchcock never settled on an individual writer with whom he completed more than one consecutive film." In his 1966 book-length interview with Hitchcock, François Truffaut suggested that, of all his movies, *Rear Window* had possibly the finest screenplay. In reply, Hitchcock dismissed Hayes as nothing more than a "radio writer who wrote the dialogue."

For his part, Woolrich complained that Hitchcock never even sent him a ticket for the opening of *Rear Window.*

Jerry and Molly and Sam

Raymond Carver

As Al saw it, there was only one solution. He had to get rid of the dog without Betty or the kids finding out about it. At night. It would have to be done at night. He would simply drive Suzy—well, someplace, later he'd decide where—open the door, push her out, drive away. The sooner the better. He felt relieved making the decision. Any action was better than no action at all, he was becoming convinced.

It was Sunday. He got up from the kitchen table where he had been eating a late breakfast by himself and stood by the sink, hands in his pockets. Nothing was going right lately. He had enough to contend with without having to worry about a stinking dog. They were laying off at Aerojet when they should be hiring. The middle of the summer, defense contracts let all over the country and Aerojet was talking of cutting back. Was cutting back, in fact, a little more every day. He was no safer than anyone else even though he'd been there two years going on three. He got along with the right people, all right, but seniority or friendship, either one, didn't mean a damn these days. If your number was up, that was that—and there was nothing anybody could do. They got ready to lay off, they laid off. Fifty, a hundred men at a time.

No one was safe, from the foreman and supers right on down to the man on the line. And three months ago, just before all the layoffs began, he'd let Betty talk him into moving into this cushy two-hundred-a-month place. Lease, with an option to buy. Shit!

Al hadn't really wanted to leave the other place. He had been comfortable enough. Who could know that two weeks after he'd move they'd start laying off? But who could know anything these days? For example, there was Jill. Jill worked in bookkeeping at Weinstock's. She was a nice girl, said she loved Al. She was just lonely, that's what she told him the first night. She didn't make it a habit, letting herself be picked up by married men, she also told him the first night. He'd met Jill about three months ago, when he was feeling depressed and jittery with all the talk of layoffs just beginning. He met her at the Town and Country, a bar not too far from his new place. They danced a little and he drove her home and they necked in the car in front of her apartment. He had not gone upstairs with her that night, though he was sure he could have. He went upstairs with her the next night.

Now he was having an *affair*, for Christ's sake, and he didn't know what to do about it. He did not want it to go on, and he did not want to break it off: you don't throw everything overboard in a storm. Al was drifting, and he knew he was drifting, and where it was all going to end he could not guess at. But he was beginning to feel he was losing control over everything. Everything. Recently, too, he had caught himself thinking about old age after he'd been constipated a few days—an affliction he had always associated with the elderly. Then there was the matter of the tiny bald spot and of his having just begun to wonder how he would comb his hair a different way. What was he going to do with his life? he wanted to know.

He was thirty-one.

All these things to contend with and then *Sandy*, his wife's younger sister, giving the kids, Alex and Mary, that mongrel dog about four months ago. He wished he'd never seen that dog. Or Sandy, either, for that matter. That bitch! She was always turning up with some shit or other that wound up costing him money, some little flimflam that went haywire after a day or two and had to be repaired, something the kids could scream over and fight over and beat the shit out of each other about. God! And then turning right around to touch him through Betty, for twenty-five bucks. The mere thought of all the twenty-five- or fifty-buck checks, and the one just a few months ago for eighty-five to make her car payment—her *car* payment, for God's sake, when he didn't even know if he was going to have a roof over his head—made him want to *kill* the goddamn dog.

Sandy! Betty and Alex and Mary! Jill! And Suzy the goddamn dog!

This was Al.

He had to start someplace—setting things in order, sorting all this out. It was time to *do* something, time for some straight thinking for a change. And he intended to start tonight.

He would coax the dog into the car undetected and, on some pretext or another, go out. Yet he hated to think of the way Betty would lower her eyes as she watched him dress, and then, later, just before he went out the door, ask him where, how long, etc., in a resigned voice that made him feel all the worse. He could never get used to the lying. Besides, he hated to use what little reserve he might have left with Betty by telling her a lie for something different from what she suspected. A wasted lie, so to speak. But he could not tell her the truth, could not say he was *not* going drinking, was *not* going calling on somebody, was instead going to do away with the goddamn dog and thus take the first step toward setting his house in order.

He ran his hand over his face, tried to put it all out of his mind for a minute. He took out a cold half quart of Lucky from the fridge and popped the aluminum top. His life had become a maze, one lie overlaid upon another until he was not sure he could untangle them if he had to.

"The goddamn dog," he said out loud.

"She doesn't have good sense!" was how Al put it. She was a sneak, besides. The moment the back door was left open and everyone gone, she'd pry open the screen, come through to the living room, and urinate on the carpet. There were at least a half dozen map-shaped stains on it right now. But her favorite place was the utility room, where she could root in the dirty clothes, so that all of the shorts and panties now had crotch or seat chewed away. And she chewed through the antenna wires on the outside of the house, and once Al pulled into the drive and found her lying in the front yard with one of his Florsheims in her mouth.

"She's crazy," he'd say. "And she's driving me crazy. I can't make it fast enough to replace it. The sonofabitch, I'm going to kill her one of these days!"

Betty tolerated the dog at greater durations, would go along apparently unruffled for a time, but suddenly she would come upon it, with fists clenched, call it a bastard, a bitch, shriek at the kids about keeping it out of their room, the living room, etc. Betty was that way with the children, too. She could go along with them just so far, let them get away with just so much, and then she would turn on them savagely and slap their faces, screaming, "Stop it! Stop it! I can't stand any more of it!"

But then Betty would say, "It's their first dog. You remember how fond you must have been of your first dog."

"My dog had brains," he would say. "It was an Irish setter!"

The afternoon passed. Betty and the kids returned from someplace or another in the car, and they all had sandwiches and potato chips on the patio. He fell asleep on the grass, and when he woke it was nearly evening.

He showered, shaved, put on slacks and a clean shirt. He felt rested but sluggish. He dressed and he thought of Jill. He thought of Betty and Alex and Mary and Sandy and Suzy. He felt drugged.

"We'll have supper pretty soon," Betty said, coming to the bathroom door and staring at him.

"That's all right. I'm not hungry. Too hot to eat," he said, fiddling with his shirt collar. "I might drive over to Carl's, shoot a few games of pool, have a couple of beers."

She said, "I see."

He said, "Jesus!"

She said, "Go ahead, I don't care."

He said, "I won't be gone long."

She said, "Go ahead, I said. I don't care."

In the garage, he said, "Goddamn you all!" and kicked the rake across the cement floor. Then he lit a cigaret and tried to get hold of himself. He picked up the rake and put it away where it belonged. He was muttering to himself, saying "Order, order," when the dog came up to the garage, sniffed around the door, and looked in.

"Here. Come here, Suzy. Here, girl," he called.

The dog wagged her tail but stayed where she was.

He went over to the cupboard above the lawn mower and took down one, then two, and finally three cans of food.

"All you want tonight, Suzy, old girl. All you can eat," he coaxed, opening up both ends of the first can and sliding the mess into the dog's dish.

He drove around for nearly an hour, not able to decide on a place. If he dropped her off in just any neighborhood and the pound were called, the dog would be back at the house in a day or two. The county pound was the first place Betty would call. He remembered reading stories about lost dogs finding their way hundreds of miles back home again. He remembered crime programs where someone saw a license number, and the thought made his heart jump. Held up to public view, without all the facts being in, it'd be a shameful thing to be caught abandoning a dog. He would have to find the right place.

He drove over near the American River. The dog needed to get out more anyway, get the feel of the wind on its back, be able to swim and wade in the river when it wanted; it was a pity to keep a dog fenced in all the time. But the fields near the levee seemed too desolate, no houses around at all. After all, he did want the dog to be found and cared for. A large old two-story house was what he had in mind, with happy, well-behaved reasonable children who needed a dog, who desperately needed a dog. But there were no old two-story houses here, not a one.

He drove back onto the highway. He had not been able to look at the dog since he'd managed to get her into the car. She lay quietly on the back seat now. But when he pulled off the road and stopped the car, she sat up and whined, looking around.

He stopped at a bar, rolled all the car windows down before he went inside. He stayed nearly an hour, drinking beer and playing the shuffleboard. He kept wondering if he should have left all the doors ajar too.

When he went back outside, Suzy sat up in the seat and rolled her lips back, showing her teeth.

He got in and started off again.

Then he thought of a place. The neighborhood where they used to live, swarming with kids and just across the line in Yolo County, that would be just the right place. If the dog were picked up, it would be taken to the Woodland Pound, not the pound in Sacramento. Just drive onto one of the streets in the old neighborhood, stop, throw a handful of the shit she ate, open the door, a little assistance in the way of a push, and out she'd go while he took off. Done! It would be done.

He stepped on it getting out there.

There were porch lights on and at three or four houses he saw men and women sitting on the front steps as he drove by. He cruised along, and when he came to his old house he slowed down almost to a stop and stared at the front door, the porch, the lighted window. He felt even more insubstantial, looking at the house. He had lived there—how long? A year, sixteen months? Before that, Chico, Red Bluff, Tacoma, Portland—where he'd met Betty—Yakima . . . Toppenish, where he was born and went to high school. Not since he was a kid, it seemed to him, had he known what it was to be free from worry and worse. He thought of summers fishing and camping in the Cascades, autumns when he'd hunt pheasants behind Sam, the setter's flashing red coat a beacon through cornfields and alfalfa meadows where the boy that he was and the dog that he had would both run like mad. He wished he could keep driving and driving tonight until he was driving onto the old bricked main street of Toppenish, turning left at the first light, then left again, stopping when he came to where his mother lived, and never, never, for any reason ever, ever leave again.

He came to the darkened end of the street. There was a large empty field straight ahead and the street turned to the right, skirting it. For almost a block there were no houses on the side nearer the field and only one house, completely dark, on the other side. He stopped the car and, without thinking any longer about what he was doing, scooped a handful of dog food up, leaned over the seat, opened the back door nearer the field, threw the stuff out, and said, "Go on, Suzy." He pushed her until she jumped down reluctantly. He leaned over farther, pulled the door shut, and drove off, slowly. Then he drove faster and faster.

He stopped at Dupee's, the first bar he came to on the way back to Sacramento. He was jumpy and perspiring. He didn't feel exactly unburdened or relieved, as he had thought he would feel. But he kept assuring himself it was a step in the right direction, that the good feeling would settle on him tomorrow. The thing to do was to wait it out.

After four beers a girl in a turtleneck sweater and sandals and carrying a suitcase sat down beside him. She set the suitcase between the stools. She seemed to know the bartender, and the bartender had something to say to her whenever he came by, once or twice stopping briefly to talk. She told Al her name was Molly, but she wouldn't let him buy her a beer. Instead, she offered to eat half a pizza.

He smiled at her, and she smiled back. He took out his cigarets and his lighter and put them on the bar.

"Pizza it is!" he said.

Later, he said, "Can I give you a lift somewhere?"

"No, thanks. I'm waiting for someone," she said.

He said, "Where you heading for?"

She said, "No place. Oh," she said, touching the suitcase with her toe, "you mean that?" laughing. "I live here in West Sac. I'm not going anyplace. It's just a washing-machine motor inside belongs to my mother. Jerry—that's the bartender—he's good at fixing things. Jerry said he'd fix it for nothing."

Al got up. He weaved a little as he leaned over her. He said, "Well, goodbye, honey. I'll see you around."

"You bet!" she said. "And thanks for the pizza. Hadn't eaten since lunch. Been trying to take some of this off." She raised her sweater, gathered a handful of flesh at the waist.

"Sure I can't give you a lift someplace?" he said.

The woman shook her head.

In the car again, driving, he reached for his cigarets and then, frantically, for his lighter, remembering leaving everything on the bar. The hell with it, he thought, let her have it. Let her put the lighter and the cigarets in the suitcase along with the washing machine. He chalked it up against the dog, one more expense. But the last, by God! It angered him now, now that he was getting things in order, that the girl hadn't been more friendly. If he'd been in a different frame of mind, he could have picked her up. But when you're depressed, it shows all over you, even the way you light a cigaret.

He decided to go see Jill. He stopped at a liquor store and bought a pint of whiskey and climbed the stairs to her apartment and he stopped at the landing to catch his breath and to clean his teeth with his tongue. He could still taste the mushrooms from the pizza, and his mouth and throat were seared from the whiskey. He realized that what he wanted to do was to go right to Jill's bathroom and use her toothbrush.

He knocked. "It's me, Al," he whispered. "Al," he said louder. He heard her feet hit the floor. She threw the lock and then tried to undo the chain as he leaned heavily against the door.

"Just a minute, honey. Al, you'll have to quit pushing—I can't unhook it. There," she said and opened the door, scanning his face as she took him by the hand.

They embraced clumsily, and he kissed her on the cheek.

"Sit down, honey. Here." She switched on a lamp and helped him to the couch. Then she touched her fingers to her curlers and said, "I'll put on some lipstick. What would you like in the meantime? Coffee? Juice? A beer? I think I have some beer. What do you have there . . . whiskey? What would you like, honey?" She stroked his hair with one hand and leaned over him, gazing into his eyes. "Poor baby, what would you like?" she said.

"Just want you to hold me," he said. "Here. Sit down. No lipstick," he said, pulling her onto his lap. "Hold. I'm falling," he said.

She put an arm around his shoulders. She said, "You come on over to the bed, baby, I'll give you what you like."

"Tell you, Jill," he said, "skating on thin ice. Crash through any minute . . . I don't know." He stared at her with a fixed, puffy expression that he could feel but not correct. "Serious," he said.

She nodded. "Don't think about anything, baby. Just relax," she said. She pulled his face to hers and kissed him on the forehead and then the lips. She turned slightly on his lap and said, "No, don't move, Al," the fingers of both hands suddenly slipping around the back of his neck and gripping his face at the same time. His eyes wobbled around the room an instant, then tried to focus on what she was doing. She held his head in place in her strong fingers. With her thumbnails she was squeezing out a blackhead to the side of his nose.

"Sit still!" she said.

"No," he said. "Don't! Stop! Not in the mood for that."

"I almost have it. Sit still, I said! . . . There, look at that. What do you think of that? Didn't know that was there, did you? Now just one more, a big one, baby. The last one," she said.

"Bathroom," he said, forcing her off, freeing his way.

At home it was all tears, confusion. Mary ran out to the car, crying, before he could get parked.

"Suzy's gone," she sobbed. "Suzy's gone. She's never coming back, Daddy, I know it. She's gone!"

My God, heart lurching, *What have I done?*

"Now don't worry, sweetheart. She's probably just off running around somewhere. She'll be back," he said.

"She isn't, Daddy, I know she isn't. Mama said we may have to get another dog."

"Wouldn't that be all right, honey?" he said. "Another dog, if Suzy doesn't come back? We'll go to the pet store—"

"I don't want another dog!" the child cried, holding onto his leg.

"Can we have a monkey, Daddy, instead of a dog?" Alex asked. "If we go to the pet store to look for a dog, can we have a monkey instead?"

"I don't want a monkey!" Mary cried. "I want Suzy."

"Everybody let go now, let Daddy in the house. Daddy has a terrible, terrible headache," he said.

Betty lifted a casserole dish from the oven. She looked tired, irritable . . . older. She didn't look at him. "The kids tell you? Suzy's gone? I've combed the neighborhood. Everywhere, I swear."

"That dog'll turn up," he said. "Probably just running around somewhere. That dog'll come back," he said.

"Seriously," she said, turning to him with her hands on her hips, "I think it's something else. I think she might have got hit by a car. I want you to drive around. The kids called her last night, and she was gone then. That's the last's been seen of her. I called the pound and described her to them, but they said all their trucks aren't in yet. I'm supposed to call again in the morning."

He went into the bathroom and could hear her still going on. He began to run the water in the sink, wondering, with a fluttery sensation in his stomach, how grave exactly was his mistake. When he turned off the faucets, he could still hear her. He kept staring at the sink.

"Did you hear me?" she called. "I want you to drive around and look for her after supper. The kids can go with you and look too . . . Al?"

"Yes, yes," he answered.

"What?" she said. "What'd you say?"

"I said yes. Yes! All right. Anything! Just let me wash up first, will you?"

She looked through from the kitchen. "Well, what in the hell is eating you? I didn't ask you to get drunk last night, did I? I've had enough of it, I can tell you! I've had a hell of a day, if you want to know. Alex waking me up at five this morning getting in with me, telling me his daddy was snoring so loud that . . . that you scared him! I saw you out there with your clothes on passed out and the room smelling to high heaven. I tell you, I've had enough of it!" She looked around the kitchen quickly, as if to seize something.

He kicked the door shut. Everything was going to hell. While he was shaving, he stopped once and held the razor in his hand and looked at himself in the mirror: his face doughy, characterless—*immoral*, that was the word. He laid the razor down. *I believe I have made the gravest mistake this time. I believe I have made the gravest mistake of all.* He brought the razor up to his throat and finished.

He did not shower, did not change clothes. "Put my supper in the oven for me," he said. "Or in the refrigerator. I'm going out. Right now," he said.

"You can wait till after supper. The kids can go with you."

"No, the hell with that. Let the kids eat supper, look around here if they want. I'm not hungry, and it'll be dark soon."

"Is everybody going crazy?" she said. "I don't know what's going to happen to us. I'm ready for a nervous breakdown. I'm ready to lose my mind. What's going to happen to the kids if I lose my mind?" She slumped against the draining board, her face crumpled, tears rolling off her cheeks. "You don't love them, anyway! You never have. It isn't the dog I'm worried about. It's us! It's us! I know you don't love me anymore—goddamn you!—but you don't even love the kids!"

"Betty, Betty!" he said. "My God!" he said. "Everything's going to be all right. I promise you," he said. "Don't worry," he said. "I promise you, things'll be all right. I'll find the dog and then things will be all right," he said.

He bounded out of the house, ducked into the bushes as he heard his children coming: the girl crying, saying, "Suzy, Suzy"; the boy saying maybe a train ran over her. When they were inside the house, he made a break for the car.

He fretted at all the lights he had to wait for, bitterly resented the time lost when he stopped for gas. The sun was low and heavy, just over the squat range of hills at the far end of the valley. At best, he had an hour of daylight.

He saw his whole life a ruin from here on in. If he had lived another fifty years—hardly likely—he felt he'd never get over it, abandoning the dog. He felt he was finished if he didn't find the dog. A man who would get rid of a little dog wasn't worth a damn. That kind of man would do anything, would stop at nothing.

He squirmed in the seat, kept staring into the swollen face of the sun as it moved lower into the hills. He knew the situation was all out of proportion now, but he couldn't help it. He knew he must somehow retrieve the dog, as the night before he had known he must lose it.

"I'm the one going crazy," he said and then nodded his head in agreement.

He came the other way this time, by the field where he had let her off, alert for any sign of movement.

"Let her be there," he said.

He stopped the car and searched the field. Then he drove on, slowly. A station wagon with the motor idling was parked in the drive of the lone house, and he saw a well-dressed woman in heels come out the front door with a little girl. They stared at him as he passed. Farther on he turned left, his eyes taking in the street and the yards on each side as far down as he could see. Nothing. Two kids with bicycles a block away stood beside a parked car.

"Hi," he said to the two boys as he pulled up alongside. "You fellows see anything of a little white dog around today? A kind of white shaggy dog? I lost one."

One boy just gazed at him. The other said, "I saw a lot of little kids playing with a dog over there this afternoon. The street the other side of this one. I don't know what kind of dog it was. It was white maybe. There was a lot of kids."

"Okay, good. Thanks," Al said. "Thank you very very much," he said.

He turned right at the end of the street. He concentrated on the street ahead. The sun had gone down now. It was nearly dark. Houses pitched side by side, trees, lawns, telephone poles, parked cars, it struck him as serene, untroubled. He could hear a man calling his children; he saw a woman in an apron step to the lighted door of her house.

"Is there still a chance for me?" Al said. He felt tears spring to his eyes. He was amazed. He couldn't help but grin at himself and shake his head as he got out his handkerchief. Then he saw a group of children coming down the street. He waved to get their attention.

"You kids see anything of a little white dog?" Al said to them.

"Oh sure," one boy said. "Is it your dog?"

Al nodded.

"We were just playing with him about a minute ago, down the street. In Terry's yard." The boy pointed. "Down the street."

"You got kids?" one of the little girls spoke up.

"I do," Al said.

"Terry said he's going to keep him. He don't have a dog," the boy said.

"I don't know," Al said. "I don't think my kids would like that. It belongs to them. It's just lost," Al said.

He drove on down the street. It was dark now, hard to see, and he began to panic again, cursing silently. He swore at what a weathervane he was, changing this way and that, one moment this, the next moment that.

He saw the dog then. He understood he had been looking at it for a time. The dog moved slowly, nosing the grass along a fence. Al got out of the car, started across the lawn, crouching forward as he walked, calling, "Suzy, Suzy, Suzy."

The dog stopped when she saw him. She raised her head. He sat down on his heels, reached out his arm, waiting. They looked at each other. She moved her tail in greeting. She lay down with her head between her front legs and regarded him. He waited. She got up. She went around the fence and out of sight.

He sat there. He thought he didn't feel so bad, all things considered. The world was full of dogs. There were dogs and there were dogs. Some dogs you just couldn't do anything with.

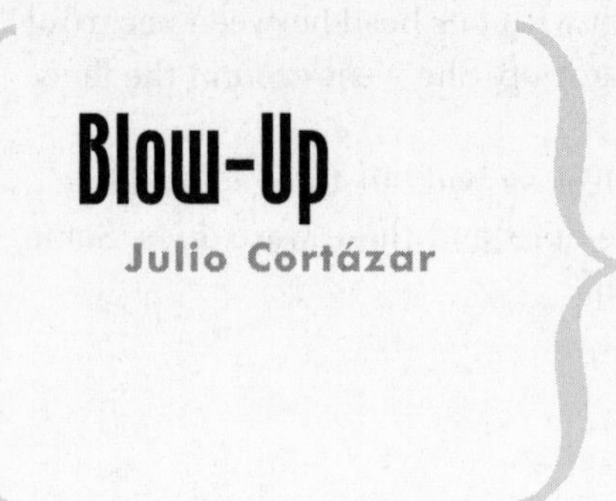

Blow-Up

Julio Cortázar

It'll never be known how this has to be told, in the first person or in the second, using the third person plural or continually inventing modes that will serve for nothing. If one might say: I will see the moon rose, or: we hurt me at the back of my eyes, and especially: you the blond woman was the clouds that race before my your his our yours their faces. What the hell.

Seated ready to tell it, if one might go to drink a bock over there, and the typewriter continue by itself (because I use the machine), that would be perfection. And that's not just a manner of speaking. Perfection, yes, because here is the aperture which must be counted also as a machine (of another sort, a Contax 1.1.2) and it is possible that one machine may know more about another machine than I, you, she—the blonde—and the clouds. But I have the dumb luck to know that if I go this Remington will sit turned to stone on top of the table with the air of being twice as quiet that mobile things have when they are not moving. So, I have to write. One of us all has to write, if this is going to get told. Better that it be me who am dead, for I'm less compromised than the rest; I who see only the clouds and can think without being distracted, write without being distracted (there goes another, with a gray edge) and remember without being distracted, I who am dead (and I'm alive, I'm not trying to fool anybody, you'll see when we get to the moment, because I have to begin some way and I've begun with this period, the last one back, the one at the beginning, which in the end is the best of the periods when you want to tell something).

All of a sudden I wonder why I have to tell this, but if one begins to wonder why he does all he does do, if one wonders why he accepts an invitation to lunch (now a pigeon's flying by and it seems to me a sparrow), or why when someone has told us a good joke immediately there starts up something like a tickling in the stomach and we are not at peace until we've gone into the office across the hall and told the joke over again; then it feels good immediately, one is fine, happy, and can get back to work. For I imagine that no one has explained this, that really the best thing is to put aside all decorum and tell it, because, after all's done, nobody is ashamed of breathing or of putting on his shoes; they're things that you do, and when something weird happens, when you find a spider in your shoe or if you take a breath and feel like a broken window, then you have to tell what's happening, tell it to the guys at the office or to the doctor. Oh, doctor, every time I take a breath. . . . Always tell it, always get rid of that tickle in the stomach that bothers you.

And now that we're finally going to tell it, let's put things a little bit in order, we'd be walking down the staircase in this house as far as Sunday, November 7, just a month back. One goes down five floors and stands then in the Sunday in the sun one would not have suspected of Paris in November, with a large appetite to walk around, to see things, to take photos (because we were photographers, I'm a photographer). I know that the most difficult thing is going to be finding a way to tell it, and I'm not afraid of repeating myself. It's going to be difficult because nobody really knows who it is telling it, if I am I or what actually occurred or what I'm seeing (clouds, and once in a while a pigeon) or if, simply, I'm telling a truth which is only my truth, and then is the truth only for my stomach, for this impulse to go running out and to finish up in some manner with, this, whatever it is.

We're going to tell it slowly, what happens in the middle of what I'm writing is coming already. If they replace me, if, so soon, I don't know what to say, if the clouds stop coming and something else starts (because it's impossible that this keep coming, clouds passing continually and occasionally a pigeon), if something out of all this. . . . And after the "if" what am I going to put if I'm going to close the sentence structure correctly? But if I begin to ask questions, I'll never tell anything, maybe to tell would be like an answer, at least for someone who's reading it.

Roberto Michel, French-Chilean, translator and in his spare time an amateur photographer, left number 11, rue Monsieur-le-Prince Sunday November 7 of the current year (now there're two small ones passing, with silver linings). He had spent three weeks working on the French version of a treatise on challenges and appeals by José Norberto Allende, professor at the University of Santiago. It's rare that there's wind in Paris, and even less seldom a wind like this that swirled around corners and rose up to whip at old wooden venetian blinds behind which astonished ladies commented variously on how unreliable the weather had been these last few years. But the sun was out also, riding the wind and friend of the cats, so there was nothing that would keep me from taking photos of the

Conservatoire and Sainte-Chapelle. It was hardly ten o'clock, and I figured that by eleven the light would be good, the best you can get in the fall; to kill some time I detoured around by the Isle Saint-Louis and started to walk along the quai D'Anjou, I stared for a bit at the hôtel de Lauzun, I recited bits from Apollinaire which always get into my head whenever I pass in front of the hôtel de Lauzun (and at that I ought to be remembering the other poet, but Michel is an obstinate beggar), and when the wind stopped all at once and the sun came out at least twice as hard (I mean warmer, but really it's the same thing), I sat down on the parapet and felt terribly happy in the Sunday morning.

One of the many ways of contesting level-zero, and one of the best, is to take photographs, an activity in which one should start becoming an adept very early in life, teach it to children since it requires discipline, aesthetic education, a good eye, and steady fingers. I'm not talking about waylaying the lie like any old reporter, snapping the stupid silhouette of the VIP leaving Number 10 Downing Street, but in all ways when one is walking about with a camera, one has almost a duty to be attentive, to not lose that abrupt and happy rebound of sun's rays off an old stone, or the pigtails-flying run of a small girl going home with a loaf of bread or a bottle of milk. Michel knew that the photographer always worked as a permutation of his personal way of seeing the world as other than the camera insidiously imposed upon it (now a large cloud is going by, almost black), but he lacked no confidence in himself, knowing that he had only to go out without the Contax to recover the keynote of distraction, the sight without a frame around it, light without the diaphragm aperture or 1/250 sec. Right now (what a word, *now,* what a dumb lie) I was able to sit quietly on the railing overlooking the river watching the red and black motorboats passing below without it occurring to me to think photographically of the scenes, nothing more than letting myself go in the letting go of objects, running immobile in the stream of time. And then the wind was not blowing.

After, I wandered down the quai de Bourbon until getting to the end of the isle where the intimate square was (intimate because it was small, not that it was hidden, it offered its whole breast to the river and the sky), I enjoyed it, a lot. Nothing there but a couple and, of course, pigeons; maybe even some of those which are flying past now so that I'm seeing them. A leap up and I settled on the wall, and let myself turn about and be caught and fixed by the sun, giving it my face and ears and hands (I kept my gloves in my pocket). I had no desire to shoot pictures, and lit a cigarette to be doing something; I think it was that moment when the match was about to touch the tobacco that I saw the young boy for the first time.

What I'd thought was a couple seemed much more now a boy with his mother, although at the same time I realized that it was not a kid and his mother, and that it was a couple in the sense that we always allegate to couples when we see them leaning up against the parapets or embracing on the benches in the squares. As I had nothing else to do, I had more than enough time to wonder why the boy was so nervous, like a young colt or a hare, sticking his hands into his pockets, taking them out immediately, one after the other, running his fingers through his hair, changing his stance, and especially why was he afraid, well, you could guess that from every gesture, a fear suffocated by his shyness, an impulse to step backwards which he telegraphed, his body standing as if it were on the edge of flight, holding itself back in a final, pitiful decorum.

All this was so clear, ten feet away—and we were alone against the parapet at the tip of the island—that at the beginning the boy's fright didn't let me see the blonde very well. Now, thinking back on it, I see her much better at that first second when I read her face (she'd turned around suddenly, swinging like a metal weathercock, and the eyes, the eyes were there), when I vaguely understood what might have been occurring to the boy and figured it would be worth the trouble to stay and watch (the wind was blowing their words away and they were speaking in a low murmur). I think that I know how to look, if it's something I know, and also that every looking oozes with mendacity, because it's that which expels us furthest outside ourselves, without the least guarantee, whereas to smell, or (but Michel rambles on to himself easily enough, there's no need to let him harangue on this way). In any case, if the likely inaccuracy can be seen beforehand, it becomes possible again to look; perhaps it suffices to choose between looking and the reality looked at, to strip things of all their unnecessary clothing. And surely all that is difficult besides.

As for the boy I remember the image before his actual body (that will clear itself up later), while now I am sure that I remember the woman's body much better than the image. She was thin and willowy, two unfair words to describe what she was, and was wearing an almost-black fur coat, almost long, almost handsome. All the morning's wind (now it was hardly a breeze and it wasn't cold) had blown through her blond hair which pared away her white, bleak face—two unfair words—and put the world at her feet and horribly alone in front of her dark eyes, her eyes fell on things like two eagles, two leaps into nothingness, two puffs of green slime. I'm not describing it. And I said two puffs of green slime.

Let's be fair, the boy was well enough dressed and was sporting yellow gloves which I would have sworn belonged to his older brother, a student of law or sociology; it was pleasant to see the fingers of the gloves sticking out of his jacket pocket. For a long time I didn't see his face, barely a profile, not stupid—a terrified bird, a Fra Filippo angel, rice pudding with milk—and the back of an adolescent who wants to take up judo and has had a scuffle or two in defense of an idea or his sister. Turning fourteen, perhaps fifteen, one would guess that he was dressed and fed by his parents but without a nickel in his pocket, having to debate with his buddies before making up his mind to buy a coffee, a cognac, a pack of cigarettes. He'd walk through the streets thinking of the girls in his class, about how good it would be to go to the movies and see the latest film, or to buy novels or neckties or bottles of liquor with green and white labels on them. At home (it would be a respectable home, lunch at noon and romantic landscapes on the walls, with a dark entryway and a mahogany umbrella stand inside the door) there'd be the slow rain of time, for studying, for being mama's hope, for looking like dad, for writing to his aunt in Avignon. So that there was a lot of walking the streets, the whole of the river for him (but without a nickel) and the mysterious city of fifteen-year-olds with its signs in doorways, its terrifying cats, a paper of fried potatoes for thirty francs, the pornographic magazine folded four ways, a solitude like the emptiness of his pockets, the eagerness for so much that was incomprehensible but illumined by a total love, by the availability analogous to the wind and the streets.

This biography was of the boy and of any boy whatsoever, but this particular one now, you could see he was insular, surrounded solely by the blonde's presence as she continued talking with him. (I'm tired of insisting, but two long ragged ones just went by. That morning I don't think I looked at the sky once, because what was happening with the boy and the woman appeared so soon I could do nothing but look at them and wait, look at them and . . .) To cut it short, the boy was agitated and one could guess without too much trouble what had just occurred a few minutes before, at most half-an-hour. The boy had come onto the tip of the island, seen the woman and thought her marvelous. The woman was waiting for that because she was there waiting for that, or maybe the boy arrived before her and she saw him from one of the balconies or from a car and got out to meet him, starting the conversation with whatever, from the beginning she was sure that he was going to be afraid and want to run off, and that, naturally, he'd stay, stiff and sullen, pretending experience and the pleasure of the adventure. The rest was easy because it was happening ten feet away from me, and anyone could have gauged the stages of the game, the derisive, competitive fencing; its major attraction was not that it was happening but in foreseeing its denouement. The boy would try to end it by pretending a date, an obligation, whatever, and would go stumbling off disconcerted, wishing he were walking with some assurance, but naked under the mocking glance which would follow him until he was out of sight. Or rather, he would stay there, fascinated or simply incapable of taking the initiative, and the woman would begin to touch his face gently, muss his hair, still talking to him voicelessly, and soon would take him by the arm to lead him off, unless he, with an uneasiness beginning to tinge the edge of desire, even his stake in the adventure, would rouse himself to put his arm around her waist and to kiss her. Any of this could have happened, though it did not, and perversely Michel waited, sitting on the railing, making the settings almost without looking at the camera, ready to take a picturesque shot of a corner of the island with an uncommon couple talking and another looking at one another.

Strange how the scene (almost nothing: two figures there mismatched in their youth) was taking on a disquieting aura. I thought it was I imposing it, and that my photo, if I shot it, would reconstitute things in their true stupidity. I would have liked to know what he was thinking, a man in a gray hat sitting at the wheel of a car parked on the dock which led up to the footbridge, and whether he was reading the paper or asleep. I had just discovered him because people inside a parked car have a tendency to disappear, they get lost in that wretched, private cage stripped of the beauty that motion and danger give it. And nevertheless, the car had been there the whole time, forming part (or deforming that part) of the isle. A car: like saying a lighted streetlamp, a park bench. Never like saying wind, sunlight, those elements always new to the skin and the eyes, and also the boy and the woman, unique, put there to change the island, to show it to me in another way. Finally, it may have been that the man with the newspaper also became aware of what was happening and would, like me, feel that malicious sensation of waiting for everything to happen. Now the woman had swung around smoothly, putting the young boy between herself and the wall, I saw them almost in profile, and he was taller, though not much taller, and yet she dominated him, it seemed like she was hovering over him (her laugh, all at once, a whip of feathers), crushing him just by being there, smiling, one hand taking a stroll through the air. Why wait any longer? Aperture at sixteen, a sighting which would not include the horrible black car, but yes, that tree, necessary to break up too much gray space. . . .

I raised the camera, pretended to study a focus which did not include them, and waited and watched closely, sure that I would finally catch the revealing expression, one that would sum it all up, life that is rhythmed by movement but which a stiff image destroys, taking time in cross section, if we do not choose the essential imperceptible fraction of it. I did not have to wait long. The woman was getting on with the job of handcuffing the boy smoothly, stripping from him what was left of his freedom a hair at a time, in an incredibly slow and delicious torture. I imagined the possible endings (now a small fluffy cloud appears, almost alone in the sky), I saw their arrival at the house (a basement apartment probably, which she would have filled with large cushions and cats) and conjectured the boy's terror and his desperate decision to play it cool and to be led off pretending there was nothing new in it for him. Closing my eyes, if I did in fact close my eyes, I set the scene: the teasing kisses, the woman mildly repelling the hands which were trying to undress her, like in novels, on a bed that would have a lilac-colored comforter, on the other hand she taking off his clothes, plainly mother and son under a milky yellow light, and everything would end up as usual, perhaps, but maybe everything would go otherwise, and the initiation of the adolescent would not happen, she would not let it happen, after a long prologue wherein the awkwardnesses, the exasperating caresses, the running of hands over bodies would be resolved in who knows what, in a separate and solitary pleasure, in a petulant denial mixed with the art of tiring and disconcerting so much poor innocence. It might go like that, it might very well go like that; that woman was not looking for the boy as a lover, and at the same time she was dominating him toward some end impossible to understand if you do not imagine it as a cruel game, the desire to desire without satisfaction, to excite herself for someone else, someone who in no way could be that kid.

Michel is guilty of making literature, of indulging in fabricated unrealities. Nothing pleases him more than to imagine exceptions to the rule, individuals outside the species, not-always-repugnant monsters. But that woman invited speculation, perhaps giving clues enough for the fantasy to hit the bull's-eye. Before she left, and now that she would fill my imaginings for several days, for I'm given to ruminating, I decided not to lose a moment more. I got it all into the view-finder (with the tree, the railing, the eleven-o'clock sun) and took the shot. In time to realize that they both had noticed and stood there looking at me, the boy surprised and as though questioning, but she was irritated, her face and body flat-footedly hostile, feeling robbed, ignominiously recorded on a small chemical image.

I might be able to tell it in much greater detail but it's not worth the trouble. The woman said that no one had the right to take a picture without permission, and demanded that I hand over the film. All this in a dry, clear voice with a good Parisian accent, which rose in color and tone with every phrase. For my part, it hardly mattered whether she got the roll of film or not, but anyone who knows me will tell you, if you want anything from me, ask nicely. With the result that I restricted myself to formulating the opinion that not only was photography in public places not prohibited, but it was looked upon with decided favor, both private and official. And while that was getting said, I noticed on the sly how the boy was falling back, sort of actively backing up though without moving, and all at once (it seemed almost incredible) he turned and broke into a run, the poor kid, thinking that he was walking off and in fact in full flight, running past the side of the car, disappearing like a gossamer filament of angel-spit in the morning air.

But filaments of angel-spittle are also called devil-spit, and Michel had to endure rather particular curses, to hear himself called meddler and imbecile, taking great pains meanwhile to smile and to abate with simple movements of his head such a hard sell. As I was beginning to get tired, I heard the car door slam. The man in the gray hat was there, looking at us. It was only at that point that I realized he was playing a part in the comedy.

He began to walk toward us, carrying in his hand the paper he had been pretending to read. What I remember best is the grimace that twisted his mouth askew, it covered his face with wrinkles, changed somewhat both in location and shape because his lips trembled and the grimace went from one side of his mouth to the other as though it were on wheels, independent and involuntary. But the rest stayed fixed, a flour-powdered clown or bloodless man, dull dry skin, eyes deepest, the nostrils black and prominently visible, blacker than the eyebrows or hair or the black necktie. Walking cautiously as though the pavement hurt his feet; I saw patent-leather shoes with such thin soles that he must have felt every roughness in the pavement. I don't know why I got down off the railing, nor very well why I decided to not give them the photo, to refuse that demand in which I guessed at their fear and cowardice. The clown and the woman consulted one another in silence: we made a perfect and unbearable triangle, something I felt compelled to break with a crack of a whip. I laughed in their faces and began to walk off, a little more slowly, I imagine, than the boy. At the level of the first houses, beside the iron footbridge, I turned around to look at them. They were not moving, but the man had dropped his newspaper; it seemed to me that the woman, her back to the parapet, ran her hands over the stone with the classical and absurd gesture of someone pursued looking for a way out.

What happened after that happened here, almost just now, in a room on the fifth floor. Several days went by before Michel developed the photos he'd taken on Sunday; his shots of the Conservatoire and of Sainte-Chapelle were all they should be. Then he found two or three proof-shots he'd forgotten, a poor attempt to catch a cat perched astonishingly on the roof of a rambling public urinal, and also the shot of the blonde and the kid. The negative was so good that he made an enlargement; the enlargement was so good that he made one very much larger, almost the size of a poster. It did not occur to him (now one wonders and wonders) that only the shots of the Conservatoire were worth so much work. Of the whole series, the snapshot of the tip of the island was the only one which interested him; he tacked up the enlargement on one wall of the room, and the first day he spent some time looking at it and remembering, that gloomy operation of comparing the memory with the gone reality; a frozen memory, like any photo, where nothing is missing, not even, and especially, nothingness, the true solidifier of the scene. There was the woman, there was the boy, the tree rigid above their heads, the sky as sharp as the stone of the parapet, clouds and stones melded into a single substance and inseparable (now one with sharp edges is going by, like a thunderhead). The first two days I accepted what I had done, from the photo itself to the enlargement on the wall, and didn't even question that every once in a while I would interrupt my translation of José Norberto Allende's treatise to encounter once more the woman's face, the dark splotches on the railing. I'm such a jerk; it had never occurred to me that when we look at a photo from the front, the eyes reproduce exactly the position and the vision of the lens; it's these things that are taken for granted and it never occurs to anyone to think about them. From my chair, with the typewriter directly in front of me, I looked at the photo ten feet away, and then it occurred to me that I had hung it exactly at the point of view of the lens. It looked very good that way; no doubt, it was the best way to appreciate a photo, though the angle from the diagonal doubtless has its pleasures and might even divulge different aspects. Every few minutes, for example when I was unable to find the way to say in good French what José Norberto Allende was saying in very good Spanish, I raised my eyes and looked at the photo; sometimes the woman would catch my eye, sometimes the boy, sometimes the pavement where a dry leaf had fallen admirably situated to heighten a lateral section. Then I rested a bit from my labors, and I enclosed myself again happily in that morning in which the photo was drenched, I recalled ironically the angry picture of the woman demanding I give her the photograph, the boy's pathetic and ridiculous flight, the entrance on the scene of the man with the white face. Basically, I was satisfied with myself; my part had not been too brilliant, and since the French have been given the gift of the sharp response, I did not see very well why I'd chosen to leave without a complete demonstration of the rights, privileges and prerogatives of citizens. The important thing, the really important thing was having helped the kid to escape in time (this in case my theorizing was correct, which was not sufficiently proven, but the running away itself seemed to show it so). Out of plain meddling, I had given him the opportunity finally to take advantage of his fright to do something useful; now he would be regretting it, feeling his honor impaired, his manhood diminished. That was better than the attentions of a woman capable of looking as she had looked at him on that island. Michel is something of a puritan at times, he believes that one should not seduce someone from a position of strength. In the last analysis, taking that photo had been a good act.

Well, it wasn't because of the good act that I looked at it between paragraphs while I was working. At that moment I didn't know the reason, the reason I had tacked the enlargement onto the wall; maybe all fatal acts happen that way, and that is the condition of their fulfillment. I don't think the almost-furtive trembling of the leaves on the tree alarmed me, I was working on a sentence and rounded it out successfully. Habits are like immense herbariums, in the end an enlargement of 32 × 28 looks like a movie screen, where, on the tip of the island, a woman is speaking with a boy and a tree is shaking its dry leaves over their heads.

But her hands were just too much. I had just translated: "In that case, the second key resides in the intrinsic nature of difficulties which societies . . ."—when I saw the woman's hand beginning to stir slowly, finger by finger. There was nothing left of me, a phrase in French which I would never have to finish, a typewriter on the floor, a chair that squeaked and shook, fog. The kid had ducked his head like boxers do when they've done all they can and are waiting for the final blow to fall; he had turned up the collar of his overcoat and seemed more a prisoner than ever, the perfect victim helping promote the catastrophe. Now the woman was talking into his ear, and her hand opened again to lay itself against his cheekbone, to caress and caress it, burning it, taking her time. The kid was less startled than he was suspicious, once or twice he poked his head over the woman's shoulder and she continued talking, saying something that made him look back every few minutes toward that area where Michel knew the car was parked and the man in the gray hat, carefully eliminated from the photo but present in the boy's eyes (how doubt that now) in the words of the woman, in the woman's hands, in the vicarious presence of the woman. When I saw the man come up, stop near them and look at them, his hands in his pockets and a stance somewhere between disgusted and demanding, the master who is about to whistle in his dog after a frolic in the square, I understood, if that was to understand, what had to happen now, what had to have happened then, what would have to happen at that moment, among these people, just where I had poked my nose in to upset an established order, interfering innocently in that which had not happened, but which was now going to happen, now was going to be fulfilled. And what I had imagined earlier was much less horrible than the reality, that woman, who was not there by herself, she was not caressing or propositioning or encouraging for her own pleasure, to lead the angel away with his tousled hair and play the tease with his terror and his eager grace. The real boss was waiting there, smiling petulantly, already certain of the business; he was not the first to send a woman in the vanguard, to bring him the prisoners manacled with flowers. The rest of it would be so simple, the car, some house or another, drinks, stimulating engravings, tardy tears, the awakening in hell. And there was nothing I could do, this time I could do absolutely nothing. My strength had been a photograph, that, there, where they were taking their revenge on me, demonstrating clearly what was going to happen. The photo had been taken, the time had run out, gone; we were so far from one another, the abusive act had certainly already taken place, the tears already shed, and the rest conjecture and sorrow. All at once the order was inverted, they were alive, moving, they were deciding and had decided, they were going to their future; and I on this side, prisoner of another time, in a room on the fifth floor, to not know who they were, that woman, that man, and that boy, to be only the lens of my camera, something fixed, rigid, incapable of intervention. It was horrible, their mocking me, deciding it before my impotent eye, mocking me, for the boy again was looking at the flour-faced clown and I had to accept the fact that he was going to say yes, that the proposition carried money with it or a gimmick, and I couldn't yell for him to run, or even open the road to him again with a new photo, a small and almost meek intervention which would ruin the framework of drool and perfume. Everything was going to resolve itself right there, at that moment; there was like an immense silence which had nothing to do with physical silence. It was stretching it out, setting itself up. I think I screamed, I screamed terribly, and that at that exact second I realized that I was beginning to move toward them, four inches, a step, another step, the tree swung its branches rhythmically in the foreground, a place where the railing was tarnished emerged from the frame, the woman's face turned toward me as though surprised, was enlarging, and then I turned a bit, I mean that the camera turned a little, and without losing sight of the woman, I began to close in on the man who was looking at me with the black holes he had in place of eyes, surprised and angered both, he looked, wanting to nail me onto the air, and at that instant I happened to see something like a large bird outside the focus that was flying in a single swoop in front of the picture, and I leaned up against the wall of my room and was happy because the boy had just managed to escape, I saw him running off, in focus again, sprinting with his hair flying in the wind, learning finally to fly across the island, to arrive at the footbridge, return to the city. For the second time he'd escaped them, for the second time I was helping him to escape, returning him to his precarious paradise. Out of breath, I stood in front of them; no need to step closer, the game was played out. Of the woman you could see just maybe a shoulder and a bit of hair, brutally cut off by the frame of the picture; but the man was directly center, his mouth half open, you could see a shaking black tongue, and he lifted his hands slowly, bringing them into the foreground, an instant still in perfect focus, and then all of him a lump that blotted out the island, the tree, and I shut my eyes, I didn't want to see any more, and I covered my face and broke into tears like an idiot.

Now there's a big white cloud, as on all these days, all this untellable time. What remains to be said is always a cloud, two clouds, or long hours of a sky perfectly clear, a very clean, clear rectangle tacked up with pins on the wall of my room. That was what I saw when I opened my eyes and dried them with my fingers: the clear sky, and then a cloud that drifted in from the left, passed gracefully and slowly across and disappeared on the right. And then another, and for a change sometimes, everything gets gray, all one enormous cloud, and suddenly the splotches of rain cracking down, for a long spell you can see it raining over the picture, like a spell of weeping reversed, and little by little, the frame becomes clear, perhaps the sun comes out, and again the clouds begin to come, two at a time, three at a time. And the pigeon; once in a while, and a sparrow or two.

Your Arkansas Traveler

Budd Schulberg

I

That was a nice little summer job on KFOX until he came along. I'd spin the platters and dead-pan the commercials, I'd read the news off the AP wire—I was a kind of transmission belt between Fox, Wyoming, and the outside world. For seventy-five a week. Just making enough to keep me in nylons and pay my way at the local beauty parlor. And doing enough to satisfy a nagging conscience.

But this isn't getting us to Lonesome Rhodes. The time is one quiet weekday morning when I have the shop pretty much to myself. There's just me and Farrell who sits there with all the little knobs and gets us on the air, hangover and all. The boss is off somewhere taking his ease. Joe Aarons, our staff-of-lifer, is out telling tradesmen their businesses will cave in if they don't hurry up advertise on KFOX. OK? Ready? Blow the trumpets. Sound the cymbals. Enter Mister Rhodes.

He's big and he's Western, but he isn't stringbean like Gary. He's kind of big all over, like a husky fullback three years after he broke training. He's got a ruddy, laughing face, the haw-haw kind. He must be well into his thirties, but he's boyish. He stands there in an unpressed brown suit and cowboy boots, shifting from one foot to another, shy-like, though something tells me deep down he is about as shy as a bulldozer. I spin one—one of my old faves, Berrigan's "Can't Get Started," and I duck to find out what brings to our wireless castle this happy big one I see through the glass.

"Ma'am," he says, "my name is Rhodes, Larry Rhodes. They call me Lonesome."

"Who calls you lonesome?" I say.

He grinned a nice warm grin. Too nice. Too warm.

"Lonesome, that's my professional name, ma'am."

"Oh, a professional. What are you a professional at?"

"Singin', ma'am. Folk singin'."

Now I know that these days you are supposed to love folk singin'. If you don't drool over "Barbara Allen," if you don't swoon to the "Blue-Tail Fly" or "The E-ri-e Canal" you are considered un-hep, unwholesome and perhaps a trifle unpatriotic. Well, I plead guilty.

I look at the big clock in the broadcasting room and I see the impatient second hand sweeping on to my next cue. So I run in to tell the waiting world of Fox, Wyoming, and environs that if they want the finest dinner they ever had for one dollar thirty-five what are they waiting for, hurry their lassies down to the Little Bluebird Grill. Then I spin Fats on his own "Ain't Misbehavin' " and I come out for another peek at Western man on the hoof.

He beams on me. "You must be a mighty smart little gal to be handlin' this here raddio station all by yourself."

"My good man," I said, "I am able to read without laughing out loud any commercial that is placed before me. I am able to pick out a group of records and point to the guy in the control room each time I want him to play one. And that is how you run a rural radio station."

"Haw," observed Lonesome Rhodes.

"I might add," I said, "that we are not in the market for live entertainment. Assuming that is what you represent. Except for the news, and once in a while an interview with a celebrity who wanders into our corral, we live on wax. We spin for our suppers."

He chuckled. Yes, warmly and nicely. He shook all over when he chuckled. He looked like Santa Claus rolled back to his middle thirties.

"You're a real five-gaited talkin' gal," he said. "Now you jest set yerself down an' try to keep still and give old Lonesome five minutes of yer invaluable time."

The way he said it and the size of him grinning down at me were not unpersuasive. What he offered was limitless confidence in his own charm. Now that you've seen him thousands of times you know what I mean.

"I brought along my *git*-tar," he said. "How can you send away from your door a fella who goes to all that trouble jest to entertain you?"

As a matter of fact we were hooked into a national soap opera called "John's Office Wife," so I was on my own for the next half-hour. "All right," I said, "entertain me."

He opened the guitar case and a *Racing Form* fell out.

"How did you do yesterday?" I said.

He shook his head and shrugged and then he grinned. "I had a tough break. Shy Lady was ready to make her move, but she couldn't find racing room."

"All right, sing," I said. "Let's have 'Home on the Range.' "

The guitar case was a large one and it also held a change of clothes and his toilet articles. "I made this myself with an old cigar box, a piece of piano wire I found in a junkyard and a little spit," he said, caressing the instrument. "Back in my home town, Riddle, Arkansas, they call me the Stradivarius of the cigar-box *git*-tar. Them folks got a heap o' culture in Riddle." He put his ear down to that god-awful-looking thing and began to tune it elaborately.

"This isn't Carnegie Hall," I said, "and I only have twenty minutes."

I hate guitars. I used to hate banjos, but I think I hate guitars more. Except for Segovia or Vincente Gomez.

"I will first sing that old folk song 'We'll Have Tea for Two If You'll Bring the Tea.' "

A Western clown, I thought to myself.

He poised his fingers over the strings and announced, "I should say at this point that I do not know how to play the *git*-tar. I sent for a home-study course, but not having a home the lessons never seem to catch up to me. A folk singer without a *git*-tar is like soft-boiled eggs without a spoon, kind of embarrassin', so I carry the *git*-tar along t' keep up appearances."

I made a fairly good job of not laughing. But he had something. To look at his big hearty puss and the way he enjoyed himself, it made you want to smile.

He started to sing one of my favorite hates, "Little Red Wing." It was only slightly awful, but it was rapidly getting worse. He broke off after a few bars and said, "If you think this is good I wish you could hear my Cousin Abernathy sing it. He does it through his nose and on a nice damp day he gets an effect that's darn near as good as playin' a comb through toilet paper."

He talked that way all through the number. He kept reminding himself of funny stories from that outrageous home town, Riddle, Arkansas. He said the riddle was how it could call itself a town when it had so few people in it. He said there was only one family in the town, his own kin, the Rhodeses. Population 372 and one half. He said the extra half was for his Great Uncle Bloomer who had two heads. "But he only had two hands and one mouth so we figured he was only entitled to one vote and one jug of corn a day. But believe me that fella's got two good heads on his shoulders. It took two of 'em to get the last word with my Aunt Lucybelle." He said there was so much intermarriage in Riddle, Arkansas, that he figured out one time his mother-in-law's kid brother was actually his stepdaddy. How he, Lonesome, ever came out so normal and intelligent he would never know, he said. He said in Riddle they called him The Perfessor because he was the only fella in town who ever got through the third grade. "And I was only fourteen at the time," he said. "The only other member of my family to be associated with an educational institution was my Great Great Uncle Wilbraham. He's been at Harvard for years. My daddy says he occupies one of the most important bottles in the medical lab, but I wouldn't swear to it because Daddy is always boasting about his kin."

And all this time in bits and snatches he's singing "Little Red Wing."

I didn't know whether it was wonderful or ghastly but I'll admit I didn't dial out. He finished with a great throbbing chord. "That is the lost chord," he said. "I picked it up in a saloon in Jackson Hole one night and I never have been able to find anybody who would own up to it. . . . Haw haw haw," he chuckled from deep in his belly. "You bring the money, Mama, I'll bring the fun."

Well, I don't know. He was outrageous. He was boisterous and effective and he had a certain animal charm that made me feel uneasy.

He was just winding up when our boss came in. He's a rich man who owns a chain of rural newspapers and affects cowboy boots and a white ten-gallon hat like Gene Autry. He is just as crazy about folk singin' as I loathe, despise and abominate it. He takes one good look at Lonesome and what he sees appeals to his Amuricanism. Now I happen to feel strongly about America, from General George to General Ike, but our boss, Jay Macdonald, loves America as if it were his own private potato patch. In his mind, he and America are practically interchangeable. You know the type. Well, he wants to know if Lonesome can sing "Bury Me Not on the Lone Prairie." Mr. Macdonald says he can always tell when it is sung right because the last line trailing off into the mournful silence invariably makes him reach for his handkerchief. Well, Lonesome gives it to him, with all the stops out. Right down to the last phrase of gooey self-pity on the Loan Pray-reeee. . . . Old Macdonald reaches for his hanky. I see this Lonesome Rhodes is no fool. He has played it very straight. Macdonald stifles a sob and says, "Dammy, I love that old song. A real true-blue Amurican song." Lonesome whips out a coarse red handkerchief and sheds a tear or two of his own.

"A-course I don' know too much about this here raddio busyness," Lonesome concedes, in what has now become a household phrase, "but it seems to me a raddio station in a hunert-per-cent Amurican community like Fox could do with a bit of its own old-fashioned Amurican singin' an' talkin'."

With eyes still damp with patriotic emotion, Macdonald allowed as to how that was so. And next thing you knew, he was allowing as to how a half-hour spot must be made in the daytime schedule for my new fellow-staffer Lonesome Rhodes.

Well, I can't build any fake suspense about a name that has become as world famous as Lonesome Rhodes'. Most of you have read *Life* and that *Time* cover story and a dozen other articles on how it all happened. Lonesome got on there for half an hour singing "Little Mohee"—just that one song for the whole program because he kept interrupting himself with funny stories, family anecdotes, homilies, recipes for pineapple upside-down cake the way his Maw made it in Riddle, Arkansas, and anything else that popped into his cagey, folksy, screwball mind.

The next day I have a new job. I am answering Lonesome Rhodes' fan mail. Seems as if half the population of Fox, Wyoming, is in his pocket. More letters in one day, says our boss, than we had been getting in three months. And I had to answer them in Lonesome's lingo. "I sure am tickled yer out there a-listenin'."

The boss ups him to three times a day for an hour. Lonesome just gets on there and drools. Anything that comes into his head, that's what the people want to hear. He's got the popular touch. A man of the people. The way he wraps himself around that mike you'd think it was his best girl or his favorite horse. He says, "Top o' the mornin' to ya, Ma—mmmm, that coffee smells good!—wish I had time to come over an' give ya a hand with them dishes," and at least three dozen housewives plunk themselves right down at their kitchen tables and write him letters about how well he understands them. Sometimes he kids the commercials and sometimes he reads them as if he were on his knees proposing. Rarely the same way twice. He's smart. That's what's wrong about him. I'm seeing quite a lot of him on the air and off, and he isn't at all the simple, fun-loving oaf he pretends. He drinks too much, and he's indiscriminate with women. I see the way he eyes all the girls when we go out together. He's not a wolf, he's King Kong. He has to prove what a helluva fella he is every five minutes. And he seems madly in love with Lonesome Rhodes. The little success he's had in Fox doesn't surprise him at all. "It's my natural magnetism," he explained, "my God-given magnetism."

"That magnetism wasn't even keeping you in beans a few weeks ago," I reminded him.

"That's because I didn't have you, Marshy," he said.

"You haven't got me now."

Not that he hadn't tried.

"But you're what's keeping me here," he said. "I was always a wanderer. My feet get itchy after a few weeks. With the singin' an' the talkin' I'm always good for a few bucks wherever I go. I play the fairgrounds and the barrelhouses. All I need to kill the people is to stay in one place. I never knew a woman good enough to stand still for. Until I found you, Marshy."

So it seems I had the love of Lonesome Rhodes. I was also responsible, in an indirect way, for elevating him from folk singer to political sage. It happened at the bar of El Rancho Gusto. The local sheriff, who was running for re-election, had had a snootful and in the dim light of the lounge he mistook me for Yvonne de Garbo or somebody. A pass took place. Lonesome Rhodes rose to defend my honor. Lonesome had had not one drink but one bottle too many and his aim was inaccurate. I sometimes wonder if his fist had ever connected with the jaw of the candidate, would he have gone on to his fabulous career. Missing the would-be sheriff left him with a king-sized frustration.

Next morning he worked it out of his system on the air. He said this fella who wanted to keep on being sheriff of a great, thriving, forward-looking community like Fox, Wyoming, didn't even deserve to be sheriff of Lonesome's home town, Riddle, Arkansas. Or maybe, he said, that's exactly what he did deserve. In Riddle, he said, the way they picked their sheriffs was they figured out which fella could best be spared from useful labor. In some places, he said, the village halfwit has to be put on town relief. But in Riddle, as an economy measure, they made a sheriff out of him. He said that is pretty much what Fox would be doing if they re-elected this poor fella of theirs.

The following day I had to answer fifty letters from listeners suggesting that Lonesome himself run for sheriff. He answered some of them on the air. He said he would have to decline the honor as he had never gotten around to learning how to read and write and he had heard that this sort of erudition came in handy if you were going to be a sheriff. He said the only difference between him and the other fella was that he, Lonesome, admitted he didn't know nuthin'.

He kept this up day after day all in good clean fun until he had that poor man crazy. And the people loved it. In fact he could just stand there picking his teeth over the microphone and the fans ate it up. For instance, one day he said into the live mike—and he wasn't kidding either: "Marshy, I'm tired today, didn't get my beauty sleep last night, hold the mike while I caulk off for a minute or two." And he handed me the mike and closed his eyes. I could have killed him. I got out a couple of letters I was answering and read them to take up the slack. But when I was half through, he mumbled, "Shhhh, Marshy, yer disturbin' my sleep, le's keep it absolutely quiet." So thirty seconds of dead time went out over KFOX. Anybody else would have been fired. But when Lonesome Rhodes did it he got fan mail.

On election night, the sheriff, whose margin last time had been 362 to 7, found himself licked for the first time in sixteen years. The fellow who won, an undertaker named Gorlick, got more votes this time than he had in the last four campaigns combined. (His seven votes in the last election had come from members of his family.) Lonesome introduced the new sheriff on his program next day by saying that Gorlick obviously was an unselfish public servant, for the better sheriff he was the less business he'd have for his undertakin' parlor.

That and some more of the same was how Lonesome got his first break in *Time.* I could hardly believe it when a local photographer phoned the station to tell us *Time* had called him to come up and get a picture of us. I say *us* because Lonesome was making a kind of assistant celebrity out of me. If he couldn't find something—in a playful mood he might pretend he had mislaid the commercial—he would call into the mike: "Marshy, Marshy—where is that forgetful girl? Neighbors, if there's anything you don't like on this here program I want you to remember it is Marshy's fault, so send your letters of complaint to her." I was always the patsy, the fall girl. So *Time* said they wanted me in the act too. The still man came up to the studio on time, but Lonesome wasn't around. That had become one of my headaches. Getting Lonesome to the studio on time. He was just a small-town star, but he was developing a talent for big-time ways. Twenty minutes before the morning show I'd find him in his room. The only way I could wake him was with a cold wet washrag right over the big, lovable, exasperating face. Lonesome Rhodes. My life work.

The *Time* piece had it pretty accurate. They called Lonesome Rhodes a younger, fatter, coarser Will Rogers in the American grain of tobacco-chewing, cracker-barrel, comic philosophers, a caricature of the folk hero who has always been able to make Americans nod their heads and grin and say, "Yep, that fella ain't so dumb as he looks!" It was hard to tell whether *Time* was putting the laurel wreath or the knock on him. You know the style. But it didn't matter. Lonesome was in. The next day I got a call from Chicago. It was the J & W Agency and they wanted Lonesome. Right away. Five hundred a week. There was nothing like him on big-time radio, the man said. A simple, lovable, plain-talking, down-to-earth American. I said Mr. Simple-Lovable would call them back.

I found the great American just where I expected to find him, in the sack in his room with a half-empty jug of blended by the bed. I said, "Get up, you slob, destiny is calling."

"Collect?" he said.

"Chicago," I said. "J & W. Five hundred cash money a week. One hour every morning. Week-ends free. And all you have to do is be your own irresistible self."

He looked at me with those big, bloodshot, roly-poly eyes. "What do you think we oughta do, Marshy?"

"*You,*" I said. "You can find yourself a new slave in Chicago."

"I'm gonna marry you in Chicago," he said. "I'm a-gonna make a honest woman of you in the Windy City, little gal."

Among his many bad habits was his way of creating the impression, through careful innuendo, that we were a team, biologically speaking. This was a figment of his imagination and designs, but since when have people ever accepted truth when nasty rumors are so much more fun? "Why talk of marriage when your heart is wrapped up in somebody else?" I said. "How could I ever replace Lonesome Rhodes in your affection?"

"Marshy, I've known some pretty good-looking broads in my get-arounds, but they always took me apart. You're not going to win any beauty contests, but you put me together. You get me up in time to go to work. You get me on and off. You keep in touch with my public. You cue me when I start repeatin' myself. You always tell me when I'm gettin' close to the line. I lean on you. So you say yes and we'll go to Chicago and make it hand over fist and you'll be the rich Mrs. Rhodes. I can't afford to lose you. You're the smartest good-lookin' gal I ever got hold of."

"Take your hand away," I said. "This is business. Shall I tell them *yes*?"

"If you're in it."

"Well, only as a job," I said, "a job I can quit when I've had enough. You understand?"

"Okay," he said, "I'll take my chances."

"So I'll tell them yes."

"Only not for five hundred. Lonesome Rhodes is not a three-figure man."

He had started at seventy-five like me and was getting a fast century now.

I called back J & W in Chicago and gave them Mr. Rhodes' estimate of his own value and they said even with that publicity from *Time* a four-figure bill was too big for a starter. I ran back to tell Lonesome (in his bathrobe drinking beer now) and he said, "I better get on the phone and talk to 'em myself." It took him an hour to pull himself into his clothes and get down to the station where he had me get on the other phone and take down what they said so he could hold them to it. Where he got that adding-machine mind I don't know, but he was never a cowhand when it came to finance. This is what Lonesome Rhodes, that simple know-nothing troubadour, suggested: That he work gratis for nothing for two weeks. At the end of that period if they want him to continue they pay him his thousand a week including back pay for the trial period. And at the end of twenty-six weeks an option for fifteen hundred for the next twenty-six weeks. "A-course I'm not tryin' t' run your busyness, gents," he Arkan-sighed, "a'm jest tryin' t' give ya an idea what a fella figures he's worth. Oh yes, an' transportation. Transportation fer my li'l ol' pardner Marshy Coulihan and yours truly."

So we flew in to Chicago and now Lonesome was on coast-to-coast. The show was called "Your Arkansas Traveler." It was pretty much the same routine that had made him the idol of Fox, Wyoming. With one important exception. That sheriff election had gone to his head. He wasn't content just to sing his old songs and tell funny stories about his family in Riddle, Arkansas, anymore. He had to hold forth. It is one of the plagues our age is heir to. No longer do disc jockeys play the music. Now they lecture you on how to solve the traffic problems of New York and improve the United Nations. That's the bug that was biting Lonesome. He was rushing in where not only angels but a majority of fools would fear to tread. I did my small best to talk him out of it and get him to know his place. But he was male-stubborn and he knew so little that any meager idea he had came to him as a world-shaking revelation that had to be shared with his public. I suppose the doctors would call it delusions of grandeur. It seems to be one of the main symptoms of the dread disease of success.

He had only been going a few days, for instance, when he interrupted the singing of "Barbara Allen" with the announcement that he was pretty sick of that song anyway and he would rather talk about the street-cleaning problem in Chicago. He said that Chicago reminded him of Riddle except that Riddle was a one-horse town and Chicago was a ten-thousand horse town and the difference between one horse and ten thousand horses ain't hay. The next day a Citizens' Clean-Up Committee was formed with Lonesome as honorary chairman. On his program next day Lonesome sang "Sweet Violets" in honor of the clean-up campaign and he said it gave him a funny feeling to be connected with "sech a projeck" because his Grandpaw Bascom used to call his paw a sissy for insisting on changing his clothes every year.

It was only a matter of weeks before Grandpaw Bascom and Cousin Abernathy and Great Great Uncle Wilbraham and the rest of Lonesome's so-called family had become public property. The famous comic-strip artist Hal Katz came to Lonesome with a deal to do a daily and Sunday strip around the Riddle characters, featuring a Lonesome-like folk singer to be called Hill-Bilious Harry. What was in it for Lonesome was a thousand a week and a percentage of subsidiary loot. So by the time the option was taken up, Lonesome, our overgrown Huck, wasn't exactly going barefoot. He was pulling down twenty-five hundred a week, not a bad living for a country boy. Lonesome was not impervious to money, either. *Au contraire*, he was decidedly pervious. He began spending it as if he had had it all his life, only more so. He lined up a pretty fancy flop at the Ambassador East and bought himself a powder-blue Cadillac that just said "Lonesome" on it. A monogram would have been too ritzy, he said. Right away he had one of those Swiss 18K calendar watches and a closet full of suits all a little baggy and country-cut but good goods. He was a folk singer, remember?

He went in for me, too. He never kept his promise about my being strictly business. He always figured the natural charm would finally overcome me. I was his one-'n-only, his indispensable can't-live-without. One night the phone woke me up and it was Lonesome getting ready to jump out the window if I didn't marry him. He said he felt confused about all the success and that I was his anchor. His anchor to reality is what I think he said. That is not exactly a compliment but I said I would think it over. I don't know if I was in love with him. Call it 90 per cent disgust and 10 per cent maternal. Oh yes, I'm the maternal type as well as the professional woman. To tell the solid truth, I was always ready to give up the high rank and all the loot whenever I found the right man. At first a girl thinks kids would be too much trouble, and then that maybe there's something to it even if it is trouble, and later that her life will not be complete without them, and finally that it is the one thing in the world she really wants. I was hovering around stage C the morning that Lonesome called. I told him to ask me at a more reasonable hour and when he was stone sober. And not to muck it up with suicide threats. What was a down-to-earth simple-grained one-hundred-and-ten-per-cent American doing with that psycho out-the-window talk? He said, "Bless you, Marshy, you do me good. Even when I'm the greatest, you'll be right alongside me."

"Lie back and get some sleep and do yourself some good," I told him.

The sponsors were awfully happy with Lonesome. He was the hottest salesman on radio-TV. He'd open with "Look down, look down that lonesome road," and then he'd slide into "Hiya, neighbors, this is yer Arkansas Traveler," and he'd have the people eating out of his big and sometimes trembling hand. He'd say, "Shucks, folks, I don't know if you'll like the stuff, maybe you got funny taste, but *I* love it, it's what makes my cheeks so rosy," and the assistant geniuses of the advertising companies would shake their heads and acknowledge Lonesome as a full-blown number-one genius. A dry cereal called Shucks came out with his picture on it. He got the idea of forming Lonesome Rhodes, Inc., so he could keep some of the gravy. It turned out he was nuts for cars—he was on a vehicular kick—so he bought a Jaguar to keep his Cadillac company. His Nielsen kept climbing until he was almost as popular as Jackie Gleason and Bishop Sheen. And when it came to getting his stuff across he could more than hold his own with both those boys. "He's got it." That was the only way the advertising brains could explain it. "He's got it," they'd say, and they would all nod their heads with a sense of accomplishment and go out to a long lunch of martinis.

Lonesome branched out from sanitation problems to advice on rent controls and diplomatic appointments. And became not only a political pundit but a good Samaritan. He built up a little department for himself called "My Brother's Keeper." During the four and one-half minutes for BK, as we called it, he would appeal for some personal cause. For instance, a little boy was dying in Meridian, Wisconsin, and his blood wasn't one of the two usual types. Lonesome told the story with all the stops out and asked for blood. Half an hour after the broadcast there had been nearly a thousand calls from all over the United States. That's what they call penetration. Lonesome was just lousy with penetration. A widow in New Jersey with nine kids had her house burn down and Lonesome asked for the dough to rebuild it. "Nobody send more'n a buck," he said. "It's us ordinary folks got to do this thing." Us ordinary folks threw in about twice as much as they needed to replace the house. Lonesome thought up a gimmick for that, too. He organized the Lonesome Rhodes Foundation. Anything over the amount he asked for specific cases went into the pot. It was a tax-exempt setup and some big names kicked in, some out of pure generosity, I suppose, and maybe some for the publicity value of having Lonesome say, "Thank you Oscar Zilch, you're good people," over the air. The foundation became kind of an obsession with Lonesome. To listen to him you would have thought that no other charities and no other humanitarianism was being perpetrated in America. Celebrities who, for one reason or another, failed to come through for the foundation became the targets of public and private abuse from Lonesome Rhodes. He would do everything from questioning the legitimacy of their birth to hinting at their involvement in the latest Communist spy ring. BK and the foundation did some good, I will admit, but at no small cost to those of us around him who had to put up with the emotional wear and tear of his playing God in a hair shirt.

It was about this time, near the end of his second twenty-six weeks, that Lonesome took his first fling into international politics. Until now he had contented himself with just telling us how to solve our domestic problems. But suddenly—I think it was from getting indigestion after eating some tainted shrimps in a Chinese restaurant—he went global. He warned the Chinese that if they didn't stop messing around with us in Korea he'd stop sending his shirts out to a Chinese laundry. Back in Riddle there was a Chinaboy who aimed to marry into Grandpaw Bascom's side of the family, he said. Grandpaw told the Chinese he couldn't marry in until he went 'n cut off his pigtail. The Chinaboy said Hokay and went out to the barn and cut off the tail of Grandpaw's favorite hawg. "That's why I sez even when ya think ya got an agreement, never trust a Chinaman," Lonesome said.

I tried to tell Lonesome I thought the story was pretty irresponsible, when we were still trying to work out a truce that would save American lives. But darned if a couple of senators didn't write in and congratulate Lonesome for his brilliantly witty analysis of "our naive if not criminally mistaken foreign policy." Lonesome was invited to address Veterans

United and the Daughters of the Constitution and to write a daily column of political jokes for a national syndicate. I don't know how many thousands wrote in after that Riddle Chinaboy joke telling Lonesome he was right and that we should break off negotiations in Korea and that this country would be a sight better off if we had a level-headed, plain-talkin' fella like Lonesome Rhodes as Secretary of State.

I tried to tell him, "Lonesome, you're fine as long as you gag your way through Old Smoky and tell your jokes about Cousin Abernathy in Riddle. But don't you think before you go handing out pronouncements on China that you should know just a little bit about what you're talking about?"

In the voice of the people, Lonesome said, "The people never know. The people is as mule-stupid as I am. We jest feel what's right."

I made a futile effort to explain: he was no more the voice of the people than I was, with my corrupted Vassar accent. In the sheep's clothing of rural Americana, he was a shrewd businessman with a sharp eye on the main chance. He was a complicated human being, an intensely self-centered one, who chose to wear the mask of the stumbling, bumbling, good-natured, "Shucks-folks-you-know-more-about-this-stuff-'n-I-do" oaf.

Like the time Lonesome made a really fine, moving talk about the noble institution of marriage. He had been singing "The Weaver's Song" and he cut into that tender ballad to ask everyone who might be contemplating divorce to try just a little harder to see the other side of the argument. "Never leave a first love just to have the last word," he murmured to the accompaniment of a few soft chords on that makeshift guitar. The response was fantastic. Some five thousand couples wrote in to tell Lonesome they were "reconsidering" and he promised the reconciled couple who wrote the best letter on why they made up that he would have them on his program and blow them to a whirlwind week-end in Chicago ("Second Honeymoon") at his own expense (tax deductible). Easy for him to say. I had to read, sort out and grade the darn letters. Such drool you never heard. Lonesome was described as a cross between the Lord Jesus and Santa Claus with the better features of both. Lonesome was getting so benevolent it was coming out his ears.

Forty-eight hours after Lonesome had come out unequivocally for marital bliss I was in my apartment working through the pile-up of letters when the phone rang. It was a woman I had never heard of before who said her name was Mrs. Rhodes. "Lonesome's mother?" I asked in my sweetest maybe-daughter-in-law-to-beish voice. "No, his wife," was the answer. "I wanna see you."

I must admit I was a little curious to see her, too.

She was about forty, in the process of getting fat, but you could see that she had been attractive once in a showy, third-rate way. Being a snob by instinct and a democrat by conviction, I tried to reject the word "coarse." But it hung over us like a low fog dampening our conversation.

"So you're Lonesome's new tootsie," she opened. "Well I hope you have more luck keeping him home than I did."

"I am simply a business associate and personal friend of Mr. Rhodes," I said, cool, collected and unconvincing.

"Come off it, miss," she said. "The floor manager on your program is my brother-in-law's first cousin. He writes me what's been going on."

"I must say that it is gracious of you to inform me that Mr. Rhodes is married," I said. "I think he might have done me the courtesy of telling me himself."

"Mr. Rhodes never did nobody no courtesies," said Mrs. Rhodes. "If you want my opinion, Mr. Rhodes is a no-good bastard."

"I have no doubt your opinion is based on considerable experience," I said.

"Not only is Mr. Rhodes a bastard," Mrs. Rhodes went on, "Mr. Rhodes is a crazy bastard. A psycho-something or other. His skull thumper told me."

"Skull thumper?"

"His mind doctor," she explained. With her index finger she described a series of sympathetic circles against her temple. "Bells in the batfry."

"I see. And may I ask just exactly what is the purpose of your visit?"

"Get Larry to shell out three thousand a month and I'll divorce him. Otherwise I not only won't divorce him, I'll make it plenty hot for the both of you."

"I am not engaged to your husband," I said. "I mean I—I suggest you discuss this matter between yourselves."

"Larry thinks he has to have every broad he sees," said Mrs. Rhodes. "And as soon as he has 'em he calls 'em tramps and leaves 'em for something new. It's part of his psycho-something or other."

"A very interesting diagnosis," I said, thanking my little stars I had never succumbed to the jovial, overgrown lap-dog passes of Lonesome Larry. "But I still suggest this is a matter between you and Mr. Rhodes."

"He's a two-timing no-goodnick," she said. "I caught him red-handed with my best girl friend. He broke my jaw."

"It seems to be working quite effectively now," I said, and showed the lady to the door.

I don't know why, it didn't really concern me except that Mrs. Rhodes' husband had proposed to me and I was curious, which Mr. Webster defines as habitually inquisitive. I called him at the Ambassador and told him I had something on my mind. "Marshy, come on over," he boomed. "Come over an' have a drink an' hear the good news. You'll be proud of me."

"You," I said. "You hypocrite. You pious bigmouth. You oracle, you."

"Marshy," he said, and he tried to laugh it away. He could commit murder with that haw-haw-haw and everybody would think he was being a laugh riot. "You just need a drink, Marshy honey."

"Something is cockeyed wrong with the world," I said.

"Why for? Why for, my lovely marshmallow?"

"The way people listen to you," I said. "The way they believe you. It's fake, it's mirrors, it's false bottoms. You and your Cadillacs and your Grandpaw Bascom. A man of the people. My derrière."

"Marshy," he said, "you're tired, you've been working too hard. You need a vacation. We'll go to Sea Island."

"Damn it, we're not a *we*," I said. "I hate you, hate what you stand for."

"What do you stand for?" he said, and the easy laughter was gone from his voice now.

"I—I don't know. Something better. Something true somewhere. I can't explain it very well. All I know is I hate phonies, sham is for the birds."

"Take it easy, Marshy. You're the boss. I carry the ball but you call the signals, you know that. Now just come over and relax with some of this good Irish drinking whiskey. Let Uncle Lonesome put a friendly arm around you and tell you how rich an' pretty you're gonna be."

Well, I went over. I tell you I wasn't in love with the man, just involved with him in some perverse professional way. He wasn't alone, he was with Tommy de Palma. De Palma was one of those advertising-agency boys. Bright. Quick. Immaculate. In the next life he'll make a good pilot fish for sharks. I don't mean to go into de Palma but I can't resist one short take: he's the kind of fellow who attaches himself to a celebrity, acts the part of the responsible friend, solemnly warns he is going to tell the truth even if it hurts, and then plays back in slightly off-beat fashion all the things the great one wants to hear. Essentially it's a business relationship, but it poses as rather an intense personal friendship. Tommy de Palma, the account executive who handled the Lonesome Rhodes-Peerless account, was now Lonesome's best friend.

Tidings of great commercial joy were being toasted with that bottle of Jameson's.

"Marshy, the busher days are over, we're moving in on the big stuff. New York! New York! Big frog in big pond department."

The plan had size, all right. Lonesome was going to do two different big shows, the ballad-singing "Arkansas Traveler" thing, and a biweekly news commentary to be called "The Cracker Barrel," Lonesome Rhodes the hayseed philosopher jest talkin' things over with his Cousin Abernathy, his Grandpaw Bascom and his Aunt Lucybelle. "We'll chew up everything from the UN to tax evasion and back to Riddle," Lonesome said. "And we'll make a lousy fortune, Marshy girl. We ain't a-goin' t' work through no advertisin' agency, neither. Why give them 15 per cent of five G's a week? We'll be our own advertisin' agency. Tommy here'll head it up for me. Its gonna be Rhodes, de Palma and Coulihan. We're partners, Marshy. Put 'er there, pardner. You'll be drawing five hundred a week for openers."

"What have you boys been smoking?" I said.

"It's a shoo-in, Marcia." De Palma took over in that sure, slick, black-knit-tie, bright-young-senior way he had. You could see him being the most enterprising prexy the Psi U's ever had. "Lonesome is the biggest thing in home entertainment today. His Nielsen is seventeen point nine. His penetration is . . ."

"Marshy," Lonesome said. "In three years I'm going to be a lousy millionaire. I'm going to have half a dozen cars. I'll have two hundred suits. I'll have a private railroad car and a yacht, maybe a plane and a big place in the country. And I'll tell the people what to eat and who to help and what to think."

"The most authentic voice of the people since Will Rogers," said Tommy de Palma.

"Bigger'n Rogers," Lonesome said. "I got more mediums to be big on. The biggest."

"The greatest," said Tommy de Palma.

"And without you, Marshy," Lonesome said, "—and that's the reason I wanted you to come over—without you, why kid myself?—I'd still be a bum."

"Let's face it," I said. "With me you're still a bum. A bum with a corny magic touch. A bum with money."

"I do a lot of good," Lonesome said. "The charities. The BK. I'm gonna start plugging a Lonesome Rhodes Summer Camp for poor city kids. Before I'm through with 'em every sucker in the country is gonna love me."

"Mrs. Rhodes doesn't love you," I said.

"That bag," he said. "That bad dream. My nemesis. She just called me."

"Some simple soul," I said. "Some spokesman for the good family life. Next time you propose to anybody you might consider getting unmarried first."

"Marshy, so help me God, I got a divorce in Mexico, but the judge got indicted for fraud, so my ex claims it didn't take. Now she thinks she's got a gun at my head. Well, OK, I'll give 'er her stinkin' three thousand a month—anything to get her off my neck. I'm nuts about you, Marshy. I can't live without you."

"On the cigar-box guitar it might sound good," I said.

De Palma rose, straightened his creases and said, "Gotta run, kiddies. Early-morning golf game with Mr. Peerless himself. Here's a good-night drink to Rhodes, de Palma and Coulihan. Dat's how dynasties are born."

Lonesome and I did a little Indian wrestling on the couch. It's a good thing I have muscles from my tennis days.

"Larry," I said, "the marriage department is one of the things I never fool with. Next thing you know we're all in one great mess. Bad for us, and not too healthy for Rhodes, de Palma and Coulihan, either."

"Then you're comin' along?"

Well, I suppose I was. If a girl is going in for careers she might as well make it a good one. It looked as if I had found a home with Lonesome Rhodes, Inc.

"Thanks, Marshy," Lonesome said. "I wouldn't tell this to anybody else, but sometimes early in the morning I get kind of scared, Marsh. Sure, I wanna be a success. I got the gimmees just about as bad as anybody, but, shucks, I never figgered on anything like this. The number-one rating and the column and the comic strip and the Grandpaw Bascom dolls and Lonesome Rhodes drinks this and smokes that and everybody hangin' on my opinion of how t' bring back the good ol' hundred-cent dollar. It's enough t' scare a fella."

Poor Lonesome. Of course these moments of self-doubt and humility were few and far between, early morning bottom-of-the-bottle lapses, but they were genuine enough while he was having them. Then they would lift like a bad headache and he'd be his old braggy, egocentric, happy St. Bernard self again. Lonesome just had a severe case of American success, that's all. I doubt if there was ever anything like it in the history of the world. For one thing it takes a free (and free-wheeling) society for a success like his, and for another it takes a particular hopped-up kind of free society. Our kind, God bless it. This is a real screwball country, if you stop to think about it. Where else would the girls be tearing the clothes off skinny, pasty-faced boys with neurotic voices like Frank Sinatra and Johnny Ray? Or making Lonesome Rhodes, an obvious concoction if ever there was one, their favorite lover-boy and social philosopher?

I tried to explain it to Lonesome, and to myself, that night. I came on with some of that stuff I had learned in school about the frontier. This country has a terrible hankering for its lost frontier, the way a mother forever mourns for a son run down by a truck when he was seven years old. The frontier song is ended, but oh how the melody lingers on. That's why we don't trust brain-trusters and professors. Lonesome said it perfectly on the air one day. "My Grandpaw Bascom never went to no school an' he was the smartest fella in the county. Everything I know I owe t' my

Granddaddy Bascom who didn' know nuthin' either. But Grandpap Bascom the ol' rascal, did say one thing . . ." And then Lonesome would sound off on some crackpot scheme and next thing I'd know there would be a bushel basket of letters to answer, saying as how it was a shame Lonesome wasn't in Washington teaching those fancy-talkin' politicians a little common sense. Once you get on that kind of a cracker-barrel American kick, you can only go up. Where it would all end I both dreaded and was fascinated to wonder.

I told him how it would be with us if I went on with him to New York. Strictly career, strictly the girl assistant, associate producer, maid of all work or whatever I was.

"I've gotta have you with me one way or another, Marshy," he said. "I know I'm great and America needs me, but without you I'd be back in Nowhereville where I came from. You're my . . ."

"Anchor," I said. "Nursemaid. Ballast. The salt in your stew."

"You can laugh," he said. "When you get way out in front like I am you need a friendly face. Without you, I'm up there all by my lonesome. I'm all alone."

"You can't sing it on the air," I said, "until I clear the rights with Berlin."

"Marshy, stay all night," he pleaded. "Twin beds. I promise I won't lay a finger on you. Brother 'n sister."

"I wouldn't trust you," I told him, "if we were lying side by side in twin coffins."

"I'm a baad boy," he said, with all his heavy charm.

"You're Huck Finn with a psychoneurosis," I scolded. "God, if your public only knew what a slender reed they were leaning on."

"That's our little secret, Marshy," he said, and gave it the deep-belly haw-haw.

I finally got away and he said, "Good night, pardner," and went back to suck on his bottle. America's Uncle Lonesome, Big Brother to all the world.

II

We moved on to New York, into a humble seven-room suite in the Waldorf Towers. There was so much work to do that I had to hire an assistant, and pretty soon she had to have an assistant. Lonesome made the cover of *Life*, with a two-page spread on Riddle, Arkansas, and one of those Luce think-pieces on "The Meaning of Lonesome Rhodes." America, in this complex age of supergovernment, overtaxation and atomic anxieties, was harking back to the simple wisdoms that had made her great, said *Life*. The mass swing to Lonesome was a sign of this harking.

Lonesome was the indisputable king of television now and his daily column, written by two of his abler press agents, was syndicated in three hundred papers. There were Lonesome Rhodes hand puppets for the kiddies and the cigar-box guitar was rapidly becoming our national instrument. The Waldorf Towers layout made Bedlam seem like Arcadia. We had a staff of writers now to devise the folksy anecdotes that Lonesome delivered so spontaneously. And there were TV and radio executives under foot all the time. And the sponsors' people, and the advertising supernumeraries, and job seekers, and the theatrical reporters, and of course the press agents. They formed their own not-so-little group of court favorites around Lonesome. They laughed at his witticisms and marveled at the way he could hold his liquor and wondered out loud if show business had ever had such a philanthropical, sagacious and all-around-helluva-fella. Lonesome's ego expanded like a giant melon. It became very difficult and rare for him to stop talking about Lonesome Rhodes. He would hold the press agents spellbound with tales of Lonesome Rhodes Foundation benevolences: how he helped a whole village of Maine fishermen starving from seasonal unemployment by setting up a cigar-box guitar factory—the fishermen were using their surplus gut and wire leaders for strings—and how he had saved the land of a sixty-year-old farmer with arthritis who was being dispossessed.

"Shucks, neighbors," he'd run off at the mouth, forgetting that these were just the hangers-on and not his great American public, "if us plain ordinary simple folks 'd just help each other a little more—think about a good-neighbor policy at home instead of way down there in those banana republics that hate our guts, anyway—why heck we wouldn't need all this alphabet soup we got in Washington. As Grandpaw Bascom used t' put it, what we need is a little more good old-fashioned Christianity and a whole lot less of this new fangled bee-you-rock-racy." Lonesome never went to church himself—Sunday mornings were always spent in what he called Hangovertown—but he was a great one for telling everybody else to get up out of bed and "show the Fellow Upstairs you haven't forgotten Him." It was as on the level as a nine-dollar bill, but at least half a dozen sects made him an Honorary Elder, and Interdenominational Faith Conferences were always presenting him with plaques and diplomas. We've got one whole closet full of the stuff. It was all done for a purpose, Lonesome's purpose, but even though behind the scenes I could see what it really was, I had to admit that he did a lot of good in his own egotistical way. The Lonesome Rhodes Summer Camp for underprivileged kids of mixed races and faiths became quite a thing. Lonesome Rhodes was far from an unmixed evil or an unmixed blessing. He had a kind of mixed-up evil genius for doing good, along with a warm-hearted gift for working evil.

Even if he had been a lot more stable than he was, it would have been superhuman for him to keep his balance with Tommy de Palma and the rest of the Towers coterie constantly at his elbow inflating his already dangerously stretched self-esteem. Lonesome only had to mention something casually into the mike, or hold it in his hand as if by accident, and the product was made. One night he happened to mention that he liked to play acey-deucey to relax from the pressure of TV rehearsals, and presto, acey-deucey started replacing canasta as the latest civilian fad. He happened to toss off the phrase "as cocky as a teen-ager driving a Jaguar" and next morning there was a brand-new Mark 7 Jag at the door, free and clear. Every gadget company in the Republic had their scouts roaming the corridors of the Waldorf hoping to inveigle Lonesome into giving them a little accidental or accidental-like publicity on the air. Everything in the world he wanted in the way of wine, women, fast cars and firearms (he had become a big gun collector with a wall full of Kentucky rifles at $400 a throw) was ponied up for him by grateful or hopeful anglers. There were always half a dozen models loping around. They used to make me feel pretty dowdy, sometimes, those numbers. Our suite with money and wine and women and worried executives and slave writers and stooges was just about as close as you can get in this country and this century to the ancient splendors of the Persian kings. I didn't know whether to laugh or cry every time I heard Lonesome (with his Cadillac and his Jaguar and his Waldorf Towers and his advertising company and his stocks and bonds and his complexes) telling his credulous listeners, "A-course I may not know what I'm a-talkin' about, I'm just one of these Arkansas farm boys with the dirt still on me. . . ." That wasn't dirt, that was money sticking to him.

The only thing the press agents and the sponsors couldn't give him was me. Not that he needed me, God knows, with all those good-looking dolls floating around, but he had got it into his greedy little head that he did. Because I was the only one who didn't come crawling and scraping, I suppose. Because I was just as sassy with him as the first day he shuffled in way back there in Fox, Wyoming, with holes in his shoes. Because I was the only one who would tell him off when he got out of line. He had fallen into the habit of going around half-cocked all the time and after one performance when he had held forth on the homespun American virtues in a voice that was unmistakably thick-tongued, I chewed him out for being a sloppy unprofessional, and threatened to walk off the job if he didn't pull himself together. We played one of those late, feverish, "I'd straighten up and fly right if only you married me" scenes. He said it looked like his agreement with the first Mrs. Rhodes was going through. She was down in the Virgin Islands having a divorce.

I said maybe. I said wait and see. I said he was a handful and there were troubles enough being his business associate without taking on the personal responsibility, too. He said he wanted a farm to get his sense of values back, to get away from the squirrel cage of television. He said he thought if he was married and settled down and had a farm, raised Black Angus and some kids, he wouldn't drink so much and be such a bastard. He said he knew I was ready to write him off as a slob but it was just this crazy pace and the fame coming down on him before he knew what hit him. He told me how he suffered from insomnia and how he talked about himself too much because deep down he knew he wasn't as great as Tommy de Palma and the rest of them talked him up. Nobody was. Deep down, he said, he was really a shy and sensitive guy. He said the brag act and the Great-I-Am bit was just a cover-up for the real Larry Rhodes. I was the only one he could admit that to, he said, and that's why he needed me and had to marry me. He'd take a high dive off the window ledge if I said no. Early hour hairdowns like this, I could almost be persuaded; there was that nice, warm St. Bernard side to him, even if it was a pretty neurotic St. Bernard. I told him I didn't warm to this high dive into no water idea. I didn't like the responsibility. I told him anybody who kept making those threats and meant them ought to have his brains examined. I even gave him the name of an analyst friend of mine.

He walked me to the door and kissed me fondly. "Marshy," he said, "if you marry me I may even soften up in my old age and get kinda liberal."

That had become a running gag with us. My common man with his two-hundred-dollar suits and his twelve-dollar neckties was about as liberal as William Howard Taft. He was all for scrapping the UN and for going back to the open shop. I used to kid him that one of these days he'd run for President, Arkansas accent, cigar-box *git*-tar and all, on a platform of child labor and the sixteen-hour day. "Shucks, back in Riddle, my Uncle Bloomer went to work in the distillery when he was seven and it sure made a man of him in a hurry. By the time he was nine his daddy made him take the pledge. Yessir, nothin' like child labor, folks, t' build self-reliance." That's my boy.

On Lonesome's next show he made a pitch about the Amurican home that was really a beaut. He sang "Home Sweet Home" and there wasn't a dry eye in the house. Nobody had done so much for the marriage business since Edward VIII tossed a kingdom away for "the woman I love." Lonesome even had Lonesome weeping. Of course if anyone had analyzed the tears he would have found them high in alcohol content. Still, Lonesome could cry with the best of them. He was one of those magnificent fakes who could overwhelm himself with his own sincerity.

The night of this telecast he flew out to Arkansas to see a football game and to judge the State drum-majorette contest. I should have mentioned—and you might have guessed—that among Lonesome's cultural hobbies was a passionate enthusiasm for drum-majoring and drum-majoretting. He was rather an accomplished amateur baton twirler himself and he had announced that he would bring the lucky winner back to appear on his program with him.

Monday morning I went out to meet the incoming plane, but Lonesome wasn't on it. I tried to phone him at his Little Rock hotel, but he had checked out. And of course he was due for a program rehearsal at three. He never showed. I could have killed him. I had to scurry around and hurry up a substitute. About fifteen minutes before we went on I got a wire from Lonesome. He was in Juarez, Mexico. He said Mary-Mae Fleckum, the winning drum-majorette, had just done him the honor of becoming Mrs. Rhodes. He added something about holding the fort.

Three days later he planed in with his Mary-Mae. She was a trim little corn-fed blonde with a provocative little can, a syrupy purr and a way of being dumb that seemed almost calculated, it was so extreme. Mary-Mae became part of the folk program. She'd appear in tight-fitting rompers, doing her cakewalk and throwing her bottom and her baton around. She could also yodel. Lonesome had really found himself a hunk of talent in this Fleckum kid. He drooled over her on and off the program. He called her his little Arkansas sweet potato.

I went in and said it was about time I took a vacation and at the end of my vacation I thought I would resign. There were any number of good TV jobs open for me now, less money but also less Lonesome Rhodes.

Lonesome took me into his private study, which looked like a medium-sized arsenal, and said he had wanted to have a heart-to-heart talk ever since he got back. I said, "Let's make it a heart talk because I can just barely make out one heart between the two of us."

"Now Marshy, now Marshy honey," he kept saying. He said it had been on his conscience to explain how he happened to marry Mary-Mae instead of me. He was afraid to marry me, he said. Last week he had been afraid not to, I reminded him. They were both true, he said, but I over-awed him. I knew more than he did and I was terribly critical. I didn't really approve of him. I made him feel small. Mary-Mae was just the opposite. Mary-Mae adored and worshipped him. For Mary-Mae being the wife of Lonesome Rhodes and living in this Waldorf penthouse with him was a Cinderella dream come true. I said, "Mary-Mae is your public in one cute little package. This is the logical culmination of the great twentieth-century love affair between Lonesome Rhodes and his mass audience."

"She's a little honey," Lonesome said.

"Sweet potatoes and honey," I said. "That's a mighty rich diet."

"I wish you weren't so bitter," Lonesome said. "You're a darned good-looking girl and you can be a lot of fun but you've got a chip on your shoulder."

"I didn't come in here to discuss my personality," I said. "That's my problem. I came to tell you good-bye and I want out."

"You can have the vacation," he said, "but then you've got to come back and work with me on a regular business basis. This thing is too big for you to quit. Lonesome Rhodes, Inc., is good for over a million a year now. Not to mention Rhodes, de Palma and Coulihan."

"It can be just Rhodes and de Palma," I said. "You two barefoot boys can buy me out. I think I'll take a job with 'Author Meets the Critics.' "

"Books," he said. Lonesome Rhodes the oracle felt he was well read when he got through the *News* and *Mirror*. "Who reads books?"

"Just a few of us," I said. "Just a few hundred thousand die-hards."

"Have fun, Marshy," Lonesome said. "Blow your stack and come on back. But don't get stuck on anybody or I'll get jealous."

Just then Mary-Mae burst in. She did a kind of jazzy military strut even when she wasn't on. "Loancie," she purred, snaking her firm golden arms around him, "I want you to take Mary-Mae down to Schrafft's for a cherry ice-cream soda with oodles of whipped-cream on top."

Lonesome patted her with distracted appreciation. "Tell Tommy to have them send you one up here right away, sweetie. Now beat it, sugar, this is business."

"I'm leaving anyway," I said. "I'm off for the Islands. So why don't you do the big thing and take her to Schrafft's? She probably never has had a chance to see life as it is lived dangerously and fatteningly on Fifth Avenue."

Mary-Mae giggled. "I can never get enough cherry ice-cream sodas."

"That's how Lonesome is about drum-majorettes," I said, wishing I could have resisted being a cat. "The two of you should be very happy."

"Thank you very much I'm sure," I heard Mrs. Rhodes say as I went out the door with my very best posture.

I went down to Cuba, to a nice informal Cuban hotel on the beach at Veradero. It was a pleasure to be away from that madhouse in the Waldorf Towers and to be rid of Lonesome Rhodes. I even met a man who interested me for the first time in years. He was one of the editors of the New York *Times* Magazine and he was well read and I liked his mind and at the same time he could be fun. We both liked the same kind of vacation, going barefoot and wearing any old thing, and we went fishing together and had good talks on the beach and in the thatch-roof bars. I wondered if I had had to get Lonesome out of my life before anything could happen to me with any other man. I wondered if an analyst would have told me that Lonesome had been a kind of father figure in my life. I was half in love with him and half driven to get rid of him. And kick him in the teeth for farewell. Anyway now that Lonesome wasn't around like a giant sponge to suck me up into his life along with all the others, I was getting along nicely.

When we went up to Havana to make the rounds one evening I ran across a copy of *Time* and that's how I saw the latest development on Lonesome. He had delivered one of his Open Letters to VIP's—this one to Churchill, telling him Great Britain should get off our gravy train and warning him that Lonesome was ready to give up on the British and advise the American people to close them out just as we would any other bankrupt outfit. America would be better off, he had told his thirty million viewers and listeners, when she stood alone, "just as we stood in the days of the war against England when we first gained our independence." If I had been around I never would have let that go through. I had been doing a fair job of x-ing out the most extreme of Lonesome's antediluvian views. And in the second place I could have told him that we weren't exactly alone in 1776. There was Lafayette, and the Polish boys Pulaski and Kosciusko. Not to mention France and Spain and half of Europe lined up against the Redcoats all over the world. It was amazing and frightening how Lonesome, this cigar-box gondolier, would sound off on global issues without the vaguest knowledge of factual or historical background. A bold know-nothing who, in the courage of his ignorance, hadn't the slightest hesitation in getting up and telling his "neighbors"—which was just everybody in America—how to run their own and the nation's business.

But what was startling about this down-with-England pitch was the official response it drew. A Labor leader in the British Parliament got up and demanded that Churchill ask Lonesome to apologize for his intemperate remarks. There was a full debate on the floor which aired Labor and Conservative views on American relations. Churchill said it was preposterous for the English even to consider interfering with American freedom of speech although naturally he deplored Mr. Lonesome Rhodes' rather uncharitable view of his British cousins. "Apparently he thinks us of an even lower order than his relations in Riddle," said the Prime Minister, thereby spreading the fame of Grandpaw Bascom and Cousin Abernathy to the far side of the Atlantic. New York papers had it on their front pages for nearly a week. Lonesome had become the darling of the Chicago *Trib*, the New York *Journal* and the *Daily News* while the *Times* and the New York *Trib* were writing polite editorials suggesting that Lonesome go home to Riddle for a while and rest up from international affairs.

One night, it must have been around three in the morning, I was enjoying one of those deep Caribbean sleeps, with the fresh warm air blowing in from the sea, when I heard someone knocking on my door. "Telayphone, pleece, long deestance." I jumped up and threw a robe around me and hurried down to the desk phone in the lobby. I was scared to death it was my old man. He hadn't been very well. But it wasn't my father. It was Lonesome Rhodes. "Lonesome, how did you know where I was staying?" That was easy, he had seen the card I had sent my assistant from Veradero and he had simply gone down the list of hotels. "Marshy," he said, "how soon can you get back to New York? You've gotta come back right away."

"Hah," I said, "or should I say *haw*?"

"No kiddin', I need ya bad, Marshy girl, I need ya real bad."

"What's happened, England declare war on you?"

"Those limey bastards. The hell with them. You shoulda heard me tonight—I really gave Churchill a piece of my mind. If there's any war declarin' t' do, I'm the one who's gonna do it. But I'll come to that in a minute. That's not why I need ya, Marshy. I need ya to live with me."

"You and I and the drum-majorette—that will be cozy."

"Mary-Mae, she's no good, Marshy. She's nuthin' but a good-for-nuthin' little tramp, Marshy. I just kicked her little ass right the hell out of here. The hell with her. It was you I wanted all the time, Marshy. I can't live without you."

"Then I'm afraid your days are numbered, Larry," I said.

"Please, Marshmallow. I'm on my knees. Right here in front of the telephone. I'm on my knees."

"If you had some white gloves you could sing 'Mammy,' " I said.

"There's a window right behind me. If you don't promise you'll come back on the next plane I'll jump out the window tonight."

"Oh, jump," I said.

"You don't believe me," he said. "You think I haven't got the guts. Well I've got the window open right now, what do you think of that? And I swear to God I am gonna use it if you don't promise to catch the next plane back."

"Lonesome," I told him, "listen. I found someone down here. The first one who's made sense to me since I got out of school. It's serious. I have a feeling it's going to work."

"Oh Jesus," Lonesome was blubbering, "what've I done that everybody should be against me? I won't be able to live if some bastard takes you away from me. I'll jump. I'll jump. I wanna die."

I thought of all the three A.M. alarms I had answered. I thought, This is a poker game and all the money is in the pot now and now is the time to call him. There was a terrible curiosity in me to see what would happen if I didn't come running. If this time I stood my own ground. I had made it too easy for him. He was an extreme personality from his shoelaces to the careless lock of hair over his forehead, and I had cushioned it for him all the way. I had toned down the views that would have made him sound like a sweet-talking Father Coughlin, and I had provided a line of emotional continuity between ex-wives and models and new wives and assorted tramps. I had been home plate, or rather the locker room where you ease up after the game, win or lose. And I had been the little cog of efficiency without which the great streamlined express breaks down. Lonesome Rhodes had been my career, my Frankenstein, my crime.

"So jump, jump," I said. "Get out of my life. Get out of everybody's life."

"Okey-doke," he shouted. 'If you tell me to do it, I'll do it. It'll be your fault."

"Jump, jump, jump," I couldn't stop saying, in a broken rage. I would never forgive him if he did, and of course I could never forgive him if he didn't.

"All right," he said. "All right. You told me, Marshy. Never forget you were the one who told me. I can't decide whether to do it tonight or wait until after my broadcast tomorrow. I have a very important broadcast tomorrow. I am going to declare war."

"Just you? Without even bothering to inform Congress?"

"The people will inform Congress," he explained. "I've had enough of these Russkies and Chinks and foreigners pushin' us around. I say it's better to get it over with now while we're strong than wait for decay to set in. Like my Cousin Abernathy used t' say . . ."

"Please," I said, "on the great American public you get away with it, but don't perpetrate that fake cousin on me."

He believed he had a Cousin Abernathy, that was the frightening part. And now he believed he *could* declare war, that was even more frightening. The screw that always had been loose in him had worked itself free and the motor was coming apart. He was saying, "If I tell the people to declare war they will flood the White House and their congressmen with letters and telegrams. The GI's will insist on going into action. Volunteer militias will rise in every town and hamlet in America. The people listen to Lonesome Rhodes. The people act with Lonesome Rhodes."

It frightened me. Maybe he was only bluffing. Trying to get a rise out of me. He knew how I felt about irresponsible amateurs with mass followings sounding off on international crises. He knew where I stood on these oracles who flunk the most elementary course in human relations but never hesitate to tell us how we could have saved those three hundred million Chinese from Communism or how to turn back the tides of Africa. So maybe this idea of declaring war was his idea of how to have fun with Marshy. But what if it was what he said it was? He had been able to bring the British to a boil. What was to stop him from bringing the whole world to the popping point? "In the Event of an Enemy Attack"—I saw those ominous billboards showing up among soft-drink and cigarette ads along American highways. I saw the fatal mushroom of atomic ruin rising above gutted, faceless cities. I saw Lonesome Rhodes as a gum-chewing Nero strumming his cigar-box *git*-tar and easing into the commercials while civilization burned.

"All right," I said. "Don't jump. I'll come. On one condition. That you hold off your war until I get there."

"Don't think you can talk me out of it, Marshy baby," he said. "I'm fed up. I'm loaded for bear."

"You're loaded, there's not much doubt about that," I said. "Now go to bed. Cool off. Sleep on the war."

"I'm sick 'n tired o' being stalled," he said. "The night before last I tried to get Joe Stalin on the phone. I figgered if Joe and I could get out behind the old woodshed together we might be able to work something out. But the big bum thinks he's too high 'n mighty to talk to me. Okay, sez I, I got an army of fifty million viewers back o' me, ready to march when I blow the whistle. I'll settle his hash."

"Take a hot bath," I said. "And then two Empirin and a phenobarbital. And stay in bed and rest until I get in."

I flew in early the next afternoon and went right to the Waldorf. Lonesome was in a terrible state. He hadn't shaved in three or four days and there was so much Irish whiskey in him that he smelled like a branch of Jameson's. Whiskey had stained his bathrobe and empty bottles made a slum of his penthouse suite.

"Marshy honey, bless you, baby," he said when I came in. "Stay here and marry me and you'll be the first lady of America. Lonesome Rhodes Clubs all over the country want me to run for President. But I'm not sure I want it. I can't do everything myself."

"Please," I said. "Just no war today. I'm simply not ready for war today."

"Marshy, honey, for you I'll do anything. I should have had my head examined for marrying that little baton-twirler from North Little Rock. The kid sure could twirl, though. One in each hand and play the harmonica at the same time. She could even do it on her toes. But I need someone worthy of me. Someone with a brain who I c'n talk to." He reached for the bottle and I could see how his hand was trembling. "Damn it, nobody hates war more'n I do. But they got me mad now. Why do I have to have all the responsibility? But if Washington is too lily-livered to act . . ."

He gulped the whiskey and staggered to his desk, pushing a jumble of papers, clippings and letters aside to find something he was looking for.

"I woulda jumped," he said. "You didn't believe me. Here—here's the note I wrote to leave behind." He picked it up and read it to me in a hoarse, maudlin voice. It told of his grief for the fine American boys having to sacrifice themselves in foreign lands. He said he was sorrowing for all his American neighbors threatened with extinction in another terrible war. "For me this whole great country of ours is just Riddle, Arkansas, multiplied," he wound it up. "Every one of you is my Cousin Abernathy, my Aunt Lucybelle, my Grandpaw Bascom. God bless you and keep you all, my beloved kinfolk and neighbors."

"But you told me you were going out the window for my sake," I protested. "Why do you drag in this other routine?"

He gave me one of those slow, inebriated winks. "My public," he said. "This is high-level BK stuff. The highest possible level. They gotta believe I love 'em to the end. Get it?"

"Yes," I said. "I think I get it."

"Smart girl," he said. "Why don't we have one more drink and then you crawl into the sack with me? The hell with everybody."

"That's not what I came back for," I said.

"Hell with everybody," he shouted. "Hell with you too if you don't be a good little girl and play house with Poppa."

His face was flushed and his eyes were crazy.

I said, "Larry, get into bed and I'll get you some sleeping pills. And for God's sake, stop drinking. I'll have the doctor come and give you a shot if you won't stop."

"Gotta put on a show at nine o'clock," he said. "Gotta declare war. *War*!" he shouted. "This means *war*!"

"Shhhh," I said, "you've got to lie down. You've got to be quiet for a while. I'll get Bert Wheeler or someone to take your place tonight. You need some sleep. Rest. Peace. Shhhhh."

He reached out his arm for me and almost lost his balance. I put my hand on his elbow to steady him. He grabbed me and we tottered together. He tried to force his mouth against mine. "Larry, for God's sake, let me go," I said. I broke away and ran down the hall. Lonesome came running heavily after me. "Hey Marshy, quit runnin'. Let's roll in the hay together." His big voice was right behind me. I had reached the marble steps leading down to the entrance hallway of the duplex suite. I ran down two steps at a time.

"Hey Marshy, let's . . ."

Then an ugly sound of hopeless protest came out of him. The staggering bulk of him had lost its balance on the top step and was floundering, hurling, thudding down. I could feel the back of his head striking the marble ledge of each step as he lurched to the bottom landing.

He made a low, broken moan and lay still. I was afraid to move him.

I ran to the phone and called Tommy de Palma. When I told him what had happened, Tommy took the name of our Lord in vain, but quite solemnly. Then he said, "Listen, Marcia. You get the hell out of there. I'll be right over and take care of everything. And never tell anybody—I mean *anybody*—how it happened."

A few hours later it was all over for Lonesome Rhodes, at least the corporeal part. A compound fracture of the skull had removed his name from the Nielsen ratings. He had become a living legend even before he lost his balance on that top step and now Tommy de Palma did a beautiful job of rounding out the myth. On all the front pages it said that Lonesome's death was due to collapsing on the stairs from overwork on his way to deliver a message of tremendous importance to his vast radio-TV audience. "We begged him to slow down, but as long as his great heart kept pumping he had to keep pitching for his fellow-Americans," Tommy was quoted. Tommy had found the suicide note and without mentioning the window business he had used the sure-fire stuff about grieving and sorrowing for the fine American boys and his fellow countrymen. "I was with him at the end and I will remember his last words as long as I live," Tommy said. I'll remember those words too, but not quite the way Tommy reported them. He used that "great country of ours is just Riddle multiplied" line and wound up with the "bless you and keep you, my beloved kinfolk and neighbors" bit.

Tommy announced that the Lonesome Rhodes Foundation would continue as a lasting memorial to this simple American. Immediately thousands of dollars poured in from all over the country to keep up the good works. Plans were drawn up for a monument to Lonesome in Riddle with his famous last words inscribed at the base of a vast likeness in bronze. Well, Tommy can have his last words. They're a little more fit for public examination than what the man really said when he was chasing me down those steps.

The funeral was the most impressive thing of its kind I have ever seen. Traffic was suspended on Fifth Avenue and the great thoroughfare was jammed for twenty blocks. Half a million people tried to pass the bier. Women grew hysterical and fainted. The Mayor was there, and General MacArthur, and a Marine Honor Guard and Ike sent personal condolences. The entire population of Riddle, Arkansas, was flown in by the publicity department of our TV network. A cowhand from Arkansas sang "Oh Bury Me Not on the Lone Prairie." A bishop spoke on the spiritual essence in Lonesome Rhodes. "He was a man of the people," said the bishop, "because he was, in the simplest and deepest and best sense, a man of God."

It was a shame Lonesome Rhodes couldn't have been there. He would have loved it. It was his kind of stuff, exactly as if it had been written for him and directed by him. He was an influence, there is no doubt of that. Look at the half-dozen minor imitators already trying to fill his boots. The film companies have started bidding for the movie rights. Already columnists are speculating as to who could play it. John Wayne? Will Rogers, Jr.? Paul Douglas? The Lonesome Rhodes Foundation is to have a considerable share of the profits. As Tommy de Palma would say, "Dat's how legends are born."

After the funeral, I walked around the corner to a bar and went in to think it over. While I had never given myself to Lonesome Rhodes, I had belonged to him. I had had a hand in shaping that legend. How could I disown it now without having to answer for myself?

Rear Window (Originally titled "It Had to Be Murder")

Cornell Woolrich

I didn't know their names. I'd never heard their voices. I didn't even know them by sight, strictly speaking, for their faces were too small to fill in with identifiable features at a distance. Yet I could have constructed a timetable of their comings and goings, their daily habits and activities. They were the rear-window dwellers around me.

Sure, I suppose it was a little bit like prying, could even have been mistaken for the fevered concentration of a Peeping Tom. That wasn't my fault, that wasn't the idea. The idea was, my movements were strictly limited just around this time. I could get from the window to the bed, and from the bed to the window, and that was all. The bay window was about the best feature my rear bedroom had in the warm weather. It was unscreened, so I had to sit with the light out or I would have had every insect in the vicinity in on me. I couldn't sleep, because I was used to getting plenty of exercise. I'd never acquired the habit of reading books to ward off boredom, so I hadn't that to turn to. Well, what should I do, sit there with my eyes tightly shuttered?

Just to pick a few at random: Straight over, and the windows square, there was a young jitter-couple, kids in their teens, only just married. It would have killed them to stay home one night. They were always in such a hurry to go, wherever it was they went, they never remembered to turn out the lights. I don't think it missed once in all the time I was watching. But they never forgot altogether, either. I was to learn to call this delayed action, as you will see. He'd always come skittering madly back in about five minutes, probably from all the way down in the street, and rush around killing the switches. Then fall over something in the dark on his way out. They gave me an inward chuckle, those two.

The next house down, the windows already narrowed a little with perspective. There was a certain light in that one that always went out each night too. Something about it, it used to make me a little sad. There was a woman living there with her child, a young widow I suppose. I'd see her put the child to bed, and then bend over and kiss her in a wistful sort of way. She'd shade the light off her and sit there painting her eyes and mouth. Then she'd go out. She'd never come back till the night was nearly spent. Once I was still up, and I looked and she was sitting there motionless with her head buried in her arms. Something about it, it used to make me a little sad.

The third one down no longer offered any insight, the windows were just slits like in a medieval battlement, due to foreshortening. That brings us around to the one on the end. In that one, frontal vision came back full-depth again, since it stood at right angles to the rest, my own included, sealing up the inner hollow all these houses backed on. I could see into it, from the rounded projection of my bay window, as freely as into a doll house with its rear wall sliced away. And scaled down to about the same size.

It was a flat building. Unlike all the rest it had been constructed originally as such, not just cut up into furnished rooms. It topped them by two stories and had rear fire escapes to show for this distinction. But it was old, evidently hadn't shown a profit. It was in the process of being modernized. Instead of clearing the entire building while the work was going on, they were doing it a flat at a time, in order to lose as little rental income as possible. Of the six rearward flats it offered to view, the topmost one had already been completed, but not yet rented. They were working on the fifth-floor one now, disturbing the peace of everyone all up and down the "inside" of the block with their hammering and sawing.

I felt sorry for the couple in the flat below. I used to wonder how they stood it with that bedlam going on above their heads. To make it worse the wife was in chronic poor health, too; I could tell that even at a distance by the listless way she moved about over there, and remained in her bathrobe without dressing. Sometimes I'd see her sitting by the window, holding her head. I used to wonder why he didn't have a doctor in to look her over, but maybe they couldn't afford it. He seemed to be out of work. Often their bedroom light was on late at night behind the drawn shade, as though she were unwell and he was sitting up with her. And one night in particular he must have had to sit up with her all night, it remained on until nearly daybreak. Not that I sat watching all that time. But the light was still burning at three in the morning, when I finally transferred from chair to bed to see if I could get a little sleep myself. And when I failed to, and hopscotched back again around dawn, it was still peering wanly out behind the tan shade.

Moments later, with the first brightening of the day, it suddenly dimmed around the edges of the shade, and then shortly afterward, not that one, but a shade in one of the other rooms—for all of them alike had been down—went up, and I saw him standing there looking out.

He was holding a cigarette in his hand. I couldn't see it, but I could tell it was that by the quick, nervous little jerks with which he kept putting his hand to his mouth, and the haze I saw rising around his head. Worried about her, I guess. I didn't blame him for that. Any husband would have been. She must have only just dropped off to sleep, after night-long suffering. And then in another hour or so, at the most, that sawing of wood and clattering of buckets was going to start in over them again. Well, it wasn't any of my business, I said to myself, but he really ought to get her out of there. If I had an ill wife on my hands . . .

He was leaning slightly out, maybe an inch past the window frame, carefully scanning the back faces of all the houses abutting on the hollow square that lay before him. You can tell, even at a distance, when a person is looking fixedly. There's something about the way the head is held. And yet his scrutiny wasn't held fixedly to any one point, it was a slow, sweeping one, moving along the houses on the opposite side from me first. When it got to the end of them, I knew it would cross over to my side and come back along there. Before it did, I withdrew several yards inside my room, to let it go safely by. I didn't want him to think I was sitting there prying into his affairs. There was still enough blue night-shade in my room to keep my slight withdrawal from catching his eye.

When I returned to my original position a moment or two later, he was gone. He had raised two more of the shades. The bedroom one was still down. I wondered vaguely why he had given that peculiar, comprehensive, semicircular stare at all the rear windows around him. There wasn't anyone at any of them, at such an hour. It wasn't important, of course. It was just a little oddity, it failed to blend in with his being worried or disturbed about his wife. When you're worried or disturbed, that's an internal preoccupation, you stare vacantly at nothing at all. When you stare around you in a great sweeping arc at windows, that betrays external preoccupation, outward interest. One doesn't quite jibe with the other. To call such a discrepancy trifling is to add to its importance. Only someone like me, stewing in a vacuum of total idleness, would have noticed it at all.

The flat remained lifeless after that, as far as could be judged by its windows. He must have either gone out or gone to bed himself. Three of the shades remained at normal height, the one masking the bedroom remained down. Sam, my day houseman, came in not long after with my eggs and morning paper, and I had that to kill time with for a while. I stopped thinking about other people's windows and staring at them.

The sun slanted down on one side of the hollow oblong all morning long, then it shifted over to the other side for the afternoon. Then it started to slip off both alike, and it was evening again—another day gone.

The lights started to come on around the quadrangle. Here and there a wall paled back, like a sounding board, a snatch of radio program that was coming in too loud. If you listened carefully you could hear an occasional clink of dishes mixed in, faint, far off. The chain of little habits that were their lives unreeled themselves. They were all bound in them tighter than the tightest straitjacket any jailer ever devised, though they all thought themselves free. The jitterbugs made their nightly dash for the great open spaces, forgot their lights, he came careening back, thumbed them out, and their place was dark until the early morning hours. The woman put her child to bed, leaned mournfully over its cot, then sat down with heavy despair to redden her mouth.

In the fourth-flour flat at right angles to the long, interior "street" the three shades had remained up, and the fourth shade had remained at full length, all day long. I hadn't been conscious of that because I hadn't particularly been looking at it, or thinking of it, until now. My eyes may have rested on those windows at times, during the day, but my thoughts had been elsewhere. It was only when a light suddenly went up in the end room behind one of the raised shades, which was their kitchen, that I realized that the shades had been untouched like that all day. That also brought something else to my mind that hadn't been in it until now: I hadn't seen the woman all day. I hadn't seen any sign of life within those windows until now.

He'd come in from outside. The entrance was at the opposite side of their kitchen, away from the window. He'd left his hat on, so I knew he'd just come in from the outside.

He didn't remove his hat. As though there was no one there to remove it for anymore. Instead, he pushed it farther to the back of his head by pronging a hand to the roots of his hair. That gesture didn't denote removal of perspiration, I knew. To do that a person makes a sidewise sweep—this was up over his forehead. It indicated some sort of harassment or uncertainty. Besides, if he'd been suffering from excess warmth, the first thing he would have done would be to take off his hat altogether.

She didn't come out to greet him. The first link, of the so-strong chain of habit, of custom, that binds us all, had snapped wide open.

She must be so ill she had remained in bed, in the room behind the lowered shade, all day. I watched. He remained where he was, two rooms away from there. Expectancy became surprise, surprise incomprehension. Funny, I thought, that he doesn't go in to her. Or at least go as far as the doorway, look in to see how she is.

Maybe she was asleep, and he didn't want to disturb her. Then immediately: but how can he know for sure that she's asleep, without at least looking in at her? He just came in by himself.

He came forward and stood there by the window, as he had at dawn. Sam had carried out my tray quite some time before, and my lights were out. I held my ground, I knew he couldn't see me within the darkness of the bay window. He stood there motionless for several minutes. And now his attitude was the proper one for inner preoccupation. He stood there looking downward at nothing, lost in thought.

He's worried about her, I said to myself, as any man would be. It's the most natural thing in the world. Funny, though, he should leave her in the dark like that, without going near her. If he's worried, then why didn't he at least look in on her on returning? Here was another of those trivial discrepancies, between inward motivation and outward indication. And just as I was thinking that, the original one, that I had noted at daybreak, repeated itself. His head went up with renewed alertness, and I could see it start to give that slow circular sweep of interrogation around the panorama of rearward windows again. True, the light was behind him this time, but there was enough of it falling on him to show me the microscopic but continuous shift of direction his head made in the process. I remained carefully immobile until the distant glance had passed me safely by. Motion attracts.

Why is he so interested in other people's windows, I wondered detachedly. And of course an effective brake to dwelling on that thought too lingeringly clamped down almost at once: Look who's talking. What about yourself?

An important difference escaped me. I wasn't worried about anything. He, presumably, was.

Down came the shades again. The lights stayed on behind their beige opaqueness. But behind the one that had remained down all along, the room remained dark.

Time went by. Hard to say how much—a quarter of an hour, twenty minutes. A cricket chirped in one of the back yards. Sam came in to see if I wanted anything before he went home for the night. I told him no, I didn't—it was all right, run along. He stood there for a minute, head down. Then I saw him shake it slightly, as if at something he didn't like. "What's the matter?" I asked.

"You know what that means? My old mammy told it to me, and she never told me a lie in her life. I never once seen it to miss, either."

"What, the cricket?"

"Any time you hear one of them things, that's a sign of death—someplace close around."

I swept the back of my hand at him. "It's somewhere close by, though. Somewhere not very far off. Got to be."

The door closed after him, and I stayed there alone in the dark.

It was a stifling night, much closer than the one before. I could hardly get a breath of air even by the open window at which I sat. I wondered how he—that unknown over there—could stand it behind those drawn shades.

Then suddenly, just as idle speculation about this whole matter was about to alight on some fixed point in my mind, crystallize into something like suspicion, up came the shades again, and off it flitted, as formless as ever and without having had a chance to come to rest on anything.

He was in the middle windows, the living room. He's taken off his coat and shirt, was bare-armed in his undershirt. He hadn't been able to stand it himself, I guess—the sultriness.

I couldn't make out what he was doing at first. He seemed to be busy in a perpendicular, up-and-down way rather than lengthwise. He remained in one place, but he kept dipping down out of sight and then straightening up into view again, at irregular intervals. It was almost like some sort of calisthenic exercise, except that the dips and rises weren't evenly timed enough for that. Sometimes he'd stay down a long time, sometimes he'd bob right up again, sometimes he'd go down two or three times in rapid succession. There was some sort of widespread black V railing him off from the window. Whatever it was, there was just a sliver of it showing above the upward inclination to which the window sill deflected my line of vision. All it did was strike off the bottom of his undershirt, to the extent of a sixteenth of an inch maybe. But I hadn't seen it there at other times, and I couldn't tell what it was.

Suddenly he left it for the first time since the shades had gone up, came out around it to the outside, stooped down into another part of the room, and straightened again with an armful of what looked like varicolored pennants at the distance at which I was. He went back behind the V and allowed them to fall across the top of it for a moment, and stay that way. He made one of his dips down out of sight and stayed that way a good while.

The "pennants" slung across the V kept changing color right in front of my eyes. I have very good sight. One moment they were white, the next red, the next blue.

Then I got it. They were a woman's dresses, and he was pulling them down to him one by one, taking the topmost one each time. Suddenly they were all gone, the V was black and bare again, and his torso had reappeared. I knew what it was now, and what he was doing. The dresses had told me. He confirmed it for me. He spread his arms to the ends of the V, I could see him heave and hitch, as if exerting pressure, and suddenly the V had folded up, become a cubed wedge. Then he made rolling motions with his whole upper body, and the wedge disappeared off to one side.

He'd been packing a trunk, packing his wife's things into a large upright trunk.

He reappeared at the kitchen window presently, stood still for a moment. I saw him draw his arms across his forehead, not once but several times, and then whip the end of it off into space. Sure, it was hot work for such a night. Then he reached up along the wall and took something down. Since it was the kitchen he was in, my imagination had to supply a cabinet and a bottle.

I could see the two or three quick passes his hand made to his mouth after that. I said to myself tolerantly: That's what nine men out of ten would do after packing a trunk—take a good stiff drink. And if the tenth didn't, it would only be because he didn't have any liquor at hand.

Then he came closer to the window again, and standing edgewise to the side of it, so that only a thin paring of his head and shoulder showed, peered watchfully out into the dark quadrilateral, along the line of windows, most of them unlighted by now, once more. He always started on the left-hand side, the side opposite mine, and made his circuit of inspection from there on around.

That was the second time in one evening I'd seen him do that. And once at daybreak, made three times altogether. I smiled mentally. You'd almost think he felt guilty about something. It was probably nothing, just an odd little habit, a quirk, that he didn't know he had himself. I had them myself, everyone does.

He withdrew into the room again, and it blacked out. His figure passed into the one that was still lighted next to it, the living room. That blacked next. It didn't surprise me that the third room, the bedroom with the drawn shade, didn't light up on his entering there. He wouldn't want to disturb her, of course—particularly if she was going away tomorrow for her health, as his packing of her trunk showed. She needed all the rest she could get, before making the trip. Simple enough for him to slip into bed in the dark.

It did surprise me, though, when a match-flare winked some time later, to have it still come from the darkened living room. He must be lying down in there, trying to sleep on a sofa or something for the night. He hadn't gone near the bedroom at all, was staying out of it altogether. That puzzled me, frankly. That was carrying solicitude almost too far.

Ten minutes or so later, there was another match-wink, still from that same living room window. He couldn't sleep.

The night brooded down on both of us alike, the curiosity-monger in the bay window, the chain-smoker in the fourth-floor flat, without giving any answer. The only sound was that interminable cricket.

I was at the window again with the first sun of the morning. Not because of him. My mattress was like a bed of hot coals. Sam found me there when he came in to get things ready for me. "You're going to be a wreck, Mr. Jeff," was all he said.

First, for a while, there was no sign of life over there. Then suddenly I saw his head bob up from somewhere down out of sight in the living room, so I knew I'd been right; he'd spent the night on a sofa or easy chair in there. Now, of course, he'd look in at her, to see how she was, find out if she felt any better. That was only common ordinary humanity. He hadn't been near her, so far as I could make out, since two nights before.

He didn't. He dressed, and he went in the opposite direction, into the kitchen, and wolfed something in there, standing up and using both hands. Then he suddenly turned and moved off side, in the direction in which I knew the flat-entrance to be, as if he had just heard some summons, like the doorbell.

Sure enough, in a moment he came back, and there were two men with him in leather aprons. Expressmen. I saw him standing by while they laboriously maneuvered that cubed black wedge out between them, in the direction they'd just come from. He did more than just stand by. He practically hovered over them, kept shifting from side to side, he was so anxious to see that it was done right.

Then he came back alone, and I saw him swipe his arm across his head, as though it was he, not they, who was all heated up from the effort.

So he was forwarding her trunk, to wherever it was she was going. That was all.

He reached up along the wall again and took something down. He was taking another drink. Two. Three. I said to myself, a little at a loss: Yes, but he hasn't just packed a trunk this time. That trunk has been standing packed and ready since last night. Where does the hard work come in? The sweat and the need for a bracer?

Now, at last, after all those hours, he finally did go in to her. I saw his form pass through the living room and go beyond, into the bedroom. Up went the shade, that had been down all this time. Then he turned his head and looked around behind him. In a certain way, a way that was unmistakable, even from where I was. Not in one certain direction, as one looks at a person. But from side to side, and up and down, and all around, as one looks at—*an empty room.*

He stepped back, bent a little, gave a fling of his arms, and an unoccupied mattress and bedding upended over the foot of a bed, stayed that way, emptily curved. A second one followed a moment later.

She wasn't in there.

They use the expression "delayed action." I found out then what it meant. For two days a sort of formless uneasiness, a disembodied suspicion, I don't know what to call it, had been flitting and volplaning around in my mind, like an insect looking for a landing place. More than once, just as it had been ready to settle, some slight thing, some slight reassuring thing, such as the raising of the shades after they had been down unnaturally long, had been enough to keep it winging aimlessly, prevent it from staying still long enough for me to recognize it. The point of contact had been there all along, waiting to receive it. Now, for some reason, within a split second after he tossed over the empty mattresses, it landed—*zoom*! And the point of contact expanded—or exploded, whatever you care to call it—into a certainty of murder.

In other words, the rational part of my mind was far behind the instinctive, subconscious part. Delayed action. Now the one had caught up to the other. The thought-message that sparked from the synchronization was: He's done something to her!

I looked down and my hand was bunching the goods over my kneecap, it was knotted so tight. I forced it open, I said to myself, steadyingly: Now wait a minute, be careful, go slow. You've seen nothing. You know nothing. You only have the negative proof that you don't see her anymore.

Sam was standing there looking over at me from the pantry way. He said accusingly: "You ain't touched a thing. And your face looks like a sheet."

It felt like one. It had that needling feeling, when the blood has left it involuntarily. It was more to get him out of the way and give myself some elbow room for undisturbed thinking, than anything else, that I said: "Sam, what's the street address of that building down there? Don't stick your head too far out and gape at it."

"Somep'n or other Benedict Avenue." He scratched his neck helpfully.

"I know that. Chase around the corner a minute and get me the exact number on it, will you?"

"Why you want to know that for?" he asked as he turned to go.

"None of your business," I said with the good-natured firmness that was all that was necessary to take care of that once and for all. I called after him just as he was closing the door: "And while you're about it, step into the entrance and see if you can tell from the mailboxes who has the fourth-floor rear. Don't get me the wrong one now. And try not to let anyone catch you at it."

He went out mumbling something that sounded like, "When a man ain't got nothing to do but just sit all day, he sure can think up the blamest things—" The door closed and I settled down to some good constructive thinking.

I said to myself: What are you really building up this monstrous supposition on? Let's see what you've got. Only that there were several little things wrong with the mechanism, the chain-belt, of their recurrent daily habits over there: 1. The lights were on all night the first night. 2. He came in later than usual the second night. 3. He left his hat on. 4. She didn't come out to greet him—she hasn't appeared since the evening before the lights were on all night. 5. He took a drink after he finished packing her trunk. But he took three stiff drinks the next morning, immediately after her trunk went out. 6. He was inwardly disturbed and worried, yet superimposed upon this was an unnatural external concern about the surrounding rear windows that was off-key. 7. He slept in the living room, didn't go near the bedroom, during the night before the departure of the trunk.

Very well. If she had been ill that first night, and he had sent her away for her health, that automatically canceled out points 1, 2, 3, 4. It left points 5 and 6 totally unimportant and unincriminating. But when it came up against 7, it hit a stumbling block.

If she went away immediately after being ill that first night, why didn't he want to sleep in their bedroom last night? Sentiment? Hardly. Two perfectly good beds in one room, only a sofa or uncomfortable easy chair in the other. Why should he stay out of there if she was already gone? Just because he missed her, was lonely? A grown man doesn't act that way. All right, then she was still in there.

Sam came back parenthetically at this point and said: "That house is number 525 Benedict Avenue. The fourth-floor rear, it got the name of Mr. and Mrs. Lars Thorwald up."

"Sh-h," I silenced, and motioned him backhand out of my ken.

"First he want it, then he don't," he grumbled philosophically, and retired to his duties.

I went ahead digging at it. But if she was still in there, in that bedroom last night, then she couldn't have gone away to the country, because I never saw her leave today. She could have left without my seeing her in the early hours of yesterday morning. I'd missed a few hours, been asleep. But this morning I had been up before he was himself, I only saw his head rear up from that sofa after I'd been at the window for some time.

To go at all she would have had to go yesterday morning. Then why had he left the bedroom shade down, left the mattresses undisturbed, until today? Above all, why had he stayed out of that room last night? That was evidence that she hadn't gone, was still in there. Then today, immediately after the trunk had been dispatched, he went in, pulled up the shade, tossed over the mattresses, and showed that she hadn't been in there. The thing was like a crazy spiral.

No, it wasn't either. *Immediately after the trunk had been dispatched—*

The trunk.

That did it.

I looked around to make sure the door was safely closed between Sam and me. My hand hovered uncertainly over the telephone dial a minute. Boyne, he'd be the one to tell about it. He was on Homicide. He had been, anyway, when I'd last seen him. I didn't want to get a flock of strange dicks and cops into my hair. I didn't want to be involved any more than I had to. Or at all, if possible.

They switched my call to the right place after a couple of wrong tries, and I got him finally.

"Look, Boyne? This is Hal Jeffries—"

"Well, where've you been the last sixty-two years?" he started to enthuse.

"We can take that up later. What I want you to do now is take down a name and address. Ready? Lars Thorwald. Five twenty-five Benedict Avenue. Fourth-floor rear. Got it?"

"Fourth-flour rear. Got it. What's it for?"

"Investigation. I've got a firm belief you'll uncover a murder there if you start digging at it. Don't call on me for anything more than that—just a conviction. There's been a man and wife living there until now. Now there's just the man. Her trunk went out early this morning. If you can find someone who saw *her* leave herself—"

Marshaled aloud like that and conveyed to somebody else, a lieutenant of detectives above all, it did sound flimsy, even to me. He said hesitantly, "Well, but—" Then he accepted it as it was. Because I was the source. I even left my window out of it completely. I could do that with him and get away with it because he'd known me for years, he didn't question my reliability. I didn't want my room all cluttered up with dicks and cops taking turns nosing out of the window in this hot weather. Let them tackle it from the front.

"Well, we'll see what we see," he said. "I'll keep you posted."

I hung up and sat back to watch and wait events. I had a grandstand seat. Or rather a grandstand seat in reverse. I could only see from behind the scenes, but not from the front. I couldn't watch Boyne go to work. I could only see the results, when and if there were any.

Nothing happened for the next few hours. The police work that I knew must be going on was as invisible as police work should be. The figure in the fourth-floor windows over there remained in sight, alone and undisturbed. He didn't go out. He was restless, but he stayed in. Once I saw him eating again—sitting down this time—and once he shaved, and once he even tried to read the paper, but he didn't stay with it long.

Little unseen wheels were in motion around him. Small and harmless as yet, preliminaries. If he knew, I wondered to myself, would he remain there quiescent like that, or would he try to bolt out and flee? That mightn't depend so much upon his guilt as upon his sense of immunity, his feeling that he could outwit them. Of his guilt I myself was already convinced, or I wouldn't have taken the step I had.

At three my phone rang. Boyne calling back. "Jeffries? Well, I don't know. Can't you give me a little more than just a bald statement like that?"

"Why?" I fenced. "Why do I have to?"

"I've had a man over there making inquiries. I've just had his report. The building superintendent and several of the neighbors all agree she left for the country, to try and regain her health, early yesterday morning."

"Wait a minute. Did any of them see her leave, according to your man?"

"No."

"Then all you've gotten is a second-hand version of an unsupported statement by him. Not an eyewitness account."

"He was met returning from the depot, after he'd bought her ticket and seen her off on the train."

"That's still an unsupported statement, once removed."

"I've sent a man down there to the station to try and check with the ticket agent if possible. After all, he should have been fairly conspicuous at that early hour. And we're keeping him under observation, of course, in the meantime, watching all his movements. The first chance we get we're going to jump in and search the place."

I had a feeling that they wouldn't find anything, even if they did.

"Don't expect anything more from me. I've dropped it in your lap. I've given you all I have to give. A name, an address, and an opinion."

"Yes, and I've always valued your opinion highly before now, Jeff—"

"But now you don't, that it?"

"Not at all. The thing is, we haven't turned up anything that seems to bear out your impression so far."

"You haven't gotten very far along, so far."

He went back to his previous cliché. "Well, we'll see what we see. Let you know later."

Another hour or so went by, and sunset came on. I saw him start to get ready to go out, over there. He put on his hat, put his hand in his pocket and stood still looking at it for a minute. Counting change, I guess. It gave me a peculiar sense of suppressed excitement, knowing they were going to come in the minute he left. I thought grimly, as I saw him take a last look around: If you've got anything to hide, brother, now's the time to hide it.

He left. A breath-holding interval of misleading emptiness descended on the flat. A three-alarm fire couldn't have pulled my eyes off those windows. Suddenly the door by which he had just left parted slightly and two men insinuated themselves, one behind the other. There they were now. They closed it behind them, separated at once, and got busy. One took the bedroom, one the kitchen and they started to work their way toward one another again from those extremes of the flat. They were thorough. I could see them going over everything from top to bottom. They took the living room together. One cased one side, the other man the other.

They'd already finished before the warning caught them. I could tell that by the way they straightened up and stood facing one another frustratedly for a minute. Then both their heads turned sharply, as at a tip-off by doorbell that he was coming back. They got out fast.

I wasn't unduly disheartened, I'd expected that. My own feeling all along had been that they wouldn't find anything incriminating around. The trunk had gone.

He came in with a mountainous brown-paper bag sitting in the curve of one arm. I watched him closely to see if he'd discover that someone had been there in his absence. Apparently he didn't. They'd been adroit about it.

He stayed in the rest of the night. Sat tight, safe and sound. He did some desultory drinking, I could see him sitting there by the window and his hand would hoist every once in a while, but not to excess. Apparently everything was under control, the tension had eased, now that—the trunk was out.

Watching him across the night, I speculated: Why doesn't he get out? If I'm right about him, and I am, why does he stick around—after it? That brought its own answer: Because he doesn't know anyone's on to him yet. He doesn't think there's any hurry. To go too soon, right after she has, would be more dangerous than to stay awhile.

The night wore on. I sat there waiting for Boyne's call. It came later than I thought it would. I picked the phone up in the dark. He was getting ready to go to bed, over there, now. He'd risen from where he'd been sitting drinking in the kitchen, and put the light out. He went into the living room, lit that. He started to pull his shirt-tail up and out of his belt. Boyne's voice was in my ear as my eyes were on him, over there. Three-cornered arrangement.

"Hello, Jeff? Listen, absolutely nothing. We searched the place while he was out—"

I nearly said, "I know you did, I saw it," but checked myself in time.

"—and didn't turn up a thing. But—" He stopped as though this was going to be important. I waited impatiently for him to go ahead.

"Downstairs in his letter box we found a post card waiting for him. We fished it up out of the slot with bent pins—"

"And?"

"And it was from his wife, written only yesterday from some farm upcountry. Here's the message we copied: 'Arrived O.K. Already feeling a little better. Love, Anna.' "

I said, faintly but stubbornly: "You say, written only yesterday. Have you proof of that? What was the postmark-date on it?"

He made a disgusted sound down in his tonsils. At me, not it. "The postmark was blurred. A corner of it got wet, and the ink smudged."

"All of it blurred?"

"The year-date," he admitted. "The hour and the month came out O.K. August. And seven-thirty P.M., it was mailed at."

This time I made the disgusted sound in my larynx. "August seven-thirty P.M.—1937 or 1939 or 1942. You have no proof how it got into that mail box, whether it came from a letter carrier's pouch or from the back of some bureau drawer!"

"Give it up, Jeff," he said. "There's such a thing as going too far."

I don't know what I would have said. That is, if I hadn't happened to have my eyes on the Thorwald flat living room windows just then. Probably very little. The post card *had* shaken me, whether I admitted it or not. But I was looking over there. The light had gone out as soon as he'd taken his shirt off. But the bedroom didn't light up. A match-flare winked from the living room, low down, as from an easy chair or sofa. With two unused beds in the bedroom, he was *still staying out of there.*

"Boyne," I said in a glassy voice, "I don't care what post cards from the other world you've turned up. I say that man has done away with his wife. Trace that trunk he shipped out. Open it up when you've located it—and I think you'll find her!"

And I hung up without waiting to hear what he was going to do about it. He didn't ring back, so I suspected he was going to give my suggestion a spin after all, in spite of his loudly proclaimed skepticism.

I stayed there by the window all night, keeping a sort of deathwatch. There were two more match-flares after the first, at about half-hour intervals. Nothing more after that. So possibly he was asleep over there. Possibly not. I had to sleep some time myself, and I finally succumbed in the flaming light of the early sun. Anything that he was going to do, he would have done under cover of darkness and not waited for broad daylight. There wouldn't be anything much to watch, for a while now. And what was there that he needed to do anymore, anyway? Nothing, just sit tight and let a little disarming time slip by.

It seemed like five minutes later that Sam came over and touched me, but it was already high noon. I said irritably, "Didn't you read that note I pinned up, for you to let me sleep?"

He said, "Yeah, but it's your old friend Inspector Boyne. I figured you'd sure want to—"

It was a personal visit this time. Boyne came into the room behind him without waiting, and without much cordiality.

I said to get rid of Sam, "Go inside and smack a couple of eggs together."

Boyne began in a galvanized-iron voice: "Jeff, what do you mean by doing anything like this to me? I've made a fool of myself, thanks to you. Sending my men out right and left on wild-goose chases. Thank God, I didn't put my foot in it any worse than I did, and have this guy picked up and brought in for questioning."

"Oh, then you don't think that's necessary?" I suggested dryly.

The look he gave me took care of that. "I'm not alone in the department, you know. There are men over me I'm accountable to for my actions. That looks great, don't it, sending one of my fellows one-half-a-day's train ride up into the sticks to some Godforsaken whistle-stop or other at departmental expense—"

"Then you located the trunk?"

"We traced it through the express agency," he said flintily.

"And you opened it?"

"We did better than that. We got in touch with the various farmhouses in the immediate locality, and Mrs. Thorwald came down to the junction in a produce-truck from one of them and opened it for him herself, with her own keys!"

Very few men have ever gotten a look from an old friend such as I got from him. At the door he said, stiff as a rifle barrel: "Just let's forget all about it, shall we? That's about the kindest thing either one of us can do for the other. You're not yourself, and I'm out a little of my own pocket money, time and temper. Let's let it go at that. If you want to telephone me in the future I'll be glad to give you my home number."

The door went *whopp!* behind him.

For about ten minutes after he stormed out my numbed mind was in a sort of straitjacket. Then it started to wriggle its way free. The hell with the police. I can't prove it to them, maybe, but I can prove it to myself, one way or the other, once and for all. Either I'm wrong or I'm right. He's got his armor on against them. But his back is naked and unprotected against me.

I called Sam in. "Whatever became of that spyglass we used to have, when we were bumming around on that cabin-cruiser that season?"

He found it someplace downstairs and came in with it, blowing on it and rubbing it along his sleeve. I let it lie idle in my lap first. I took a piece of paper and a pencil and wrote six words on it: *What have you done with her?*

I sealed it in an envelope and left the envelope blank. I said to Sam: "Now here's what I want you to do, and I want you to be slick about it. You take this, go in that building 525, climb the stairs to the fourth-floor rear, and ease it under the door. You're fast, at least you used to be. Let's see if you're fast enough to keep from being caught at it. Then when you get safely down again, give the outside doorbell a little poke, to attract attention."

His mouth started to open.

"And don't ask me any questions, you understand? I'm not fooling."

He went, and I got the spyglass ready.

I got him in the right focus after a minute or two. A face leaped up, and I was really seeing him for the first time. Dark-haired, but unmistakable Scandinavian ancestry. Looked like a sinewy customer, although he didn't run to much bulk.

About five minutes went by. His head turned sharply, profile-wards. That was the bell-poke, right there. The note must be in already.

He gave me the back of his head as he went back toward the flat-door. The lens could follow him all the way to the rear, where my unaided eyes hadn't been able to before.

He opened the door first, missed seeing it, looked out on a level. He closed it. Then he dipped, straightened up. He had it. I could see him turning it this way and that.

He shifted in, away from the door, nearer the window. He thought danger lay near the door, safety away from it. He didn't know it was the other way around, the deeper into his own rooms he retreated the greater the danger.

He'd torn it open, he was reading it. God, how I watched his expression. My eyes clung to it like leeches. There was a sudden widening, a pulling—the whole skin of his face seemed to stretch back behind the ears, narrowing his eyes to Mongoloids. Shock. Panic. His hand pushed out and found the wall, and he braced himself with it. Then he went back toward the door again slowly. I could see him creeping up on it, stalking it as though it were something alive. He opened it so slenderly you couldn't see it at all, peered fearfully through the crack. Then he closed it, and he came back, zigzag, off balance from sheer reflex dismay. He toppled into a chair and snatched up a drink. Out of the bottle neck itself this time. And even while he was holding it to his lips, his head was turned looking over his shoulder at the door that had suddenly thrown his secret in his face.

I put the glass down.

Guilty! Guilty as all hell, and the police be damned!

My hand started toward the phone, came back again. What was the use? They wouldn't listen now any more than they had before. "You should have seen his face, etc." And I could heard Boyne's answer: "Anyone gets a jolt from an anonymous letter, true or false. You would yourself." They had a real live Mrs. Thorwald to show me—or thought they had. I'd have to show them the dead one, to prove that they both weren't one and the same. I, from my window, had to show them a body.

Well, he'd have to show me first.

It took hours before I got it. I kept pegging away at it, pegging away at it, while the afternoon wore away. Meanwhile he was pacing back and forth there like a caged panther. Two minds with but one thought, turned inside-out in my case. How to keep it hidden, how to see that it wasn't kept hidden.

I was afraid he might try to light out, but if he intended doing that he was going to wait until after dark, apparently, so I had a little time yet. Possibly he didn't want to himself, unless he was driven to it—still felt that it was more dangerous than to stay.

The customary sights and sounds around me went on unnoticed, while the main stream of my thoughts pounded like a torrent against that one obstacle stubbornly damming them up: how to get him to give the location away to me, so that I could give it away in turn to the police.

I was dimly conscious, I remember, of the landlord or somebody bringing in a prospective tenant to look at the sixth-floor apartment, the one that had already been finished. This was two over Thorwald's; they were still at work on the in-between one. At one point an odd little bit of synchronization, completely accidental of course, cropped up. Landlord and tenant both happened to be near the living room windows on the sixth at the same moment that Thorwald was near those on the fourth. Both parties moved onward simultaneously into the kitchen from there, and, passing the blind spot on the wall, appeared next at the kitchen windows. It was uncanny, they were almost like precision-strollers or puppets manipulated on one and the same string. It probably wouldn't have happened again just like that in another fifty years. Immediately afterwards they digressed, never to repeat themselves like that again.

The thing was, something about it had disturbed me. There had been some slight flaw or hitch to mar its smoothness. I tried for a moment or two to figure out what it had been, and couldn't. The landlord and tenant had gone now, and only Thorwald was in sight. My unaided memory wasn't enough to recapture it for me. My eyesight might have if it had been repeated, but it wasn't.

It sank into my subconscious, to ferment there like yeast, while I went back to the main problem at hand.

I got it finally. It was well after dark, but I finally hit on a way. It mightn't work, it was cumbersome and roundabout, but it was the only way I could think of. An alarmed turn of the head, a quick precautionary step in one certain direction, was all I needed. And to get this brief, flickering, transitory give-away, I needed two phone calls and an absence of about half an hour on his part between them.

I leafed a directory by matchlight until I'd found what I wanted: *Thorwald, Lars, 525 Bndct. . . . SWansea 5-2114.*

I blew out the match, picked up the phone in the dark. It was like television. I could see to the other end of my call, only not along the wire but by a direct channel of vision from window to window.

He said, "Hullo?" gruffly.

I thought: How strange this is. I've been accusing him of murder for three days straight, and only now I'm hearing his voice for the first time.

I didn't try to disguise my own voice. After all, he'd never see me and I'd never see him. I said: "You got my note?"

He said guardedly: "Who is this?"

"Just somebody who happens to know."

He said craftily: "Know what?"

"Know what you know. You and I, we're the only ones."

He controlled himself well. I didn't hear a sound. But he didn't know he was open another way too. I had the glass balanced there at proper height on two large books on the sill. Through the window I saw him pull open the collar of his shirt as though its stricture was intolerable. Then he backed his hand over his eyes like you do when there's a light blinding you.

His voice came back firmly. "I don't know what you're talking about."

"Business, that's what I'm talking about. It should be worth something to me, shouldn't it? To keep it from going any further." I wanted to keep him from catching on that it was the windows. I still needed them. I needed them now more than ever. "You weren't very careful about your door the other night. Or maybe the draft swung it open a little."

That hit him where he lived. Even the stomach-heave reached me over the wire. "You didn't see anything. There wasn't anything to see."

"That's up to you. Why should I go to the police?" I coughed a little. "If it would pay me not to."

"Oh," he said. And there was relief of a sort in it. "D'you want to see me? Is that it?"

"That would be the best way, wouldn't it? How much can you bring with you for now?"

"I've only got about seventy dollars around here."

"All right then we can arrange the rest for later. Do you know where Lakeside Park is? I'm near there now. Suppose we make it there." That was about thirty minutes away. Fifteen there and fifteen back. "There's a little pavilion as you go in."

"How many of you are there?" he asked cautiously.

"Just me. It pays to keep things to yourself. That way you don't have to divvy up."

He seemed to like that too. "I'll take a run out," he said, "just to see what it's all about."

I watched him more closely than ever, after he'd hung up. He flitted straight through to the end room, the bedroom, that he didn't go near anymore. He disappeared into a clothes-closet in there, stayed a minute, came out again. He must have taken something out of a hidden cranny or niche in there that even the dicks had missed. I could tell by the piston-like motion of his hand, just before it disappeared inside his coat, what it was. A gun.

It's a good thing, I thought, I'm not out there in Lakeside Park waiting for my seventy dollars.

The place blacked and he was on his way.

I called Sam in. "I want you to do something for me that's a little risky. In fact, damn risky. You might break a leg, or you might get shot, or you might even get pinched. We've been together ten years, and I wouldn't ask you anything like that if I could do it myself. But I can't, and it's got to be done." Then I told him. "Go out the back way, cross the backyard fences, and see if you can get into that fourth-floor flat up the fire escape. He's left one of the windows down a little from the top."

"What do you want me to look for?"

"Nothing." The police had been there already, so what was the good of that? "There are three rooms over there. I want you to disturb everything just a little bit, in all three, to show someone's been in there. Turn up the edge of each rug a little, shift every chair and table around a little, leave the closet doors standing out. Don't pass up a thing. Here, keep your eyes on this." I took off my own wristwatch, strapped it on him. "You've got twenty-five minutes, starting from now. If you stay within those twenty-five minutes, nothing will happen to you. When you see they're up, don't wait any longer, get out and get out fast."

"Climb back down?"

"No." He wouldn't remember, in his excitement, if he'd left the windows up or not. And I didn't want him to connect danger with the back of his place, but with the front. I wanted to keep my own window out of it. "Latch the window down tight, let yourself out the door, and beat it out of the building the front way, for your life!"

"I'm just an easy mark for you," he said ruefully, but he went.

He came out through our own basement door below me, and scrambled over the fences. If anyone had challenged him from one of the surrounding windows, I was going to backstop for him, explain I'd sent him down to look for something. But no one did. He made it pretty good for anyone his age. He isn't so young anymore. Even the fire escape backing the flat, which was drawn up short, he managed to contact by standing up on something. He got in, lit the light, looked over at me. I motioned him to go ahead, not weaken.

I watched him at it. There wasn't any way I could protect him now that he was in there. Even Thorwald would be within his rights in shooting him down—this was break and entry. I had to stay in back behind the scenes, like I had been all along. I couldn't get out in front of him as a lookout and shield him. Even the dicks had a lookout posted.

He must have been tense, doing it. I was twice as tense, watching him do it. The twenty-five minutes took fifty to go by. Finally, he came over to the window, latched it fast. The lights went, and he was out. He'd made it. I blew out a bellyful of breath that was twenty-five minutes old.

I heard him keying the street door, and when he came up I said warningly: "Leave the light out in here. Go and build yourself a great big two-story whiskey punch; you're as close to white as you'll ever be."

Thorwald came back twenty-nine minutes after he'd left for Lakeside Park. A pretty slim margin to hang a man's life on. So now for the finale of the long-winded business, and here was hoping. I got my second phone call in before he had time to notice anything amiss. It was tricky timing but I'd been sitting there with the receiver ready in my hand, dialing the number over and over, then killing it each time. He came in on the 2 of 5-2114, and I saved that much time. The ring started before his hand came away from the light switch.

This was the one that was going to tell the story.

"You were supposed to bring money, not a gun; that's why I didn't show up." I saw the jolt that threw into him. The window still had to stay out of it. "I saw you tap the inside of your coat, where you had it, as you came out on the street." Maybe he hadn't, but he wouldn't remember now whether he had or not. You usually do when you're packing a gun and aren't a habitual carrier.

"Too bad you had your trip out and back for nothing. I didn't waste my time while you were gone, though. I know more now than I knew before." This was the important part. I had the glass up and I was practically fluoroscoping him. "I've found out where—it is. You know what I mean. I know now where you've got—it. I was there while you were out."

Not a word. Just quick breathing.

"Don't you believe me? Look around. Put the receiver down and take a look for yourself. I found it."

He put it down, moved as far as the living room entrance, and touched off the lights. He just looked around him once, in a sweeping, all-embracing stare, that didn't come to a head on any one fixed point, didn't center at all.

He was smiling grimly when he came back to the phone. All he said, softly and with malignant satisfaction, was: "You're a liar."

Then I saw him lay the receiver down and take his hand off it. I hung up at my end.

The test had failed. And yet it hadn't. He hadn't given the location away as I'd hoped he would. And yet that "You're a liar" was a tacit admission that it was there to be found, somewhere around him, somewhere on those premises. In such a good place that he didn't have to worry about it, didn't even have to look to make sure.

So there was a kind of sterile victory in my defeat. But it wasn't worth a damn to me.

He was standing there with his back to me, and I couldn't see what he was doing. I knew the phone was somewhere in front of him, but I thought he was just standing there pensive behind it. His head was slightly lowered, that was all. I'd hung up at my end. I didn't even see his elbow move. And if his index finger did, I couldn't see it.

He stood like that a moment or two, then finally he moved aside. The lights went out over there; I lost him. He was careful not even to strike matches, like he sometimes did in the dark.

My mind no longer distracted by having him to look at, I turned to trying to recapture something else—that troublesome little hitch in synchronization that had occurred this afternoon, when the renting agent and he both moved simultaneously from one window to the next. The closest I could get was this: it was like when you're looking at someone through a pane of imperfect glass, and a flaw in the glass distorts the symmetry of the reflected image for a second, until it has gone on past that point. Yet that wouldn't do, that was not it. The windows had been open and there had been no glass between. And I hadn't been using the lens at the time.

My phone rang. Boyne, I supposed. It wouldn't be anyone else at this hour. Maybe, after reflecting on the way he'd jumped all over me—I said "Hello" unguardedly, in my own normal voice.

There wasn't any answer.

I said: "Hello? Hello? Hello?" I kept giving away samples of my voice. There wasn't a sound from first to last.

I hung up finally. It was still dark over there, I noticed.

Sam looked in to check out. He was a bit thick-tongued from his restorative drink. He said something about "Awri' if I go now?" I half heard him. I was trying to figure out another way of trapping *him* over there into giving away the right spot. I motioned my consent absently.

He went a little unsteadily down the stairs to the ground floor and after a delaying moment or two I heard the street door close after him. Poor Sam, he wasn't much used to liquor.

I was left alone in the house, one chair the limit of my freedom of movement.

Suddenly a light went on over there again, just momentarily, to go right out again afterwards. He must have needed it for something, to locate something that he had already been looking for and found he wasn't able to put his hands on readily without it. He found it, whatever it was, almost immediately, and moved back at once to put the lights out again. As he turned to do so, I saw him give a glance out the window. He didn't come to the window to do it, he just shot it out in passing.

Something about it struck me as different from any of the others I'd seen him give in all the time I'd been watching him. If you can qualify such an elusive thing as a glance, I would have termed it a glance with purpose. It was certainly anything but vacant or random, it had a bright spark of fixity in it. It wasn't one of those precautionary sweeps I'd seen him give, either. It hadn't started over on the other side and worked its way around to my side, the right. It had hit dead-center at my bay window, for just a split second while it lasted, and then was gone again. And the lights were gone, and he was gone.

Sometimes your senses take things in without your mind translating them into their proper meaning. My eyes saw that look. My mind refused to smelter it properly. "It was meaningless," I thought. "An unintentional bull's-eye, that just happened to hit square over here, as he went toward the lights on his way out."

Delayed action. A wordless ring of the phone. To test a voice? A period of bated darkness following that, in which two could have played at the same game—stalking one another's window-squares, unseen. A last-moment flicker of the lights, that was bad strategy but unavoidable. A parting glance, radioactive with malignant intention. All these things sank in without fusing. My eyes did their job, it was my mind that didn't—or at least took its time about it.

Seconds went by in packages of sixty. It was very still around the familiar quadrangle formed by the back of the houses. Sort of a breathless stillness. And then a sound came into it, starting up from nowhere, nothing. The unmistakable, spaced clicking a cricket makes in the silence of the night. I thought of Sam's superstition about them, that he claimed had never failed to fulfill itself yet. If that was the case, it looked bad for somebody in one of these slumbering houses around here—

Sam had been gone only about ten minutes. And now he was back again, he must have forgotten something. That drink was responsible. Maybe his hat, or maybe even the key to his own quarters uptown. He knew I couldn't come down and let him in, and he was trying to be quiet about it, thinking perhaps I'd dozed off. All I could hear was this faint jiggling down at the lock of the front door. It was one of those old-fashioned stoop houses, with an outer pair of storm doors that were allowed to swing free all night, and then a small vestibule, and then the inner door, worked by a simple iron key. The liquor had made his hand a little unreliable, although he'd had this difficulty once or twice before, even without it. A match would have helped him find the keyhole quicker, but then, Sam doesn't smoke. I knew he wasn't likely to have one on him.

The sound had stopped now. He must have given up, gone away again, decided to let whatever it was go until tomorrow. He hadn't gotten in, because I knew his noisy way of letting doors coast shut by themselves too well, and there hadn't been any sound of that sort, that loose slap he always made.

Then suddenly it exploded. Why at this particular moment, I don't know. That was some mystery of the inner workings of my own mind. It flashed like waiting gunpowder which a spark has finally reached along a slow train. Drove all thought of Sam, and the front door, and this and that completely out of my head. It had been waiting there since mid-afternoon today, and only now— More of that delayed action. Damn that delayed action.

The renting agent and Thorwald had both started from the living room window. An intervening gap of blind wall, and both had reappeared at the kitchen window, still one above the other. But some sort of a hitch or flaw or jump had taken place, right there, that bothered me. The eye is a reliable surveyor. There wasn't anything the matter with their timing, it was with their parallel-ness, or whatever the word is. The hitch had been vertical, not horizontal. There had been an upward "jump."

Now I had it, now I knew. And it couldn't wait. It was too good. They wanted a body? Now I had one for them.

Sore or not, Boyne would have to listen to me now. I didn't waste any time, I dialed the precinct-house then and there in the dark, working the slots in my lap by memory alone. They didn't make much noise going around, just a light click. Not even as distinct as that cricket out there—

"He went home long ago," the desk sergeant said.

This couldn't wait. "All right, give me his home phone number."

He took a minute, came back again. "Trafalgar," he said. Then nothing more.

"Well? Trafalgar what?" Not a sound.

"Hello? Hello?" I tapped it. "Operator, I've been cut off. Give me that party again." I couldn't get her either.

I hadn't been cut off. My wire had been cut. That had been too sudden, right in the middle of— And to be cut like that it would have to be done somewhere right here inside the house with me. Outside it went underground.

Delayed action. This time final, fatal, altogether too late. A voiceless ring of the phone. A direction-finder of a look from over there. "Sam" seemingly trying to get in a while ago.

Surely, death was somewhere inside the house here with me. And I couldn't move, I couldn't get up out of this chair. Even if I had gotten through to Boyne just now, that would have been too late. There wasn't time enough now for one of those camera-finishes in this. I could have shouted out the window to that gallery of sleeping rear-window neighbors around me, I supposed. It would have brought them to their windows. It couldn't have brought them over here in time. By the time they had even figured which particular house it was coming from, it would stop again, be over with. I didn't open my mouth. Not because I was brave, but because it was so obviously useless.

He'd be up in a minute. He must be on the stairs now, although I couldn't hear him. Not even a creak. A creak would have been a relief, would have placed him. This was like being shut up in the dark with the silence of a gliding, coiling cobra somewhere around you.

There wasn't a weapon in the place with me. There were books there on the wall, in the dark, within reach. Me, who never read. The former owner's books. There was a bust of Rousseau or Montesquieu, I'd never been able to decide which, one of those gents with flowing manes, topping them. It was a monstrosity, bisque clay, but it too dated from before my occupancy.

I arched my middle upward from the chair seat and clawed desperately up at it. Twice my fingertips slipped off it, then at the third raking I got it to teeter, and the fourth brought it down into my lap, pushing me down into the chair. There was a steamer rug under me. I didn't need it around me in this weather, I'd been using it to soften the seat of the chair. I tugged it out from under and mantled it around me like an Indian brave's blanket. Then I squirmed far down in the chair, let my head and one shoulder dangle out over the arm, on the side next to the wall. I hoisted the bust to my other, upward shoulder, balanced it there precariously for a second head, blanket tucked around its ears. From the back, in the dark, it would look—I hoped—

I proceeded to breathe adenoidally, like someone in heavy upright sleep.

It wasn't hard. My own breath was coming nearly that labored anyway, from tension.

He was good with knobs and hinges and things. I never heard the door open, and this one, unlike the one downstairs, was right behind me. A little eddy of air puffed through the dark at me. I could feel it because my scalp, the real one, was all wet at the roots of the hair right then.

If it was going to be a knife or head-blow, the dodge might give me a second chance, that was the most I could hope for, I knew. My arms and shoulders are hefty. I'd bring him down on me in a bear-hug after the first slash or drive, and break his neck or collarbone against me. If it was going to be a gun, he'd get me anyway in the end. A difference of a few seconds. He had a gun, I knew, that he was going to use on me in the open, over at Lakeside Park. I was hoping that here, indoors, in order to make his own escape more practicable—

Time was up.

The flash of the shot lit up the room for a second, it was so dark. Or at least the corners of it, like flickering weak lightning. The bust bounced on my shoulder and disintegrated into chunks.

I thought he was jumping up and down on the floor for a minute with frustrated rage. Then when I saw him dart by me and lean over the window sill to look for a way out, the sound transferred itself rearwards and downwards, became a pummeling with hoof and hip at the street door. The camera-finish after all. But he still could have killed me five times.

I flung my body down into the narrow crevice between chair arm and wall, but my legs were still up, and so was my head and that one shoulder.

He whirled, fired at me so close that it was like looking a sunrise in the face. I didn't feel it, so—it hadn't hit.

"You—" I heard him grunt to himself. I think it was the last thing he said. The rest of his life was all action, not verbal.

He flung over the sill on one arm and dropped into the yard. Two-story drop. He made it because he missed the cement, landed on the sod-strip in the middle. I jacked myself up over the chair arm and flung myself bodily forward at the window, nearly hitting it chin first.

He went all right. When life depends on it, you go. He took the first fence, rolled over that bellywards. He went over the second like a cat, hands and feet pointed together in a spring. Then he was back in the rear yard of his own building. He got up on something, just about like Sam had— The rest was all footwork, with quick little corkscrew twists at each landing stage. Sam had latched his windows down when he was over there, but he'd reopened one of them for ventilation on his return. His whole life depended now on that casual unthinking act—

Second, third. He was up to his own windows. He'd made it. Something went wrong. He veered out away from them in another pretzel-twist, flashed up toward the fifth, the one above. Something sparked in the darkness of one of his own windows, where he'd been just now, and a shot thudded heavily out around the quadrangle-enclosure like a big bass drum.

He passed the fifth, the sixth, got up to the roof. He'd made it a second time. Gee, he loved life! The guys in his own windows couldn't get him, he was over them in a straight line and there was too much fire escape interlacing in the way.

I was too busy watching him to watch what was going on around me. Suddenly Boyne was next to me, sighing. I heard him mutter: "I almost hate to do this, he's got to fall so far."

He was balanced on the roof parapet up there, with a star right over his head. An unlucky star. He stayed a minute too long, trying to kill before he was killed. Or maybe he was killed, and knew it.

A shot cracked, high up against the sky, the window pane flew apart all over the two of us, and one of the books snapped right behind me.

Boyne didn't say anything more about hating to do it. My face was pressing outward against his arm. The recoil of his elbow jarred my teeth. I blew a clearing through the smoke to watch him go.

It was pretty horrible. He took a minute to show anything, standing up there on the parapet. Then he let his gun go, as if to say: "I won't need it anymore." Then he went after it. He missed the fire escape entirely, came all the way down on the outside. He landed so far out he hit one of the projecting planks, down there out of sight. It bounced his body up, like a springboard. Then it landed again—for good. And that was all.

I said to Boyne: "I got it. I got it finally. The fifth-floor flat, the one over his, that they're still working on. The cement kitchen floor, raised above the level of the other rooms. They wanted to comply with the fire laws and also obtain a dropped living room effect, as cheaply as possible. Dig it up—"

He went right over then and there, down through the basement and over the fences to save time. The electricity wasn't turned on yet in that one, they had to use their torches. It didn't take them long at that, once they'd got started. In about half an hour he came to the window and wig-wagged over for my benefit. It meant yes.

He didn't come over until nearly eight in the morning; after they'd tidied up and taken them away. Both away, the hot dead and the cold dead. He said: "Jeff, I take it all back. That damn fool that I sent up there about the trunk—well, it wasn't his fault, in a way. I'm to blame. He didn't have orders to check on the woman's description, only on the contents of the trunk. He came back and touched on it in a general way. I go home and I'm in bed already and suddenly pop! into my brain—one of the tenants I questioned two whole days ago had given us a few details and they didn't tally with his on several important points. Talk about being slow to catch on!"

"I've had that all the way through this damn thing," I admitted ruefully. "I call it delayed action. It nearly killed me."

"I'm a police officer and you're not."

"That how you happened to shine at the right time?"

"Sure. We came over to pick him up for questioning. I left them planted there when we saw he wasn't in, and came on over here by myself to square it up with you while we were waiting. How did you happen to hit on that cement floor?"

I told him about the freak synchronization. "The renting agent showed up taller at the kitchen window in proportion to Thorwald, than he had been a moment before when both were at the living room windows together. It was no secret that they were putting in cement floors, topped by a cork composition, and raising them considerable. But it took on new meaning. Since the top floor one has been finished for some time, it had to be the fifth. Here's the way I lined up, just in theory. She's been in ill health for years, and he's been out of work, and he got sick of that and of her both. Met this other—"

"She'll be here later today, they're bringing her down under arrest."

"He probably insured her for all he could get, and then started to poison her slowly, trying not to leave any trace. I imagine—and remember, this is pure conjecture—she caught him at it that night the light was on all night. Caught on in some way, or caught him in the act. He lost his head, and did the very thing he had wanted all along to avoid doing. Killed her by violence—strangulation or a blow. The rest had to be hastily improvised. He got a better break than he deserved at that. He thought of the apartment upstairs, went up and looked around. They'd just finished laying the floor, the cement hadn't hardened yet, and the materials were still around. He gouged a trough out of it just wide enough to take her body, put her in it, mixed fresh cement and re-cemented over her, possibly raising the general level of the flooring an inch or two so that she'd be safely covered. A permanent, odorless coffin. Next day the workmen came back, laid down the cork surfacing on top of it without noticing anything; I suppose he'd used one of their own trowels to smooth it. Then he sent his accessory upstate fast, near where his wife had been several summers before, but to a different farmhouse where she wouldn't be recognized, along with the trunk keys. Sent the trunk up after her, and dropped himself an already used post card into his mailbox, with the year-date blurred. In a week or two she would have probably committed 'suicide' up there as Mrs. Anna Thorwald. Despondency due to ill health. Written him a farewell note and left her clothes beside some body of deep water. It was risky, but they might have succeeded in collecting the insurance at that."

By nine Boyne and the rest had gone. I was still sitting there in the chair, too keyed up to sleep. Sam came in and said: "Here's Doc Preston."

He showed up rubbing his hands, in that way he has. "Guess we can take that cast off your leg now. You must be tired of sitting there all day doing nothing."

PART II

SCIENCE FICTION:

KUBRICK AND SPIELBERG, SPIELBERG AND KUBRICK

"The Sentinel"
by Arthur C. Clarke

2001: A Space Odyssey, directed by Stanley Kubrick, 1968

"Supertoys Last All Summer Long"
by Brian Aldiss

A.I. Artificial Intelligence, directed by Steven Spielberg and Stanley Kubrick, 2001

"The Minority Report"
by Philip K. Dick

Minority Report, directed by Steven Spielberg, 2002

You can belong, too, if you like to spend your days wondering about the nature of reality and the deceptiveness of time. Or if you're interested in extrapolating the latest scientific theory in an effort to assuage your cosmic loneliness. Or if you think a lot about the desirability of artificial intelligence and cloning but can't decide whether it's a good way to achieve utopia. You'll have to suffer the label of geek. Your work may not be appreciated in your lifetime—or ever. You can't care too much about money (unless you work in the movies). And you can't slip and say you're into "sci-fi," because it's "SF" to everyone who matters. But if you meet these criteria and can tell a good story—written or visual—you will probably be welcomed into the very small and very chummy club of science fiction professionals. So chummy, in fact, that its members practically finish one another's sentences—or movies, as the case may be. Brian Aldiss spent two years writing a screenplay based on Philip K. Dick's novel *Martian Time-Slip.* Arthur C. Clarke worked on the screenplay for *A.I. Artificial Intelligence*, based on Aldiss's story "Supertoys Last All Summer Long." And of course, Steven Spielberg filmed *A.I.* based on the work Stanley Kubrick (and many others) did on that project before Kubrick's death.

But before all that there was Kubrick's first groundbreaking science fiction tour de force, *2001: A Space Odyssey.* When Kubrick decided his follow-up to *Dr. Strangelove* would be SF, he did the same thing as always: read copiously. "The hardest thing for me," he once said, ". . . is finding the story. It's much harder than financing, writing the script, making the film, editing it, whatever. . . . When I'm looking for a story, I read an average of about five hours each day." His first choice for collaborator was Arthur C. Clarke. Later, Clarke said: "When I met Stanley Kubrick for the first time . . . he had already absorbed an immense amount of science fact and science fiction, and was in some danger of believing in flying saucers; I felt I had arrived just in time to save him from this gruesome fate." They started their project (private title: *How the Solar System Was Won*) with six of Clarke's stories as a baseline, then began brainstorming an average of five hours a day. In the end, they narrowed the source material down to

"The Sentinel," and Clarke bought back the other five stories. Clarke describes "The Sentinel" as a "mood piece," one of his earliest stories to explore what became a familiar theme: the hope "that humanity's loneliness in the universe will be remedied by contact with other-world living beings."

People who have worked with Kubrick describe it as a little like being swallowed up by a cold and intelligent creature with many tentacles and a passion for late-night phone calls. Clarke kept a diary of their progress: *July 9. Spent much of the day teaching Stanley to use the slide rule—he's fascinated. July 10. Joined Stanley to discuss plot development, but spent almost all the time arguing about Cantor's Theory of Transfinite Groups. . . . July 11. Now have everything—except the plot.* Admittedly, Kubrick and Clarke took an unusual approach. Rather than immediately tackling a screenplay—"about the least ideal way of communicating information, especially if it's visual or emotional" (according to Kubrick)—Kubrick suggested they expand the story into a novel. Instead of a novel, though, they ended up with what Kubrick later called a "fifty-thousand-word prose 'thing.'" At this point, work on the novel and screenplay became concurrent, with Clarke taking ownership of the novel and Kubrick the screenplay, but with each giving feedback on the other's work. Clarke, who was occasionally frustrated by this process—he had hoped the novel would precede the movie—ended up making his final revisions to the novel "after we had seen the rushes based on the screenplay based on earlier versions of the novel . . . and so on."

They may have appeared to be a mismatched couple—Clarke the dapper English gentleman and Kubrick the wild-eyed, iconoclastic Bronxite—but they had two important things in common. Both were information junkies and both had hubris to spare—each was looking for a metaphor to explain the universe. Kubrick favored fairy tales and myths. Clarke was partial to symbols. In the end, Kubrick decided that the best way to convey his ideas was to let the film work as a series of deliberately ambiguous images. Out went the explanatory voiceovers he and Clarke had written. "I tried to create a visual experience," Kubrick said, ". . . that bypasses verbalized pigeonholing and directly penetrates the subconscious with an emotional and philosophic content."

At first, many people found his approach baffling. The *New York Times* labeled it "somewhere between hypnotic and immensely boring." Pauline Kael said, "It's a bad, bad sign when a movie director begins to think of himself as a myth-maker, and this limp myth of a grand plan that justifies slaughter and ends with resurrection has been around before." The audience at the film's premier didn't know what to think; many of them laughed at the opening "Dawn of Man" sequence. The film eventually found its audience, though—particularly among potheads—and it became a pop-culture phenomenon cleverly advertised as the "ultimate trip." Now one of the highest-grossing films of all time, it is widely considered a masterpiece. It is also one of the best examples of a director playing magician, with the resulting adaptation a complete visual reinvention. Many of Kubrick's technical innovations have become standard practice today. "I think it gives you the opportunity of seeing two attempts in two different mediums, print and film, to express the same basic concept and story," Kubrick said. "In both cases, of course, the treatment must accommodate to the necessities of the medium."

The success of *2001* made Clarke both rich and famous, a rare thing among SF practitioners. He has also racked up an impressive number of awards in his long career, including Nebulas and Hugos, and a 1994 Nobel Peace Prize nomination for his early work with satellite technology. He was awarded the title of Grand Master by Science Fiction Writers of America and was knighted by Queen Elizabeth in 1997. Sir Clarke is not shy about talking about his accomplishments—*ego* is a word that comes up often in reference to him—but he also has an altruistic side. From his base in Sri Lanka, where he has lived since 1956, he has set up (and partially financed) the Arthur C. Clarke Centre for Modern Technologies, an organization dedicated to the development of cheap communication systems tailored to the agricultural needs of the Third World. According to his colleague Brian Aldiss: "Such a project harnesses expensive space technologies in a way which answers those critics who have argued that it is immoral to waste funds on the romantic gesture of spaceflight when problems of poverty, illness, and hunger remain in the world. That advanced technology would eventually benefit all of Mankind has always been Clarke's belief—perhaps naïve, but visionaries often function more effectively for a touch of naïveté about them."

Aldiss himself has remained in England, and the difference between the two men can be glimpsed in this entry from his autobiography: "When Arthur C. Clarke wrote from Sri Lanka to tell me of all the important events in which he was taking part, I wrote back telling him that Margaret and I had just bought a pound of sausages in Abingdon." Where Clarke looks outward, Aldiss looks inward—and this, according to Aldiss, was exactly the trouble with Kubrick's adaptation of his story "Supertoys Last All Summer Long." "I had refused to see my vignette as a full-scale motion picture. Stanley reassured me. . . . [H]e had taken Arthur C. Clarke's short story . . . and made it into a major picture. We could do the same with my story. Only later did I see the flaw in this line of reasoning: while Arthur's story looks . . . to the solar system, my story looks inward."

Like Clarke, Aldiss is a Grand Master with multiple Nebulas and Hugos to his credit. His path is a singular one, though. It sometimes intersects with mainstream SF but is just as likely to go off in another direction entirely. He's written mainstream fiction, travelogues, poetry, humorous essays, and several memoirs, as well as a couple of stylistically experimental SF novels. Despite his forays into other territories, Aldiss has proven himself to be one of SF's greatest ambassadors. He's adept at the improvisatory public conversations and monologues that are part and parcel of SF's fandom, and even went so far as to create a show, *Science Fiction Blues: The Show That Brian Aldiss Took on the Road.* His biggest contribution to the understanding of SF, though, is *The Trillion Year Spree* (formerly *The Billion Year Spree*), a history and critical analysis of the genre, unprecedented in both range and depth. Characteristically, he avoids mention of his own fiction, but elsewhere he has expressed his preference for stories that deal with people and society over those that are filled only with technology or ideas. "The use of the future is a metaphor for today," he has said, "a mirror in which we see an abstract of our present homes and woes."

Aldiss views "Supertoys" as just such a mirror: a simple tale about a boy who cannot please his mother. But domestic drama, even involving androids, is not Kubrickian material. Nor was simplicity his forte. For years Aldiss reported to "Castle Kubrick" and made vain and often far-fetched attempts to adapt his story. "We spent some while turning 'Supertoys' into a concentration camp story," Aldiss remembers. "It seemed to me an outré path to take, even while I recognized that outré paths were his strong point." He was not taken with Kubrick's fairy-tale approach either. "His idea of inserting a Blue Fairy—for he had overdosed on *Pinocchio*—was anathema to me." Not surprisingly, the two men eventually parted ways. "My belief," Adiss says, "is that he was basically mistaken. Obsessed with the big blockbuster SF movies of the time, he was determined to take my sorrowing domestic scene out into the galaxy."

Kubrick continued to work on the story without Aldiss—and continued to have trouble. He enlisted new SF talent, including Arthur C. Clarke, Ian Watson, and Bob Shaw. He commissioned thousands of sketches and storyboards. In 1994, he enticed Steven Spielberg to work on it with him, with Spielberg to direct their coauthored script. "Stanley wanted a screenplay written in England," Spielberg remembers, "which meant Stanley would have had about ninety-nine percent control. . . ." Wisely, Spielberg extracted himself, and in 1995 Kubrick placed *A.I.* on a shelf and moved on to *Eyes Wide Shut.* He still continued to talk to Spielberg about it, though. According to Jan Harlan, Kubrick's brother-in-law and business partner, "Stanley thought Spielberg might be the right person to direct this for several reasons. Using a real child actor is possible for Steven, who would shoot this film in twenty weeks while Stanley knew he would take years." And Spielberg is a wizard with special effects. In 1999, Kubrick died unexpectedly, after having spent the better part of two decades on the project. Spielberg decided to direct the film as a tribute to him. But not before rewriting it. Again.

By then he had access to two additional stories that Aldiss had written to complete the "Supertoys" cycle. "I was like an archaeologist," Spielberg says, "picking up the pieces of a civilization, putting Stanley's picture back together again." An apt comparison, given the strata of material available. Another challenge was that of style: Spielberg's couldn't have been more different from Kubrick's. When the film was finished, some in the audience found the combination interesting and demanding—others didn't. *Newsweek*: "The result is fascinating—a rich, strange, problematical movie full of wild tonal shifts and bravura moviemaking." *San Francisco Chronicle*: "By the end, *A.I.* exhibits all its creators' bad traits and none of the good. So we end up with the structureless, meandering, slow-motion endlessness of Kubrick combined with the fuzzy, cuddly mindlessness of Spielberg." Like it or hate it, though, it's absolutely unique.

With *Minority Report,* Spielberg was able to let go of "Stanley's ghost and his conscience and his friendship haunting me." But he had another ghost to contend with: Philip K. Dick's. Since his death in 1982, Dick has become SF's totemic figure—part seer, part shaman. Societies and clubs discuss and dissect his ideas. They distribute newsletters and FAQs. Libraries struggle to keep his books on their shelves; they are frequently stolen or never returned. Web sites, dissertations, and movie adaptations (*Blade Runner, Total Recall, Paycheck*) continue to proliferate. All of this would have surprised, annoyed, and probably even frightened Dick. His troubles were many: He was agoraphobic, paranoid, and haunted by a childhood diagnosis of schizophrenia. Add to this an indulgence in drugs of various sorts and you have SF's mad genius. "The Minority Report," published in 1956 in *Fantastic Universe,* is from Dick's earliest period, when he was madly cranking out stories. (In 1953, he sold fifteen stories in one month.) It contains an early iteration of several Dickian themes, including the possibility of alternate realities, multiple time-paths, and the hypersensitivity of "abnormal" persons. Like his story's mutants, Dick considered himself occasionally precognitive, and in several essays he explored the connection between precognition and mental illness. In one essay, he stated: "The mentally ill person at one time or another *knew too much.*" In another, he suggests that what distinguishes the schizophrenic is the element of time: "The schizophrenic is having it all now. . . . The whole can of film has descended on him, whereas we watch it progress frame by frame."

Although Spielberg has referred to "Minority Report" as a "gourmet popcorn movie," *weird* displaces his trademark *wonder.* "I just go along with the subject matter that interests me, and I try to acquit it in a way that is not going to play against the original intention of the story. Philip K. Dick is dark." Dick became even darker—personally and professionally—as time passed. His stories, including "Minority Report," rarely contain the complexly flawed protagonists of his novels. Nor his obsession with drug-induced states and radical political trends. That all came later. But Spielberg has also darkened with age. Beginning with *Amistad,* he feels that his films have become more grimly courageous: "There's been a, well, I'm not sure I'd call it skepticism, but a being unafraid of the dark truth, the difficult realities."

The film *Minority Report* contains a darkness (mixed with humor) that is more consistent with Dick himself, and his later work, than with the story. "We live in a society," Dick wrote in 1978, "in which spurious realities are manufactured by the media, by governments, by big corporations, by religious groups, political groups. . . . I ask, in my writing, What is real? Because unceasingly we are bombarded with pseudorealities manufactured by very sophisticated people using very sophisticated electronic mechanisms. I do not distrust their motives. I distrust their power." John Underkoffler, one of the "futurists" who worked on *Minority Report,* says of Dick, "He was one of the few guys back in the fifties who knew the truth about technology. . . . That's what makes him continue to be relevant where other authors of the same era—their shiny spaceships and ray guns look a little tarnished right now." Would Dick have foreseen retina-scan ads or robotic search spiders? Probably not. He was more concerned with ideas than with gadgetry. But the ubiquitous and invasive advertising in Spielberg's film is certainly consistent with his vision. So are the right-to-privacy issues addressed there (although, surprisingly, they are not the focus of his story). Dick purists can complain if they want to. "They never have to say it's better than the book," says Spielberg. "If they can at least say 'I was really engaged,' then I feel I've done my job."

For all its popularity, SF continues to be a small, varied, and tangled society. (The budget for *Minority Report* was rumored to be around $80 million. That of *A.I.,* somewhere around $100 million. With numbers that high, it's a playground only a few can afford.) There is one thing all SF practitioners have in common, though: a wide-ranging curiosity of the sort that asks, "My God—what if..." And everything is fodder for their questioning.* So maybe it's not out of line to ask what might have happened if Clarke had worked on a novel that Dick had adapted into a screenplay that Spielberg had storyboarded and Kubrick had filmed. Or if...

* Dick's list of the most productive sources for SF ideas includes psychology journals, the works of C. G. Jung, Oriental writings on Zen Buddhism and Taoism, historical and medieval works (especially those dealing with crafts, such as glassblowing), Greek philosophy, Roman literature of every sort, Persian religious texts, Renaissance studies on the theory of art, and German dramatic writings of the Romantic period.

The Sentinel

Arthur C. Clarke

The next time you see the full moon high in the south, look carefully at its right-hand edge and let your eye travel upward along the curve of the disk. Round about two o'clock you will notice a small, dark oval: anyone with normal eyesight can find it quite easily. It is the great walled plain, one of the finest on the Moon, known as the Mare Crisium—the Sea of Crises. Three hundred miles in diameter, and almost completely surrounded by a ring of magnificent mountains, it had never been explored until we entered it in the late summer of 1996.

Our expedition was a large one. We had two heavy freighters which had flown our supplies and equipment from the main lunar base in the Mare Serenitatis, five hundred miles away. There were also three small rockets which were intended for short-range transport over regions which our surface vehicles couldn't cross. Luckily, most of the Mare Crisium is very flat. There are none of the great crevasses so common and so dangerous elsewhere, and very few craters or mountains of any size. As far as we could tell, our powerful Caterpillar tractors would have no difficulty in taking us wherever we wished to go.

I was geologist—or selenologist, if you want to be pedantic—in charge of the group exploring the southern region of the Mare. We had crossed a hundred miles of it in a week, skirting the foothills of the mountains along the shore of what was once the ancient sea, some thousand million years before. When life was beginning on Earth, it was already dying here. The waters were retreating down the flanks of those stupendous cliffs, retreating into the empty heart of the Moon. Over the land which we were crossing, the tideless ocean had once been half a mile deep, and now the only trace of moisture was the hoarfrost one could sometimes find in caves which the searing sunlight never penetrated.

We had begun our journey early in the slow lunar dawn, and still had almost a week of Earth-time before nightfall. Half a dozen times a day we would leave our vehicle and go outside in the space suits to hunt for interesting minerals, or to place markers for the guidance of future travelers. It was an uneventful routine. There is nothing hazardous or even particularly exciting about lunar exploration. We could live comfortably for a month in our pressurized tractors, and if we ran into trouble, we could always radio for help and sit tight until one of the spaceships came to our rescue.

I said just now that there was nothing exciting about lunar exploration, but of course that isn't true. One could never grow tired of those incredible mountains, so much more rugged than the gentle hills of Earth. We never knew, as we rounded the capes and promontories of that vanished sea, what new splendors would be revealed to us. The whole southern curve of the Mare Crisium is a vast delta where a score of rivers once found their way into the ocean, fed perhaps by the torrential rains that must have lashed the mountains in the brief volcanic age when the Moon was young. Each of these ancient valleys was an invitation, challenging us to climb into the unknown uplands beyond. But we had a hundred miles still to cover, and could only look longingly at the heights which others must scale.

We kept Earth-time aboard the tractor, and precisely at 22:00 hours the final radio message would be sent out to Base and we would close down for the day. Outside, the rocks would still be burning beneath the almost vertical sun, but to us it would be night until we awoke again eight hours later. Then one of us would prepare breakfast, there would be a great buzzing of electric razors and someone would switch on the shortwave radio from Earth. Indeed, when the smell of frying sausages began to fill the cabin, it was sometimes hard to believe that we were not back on our own world—everything was so normal and homely, apart from the feeling of decreased weight and the unnatural slowness with which objects fell.

It was my turn to prepare breakfast in the corner of the main cabin that served as a galley. I can remember that moment quite vividly after all these years, for the radio had just played one of my favorite melodies, the old Welsh air "David of the White Rock." Our driver was already outside in his space suit, inspecting our Caterpillar treads. My assistant, Louis Garnett, was up forward in the control position, making some belated entries in yesterday's log.

As I stood by the frying pan, waiting, like any terrestrial housewife, for the sausages to brown, I let my gaze wander idly over the mountain walls which covered the whole of the southern horizon, marching out of sight to east and west below the curve of the Moon. They seemed only a mile or two from the tractor, but I knew that the nearest was twenty miles away. On the Moon, of course, there is no loss of detail with distance—none of that almost imperceptible haziness which softens and sometimes transfigures all far-off things on Earth.

Those mountains were ten thousand feet high, and they climbed steeply out of the plain as if ages ago some subterranean eruption had smashed them skyward through the molten crust. The base of even the nearest was hidden from sight by the steeply curving surface of the plain, for the Moon is a very little world, and from where I was standing the horizon was only two miles away.

I lifted my eyes toward the peaks which no man had ever climbed, the peaks which, before the coming of terrestrial life, had watched the retreating oceans sink sullenly into their graves, taking with them the hope and the morning promise of a world. The sunlight was beating against those ramparts with a glare that hurt the eyes, yet only a little way above them the stars were shining steadily in a sky blacker than a winter midnight on Earth.

I was turning away when my eye caught a metallic glitter high on the ridge of a great promontory thrusting out into the sea thirty miles to the west. It was a dimensionless point of light, as if a star had been clawed from the sky by one of those cruel peaks, and I imagined that some smooth rock surface was catching the sunlight and heliographing it straight into my eyes. Such things were not uncommon. When the Moon is in her second quarter, observers on Earth can sometimes see the great ranges in the Oceanus Procellarum burning with a blue-white iridescence as the sunlight flashes from their slopes and leaps again from world to world. But I was curious to know what kind of rock could be shining so brightly up there, and I climbed into the observation turret and swung our four-inch telescope round to the west.

I could see just enough to tantalize me. Clear and sharp in the field of vision, the mountain peaks seemed only half a mile away, but whatever was catching the sunlight was still too small to be resolved. Yet it seemed to have an elusive symmetry, and the summit upon which it rested was curiously flat. I stared for a long time at that glittering enigma, straining my eyes into space, until presently a smell of burning from the galley told me that our breakfast sausages had made their quarter-million-mile journey in vain.

All that morning we argued our way across the Mare Crisium while the western mountains reared higher in the sky. Even when we were out prospecting in the space suits, the discussion would continue over the radio. It was absolutely certain, my companions argued, that there had never been any form of intelligent life on the Moon. The only living things that had ever existed there were a few primitive plants and their slightly less degenerate ancestors. I knew that as well as anyone, but there are times when a scientist must not be afraid to make a fool of himself.

"Listen," I said at last, "I'm going up there, if only for my own peace of mind. That mountain's less than twelve thousand feet high—that's only two thousand under Earth gravity—and I can make the trip in twenty hours at the outside. I've always wanted to go up into those hills, anyway, and this gives me an excellent excuse."

"If you don't break your neck," said Garnett, "you'll be the laughing-stock of the expedition when we get back to Base. That mountain will probably be called Wilson's Folly from now on."

"I won't break my neck," I said firmly. "Who was the first man to climb Pico and Helicon?"

"But weren't you rather younger in those days?" asked Louis gently.

"That," I said with great dignity, "is as good a reason as any for going."

We went to bed early that night, after driving the tractor to within half a mile of the promontory. Garnett was coming with me in the morning; he was a good climber, and had often been with me on such exploits before. Our driver was only too glad to be left in charge of the machine.

At first sight, those cliffs seemed completely unscalable, but to anyone with a good head for heights, climbing is easy on a world where all weights are only a sixth of their normal value. The real danger in lunar mountaineering lies in overconfidence; a six-hundred-foot drop on the Moon can kill you just as thoroughly as a hundred-foot fall on Earth.

We made our first halt on a wide ledge about four thousand feet above the plain. Climbing had not been very difficult, but my limbs were stiff with the unaccustomed effort, and I was glad of the rest. We could still see the tractor as a tiny metal insect far down at the foot of the cliff, and we reported our progress to the driver before starting on the next ascent.

Inside our suits it was comfortably cool, for the refrigeration units were fighting the fierce sun and carrying away the body heat of our exertions. We seldom spoke to each other, except to pass climbing instructions and to discuss our best plan of ascent. I do not know what Garnett was thinking, probably that this was the craziest goose chase he had ever embarked upon. I more than half agreed with him, but the joy of climbing, the knowledge that no man had ever gone this way before, and the exhilaration of the steadily widening landscape gave me all the reward I needed.

I do not think I was particularly excited when I saw in front of us the wall of rock I had first inspected through the telescope from thirty miles away. It would level off about fifty feet above our heads, and there on the plateau would be the thing that had lured me over these barren wastes. It would be, almost certainly, nothing more than a boulder splintered ages ago by a falling meteor, and with its cleavage planes still fresh and bright in this incorruptible, unchanging silence.

There were no handholds on the rock face, and we had to use a grapnel. My tired arms seemed to gain new strength as I swung the three-pronged metal anchor round my head and sent it sailing slowly back when we pulled the rope. On the third attempt, the prongs gripped firmly and our combined weights could not shift it.

Garnett looked at me anxiously. I could tell that he wanted to go first, but I smiled back at him through the glass of my helmet and shook my head. Slowly, taking my time, I began the final ascent.

Even with my space suit, I weighed only forty pounds here, so I pulled myself up hand over hand without bothering to use my feet. At the rim I paused and waved to my companion, then I scrambled over the edge and stood upright, staring ahead of me.

You must understand that until this very moment I had been almost completely convinced that there could be nothing strange or unusual for me to find here. Almost, but not quite; it was that haunting doubt that had driven me forward. Well, it was a doubt no longer, but the haunting had scarcely begun.

I was standing on a plateau perhaps a hundred feet across. It had once been smooth—too smooth to be natural—but falling meteors had pitted and scored its surface through immeasurable eons. It had been leveled to support a glittering, roughly pyramidal structure, twice as high as a man, that was set in the rock like a gigantic, many faceted jewel.

Probably no emotion at all filled my mind in those first few seconds. Then I felt a great lifting of my heart, and a strange inexpressible joy. For I loved the Moon, and now I knew that the creeping moss of Aristarchus and Eratosthenes was not the only life she had brought forth in her youth. The old, discredited dream of the first explorers was true. There had, after all, been a lunar civilization—and I was the first to find it. That I had come perhaps a hundred million years too late did not distress me; it was enough to have come at all.

My mind was beginning to function normally, to analyze and to ask questions. Was this a building, a shrine—or something for which my language had no name? If a building, then why was it erected in so uniquely inaccessible a spot? I wondered if it might be a temple, and I could picture the adepts of some strange priesthood calling on their gods to preserve them as the life of the Moon ebbed with the dying oceans, and calling on their god in vain.

I took a dozen steps forward to examine the thing more closely, but some sense of caution kept me from going too near. I knew a little of archeology, and tried to guess the cultural level of the civilization that must have smoothed this mountain and raised the glittering mirror surfaces that still dazzled my eyes.

The Egyptians could have done it, I thought, if their workmen had possessed whatever strange materials these far more ancient architects had used. Because of the thing's smallness, it did not occur to me that I might be looking at the handiwork of a race more advanced than my own. The idea that the Moon had possessed intelligence at all was still almost too tremendous to grasp, and my pride would not let me take the final, humiliating plunge.

And then I noticed something that set the scalp crawling at the back of my neck—something so trivial and so innocent that many would never have noticed it at all. I have said that the plateau was scarred by meteors; it was also coated inches deep with the cosmic dust that is always filtering down upon the surface of any world where there are no winds to disturb it. Yet the dust and the meteor scratches ended quite abruptly in a wide circle enclosing the little pyramid, as though an invisible wall was protecting it from the ravages of time and the slow but ceaseless bombardment from space.

There was someone shouting in my earphones, and I realized that Garnett had been calling me for some time. I walked unsteadily to the edge of the cliff and signaled him to join me, not trusting myself to speak. Then I went back toward the circle in the dust. I picked up a fragment of splintered rock and tossed it gently toward the shining enigma. If the pebble had vanished at that invisible barrier, I should not have been surprised, but it seemed to hit a smooth, hemispheric surface and slide gently to the ground.

I knew then that I was looking at nothing that could be matched in the antiquity of my own race. This was not a building, but a machine, protecting itself with forces that had challenged Eternity. Those forces, whatever they might be, were still operating, and perhaps I had already come too close. I thought of all the radiations man had trapped and tamed in the past century. For all I knew, I might be as irrevocably doomed as if I had stepped into the deadly, silent aura of an unshielded atomic pile.

I remember turning then toward Garnett, who had joined me and was now standing motionless at my side. He seemed quite oblivious to me, so I did not disturb him, but I walked to the edge of the cliff in an effort to marshal my thoughts. There below me lay the Mare Crisium—Sea of Crises, indeed—strange and weird to most men, but reassuringly familiar to me. I lifted my eyes toward the crescent Earth, lying in her cradle of stars, and I wondered what her clouds had covered when these unknown builders had finished their work. Was it the steaming jungle of the Carboniferous, the bleak shoreline over which the first amphibians must crawl to conquer the land—or, earlier still, the loneliness before the coming of life?

Do not ask me why I did not guess the truth sooner—the truth that seems so obvious now. In the first excitement of my discovery, I had assumed without question that this crystalline apparition had been built by some race belonging to the Moon's remote past, but suddenly, and with overwhelming force, the belief came to me that it was as alien to the Moon as I myself.

In twenty years we had found no trace of life but a few degenerate plants. No lunar civilization, whatever its doom, could have left but a single token of its existence.

I looked at the shining pyramid again, and the more I looked, the more remote it seemed from anything that had to do with the Moon. And suddenly I felt myself shaking with a foolish, hysterical laughter, brought on by excitement and overexertion: For I had imagined that the little pyramid was speaking to me and was saying, "Sorry, I'm a stranger here myself."

It has taken us twenty years to crack that invisible shield and to reach the machine inside those crystal walls. What we could not understand, we broke at last with the savage might of atomic power and now I have seen the fragments of the lovely, glittering thing I found up there on the mountain.

They are meaningless. The mechanisms—if indeed they are mechanisms—of the pyramid belong to a technology that lies far beyond our horizon, perhaps to the technology of paraphysical forces.

The mystery haunts us all the more now that the other planets have been reached and we know that only Earth has ever been the home of intelligent life in our Universe. Nor could any lost civilization of our own world have built that machine, for the thickness of the meteoric dust on the plateau had enabled us to measure its age. It was set there upon its mountain before life had emerged from the seas of Earth.

When our world was half its present age, *something* from the stars swept through the Solar System, left this token of its passage, and went again upon its way. Until we destroyed it, that machine was still fulfilling the purpose of its builders; and as to that purpose, here is my guess.

Nearly a hundred thousand million stars are turning in the circle of the Milky Way, and long ago other races on the worlds of other suns must have scaled and passed the heights that we have reached. Think of such civilizations, far back in time against the fading afterglow of Creation, masters of a universe so young that life as yet had come only to a handful of worlds. Theirs would have been a loneliness we cannot imagine, the loneliness of gods looking out across infinity and finding none to share their thoughts.

They must have searched the star clusters as we have searched the planets. Everywhere there would be worlds, but they would be empty or peopled with crawling, mindless things. Such was our own Earth, the smoke of the great volcanoes still staining the skies, when that first ship of the peoples of the dawn came sliding in from the abyss beyond Pluto. It passed the frozen outer worlds, knowing that life could play no part in their destinies. It came to rest among the inner planets, warming themselves around the fire of the Sun and waiting for their stories to begin.

Those wanderers must have looked on Earth, circling safely in the narrow zone between fire and ice, and must have guessed that it was the favorite of the Sun's children. Here, in the distant future, would be intelligence; but there were countless stars before them still, and they might never come this way again.

So they left a sentinel, one of millions they scattered throughout the Universe, watching over all worlds with the promise of life. It was a beacon that down the ages patiently signaled the fact that no one had discovered it.

Perhaps you understand now why that crystal pyramid was set upon the Moon instead of on the Earth. Its builders were not concerned with races still struggling up from savagery. They would be interested in our civilization only if we proved our fitness to survive—by crossing space and so escaping from the Earth, our cradle. That is the challenge that all intelligent races must meet, sooner or later. It is a double challenge, for it depends in turn upon the conquest of atomic energy and the last choice between life and death.

Once we had passed that crisis, it was only a matter of time before we found the pyramid and forced it open. Now its signals have ceased, and those whose duty it is will be turning their minds upon Earth. Perhaps they wish to help our infant civilization. But they must be very, very old, and the old are often insanely jealous of the young.

I can never look now at the Milky Way without wondering from which of those banked clouds of stars the emissaries are coming. If you will pardon so commonplace a simile, we have set off the fire alarm and have nothing to do but wait.

I do not think we will have to wait for long.

Supertoys Last All Summer Long

Brian Aldiss

In Mrs. Swinton's garden, it was always summer. The lovely almond trees stood about it in perpetual leaf. Monica Swinton plucked a saffron-colored rose and showed it to David.

"Isn't it lovely?" she said.

David looked up at her and grinned without replying. Seizing the flower, he ran with it across the lawn and disappeared behind the kennel where the mowervator crouched, ready to cut or sweep or roll when the moment dictated. She stood alone on her impeccable plastic gravel path.

She had tried to love him.

When she made up her mind to follow the boy, she found him in the courtyard floating the rose in his paddling pool. He stood in the pool engrossed, still wearing his sandals.

"David, darling, do you have to be so awful? Come in at once and change your shoes and socks."

He went with her without protest into the house, his dark head bobbing at the level of her waist. At the age of three, he showed no fear of the ultrasonic dryer in the kitchen. But before his mother could reach for a pair of slippers, he wriggled away and was gone into the silence of the house.

He would probably be looking for Teddy.

Monica Swinton, twenty-nine, of graceful shape and lambent eye, went and sat in her living room, arranging her limbs with taste. She began by sitting and thinking; soon she was just sitting. Time waited on her shoulder with the maniac slowth it reserves for children, the insane, and wives whose husbands are away improving the world. Almost by reflex, she reached out and changed the wavelength of her windows. The garden faded; in its place, the city center rose by her left hand, full of crowding people, blowboats, and buildings (but she kept the sound down). She remained alone. An overcrowded world is the ideal place in which to be lonely.

• • •

The directors of Synthank were eating an enormous luncheon to celebrate the launching of their new product. Some of them wore the plastic face-masks popular at the time. All were elegantly slender, despite the rich food and drink they were putting away. Their wives were elegantly slender, despite the food and drink they too were putting away. An earlier and less sophisticated generation would have regarded them as beautiful people, apart from their eyes.

Henry Swinton, Managing Director of Synthank, was about to make a speech.

"I'm sorry your wife couldn't be with us to hear you," his neighbor said.

"Monica prefers to stay at home thinking beautiful thoughts," said Swinton, maintaining a smile.

"One would expect such a beautiful woman to have beautiful thoughts," said the neighbor.

Take your mind off my wife, you bastard, thought Swinton, still smiling.

He rose to make his speech amid applause.

After a couple of jokes, he said, "Today marks a real breakthrough for the company. It is now almost ten years since we put our first synthetic life-forms on the world market. You all know what a success they have been, particularly the miniature dinosaurs. But none of them had intelligence.

"It seems like a paradox that in this day and age we can create life but not intelligence. Our first selling line, the Crosswell Tape, sells best of all, and is the most stupid of all." Everyone laughed.

"Though three-quarters of the overcrowded world are starving, we are lucky here to have more than enough, thanks to population control. Obesity's our problem, not malnutrition. I guess there's nobody round this table who doesn't have a Crosswell working for him in the small intestine, a perfectly safe parasite tape-worm that enables its host to eat up to fifty percent more food and still keep his or her figure. Right?" General nods of agreement.

"Our miniature dinosaurs are almost equally stupid. Today, we launch an intelligent synthetic life-form—a full-size serving-man.

"Not only does he have intelligence, he has a controlled amount of intelligence. We believe people would be afraid of a being with a human brain. Our serving-man has a small computer in his cranium.

"There have been mechanicals on the market with mini-computers for brains—plastic things without life, super-toys—but we have at last found a way to link computer circuitry with synthetic flesh."

David sat by the long window of his nursery, wrestling with paper and pencil. Finally, he stopped writing and began to roll the pencil up and down the slope of the desk-lid. "Teddy!" he said.

Teddy lay on the bed against the wall, under a book with moving pictures and a giant plastic soldier. The speech-pattern of his master's voice activated him and he sat up. "Teddy, I can't think what to say!"

Climbing off the bed, the bear walked stiffly over to cling to the boy's leg. David lifted him and set him on the desk.

"What have you said so far?"

"I've said—" He picked up his letter and stared hard at it. "I've said, 'Dear Mummy, I hope you're well just now. I love you. . . .' "

There was a long silence, until the bear said, "That sounds fine. Go downstairs and give it to her."

Another long silence.

"It isn't quite right. She won't understand."

Inside the bear, a small computer worked through its program of possibilities.

"Why not do it again in crayon?"

When David did not answer, the bear repeated his suggestion. "Why not do it again in crayon?"

David was staring out of the window. "Teddy, you know what I was thinking? How do you tell what are real things from what aren't real things?"

The bear shuffled its alternatives. "Real things are good."

"I wonder if time is good."

"I don't think Mummy likes time very much. The other day, lots of days ago, she said that time went by her. Is time real, Teddy?"

"Clocks tell the time. Clocks are real. Mummy has clocks so she must like them. She has a clock on her wrist next to her dial."

David started to draw a jumbo jet on the back of his letter. "You and I are real, Teddy, aren't we?"

The bear's eyes regarded the boy unflinchingly. "You and I are real, David." It specialized in comfort.

Monica walked slowly about the house. It was almost time for the afternoon post to come over the wire. She punched the Post Office number on the dial on her wrist but nothing came through. A few minutes more.

She could take up her painting. Or she could dial her friends. Or she could wait till Henry came home. Or she could go up and play with David. . . .

She walked out into the hall and to the bottom of the stairs.

"David!"

No answer. She called again and a third time.

"Teddy!" she called, in sharper tones.

"Yes, Mummy!" After a moment's pause, Teddy's head of golden fur appeared at the top of the stairs.

"Is David in his room, Teddy?"

"David went into the garden, Mummy."

"Come down here, Teddy!"

She stood impassively, watching the little furry figure as it climbed down from step to step on its stubby limbs. When it reached the bottom, she picked it up and carried it into the living room. It lay unmoving in her arms, staring up at her. She could feel just the slightest vibration from its motor.

"Stand there, Teddy. I want to talk to you." She set him down on a tabletop, and he stood as she requested, arms set forward and open in the eternal gesture of embrace. "Teddy, did David tell you to tell me he had gone into the garden?"

The circuits of the bear's brain were too simple for artifice. "Yes, Mummy."

"So you lied to me."

"Yes, Mummy."

"Stop calling me Mummy! Why is David avoiding me? He's not afraid of me, is he?"

"No. He loves you."

"Why can't we communicate?"

"David's upstairs."

The answer stopped her dead. Why waste time talking to this machine? Why not simply go upstairs and scoop David into her arms and talk to him, as a loving mother should to a loving son? She heard the sheer weight of silence in the house, with a different quality of silence pouring out of every room. On the upper landing, something was moving very silently—David, trying to hide away from her. . . .

He was nearing the end of his speech now. The guests were attentive; so was the Press, lining two walls of the banqueting chamber, recording Henry's words and occasionally photographing him.

"Our serving-man will be, in many senses, a product of the computer. Without computers, we could never have worked through the sophisticated biochemics that go into synthetic flesh. The serving-man will also be an extension of the computer—for he will contain a computer in his own head, a microminiaturized computer capable of dealing with almost any situation he may encounter in the home. With reservations, of course." Laughter at this; many of those present knew the heated debate that had engulfed the Synthank boardroom before the decision had finally been taken to leave the serving-man neuter under his flawless uniform.

"Amid all the triumphs of our civilization—yes, and amid the crushing problems of overpopulation too—it is sad to reflect how many millions of people suffer from increasing loneliness and isolation. Our serving-man will be a boon to them; he will always answer, and the most vapid conversation cannot bore him.

"For the future, we plan more models, male and female—some of them without the limitations of this first one, I promise you!—of more advanced design, true bioelectronic beings.

"Not only will they possess their own computer, capable of individual programming; they will be linked to the World Data Network. Thus everyone will be able to enjoy the equivalent of an Einstein in their own homes. Personal isolation will then be banished forever!"

He sat down to enthusiastic applause. Even the synthetic serving-man, sitting at the table dressed in an unostentatious suit, applauded with gusto.

Dragging his satchel, David crept round the side of the house. He climbed on to the ornamental seat under the living-room window and peeped cautiously in.

His mother stood in the middle of the room. Her face was blank; its lack of expression scared him. He watched fascinated. He did not move; she did not move. Time might have stopped, as it had stopped in the garden.

At last she turned and left the room. After waiting a moment, David tapped on the window. Teddy looked round, saw him, tumbled off the table, and came over to the window. Fumbling with his paws, he eventually got it open.

They looked at each other.

"I'm no good, Teddy. Let's run away!"

"You're a very good boy. Your Mummy loves you."

Slowly, he shook his head. "If she loved me, then why can't I talk to her?"

"You're being silly, David. Mummy's lonely. That's why she had you."

"She's got Daddy. I've got nobody 'cept you, and I'm lonely."

Teddy gave him a friendly cuff over the head. "If you feel so bad, you'd better go to the psychiatrist again."

"I hate that old psychiatrist—he makes me feel I'm not real." He started to run across the lawn. The bear toppled out of the window and followed as fast as its stubby legs would allow.

Monica Swinton was up in the nursery. She called to her son once and then stood there, undecided. All was silent.

Crayons lay on his desk. Obeying a sudden impulse, she went over to the desk and opened it. Dozens of pieces of paper lay inside. Many of them were written in crayon in David's clumsy writing, with each letter picked out in a color different from the letter preceding it. None of the messages was finished.

"My dear Mummy, How are you really, do you love me as much—"

"Dear Mummy, I love you and Daddy and the sun is shining—"

"Dear dear Mummy, Teddy's helping me write to you. I love you and Teddy—"

"Darling Mummy, I'm your one and only son and I love you so much that some times—"

"Dear Mummy, you're really my Mummy and I hate Teddy—"

"Darling Mummy, guess how much I love—"

"Dear Mummy, I'm your little boy not Teddy and I love you but Teddy—"

"Dear Mummy, this is a letter to you just to say how much how ever so much—"

Monica dropped the pieces of paper and burst out crying. In their gay inaccurate colors, the letters fanned out and settled on the floor.

Henry Swinton caught the express home in high spirits, and occasionally said a word to the synthetic serving-man he was taking home with him. The serving-man answered politely and punctually, although his answers were not always entirely relevant by human standards.

The Swintons lived in one of the ritziest city-blocks, half a kilometer above the ground. Embedded in other apartments, their apartment had no windows to the outside; nobody wanted to see the overcrowded external world. Henry unlocked the door with his retina pattern-scanner and walked in, followed by the serving-man.

At once, Henry was surrounded by the friendly illusion of gardens set in eternal summer. It was amazing what Whologram could do to create huge mirages in small spaces. Behind its roses and wisteria stood their house; the deception was complete: a Georgian mansion appeared to welcome him.

"How do you like it?" he asked the serving-man.

"Roses occasionally suffer from black spot."

"These roses are guaranteed free from any imperfections."

"It is always advisable to purchase goods with guarantees, even if they cost slightly more."

"Thanks for the information," Henry said dryly. Synthetic life-forms were less than ten years old, the old android mechanicals less than sixteen; the faults of their systems were still being ironed out, year by year.

He opened the door and called to Monica.

She came out of the sitting-room immediately and flung her arms round him, kissing him ardently on cheek and lips. Henry was amazed.

Pulling back to look at her face, he saw how she seemed to generate light and beauty. It was months since he had seen her so excited. Instinctively, he clasped her tighter.

"Darling, what's happened?"

"Henry, Henry—oh, my darling, I was in despair . . . but I've just dialed the afternoon post and—you'll never believe it! Oh, it's wonderful!"

"For heaven's sake, woman, what's wonderful?"

He caught a glimpse of the heading on the photostat in her hand, still moist from the wall-receiver: Ministry of Population. He felt the color drain from his face in sudden shock and hope.

"Monica . . . Oh . . . Don't tell me our number's come up!"

"Yes, my darling, yes, we've won this week's parenthood lottery! We can go ahead and conceive a child at once!"

He let out a yell of joy. They danced round the room. Pressure of population was such that reproduction had to be strict, controlled. Childbirth required government permission. For this moment, they had waited four years. Incoherently they cried their delight.

They paused at last, gasping, and stood in the middle of the room to laugh at each other's happiness. When she had come down from the nursery, Monica had de-opaqued the windows, so that they now revealed the vista of garden beyond. Artificial sunlight was growing long and golden across the lawn—and David and Teddy were staring through the window at them.

Seeing their faces, Henry and his wife grew serious.

"What do we do about them?" Henry asked.

"Teddy's no trouble. He works well."

"Is David malfunctioning?"

"His verbal communication-center is still giving trouble. I think he'll have to go back to the factory again."

"Okay. We'll see how he does before the baby's born. Which reminds me—I have a surprise for you: help just when help is needed! Come into the hall and see what I've got."

As the two adults disappeared from the room, boy and bear sat down beneath the standard roses.

"Teddy—I suppose Mummy and Daddy are real, aren't they?"

Teddy said, "You ask such silly questions, David. Nobody knows what 'real' really means. Let's go indoors."

"First I'm going to have another rose!" Plucking a bright pink flower, he carried it with him into the house. It could lie on the pillow as he went to sleep. Its beauty and softness reminded him of Mummy.

The Minority Report

Philip K. Dick

I

The first thought Anderton had when he saw the young man was: *I'm getting bald. Bald and fat and old.* But he didn't say it aloud. Instead, he pushed back his chair, got to his feet, and came resolutely around the side of his desk, his right hand rigidly extended. Smiling with forced amiability, he shook hands with the young man.

"Witwer?" he asked, managing to make this query sound gracious.

"That's right," the young man said. "But the name's Ed to you, of course. That is, if you share my dislike for needless formality." The look on his blond overly-confident face showed that he considered the matter settled. It would be Ed and John: Everything would be agreeably cooperative right from the start.

"Did you have much trouble finding the building?" Anderton asked guardedly, ignoring the too-friendly overture. Good God, he had to hold on to something. Fear touched him and he began to sweat. Witwer was moving around the office as if he already owned it—as if he were measuring it for size. Couldn't he wait a couple of days—a decent interval?

"No trouble," Witwer answered blithely, his hands in his pockets. Eagerly, he examined the voluminous files that lined the wall. "I'm not coming into your agency blind, you understand. I have quite a few ideas of my own about the way Precrime is run."

Shakily, Anderton lit his pipe. "How is it run? I should like to know."

"Not badly," Witwer said. "In fact, quite well."

Anderton regarded him steadily. "Is that your private opinion? Or is it just cant?"

Witwer met his gaze guilelessly. "Private and public. The Senate's pleased with your work. In fact, they're enthusiastic." He added, "As enthusiastic as very old men can be."

Anderton winced, but outwardly he remained impassive. It cost him an effort, though. He wondered what Witwer really thought. What was actually going on in that closecropped skull? The young man's eyes were blue, bright—and disturbingly clever. Witwer was nobody's fool. And obviously he had a great deal of ambition.

"As I understand it," Anderton said cautiously, "you're going to be my assistant until I retire."

"That's my understanding, too," the other replied, without an instant's hesitation.

"Which may be this year, or next year—or ten years from now." The pipe in Anderton's hand trembled. "I'm under no compulsion to retire. I founded Precrime and I can stay on here as long as I want. It's purely *my* decision."

Witwer nodded, his expression still guileless. "Of course."

With an effort, Anderton cooled down a trifle. "I merely wanted to get things straight."

"From the start," Witwer agreed. "You're the boss. What you say goes." With every evidence of sincerity, he asked: "Would you care to show me the organization? I'd like to familiarize myself with the general routine as soon as possible."

As they walked along the busy, yellow-lit tiers of offices, Anderton said, "You're acquainted with the theory of precrime, of course. I presume we can take that for granted."

"I have the information publicly available," Witwer replied. "With the aid of your precog mutants, you've boldly and successfully abolished the postcrime punitive system of jails and fines. As we all realize, punishment was never much of a deterrent, and could scarcely have afforded comfort to a victim already dead."

They had come to the descent lift. As it carried them swiftly downward, Anderton said: "You've probably grasped the basic legalistic drawback to precrime methodology. We're taking in individuals who have broken no law."

"But they surely will," Witwer affirmed with conviction.

"Happily they *don't*—because we get them first, before they can commit an act of violence. So the commission of the crime itself is absolute metaphysics. We claim they're culpable. They, on the other hand, eternally claim they're innocent. And, in a sense, they are innocent."

The lift let them out, and they again paced down a yellow corridor. "In our society we have no major crimes," Anderton went on, "but we do have a detention camp full of would-be criminals."

Doors opened and closed, and they were in the analytical wing. Ahead of them rose impressive banks of equipment—the data-receptors, and the computing mechanisms that studied and restructured the incoming material. And beyond the machinery sat the three precogs, almost lost to view in the maze of wiring.

"There they are," Anderton said dryly. "What do you think of them?"

In the gloomy half-darkness the three idiots sat babbling. Every incoherent utterance, every random syllable, was analyzed, compared, reassembled in the form of visual symbols, transcribed on conventional punchcards, and ejected into various coded slots. All day long the idiots babbled, imprisoned in their special high-backed chairs, held in one rigid position by metal bands, and bundles of wiring, clamps. Their physical needs were taken care of automatically. They had no spiritual needs. Vegetable-like, they muttered and dozed and existed. Their minds were dull, confused, lost in shadows.

But not the shadows of today. The three gibbering, fumbling creatures, with their enlarged heads and wasted bodies, were contemplating the future. The analytical machinery was recording prophecies, and as the three precog idiots talked, the machinery carefully listened.

For the first time, Witwer's face lost its breezy confidence. A sick dismayed expression crept into his eyes, a mixture of shame and moral shock. "It's not—pleasant," he murmured. "I didn't realize they were so—" He groped in his mind for the right word, gesticulating. "So—deformed."

"Deformed and retarded," Anderton instantly agreed. "Especially the girl, there. Donna is forty-five years old. But she looks about ten. The talent absorbs everything; the esp-lobe shrivels the balance of the frontal area. But what do we care? We get their prophecies. They pass on what we need. They don't understand any of it, but *we* do."

Subdued, Witwer crossed the room to the machinery. From a slot he collected a stack of cards. "Are these names that have come up?" he asked.

"Obviously." Frowning, Anderton took the stack from him. "I haven't had a chance to examine them," he explained, impatiently concealing his annoyance.

Fascinated, Witwer watched the machinery pop a fresh card into the now empty slot. It was followed by a second—and a third. From the whirring disks came one card after another. "The precogs must see quite far into the future," Witwer exclaimed.

"They see a quite limited span," Anderton informed him. "One week or two ahead at the very most. Much of their data is worthless to us—simply not relevant to our line. We pass it on to the appropriate agencies. And they in turn trade data with us. Every important bureau has its cellar of treasured *monkeys.*"

"Monkeys?" Witwer stared at him uneasily. "Oh, yes, I understand. See no evil, speak no evil, et cetera. Very amusing."

"Very *apt.*" Automatically, Anderton collected the fresh cards which had been turned up by the spinning machinery. "Some of these names will be totally discarded. And most of the remainder record petty crimes: thefts, income tax evasion, assault, extortion. As I'm sure you know, Precrime has cut down felonies by ninety-nine and decimal point eight percent. We seldom get actual murder or treason. After all, the culprit knows we'll confine him in the detention camp a week before he gets a chance to commit the crime."

"When was the last time an actual murder was committed?" Witwer asked.

"Five years ago," Anderton said, pride in his voice.

"How did it happen?"

"The criminal escaped our teams. We had his name—in fact, we had all the details of his crime, including the victim's name. We knew the exact moment, the location of the planned act of violence. But in spite of us he was able to carry it out." Anderton shrugged. "After all, we can't get all of them." He riffled the cards. "But we do get most."

"One murder in five years." Witwer's confidence was returning. "Quite an impressive record . . . something to be proud of."

Quietly Anderton said: "I am proud. Thirty years ago I worked out the theory—back in the days when the self-seekers were thinking in terms of quick raids on the stock market. I saw something legitimate ahead—something of tremendous social value."

He tossed the packet of cards to Wally Page, his subordinate in charge of the monkey block. "See which ones we want," he told him. "Use your own judgment."

As Page disappeared with the cards, Witwer said thoughtfully: "It's a big responsibility."

"Yes, it is," agreed Anderton. "If we let one criminal escape—as we did five years ago—we've got a human life on our conscience. We're solely responsible. If we slip up, somebody dies." Bitterly, he jerked three new cards from the slot. "It's a public trust."

"Are you ever tempted to—" Witwer hesitated. "I mean, some of the men you pick up must offer you plenty."

"It wouldn't do any good. A duplicate file of cards pops out at Army GHQ. It's check and balance. They can keep their eye on us as continuously as they wish." Anderton glanced briefly at the top card. "So even if we wanted to accept a—"

He broke off, his lips tightening.

"What's the matter?" Witwer asked curiously.

Carefully, Anderton folded up the top card and put it away in his pocket. "Nothing," he muttered. "Nothing at all."

The harshness in his voice brought a flush to Witwer's face. "You really don't like me," he observed.

"True," Anderton admitted. "I don't. But—"

He couldn't believe he disliked the young man that much. It didn't seem possible: it *wasn't* possible. Something was wrong. Dazed, he tried to steady his tumbling mind.

On the card was his name. Line one—an already accused future murderer! According to the code punches, Precrime Commissioner John A. Anderton was going to kill a man—and within the next week.

With absolute, overwhelming conviction, he didn't believe it.

II

In the outer office, talking to Page, stood Anderton's slim and attractive young wife, Lisa. She was engaged in a sharp, animated discussion of policy, and barely glanced up as Witwer and her husband entered.

"Hello, darling," Anderton said.

Witwer remained silent. But his pale eyes flickered slightly as they rested on the brown-haired woman in her trim police uniform. Lisa was now an executive official of Precrime but once, Witwer knew, she had been Anderton's secretary.

Noticing the interest on Witwer's face Anderton paused and reflected. To plant the card in the machines would require an accomplice on the inside—someone who was closely connected with Precrime and had access to the analytical equipment. Lisa was an improbable element. But the possibility did exist.

Of course, the conspiracy could be large-scale and elaborate, involving far more than a "rigged" card inserted somewhere along the line. The original data itself might have been tampered with. Actually, there was no telling how far back the alteration went. His original impulse—to tear open the machines and remove all the data—was uselessly primitive. Probably the tapes agreed with the card: He would only incriminate himself further.

He had approximately twenty-four hours. Then, the Army people would check over their cards and discover the discrepancy. They would find in their files a duplicate of the card he had appropriated. They had only one of two copies, which meant that the folded card in his pocket might just as well be lying on Page's desk in plain view of everyone.

From outside of the building came the drone of police cars starting out on their routine round-ups. How many hours would elapse before one of them pulled up in front of *his* house?

"What's the matter, darling?" Lisa asked him uneasily. "You look as if you've just seen a ghost. Are you all right?"

"I'm fine," he assured her.

Lisa suddenly seemed to become aware of Ed Witwer's admiring scrutiny. "Is this gentleman your new co-worker, darling?" she asked.

Warily, Anderton introduced his new associate. Lisa smiled in a friendly greeting. Did a covert awareness pass between them? He couldn't tell. God, he was beginning to suspect everybody—not only his wife and Witwer, but a dozen members of his staff.

"Are you from New York?" Lisa asked.

"No," Witwer replied. "I've lived most of my life in Chicago. I'm staying at a hotel—one of the big downtown hotels. Wait—I have the name written on a card somewhere."

While he self-consciously searched his pockets, Lisa suggested: "Perhaps you'd like to have dinner with us. We'll be working in close cooperation, and I really think we ought to get better acquainted."

Startled, Anderton backed off. What were the chances of his wife's friendliness being benign, accidental? Witwer would be present the balance of the evening, and would now have an excuse to trail along to Anderton's private residence. Profoundly disturbed, he turned impulsively, and moved toward the door.

"Where are you going?" Lisa asked, astonished.

"Back to the money block," he told her. "I want to check over some rather puzzling data tapes before the Army sees them." He was out in the corridor before she could think of a plausible reason for detaining him.

Rapidly, he made his way to the ramp at its far end. He was striding down the outside stairs toward the public sidewalk, when Lisa appeared breathlessly behind him.

"What on earth has come over you?" Catching hold of his arm, she moved quickly in front of him. "I *knew* you were leaving," she exclaimed, blocking his way. "What's wrong with you? Everybody thinks you're—" She checked herself. "I mean, you're acting so erratically."

People surged by them—the usual afternoon crowd. Ignoring them, Anderton pried his wife's fingers from his arm. "I'm getting out," he told her. "While there's still time."

"But—*why*?"

"I'm being framed—deliberately and maliciously. This creature is out to get my job. The Senate is getting at me *through* him."

Lisa gazed up at him, bewildered. "But he seems like such a nice young man."

"Nice as a water moccasin."

Lisa's dismay turned to disbelief. "I don't believe it. Darling, all this strain you've been under—" Smiling uncertainly, she faltered: "It's not really credible that Ed Witwer is trying to frame you. How could he, even if he wanted to? Surely Ed wouldn't—"

"Ed?"

"That's his name, isn't it?"

Her brown eyes flashed in startled, wildly incredulous protest. "Good heavens, you're suspicious of everybody. You actually believe I'm mixed up with it in some way, don't you?"

He considered. "I'm not sure."

She drew closer to him, her eyes accusing. "That's not true. You really believe it. Maybe you *ought* to go away for a few weeks. You desperately need a rest. All this tension and trauma, a younger man coming in. You're acting paranoiac. Can't you see that? People plotting against you. Tell me, do you have any actual proof?"

Anderton removed his wallet and took out the folded card. "Examine this carefully," he said, handing it to her.

The color drained out of her face, and she gave a little harsh, dry gasp.

"The set-up is fairly obvious," Anderton told her, as levelly as he could. "This will give Witwer a legal pretext to remove me right now. He won't have to wait until I resign." Grimly, he added: "They know I'm good for a few years yet."

"But—"

"It will end the check and balance system. Precrime will no longer be an independent agency. The Senate will control the police, and after that—" His lips tightened. "They'll absorb the Army too. Well, it's outwardly logical enough. *Of course* I feel hostility and resentment toward Witwer—of course I have a motive.

"Nobody likes to be replaced by a younger man, and find himself turned out to pasture. It's all really quite plausible—except that I haven't the remotest intention of killing Witwer. But I can't prove that. So what can I do?"

Mutely, her face very white, Lisa shook her head. "I—I don't know. Darling, if only—"

"Right now," Anderton said abruptly, "I'm going home to pack my things. That's about as far ahead as I can plan."

"You're really going to—to try to hide out?"

"I am. As far as the Centaurian-colony planets, if necessary. It's been done successfully before, and I have a twenty-four-hour start." He turned resolutely. "Go back inside. There's no point in your coming with me."

"Did you imagine I would?" Lisa asked huskily.

Startled, Anderton stared at her. "Wouldn't you?" Then with amazement, he murmured: "No, I can see you don't believe me. You still think

I'm imagining all this." He jabbed savagely at the card. "Even with that evidence you still aren't convinced."

"No," Lisa agreed quickly, "I'm not. You didn't look at it closely enough, darling. Ed Witwer's name isn't on it."

Incredulous, Anderton took the card from her.

"Nobody says you're going to kill Ed Witwer," Lisa continued rapidly, in a thin, brittle voice. "The card *must* be genuine, understand? And it has nothing to do with Ed. He's not plotting against you and neither is anybody else."

Too confused to reply, Anderton stood studying the card. She was right. Ed Witwer was not listed as his victim. On line five, the machine had neatly stamped another name.

LEOPOLD KAPLAN

Numbly, he pocketed the card. He had never heard of the man in his life.

III

The house was cool and deserted, and almost immediately Anderton began making preparations for his journey. While he packed, frantic thoughts passed through his mind.

Possibly he was wrong about Witwer—but how could he be sure? In any event, the conspiracy against him was far more complex than he had realized. Witwer, in the overall picture, might be merely an insignificant puppet animated by someone else—by some distant, indistinct figure only vaguely visible in the background.

It had been a mistake to show the card to Lisa. Undoubtedly, she would describe it in detail to Witwer. He'd never get off Earth, never have an opportunity to find out what life on a frontier planet might be like.

While he was thus preoccupied, a board creaked behind him. He turned from the bed, clutching a weather-stained winter sports jacket, to face the muzzle of a gray-blue A-pistol.

"It didn't take you long," he said, staring with bitterness at the tightlipped, heavyset man in a brown overcoat who stood holding the gun in his gloved hand. "Didn't she even hesitate?"

The intruder's face registered no response. "I don't know what you're talking about," he said. "Come along with me."

Startled, Anderton laid down the sports jacket. "You're not from my agency? You're not a police officer?"

Protesting and astonished, he was hustled outside the house to a waiting limousine. Instantly three heavily armed men closed in behind him. The door slammed and the car shot off down the highway, away from the city. Impassive and remote, the faces around him jogged with the motion of the speeding vehicle as open fields, dark and somber, swept past.

Anderton was still trying futilely to grasp the implications of what had happened, when the car came to a rutted side road, turned off, and descended into a gloomy sub-surface garage. Someone shouted an order. The heavy metal lock grated shut and overhead lights blinked on. The driver turned off the car motor.

"You'll have reason to regret this," Anderton warned hoarsely, as they dragged him from the car. "Do you realize who I am?"

"We realize," the man in the brown overcoat said.

At gun-point, Anderton was marched upstairs, from the clammy silence of the garage into a deep-carpeted hallway. He was, apparently, in a luxurious private residence, set out in the war-devoured rural area. At the far end of the hallway he could make out a room—a book-lined study simply but tastefully furnished. In a circle of lamplight, his face partly in shadows, a man he had never met sat waiting for him.

As Anderton approached, the man nervously slipped a pair of rimless glasses in place, snapped the case shut, and moistened his dry lips. He was elderly, perhaps seventy or older, and under his arm was a slim silver cane. His body was thin, wiry, his attitude curiously rigid. What little hair he had was dusty brown—a carefully-smoothed sheen of neutral color above his pale, bony skull. Only his eyes seemed really alert.

"Is this Anderton?" he inquired querulously, turning to the man in the brown overcoat. "Where did you pick him up?"

"At his home," the other replied. "He was packing—as we expected."

The man at the desk shivered visibly. "Packing." He took off his glasses and jerkily returned them to their case. "Look here," he said bluntly to Anderton, "what's the matter with you? Are you hopelessly insane? How could you kill a man you've never met?"

The old man, Anderton suddenly realized, was Leopold Kaplan.

"First, I'll ask you a question," Anderton countered rapidly. "Do you realize what you've done? I'm Commissioner of Police. I can have you sent up for twenty years."

He was going to say more, but a sudden wonder cut him short.

"How did you find out?" he demanded. Involuntarily, his hand went to his pocket, where the folded card was hidden. "It won't be for another—"

"I wasn't notified through your agency," Kaplan broke in, with angry impatience. "The fact that you've never heard of me doesn't surprise me too much. Leopold Kaplan, General of the Army of the Federated Westbloc Alliance." Begrudgingly, he added. "Retired, since the end of the Anglo-Chinese War, and the abolishment of AFWA."

It made sense. Anderton had suspected that the Army processed its duplicate cards immediately, for its own protection. Relaxing somewhat, he demanded: "Well? You've got me here. What next?"

"Evidently," Kaplan said, "I'm not going to have you destroyed, or it would have shown up on one of those miserable little cards. I'm curious about you. It seemed incredible to me that a man of your stature could contemplate the cold-blooded murder of a total stranger. There must be something more here. Frankly, I'm puzzled. If it represented some kind of Police strategy—" He shrugged his thin shoulders. "Surely you wouldn't have permitted the duplicate card to reach us."

"Unless," one of his men suggested, "it's a deliberate plant."

Kaplan raised his bright, bird-like eyes and scrutinized Anderton. "What do you have to say?"

"That's exactly what it is," Anderton said, quick to see the advantage of stating frankly what he believed to be the simple truth. "The prediction on the card was deliberately fabricated by a clique inside the police agency. The card is prepared and I'm netted. I'm relieved of my authority automatically. My assistant steps in and claims he prevented the murder in the usual efficient Precrime manner. Needless to say, there is no murder or intent to murder."

"I agree with you that there will be no murder," Kaplan affirmed grimly. "You'll be in police custody. I intend to make certain of that."

Horrified, Anderton protested. "You're taking me back there? If I'm in custody, I'll never be able to prove—"

"I don't care what you prove or don't prove," Kaplan interrupted. "All I'm interested in is having you out of the way." Frigidly, he added: "For my own protection."

"He was getting ready to leave," one of the men asserted.

"That's right," Anderton said, sweating. "As soon as they get hold of me I'll be confined in the detention camp. Witwer will take over—lock, stock, and barrel." His face darkened. "And my wife. They're acting in concert, apparently."

For a moment Kaplan seemed to waver. "It's possible," he conceded, regarding Anderton steadily. Then he shook his head. "I can't take the chance. If this is a frame against you, I'm sorry. But it's simply not my affair." He smiled slightly. "However, I wish you luck." To the men he said: "Take him to the police building and turn him over to the highest authority." He mentioned the name of the acting commissioner, and waited for Anderton's reaction.

"Witwer!" Anderton echoed, incredulous.

Still smiling slightly, Kaplan turned and clicked on the console radio in the study. "Witwer has already assumed authority. Obviously, he's going to create quite an affair out of this."

There was a brief static hum, and then, abruptly, the radio blared out into the room—a noisy professional voice, reading a prepared announcement.

". . . All citizens are warned not to shelter or in any fashion aid or assist this dangerous marginal individual. The extraordinary circumstance of an escaped criminal at liberty and in a position to commit an act of violence is unique in modern times. All citizens are hereby notified that legal statutes still in force implicate any and all persons failing to cooperate fully with the police in their task of apprehending John Allison Anderton. To repeat: The Precrime Agency of the Federal Westbloc Government is in the process of locating and neutralizing its former Commissioner, John Allison Anderton, who, through the methodology of the Precrime system, is hereby declared a potential murderer and as such forfeits his rights to freedom and all its privileges."

"It didn't take him long," Anderton muttered, appalled. Kaplan snapped off the radio and the voice vanished.

"Lisa must have gone directly to him," Anderton speculated bitterly.

"Why should he wait?" Kaplan asked. "You made your intentions clear."

He nodded to his men. "Take him back to town. I feel uneasy having him so close. In that respect I concur with Commissioner Witwer. I want him neutralized as soon as possible."

IV

Cold, light rain beat against the pavement, as the car moved through the dark streets of New York City toward the police building.

"You can see his point," one of the men said to Anderton. "If you were in his place you'd act just as decisively."

Sullen and resentful, Anderton stared straight ahead.

"Anyhow," the man went on, "you're just one of many. Thousands of people have gone to that detention camp. You won't be lonely. As a matter of fact, you may not want to leave."

Helplessly, Anderton watched pedestrians hurrying along the rain-swept sidewalks. He felt no strong emotion. He was aware only of an overpowering fatigue. Dully, he checked off the street numbers: they were getting near the police station.

"This Witwer seems to know how to take advantage of an opportunity," one of the men observed conversationally. "Did you ever meet him?"

"Briefly," Anderton answered.

"He wanted your job—so he framed you. Are you sure of that?"

Anderton grimaced. "Does it matter?"

"I was just curious." The man eyed him languidly. "So you're the ex-Commissioner of Police. People in the camp will be glad to see you coming. They'll remember you."

"No doubt," Anderton agreed.

"Witwer sure didn't waste any time. Kaplan's lucky—with an official like that in charge." The man looked at Anderton almost pleadingly. "You're really convinced it's a plot, eh?"

"Of course."

"You wouldn't harm a hair of Kaplan's head? For the first time in history, Precrime goes wrong? An innocent man is framed by one of those cards. Maybe there've been other innocent people—right?"

"It's quite possible," Anderton admitted listlessly.

"Maybe the whole system can break down. Sure, you're not going to commit a murder—and maybe none of them were. Is that why you told Kaplan you wanted to keep yourself outside? Were you hoping to prove the system wrong? I've got an open mind, if you want to talk about it."

Another man leaned over, and asked, "Just between the two of us, is there really anything to this plot stuff? Are you really being framed?"

Anderton sighed. At that point he wasn't certain himself. Perhaps he was trapped in a closed, meaningless time-circle with no motive and no beginning. In fact, he was almost ready to concede that he was the victim of a weary, neurotic fantasy, spawned by growing insecurity. Without a fight, he was willing to give himself up. A fast weight of exhaustion lay upon him. He was struggling against the impossible—and all the cards were stacked against him.

The sharp squeal of tires roused him. Frantically, the driver struggled to control the car, tugging at the wheel and slamming on the brakes, as a massive bread truck loomed up from the fog and ran directly across the lane ahead. Had he gunned the motor instead he might have saved himself. But too late he realized his error. The car skidded, lurched, hesitated for a brief instant, and then smashed head on into the bread truck.

Under Anderton the seat lifted up and flung him face-forward against the door. Pain, sudden, intolerable, seemed to burst in his brain as he lay gasping and trying feebly to pull himself to his knees. Somewhere the crackle of fire echoed dismally, a patch of hissing brilliance winking in the swirls of mist making their way into the twisted hulk of the car.

Hands from outside the car reached for him. Slowly he became aware that he was being dragged through the rent that had been the door. A heavy seat cushion was shoved brusquely aside, and all at once he found himself on his feet, leaning heavily against a dark shape and being guided into the shadows of an alley a short distance from the car.

In the distance, police sirens wailed.

"You'll live," a voice grated in his ear, low and urgent. It was a voice he had never heard before, as unfamiliar and harsh as the rain beating into his face. "Can you hear what I'm saying?"

"Yes," Anderton acknowledged. He plucked aimlessly at the ripped sleeve of his shirt. A cut on his cheek was beginning to throb. Confused, he tried to orient himself. "You're not—"

"Stop talking and listen." The man was heavyset, almost fat. Now his big hands held Anderton propped against the wet brick wall of the building, out of the rain and the flickering light of the burning car. "We had to do it that way," he said. "It was the only alternative. We didn't have much time. We thought Kaplan would keep you at his place longer."

"Who are you?" Anderton managed.

The moist, rain-streaked face twisted into a humorless grin. "My name's Fleming. You'll see me again. We have about five seconds before the police get here. Then we're back where we started." A flat packet was stuffed into Anderton's hands. "That's enough loot to keep you going. And there's a full set of identification in there. We'll contact you from time to time." His grin increased and became a nervous chuckle. "Until you've proved your point."

Anderton blinked. "It is a frameup, then?"

"Of course." Sharply, the man swore. "You mean they got you to believe it, too?"

"I thought—" Anderton had trouble talking; one of his front teeth seemed to be loose. "Hostility toward Witwer . . . replaced, my wife and a younger man, natural resentment . . ."

"Don't kid yourself," the other said. "You know better than that. This whole business was worked out carefully. They had every phase of it under control. The card was set to pop the day Witwer appeared. They've already got the first part wrapped up. Witwer is Commissioner, and you're a hunted criminal."

"Who's behind it?"

"Your wife."

Anderton's head spun. "You're positive?"

The man laughed. "You bet your life." He glanced quickly around. "Here come the police. Take off down this alley. Grab a bus, get yourself into the slum section, rent a room and buy a stack of magazines to keep you busy. Get other clothes— You're smart enough to take care of yourself. Don't try to leave Earth. They've got all the intersystem transports screened. If you can keep low for the next seven days, you're made."

"Who are you?" Anderton demanded.

Fleming let go of him. Cautiously, he moved to the entrance of the alley and peered out. The first police car had come to rest on the damp pavement;

its motor spinning tinnily, it crept suspiciously toward the smoldering ruin that had been Kaplan's car. Inside the wreck the squad of men was stirring feebly, beginning to creep painfully through the tangle of steel and plastic out into the cold rain.

"Consider us a protective society," Fleming said softly, his plump, expressionless face shining with moisture. "A sort of police force that watches the police. To see," he added, "that everything stays on an even keel."

His thick hand shot out. Stumbling, Anderton was knocked away from him, half-falling into the shadows and damp debris that littered the alley.

"Get going," Fleming told him sharply. "And don't discard that packet." As Anderton felt his way hesitantly toward the far exit of the alley, the man's last words drifted to him. "Study it carefully and you may still survive."

V

The identification cards described him as Ernest Temple, an unemployed electrician, drawing a weekly subsistence from the State of New York, with a wife and four children in Buffalo and less than a hundred dollars in assets. A sweat-stained green card gave him permission to travel and to maintain no fixed address. A man looking for work needed to travel. He might have to go a long way.

As he rode across town in the almost empty bus, Anderton studied the description of Ernest Temple. Obviously, the cards had been made out with him in mind, for all the measurements fitted. After a time he wondered about the fingerprints and the brainwave pattern. They couldn't possibly stand comparison. The walletful of cards would get him past only the most cursory examinations.

But it was something. And with the ID cards came ten thousand dollars in bills. He pocketed the money and cards, then turned to the neatly-typed message in which they had been enclosed.

At first he could make no sense of it. For a long time he studied it, perplexed.

The existence of a majority logically implies
A corresponding minority.

The bus had entered the vast slum region, the tumbled miles of cheap hotels and broken-down tenements that had sprung up after the mass destruction of the war. It slowed to a stop, and Anderton got to his feet. A few passengers idly observed his cut cheek and damaged clothing. Ignoring them, he stepped down onto the rain-swept curb.

Beyond collecting the money due him, the hotel clerk was not interested. Anderton climbed the stairs to the second floor and entered the narrow, musty-smelling room that now belonged to him. Gratefully, he locked the door and pulled down the window shades. The room was small but clean. Bed, dresser, scenic calendar, chair, lamp, a radio with a slot for the insertion of quarters.

He dropped a quarter into it and threw himself heavily down on the bed. All main stations carried the police bulletin. It was novel, exciting, something unknown to the present generation. An escaped criminal! The public was avidly interested.

". . . this man has used the advantage of this high position to carry out an initial escape," the announcer was saying, with professional indignation. "Because of his high office he had access to the previewed data and the trust placed in him permitted him to evade the normal process of detection and re-location. During the period of his tenure he exercised his authority to send countless potentially guilty individuals to their proper confinement, thus sparing the lives of innocent victims. This man, John Allison Anderton, was instrumental in the original creation of the Precrime system, the prophylactic pre-detection of criminals through the ingenious use of mutant precogs, capable of previewing future events and transferring orally that data to analytical machinery. These three precogs, in their vital function . . ."

The voice faded out as he left the room and entered the tiny bathroom. There, he stripped off his coat, and shirt, and ran hot water in the wash bowl. He began bathing the cut on his cheek. At the drugstore on the corner he had bought iodine and Band-Aids, a razor, comb, toothbrush, and other small things he would need. The next morning he intended to find a second-hand clothing store and buy more suitable clothing. After all, he was now an unemployed electrician, not an accident-damaged Commissioner of Police.

In the other room the radio blared on. Only subconsciously aware of it, he stood in front of the cracked mirror, examining a broken tooth.

". . . the system of three precogs finds its genesis in the computers of the middle decades of this century. How are the results of an electronic computer checked? By feeding the data to a second computer of identical design. But two computers are not sufficient. If each computer arrived at a different answer it is impossible to tell *a priori* which is correct. The solution, based on a careful study of statistical method, is to utilize a third computer to check the result of the first two. In this manner, a so-called majority report is obtained. It can be assumed with fair probability that the agreement of two out of three computers indicates which of the alternative results is accurate. It would not be likely that two computers would arrive at identically incorrect solutions—"

Anderton dropped the towel he was clutching and raced into the other room. Trembling, he bent to catch the blaring words of the radio.

". . . unanimity of all three precogs is a hoped-for but seldom-achieved phenomenon, acting-Commissioner Witwer explains. It is much more common to obtain a collaborative majority report of two precogs, plus a minority report of some slight variation, usually with reference to time and place, from the third mutant. This is explained by the theory of *multiple-futures.* If only one time-path existed, precognitive information would be of no importance, since no possibility would exist, in possessing this information, of altering the future. In the Precrime Agency's work we must first of all assume—"

Frantically, Anderton paced around the tiny room. Majority report—only two of the precogs had concurred on the material underlying the card. That was the meaning of the message enclosed within the packet. The report of the third precog, the minority report, was somehow of importance.

Why?

His watch told him that it was after midnight. Page would be off duty. He wouldn't be back in the monkey block until the next afternoon. It was a slim chance, but worth taking. Maybe Page would cover for him, and maybe not. He would have to risk it.

He had to see the minority report.

VI

Between noon and one o'clock the rubbish-littered streets swarmed with people. He chose that time, the busiest part of the day, to make his call. Selecting a phone booth in a patron-teeming super drugstore, he dialed the familiar police number and stood holding the cold receiver to his ear. Deliberately, he had selected the aud, not the vid line: in spite of his second-hand clothing and seedy, unshaven appearance, he might be recognized.

The receptionist was new to him. Cautiously, he gave Page's extension. If Witwer were removing the regular staff and putting in his satellites, he might find himself talking to a total stranger.

"Hello," Page's gruff voice came.

Relieved, Anderton glanced around. Nobody was paying any attention to him. The shoppers wandered among the merchandise, going about their daily routines. "Can you talk?" he asked. "Or are you tied up?"

There was a moment of silence. He could picture Page's mild face torn with uncertainty as he wildly tried to decide what to do. At last came halting words. "Why—are you calling here?"

Ignoring the question, Anderton said, "I didn't recognize the receptionist. New personnel?"

"Brand-new," Page agreed, in a thick strangled voice. "Big turnovers, these days."

"So I hear." Tensely, Anderton asked, "How's your job? Still safe?"

"Wait a minute." The receiver was put down and the muffled sound of steps came in Anderton's ear. It was followed by the quick slam of a door being hastily shut. Page returned. "We can talk better now," he said hoarsely.

"How much better?"

"Not a great deal. Where are you?"

"Strolling through Central Park," Anderton said. "Enjoying the sunlight." For all he knew, Page had gone to make sure the line-tap was in place. Right now, an airborne police team was probably on its way. But he had to take the chance. "I'm in a new field," he said curtly. "I'm an electrician these days."

"Oh?" Page said, baffled.

"I thought maybe you had some work for me. If it can be arranged, I'd like to drop by and examine your basic computing equipment. Especially the data and analytical banks in the monkey block."

After a pause, Page said: "It—might be arranged. If it's really important."

"It is," Anderton assured him. "When would be best for you?"

"Well," Page said, struggling. "I'm having a repair team come in to look at the intercom equipment. The acting-Commissioner wants it improved, so he can operate quicker. You might trail along."

"I'll do that. About when?"

"Say four o'clock. Entrance B, level 6. I'll—meet you."

"Fine," Anderton agreed, already starting to hang up. "I hope you're still in charge when I get there."

He hung up and rapidly left the booth. A moment later he was pushing through the dense pack of people crammed into the nearby cafeteria. Nobody would locate him there.

He had three and a half hours to wait. And it was going to seem a lot longer. It proved to be the longest wait of his life before he finally met Page as arranged.

The first thing Page said was: "You're out of your mind. Why in hell did you come back?"

"I'm not back for long." Tautly, Anderton prowled around the monkey block, systematically locking one door after another. "Don't let anybody in. I can't take chances."

"You should have quit when you were ahead." In an agony of apprehension, Page followed after him. "Witwer is making hay, hand over fist. He's got the whole country screaming for your blood."

Ignoring him, Anderton snapped open the main control bank of the analytical machinery. "Which of the three monkeys gave the minority report?"

"Don't question me—I'm getting out." On his way to the door Page halted briefly, pointed to the middle figure, and then disappeared. The door closed; Anderton was alone.

The middle one. He knew that one well. The dwarfed, hunched-over figure had sat buried in its wiring and relays for fifteen years. As Anderton approached, it didn't look up. With eyes glazed and blank, it contemplated a world that did not yet exist, blind to the physical reality that lay around it.

"Jerry" was twenty-four years old. Originally, he had been classified as a hydrocephalic idiot but when he reached the age of six the psych testers had identified the precog talent, buried under the layers of tissue corrosion. Placed in a government-operated training school, the latent talent had been cultivated. By the time he was nine the talent had advanced to a useful stage. "Jerry," however, remained in the aimless chaos of idiocy; the burgeoning faculty had absorbed the totality of his personality.

Squatting down, Anderton began disassembling the protective shields that guarded the tape-reels stored in the analytical machinery. Using schematics, he traced the leads back from the final stages of the integrated computers, to the point where "Jerry's" individual equipment branched off. Within minutes he was shakily lifting out two half-hour tapes: recent rejected data not fused with majority reports. Consulting the code chart, he selected the section of tape which referred to his particular card.

A tape scanner was mounted nearby. Holding his breath, he inserted the tape, activated the transport, and listened. It took only a second. From the first statement of the report it was clear what had happened. He had what he wanted; he could stop looking.

"Jerry's" vision was misphased. Because of the erratic nature of precognition, he was examining a time-area slightly different from that of his companions. For him, the report that Anderton would commit a murder was an event to be integrated along with everything else. That assertion—and Anderton's reaction—was one more piece of datum.

Obviously, "Jerry's" report superseded the majority report. Having been informed that he would commit a murder, Anderton would change his mind and not do so. The preview of the murder had cancelled out the murder; prophylaxis had occurred simply in his being informed. Already, a new time-path had been created. But "Jerry" was outvoted.

Trembling, Anderton rewound the tape and clicked on the recording head. At high speed he made a copy of the report, restored the original, and removed the duplicate from the transport. Here was the proof that the card was invalid: *obsolete.* All he had to do was show Witwer. . . .

His own stupidity amazed him. Undoubtedly, Witwer had seen the report; and in spite of it, had assumed the job of Commissioner, had kept the police teams out. Witwer didn't intend to back down; he wasn't concerned with Anderton's innocence.

What, then, could he do? Who else would be interested?

"You damn fool!" a voice behind him grated, wild with anxiety.

Quickly, he turned. His wife stood at one of the doors, in her police uniform, her eyes frantic with dismay. "Don't worry," he told her briefly, displaying the reel of tape. "I'm leaving."

Her face distorted, Lisa rushed frantically up to him. "Page said you were here, but I couldn't believe it. He shouldn't have let you in. He just doesn't understand what you are."

"What am I?" Anderton inquired caustically. "Before you answer, maybe you better listen to this tape."

"I don't want to listen to it! I just want you to get out of here! Ed Witwer knows somebody's down here. Page is trying to keep him occupied, but—" She broke off, her head turned stiffly to one side. "He's here now! He's going to force his way in."

"Haven't you got any influence? Be gracious and charming. He'll probably forget about me."

Lisa looked at him in bitter reproach. "There's a ship parked on the roof. If you want to get away. . . ." Her voice choked and for an instant she was silent. Then she said, "I'll be taking off in a minute or so. If you want to come—"

"I'll come," Anderton said. He had no other choice. He had secured his tape, his proof, but he hadn't worked out any method of leaving. Gladly, he hurried after the slim figure of his wife as she strode from the block, through a side door and down a supply corridor, her heels clicking loudly in the deserted gloom.

"It's a good fast ship," she told him over her shoulder. "It's emergency-fueled—ready to go. I was going to supervise some of the teams."

VII

Behind the wheel of the high-velocity police cruiser, Anderton outlined what the minority report tape contained. Lisa listened without comment, her face pinched and strained, her hands clasped tensely in her lap. Below the ship, the war-ravaged rural countryside spread out like a relief map, the vacant regions between cities crater-pitted and dotted with the ruins of farms and small industrial plants.

"I wonder," she said, when he had finished, "how many times this has happened before."

"A minority report? A great many times."

"I mean, one precog misphased. Using the report of the others as data—superseding them." Her eyes dark and serious, she added, "Perhaps a lot of the people in the camps are like you."

"No," Anderton insisted. But he was beginning to feel uneasy about it, too. "I was in a position to see the card, to get a look at the report. That's what did it."

"But—" Lisa gestured significantly. "Perhaps all of them would have reacted that way. We could have told them the truth."

"It would have been too great a risk," he answered stubbornly.

Lisa laughed sharply. "Risk? Chance? Uncertainty? With precogs around?"

Anderton concentrated on steering the fast little ship. "This is a unique case," he repeated. "And we have an immediate problem. We can tackle the theoretical aspects later on. I have to get this tape to the proper people—before your bright young friend demolishes it."

"You're taking it to Kaplan?"

"I certainly am." He tapped the reel of tape which lay on the seat between them. "He'll be interested. Proof that his life isn't in danger ought to be of vital concern to him."

From her purse, Lisa shakily got out her cigarette case. "And you think he'll help you."

"He may—or he may not. It's a chance worth taking."

"How did you manage to go underground so quickly?" Lisa asked. "A completely effective disguise is difficult to obtain."

"All it takes is money," he answered evasively.

As she smoked, Lisa pondered. "Probably Kaplan will protect you," she said. "He's quite powerful."

"I thought he was only a retired general."

"Technically—that's what he is. But Witwer got out the dossier on him. Kaplan heads an unusual kind of exclusive veterans' organization. It's actually a kind of club, with a few restricted members. High officers only—an international class from both sides of the war. Here in New York they maintain a great mansion of a house, three glossy-paper publications, and occasional TV coverage that costs them a small fortune."

"What are you trying to say?"

"Only this. You've convinced me that you're innocent. I mean, it's obvious that you *won't* commit a murder. But you must realize now that the original report, the majority report, *was not a fake.* Nobody falsified it. Ed Witwer didn't create it. There's no plot against you, and there never was. If you're going to accept this minority report as genuine, you'll have to accept the majority one, also."

Reluctantly, he agreed. "I suppose so."

"Ed Witwer," Lisa continued, "is acting in complete good faith. He really believes you're a potential criminal—and why not? He's got the majority report sitting on his desk, but you have that card folded up in your pocket."

"I destroyed it," Anderton said, quietly.

Lisa leaned earnestly toward him. "Ed Witwer isn't motivated by any desire to get your job," she said. "He's motivated by the same desire that has always dominated you. He believes in Precrime. He wants the system to continue. I've talked to him and I'm convinced he's telling the truth."

Anderton asked, "Do you want me to take this reel to Witwer? If I do—he'll destroy it."

"Nonsense," Lisa retorted. "The originals have been in his hands from the start. He could have destroyed them any time he wished."

"That's true," Anderton conceded. "Quite possibly he didn't know."

"Of course he didn't. Look at it this way. If Kaplan gets hold of that tape, the police will be discredited. Can't you see why? It would prove that the majority report was in error. Ed Witwer is absolutely right. You have to be taken in—if Precrime is to survive. You're thinking of your own safety. But think for a moment, about the system." Leaning over, she stubbed out her cigarette and fumbled in her purse for another. "Which means more to you—your own personal safety or the existence of the system?"

"My safety," Anderton answered, without hesitation.

"You're positive?"

"If the system can survive only by imprisoning innocent people, then it deserves to be destroyed. My personal safety is important because I'm a human being. And furthermore—"

From her purse, Lisa got out an incredibly tiny pistol. "I believe," she told him huskily, "that I have my finger on the firing release. I've never used a weapon like this before. But I'm willing to try."

After a pause, Anderton asked: "You want me to turn the ship around? Is that it?"

"Yes, back to the police building. I'm sorry. If you could put the good of the system above your own selfish—"

"Keep your sermon," Anderton told her. "I'll take the ship back. But I'm not going to listen to your defense of a code of behavior no intelligent man could subscribe to."

Lisa's lips pressed into a thin, bloodless line. Holding the pistol tightly, she sat facing him, her eyes fixed intently on him as he swung the ship in a broad arc. A few loose articles rattled from the glove compartment as the little craft turned on a radical slant, one wing rising majestically until it pointed straight up.

Both Anderton and his wife were supported by the constraining metal arms of their seats. But not so the third member of the party.

Out of the corner of his eye, Anderton saw a flash of motion. A sound came simultaneously, the clawing struggle of a large man as he abruptly lost his footing and plunged into the reinforced wall of the ship. What followed happened quickly. Fleming scrambled instantly to his feet, lurching and wary, one arm lashing out for the woman's pistol. Anderton was too startled to cry out. Lisa turned, saw the man—and screamed. Fleming knocked the gun from her hand, sending it clattering to the floor.

Grunting, Fleming shoved her aside and retrieved the gun. "Sorry," he gasped, straightening up as best he could. "I thought she might talk more. That's why I waited."

"You were here when—" Anderton began—and stopped. It was obvious that Fleming and his men had kept him under surveillance. The existence of Lisa's ship had been duly noted and factored in, and while Lisa had debated whether it would be wise to fly him to safety, Fleming had crept into the storage compartment of the ship.

"Perhaps," Fleming said, "you'd better give me that reel of tape." His moist, clumsy fingers groped for it. "You're right—Witwer would have melted it down to a puddle."

"Kaplan, too?" Anderton asked numbly, still dazed by the appearance of the man.

"Kaplan is working directly with Witwer. That's why his name showed on line five of the card. Which one of them is the actual boss, we can't tell. Possibly neither." Fleming tossed the tiny pistol away and got out his own heavy-duty military weapon. "You pulled a real flub in taking off with this woman. I told you she was back of the whole thing."

"I can't believe that," Anderton protested. "If she—"

"You've got no sense. This ship was warmed up by Witwer's order. They wanted to fly you out of the building so that we couldn't get to you. With you on your own, separated from us, you didn't stand a chance."

A strange look passed over Lisa's stricken features. "It's not true," she whispered. "Witwer never saw this ship. I was going to supervise—"

"You almost got away with it," Fleming interrupted inexorably. "We'll be lucky if a police patrol ship isn't hanging on us. There wasn't time to check." He squatted down as he spoke, directly behind the woman's chair. "The first thing is to get this woman out of the way. We'll have to drag you completely out of this area. Page tipped off Witwer on your new disguise, and you can be sure it has been widely broadcast."

Still crouching, Fleming seized hold of Lisa. Tossing his heavy gun to Anderton, he expertly tilted her chin up until her temple was shoved back against the seat. Lisa clawed frantically at him; a thin, terrified wail rose in her throat. Ignoring her, Fleming closed his great hands around her neck and began relentlessly to squeeze.

"No bullet wound," he explained, gasping. "She's going to fall out—natural accident. It happens all the time. But in this case, her neck will be broken *first*."

It seemed strange that Anderton waited so long. As it was, Fleming's thick fingers were cruelly embedded in the woman's pale flesh before he lifted the butt of the heavy-duty pistol and brought it down on the back of Fleming's skull. The monstrous hands relaxed. Staggered, Fleming's head fell forward and he sagged against the wall of the ship. Trying feebly to collect himself, he began dragging his body upward. Anderton hit him again, this time above the left eye. He fell back, and lay still.

Struggling to breathe, Lisa remained for a moment huddled over, her body swaying back and forth. Then, gradually, the color crept back into her face.

"Can you take the controls?" Anderton asked, shaking her, his voice urgent.

"Yes, I think so." Almost mechanically she reached for the wheel. "I'll be all right. Don't worry about me."

"This pistol," Anderton said, "is Army ordnance issue. But it's not from the war. It's one of the useful new ones they've developed. I could be a long way off but there's just a chance—"

He climbed back to where Fleming lay spread out on the deck. Trying not to touch the man's head, he tore open his coat and rummaged in his pockets. A moment later Fleming's sweat-sodden wallet rested in his hands.

Tod Fleming, according to his identification, was an Army Major attached to the Internal Intelligence Department of Military Information. Among the various papers was a document signed by General Leopold Kaplan, stating that Fleming was under the special protection of his own group—the International Veterans' League.

Fleming and his men were operating under Kaplan's orders. The bread truck, the accident, had been deliberately rigged.

It meant that Kaplan had deliberately kept him out of police hands. The plan went back to the original contact in his home, when Kaplan's men had picked him up as he was packing. Incredulous, he realized what had really happened. Even then, they were making sure they got him before the police. From the start, it had been an elaborate strategy to make certain that Witwer would fail to arrest him.

"You were telling the truth," Anderton said to his wife, as he climbed back in the seat. "Can we get hold of Witwer?"

Mutely, she nodded. Indicating the communications circuit of the dashboard, she asked: "What—did you find?"

"Get Witwer for me. I want to talk to him as soon as I can. It's very urgent."

Jerkily, she dialed, got the closed-channel mechanical circuit, and raised police headquarters in New York. A visual panorama of petty police officials flashed by before a tiny replica of Ed Witwer's features appeared on the screen.

"Remember me?" Anderton asked him.

Witwer blanched. "Good God. What happened? Lisa, are you bringing him in?" Abruptly his eyes fastened on the gun in Anderton's hands. "Look," he said savagely, "don't do anything to her. Whatever you may think, she's not responsible."

"I've already found that out," Anderton answered. "Can you get a fix on us? We may need protection getting back."

"Back!" Witwer gazed at him unbelievingly. "You're coming in? You're giving yourself up?"

"I am, yes." Speaking rapidly, urgently, Anderton added, "There's something you must do immediately. Close off the monkey block. Make certain nobody gets it—Page or anyone else. *Especially Army people.*"

"Kaplan," the miniature image said.

"What about him?"

"He was here. He—he just left."

Anderton's heart stopped beating. "What was he doing?"

"Picking up data. Transcribing duplicates of our precog reports on you. He insisted he wanted them solely for his protection."

"Then he's already got it," Anderton said. "It's too late."

Alarmed, Witwer almost shouted: "Just what do you mean? What's happening?"

"I'll tell you," Anderton said heavily, "when I get back to my office."

VIII

Witwer met him on the roof of the police building. As the small ship came to rest, a cloud of escort ships dipped their fins and sped off. Anderton immediately approached the blond-haired young man.

"You've got what you wanted," he told him. "You can lock me up, and send me to the detention camp. But that won't be enough."

Witwer's blue eyes were pale with uncertainty. "I'm afraid I don't understand—"

"It's not my fault. I should never have left the police building. Where's Wally Page?"

"We've already clamped down on him," Witwer replied. "He won't give us any trouble."

Anderton's face was grim.

"You're holding him for the wrong reason," he said. "Letting me into the monkey block was no crime. But passing information to Army is. You've had an Army plant working here." He corrected himself, a little lamely, "I mean, I have."

"I've called back the order on you. Now the teams are looking for Kaplan."

"Any luck?"

"He left here in an Army truck. We followed him, but the truck got into a militarized Barracks. Now they've got a big wartime R-3 tank blocking the street. It would be civil war to move it aside."

Slowly, hesitantly, Lisa made her way from the ship. She was still pale and shaken and on her throat an ugly bruise was forming.

"What happened to you?" Witwer demanded. Then he caught sight of Fleming's inert form lying spread out inside. Facing Anderton squarely, he said: "Then you've finally stopped pretending this is some conspiracy of mine."

"I have."

"You don't think I'm—" he made a disgusted face. "*Plotting* to get your job."

"Sure you are. Everybody is guilty of that sort of thing. And I'm plotting to keep it. But this is something else—and you're not responsible."

"Why do you assert," Witwer inquired, "that it's too late to turn yourself in? My God, we'll put you in the camp. The week will pass and Kaplan will still be alive."

"He'll be alive, yes," Anderton conceded. "But he can prove he'd be just as alive if I were walking the streets. He has information that proves the majority report is obsolete. He can break the Precrime system." He finished, "Heads or tails, he wins—and we lose. The Army discredits us; their strategy paid off."

"But why are they risking so much? What exactly do they want?"

"After the Anglo-Chinese War, the Army lost out. It isn't what it was in the good old AFWA days. They ran the complete show, both military and domestic. And they did their own police work."

"Like Fleming," Lisa said faintly.

"After the war, the Westbloc was demilitarized. Officers like Kaplan were retired and discarded. Nobody likes that." Anderton grimaced. "I can sympathize with him. He's not the only one. But we couldn't keep on running things that way. We had to divide up the authority."

"You say Kaplan has won," Witwer said. "Isn't there anything we can do?"

"I'm not going to kill him. We know it and he knows it. Probably he'll come around and offer us some kind of deal. We'll continue to function, but the Senate will abolish our real pull. You wouldn't like that, would you?"

"I should say not," Witwer answered emphatically. "One of these days I'm going to be running this agency." He flushed. "Not immediately, of course."

Anderton's expression was somber. "It's too bad you publicized the majority report. If you had kept it quiet, we could cautiously draw it back in. But everybody's heard about it. We can't retract it now."

"I guess not," Witwer admitted awkwardly. "Maybe I—don't have this job down as neatly as I imagined."

"You will, in time. You'll be a good police officer. You believe in the status quo. But learn to take it easy." Anderton moved away from them. "I'm going to study the data tapes of the majority report. I want to find out exactly how I was supposed to kill Kaplan." Reflectively, he finished: "It might give me some ideas."

The data tapes of the precogs "Donna" and "Mike" were separately stored. Choosing the machinery responsible for the analysis of "Donna," he opened the protective shield and laid out the contents. As before, the code informed him which reels were relevant and in a moment he had the tape-transport mechanism in operation.

It was approximately what he had suspected. This was the material utilized by "Jerry"—the superseded time-path. In it Kaplan's Military Intelligence agents kidnapped Anderton as he drove home from work. Taken to Kaplan's villa, the organization GHQ of the International Veterans' League. Anderton was given an ultimatum: voluntarily disband the Precrime system or face open hostilities with Army.

In this discarded time-path, Anderton, as Police Commissioner, had turned to the Senate for support. No support was forthcoming. To avoid civil war, the Senate had ratified the dismemberment of the police system, and decreed a return to military law "to cope with the emergency." Taking a corps of fanatic police, Anderton had located Kaplan and shot him, along with other officials of the Veterans' League. Only Kaplan had died. The others had been patched up. And the coup had been successful.

This was "Donna." He rewound the tape and turned to the material previewed by "Mike." It would be identical; both precogs had combined to present a unified picture. "Mike" began as "Donna" had begun: Anderton had become aware of Kaplan's plot against the police. But something was wrong. Puzzled, he ran the tape back to the beginning. Incomprehensibly, it didn't jibe. Again he replayed the tape, listening intently.

The "Mike" report was quite different from the "Donna" report.

An hour later, he had finished his examination, put away the tapes, and left the monkey block. As soon as he emerged, Witwer asked, "What's the matter? I can see something's wrong."

"No," Anderton answered slowly, still deep in thought. "Not exactly wrong." A sound came to his ears. He walked vaguely over to the window and peered out.

The street was crammed with people. Moving down the center lane was a four-column line of uniformed troops. Rifles, helmets . . . marching in their dingy wartime uniforms, carrying the cherished pennants of AFWA flapping in the cold afternoon wind.

"An Army rally," Witwer explained bleakly. "I was wrong. They're not going to make a deal with us. Why should they? Kaplan's going to make it public."

Anderton felt no surprise. "He's going to read the minority report?"

"Apparently. They're going to demand the Senate disband us, and take away our authority. They're going to claim we've been arresting innocent men—nocturnal police raids, that sort of thing. Rule by terror."

"You suppose the Senate will yield?"

Witwer hesitated. "I wouldn't want to guess."

"I'll guess," Anderton said. "They will. That business out there fits with what I learned downstairs. We've got ourselves boxed in and there's only one direction we can go. Whether we like it or not, we'll have to take it." His eyes had a steely glint.

Apprehensively, Witwer asked: "What is it?"

"Once I say it, you'll wonder why you didn't invent it. Very obviously, I'm going to have to fulfill the publicized report. I'm going to have to kill Kaplan. That's the only way we can keep them from discrediting us."

"But," Witwer said, astonished, "the majority report has been superseded."

"I can do it," Anderton informed him, "but it's going to cost. You're familiar with the statutes governing first-degree murder?"

"Life imprisonment."

"At least. Probably, you could pull a few wires and get it commuted to exile. I could be sent to one of the colony planets, the good old frontier."

"Would you—prefer that?"

"Hell, no," Anderton said heartily. "But it would be the lesser of the two evils. And it's got to be done."

"I don't see how you can kill Kaplan."

Anderton got out the heavy-duty military weapon Fleming had tossed to him. "I'll use this."

"They won't stop you?"

"Why should they? They've got that minority report that says I've changed my mind."

"Then the minority report is incorrect?"

"No," Anderton said, "it's absolutely correct. But I'm going to murder Kaplan anyhow."

IX

He had never killed a man. He had never even seen a man killed. And he had been Police Commissioner for thirty years. For this generation, deliberate murder had died out. It simply didn't happen.

A police car carried him to within a block of the Army rally. There, in the shadows of the back seat, he painstakingly examined the pistol Fleming had provided him. It seemed to be intact. Actually, there was no doubt of the outcome. He was absolutely certain of what would happen within the next half hour. Putting the pistol back together, he opened the door of the parked car and stepped warily out.

Nobody paid the slightest attention to him. Surging masses of people pushed eagerly forward, trying to get within hearing distance of the rally. Army uniforms predominated and at the perimeter of the cleared area, a line of tanks and major weapons was displayed—formidable armament still in production.

Army had erected a metal speaker's stand and ascending steps. Behind the stand hung the vast AFWA banner, emblem of the combined powers that had fought in the war. By a curious corrosion of time, the AFWA Veterans' League included officers from the wartime enemy. But a general was a general and fine distinctions had faded over the years.

Occupying the first rows of seats sat the high brass of the AFWA command. Behind them came junior commissioned officers. Regimental banners swirled in a variety of colors and symbols. In fact, the occasion had taken on the aspect of a festive pageant. On the raised stand itself sat stern-faced dignitaries of the Veterans' League, all of them tense with expectancy. At the extreme edges, almost unnoticed, waited a few police units, ostensibly to keep order. Actually, they were informants making observations. If order were kept, the Army would maintain it.

The late-afternoon wind carried the muffled booming of many people packed tightly together. As Anderton made his way through the dense mob he was engulfed by the solid presence of humanity. An eager sense of anticipation held everybody rigid. The crowd seemed to sense that something spectacular was on the way. With difficulty, Anderton forced his way past the rows of seats and over to the tight knot of Army officials at the edge of the platform.

Kaplan was among them. But he was now General Kaplan.

The vest, the gold pocket watch, the cane, the conservative business suit—all were gone. For this event, Kaplan had got his old uniform from its mothballs. Straight and impressive, he stood surrounded by what had been his general staff. He wore his service bars, his medals, his boots, his decorative short-sword, and his visored cap. It was amazing how transformed a bald man became under the stark potency of an officer's peaked and visored cap.

Noticing Anderton, General Kaplan broke away from the group and strode to where the younger man was standing. The expression on his thin, mobile countenance showed how incredulously glad he was to see the Commissioner of Police.

"This is a surprise," he informed Anderton, holding out his small gray-gloved hand. "It was my impression you had been taken in by the acting Commissioner."

"I'm still out," Anderton answered shortly, shaking hands. "After all, Witwer has that same reel of tape." He indicated the package Kaplan clutched in his steely fingers and met the man's gaze confidently.

In spite of his nervousness, General Kaplan was in good humor. "This is a great occasion for the Army," he revealed. "You'll be glad to hear I'm going to give the public a full account of the spurious charge brought against you."

"Fine," Anderton answered noncommittally.

"It will be made clear that you were unjustly accused." General Kaplan was trying to discover what Anderton knew. "Did Fleming have an opportunity to acquaint you with the situation?"

"To some degree," Anderton replied. "You're going to read only the minority report? That's all you've got there?"

"I'm going to compare it to the majority report." General Kaplan signaled an aide and a leather briefcase was produced. "Everything is here—all the evidence we need," he said. "You don't mind being an example, do you? Your case symbolizes the unjust arrests of countless individuals." Stiffly, General Kaplan examined his wristwatch. "I must begin. Will you join me on the platform?"

"Why?"

Coldly, but with a kind of repressed vehemence, General Kaplan said: "So they can see the living proof. You and I together—the killer and his victim. Standing side by side, exposing the whole sinister fraud which the police have been operating."

"Gladly," Anderton agreed. "What are we waiting for?"

Disconcerted, General Kaplan moved toward the platform. Again, he glanced uneasily at Anderton, as if visibly wondering why he had appeared and what he really knew. His uncertainty grew as Anderton willingly mounted the steps of the platform and found himself a seat directly beside the speaker's podium.

"You fully comprehend what I'm going to be saying?" General Kaplan demanded. "The exposure will have considerable repercussions. It may cause the Senate to reconsider the basic validity of the Precrime system."

"I understand," Anderton answered, arms folded. "Let's go."

A hush had descended on the crowd. But there was a restless, eager stirring when General Kaplan obtained the briefcase and began arranging his material in front of him.

"The man sitting at my side," he began, in a clean, clipped voice, "is familiar to you all. You may be surprised to see him, for until recently he was described by the police as a dangerous killer."

The eyes of the crowd focused on Anderton. Avidly, they peered at the only potential killer they had ever been privileged to see at close range.

"Within the last few hours, however," General Kaplan continued, "the police order for his arrest has been cancelled; because former Commissioner Anderton voluntarily gave himself up? No, that is not strictly accurate. He is sitting here. He has not given himself up, but the police are no longer interested in him. John Allison Anderton is innocent of any crime in the past, present, and future. The allegations against him were patent frauds, diabolical distortions of a contaminated penal system based on a false premise—a vast, impersonal engine of destruction grinding men and women to their doom."

Fascinated, the crowd glanced from Kaplan to Anderton. Everyone was familiar with the basic situation.

"Many men have been seized and imprisoned under the so-called prophylactic Precrime structure," General Kaplan continued, his voice gaining feeling and strength. "Accused not of crimes they have committed, *but of crimes they will commit.* It is asserted that these men, if allowed to remain free, will at some future time commit felonies.

"But there can be no valid knowledge about the future. As soon as precognitive information is obtained, it cancels itself out. The assertion that this man will commit a future crime is paradoxical. The very act of possessing this data renders it spurious. In every case, without exception, the report of the three police precogs has invalidated their own data. If no arrests had been made, there would still have been no crimes committed."

Anderton listened idly, only half-hearing the words. The crowd, however, listened with great interest. General Kaplan was now gathering up a summary made from the minority report. He explained what it was and how it had come into existence.

From his coat pocket, Anderton slipped out his gun and held it in his lap. Already, Kaplan was laying aside the minority report, the precognitive material obtained from "Jerry." His lean, bony fingers groped for the summary of first, "Donna," and after that, "Mike."

"This was the original majority report," he explained. "The assertion made by the first two precogs, that Anderton would commit a murder. Now here is the automatically invalidated material. I shall read it to you." He whipped out his rimless glasses, fitted them to his nose, and started slowly to read.

A queer expression appeared on his face. He halted, stammered, and abruptly broke off. The papers fluttered from his hands. Like a cornered animal, he spun, crouched, and dashed from the speaker's stand.

For an instant his distorted face flashed past Anderton. On his feet now, Anderton raised the gun, stepped quickly forward, and fired. Tangled up in the rows of feet projecting from the chairs that filled the platform, Kaplan gave a single shrill shriek of agony and fright. Like a ruined bird, he tumbled, fluttering and flailing, from the platform to the ground below. Anderton stepped to the railing, but it was already over.

Kaplan, as the majority report had asserted, was dead. His thin chest was a smoking cavity of darkness, crumbling ash that broke loose as the body lay twitching.

Sickened, Anderton turned away, and moved quickly between the rising figures of stunned Army officers. The gun, which he still held, guaranteed that he would not be interfered with. He leaped from the platform and edged into the chaotic mass of people at its base. Stricken, horrified, they struggled to see what had happened. The incident, occurring before their very eyes, was incomprehensible. It would take time for the acceptance to replace blind terror.

At the periphery of the crowd, Anderton was seized by the waiting police. "You're lucky to get out," one of them whispered to him as the car crept cautiously ahead.

"I guess I am," Anderton replied remotely. He settled back and tried to compose himself. He was trembling and dizzy. Abruptly, he leaned forward and was violently sick.

"The poor devil," one of the cops murmured sympathetically.

Through the swirls of misery and nausea, Anderton was unable to tell whether the cop was referring to Kaplan or himself.

X

Four burly policemen assisted Lisa and John Anderton in the packing and loading of their possessions. In fifty years, the ex-Commissioner of Police had accumulated a vast collection of material goods. Somber and pensive, he stood watching the procession of crates on their way to the waiting trucks.

By truck they would go directly to the field—and from there to Centaurus X by inter-system transport. A long trip for an old man. But he wouldn't have to make it back.

"There goes the second from the last crate," Lisa declared, absorbed and preoccupied by the task. In a sweater and slacks, she roamed through the barren rooms, checking on last-minute details. "I suppose we won't be able to use these new atronic appliances. They're still using electricity on Centten."

"I hope you don't care too much," Anderton said.

"We'll get used to it," Lisa replied, and gave him a fleeting smile. "Won't we?"

"I hope so. You're positive you'll have no regrets. If I thought—"

"No regrets," Lisa assured him. "Now suppose you help me with this crate."

As they boarded the lead truck, Witwer drove up in a patrol car. He leaped out and hurried up to them, his face looking strangely haggard. "Before you take off," he said to Anderton, "you'll have to give me a breakdown on the situation with the precogs. I'm getting inquiries from the Senate. They want to find out if the middle report, the retraction, was an error—or what." Confusedly, he finished: "I still can't explain it. The minority report was wrong, wasn't it?"

"Which minority report?" Anderton inquired, amused.

Witwer blinked. "Then that *is* it. I might have known."

Seated in the cabin of the truck, Anderton got out his pipe and shook tobacco into it. With Lisa's lighter he ignited the tobacco and began operations. Lisa had gone back to the house, wanting to be sure nothing vital had been overlooked.

"There were three minority reports," he told Witwer, enjoying the young man's confusion. Someday, Witwer would learn not to wade into situations he didn't fully understand. Satisfaction was Anderton's final emotion. Old and worn-out as he was, he had been the only one to grasp the real nature of the problem.

"The three reports were consecutive," he explained. "The first was 'Donna.' In that time-path, Kaplan told me of the plot, and I promptly murdered him. 'Jerry,' phased slightly ahead of 'Donna,' used her report as data. He factored in my knowledge of the report. In that, the second time-path, all I wanted to do was to keep my job. It wasn't Kaplan I wanted to kill. It was my own position and life I was interested in."

"And 'Mike' was the third report? That came *after* the minority report?" Witwer corrected himself. "I mean, it came last?"

" 'Mike' was the last of the three, yes. Faced with the knowledge of the first report, I had decided *not* to kill Kaplan. That produced report two. But faced with *that* report, I changed my mind back. Report two, situation two, was the situation Kaplan wanted to create. It was to the advantage of the police to recreate position one. And by that time I was thinking of the police. I had figured out what Kaplan was doing. The third report invalidated the second one in the same way the second one invalidated the first. That brought us back where we started from."

Lisa came over, breathless and gasping. "Let's go—we're all finished here." Lithe and agile, she ascended the metal rungs of the truck and squeezed in beside her husband and the driver. The latter obediently started up his truck and the others followed.

"Each report was different," Anderton concluded. "Each was unique. But two of them agreed on one point. If left free, I would kill Kaplan. That created the illusion of a majority report. Actually, that's all it was—an illusion. 'Donna' and 'Mike' previewed the same event—but in two totally different time-paths, occurring under totally different situations. 'Donna' and 'Jerry,' the so-called minority report and half of the majority report, were incorrect. Of the three, 'Mike' was correct—since no report came after his, to invalidate him. That sums it up."

Anxiously, Witwer trotted along beside the truck, his smooth, blond face creased with worry. "Will it happen again? Should we overhaul the setup?"

"It can happen in only one circumstance," Anderton said. "My case was unique, since I had access to the data. It could happen again—but only to the next Police Commissioner. So watch your step." Briefly, he grinned, deriving no inconsiderable comfort from Witwer's strained expression. Beside him, Lisa's red lips twitched and her hand reached out and closed over his.

"Better keep your eyes open," he informed young Witwer. "It might happen to you at any time."

PART III

HORROR:

CUE THE GORE

"Spurs"
by Tod Robbins

Freaks, directed by Tod Browning, 1932

"The Fly"
by George Langelaan

The Fly, directed by Kurt Neumann, 1958

The Fly, directed by David Cronenberg, 1986

"Herbert West—Reanimator: Six Shots by Moonlight"
by H. P. Lovecraft

Re-Animator, directed by Stuart Gordon, 1985

By today's slash-and-spatter standards, the stories here are relatively tame. H. P. Lovecraft, author of "Herbert West—Reanimator," aimed his work at a relatively small audience, people who were still able to "tremble at the thought of the hidden and fathomless worlds of strange life." The narrator of George Langelaan's "The Fly" is genteel, the horror he describes understated. Tod Robbins's "Spurs," with its masochistic and misogynistic protagonist, is slightly less subtle—yet the story manages to escape trespass because of its fable-like narration. But, oh, the movie adaptations! From this relatively benign material, the filmmakers go over the top, flirting with taboos, perverting formulas, and flaunting their bad taste.

Freaks, adapted from Clarence Aaron "Tod" Robbins's "Spurs," shocked and disgusted the American public and was even banned in Great Britain until 1963. Cast with people with real deformities, the movie was advertised as "A Horde of Caricatures of Creation!" Critical response was mixed. The *New York Times* withheld judgment: "*Freaks* is no normal program film, but whether it deserves the title of abnormal is a matter of personal opinion." The rest of the country was not as generous as New York City, and Browning's career was ruined. Prior to *Freaks* he was at the top of the horror heap, having collaborated with Lon Chaney on ten films and recently directed Bela Lugosi in *Dracula*. After *Freaks*, he was relegated to lesser pictures without the autonomy to pursue his own bizarre vision. In the 1960s, after his death, *Freaks* was rediscovered—and this time many in the audiences weren't frightened or repulsed. Instead, they found the film sensitive and generous. As Ivan Butler wrote in *Horror in the Cinema* (1970), "Browning has turned the popular convention of horror topsy-turvy. It is the ordinary, the apparently normal, the beautiful which horrify—the monstrous and distorted which compel our respect, our sympathy, ultimately our affection. The visible beauty conceals the unseen evil, the visible horror is the real goodness."*

* The cast didn't necessarily go along with this reassessment. According to David Skal, author of *The Monster Show: A Cultural History of Horror*, "Only two, Johnny Eck and Angelo Rossitto, maintained any affection for the director in later years."

"Spurs" was recommended to Browning by Harry Earles, the midget actor who had starred in a previous Browning/Chaney vehicle, *The Unholy Three* (1925), based on Robbins's novel of the same name. The story, which is set in a French circus, seemed made to order for Browning, who set many of his films in a circus environment, having himself run away from home at sixteen to join the Manhattan Fair and Carnival Company. There, he performed as "The Living Hypnotic Corpse," pretending to be buried alive for up to two days at a time in a box with a secret ventilating system. (He also briefly performed as a clown with the Ringling Brothers Circus and later as a contortionist/clown/singer/dancer/comic in vaudeville.) With several other writers, Browning set about adapting the story to fit his own peculiar aesthetic—an emphasis on mutilated characters whose physical state mirrors their mental or spiritual decline. (One of his earlier silent films, *The Unknown*, features Chaney as a circus knife thrower who pretends to have no arms, then undergoes an actual amputation of both limbs to avoid suspicion as a murderer.) When Irving Thalberg, who had championed the project, was shown the script he reportedly covered his head with his hands and groaned, "I asked for something horrifying and I got it." Browning changed the tone of Robbins's story from allegorical to realistic and replaced Robbins's stock circus characters with the most photogenically deformed sideshow performers available. The result is a film that is often called a semi-documentary, an unrepeatable subgenre of one.

Robbins was paid $8,000—a substantial sum, especially in 1929—for the rights to "Spurs," but as heir to a Brooklyn fortune, he was never in need of money. An athlete and society gadabout, Robbins first hit the society pages in 1909 when he eloped while still in college. Over the years, the *New York Times* covered his various marriages and divorces, but, tellingly, never reviewed one of his books. Early in his career he wrote prolifically, starting with novels and a book of poetry, then becoming a regular contributor to the Munsey pulps. (Frank Munsey introduced the first "pulp" magazine when he slashed the price of one of his magazines from 25 cents to 10 cents by printing it on cheaper paper made from pulpwood scraps.) Robbins published "Spurs" in *Munsey's* magazine near the end of his pulp career.

Always drawn to dark subjects, Robbins first wrote a novel of psychological horror, *Mysterious Martin*, featured a man with a compelling need to know how it feels to commit murder. Later, his pulp work specialized in the *conte cruel*, a type of story following in the vein of French author Villiers de L'Isle-Adam's classic story collection, *Contes Cruels* (1883, English title *Sar-*

donic Stories).* "Spurs," a sadistic revenge fantasy as well as a horrifying parable of love and marriage, falls in this category. Whether it is sheer invention or involves self-analysis on Robbins's part may be unfair speculation—but it is interesting to note that Robbins, like his protagonist Jacques, was a "small but powerful man" who inherited a fortune and had a lifetime of trouble with women. (He ultimately married six times.) A globetrotter and Francophile, he lived most of his life on the French Riviera. When he refused to leave France during World War II he was captured by the Germans and imprisoned in a concentration camp. He died in 1949.

George Langelaan, author of "The Fly," is another writer whose life provides an uncanny parallel to his story. As a British intelligence agent during World War II, he underwent plastic surgery to have his features altered so that he could move freely through Nazi-occupied France—but unlike his character André, Langelaan had a physical transformation that proved to be a positive one. Prior to the surgery he had been especially easy to recognize because of his large and awkwardly angled ears; afterwards he thought his ears "elegant." In his memoir, *The Masks of War*, he describes his two operations, as well as his transformation from bungling journalist to MacGyver-like warrior: "If you know how . . . a newspaper folded in a certain way can be as murderous as a hammer." He also learned how to make invisible ink, stop an express train with an overcoat, kill an enraged dog with his bare hands, and forge signatures with the aid of an egg. Despite such skills, he was captured and imprisoned by the Vichy police but ultimately managed to escape into Spain.

In "The Fly" Langelaan puts a spin on Robert Louis Stevenson's "Dr. Jekyl and Mr. Hyde," but with a modern sigh. "Telephones and telephone bells have always made me uneasy," the narrator begins, and, not surprisingly, the fateful "transmitter" turns out to be a souped-up phone booth. Kurt Neumann's 1958 adaptation retains this sentiment of dissatisfaction with progress, but screenwriter James Clavell *(Shogun)* escalates the debate. The film is a strange combination of kitsch and serious message. According to Vincent Price's daughter, Price and Herbert Marshall laughed until they cried while filming the "Help me!" scene near the end of the movie. But at the same time Clavell molded the story into a thinly veiled Cold War metaphor. "There are some things that should be left alone," Hélène tells her scientist husband, a message that didn't go unnoticed. "This is quite a little picture," said the *New York Times*. "Even with

* Although the term *conte cruel* is sometimes used to classify nonsupernatural horror, or merely cruel tales, *contes cruels* are more accurately defined as fantasies that draw uniquely sharp attention to the cruelties of fate, usually with nasty climactic twists.

the laboratory absurdities, it holds an interesting philosophy about man's tampering with the unknown."

One of the first things Canadian director David Cronenberg did when he tackled the script for his 1986 remake of *The Fly* was to jettison the Cold War rhetoric. "The idea that the scientist . . . must destroy what he's invented because there are things we must not know was ludicrous. Even in 1958 that theory didn't hold water but it was slightly more convincing then because of the relative naïveté of the times." Instead, Cronenberg fit the story into his own evolving aesthetic. "There was something about *The Fly* story that was much more universal to me: aging and death—something all of us have to deal with." Also central to his version is a wrenching romance—"Every love story must end tragically"—that probably accounts for the movie's popular success. Prior to *The Fly*, Cronenberg was considered by most to be a maker of senseless splatter films. Robert Fulford's review of *Shivers* for *Saturday Night* magazine began with the headline "You Should Know How Bad This Film Is. After All, You Paid For It." In it, he disparaged the fact that Cronenberg received a grant from the Canadian government. After *Shivers* came *Rabid* (starring porn star Marilyn Chambers), *Scanners* (the exploding head movie), and *Videodrome* (involving video tapes and bodily apertures). But *The Fly* brought Cronenberg into the mainstream.

Well, at least as far into the mainstream as he is likely to venture. Still, Cronenberg doesn't think of himself as a director of horror films, but as someone who is exploring thematic concerns—concerns that have been surprisingly consistent throughout his career. He hopes that audiences will see that all of his films, taken together, are "like chapters in an ongoing book." A book about separation, disintegration, death, dying, technology, and even the meaning of life. "I never thought I was doing the same thing as directors like John Carpenter, George Romero, and sometimes even Hitchcock. . . ." Cronenberg has said. "We're after a different game. The filmmaking process is a very personal one to me; I mean it really is a personal kind of communication. It's not as though it's a study of fear or any of that stuff."

For H. P. Lovecraft, author of "Herbert West—Reanimator," it *is* all about the study of fear. "The oldest and strongest emotion of mankind is fear, and the oldest and strongest kind of fear is fear of the unknown." So begins *Supernatural Horror in Literature*, Lovecraft's book-length treatise and defense of the genre. In horror circles, Lovecraft has been highly influential. Joyce Carol Oates observed in her introduction to *American Gothic Tales*, "If there is a single gothic-grotesque writer of the American twentieth century to be compared with Poe, it is H. P. Lovecraft." Scores of followers have catalogued every available aspect of his life, although it was not an outwardly exciting one. He dropped out of high school because of extended absences brought about by illness. He lived with his domineering, possibly schizophrenic mother until she was removed to an asylum when he was twenty-nine. He ventured away from Providence, Rhode Island, only once, for a two-year sojourn in New York. When he returned, he wrote, "There *is* no other place for me. My world is Providence." (He also said, "New York is no place for a white man to live," an indication of the muffled racism that appears in "Six Shots by Moonlight.") Lovecraft married briefly but had, apparently, little interest in sex or romance. He worked sporadically as a ghost writer and poetry editor. And of course, he wrote stories.

Lovecraft's was a life of the mind. His most famous story, "The Call of Cthulhu," his first story to deal with the Cthulhu Mythos, might also be called "The Secret History of the Earth." In it, Lovecraft chronicles the world's mythic past, which sensitive souls—artists and writers—encounter in strange dreams. Not surprisingly, much of this story emerged from his own dreams. Lovecraft's work, especially the Cthulhu Mythos, has captured the imagination of countless devotees and inspired volumes of imitations. But many find his prose too florid, his storytelling awkward and juvenile. "Herbert West" sits for many on the cusp of this debate. Did Lovecraft intend these stories—a series of six, including "Six Shots by Moonlight," published in *Home Brew* in 1922—as parody or serious horror? Are they, as one critic has asked, "a marvelous *jeu d'esprit* or one of the worst things Lovecraft wrote?"

This same uncertainty—is it an intentional spoof?—applies to Stuart Gordon's gristle-and-gore adaptation, *Re-Animator*. Gordon was a Lovecraft fan, having read him since he was a teenager. When he and associates began talking about making a Frankenstein film, someone suggested he read "Herbert West." He found a copy at the public library—"an old pulp magazine that literally was crumbling in my hands as I turned the pages"—and that was that. In her mostly positive review of *Re-Animator*, Janet Maslin points out that the film "even has a sense of humor, albeit one that would be lost on 99.9 percent of any ordinary movie-going crowd." Gordon claims that black humor is built into all of his films, but Jeffrey Combs, who played Herbert West, admitted in an interview that "Stuart had no intention to insert humor in it, not to that extent, at least. His will was to make a dramatic horror film, but I don't think he was disappointed when he saw the audience's reaction to it." Yet it's hard to believe that the humor in a movie as self-reflexive as *Re-Animator* was unintentional. What *is* certain is that Gordon is primarily interested in trying to make films that disturb people. When *Re-Animator* received an R rating, Gordon and crew asked the Motion Picture Association of

America (MPAA) to take it back. "They said that was the first time anyone had ever requested that! But they did it. They took back the R and let us release the unrated version." The money shot—how to delicately word it?—of a disembodied head pleasuring a bound young woman was also intentionally over the top. "Horror movies have always had a certain element of sexuality," Gordon explained. "There's always the scene of the monster carrying the girl in the negligee off to the swamp, or something. However, they never show you exactly what he's gonna do with her once they get there. So in *Re-Animator*, we did."

Browning, Neumann, Cronenberg, Gordon—you can call them schlockmeisters, kings of kitsch, or barons of blood. Or you can admire them for their cheek, as the jury at the Cannes Film Festival did recently when they awarded Cronenberg a prize for "audacity." After all, artists make it their business to dance naked for their audiences: Alcoholic confessions fuel much of the work of F. Scott Fitzgerald and Raymond Carver, drug addiction that of Denis Johnson, misanthropic musings the comics of Harvey Pekar. But in dealing with taboos and trespasses, practitioners of the horror genre go a step further. They direct light on our unspoken (and unspeakable) fears, fascinations, and even fetishes. And yes, it's uncomfortable.

Spurs

Tod Robbins

I

Jacques Courbé was a romanticist. He measured only twenty-eight inches from the soles of his diminutive feet to the crown of his head; but there were times, as he rode into the arena on his gallant charger, St. Eustache, when he felt himself a doughty knight of old about to do battle for his lady.

What matter that St. Eustache was not a gallant charger except in his master's imagination—not even a pony, indeed, but a large dog of a nondescript breed, with the long snout and upstanding ears of a wolf? What matter that Monsieur Courbé's entrance was invariably greeted with shouts of derisive laughter and bombardments of banana skins and orange peel? What matter that he had no lady and that his daring deeds were severely curtailed to a mimicry of the bareback riders who preceded him? What mattered all of these things to the tiny man who lived in dreams and who resolutely closed his shoe-button eyes to the drab realities of life?

The dwarf had no friends among the other freaks in Copo's Circus. They considered him ill-tempered and egotistical, and he loathed them for their acceptance of things as they were. Imagination was the armour that protected him from the curious glances of a cruel, gaping world, from the stinging lash of ridicule, from the bombardments of banana skins and orange peel. Without it, he must have shriveled up and died. But these others? Ah, they had no armour except their own thick hides! The door that opened on the kingdom of imagination was closed and locked to them; and although they did not wish to open this door, although they did not miss what lay beyond it, they resented and mistrusted anyone who possessed the key.

Now it came about, after many humiliating performances in the arena, made palatable only by dreams, that love entered the circus tent and beckoned commandingly to Monsieur Jacques Courbé. In an instant the dwarf was engulfed in a sea of wild tumultuous passion.

Mademoiselle Jeanne Marie was a daring bareback rider. It made Monsieur Jacques Courbé's tiny heart stand still to see her that first night of her appearance in the arena, performing brilliantly on the broad back of her aged mare, Sappho. A tall, blond woman of the amazon type, she had round eyes of baby blue which held no spark of her avaricious peasant's soul, carmine lips and cheeks, large white teeth which flashed continually in a smile and hands which, when doubled up, were nearly the size of the dwarf's head.

Her partner in the act was Simon Lafleur, the Romeo of the circus tent—a swarthy, Herculean young man with bold black eyes and hair that glistened with grease like the back of Solon, the trained seal.

From the first performance Monsieur Jacques Courbé loved Mademoiselle Jeanne Marie. All his tiny body was shaken with longing for her. Her buxom charms, so generously revealed in tights and spangles, made him flush and cast down his eyes. The familiarities allowed to Simon Lafleur, the bodily acrobatic contacts of the two performers, made the dwarf's blood boil. Mounted on St. Eustache, awaiting his turn at the entrance, he would grind his teeth in impotent rage to see Simon circling round and round the ring, standing proudly on the back of Sappho and holding Mademoiselle Jeanne Marie in an ecstatic embrace, while she kicked one shapely bespangled leg skyward.

"Ah, the dog!" Monsieur Jacques Courbé would mutter. "Some day I shall teach this hulking stable-boy his place! *Ma foi*, I will clip his ears for him!"

St. Eustache did not share his master's admiration for Mademoiselle Jeanne Marie. From the first he evinced his hearty detestation for her by low growls and a ferocious display of long, sharp fangs. It was little consolation for the dwarf to know that St. Eustache showed still more marked signs of rage when Simon Lafleur approached him. It pained Monsieur Jacques Courbé to think that his gallant charger, his sole companion, his bedfellow, should not also love and admire the splendid giantess who each night risked life and limb before the awed populace. Often, when they were alone together, he would chide St. Eustache on his churlishness.

"Ah, you devil of a dog!" the dwarf would cry. "Why must you always growl and show your ugly teeth when the lovely Jeanne Marie condescends to notice you? Have you no feelings under your tough hide? Cur, she is an angel and you snarl at her! Do you not remember how I found you, a starving puppy in a Paris gutter? And now you must threaten the hand of my princess! So this is your gratitude, great hairy pig!"

Monsieur Jacques Courbé had one living relative—not a dwarf, like himself, but a fine figure of a man, a prosperous farmer living just outside the town of Roubaix. The elder Courbé had never married and so one day, when he was found dead from heart failure, his tiny nephew—for whom, it must be confessed, the farmer had always felt an instinctive aversion—fell heir to a comfortable property. When the tidings were brought to him the dwarf threw both arms about the shaggy neck of St. Eustache and cried out:

"Ah, now we can retire, marry and settle down, old friend! I am worth many times my weight in gold!"

That evening, as Mademoiselle Jeanne Marie was changing her gaudy costume after the performance, a light tap sounded on the door.

"Enter!" she called, believing it to be Simon Lafleur, who had promised to take her that evening to the Sign of the Wild Boar for a glass of wine to wash the sawdust out of her throat. "Enter, *mon chéri*!"

The door swung slowly open and in stepped Monsieur Jacques Courbé, very proud and upright, in the silks and laces of a courtier, with a tiny gold-hilted sword swinging at his hip. Up he came, his shoe-button eyes all a-glitter to see the more than partially revealed charms of his robust lady. Up he came to within a yard of where she sat, and down on one knee he went and pressed his lips to her red-slippered foot.

"Oh, most beautiful and daring lady," he cried, in a voice as shrill as a pin scratching on a window-pane, "will you not take mercy on the unfortunate Jacques Courbé? He is hungry for your smiles, he is starving for your lips! All night long he tosses on his couch and dreams of Jeanne Marie!"

"What play-acting is this, my brave little fellow?" she asked, bending down with the smile of an ogress. "Has Simon Lafleur sent you to tease me?"

"May the black plague have Simon!" the dwarf cried, his eyes seeming to flash blue sparks. "I am not play-acting. It is only too true that I love you, mademoiselle, that I wish to make you my lady. And now that I have a fortune, not that—" He broke off suddenly and his face resembled a withered apple. "What is this, mademoiselle?" he said, in the low, droning tone of a hornet about to sting. "Do you laugh at my love? I warn you, mademoiselle—do not laugh at Jacques Courbé!"

Mademoiselle Jeanne Marie's large, florid face had turned purple from suppressed merriment. Her lips twitched at the corners. It was all she could do not to burst out into a roar of laughter.

Why, the ridiculous little manikin was serious in his love-making! This pocket-sized edition of a courtier was proposing marriage to her! He, this splinter of a fellow, wished to make her his wife! Why, she could carry him about on her shoulder like a trained marmoset!

What a joke this was—what a colossal, corset-creaking joke! Wait till she told Simon Lafleur! She could fairly see him throw back his sleek head, open his mouth to its widest dimensions and shake with silent laughter. But *she* must not laugh—not now. First she must listen to everything the dwarf had to say, draw all the sweetness out of this bonbon of humour before she crushed it under the heel of ridicule.

"I am not laughing," she managed to say. "You have taken me by surprise. I never thought, I never even guessed—"

"That is well, mademoiselle," the dwarf broke in. "I do not tolerate laughter. In the arena I am paid to make laughter, but these others pay to laugh at *me*. I always make people pay to laugh at me."

"But do I understand you aright, Monsieur Courbé? Are you proposing an honourable marriage?"

The dwarf rested his hand on his heart and bowed. "Yes, mademoiselle, an honourable marriage, and the wherewithal to keep the wolf from the door. A week ago my uncle died and left me a large estate. We shall have a servant to wait on our wants, a horse and carriage, food and wine of the best, and leisure to amuse ourselves. And you? Why, you will be a fine lady! I will clothe that beautiful big body of yours with silks and laces! You will be as happy, mademoiselle, as a cherry tree in June!"

The dark blood slowly receded from Mademoiselle Jeanne Marie's full cheeks, her lips no longer twitched at the corners, her eyes had narrowed slightly. She had been a bareback rider for years and she was weary of it. The life of the circus tent had lost its tinsel. She loved the dashing Simon Lafleur, but she knew well enough that this Romeo in tights would never espouse a dowerless girl.

The dwarf's words had woven themselves into a rich mental tapestry. She saw herself a proud lady, ruling over a country estate, and later welcoming Simon Lafleur with all the luxuries that were so near his heart. Simon would be overjoyed to marry into a country estate. These pygmies were a puny lot. They died young! She would do nothing to hasten the end of Jacques Courbé. No, she would be kindness itself to the poor little fellow, but, on the other hand, she would not lose her beauty mourning for him.

"Nothing that you wish shall be withheld from you as long as you love me, mademoiselle," the dwarf continued. "Your answer?"

Mademoiselle Jeanne Marie bent forward and, with a single movement of her powerful arms, raised Monsieur Jacques Courbé and placed him on her knee. For an ecstatic instant she held him thus, as if he were a large French doll, with his tiny sword cocked coquettishly out behind. Then she planted on his cheek a huge kiss that covered his entire face from chin to brow.

"I am yours!" she murmured, pressing him to her ample bosom. "From the first I love you, Monsieur Jacques Courbé!"

2

The wedding of Mademoiselle Jeanne Marie was celebrated in the town of Roubaix, where Copo's Circus had taken up its temporary quarters. Following the ceremony, a feast was served in one of the tents, which was attended by a whole galaxy of celebrities.

The bridegroom, his dark little face flushed with happiness and wine, sat at the head of the board. His chin was just above the tablecloth, so that his head looked like a large orange that had rolled off the fruit-dish. Immediately beneath his dangling feet, St. Eustache, who had more than once evinced by deep growls his disapproval of the proceedings, now worried a bone with quick, sly glances from time to time at the plump legs of his new mistress. Papa Copo was on the dwarf's right, his large round face as red and benevolent as a harvest moon. Next to him sat Griffo, the giraffe boy, who was covered with spots, and whose neck was so long that he looked down on all the rest, including Monsieur Hercule Hippo, the giant. The rest of the company included Mademoiselle Lupa, who had sharp white teeth of an incredible length, and who growled when she tried to talk; the tiresome Monsieur Jejongle, who insisted on juggling fruit, plates and knives, although the whole company was heartily sick of his tricks; Madame Samson, with her trained baby boa constrictors coiled about her neck and peeping out timidly, one above each ear; Simon Lafleur and a score of others.

The bareback rider had laughed silently and almost continually ever since Jeanne Marie had told him of her engagement. Now he sat next to her in his crimson tights. His black hair was brushed back from his forehead and so glistened with grease that it reflected the lights overhead, like a burnished helmet. From time to time he tossed off a brimming goblet of Burgundy, nudged the bride in the ribs with his elbow and threw back his sleek head in another silent outburst of laughter.

"And you are sure that you will not forget me, Simon?" she whispered. "It may be some time before I can get the little ape's money."

"Forget you, Jeanne?" he muttered. "By all the dancing devils in champagne, never! I will wait as patiently as Job till you have fed that mouse some poisoned cheese. But what will you do with him in the meantime, Jeanne? You must allow him no liberties. I grind my teeth to think of you in his arms!"

The bride smiled and regarded her diminutive husband with an appraising glance. What an atom of a man! And yet life might linger in his bones for a long time to come. Monsieur Jacques Courbé had allowed himself only one glass of wine and yet he was far gone into intoxication. His tiny face was suffused with blood and he stared at Simon Lafleur belligerently. Did he suspect the truth?

"Your husband is flushed with wine!" the bareback rider whispered. "*Ma foi, madame,* later he may knock you about! Possibly he is a dangerous fellow in his cups. Should he maltreat you, Jeanne, do not forget that you have a protector in Simon Lafleur."

"You clown!" Jeanne Marie rolled her large eyes roguishly and laid her hand for an instant on the bareback rider's knee. "Simon, I could crack his skull between my finger and thumb, like this hickory nut!" She paused to illustrate her example, and then added reflectively: "And, perhaps, I shall do that very thing, if he attempts any familiarities. Ugh! The little ape turns my stomach!"

By now the wedding guests were beginning to show the effects of their potations. This was especially marked in the case of Monsieur Jacques's associates in the sideshow.

Griffo, the giraffe boy, had closed his large brown eyes and was swaying his small head languidly above the assembly, while a slightly supercilious expression drew his lips down at the corners. Monsieur Hercule Hippo, swollen out by his libations to even more colossal proportions, was repeating over and over: "I tell you I am not like other men. When I walk, the earth trembles!" Mademoiselle Lupa, her hairy upper lip lifted above her long white teeth, was gnawing at a bone, growling unintelligible phrases to herself and shooting savage, suspicious glances at her companions. Monsieur Jejongle's hands had grown unsteady and, as he insisted on juggling the knives and plates of each new course, broken bits of crockery littered the floor. Madame Samson, uncoiling her necklace of baby boa constrictors, was feeding them lumps of sugar soaked in rum. Monsieur Jacques Courbé had finished his second glass of wine and was surveying the whispering Simon Lafleur through narrowed eyes.

There can be no genial companionship among great egotists who have drunk too much. Each one of these human oddities thought that he or she alone was responsible for the crowds that daily gathered at Copo's Circus; so now, heated with the good Burgundy, they were not slow in asserting themselves. Their separate egos rattled angrily together, like so many pebbles in a bag. Here was gunpowder which needed only a spark.

"I am big—a very big man!" Monsieur Hercule Hippo said sleepily. "Women love me. The pretty little creatures leave their pygmy husbands, so that they may come and stare at Hercule Hippo of Copo's Circus. Ha, and when they return home, they laugh at other men always! 'You may kiss me again when you grow up,' they tell their sweethearts."

"Fat bullock, here is one woman who has no love for you!" cried Mademoiselle Lupa, glaring sidewise at the giant over her bone. "That great carcass of yours is only so much food gone to waste. You have cheated the butcher, my friend. Fool, women do not come to see *you*! As well might they stare at the cattle being led through the street. Ah, no, they come from far and near to see one of their own sex who is not a cat!"

"Quite right," cried Papa Copo in a conciliatory tone, smiling and rubbing his hands together. "Not a cat, mademoiselle, but a wolf. Ah, you have a sense of humour! How droll!"

"I *have* a sense of humour," Mademoiselle Lupa agreed, returning to her bone, "and also sharp teeth. Let the erring hand not stray too near!"

"You, Monsieur Hippo and Mademoiselle Lupa, are both wrong," said a voice which seemed to come from the roof. "Surely it is none other than me whom the people come to stare at!"

All raised their eyes to the supercilious face of Griffo, the giraffe boy, which swayed slowly from side to side on its long pipe-stem neck. It was he who had spoken, although his eyes were still closed.

"Of all the colossal impudence!" cried the matronly Madame Samson. "As if my little dears had nothing to say on the subject!" She picked up the two baby boa constrictors, which lay in drunken slumber on her lap, and shook them like whips at the wedding guests. "Papa Copo knows only too well that it is on account of these little charmers, Mark Antony and Cleopatra, that the sideshow is so well attended!"

The circus owner, thus directly appealed to, frowned in perplexity. He felt himself in quandary. These freaks of his were difficult to handle. Why had he been fool enough to come to Monsieur Jacques Courbé's wedding feast? Whatever he said would be used against him.

As Papa Copo hesitated, his round face wreathed in ingratiating smiles, the long deferred spark suddenly alighted in the powder. It all came about on account of the carelessness of Monsieur Jejongle, who had become engrossed in the conversation and wished to put in a word for himself. Absent-mindedly juggling two heavy plates and a spoon, he said in a petulant tone: "You all appear to forget *me*!"

Scarcely were the words out of his mouth when one of the heavy plates descended with a crash on the thick skull of Monsieur Hippo and Monsieur Jejongle was instantly remembered. Indeed, he was more than remembered, for the giant, already irritated to the boiling-point by Mademoiselle Lupa's insults, at this new affront struck out savagely past her and knocked the juggler head-over-heels under the table.

Mademoiselle Lupa, always quick-tempered and especially so when her attention was focused on a juicy chicken bone, evidently considered her dinner companion's conduct far from decorous and promptly inserted her sharp teeth in the offending hand that had administered the blow. Monsieur Hippo, squealing from rage and pain like a wounded elephant, bounded to his feet, overturning the table.

Pandemonium followed. Every freak's hands, teeth, feet, were turned against the others. Above the shouts, screams, growls and hisses of the combat, Papa Copo's voice could be heard bellowing for peace:

"Ah, my children, my children! This is no way to behave! Calm yourselves, I pray you! Mademoiselle Lupa, remember that you are a lady as well as a wolf!"

There is no doubt that Monsieur Jacques Courbé would have suffered most in this undignified fracas had it not been for St. Eustache, who had stationed himself over his tiny master and who now drove off all would-be assailants. As it was, Griffo, the unfortunate giraffe boy, was the most defenceless and therefore became the victim. His small, round head swayed back and forth to blows like a punching bag. He was bitten by Mademoiselle Lupa, buffeted by Monsieur Hippo, kicked by Monsieur Jejongle, clawed by Madame Samson, and nearly strangled by both the baby boa constrictors, which had wound themselves about his neck like hangmen's nooses. Undoubtedly, he would have fallen victim to circumstances had it not been for Simon Lafleur, the bride and half a dozen of her acrobatic friends, whom Papa Copo had implored to restore peace. Roaring with laughter, they sprang forward and tore the combatants apart.

Monsieur Jacques Courbé was found sitting grimly under a fold of the tablecloth. He held a broken bottle of wine in one hand. The dwarf was very drunk and in a towering rage. As Simon Lafleur approached with one of his silent laughs, Monsieur Jacques Courbé hurled the bottle at his head.

"Ah, the little wasp!" the bareback rider cried, picking up the dwarf by his waistband. "Here is your fine husband, Jeanne! Take him away before he does me some mischief. *Parbleu,* he is a bloodthirsty fellow in his cups!"

The bride approached, her blond face crimson from wine and laughter. Now that she was safely married to a country estate she took no more pains to conceal her true feelings.

"Oh, *la, la*!" she cried, seizing the struggling dwarf and holding him forcibly on her shoulder. "What a temper the little ape has! Well, we shall spank it out of him before long!"

"Let me down!" Monsieur Jacques Courbé screamed in a paroxysm of fury. "You will regret this, madame! Let me down, I say!"

But the stalwart bride shook her head. "No, no my little one!" she laughed. "You cannot escape your wife so easily! What, you would fly from my arms before the honeymoon!"

"Let me down!" he cried again. "Can't you see that they are laughing at me?"

"And why should they not laugh, my little ape? Let them laugh, if they will, but I will not put you down. No, I will carry you thus, perched on my shoulder, to the farm. It will set a precedent which brides of the future may find a certain difficulty in following!"

"But the farm is quite a distance from here, my Jeanne," said Simon Lafleur. "You are as strong as an ox and he is only marmoset, still, I will wager a bottle of Burgundy that you set him down by the roadside."

"Done, Simon!" the bride cried, with a flash of her strong white teeth. "You shall lose your wager, for I swear that I could carry my little ape from one end of France to the other!"

Monsieur Jacques Courbé no longer struggled. He now sat bolt upright on his bride's broad shoulder. From the flaming peaks of blind passion he had fallen into an abyss of cold fury. His love was dead but some quite alien emotion was rearing an evil head from its ashes.

"So, madame, you could carry me from one end of France to the other!" he droned in a monotonous undertone. "From one end of France to the other! I will remember that always, madame!"

"Come!" cried the bride suddenly. "I am off. Do you and the others, Simon, follow to see me win my wager."

They all trooped out of the tent. A full moon rode the heavens and showed the road, lying as white and straight through the meadows as the parting in Simon Lafleur's black, oily hair. The bride, still holding the diminutive bridegroom on her shoulder, burst out into song as she strode forward. The wedding guests followed. Some walked none too steadily. Griffo, the giraffe boy, staggered pitifully on his long, thin legs. Papa Copo alone remained behind.

"What a strange world!" he muttered, standing in the tent door and following them with his round blue eyes. "Ah, these children of mine are difficult at times—very difficult!"

3

A year had rolled by since the marriage of Mademoiselle Jeanne Marie and Monsieur Jacques Courbé. Copo's Circus had once more taken up its quarters in the town of Roubaix. For more than a week the country people for miles around had flocked to the side-show to get a peep at Griffo, the giraffe boy; Monsieur Hercule Hippo, the giant; Mademoiselle Lupa, the wolf lady; Madame Samson, with her baby boa constrictors; and Monsieur Jejongle, the famous juggler. Each was still firmly convinced that he or she alone was responsible for the popularity of the circus.

Simon Lafleur sat in his lodgings at the Sign of the Wild Boar. He wore nothing but red tights. His powerful torso, stripped to the waist, glistened with oil. He was kneading his biceps tenderly with some strong-smelling fluid.

Suddenly there came the sound of heavy, laborious footsteps on the stairs. Simon Lafleur looked up. His rather gloomy expression lifted, giving place to the brilliant smile that had won for him the hearts of so many lady acrobats.

"Ah, this is Marcelle!" he told himself. "Or perhaps it is Rose, the English girl; or, yet again, little Francesca, although she walks more lightly. Well, no matter—whoever it is, I will welcome her!"

But now the lagging, heavy footfalls were in the hall and, a moment later, they came to a halt outside the door. There was a timid knock.

Simon Lafleur's brilliant smile broadened. "Perhaps some new admirer who needs encouragement," he told himself. But aloud he said: "Enter, mademoiselle!"

The door swung slowly open and revealed the visitor. She was a tall, gaunt woman dressed like a peasant. The wind had blown her hair into her eyes. Now she raised a large, toil-worn hand, brushed it back across her forehead and looked long and attentively at the bareback rider.

"You do not remember me?" she said at length.

Two lines of perplexity appeared above Simon Lafleur's Roman nose; he slowly shook his head. He, who had known so many women in his time, was now at a loss. Was it a fair question to ask a man who was no longer a boy and who had lived? Women change so in a brief time! Now this bag of bones might at one time have appeared desirable to him.

Parbleu! Fate was a conjurer! She waved her wand and beautiful women were transformed into hags, jewels into pebbles, silks and laces into hempen cords. The brave fellow who danced tonight at the prince's ball might tomorrow dance more lightly on the gallows tree. The thing was to live and die with a full belly. To digest all that one could—that was life!

"You do not remember me?" she said again.

Simon Lafleur once more shook his sleek, black head. "I have a poor memory for faces, madame," he said politely. "It is my misfortune, when there are such beautiful faces."

"Ah, but you should have remembered, Simon!" the woman cried, a sob rising up in her throat. "We were very close together, you and I. Do you not remember Jeanne Marie?"

"Jeanne Marie!" the bareback rider cried. "Jeanne Marie, who married a marmoset and a country estate? Don't tell me, madame, that you—"

He broke off and stared at her, open-mouthed. His sharp black eyes wandered from the wisps of wet, straggling hair down her gaunt person till they rested at last on her thick cowhide boots, encrusted with layer on layer of mud from the countryside.

"It is impossible!" he said at last.

"It is indeed Jeanne Marie," the woman answered, "or what is left of her. Ah, Simon, what a life he has led me! I have been merely a beast of burden! There are no ignominies which he has not made me suffer!"

"To whom do you refer?" Simon Lafleur demanded. "Surely you cannot mean that pocket edition husband of yours—that dwarf, Jacques Courbé?"

"Ah, but I do, Simon! Alas, he has broken me!"

"He—that toothpick of a man?" the bareback rider cried, with one of his silent laughs. "Why it is impossible! As you once said yourself, Jeanne, you could crack his skull between finger and thumb like a hickory nut!"

"So I thought once. Ah, but I did not know him then, Simon! Because he was so small, I thought I could do with him as I liked. It seemed to me that I was marrying a manikin. 'I will play Punch and Judy with this little fellow,' I said to myself. Simon you may imagine my surprise when he began playing Punch and Judy with me!"

"But I do not understand, Jeanne. Surely at any time you could have slapped him into obedience!"

"Perhaps," she assented wearily, "had it not been for St. Eustache. From the first that wolf dog of his hated me. If I so much as answered his master back, he would show his teeth. Once, at the beginning, when I raised my hand to cuff Jacques Courbé, he sprang at my throat and would have torn me limb from limb had not the dwarf called him off. I was a strong woman, but even then I was no match for a wolf!"

"There was poison, was there not?" Simon Lafleur suggested.

"Ah, yes, I, too, thought of poison, but it was of no avail. St. Eustache would eat nothing that I gave him and the dwarf forced me to taste first of all food that was placed before him and his dog. Unless I myself wished to die, there was no way of poisoning either of them."

"My poor girl!" the bareback rider said, pityingly. "I begin to understand, but sit down and tell me everything. This is a revelation to me, after seeing you stalking homeward so triumphantly with your bridegroom on your shoulder. You must begin at the beginning."

"It was just because I carried him thus on my shoulder that I have had to suffer so cruelly," she said, seating herself on the only other chair the room afforded. "He has never forgiven me the insult which he says I put upon him. Do you remember how I boasted that I could carry him from one end of France to the other?"

"I remember. Well, Jeanne?"

"Well, Simon, the little demon has figured out the exact distance in leagues. Each morning, rain or shine, we sally out of the house—he on my back, the wolf dog at my heels—and I tramp along the dusty roads till my bones tremble beneath me from fatigue. If I so much as slacken my pace, if I falter, he goads me with his cruel little golden spurs, while, at the same time, St. Eustache nips my ankles. When we return home, he strikes so many leagues off a score which he says is the number of leagues from one end of France to the other. Not half that distance has been covered and I am no longer a strong woman, Simon. Look at these shoes!"

She held up one of her feet for his inspection. The sole of the cowhide boot had been worn through; Simon Lafleur caught a glimpse of bruised flesh caked with the mire of the highway.

"This is the third pair that I have had," she continued hoarsely. "Now he tells me that the price of shoe leather is too high, that I shall have to finish my pilgrimage barefooted."

"But why do you put up with all this, Jeanne?" Simon Lafleur asked angrily. "You, who have a carriage and a servant, should not walk at all!"

"At first there was a carriage and a servant," she said, wiping the tears from her eyes with the back of her hand, "but they did not last a week. He sent the servant about his business and sold the carriage at a nearby fair. Now there is no one but me to wait on him and his dog."

"But the neighbors?" Simon Lafleur persisted. "Surely you could appeal to them?"

"We have no near neighbors, the farm is quite isolated. I would have run away many months ago if I could have escaped unnoticed, but they keep a continual watch on me. Once I tried, but I hadn't traveled more than a league before the wolf dog was snapping at my ankles. He drove me back to the farm and the following day I was compelled to carry the little fiend till I fell from sheer exhaustion."

"But tonight you got away?"

"Yes," she said, with a quick, frightened glance at the door. "Tonight I slipped out while they were both sleeping and came here to you. I knew that you would protect me, Simon, because of what we have been to each other. Get Papa Copo to take me back in the circus and I will work my fingers to the bone! Save me, Simon!"

Jeanne Marie could no longer suppress her sobs. They rose in her throat, choking her, making her incapable of further speech.

"Calm yourself, Jeanne," Simon Lafleur said soothingly. "I will do what I can for you. I shall have a talk with Papa Copo tomorrow. Of course, you are no longer the same woman that you were a year ago. You have aged since then, but perhaps our good Papa Copo could find you something to do."

He broke off and eyed her intently. She had stiffened in the chair, her face, even under its coat of grime, had gone a sickly white.

"What troubles you, Jeanne?" he asked a trifle breathlessly.

"Hush!" she said, with a finger to her lips. "Listen!"

Simon Lafleur could hear nothing but the tapping of the rain on the roof and the sighing of the wind through the trees. An unusual silence seemed to pervade the Sign of the Wild Boar.

"Now don't you hear it?" she cried with an inarticulate gasp. "Simon, it is in the house—it is on the stairs!"

At last the bareback rider's less sensitive ears caught the sound his companion had heard a full minute before. It was a steady *pit-pat, pit-pat,* on the stairs, hard to dissociate from the drip of the rain from the eaves, but each instant it came nearer, grew more distinct.

"Oh, save me, Simon, save me!" Jeanne Marie cried, throwing herself at his feet and clasping him about the knees. "Save me! It is St. Eustache!"

"Nonsense, woman!" the bareback rider said angrily, but nevertheless he rose. "There are other dogs in the world. On the second landing there is a blind fellow who owns a dog. Perhaps it is he you hear."

"No, no—it is St. Eustache's step! My God, if you had lived with him a year, you would know it, too! Close the door and lock it!"

"That I will not," Simon Lafleur said contemptuously. "Do you think I am frightened so easily? If it is the wolf dog, so much the worse for him. He will not be the first cur I have choked to death with these two hands!"

Pit-pat, pit-pat—it was on the second landing. *Pit-pat, pit-pat*—now it was in the corridor, and coming fast. *Pit-pat*—all at once it stopped.

There was a moment's breathless silence and then into the room trotted St. Eustache. Monsieur Jacques Courbé sat astride the dog's broad back, as he had so often done in the circus ring. He held a tiny drawn sword, his shoe-button eyes seemed to reflect its steely glitter.

The dwarf brought the dog to a halt in the middle of the room and took in, at a single glance, the prostrate figure of Jeanne Marie. St. Eustache, too, seemed to take silent note of it. The stiff hair on his back rose up, he showed his long white fangs hungrily and his eyes glowed like two live coals.

"So I find you thus, madame!" Monsieur Jacques Courbé said at last. "It is fortunate that I have a charger here who can scent out my enemies as well as hunt them down in the open. Without him, I might have had some difficulty in discovering you. Well, the little game is up. I find you with your lover!"

"Simon Lafleur is not my lover!" she sobbed. "I have not seen him once since I married you until tonight! I swear it!"

"Once is enough," the dwarf said grimly. "The impudent stable-boy must be chastised."

"Oh, spare him!" Jeanne Marie implored. "Do not harm him, I beg of you! It is not his fault that I came! I—"

But at this point Simon Lafleur drowned her out in a roar of laughter.

"Ho, ho!" he roared, putting his hands on his hips. "You would chastise me, eh? *Nom d'un chien!* Don't try your circus tricks on *me*! Why hop-o-my-thumb, you who ride on a dog's back like a flea, out of this room before I squash you! Begone, melt, fade away!" He paused, expanded his barrel-like chest, puffed out his cheeks and blew a great breath at the dwarf. "Blow away, insect," he bellowed, "lest I put my heel on you!"

Monsieur Jacques Courbé was unmoved by this torrent of abuse. He sat very upright on St. Eustache's back, his tiny sword resting on his tiny shoulder.

"Are you done?" he said at last, when the bareback rider had run dry of invectives. "Very well, monsieur! Prepare to receive cavalry!" He paused for an instant, then added in a high, clear voice: "Get him, St. Eustache!"

The dog crouched and, at almost the same moment, sprang at Simon Lafleur. The bareback rider had no time to avoid him and his tiny rider. Almost instantaneously the three of them had come to death grips. It was a gory business.

Simon Lafleur, strong man as he was, was bowled over by the wolf dog's unexpected leap. St. Eustache's clashing jaws closed on his right arm and crushed it to the bone. A moment later the dwarf, still clinging to his dog's back, thrust the point of his tiny sword into the body of the prostrate bareback rider.

Simon Lafleur struggled valiantly, but to no purpose. Now he felt the fetid breath of the dog fanning his neck and the wasp-like sting of the dwarf's blade, which at this time found a mortal spot. A convulsive tremor shook him and he rolled over on his back. The circus Romeo was dead.

Monsieur Jacques Courbé cleansed his sword on a kerchief of lace, dismounted and approached Jeanne Marie. She was still crouching on the floor, her eyes closed, her head held tightly between both hands. The dwarf touched her imperiously on the broad shoulder which had so often carried him.

"Madame," he said, "we can now return home. You must be more careful hereafter. *Ma foi,* it is an ungentlemanly business cutting the throats of stable-boys!"

She rose to her feet, like a large trained animal at the word of command.

"You wish to be carried?" she said between livid lips.

"Ah, that is true, madame," he murmured. "I was forgetting our little wager. Ah, yes! Well, you are to be congratulated, madame—you have covered nearly half the distance."

"Nearly half the distance," she repeated in a lifeless voice.

"Yes, madame," Monsieur Jacques Courbé continued. "I fancy that you will be quite a docile wife by the time you have done." He paused and then added reflectively, "It is truly remarkable how speedily one can ride the devil out of a woman—with spurs!"

Papa Copo had been spending a convivial evening at the Sign of the Wild Boar. As he stepped out into the street he saw three familiar figures preceding him—a tall woman, a tiny man and a large dog with upstanding ears. The woman carried the man on her shoulder, the dog trotted at her heels.

The circus owner came to a halt and stared after them. His round eyes were full of childish astonishment.

"Can it be?" he murmured. "Yes, it is! Three old friends! And so Jeanne Marie still carries him! Ah, but she should not poke fun at Monsieur Jacques Courbé! He is so sensitive; but, alas, they are the kind that are always henpecked!"

The Fly

George Langelaan

Telephones and telephone bells have always made me uneasy. Years ago, when they were mostly wall fixtures, I disliked them, but nowadays, when they are planted in every nook and corner, they are a downright intrusion. We have a saying in France that a coalman is master in his own house; with the telephone that is no longer true, and I suspect that even the Englishman is no longer king in his own castle.

At the office, the sudden ringing of the telephone annoys me. It means that, no matter what I am doing, in spite of the switchboard operator, in spite of my secretary, in spite of doors and walls, some unknown person is coming into the room and on to my desk to talk right into my very ear, confidentially—whether I like it or not. At home, the feeling is still more disagreeable, but the worst is when the telephone rings in the dead of night. If anyone could see me turn on the light and get up blinking to answer it, I suppose I would look like any other sleepy man annoyed at being disturbed. The truth in such a case, however, is that I am struggling against panic, fighting down a feeling that a stranger has broken into the house and is in my bedroom. By the time I manage to grab the receiver and say: *"Ici Monsieur Delambre. Je vous écoute,"* I am outwardly calm, but I only get back to a more normal state when I know what is wanted of me.

The effort at dominating a purely animal reaction and fear had become so effective that when my sister-in-law called me at two in the morning, asking me to come over, but first to warn the police that she had just killed my brother, I quietly asked her how and why she had killed André.

"But, François! . . . I can't explain all that over the telephone. Please call the police and come quickly."

"Maybe I had better see you first, Hélène."

"No, you'd better call the police first; otherwise they will start asking you all sorts of awkward questions. They'll have enough trouble as it is to believe that I did it alone.... And, by the way, I suppose you ought to tell them that André... André's body is down at the factory. They may want to go there first."

"Did you say that André is at the factory?"

"Yes... under the steam hammer."

"Under the what?"

"The steam hammer! But don't ask so many questions. Please come quickly, François! Please understand that I'm afraid... that my nerves won't stand it much longer!"

Have you ever tried to explain to a sleepy police officer that your sister-in-law has just phoned to say that she has killed your brother with a steam hammer? I tried to repeat my explanation, but he would not let me.

"*Oui*, monsieur, *oui*, I hear... but who are you? What is your name? Where do you live? I said, where do you live!"

It was then that Commissaire Charas took over the line and the whole business. He at least seemed to understand everything. Would I wait for him? Yes, he would pick me up and take me over to my brother's house. When? In five or ten minutes.

I had just managed to pull on my trousers, wriggle into a sweater and grab a hat and coat, when a black Citroen, headlights blazing, pulled up at the door.

"I assume you have a night watchman at your factory, Monsieur Delambre. Has he called you?" asked Commissaire Charas, letting in the clutch as I sat down beside him and slammed the door of the car.

"No, he hasn't. Though of course my brother could have entered the factory through his laboratory where he often works late at night... all night sometimes."

"Is Professor Delambre's work connected with your business?"

"No, my brother is, or was, doing research work for the Ministère de l'Air. As he wanted to be away from Paris and yet within reach of where skilled workmen could fix up or make gadgets big and small for his experiments, I offered him one of the old workshops of the factory and he came to live in the first house built by our grandfather on the top of the hill at the back of the factory."

"Yes, I see. Did he talk about his work? What sort of research work?"

"He rarely talked about it, you know; I suppose the Air Ministry could tell you. I only know that he was about to carry out a number of experiments he had been preparing for some months, something to do with the disintegration of matter, he told me."

Barely slowing down, the commissaire swung the car off the road, slid it through the open factory gate and pulled up sharp by a policeman apparently expecting him.

I did not need to hear the policeman's confirmation. I knew now that my brother was dead; it seemed that I had been told years ago. Shaking like a leaf, I scrambled out after the commissaire.

Another policeman stepped out of a doorway and led us towards one of the shops where all the lights had been turned on. More policemen were standing by the hammer, watching two men setting up a camera. It was tilted downwards, and I made an effort to look.

It was far less horrid than I had expected. Though I had never seen my brother drunk, he looked just as if he were sleeping off a terrific binge, flat on his stomach across the narrow line on which the white-hot slabs of metal were rolled up to the hammer. I saw at a glance that his head and arm could only be a flattened mess, but that seemed quite impossible; it looked as if he had somehow pushed his head and arm right into the metallic mass of the hammer.

Having talked to his colleagues, the commissaire turned towards me:

"How can we raise the hammer, Monsieur Delambre?"

"I'll raise it for you."

"Would you like us to get one of your men over?"

"No, I'll be all right. Look, here is the switchboard. It was originally a steam hammer, but everything is worked electrically here now. Look commissaire, the hammer has been set at fifty tons and its impact at zero."

"At zero . . . ?"

"Yes, level with the ground if you prefer. It is also set for single strokes, which means that it has to be raised after each blow. I know what Hélène, my sister-in-law, will have to say about all this, but one thing I am sure of: she certainly did not know how to set and operate the hammer."

"Perhaps it was set that way last night when work stopped?"

"Certainly not. The drop is never set at zero, monsieur le commissaire."

"I see. Can it be raised gently?"

"No. The speed of the upstroke cannot be regulated. But in any case it is not very fast when the hammer is set for single strokes."

"Right. Will you show me what to do? It won't be very nice to watch, you know."

"No, no, monsieur le commissaire. I'll be all right."

"All set?" asked the commissaire of the others. "All right then, Monsieur Delambre. Whenever you like."

Watching my brother's back, I slowly but firmly pushed the upstroke button.

The unusual silence of the factory was broken by the sigh of compressed air rushing into the cylinders, a sigh that always makes me think of a giant taking a deep breath before solemnly socking another giant, and the steel mass of the hammer shuddered and then rose swiftly. I also heard the sucking sound as it left the metal base and thought I was going to panic when I saw André's body heave forward as a sickly gush of blood poured all over the ghastly mess bared by the hammer.

"No danger of it coming down again, Monsieur Delambre?"

"No, none whatever," I mumbled as I threw the safety switch and, turning around, I was violently sick in front of a young green-faced policeman.

For weeks after, Commissaire Charas worked on the case, listening, questioning, running all over the place, making out reports, telegraphing and telephoning right and left. Later, we became quite friendly and he owned up that he had for a long time considered me as suspect number one, but had finally given up on that idea because, not only was there no clue of any sort, there was not even a motive.

Hélène, my sister-in-law, was so calm throughout the whole business that the doctors finally confirmed what I had long considered the only possible solution: that she was mad. That being the case, there was of course no trial.

My brother's wife never tried to defend herself in any way and even got quite annoyed when she realized that people thought her mad, and this of course was considered proof that she was indeed mad. She owned up to the murder of her husband and proved easily that she knew how to handle the hammer; but she would never say why, exactly how, or under what circumstances she had killed my brother. The great mystery was how and why had my brother so obligingly stuck his head under the hammer, the only possible explanation for his part in the drama.

The night watchman had heard the hammer all right; he had even heard it twice, he claimed. This was strange, and the stroke counter, which was always set back to nought after a job, seemed to prove him right, since it marked the figure two. Also, the foreman in charge of the hammer confirmed that after cleaning up the day before the murder, he had as usual turned the stroke counter back to nought. In spite of this, Hélène maintained that she had only used the hammer once, and this seemed just another proof of her insanity.

Commissaire Charas, who had been put in charge of the case, at first wondered if the victim were really my brother. But of that there was no possible doubt, if only because of the great scar running from his knee to his thigh, the result of a shell that had landed within a few feet of him during the retreat in 1940; and there were also the fingerprints of his left hand which corresponded to those found all over his laboratory and his personal belongings in the house.

A guard had been put on his laboratory and the next day half a dozen officials came down from the Air Ministry. They went through all his papers and took away some of his instruments, but before leaving, they told the commissaire that the most interesting documents and instruments had been destroyed.

The Lyons police laboratory, one of the most famous in the world, reported that André's head had been wrapped in a piece of velvet when it was crushed by the hammer, and one day Commissaire Charas showed me a tattered drapery which I immediately recognized as the brown velvet cloth I had seen on a table in my brother's laboratory, the one on which his meals were served when he could not leave his work.

After only a very few days in prison, Hélène had been transferred to a nearby asylum, one of the three in France where insane criminals are taken care of. My nephew Henri, a boy of six, the very image of his father, was entrusted to me, and eventually all legal arrangements were made for me to become his guardian and tutor.

Hélène, one of the quietest patients of the asylum, was allowed visitors and I went to see her on Sundays. Once or twice the commissaire had accompanied me and, later, I learned that he had also visited Hélène alone. But we were never able to obtain any information from my sister-in-law, who seemed to have become utterly indifferent. She rarely answered my questions and hardly ever those of the commissaire. She spent a lot of her time sewing, but her favourite pastime seemed to be catching flies which she invariably released unharmed after having examined them carefully.

Hélène only had one fit of raving—more like a nervous breakdown than a fit, said the doctor who had administered morphia to quieten her—the day she saw a nurse swatting flies.

The day after Hélène's one and only fit, Commissaire Charas came to see me.

"I have a strange feeling that there lies the key to the whole business, Monsieur Delambre," he said.

I did not ask him how it was that he already knew all about Hélène's fit.

"I do not follow you, commissaire. Poor Madame Delambre could have shown an exceptional interest for anything else, really. Don't you think that flies just happen to be the border-subjects of her tendency to raving?"

"Do you believe she is really mad?" he asked.

"My dear commissaire, I don't see how there can be any doubt. Do you doubt it?"

"I don't know. In spite of all the doctors say, I have the impression that Madame Delambre has a very clear brain . . . even when catching flies."

"Supposing you were right, how would you explain her attitude with regard to her little boy? She never seems to consider him as her own child."

"You know, Monsieur Delambre, I have thought about that also. She may be trying to protect him. Perhaps she fears the boy or, for all we know, hates him?"

"I'm afraid I don't understand, my dear commissaire."

"Have you noticed, for instance, that she never catches flies when the boy is there?"

"No. But come to think of it, you are quite right. Yes, that is strange.... Still, I fail to understand."

"So do I, Monsieur Delambre. And I'm very much afraid that we shall never understand, unless perhaps your sister-in-law should *get better*."

"The doctors seem to think that there is no hope of any sort, you know."

"Yes. Do you know if your brother ever experimented with flies?"

"I really don't know, but I should think so. Have you asked the Air Ministry people? They knew all about the work."

"Yes, and they laughed at me."

"I can understand that."

"You are very fortunate to understand anything, Monsieur Delambre. I do not... but I hope to someday."

"Tell me, Uncle, do flies live a long time?"

We were just finishing our lunch and, following an established tradition between us, I was just pouring some wine into Henri's glass for him to dip a biscuit in.

Had Henri not been staring at his glass gradually being filled to the brim, something in my look might have frightened him.

This was the first time that he had ever mentioned flies, and I shuddered at the thought that Commissaire Charas might quite easily have been present. I could imagine the glint in his eye as he would have answered my nephew's question with another question. I could almost hear him saying:

"I don't know, Henri. Why do you ask?"

"Because I have again seen the fly that Maman was looking for."

And it was only after drinking off Henri's own glass of wine that I realized that he had answered my spoken thought.

"I did not know that your mother was looking for a fly."

"Yes, she was. It has grown quite a lot, but I recognized it all right."

"Where did you see this fly, Henri, and... how did you recognize it?"

"This morning on your desk, Uncle François. Its head is white instead of black, and it has a funny sort of leg."

Feeling more and more like Commissaire Charas, but trying to look unconcerned, I went on:

"And when did you see this fly for the first time?"

"The day that Papa went away. I had caught it, but Maman made me let it go. And then after, she wanted me to find it again. She'd changed her mind," and shrugging his shoulders just as my brother used to, he added, "you know how women are."

"I think that fly must have died long ago, and you must be mistaken, Henri," I said, getting up and walking to the door.

But as soon as I was out of the dining room, I ran up the stairs to my study. There was no fly anywhere to be seen.

I was bothered, far more than I cared to even think about. Henri had just proved that Charas was really closer to a clue than it had seemed when he told me about his thoughts concerning Hélène's pastime.

For the first time I wondered if Charas did not really know much more than he let on. For the first time also, I wondered about Hélène. Was she really insane? A strange horrid feeling was growing on me, and the more I thought about it, the more I felt that, somehow, Charas was right: Hélène was *getting away with it*!

What could possibly have been the reason for such a monstrous crime? What had led up to it? Just what had happened?

I thought of all the hundreds of questions that Charas had put to Hélène, sometimes gently like a nurse trying to soothe, sometimes stern and cold, sometimes barking them furiously. Hélène had answered very few, always in a calm quiet voice and never seeming to pay any attention to the way in which the question had been put. Though dazed, she had seemed perfectly sane then.

Refined, well-bred, and well-read, Charas was more than just an intelligent police official. He was a keen psychologist and had an amazing way of smelling out a fib or an erroneous statement even before it was uttered. I knew that he had accepted as true the few answers she had given him. But then there had been all those questions which she had never answered: the most direct and important ones. From the very beginning, Hélène had adopted a very simple system. "I cannot answer that question," she would say in her low, quiet voice. And that was that! The repetition of the same question never seemed to annoy her. In all the hours of questioning that she underwent, Hélène did not once point out to the commissaire that he had already asked her this or that. She would simply say, "I cannot answer that question," as though it was the very first time that that particular question had been asked and the very first time she had made that answer.

This cliché had become the formidable barrier beyond which Commissaire Charas could not even get a glimpse, an idea of what Hélène might be thinking. She had very willingly answered all questions about her life with my brother—which seemed a happy and uneventful one—up to the time of his end. About his death, however, all that she would say was that she had killed him with the steam hammer, but she refused to say why, what had led up to the drama and how she got my brother to put his head under it. She never actually refused outright; she would just go bland and, with no apparent emotion, would switch over to, "I cannot answer that question."

Hélène, as I have said, had shown the commissaire that she knew how to set and operate the steam hammer.

Charas could only find one single fact which did not coincide with Hélène's declarations, the fact that the hammer had been used twice. Charas was no longer willing to attribute this to insanity. That evident flaw in Hélène's stonewall defense seemed a crack which the commissaire might possibly enlarge. But my sister-in-law finally cemented it by acknowledging:

"All right, I lied to you. I did use the hammer twice. But do not ask me why, because I cannot tell you."

"Is that your only . . . misstatement, Madame Delambre?" the commissaire had asked. Trying to follow up what looked at last like an advantage.

"It is . . . and you know it, monsieur le commissaire."

And, annoyed, Charas had seen that Hélène could read him like an open book.

I had thought of calling on the commissaire, but the knowledge that he would inevitably start questioning Henri made me hesitate. Another reason also made me hesitate, a vague sort of fear that he would look for and find the fly Henri had talked of. And that annoyed me a good deal because I could find no satisfactory explanation for that particular fear.

André was definitely not the absent-minded sort of professor who walks about in pouring rain with a rolled umbrella under his arm. He was human, had a keen sense of humour, loved children and animals and could not bear to see anyone suffer. I had often seen him drop his work to watch a parade of the local fire brigade, or see the Tour de France cyclists go by, or even follow a circus parade all around the village. He liked games of logic and precision, such as billiards and tennis, bridge and chess.

How was it then possible to explain his death? What could have made him put his head under that hammer? It could hardly have been the result of some stupid bet or a test of courage. He hated betting and had no patience with those who indulged in it. Whenever he heard a bet proposed, he would invariably remind all present that, after all, a bet was but a contract between a fool and a swindler, even if it turned out to be a toss-up as to which was which.

It seemed there were only two possible explanations for André's death.

Either he had gone mad, or else he had a reason for letting his wife kill him in such a strange and terrible way. And just what could have been his wife's role in all this? They surely could not have both been insane?

Having finally decided not to tell Charas about my nephew's innocent revelations, I thought I myself would try to question Hélène.

She seemed to have been expecting my visit, for she came into the parlour almost as soon as I had made myself known to the matron and been allowed inside.

"I wanted to show you my garden," explained Hélène as I looked at the coat slung over her shoulders.

As one of the "reasonable" inmates, she was allowed to go into the garden during certain hours of the day. She had asked for and obtained the right to a little patch of ground where she could grow flowers, and I had sent her seeds and some rosebushes out of my garden.

She took me straight to a rustic wooden bench which had been made in the men's workshop and only just set up under a tree close to her little patch of ground.

Searching for the right way to broach the subject of André's death, I sat for a while tracing vague designs on the ground with the end of my umbrella.

"François, I want to ask you something," said Hélène after a while.

"Anything I can do for you, Hélène?"

"No, just something I want to know. Do flies live very long?"

Staring at her, I was about to say that her boy had asked the very same question a few hours earlier when I suddenly realized that here was the opening I had been searching for and perhaps even the possibility of striking a great blow, a blow perhaps powerful enough to shatter her stonewall defense, be it sane or insane.

Watching her carefully, I replied:

"I don't really know, Hélène, but the fly you were looking for was in my study this morning."

No doubt about it, I had struck a shattering blow. She swung her head round with such force that I heard the bones crack in her neck. She opened her mouth, but said not a word, only her eyes seemed to be screaming with fear.

Yes, it was evident that I had crashed through something, but what? Undoubtedly, the commissaire would have known what to do with such an advantage; I did not. All I knew was that he would never have given her time to think, to recuperate, but all I could do, and even that was a strain, was to maintain my best poker face, hoping against hope that Hélène's defenses would go on crumbling.

She must have gone quite a while without breathing, because she suddenly gasped and put both her hands over her still open mouth.

"François . . . Did you kill it?" she whispered, her eyes no longer fixed, but searching every inch of my face.

"No."

"You have it then. . . . You have it on you! Give it to me!" she almost shouted, touching me with both her hands, and I knew that had she felt strong enough, she would have tried to search me.

"No, Hélène, I haven't got it."

"But you know now. . . . You have guessed, haven't you?"

"No, Hélène. I only know one thing, and that is that you are not insane. But I mean to know all, Hélène, and somehow I am going to find out. You can choose: either you tell me everything and I'll see what is to be done, or . . ."

"Or what? Say! Say it!"

"I was going to say it, Hélène . . . or I assure you that your friend the commissaire will have that fly first thing tomorrow morning."

She remained quite still, looking down at the palms of her hands on her lap and although it was getting chilly, her forehead and hands were moist. Without even brushing aside a wisp of long brown hair blown across her mouth by the breeze, she murmured:

"If I tell you . . . will you promise to destroy that fly before doing anything else?"

"No, Hélène, I can make no such promise before knowing."

"But François, you must understand. I promised André that fly would be destroyed. That promise must be kept and I can say nothing until it is."

I could sense the deadlock ahead. I was not yet losing ground, but I was losing the initiative. I tried a shot in the dark:

"Hélène, of course you understand that as soon as the police examine that fly, they will know that you are not insane, and then . . ."

"François, no! For Henri's sake! Don't you see? I was expecting that fly; I was hoping it would find me here but it couldn't know what had become of me. What else could it do but go to others it loves, to Henri, to you . . . you who might know and understand what was to be done."

Was she really mad, or was she simulating again? But mad or not, she was cornered. Wondering how to follow up and how to land the knockout blow without running the risk of seeing her slip away out of reach, I said very quietly:

"Tell me all, Hélène. I can then protect your boy."

"Protect my boy from what? Don't you understand that if I am here, it is merely so that Henri won't be the son of a woman who was guillotined for having murdered his father? Don't you understand that I would by far prefer the guillotine to the living death of this lunatic asylum?"

"I understand, Hélène, and I'll do my best for the boy whether you tell me or not. If you refuse to tell me, I'll still do the best I can to protect Henri, but you must understand that the game will be out of my hands, because Commissaire Charas will have the fly."

"But why must you know?" said, rather than asked, my sister-in-law, struggling to control her temper.

"Because I must and will know how and why my brother died, Hélène."

"All right. Take me back to the . . . house. I'll give you what your commissaire would call my 'confession.' "

"Do you mean to say that you have written it!"

"Yes. It was not really meant for you, but more likely for *your friend*, the commissaire. I had foreseen that, sooner or later, he would get too close to the truth."

"You then have no objection to his reading it?"

"You will act as you think fit, François. Wait for me a minute."

Leaving me at the door of the parlour, Hélène ran upstairs to her room. In less than a minute she was back with a large brown envelope.

"Listen, François; you are not nearly as bright as was your poor brother, but you are not unintelligent. All I ask is that you read this alone. After that, you may do as you wish."

"That I promise you, Hélène," I said, taking the precious envelope. "I'll read it tonight and although tomorrow is not a visiting day, I'll come down to see you."

"Just as you like," said my sister-in-law without even saying goodbye as she went back upstairs.

It was only on reaching home, as I walked from the garage to the house, that I read the inscription on the envelope:

To Whom It May Concern
(Probably Commissaire Charas)

Having told the servants that I would have only a light supper, to be served immediately in my study, and that I was not to be disturbed after, I ran upstairs, threw Hélène's envelope on my desk and made another careful search of the room before closing the shutters and drawing the curtains. All I could find was a long-since-dead mosquito stuck to the wall near the ceiling.

Having motioned to the servant to put her tray down on a table by the fireplace, I poured myself a glass of wine and locked the door behind her. I then disconnected the telephone—I always did this now at night—and turned out all the lights but the lamp on my desk.

Slitting open Hélène's fat envelope, I extracted a thick wad of closely written pages. I read the following lines neatly centered in the middle of the top page:

> This is not a confession because, although I killed my husband, I am not a murderess. I simply and very faithfully carried out his last wish by crushing his head and right arm under the steam hammer at his brother's factory.

Without even touching the glass of wine by my elbow, I turned the page and started reading.

For very nearly a year before his death (the manuscript began), my husband had told me of some of his experiments. He knew full well that his colleagues of the Air Ministry would have forbidden some of them as too dangerous, but he was keen on obtaining positive results before reporting his discovery.

Whereas the only sound and pictures had been, so far, transmitted through space by radio and television, André claimed to have discovered a way of transmitting matter. Matter, any solid object, placed in his "transmitter" was instantly disintegrated and reintegrated in a special receiving set.

André considered his discovery as perhaps the most important since that of the wheel sawn off the end of a tree trunk. He reckoned that the transmission of matter by instantaneous "disintegration-reintegration" would completely change life as we had known it so far. It would mean the end of all means of transport, not only of goods including food, but also of human beings. André, the practical scientist who never allowed theories or daydreams to get the better of him, already foresaw the time when there would no longer be any aeroplanes, ships, trains, or cars, and therefore, no longer any roads or railway lines, ports, airports, or stations. All that would be replaced by matter transmitting-and-receiving-stations throughout the world. Travelers and goods would be placed in special cabins and, at a given signal, would simply disappear and reappear almost immediately at the chosen receiving station.

André's receiving set was only a few feet away from his transmitter, in an adjoining room of his laboratory, and he at first ran into all sorts of snags. His first successful experiment was carried out with an ashtray taken from his desk, a souvenir we had brought back from a trip to London.

That was the first time he told me about his experiments and I had no idea of what he was talking about the day he came dashing into the house and threw the ashtray in my lap.

"Hélène, look! For a fraction of a second, a bare ten-millionth of a second, that ashtray has been completely disintegrated. For one little moment it no longer existed! Gone! Nothing left, absolutely nothing! Only atoms traveling through space at the speed of light! And the moment after, the atoms were once more gathered together in the shape of an ashtray!"

"André, please . . . please! What on earth are you raving about?"

He started sketching all over a letter I had been writing. He laughed at my wry face, swept all my letters off the table and said:

"You don't understand? Right? Let's start all over again. Hélène, do you remember I once read you an article about the mysterious flying stones that seem to come from nowhere in particular, and which are said occasionally to fall in certain houses in India? They come flying in as though thrown from outside, in spite of closed doors and windows."

"Yes, I remember. I also remember that Professor Augier, your friend of the Collège de France, who had come down for few days, remarked that if there was no trickery about it, the only possible explanation was that the stones had been disintegrated after having been thrown from outside, come through the walls, and then been reintegrated before hitting the floor of the opposite walls."

"That's right. And I added that there was, of course, one other possibility, namely the momentary and partial disintegration of the walls as the stone or stones came through."

"Yes, André. I remember all that, and I suppose you also remember that I failed to understand, and that you got quite annoyed. Well, I still do not understand why and how, even disintegrated, stones should be able to come through a wall or a closed door."

"But it is possible, Hélène, because the atoms that make up matter are not close together like the bricks of a wall. They are separated by relative immensities of space."

"Do you mean to say that you have disintegrated that ashtray and then put it together again after pushing it through something?"

"Precisely, Hélène. I projected it through the wall that separates my transmitter from my receiving set."

"And would it be foolish to ask how humanity is to benefit from ashtrays that can go through walls?"

André seemed quite offended, but he soon saw that I was only teasing and again waxing enthusiastic, he told me of some of the possibilities of his discovery.

"Isn't it wonderful, Hélène?" he finally gasped, out of breath.

"Yes, André. But I hope you won't ever transmit me; I'd be too much afraid of coming out the other end like your ashtray."

"What do you mean?"

"Do you remember what was written under that ashtray?"

"Yes, of course; Made in Japan. That was the great joke of our typically British souvenir."

"The words are still there André; but . . . look!"

He took the ashtray out of my hands, frowned, and walked over to the window. Then he went quite pale, and I knew that he had seen what had proved to me that he had indeed carried out a strange experiment.

The three words were still there, but reversed and reading:

Made in Japan

Without a word, having completely forgotten me, André rushed off to his laboratory. I only saw him the next morning, tired and unshaven after a whole night's work.

A few days later, André had a new reverse which put him out of sorts and made him fussy and grumpy for several weeks. I stood it patiently enough for a while, but being myself bad-tempered one evening, we had a silly row over some futile thing, and I reproached him for his moroseness.

"I'm sorry, *chérie.* I've been working my way through a maze of problems and have given you all a very rough time. You see, my very first experiment with a live animal proved a complete fiasco."

"André! You tried that experiment with Dandelo, didn't you?"

"Yes. How did you know?" he answered sheepishly. "He disintegrated perfectly, but he never reappeared in the receiving set."

"Oh, André! What became of him then?"

"Nothing . . . there is no more Dandelo; only the dispersed atoms of a cat wandering, God knows where, in the universe."

Dandelo was a small white cat the cook had found one morning in the garden and which we had promptly adopted. Now I knew how it had disappeared and was quite angry about the whole thing, but my husband was so miserable over it all that I said nothing.

I saw little of my husband during the next few weeks. He had most of his meals sent down to the laboratory. I would often wake up in the morning and find his bed unslept in. Sometimes, if he had come in very late, I would find that storm-swept appearance which only a man can give a bedroom by getting up very early and fumbling around in the dark.

One evening he came home to dinner all smiles, and I knew that his troubles were over. His face dropped, however, when he saw I was dressed for going out.

"Oh. Were you going out, Hélène?"

"Yes, the Drillons invited me for a game of bridge, but I can easily phone them and put it off."

"No, it's all right."

"It isn't all right. Out with it, dear!"

"Well, I've at last got everything perfect and I wanted you to be the first to see the miracle."

"*Magnifique*, André! Of course I'll be delighted."

Having telephoned our neighbors to say how sorry I was and so forth, I ran down to the kitchen and told the cook that she had exactly ten minutes in which to prepare a "celebration dinner."

"An excellent idea, Hélène," said my husband when the maid appeared with the champagne after our candlelight dinner. "We'll celebrate with reintegrated champagne!" and taking the tray from the maid's hands, he led the way down to the laboratory.

"Do you think it will be as good as before its disintegration?" I asked, holding the tray while he opened the door and switched on the lights.

"Have no fear. You'll see! Just bring it here, will you," he said, opening the door of a telephone call box he had bought and which had been transformed into what he called a transmitter. "Put it down on that now," he added, putting a stool inside the box.

Having carefully closed the door, he took me to the other end of the room and handed me a pair of very dark sunglasses. He put on another pair and walked back to the switchboard by the transmitter.

"Ready, Hélène?" said my husband, turning out all the lights. "Don't remove your glasses till I give the word."

"I won't budge, André, go on," I told him, my eyes fixed on the tray which I could just see in a greenish shimmering light through the glass-paneled door of the telephone booth.

"Right," said André, throwing a switch.

The whole room was brilliantly illuminated by an orange flash. Inside the cabin I had seen a crackling ball of fire and felt its heat on my face, neck, and hands. The whole thing lasted but a fraction of a second, and I found myself blinking at green-edged black holes like those one sees after having stared at the sun.

"*Et voilà*! You can take off your glasses, Hélène!"

A little theatrically perhaps, my husband opened the door of the cabin. Though André had told me what to expect, I was astonished to find that the champagne, glasses, tray, and stool were no longer there.

André ceremoniously led me by the hand into the next room in a corner of which stood a second telephone booth. Opening the door wide, he triumphantly lifted the champagne tray off the stool.

Feeling somewhat like the good-natured kind-member-of-the-audience that has been dragged onto the music hall stage by the magician, I repressed from saying, "All done with mirrors," which I knew would have annoyed my husband.

"Sure it's not dangerous to drink?" I asked as the cork popped.

"Absolutely sure, Hélène," he said, handing me a glass. "But that was nothing. Drink this off and I'll show you something much more astounding."

We went back into the other room.

"Oh, André! Remember poor Dandelo!"

"This is only a guinea pig, Hélène. But I'm positive it will go through all right."

He set the furry beast down on the green enameled floor of the booth and quickly closed the door. I again put on my dark glasses and saw and felt the vivid crackling flash.

Without waiting for André to open the door, I rushed into the next room where the lights were still on and looked into the receiving booth.

"Oh, André! *Chéri!* He's all right!" I shouted excitedly, watching the little animal trotting round and round. "It's wonderful, André. It works! You've succeeded!"

"I hope so, but I must be patient. I'll know for sure in a few weeks' time."

"What do you mean? Look! He's as full of life as when you put him in the other cabin."

"Yes, so he seems. But we'll have to see if all his organs are intact, and that will take some time. If that little beast is still full of life in a month's time, we then consider the experiment a success."

I begged André to let me take care of the guinea pig.

"All right, but don't kill it by overfeeding," he agreed with a grin for my enthusiasm.

Though not allowed to take Hop-la—the name I had given the guinea pig—out of its box in the laboratory, I had tied a pink ribbon round his neck and was allowed to feed it twice a day.

Hop-la soon got used to its pink ribbon and became quite a tame little pet, but that month of waiting seemed like a year.

And then one day, André put Miquette, our cocker spaniel, into his "transmitter." He had not told me beforehand, knowing full well that I would never have agreed to such an experiment with our dog. But when he did tell me, Miquette had been successfully transmitted half-a-dozen times and seemed to be enjoying the operation thoroughly; no sooner was she let out of the "reintegrator" than she dashed madly into the next room, scratching at the "transmitter" door to have "another go," as André called it.

I now expected that my husband would invite some of his old colleagues and Air Ministry specialists to come down. He usually did this when he had finished a research job and, before handing them long detailed reports which he always typed himself, he would carry out an experiment or two before them. But this time, he just went on working. One morning I finally asked him when he intended throwing his usual "surprise party," as we called it.

"No, Hélène, not for a long while yet. This discovery is much too important. I have an awful lot of work to do on it still. Do you realize that there are some parts of the transmission proper which I do not yet myself fully understand? It works all right, but you see, I can't just say to all these eminent professors that I do this and that and, poof, it works! I must be able to explain how and why it works. And what is even more important, I must be ready and able to refute every destructive argument they will not fail to trot out, as they usually do when faced with anything really good."

I was occasionally invited down to the laboratory to witness some new experiment, but I never went unless André invited me, and only talked about his work if he broached the subject first. Of course it never occurred to me that he would, at that stage at least, have tried an experiment with a human being; though, had I thought about it—knowing André—it would have been obvious that he would never have allowed anyone into the "transmitter" before he had been through to test it first. It was only after the accident that I discovered he had duplicated all his switches inside the disintegration booth, so that he could try it out by himself.

The morning André tried this terrible experiment, he did not show up for lunch. I sent the maid down with a tray, but she brought it back with a note she had found pinned outside the laboratory door: "Do not disturb me, I am working."

He did occasionally pin such notes on his door and, though I noticed it, I paid no particular attention to the unusually large handwriting of his note.

It was just after that, as I was drinking my coffee, that Henri came bouncing into the room to say that he had caught a funny fly, and would I like to see it. Refusing even to look at his closed fist, I ordered him to release it immediately.

"But Maman, it has such a funny white head!"

Marching the boy over to the open window, I told him to release the fly immediately, which he did. I knew that Henri had caught the fly merely because he thought it looked curious or different from other flies, but I also knew that his father would never stand for any form of cruelty to animals, and that there would be a fuss should he discover that our son had put a fly in a box or a bottle.

At dinnertime that evening, André had still not shown up and, a little worried, I ran down to the laboratory and knocked at the door.

He did not answer my knock, but I heard him moving around and a moment later he slipped a note under the door. It was typewritten:

Hélène, I am having trouble. Put the boy to bed and come back in an hour's time. A.

Frightened, I knocked and called, but André did not seem to pay any attention and, vaguely reassured by the familiar noise of his typewriter, I went back to the house.

Having put Henri to bed, I returned to the laboratory, where I found another note slipped under the door. My hand shook as I picked it up because I knew by then that something must be radically wrong. I read:

Hélène, first of all I count on you not to lose your nerve or do anything rash because you alone can help me. I have had a serious accident. I am not in any particular danger for the time being though it is a matter of life and death. It is useless calling to me or saying anything. I cannot answer, I cannot speak. I want you to do exactly and very carefully all that I ask. After having knocked three times to show that you understand and agree, fetch me a bowl of milk laced with rum. I have had nothing all day and can do with it.

Shaking with fear, not knowing what to think and repressing a furious desire to call André and bang away until he opened the door, I knocked three times as requested and ran all the way home to fetch what he wanted.

In less than five minutes I was back. Another note had been slipped under the door:

Hélène, follow these instructions carefully. When you knock I'll open the door. You are to walk over to my desk and put down the bowl of milk. You will then go into the other room where the receiver is. Look carefully and try to find a fly which ought to be there but which I am unable to find. Unfortunately, I cannot see small things very easily.

Before you come in you must promise to obey me implicitly. Do not look at me and remember that talking is quite useless. I cannot answer. Knock again three times and that will mean I have your promise. My life depends entirely on the help you can give me.

I had to wait a while to pull myself together, and then I knocked slowly three times.

I heard André shuffling behind the door, then his hand fumbling with the lock, and the door opened.

Out of the corner of my eye, I saw that he was standing behind the door, but without looking round, I carried the bowl of milk to his desk. He was evidently watching me and I had to at all costs appear calm and collected.

"*Chéri,* you can count on me," I said gently, and putting the bowl down under his desk lamp, the only one alight, I walked into the next room where all the lights were blazing.

My first impression was that some sort of hurricane must have blown out of the receiving booth. Papers were scattered in every direction, a whole row of test tubes lay smashed in a corner, chairs and stools were upset and one of the window curtains hung half torn from its bent rod. In a large enamel basin on the floor a heap of burned documents was still smoldering.

I knew that I would not find the fly André wanted me to look for. Women know things that men only suppose by reasoning and deduction; it is a form of knowledge very rarely accessible to them and which they disparagingly call intuition. I already knew that the fly André wanted was the one which Henri had caught and which I had made him release.

I heard André shuffling around in the next room, and then a strange gurgling and sucking as though he had trouble in drinking his milk.

"André, there is no fly here. Can you give me any sort of indication that might help? If you can't speak, rap or something . . . you know once for yes, twice for no."

I had tried to control my voice and speak as though perfectly calm, but I had to choke down a sob of desperation when he rapped twice for "no."

"May I come to you, André? I don't know what can have happened, but whatever it is, I'll be courageous, dear."

After a moment of silent hesitation, he tapped once on his desk.

At the door I stopped aghast at the sight of André standing with his head and shoulders covered by the brown velvet cloth he had taken from a table by his desk, the table on which he usually ate when he did not want to leave his work. Suppressing a laugh that might easily have turned to sobbing, I said:

"André, we'll search thoroughly tomorrow, by daylight. Why don't you go to bed? I'll lead you to the guest room if you like, and won't let anyone else see you."

His left hand tapped the desk twice.

"Do you need a doctor, André?"

"No," he rapped.

"Would you like to call up Professor Augier? He might be of more help . . ."

Twice he rapped "no" sharply. I did not know what to do or say. And then I told him:

"Henri caught a fly this morning which he wanted to show me, but I made him release it. Could it have been the one you are looking for? I didn't see it, but the boy said its head was white."

André emitted a strange metallic sigh, and I just had time to bite my fingers fiercely in order not to scream. He had let his right arm drop, and instead of his long-fingered muscular hand, a gray stick with little buds on it like the branch of a tree hung out of his sleeve almost down to his knee.

"André, *mon chéri*, tell me what happened. I might be of more help to you if I knew, André . . . oh, it's terrible!" I sobbed, unable to control myself.

Having rapped once for yes, he pointed to the door with his left hand.

I stepped out and sank down crying as he locked the door behind me. He was typing again and I waited. At last he shuffled to the door and slid a sheet of paper under it.

Hélène, come back in the morning. I must think and will have typed out an explanation for you. Take one of my sleeping tablets and go straight to bed. I need you fresh and strong tomorrow, *ma pauvre chérie*. A.

"Do you want anything for the night, André?" I shouted through the door.

He knocked twice for no, and a little later I heard the typewriter again.

The sun full on my face woke me up with a start. I had set the alarm clock for five but had not heard it, probably because of the sleeping tablets. I had indeed slept like a log, without a dream. Now I was back in my living nightmare and crying like a child I sprang out of bed. It was just on seven!

Rushing into the kitchen, without a word for the startled servants, I rapidly prepared a tray-load of coffee, bread, and butter with which I ran down to the laboratory.

André opened the door as soon as I knocked and closed it again as I carried the tray to his desk. His head was still covered, but I saw from his crumpled suit and his open camp bed that he must have at least tried to rest.

On his desk lay a typewritten sheet for me which I picked up. André opened the other door, and taking this to mean that he wanted to be left alone, I walked into the next room. He pushed the door to, and I heard him pouring out the coffee as I read:

Do you remember the ashtray experiment? I have had a similar accident. I transmitted myself successfully the night before last. During a second

experiment yesterday a fly which I did not see must have got into the disintegrator. My only hope is to find that fly and go through again with it. Please search for it carefully since, if it is not found, I shall have to find a way of putting an end to all this.

If only André had been more explicit! I shuddered at the thought that he must be terribly disfigured and then cried softly as I imagined his face inside-out, or perhaps his eyes in place of his ears, or his mouth at the back of his neck, or worse!

André must be saved! For that, the fly must be found!

Pulling myself together, I said:

"André, may I come in?"

He opened the door.

"André, don't despair; I am going to find that fly. It is no longer in the laboratory, but it cannot be very far. I suppose you're disfigured, perhaps terribly so, but there can be no question of putting an end to all this, as you say in your note; that I will never stand for. If necessary, if you do not wish to be seen, I'll make you a mask or a cowl so that you can go on with your work until you get well again. If you cannot work, I'll call Professor Augier, and he and all your other friends will save you, André."

Again I heard that curious metallic sigh as he rapped violently on his desk.

"André, don't be annoyed; please be calm. I won't do anything without first consulting you, but you must rely on me, have faith in me and let me help you as best I can. Are you terribly disfigured, dear? Can't you let me see your face? I won't be afraid. . . . I am your wife you know."

But my husband again rapped a decisive "no" and pointed to the door.

"All right. I am going to search for the fly now, but promise me you won't do anything foolish; promise you won't do anything rash or dangerous without first letting me know all about it!"

He extended his left hand, and I knew I had his promise.

I will never forget that ceaseless daylong hunt for a fly. Back home, I turned the house inside out and made all the servants join in the search. I told them that a fly had escaped from the Professor's laboratory and that it must be captured alive, but it was evident they already thought me crazy. They said so to the police later, and that day's hunt for a fly most probably saved me from the guillotine later.

I questioned Henri, and as he failed to understand right away what I was talking about, I shook him and slapped him and made him cry in front of the round-eyed maids. Realizing that I must not let myself go, I kissed and petted the poor boy and at last made him understand what I wanted of him. Yes, he remembered, he had found the fly just by the kitchen window; yes, he had released it immediately as told to.

Even in summertime we had very few flies because our house is on the top of a hill and the slightest breeze coming across the valley blows round it. In spite of that, I managed to catch dozens of flies that day. On all the window sills and all over the garden I had put saucers of milk, sugar, jam, meat—all the things likely to attract flies. Of all those we caught, and many others which we failed to catch but which I saw, none resembled the one Henri had caught the day before. One by one, with a magnifying glass, I examined every unusual fly, but none had anything like a white head.

At lunchtime, I ran down to André with some milk and mashed potatoes. I also took some of the flies we had caught, but he gave me to understand that they could be of no possible use to him.

"If that fly has not been found by tonight, André, we'll have to see what is to be done. And this is what I propose: I'll sit in the next room. When you can't answer by the yes-no method of rapping, you'll type out whatever you want to say and then slip it under the door. Agreed?"

"Yes," rapped André.

By nightfall we had still not found the fly. At dinnertime, as I prepared André's tray, I broke down and sobbed in the kitchen in front of the silent servants. My maid thought that I had had a row with my husband, probably about the mislaid fly, but I learned later that the cook was already quite sure that I was out of my mind.

Without a word, I picked up the tray and then put it down again as I stopped by the telephone. That this was really a matter of life and death for André, I had no doubt. Neither did I doubt that he fully intended committing suicide, unless I could make him change his mind, or at least put off such a drastic decision. Would I be strong enough? He would never forgive me for not keeping a promise, but under the circumstances, did that really matter? To the devil with promises and honor! At all costs André must be saved! And having thus made up my mind, I looked up and dialed Professor Augier's number.

"The professor is away and will not be back before the end of the week," said a polite neutral voice at the other end of the line.

That was that! I would have to fight alone and fight I would. I would save André come what may.

All my nervousness had disappeared as André let me in and, after putting the tray of food down on his desk, I went into the other room, as agreed.

"The first thing I want to know," I said as he closed the door behind me, "is what happened exactly. Can you please tell me, André?"

I waited patiently while he typed an answer which he pushed under the door a little later.

> Hélène, I would rather not tell you. Since go I must, I would rather you remember me as I was before. I must destroy myself in such a way that none can possibly know what has happened to me. I have of course thought of simply disintegrating myself in my transmitter, but I had better not because, sooner or later, I might find myself reintegrated. Someday, somewhere, some scientist is sure to make the same discovery. I have therefore thought of a way which is neither simple nor easy, but you can and will help me.

For several minutes I wondered if André had not simply gone stark raving mad.

"André," I said at last, "whatever you may have chosen or thought of, I cannot and will never accept such a cowardly solution. No matter how awful the result of your experiment or accident, you are alive, you are a man, a brain . . . and you have a soul. You have no right to destroy yourself. You know that!"

> I am alive all right, but I am already no longer a man. As to my brain or intelligence, it may disappear at any moment. As it is, it is no longer intact. And there can be no soul without intelligence . . . and you know that!

"Then you must tell the other scientists about your discovery. They will help you and save you, André!"

I staggered back frightened as he angrily thumped the door twice.

"André . . . Why? Why do you refuse the aid you know they would give you with all their hearts?"

A dozen furious knocks shook the door and made me understand that my husband would never accept such a solution. I had to find other arguments.

For hours, it seemed, I talked to him about our boy, about me, about his family, about his duty to us and to the rest of humanity. He made no reply of any sort. At last I cried:

"André . . . do you hear me?"

"Yes," he knocked very gently.

"Well, listen then. I have another idea. You remember your first experiment with the ashtray? . . . Well, do you think that if you had put it through again a second time, it might possibly have come out with the letters turned back the right way?"

Before I had finished speaking, André was busily typing and a moment later I read his answer:

I have already thought of that, and that is why I needed the fly. It has got to go through with me. There is no hope otherwise.

"Try all the same, André. You never know!"

I have tried seven times already, was the typewritten reply I got to that.

"André! Try again, please!"

The answer this time gave me a flutter of hope, because no woman has ever understood, or will ever understand, how a man about to die can possibly consider anything funny.

I deeply admire your delicious feminine logic. We could go on doing this experiment until doomsday. However, just to give you that pleasure, probably the very last I shall ever be able to give you, I will try once more. If you cannot find the dark glasses, turn your back to the machine and press your hands over your eyes. Let me know when you are ready.

"Ready, André!" I shouted without even looking for the glasses and following his instructions.

I heard him moving around and then opening and closing the door of his "disintegrator." After what seemed a very long wait, but probably was not more than a minute or so, I heard a violent crackling noise and perceived a bright flash through my eyelids and fingers.

I turned around as the cabin door opened.

His head and shoulders still covered with the brown velvet carpet, André was gingerly stepping out of it.

"How do you feel, André? Any difference?" I asked, touching his arm.

He tried to step away from me and caught his foot in one of the stools which I had not troubled to pick up. He made a violent effort to regain his balance, and the velvet cloth slowly slid off his shoulders and head as he fell heavily backwards.

The horror was too much for me, too unexpected. As a matter of fact, I am sure that, even had I known, the horror impact could hardly have been less powerful. Trying to push both hands into my mouth to stifle my screams and although my fingers were bleeding, I screamed again and again. I could not take my eyes off him, I could not even close them, and yet I knew that if I looked at the horror much longer, I would go on screaming for the rest of my life.

Slowly, the monster, the thing that had been my husband, covered its head, got up and groped its way to the door and passed it. Though still screaming, I was able to close my eyes.

I who had ever been a true Catholic, who believed in God and another, better life hereafter, have today but one hope: that when I die, I really die, and that there may be no afterlife of any sort because if there is, then I shall never forget! Day and night, awake or asleep, I see it, and I know that I am condemned to see it forever, even perhaps into oblivion!

Until I am totally extinct, nothing can, nothing will ever make me forget that dreadful white hairy head with its low flat skull and its two pointed ears. Pink and moist, the nose was also that of a cat, a huge cat. But the eyes! Or rather, where the eyes should have been were two brown bumps the size of saucers. Instead of a mouth, animal or human, there was a long hairy vertical slit from which hung a black quivering trunk that widened at the end, trumpetlike, and from which saliva kept dripping.

I must have fainted, because I found myself flat on my stomach on the cold cement floor of the laboratory, staring at the closed door behind which I could hear the noise of André's typewriter.

Numb, numb and empty, I must have looked as people do immediately after a terrible accident, before they fully understand what has happened. I could only think of a man I had once seen on the platform of a railway station, quite conscious, and looking stupidly at his leg still on the line where the train had just passed.

My throat was aching terribly, and that made me wonder if my vocal cords had not perhaps been torn, and whether I would ever be able to speak again.

The noise of the typewriter suddenly stopped and I felt I was going to scream again as something touched the door and a sheet of paper slid from under it.

Shivering with fear and disgust, I crawled over to where I could read it without touching it:

> **Now you understand. That last experiment was a new disaster, my poor Hélène. I suppose you recognized part of Dandelo's head. When I went into the disintegrator just now, my head was only that of a fly. I now only have its eyes and mouth left. The rest has been replaced by parts of the cat's head. Poor Dandelo whose atoms had never come together. You see now that there can only be one possible solution, don't you? I must disappear. Knock on the door when you are ready and I shall explain what you have to do.**

Of course he was right, and it had been wrong and cruel of me to insist on a new experiment. And I knew that there was now no possible hope, that any further experiments could only bring about worse results.

Getting up dazed, I went to the door and tried to speak, but no sound came out of my throat . . . so I knocked once!

You can of course guess the rest. He explained his plan in short type-written notes, and I agreed, I agreed to everything!

My head on fire, but shivering with cold, like an automaton, I followed him into the silent factory. In my hand was a full page of explanation: what I had to know about the steam hammer.

Without stopping or looking back, he pointed to the switchboard that controlled the steam hammer as he passed it. I went no further and watched him come to a halt before the terrible instrument.

He knelt down, carefully wrapped the cloth round his head, and then stretched out flat on the ground.

It was not difficult. I was not killing my husband. André, poor André had gone long ago, years ago, it seemed. I was merely carrying out his last wish . . . and mine.

Without hesitating, my eyes on the long still body, I firmly pushed the "stroke" button right in. The great metallic mass seemed to drop slowly. It was not so much the resounding clang of the hammer that made me jump as the sharp cracking which I had distinctly heard at the same time. My hus . . . the thing's body shook a second and then lay still.

It was then I noticed that he had forgotten to put his right arm, his fly-leg, under the hammer. The police would never understand but the scientists would, and they must not! That had been André's last wish, also!

I had to do it and quickly, too; the night watchman must have heard the hammer and would be round any moment. I pushed the other button and the hammer slowly rose. Seeing but trying not to look, I ran up, leaned down, lifted and moved forward the right arm which seemed terribly light. Back at the switchboard, again I pushed the red button, and down came the hammer a second time. Then I ran all the way home.

You know the rest and can now do whatever you think right.

So ended Hélène's manuscript.

The following day I telephoned Commissaire Charas to invite him to dinner.

"With pleasure, Monsieur Delambre. Allow me, however, to ask: is it the commissaire you are inviting, or just Monsieur Charas?"

"Have you any preference?"

"No, not at the present moment."

"Well then, make it whichever you like. Will eight o'clock suit you?"

Although it was raining, the commissaire arrived on foot that evening.

"Since you did not come tearing up to the door in your black Citroen, I take it you have opted for Monsieur Charas, off duty?"

"I left the car up a side street," mumbled the commissaire with a grin as a maid staggered under the weight of his raincoat.

"Merci," he said a minute later as I handed him a glass of Pernod, into which he tipped a few drops of water, watching it turn the golden amber liquid to pale blue milk.

"You heard about my poor sister-in-law?"

"Yes, shortly after you telephoned me this morning. I am sorry, but perhaps it was all for the best. Being already in charge of your brother's case, the inquiry automatically comes to me."

"I suppose it was suicide."

"Without a doubt. Cyanide the doctors say quite rightly; I found a second tablet in the unstitched hem of her dress."

"Monsieur est servi," announced the maid.

"I would like to show you a very curious document afterwards, Charas."

"Ah, yes. I heard that Madame Delambre had been writing a lot, but we could find nothing beyond the short note informing us that she was committing suicide."

During our tête-à-tête dinner, we talked politics, books and films, and the local football club of which the commissaire was a keen supporter.

After dinner, I took him up to my study where a bright fire—a habit I had picked up in England during the war—was burning.

Without even asking him, I handed him his brandy and mixed myself what he called "crushed-bug juice in soda water"—his appreciation of whisky.

"I would like you to read this, Charas; first because it was partly intended for you and, secondly, because it will interest you. If you think Commissaire Charas has no objection, I would like to burn it after."

Without a word, he took the wad of sheets Hélène had given me the day before and settled down to read them.

"What do you think of it all?" I asked some twenty minutes later as he carefully folded Hélène's manuscript, slipped it into the brown envelope, and put it into the fire.

Charas watched the flames licking the envelope from which wisps of gray smoke were escaping, and it was only when it burst into flames that he said, slowly raising his eyes to mine:

"I think it proves very definitely that Madame Delambre was quite insane."

For a long while we watched the fire eating up Hélène's "confession."

"A funny thing happened to me this morning, Charas. I went to the cemetery, where my brother is buried. It was quite empty and I was alone."

"Not quite, Monsieur Delambre. I was there, but I did not want to disturb you."

"Then you saw me . . ."

"Yes, I saw you bury a matchbox."

"Do you know what was in it?"

"A fly, I suppose."

"Yes, I had found it early this morning, caught in a spider's web in the garden."

"Was it dead?"

"No, not quite. I . . . crushed it . . . between two stones. Its head was . . . white . . . all white."

Herbert West—Reanimator: Six Shots by Moonlight

H. P. Lovecraft

It is uncommon to fire all six shots of a revolver with great suddenness when one would probably be sufficient, but many things in the life of Herbert West were uncommon. It is, for instance, not often that a young physician leaving college is obliged to conceal the principles which guide his selection of a home and office, yet that was the case with Herbert West. When he and I obtained our degrees at the medical school of Miskatonic University, and sought to relieve our poverty by setting up as general practitioners, we took great care not to say that we chose our house because it was fairly well isolated, and as near as possible to the potter's field.

Reticence such as this is seldom without cause, nor indeed was ours; for our requirements were those resulting from a life-work distinctly unpopular. Outwardly we were doctors only, but beneath the surface were aims of far greater and more terrible moment—for the essence of Herbert West's existence was a quest amid black and forbidden realms of the unknown, in which he hoped to uncover the secret of life and restore to perpetual animation the graveyard's cold clay. Such a quest demands strange materials, among them fresh bodies; and in order to keep supplied with these indispensable things one must live quietly and not far from a place of informal interment.

West and I had met in college, and I had been the only one to sympathize with his hideous experiments. Gradually I had come to be his inseparable assistant, and now that we were out of college we had to keep together. It was not easy to find a good opening for two doctors in company, but finally the influence of the university secured us a practice in Bolton—a factory town near Arkham, the seat of the college. The Bolton Worsted Mills are the largest in the Miskatonic Valley, and their polyglot employees are never popular as patients with the local physicians. We chose our house with the greatest care, seizing at last on a rather run-down cottage near the end of Pond Street; five numbers from the closest neighbor, and separated from the local potter's field by only a stretch of meadow land, bisected by a narrow neck of the rather dense forest which lies to the north. The distance was greater than we wished, but we could get no nearer house without going on the other side of the field, wholly out of the factory district. We were not much displeased, however, since there were no people between us and our sinister source of supplies. The walk was a trifle long, but we could haul our silent specimens undisturbed.

Our practice was surprisingly large from the very first—large enough to please most young doctors, and large enough to prove a bore and a burden to students whose real interest lay elsewhere. The mill-hands were of somewhat turbulent inclinations; and besides their many natural needs, their frequent clashes and stabbing affrays gave us plenty to do. But what actually absorbed our minds was the secret laboratory we had fitted up in the cellar—the laboratory with the long table under the electric lights, where in the small hours of the morning we often injected West's various solutions into the veins of things we dragged from the potter's field. West was experimenting madly to find something which would start man's vital motions anew after they had been stopped by the thing we call death, but had encountered the most ghastly obstacles. The solution had to be differently compounded for different types—what would serve for guinea-pigs would not serve for human beings, and different human specimens required large modifications.

The bodies had to be exceedingly fresh, or the slight decomposition of brain tissue would render perfect reanimation impossible. Indeed, the greatest problem was to get them fresh enough—West had had horrible experiences during his secret college researches with corpses of doubtful vintage. The results of partial or imperfect animation were much more hideous than were the total failures, and we both held fearsome recollections of such things. Ever since our first daemonic session in the deserted farmhouse on Meadow Hill in Arkham, we had felt a brooding menace; and West, though a calm, blond, blue-eyed scientific automaton in most respects, often confessed to a shuddering sensation of stealthy pursuit. He half felt that he was followed—a psychological delusion of shaken nerves, enhanced by the undeniably disturbing fact that at least one of our reanimated specimens was still alive—a frightful carnivorous thing in a padded cell at Sefton. Then there was another—our first—whose exact fate we had never learned.

We had fair luck with specimens in Bolton—much better than in Arkham. We had not been settled a week before we got an accident victim on the very night of burial, and made it open its eyes with an amazingly rational expression before the solution failed. It had lost an arm—

if it had been a perfect body we might have succeeded better. Between then and the next January we secured three more; one total failure, one case of marked muscular motion, and one rather shivery thing—it rose of itself and uttered a sound. Then came a period when luck was poor; interments fell off, and those that did occur were of specimens either too diseased or too maimed for use. We kept track of all the deaths and their circumstances with systematic care.

One March night, however, we unexpectedly obtained a specimen which did not come from the potter's field. In Bolton the prevailing spirit of Puritanism had outlawed the sport of boxing—with the usual result. Surreptitious and ill-conducted bouts among the mill-workers were common, and occasionally professional talent of low grade was imported. This late winter night there had been such a match; evidently with disastrous results, since two timorous Poles had come to us with incoherently whispered entreaties to attend to a very secret and desperate case. We followed them to an abandoned barn, where the remnants of a crowd of frightened foreigners were watching a silent black form on the floor.

The match had been between Kid O'Brien—a lubbery and now quaking youth with a most un-Hibernian hooked nose—and Buck Robinson, "The Harlem Smoke." The negro had been knocked out, and a moment's examination showed us that he would permanently remain so. He was a loathsome, gorilla-like thing, with abnormally long arms which I could not help calling fore legs, and a face that conjured up thoughts of unspeakable Congo secrets and tom-tom poundings under an eerie moon. The body must have looked even worse in life—but the world holds many ugly things. Fear was upon the whole pitiful crowd, for they did not know what the law would exact of them if the affair were not hushed up; and they were grateful when West, in spite of my involuntary shudders, offered to get rid of the thing quietly—for a purpose I knew too well.

There was bright moonlight over the snowless landscape, but we dressed the thing and carried it home between us through the deserted streets and meadows, as we had carried a similar thing one horrible night in Arkham. We approached the house from the field in the rear, took the specimen in the back door and down the cellar stairs, and prepared it for the usual experiment. Our fear of the police was absurdly great, though we had timed our trip to avoid the solitary patrolman of that section.

The result was wearily anticlimactic. Ghastly as our prize appeared, it was wholly unresponsive to every solution we injected in its black arm; solutions prepared from experience with white specimens only. So as the hour grew dangerously near to dawn, we did as we had done with the others—dragged the thing across the meadows to the neck of the woods near the potter's field, and buried it there in the best sort of grave the frozen ground would furnish. The grave was not very deep, but fully as good as that of the previous specimen—the thing which had risen of itself and uttered a sound. In the light of our dark lanterns we carefully covered it with leaves and dead vines, fairly certain that the police would never find it in a forest so dim and dense.

The next day I was increasingly apprehensive about the police, for a patient brought rumours of a suspected fight and death. West had still another source of worry, for he had been called in the afternoon to a case which ended very threateningly. An Italian woman had become hysterical over her missing child—a lad of five who had strayed off early in the morning and failed to appear for dinner—and had developed symptoms highly alarming in view of an always weak heart. It was a very foolish hysteria, for the boy had often run away before; but Italian peasants are exceedingly superstitious, and this woman seemed as much harassed by omens as by facts. About seven o'clock in the evening she died, and her frantic husband had made a frightful scene in his efforts to kill West, whom he wildly blamed for not saving her life. Friends had held him when he drew a stiletto, but West departed amidst his inhuman shrieks, curses, and oaths of vengeance. In his latest affliction the fellow seemed to have forgotten his child, who was still missing as the night advanced. There was some talk of searching the woods, but most of the family's friends were busy with the dead woman and the screaming man. Altogether, the nervous strain upon West must have been tremendous. Thoughts of the police and of the mad Italian both weighed heavily.

We retired about eleven, but I did not sleep well. Bolton had a surprisingly good police force for so small a town, and I could not help fearing the mess which would ensue if the affair of the night before were ever tracked down. It might mean the end of all our local work—and perhaps prison for both West and me. I did not like those rumours of a fight which were floating about. After the clock struck three the moon shone in my eyes, but I turned over without rising to pull down the shade. Then came the steady rattling at the back door.

I lay still and somewhat dazed, but before long heard West's rap on my door. He was clad in a dressing-gown and slippers, and had in his hands a revolver and an electric flashlight. From the revolver I knew that he was thinking more of the crazed Italian than of the police.

"We'd better both go," he whispered. "It wouldn't do not to answer it anyway, and it may be a patient—it would be like one of those fools to try the back door."

So we both went down the stairs on tiptoe, with a fear partly justified and partly that which comes only from the soul of the weird small hours. The rattling continued, growing somewhat louder. When we reached the door I cautiously unbolted it and threw it open, and as the moon streamed revealingly down on the form silhouetted there, West did a peculiar thing. Despite the obvious danger of attracting notice and bringing down on our heads the dreaded police investigation—a thing which after all was mercifully averted by the relative isolation of our cottage—my friend suddenly, excitedly, and unnecessarily emptied all six chambers of his revolver into the nocturnal visitor.

For that visitor was neither Italian nor policeman. Looming hideously against the spectral moon was a gigantic misshapen thing not to be imagined save in nightmares—a glassy-eyed, ink-black apparition nearly on all fours, covered with bits of mould, leaves, and vines, foul with caked blood, and having between its glistening teeth a snow-white, terrible, cylindrical object terminating in a tiny hand.

PART IV

WESTERNS:

"TONTO"
MEANS "FOOL"
IN SPANISH

"Stage to Lordsburg"
by Ernest Haycox

Stagecoach, directed by John Ford, 1939

"A Man Called Horse"
by Dorothy M. Johnson

A Man Called Horse, directed by Elliot Silverstein, 1970

"This Is What It Means to Say Phoenix, Arizona"
by Sherman Alexie

Smoke Signals, directed by Chris Eyre, 1998

"TONTO" MEANS "FOOL" IN SPANISH

The Western is the Madonna of film genres: It has—despite myriad naysayers and death-knellers—stuck around by continually reinventing itself. As Scott Simmon points out in *The Invention of the Western Film*, the genre was rumored dead as early as 1911, when an article in *Nickelodeon* declared, "The old thrills are exhausted and people want something new. It is just simply the case of a gold mine that has been worked to the limit and can give no more desirable ore." Obviously *Nickelodeon* was wrong. Westerns have risen from the dead over and over, and each time they look a little different. They've moved geographically, from the early silents filmed on the East Coast to the more recognizable desert Western. They've explored variation in story lines, from epics *(Dances with Wolves)* to spoofs *(Cat Ballou)* to biopics *(Buffalo Bill)*. They've experimented with heroes, from laconic gun-slinging loners *(High Noon)* to calculating tricksters *(My Name Is Nobody)*. And, maybe most important, they've attempted time and again to come to grips with the role Native Americans have played in the Western myth.

By the time director John Ford came upon Ernest Haycox's 1937 story "Stage to Lordsburg," Western films were on the wane again and were rarely more than low-budget B offerings made for juvenile audiences. Ford bought the story for about $2,500 but then couldn't get his movie financed. "After the studio heads read it, they said to me, 'But this is a Western! People don't make Westerns anymore!' " It took him a year to locate financing through Walter Wanger, an independent producer releasing through United Artists. Ford filmed *Stagecoach* in Monument Valley, Arizona (Navajo land), a decision he said he made to help the Navajos: "I used to stay occasionally with a chap who ran the trading post, and he said, 'You know, the Navajos are starving. I understand you're going to do a Western. If you come up there and do it, you'd probably save a lot of lives.' I think we left about $500,000 there." (This, of course, means that the Apaches in the film were played by Navajos.) In all, Ford filmed ten movies in Monument Valley and was very proud that the Navajos appointed him honorary Sachem (chief) with the name Great Soldier.

A director's director, Ford was a cinematic stylist studied by the likes of Orson Welles, Elia Kazan, Akira Kurosawa, Ingmar Bergman, François Truffaut, and Frank Capra. According to cinematographer William Clothier, "Ford knew more about photography than any other man who ever worked in the movies," and he took full advantage of Monument Valley's harsh, open landscape. Visually, *Stagecoach* was like nothing that had been seen before, and it lifted the genre (and John Wayne) to the A list. The *New York Times* raved, "In one superbly expansive gesture . . . John Ford has swept aside ten years of artifice and talkie compromise and has made a motion picture that sings a song of camera." He also transcended the stock characters found in previous Westerns, fleshing out Haycox's story by providing motivations and backstory for each of the characters. But, as in Haycox's story, the Indians in the film are savage and indistinguishable, serving only as a source of conflict or plot device—and for this (and the content of other, less politically benign, films like *The Searchers*) he has received much criticism. Perhaps a bit unfairly.

Ford preferred to adapt short stories, as he told Peter Bogdanovich in a 1966 interview: "I don't like to do books or plays. I prefer to take a short story and expand it, rather than take a novel and try to condense. But it *has* become more difficult to get a good *story*." Because of Ford's reputation as an auteur, his reliance on the short-story market is rarely noted. Many of his adaptations, like *Stagecoach*, are faithful to the source's original story line; likewise, the elements of racism of which he has been accused were often already present in the stories. In fact, many, if not most, Westerns drew from literary sources, and one of the most interesting influences on this genre is the shift in editorial policies after the publication of Zane Grey's *The Vanishing American* (1925).

In the forty or so years after the Plains wars, fiction, like film, was still making up its mind about the Indians. Grey, a bestselling author of the day, was one of those sympathetic to their plight, and the protagonist of his novel was a full-blooded Indian in love with a white woman. The novel was serialized in *The Ladies Home Journal*, and its handling of miscegenation, as well as its unfavorable depiction of missionaries, caused a public outcry. The furor resulted in a new editorial policy at Curtis Publications, which owned both *The Ladies Home Journal* and *The Saturday Evening Post*. This policy, which has often been called "anti-Indian," was at the very least unsympathetic toward Native Americans.* For their part, Harper

* The exact nature of this policy is difficult to pin down, as the editors were seemingly consistent in their inconsistency. According to *The Native American in Short Fiction in the "Saturday Evening Post,"* the red man is represented as an "unambiguous adversary to the heroic white man" in more than half of the 265 stories published between 1897 and 1968. The Indian is a "sympathetic protagonist" in fewer than ten percent.

and Brothers would not publish the novel in book form until Grey removed offending passages and changed the ending so that the Indian hero did not marry his white sweetheart. Grey was also forced to rewrite the screen adaptation he was working on in order to make it more palatable. In a letter to his publishers, Grey wrote, "This is the first time in my life that I have been driven away from the truth, from honor and ideals, and in this case, from telling the world of the tragedy of the Indian. It is a melancholy thing. I wonder what effect it will have on me."

It's difficult to overstate the effect this incident must have had on the entire genre of Western fiction, and ultimately film. Which brings us to "Stage to Lordsburg" by Ernest Haycox, published in *Collier's* in 1937. From the beginning Haycox was talented but pragmatic. As a starving young writer he'd been advised by an editor, "Learn to write a Western. Once you have mastered that, the rest is up to you." And he did. For nearly three decades—from the mid-1920s to the mid-1940s—Haycox's frontier stories and serials were staples, first in the pulps, then later in *Collier's* and *The Saturday Evening Post.* During this period of his career, he worked within the established Western formulas—and within the established editorial policies of the day. Haycox's editors at *Collier's* allowed him considerable latitude in subject and technique, but they discouraged him from straying from the successful Western formula. "Stage to Lordsburg" is typical for its day. It begins by immediately establishing the Apaches as hostile, a conflict that is not delineated but simply exists as part of the donnée. Likewise, the Indians aren't characters; they're a force similar to an act of nature.

Although Haycox didn't reinvent the genre, his contributions are considerable, chief among them an attempt at historical accuracy (not necessarily a requirement at the time, or even now). History was Haycox's passion, and in the mid-'40s he gave up his lucrative career as a commercial writer and devoted himself to writing nonformulaic novels about Oregon history. Unfortunately, he found it difficult to break the habit of years of genre work—some believe he was just hitting his stride as a serious novelist when he died of cancer at the age of fifty-one. His admirers were many. Gertrude Stein recommended his novels and lent copies to friends. Ernest Hemingway said that even when he wasn't reading much fiction, he would go out of his way for a Haycox story in the *Post.* And among writers of the genre, he was, and is, deeply admired. Western author D. B. Newton claims, "Haycox very nearly succeeded, singlehandedly, in doing for the standard Western what Hammett and Chandler did for the private eye detective story—made it respectable."

In the 1940s, the confines of Western fiction began to expand, and one of the first revisionist short-story writers was Dorothy Johnson. Johnson wouldn't have used the term "revisionist," though. When asked what school of writing she belonged to, she replied, "The Disreputable School—when I was writing Western short stories anyone who wrote Westerns was not quite respectable." She referred to one of her techniques—a method of fracturing the formula—as "the switch." It involved turning a situation or cliché around and looking at it another way. For example, what if the hero of a Western isn't bold or brave? What if he isn't even a good shot? And furthermore, what if he only thinks he killed the villain, but it's someone else's shot that really did it? (Western buffs will recognize this as the premise for "The Man Who Shot Liberty Valence.") "A Man Called Horse" was the result of a different kind of "what if?" After reading *The Crow Indians*, written by Robert Lowie, an American anthropologist who lived among the Crow and collected their stories, Johnson began to wonder how a stranger could survive among the Crow without having first read Lowie's book. She wrote "Horse" to work out the answer. In it, Johnson strikes a delicate balance. Her Crow are both cruel and kind, and among them a spoiled and calculating white man finds self-respect. What is astonishing is that, given this now-familiar scenario, Johnson manages to avoid the noble savage stereotype, as well as any hint of pre–New Age Native American mysticism. In 1984, "Horse" was voted the "best Western story of all time" by one hundred members of the Western Writers of America.

Johnson began researching the West while living in New York City and working as a journalist, then later as managing editor of *The Woman* magazine. She was homesick for Montana, where she'd grown up, and spent her free time in museums and libraries, researching the Plains Indians. Much of this background was used in her first book of Western stories, *Indian Country* (1953), which contains "Horse." "To write about the West wasn't just some decision I sat down and made," she said. "It was just something I happened to want to know about. Anytime I write anything that isn't the West of the nineteenth century I'm sort of off my track." With *Indian Country* she became not only one of the first women to enter the male-dominated field of literary Westerns, but one of the first to explore, with a historian's objectivity, the culture clash between the white and Indian worlds. (In 1959, she became one of the few white people honored as an adoptive member of the Blackfoot tribe. They gave her the name Princess Kills-Both-Places.) While some place her work in the pastoral tradition alongside Willa Cather's, she's been largely overlooked by critics. Her own ambitions were modest: to write well and profitably, and create "crackin' good stories about real people, courageous people."

If Johnson's "A Man Called Horse" is based on a lifetime of research, its 1970 adaptation isn't as meticulous. Ward Churchill, a Native American activist and author, points out its many inconsistencies: "This droll adventure, promoted as 'the most authentic description of North American Indian life ever filmed,' depicts a people whose language is Lakota, whose hairstyles range from Assiniboin through Nez Perce to Comanche, whose tipi design is Crow, and whose Sun Dance ceremony and lodge in which it is held are both typically Mandan." The film, directed by Elliot Silverstein (*Cat Ballou,* 1965), widely publicized its accuracy. A few reviewers were skeptical, but many responded like Louise Sweeney of the *Christian Science Monitor.* "*A Man Called Horse* does have a documentary kind of realism, for several reasons. . . . This realism is due in large part to its stress on the primitive and savage aspects of tribal life. Production notes emphasize the amount of anthropological and historical research done, as well as the use of members of the Rosebud Sioux Reservation in feature roles and behind the scenes, creating accurate costumes, teepees, and weapons."* (Few viewers today would accuse *Horse* of much realism at all, let alone documentary realism. It's not a film that has held up at all well.)

Maybe the makers of *Horse* perpetrated a hoax by intentionally misleading the public, as some people believe; probably they were simply careless and misguided. For the most part, Hollywood has been earnest in its attempts to reexamine the role of the Native American. For example, few who have heard Kevin Costner speak about *Dances with Wolves* (1990) can doubt his good intentions, or his attempt to incorporate the decade's emphasis on political correctness. But, while conceding that *Wolves* was well intentioned and succeeds on a number of levels, many Native American critics still feel a basic issue is at stake. Native American author and critic Jacquelyn Kilpatrick voices this concern when she says, "The main flaw remains the problem of appropriation of identity; John Dunbar [*Wolves'* protagonist] is the white narrator of an Indian existence."

Fortunately, for the first time, Native American storytellers are in a position to tell their own stories, and at the forefront of this movement is American Indian author Sherman Alexie. For him, issues of identity and how the media have portrayed American Indians (a term he prefers over "Native American") is not one that subtly informs his work. It is *the* issue that galvanizes it. Don't think that the title of his book of stories, *The Lone Ranger and Tonto Fistfight in Heaven,* which contains the story "This Is What It

* Perhaps there was a disconnect between the filmmakers and the marketing department. In *The American West in Film: Critical Approaches to the Western,* Jon Tuska tells of a chance meeting with Jack DeWitt, who wrote the screenplay for *A Man Called Horse.* Tuska asked about a few of the elements of dramatic license: why, for example, the Crow in Johnson's story became Sioux; why the Mandan ceremony was portrayed as the Sioux Sun Dance; why Richard Harris, as Horse, teaches the Sioux British military tactics. DeWitt's reply was that he based the teaching episode on *Lawrence of Arabia,* and as for the rest, ". . . at this late date, who cares?"

Means to Say Phoenix, Arizona," is just a catchy play on words. Alexie is doing everything he can to wrestle down the old stereotypes. He writes prolifically, determined to change perceptions of the Indian culture. "We're either portrayed as the noble savage or the ignoble savage," Alexie has said. "In most people's minds, we only exist in the nineteenth century." He writes poetry, short stories, novels, essays, and screenplays—all with the aim of setting the record straight. "So much has been taken from us," he says in *The Unauthorized Autobiography of Me*, "that we hold on to the smallest things left with all the strength we have." Or, put another way, "Poetry = Anger × Imagination."

If Alexie is angry, he is also funny. In 1999, he made his stand-up debut at a comedy festival, joking about "crazy white people" who expect him to "read coyote stories, speak in a slow monotone and stare off into the distance constantly receiving visions." He talks about the persistence of Indian stereotypes: "Just look at the sports teams. You can have the Washington Redskins and this Indian with a big nose and big lips running around. How would you feel if it was the Washington Rabbis and you had a guy with braids running around throwing bagels? Or the Washington Jesuits with some guy handing out communion wafers. It wouldn't happen. So it's an insult. It's proof of the way we get ignored." Alexie has gone on the record with his opinion of the best and worst movie depictions of American Indians. The best (in alphabetical order): *Exiles* (1961); *Heat* (1995); *Little Big Man* (1970); *One Flew over the Cuckoo's Nest* (1975): "I still think the Indian was the hero"; *Soldier Blue* (1970). The worst: *Dances with Wolves* (1990): "Would have been a great movie if the cavalry had caught him"; *F Troop:* "Twelve Sambos running around"; *The Searchers* (1956); *Thunderheart* (1992); and any film featuring Tonto: "Tonto is the one who started it all . . . the monosyllabic stoic Indian stereotype."

Smoke Signals—inspired by "Phoenix, Arizona" and several other stories in *The Lone Ranger and Tonto*—was the first movie written, directed, and produced by Native Americans. And, as Alexie likes to add, "The Indians weren't played by Italians with long hair." The film was developed at the Sundance Institute, which allowed Chris Eyre, the director, the freedom to experiment without the usual financial pressures. The movie premiered at the Sundance Festival in 1998, where it received the Audience Award for Dramatic Films, the Filmmakers Trophy, and a nomination for the Grand Jury Prize. The filmmakers were unapologetic about their agenda. Alexie, who wrote the screenplay and was one of the coproducers, said, "I want everyone in the world to see this movie. I'm not interested in making movies that don't appeal to a lot of people. . . . Perhaps now, based on the success of this film, Indian filmmakers can get a little more adventurous and still find an audience." Naturally, the film received some criticism among Native

Americans for its blatant attempt to appeal to mainstream audiences. But this criticism is tempered by the knowledge that, even in the independent film community, such films are difficult to finance, make, and distribute. (After all, how many people recognize the names of other recent Native American filmmakers, like Victor Masayesva, Aaron Carr, and George Burdeau?)

Maybe Westerns today *are* like a cat that has finally used up all its lives. In 2003, Western film scholar Scott Simmon seemed to be suggesting this when he concluded, "The many premature obituaries for the Western film . . . might warn us off such a pronouncement, but the genre is beginning to feel clinically dead, especially if a living genre requires a critical mass of productions." Then again, maybe the Western has one life left, one that involves the Indians finally telling their own story.

Stage to Lordsburg

Ernest Haycox

This was one of those years in the Territory when Apache smoke signals spiraled up from the stony mountain summits and many a ranch cabin lay as a square of blackened ashes on the ground and the departure of a stage from Tonto was the beginning of an adventure that had no certain happy ending. . . .

The stage and its six horses waited in front of Weilner's store on the north side of Tonto's square. Happy Stuart was on the box, the ribbons between his fingers and one foot teetering on the brake. John Strang rode shotgun guard and an escort of ten cavalrymen waited behind the coach, half asleep in their saddles.

At four-thirty in the morning this high air was quite cold, though the sun had begun to flush the sky eastward. A small crowd stood in the square, presenting their final messages to the passengers now entering the coach. There was a girl going down to marry an infantry officer, a whisky drummer from St. Louis, an Englishman all length and bony corners and bearing with him an enormous sporting rifle, a gambler, a solid-shouldered cattleman on his way to New Mexico and a blond young man upon whom both Happy Stuart and the shotgun guard placed a narrow-eyed interest.

This seemed all until the blond man drew back from the coach door; and then a girl known commonly throughout the Territory as Henriette came quietly from the crowd. She was small and quiet, with a touch of paleness in her cheeks and her quite dark eyes lifted at the blond man's unexpected courtesy, showing surprise. There was this moment of delay and then the girl caught up her dress and stepped into the coach.

Men in the crowd were smiling but the blond one turned, his motion like the swift cut of a knife, and his attention covered that group until the smiling quit. He was tall, hollow-flanked, and definitely stamped by the guns slung low on his hips. But it wasn't the guns alone; something in his face, so watchful and so smooth, also showed his trade. Afterwards he got into the coach and slammed the door.

Happy Stuart kicked off the brakes and yelled, "Hi!" Tonto's people were calling out their last farewells and the six horses broke into a trot and the stage lunged on its fore and aft springs and rolled from town with dust dripping off its wheels like water, the cavalrymen trotting briskly behind. So they tipped down the long grade, bound on a journey no stage had attempted during the last forty-five days. Out below in the desert's distance stood the relay stations they hoped to reach and pass. Between lay a country swept empty by the quick raids of Geronimo's men.

The Englishman, the gambler and the blond man sat jammed together in the forward seat, riding backward to the course of the stage. The drummer and the cattleman occupied the uncomfortable middle bench; the two women shared the rear seat. The cattleman faced Henriette, his knees almost touching her. He had one arm hooked over the door's window sill to steady himself. A huge gold nugget slid gently back and forth along the watch chain slung across his wide chest and a chunk of black hair lay below his hat. His eyes considered Henriette, reading something in the girl that caused him to show her a deliberate smile. Henriette dropped her glance to the gloved tips of her fingers, cheeks unstirred.

They were all strangers packed closely together, with nothing in common save a destination. Yet the cattleman's smile and the boldness of his glance were something as audible as speech, noted by everyone except the Englishman, who sat bolt upright with his stony indifference. The army girl, tall and calmly pretty, threw a quick side glance at Henriette and afterwards looked away with a touch of color. The gambler saw this interchange of glances and showed the cattleman an irritated attention. The whisky drummer's eyes narrowed a little and some inward cynicism made a faint change on his lips. He removed his hat to show a bald head already beginning to sweat; his cigar smoke turned the coach cloudy and ashes kept dropping on his vest.

The blond man had observed Henriette's glance drop from the cattleman; he tipped his hat well over his face and watched her—not boldly but as though he were puzzled. Once her glance lifted and touched him. But he had been on guard against that and was quick to look away.

The army girl coughed gently behind her hand, whereupon the gambler tapped the whisky drummer on the shoulder. "Get rid of that." The drummer appeared startled. He grumbled, "Beg pardon," and tossed the smoke through the window.

All this while the coach went rushing down the ceaseless turns of the mountain road, rocking on its fore and aft springs, its heavy wheels slamming through the road ruts and whining on the curves. Occasionally the strident yell of Happy Stuart washed back. "Hi, Nellie! By God—!" The whisky drummer braced himself against the door and closed his eyes.

Three hours from Tonto the road, making a last round sweep, let them down upon the flat desert. Here the stage stopped and the men got out to stretch. The gambler spoke to the army girl, gently: "Perhaps you would find my seat more comfortable." The army girl said "Thank you," and changed over. The cavalry sergeant rode up to the stage, speaking to Happy Stuart.

"We'll be goin' back now—and good luck to ye."

The men piled in, the gambler taking the place beside Henriette. The blond man drew his long legs together to give the army girl more room, and watched Henriette's face with a soft, quiet care. A hard sun beat fully on the coach and dust began to whip up like fine smoke. Without escort they rolled across a flat earth broken only by a cacti standing against a dazzling light. In the far distance, behind a blue heat haze, lay the faint suggestion of mountains.

The cattleman reached up and tugged at the ends of his mustache and smiled at Henriette. The army girl spoke to the blond man. "How far is it to the noon station?" The blond man said courteously: "Twenty miles." The gambler watched the army girl with the strictness of his face relaxing, as though the run of her voice reminded him of things long forgotten.

The miles fell behind and the smell of alkali dust got thicker. Henriette rested against the corner of the coach, her eyes dropped to the tips of her gloves. She made an enigmatic, disinterested shape there; she seemed past stirring, beyond laughter. She was young, yet she had a knowledge that put the cattleman and the gambler and the drummer and the army girl in their exact places; and she knew why the gambler had offered the army girl his seat. The army girl was in one world and she was in another, as everyone in the coach understood. It had no effect on her for this was a distinction she had learned long ago. Only the blond man broke through her indifference. His name was Malpais Bill and she could see the wildness in the corners of his eyes and in the long crease of his lips; it was a stamp that would never come off. Yet something flowed out of him toward her that was different than the predatory curiosity of other men; something unobtrusively gallant, unexpectedly gentle.

Upon the box Happy Stuart pointed to the hazy outline two miles away. "Injuns ain't burned that anyhow." The sun was directly overhead, turning the light of the world a cruel brass-yellow. The crooked crack of a dry wash opened across the two deep ruts that made this road. Strang shifted the gun in his lap. "What's Malpais Bill ridin' in with us for?"

"I guess I wouldn't ask him," returned Happy Stuart and studied the wash with a troubled eye. The road fell into it roughly and he got a tighter grip on his reins and yelled: "Hang on! Hi, Nellie! God damn you, hi!" The six horses plunged down the rough side of the wash and for a moment the coach stood alone, high and lonely on the break, and then went reeling over the rim. It struck the gravel with a roar, the front wheels bouncing and the back wheels skewing around. The horses faltered but Happy Stuart cursed at his leaders and got them into a run again. The horses lunged up the far side of the wash two and two, their muscles bunching and the soft dirt flying in yellow clouds. The front wheels struck solidly and something cracked like a pistol shot; the stage rose out of the wash, teetered crosswise and then fell ponderously on its side, splintering the coach panels.

Johnny Strang jumped clear. Happy Stuart hung to the handrail with one hand and hauled on the reins with the other; and stood up while the passengers crawled through the upper door. All the men, except the whisky drummer, put their shoulders to the coach and heaved it upright again. The whisky drummer stood strangely in the bright sunlight shaking his head dumbly while the others climbed back in. Happy Stuart said, "All right, brother, git aboard."

The drummer climbed in slowly and the stage ran on. There was a low, gray 'dobe relay station squatted on the desert dead ahead with a scatter of corrals about it and a flag hanging limp on a crooked pole. Men came out of the 'dobe's dark interior and stood in the shade of the porch gallery. Happy Stuart rolled up and stopped. He said to a lanky man: "Hi, Mack. Where's the Goddamned Injuns?"

The passengers were filing into the 'dobe's dining room. The lanky one drawled: "You'll see 'em before tomorrow night." Hostlers came up to change horses.

The little dining room was cool after the coach, cool and still. A fat Mexican woman ran in and out with the food platters. Happy Stuart said: "Ten minutes," and brushed the alkali dust from his mouth and fell to eating.

The long-jawed Mack said: "Catlin's ranch burned last night. Was a troop of cavalry around here yesterday. Came and went. You'll git to the Gap tonight all right but I do' know about the mountains beyond. A little trouble?"

"A little," said Happy, briefly, and rose. This was the end of rest. The passengers followed, with the whisky drummer straggling at the rear, reaching deeply for the wind. The coach rolled away again, Mack's voice pursuing them. "Hit it a lick, Happy, if you see any dust rollin' out of the east."

Heat had condensed in the coach and the little wind fanned up by the run of the horses was stifling to the lungs; the desert floor projected its white glitter endlessly away until lost in the smoky haze. The cattleman's knees bumped Henriette gently and he kept watching her, a celluloid toothpick dropped between his lips. Happy Stuart's voice ran back, profane and urgent, keeping the speed of the coach constant through the ruts. The whisky drummer's eyes were round and strained and his mouth was open and all the color had gone out of his face. The gambler observed this without expression and without care; and once the cattleman, feeling the sag of the whisky drummer's shoulder, shoved him away. The Englishman sat bolt upright, staring emotionlessly at the passing desert. The army girl spoke to Malpais Bill: "What is the next stop?"

"Gap Creek."

"Will we meet soldiers there?"

He said: "I expect we'll have an escort over the hills into Lordsburg."

And at four o'clock of this furnace-hot afternoon the whisky drummer made a feeble gesture with one hand and fell forward into the gambler's lap.

The cattleman shrugged his shoulders and put a head through the window, calling up to Happy Stuart: "Wait a minute." When the stage stopped everybody climbed out and the blond man helped the gambler lay the whisky drummer in the sweltering patch of shade created by the coach. Neither Happy Stuart nor the shotgun guard bothered to get down. The whisky drummer's lips moved a little but nobody said anything and nobody knew what to do—until Henriette stepped forward.

She dropped to the ground, lifting the whisky drummer's shoulders and head against her breasts. He opened his eyes and there was something in them that they could all see, like relief and ease, like gratefulness. She murmured: "You are all right," and her smile was soft and pleasant, turning her lips maternal. There was this wisdom in her, this knowledge of the fears that men concealed behind their manners, the deep hungers that rode them so savagely, and the loneliness that drove them to women of her kind. She repeated, "You are all right," and watched this whisky drummer's eyes lose the wildness of what he knew.

The army girl's face showed shock. The gambler and the cattleman looked down at the whisky drummer quite impersonally. The blond man watched Henriette through lids half closed, but the flare of a powerful interest broke the severe lines of his cheeks. He held a cigarette between his fingers; he had forgotten it.

Happy Stuart said: "We can't stay here."

The gambler bent down to catch the whisky drummer under the arms. Henriette rose and said, "Bring him to me," and got into the coach. The blond man and the gambler lifted the drummer through the door so that he was lying along the back seat, cushioned on Henriette's lap. They all got in and the coach rolled on. The drummer groaned a little, whispering: "Thanks—thanks," and the blond man, searching Henriette's face for every shred of expression, drew a gusty breath.

They went on like this, the big wheels pounding the ruts of the road while a lowering sun blazed through the coach windows. The mountain bulwarks began to march nearer, more definite in the blue fog. The cattleman's eyes were small and brilliant and touched Henriette personally, but the gambler bent toward Henriette to say: "If you are tired—"

"No," she said. "No. He's dead."

The army girl stifled a small cry. The gambler bent nearer the whisky drummer, and then they were all looking at Henriette; even the Englishman stared at her for a moment, faint curiosity in his eyes. She was remotely smiling, her lips broad and soft. She held the drummer's head with both her hands and continued to hold him like that until, at the swift fall of dusk, they rolled across the last of the desert floor and drew up before Gap Station.

The cattleman kicked open the door and stepped out, grunting as his stiff legs touched the ground. The gambler pulled the drummer up so that Henriette could leave. They all came out, their bones tired from the shaking. Happy Stuart climbed from the box, his face a gray mask of alkali and his eyes bloodshot. He said: "Who's dead?" and looked into the coach. People sauntered from the station yard, walking with the indolence of twilight. Happy Stuart said, "Well, he won't worry about tomorrow," and turned away.

A short man with a tremendous stomach shuffled through the dusk. He said: "Wasn't sure you'd try to git through yet, Happy."

"Where's the soldiers for tomorrow?"

"Other side of the mountains. Everybody's chased out. What ain't forted up here was sent to Lordsburg. You men will bunk in the barn. I'll make out for the ladies somehow." He looked at the army girl and he appraised Henriette instantly. His eyes slid on to Malpais Bill standing in the background and recognition stirred him then and made his voice careful. "Hello, Bill. What brings you this way?"

Malpais Bill's cigarette glowed in the gathering dusk and Henriette caught the brief image of his face, serene and watchful. Malpais Bill's tone was easy, it was soft. "Just the trip."

They were moving on toward the frame house whose corners seemed to extend indefinitely into a series of attached sheds. Lights glimmered in the windows and men moved around the place, idly talking. The unhitched horses went away at a trot. The tall girl walked into the station's big room, to face a soldier in a disheveled uniform.

He said: "Miss Robertson? Lieutenant Hauser was to have met you here. He is at Lordsburg. He was wounded in a brush with the Apaches last night."

The tall army girl stood very still. She said: "Badly?"

"Well," said the soldier, "yes."

The fat man came in, drawing deeply for wind. "Too bad—too bad. Ladies, I'll show you the rooms, such as I got."

Henriette's dove-colored dress blended with the background shadows. She was watching the tall army girl's face whiten. But there was a strength in the army girl, a fortitude that made her think of the soldier. For she said quietly, "You must have had a bad trip."

"Nothing—nothing at all," said the soldier and left the room. The gambler was here, his thin face turning to the army girl with a strained expression, as though he were remembering painful things. Malpais Bill had halted in the doorway, studying the softness and the humility of Henriette's cheeks. Afterwards both women followed the fat host of Gap Station along a narrow hall to their quarters.

Malpais Bill wheeled out and stood indolently against the wall of this desert station, his glace quick and watchful in the way it touched all the men loitering along the yard, his ears weighing all the night-softened voices. Heat died from the earth and a definite chill rolled down the mountain hulking so high behind the house. The soldier was in his saddle, murmuring drowsily to Happy Stuart.

"Well, Lordsburg is a long ways off and the damn' mountains are squirmin' with Apaches. You won't have any cavalry escort tomorrow. The troops are all in the field."

Malpais Bill listened to the hoofbeats of the soldier's horse fade out, remembering the loneliness of a man in those dark mountain passes, and went back to the saloon at the end of the station. This was a low-ceilinged shed with a dirt floor and whitewashed walls that once had been part of a stable. Three men stood under a lantern in the middle of this little place, the light of the lantern palely shining in the rounds of their eyes as they watched him. At the far end of the bar the cattleman and the gambler drank in taciturn silence. Malpais Bill took his whisky when the bottle came, and noted the barkeep's obscure glance. Gap's host put in his head and wheezed, "Second table," and the other men in here began to move out. The barkeep's words rubbed together, one tone above a whisper. "Better not ride into Lordsburg. Plummer and Shanley are there."

Malpais Bill's lips were stretched to the long edge of laughter and there was a shine like wildness in his eyes. He said, "Thanks, friend," and went into the dining room.

When he came back to the yard night lay wild and deep across the desert and the moonlight was a frozen silver that touched but could not dissolve the world's incredible blackness. The girl Henriette walked along the Tonto road, swaying gently in the vague shadows. He went that way, the click of his heels on the hard earth bringing her around.

Her face was clear and strange and incurious in the night, as though she waited for something to come, and knew what it would be. But he said: "You're too far from the house. Apaches like to crawl down next to a settlement and wait for strays."

She was indifferent, unafraid. Her voice was cool and he could hear the faint loneliness in it, the fatalism that made her words so even. "There's a wind coming up, so soft and good."

He took off his hat, long legs braced, and his eyes were both attentive and puzzled. His blond hair glowed in the fugitive light.

She said in a deep breath: "Why do you do that?"

His lips were restless and the sing and rush of strong feeling was like a current of quick wind around him. "You have folks in Lordsburg?"

She spoke in a direct, patient way as though explaining something he should have known without asking, "I run a house in Lordsburg."

"No," he said. "It wasn't what I asked."

"My folks are dead—I think. There was a massacre in the Superstition Mountains when I was young."

He stood with his head bowed, his mind reaching back to fill in that gap of her life. There was a hardness and a rawness to this land and little sympathy for the weak. She had survived and had paid for her survival, and looked at him now in a silent way that offered no explanations or apologies for whatever had been; she was still a pretty girl with the dead patience of all the past years in her eyes, in the expressiveness of her lips.

He said: "Over in the Tonto Basin is a pretty land. I've got a piece of ranch there—with a house half built."

"If that's your country why are you here?"

His lips laughed and the rashness in him glowed hot again and he seemed to grow taller in the moonlight. "A debt to collect."

"That's why you're going to Lordsburg? You will never get through collecting those kinds of debts. Everybody in the Territory knows you. Once you were just a rancher. Then you tried to wipe out a grudge and then there was a bigger one to wipe out—and the debt kept growing and more men are waiting to kill you. Someday a man will. You'd better run away from the debts."

His bright smile kept constant, and presently she lifted her shoulders with resignation. "No," she murmured, "you won't run." He could see the sweetness of her lips and the way her eyes were sad for him; he could see in them the patience he had never learned.

He said, "We'd better go back," and turned her with his arm. They went across the yard in silence, hearing the undertone of men's drawling talk roll out of the shadows, seeing the glow of men's pipes in the dark corners. Malpais Bill stopped and watched her go through the station door; she turned to look at him once more, her eyes all dark and her lips softly sober, and then passed down the narrow corridor to her own quarters. Beyond her window, in the yard, a man was murmuring to another man: "Plummer and Shanley are in Lordsburg. Malpais Bill knows it." Through the thin partition of the adjoining room she heard the army girl crying with a suppressed, uncontrollable regularity. Henriette stared at the dark wall, her shoulders and head bowed; and afterwards returned to the hall and knocked on the army girl's door and went in.

Six fresh horses fiddled in front of the coach and the fat host of Gap Station came across the yard swinging a lantern against the dead, bitter black. All the passengers filed sleep-dulled and miserable from the house. Johnny Strang slammed the express box in the boot and Happy Stuart gruffly said: "All right, folks."

The passengers climbed in. The cattleman came up and Malpais Bill drawled: "Take the corner spot, mister," and got in, closing the door. The Gap host grumbled: "If they don't jump you on the long grade you'll be all right. You're safe when you get to Schrieber's ranch." Happy's bronze voice shocked the black stillness and the coach lurched forward, its leather springs squealing.

They rode for an hour in this complete darkness, chilled and uncomfortable and half asleep, feeling the coach drag on a heavy-climbing grade. Gray dawn cracked through, followed by a sunless light rushing all across the flat desert now far below. The road looped from one barren shoulder to another and at sunup they had reached the first bench and were slamming full speed along a boulder-strewn flat. The cattleman sat in the forward corner, the left corner of his mouth swollen and crushed, and when Henriette saw that her glance slid to Malpais Bill's knuckles. The army girl had her eyes closed, her shoulders pressing against the Englishman, who remained bolt upright with the sporting gun between his knees. Beside Henriette the gambler seemed to sleep, and on the middle bench Malpais Bill watched the land go by with a thin vigilance.

At ten they were rising again, with juniper and scrub pine showing on the slopes and the desert below them filling with the powdered haze of another hot day. By noon they reached the summit of the range and swung to follow its narrow rock-ribbed meadows. The gambler, long motionless, shifted his feet and caught the army girl's eyes.

"Schrieber's is directly ahead. We are past the worst of it."

The blond man looked around at the gambler, making no comment; and it was then that Henriette caught the smell of smoke in the windless air. Happy Stuart was cursing once more and the brake blocks began to cry. Looking through the angled vista of the window panel Henriette saw a clay and rock chimney standing up like a gaunt skeleton against the day's light. The house that had been there was a black patch on the ground, smoke still rising from pieces that had not been completely burnt.

The stage stopped and all the men were instantly out. An iron stove squatted on the earth, with one section of pipe stuck upright to it. Fire licked lazily along the collapsed fragments of what had been a trunk. Beyond the location of the house, at the foot of a corral, lay two nude figures grotesquely bald, with deliberate knife slashes marking their bodies. Happy Stuart went over there and had his look; and came back.

"Schriebers. Well—"

Malpais Bill said: "This morning about daylight." He looked at the gambler, at the cattleman, at the Englishman who showed no emotion. "Get back in the coach." He climbed to the coach's top, flattening himself full length there. Happy Stuart and Strang took their places again. The horses broke into a run.

The gambler said to the army girl: "You're pretty safe between those two fellows," and hauled a .44 from a back pocket and laid it over his lap. He considered Henriette more carefully than before, his taciturnity breaking. He said: "How old are you?"

Her shoulders rose and fell, which was the only answer. But the gambler said gently, "Young enough to be my daughter. It is a rotten world. When I call to you, lie down on the floor."

The Englishman had pulled the rifle from between his knees and laid it across the sill of the window on his side. The cattleman swept back the skirt of his coat to clear the holster of his gun.

The little flinty summit meadows grew narrower, with shoulders of gray rock closing in upon the road. The coach wheels slammed against the stony ruts and bounced high and fell again with a jar the springs could not soften. Happy Stuart's howl ran steadily above this rattle and rush. Fine dust turned all things gray.

Henriette sat with her eyes pinned to the gloved tips of her fingers, remembering the tall shape of Malpais Bill cut against the moonlight of Gap Station. He had smiled at her as a man might smile at any desirable woman, with the sweep and swing of laughter in his voice; and his eyes had been gentle. The gambler spoke very quietly and she didn't hear him until his fingers gripped her arm. He said again, not raising his voice: "Get down."

Henriette dropped to her knees, hearing gunfire blast through the rush and run of the coach. Happy Stuart ceased to yell and the army girl's eyes were round and dark. The walls of the canyon had tapered off. Looking upward through the window on the gambler's side, Henriette saw the weaving figure of an Apache warrior reel nakedly on a calico pony and rush by with a rifle raised and pointed in his bony elbows. The gambler took a cool aim; the stockman fired and aimed again. The Englishman's sporting rifle blasted heavy echoes through the coach, hurting her ears, and the smell of powder got rank and bitter. The blond man's boots scraped the coach top and round small holes began to dimple the paneling as the Apache bullets struck. An Indian came boldly abreast the coach and made a target that couldn't be missed. The cattleman dropped him with one shot. The wheels screamed as they slowed around the sharp ruts and the whole heavy superstructure of the coach bounced high into the air. Then they were rushing downgrade.

The gambler said quietly, "You had better take this," handing Henriette his gun. He leaned against the door with his small hands gripping the sill. Pallor loosened his cheeks. He said to the army girl: "Be sure and keep between those gentlemen," and looked at her with a way that was desperate and forlorn and dropped his head to the window sill.

Henriette saw the bluff rise up and close in like a yellow wall. They were rolling down the mountain without a brake. Gunfire fell off and the crying of the Indians faded back. Coming up from her knees then she saw the desert's flat surface far below, with the angular pattern of Lordsburg vaguely on the far borders of the heat fog. There was no more firing and Happy Stuart's voice lifted again and the brakes were screaming on the wheels, and going off, and screaming again. The Englishman stared out of the window sullenly; the army girl seemed in a deep desperate dream; the cattleman's face was shining with a strange sweat. Henriette reached over to pull the gambler up, but he had an unnatural weight to him and slid into the far corner. She saw that he was dead.

At five o'clock that long afternoon the stage threaded Lordsburg's narrow streets of 'dobe and frame houses, came upon the center square and stopped before a crowd of people gathered in the smoky heat. The passengers crawled out stiffly. A Mexican boy ran up to see the dead gambler and began to yell his news in shrill Mexican. Malpais Bill climbed off the top, but Happy Stuart sat back on his seat and stared taciturnly at the crowd. Henriette noticed then that the shotgun messenger was gone.

A gray man in a sleazy white suit called up to Happy. "Well, you got through."

Happy Stuart said: "Yeah. We got through."

An officer stepped through the crowd, smiling at the army girl. He took her arm and said, "Miss Robertson, I believe Lieutenant Hauser is quite all right. I will get your luggage—"

The army girl was crying then, definitely. They were all standing around, bone-weary and shaken. Malpais Bill remained by the wheel of the coach, his cheeks hard against the sunlight and his eyes riveted on a pair of men standing under the board awning of an adjoining store. Henriette observed the manner of their waiting and knew why they were there. The blond man's eyes, she noticed, were very blue and flame burned brilliantly in them. The army girl turned to Henriette, tears in her eyes. She murmured: "If there is anything I can ever do for you—"

But Henriette stepped back, shaking her head. This was Lordsburg and everybody knew her place except the army girl. Henriette said formally, "Good-bye," noting how still and expectant the two men under the awning remained. She swung toward the blond man and said, "Would you carry my valise?"

Malpais Bill looked at her, laughter remote in his eyes, and reached into the luggage pile and got her battered valise. He was still smiling as he went beside her, through the crowd and past the two waiting men. But when they turned into an anonymous and dusty little side street of town, where the houses all sat shoulder to shoulder without grace or dignity, he had turned sober. He said: "I am obliged to you. But I'll have to go back there."

They were in front of a house no different from its neighbors; they had stopped at its door. She could see his eyes travel this street and comprehend its meaning and the kind of traffic it bore. But he was saying in that gentle, melody-making tone:

"I have watched you for two days." He stopped, searching his mind to find the thing he wanted to say. It came out swiftly. "God made you a woman. The Tonto is a pretty country."

Her answer was quite barren of feeling. "No. I am known all through the Territory. But I can remember that you asked me."

He said: "No other reason?" She didn't answer but something in her eyes pulled his face together. He took off his hat and it seemed to her he was looking through this hot day to that far-off country and seeing it fresh and desirable. He murmured: "A man can escape nothing. I have got to do this. But I will be back."

He went along the narrow street, made a quick turn at the end of it, and disappeared. Heat rolled like a heavy wave over Lordsburg's housetops and the smell of dust was very sharp. She lifted her valise, and dropped it and stood like that, mute and grave before the door of her dismal house. She was remembering how tall he had been against the moonlight at Gap Station.

There were four swift shots beating furiously along the sultry quiet, and a shout, and afterwards a longer and longer silence. She put one hand against the door to steady herself, and knew that those shots marked the end of a man, and the end of hope. He would never come back; he would never stand over here in the moonlight with the long gentle smile on his lips and with the swing of life in his casual tone. She was thinking of all that humbly and with the patience life had beaten into her.

She was thinking of all that when she heard the strike of boots on the street's packed earth; and turned to see him, high and square in the muddy sunlight, coming toward her with his smile.

A Man Called Horse

Dorothy M. Johnson

He was a young man of good family, as the phrase went in the New England of a hundred-odd years ago, and the reasons for his bitter discontent were unclear, even to himself. He grew up in the gracious old Boston home under his grandmother's care, for his mother had died in giving him birth; and all his life he had known every comfort and privilege his father's wealth could provide.

But still there was the discontent, which puzzled him because he could not even define it. He wanted to live among his equals—people who were no better than he and no worse either. That was as close as he could come to describing the source of his unhappiness in Boston and his restless desire to go somewhere else.

In the year 1845, he left home and went out West, far beyond the country's creeping frontier, where he hoped to find his equals. He had the idea that in Indian country, where there was danger, all white men were kings, and he wanted to be one of them. But he found, in the West as in Boston, that the men he respected were still his superiors, even if they could not read, and those he did not respect weren't worth talking to.

He did have money, however, and he could hire the men he respected. He hired four of them, to cook and hunt and guide and be his companions, but he found them not friendly.

They were apart from him and he was still alone. He still brooded about his status in the world, longing for his equals.

On a day in June, he learned what it was to have no status at all. He became a captive of a small raiding party of Crow Indians.

He heard gunfire and the brief shouts of his companions around the bend of the creek just before they died, but he never saw their bodies. He had no chance to fight, because he was naked and unarmed, bathing in the creek, when a Crow warrior seized and held him.

His captor let him go at last, let him run. Then the lot of them rode him down for sport, striking him with their coup sticks. They carried the dripping scalps of his companions and one had skinned off Baptiste's black beard as well, for a trophy.

They took him along in a matter-of-fact way, as they took the captured horses. He was unshod and naked as the horses were, and like them he had a rawhide thong around his neck. So long as he didn't fall down, the Crows ignored him.

On the second day they gave him his breeches. His feet were too swollen for his boots, but one of the Indians threw him a pair of moccasins that had belonged to the halfbreed, Henri, who was dead back at the creek. The captive wore the moccasins gratefully. The third day they let him ride one of the spare horses so the party could move faster, and on that day they came in sight of their camp.

He thought of trying to escape, hoping he might be killed in flight rather than by slow torture in the camp, but he never had a chance to try. They were more familiar with escape than he was and, knowing what to expect, they forestalled it. The only other time he had tried to escape from anyone, he had succeeded. When he had left his home in Boston, his father had raged and his grandmother had cried, but they could not talk him out of his intention.

The men of the Crow raiding party didn't bother with talk.

Before riding into camp they stopped and dressed in their regalia, and in parts of their victim's clothing; they painted their faces black. Then, leading the white man by the rawhide around his neck as though he were a horse, they rode down toward the tepee circle, shouting and singing, brandishing their weapons. He was unconscious when they got there; he fell and was dragged.

He lay dazed and battered near a tepee while the noisy, busy life of the camp swarmed around him and Indians came to stare. Thirst consumed him, and when it rained he lapped rain water from the ground like a dog. A scrawny, shrieking, eternally busy old woman with ragged graying hair threw a chunk of meat on the grass, and he fought the dogs for it.

When his head cleared, he was angry, although anger was an emotion he knew he could not afford.

It was better when I was a horse, he thought—when they led me by the rawhide around my neck. I won't be a dog, no matter what!

The hag gave him stinking, rancid grease and let him figure out what it was for. He applied it gingerly to his bruises and sun-seared body.

Now, he thought, I smell like the rest of them.

While he was healing, he considered coldly the advantages of being a horse. A man would be humiliated, and sooner or later he would strike back and that would be the end of him. But a horse had only to be docile. Very well, he would learn to do without pride.

He understood that he was the property of the screaming old woman, a fine gift from her son, one that she liked to show off. She did more yelling at him than at anyone else, probably to impress the neighbors so they would not forget what a great and generous man her son was. She was bossy and proud, a dreadful sag of skin and bones, and she was a devilish hard worker.

The white man, who now thought of himself as a horse, forgot sometimes to worry about his danger. He kept making mental notes of things to tell his own people in Boston about this hideous adventure. He would go back a hero, and he would say, "Grandmother, let me fetch your shawl. I've been accustomed to doing little errands for another lady about your age."

Two girls lived in the tepee with the old hag and her warrior son. One of them, the white man concluded, was his captor's wife and the other was his little sister. The daughter-in-law was smug and spoiled. Being beloved, she did not have to be useful. The younger girl had bright, wandering eyes. Often enough they wandered to the white man who was pretending to be a horse.

The two girls worked when the old woman put them at it, but they were always running off to do something they enjoyed more. There were games and noisy contests, and there was much laughter. But not for the white man. He was finding out what loneliness could be.

That was a rich summer on the plains, with plenty of buffalo for meat and clothing and the making of tepees. The Crows were wealthy in horses, prosperous and contented. If their men had not been so avid for glory, the white man thought, there would have been a lot more of them. But they went out of their way to court death, and when one of them met it, the whole camp mourned extravagantly and cried to their God for vengeance.

The captive was a horse all summer, a docile bearer of burdens, careful and patient. He kept reminding himself that he had to be better-natured than other horses, because he could not lash out with hoofs or teeth. Helping the old woman load up the horses for travel, he yanked at a pack and said, "Whoa, brother. It goes easier when you don't fight."

The horse gave him a big-eyed stare as if it understood his language—a comforting thought, because nobody else did. But even among the horses he felt unequal. They were able to look out for themselves if they escaped. He would simply starve. He was envious still, even among the horses.

Humbly he fetched and carried. Sometimes he even offered to help, but he had not the skill for the endless work of the women, and he was not trusted to hunt with the men, the providers.

When the camp moved, he carried a pack trudging with the women. Even the dogs worked then, pulling small burdens on travois of sticks.

The Indian who had captured him lived like a lord, as he had a right to do. He hunted with his peers, attended long ceremonial meetings with much chanting and dancing, and lounged in the shade with his smug bride. He had only two responsibilities: to kill buffalo and to gain glory. The white man was so far beneath him in status that the Indian did not even think of envy.

One day several things happened that made the captive think he might sometime become a man again. That was the day when he began to understand their language. For four months he had heard it, day and night, the joy and the mourning, the ritual chanting and sun prayers, the squabbles and the deliberations. None of it meant anything to him at all.

But on that important day in early fall the two young women set out for the river, and one of them called over her shoulder to the old woman. The white man was startled. She had said she was going to bathe. His understanding was so sudden that he felt as if his ears had come unstopped. Listening to the racket of the camp, he heard fragment of meaning instead of gabble.

On that same important day the old woman brought a pair of new moccasins out of the tepee and tossed them on the ground before him. He could not believe she would do anything for him because of kindness, but giving him moccasins was one way of looking after her property.

In thanking her, he dared greatly. He picked a little handful of fading fall flowers and took them to her as she squatted in front of her tepee, scraping a buffalo hide with a tool made from a piece of iron tied to a bone. Her hands were hideous—most of the fingers had the first joint missing. He bowed solemnly and offered the flowers.

She glared at him from beneath the short, ragged tangle of her hair. She stared at the flowers, knocked them out of his hand and went running to the next tepee, squalling the story. He heard her and the other women screaming with laughter.

The white man squared his shoulders and walked boldly over to watch three small boys shooting arrows at a target. He said in English, "Show me how to do that, will you?"

They frowned, but he held out his hand as if there could be no doubt. One of them gave him a bow and one arrow, and they snickered when he missed.

The people were easily amused, except when they were angry. They were amused, at him, playing with the little boys. A few days later he asked the hag, with gestures, for a bow that her son had just discarded, a man-size bow of horn. He scavenged for old arrows. The old woman cackled at his marksmanship and called her neighbors to enjoy the fun.

When he could understand words, he could identify his people by their names. The old woman was Greasy Hand, and her daughter was Pretty Calf. The other young woman's name was not clear to him, for the words were not in his vocabulary. The man who had captured him was Yellow Robe.

Once he could understand, he could begin to talk a little, and then he was less lonely. Nobody had been able to see any reason for talking to him, since he would not understand anyway. He asked the old woman, "What is my name?" Until he knew it, he was incomplete. She shrugged to let him know he had none.

He told her in the Crow language, "My name is Horse." He repeated it, and she nodded. After that they called him Horse when they called him anything. Nobody cared except the white man himself.

They trusted him enough to let him stray out of camp, so that he might have got away and, by unimaginable good luck, might have reached a trading post or a fort, but winter was too close. He did not dare leave without a horse; he needed clothing and a better hunting weapon than he had, and more certain skill in using it. He did not dare steal, for then they would surely have pursued him, and just as certainly they would have caught him. Remembering the warmth of the home that was waiting in Boston, he settled down for the winter.

On a cold night he crept into the tepee after the others had gone to bed. Even a horse might try to find shelter from the wind. The old woman grumbled, but without conviction. She did not put him out.

They tolerated him, back in the shadows, so long as he did not get in the way.

He began to understand how the family that owned him differed from the others. Fate had been cruel to them. In a short, sharp argument among the old women, one of them derided Greasy Hand by sneering, "You have no relatives!" and Greasy Hand raved for minutes of the deeds of her father and uncles and brothers. And she had had four sons, she reminded her detractor—who answered with scorn, "Where are they?"

Later the white man found her moaning and whimpering to herself, rocking back and forth on her haunches, staring at her mutilated hands. By that time he understood. A mourner often chopped off a finger joint. Old Greasy Hand had mourned often. For the first time he felt a twinge of pity, but he put it aside as another emotion, like anger, that he could not afford. He thought: What tales I will tell when I get home!

He wrinkled his nose in disdain. The camp stank of animals and meat and rancid grease. He looked down at his naked, shivering legs and was startled, remembering that he was still only a horse.

He could not trust the old woman. She fed him only because a starved slave would die and not be worth boasting about. Just how fitful her temper was he saw on the day when she got tired of stumbling over one of the hundred dogs that infested the camp. This was one of her own dogs, a large, strong one that pulled a baggage travois when the tribe moved camp.

Countless times he had seen her kick the beast as it lay sleeping in front of the tepee, in her way. The dog always moved, with a yelp, but it always got in the way again. One day she gave the dog its usual kick and then stood scolding at it while the animal rolled its eyes sleepily. The old woman suddenly picked up her axe and cut the dog's head off with one blow. Looking well satisfied with herself, she beckoned her slave to remove the body.

It could have been me, he thought, if I were a dog. But I'm a horse.

His hope of life lay with the girl, Pretty Calf. He set about courting her, realizing how desperately poor he was both in property and honor. He owned no horse, no weapon but the old bow and the battered arrows. He had nothing to give away and he needed gifts, because he did not dare seduce the girl.

One of the customs of courtship involved sending a gift of horses to a girl's older brother and bestowing much buffalo meat upon her mother. The white man could not wait for some far-off time when he might have either horses or meat to give away. And his courtship had to be secret. It was not for him to stroll past the groups of watchful girls, blowing a flute made of an eagle's wing bone, as the flirtatious young bucks did.

He could not ride past Pretty Calf's tepee, painted and bedizened; he had no horse, no finery.

Back home, he remembered, I could marry just about any girl I'd want to. But he wasted little time thinking about that. A future was something to be earned.

The most he dared do was wink at Pretty Calf now and then, or state his admiration while she giggled and hid her face. The least he dared do to win his bride was to elope with her, but he had to give her a horse to put the seal of tribal approval on that. And he had no horse until he killed a man to get one. . . .

His opportunity came in early spring. He was casually accepted by that time. He did not belong, but he was amusing to the Crows, like a strange pet, or they would not have fed him through the winter.

His chance came when he was hunting small game with three young boys who were his guards as well as scornful companions. Rabbits and birds were of no account in a camp well fed on buffalo meat, but they made good targets.

His party walked far that day. All of them at once saw the two horses in a sheltered coulee. The boys and the man crawled forward on their bellies, and then they saw an Indian who lay on the ground, moaning, a lone traveler. From the way the boys inched forward, Horse knew the man was fair prey—a member of some enemy tribe.

This is the way the captive white man acquired wealth and honor to win a bride and save his life: He shot an arrow into the sick man, a split second ahead of one of his small companions, and dashed forward to strike the still-groaning man with his bow, to count first coup. Then he seized the hobbled horses.

By the time he had the horses secure, and with them his hope for freedom, the boys had followed, counting coup with gestures and shrieks they had practiced since boyhood, and one of them had the scalp. The white man was grimly amused to see the boy double up with sudden nausea when he had the thing in his hand. . . .

There was a hubbub in the camp when they rode in that evening, two of them on each horse. The captive was noticed. Indians who had ignored him as a slave stared at the brave man who had struck first coup and had stolen horses.

The hubbub lasted all night, as fathers boasted loudly of their young sons' exploits. The white man was called upon to settle an argument between two fierce boys as to which of them had struck second coup and which must be satisfied with third. After much talk that went over his head, he solemnly pointed at the nearest boy. He didn't know which boy it was and didn't care, but the boy did.

The white man had watched warriors in their triumph. He knew what to do. Modesty about achievements had no place among the Crow people. When a man did something big, he told about it.

The white man smeared his face with grease and charcoal. He walked inside the tepee circle, chanting and singing. He used his own language.

"You heathens, you savages," he shouted. "I'm going to get out of here someday! I am going to get away!" The Crow people listened respectfully. In the Crow tongue he shouted, "Horse! I am Horse!" and they nodded.

He had a right to boast, and he had two horses. Before dawn, the white man and his bride were sheltered beyond a far hill, and he was telling her, "I love you, little lady. I love you."

She looked at him with her great dark eyes, and he thought she understood his English words—or as much as she needed to understand.

"You are my treasure," he said, "more precious than jewels, better than fine gold. I am going to call you Freedom."

When they returned to camp two days later, he was bold but worried. His ace, he suspected, might not be high enough in the game he was playing without being sure of the rules. But it served.

Old Greasy Hand raged—but not at him. She complained loudly that her daughter had let herself go too cheap. But the marriage was as good as any Crow marriage. He had paid a horse.

He learned the language faster after that, from Pretty Calf, whom he sometimes called Freedom. He learned that his attentive, adoring bride was fourteen years old.

One thing he had not guessed was the difference that being Pretty Calf's husband would make in his relationship to her mother and brother. He had hoped only to make his position a little safer, but he had not expected to be treated with dignity. Greasy Hand no longer spoke to him at all. When the white man spoke to her, his bride murmured in dismay, explaining at great length that he must never do that. There could be no conversation between a man and his mother-in-law. He could not even mention a word that was part of her name.

Having improved his status so magnificently, he felt no need for hurry in getting away. Now that he had a woman, he had as good a chance to be rich as any man. Pretty Calf waited on him; she seldom ran off to play games with other young girls, but took pride in learning from her mother the many women's skills of tanning hides and making clothing and preparing food.

He was no more a horse but a kind of man, a half-Indian, still poor and unskilled but laden with honors, clinging to the buckskin fringes of Crow society.

Escape could wait until he could manage it in comfort, with fit clothing and a good horse, with hunting weapons. Escape could wait until the camp moved near some trading post. He did not plan how he would get home. He dreamed of being there all at once, and of telling stories nobody would believe. There was no hurry.

Pretty Calf delighted in educating him. He began to understand tribal arrangements, customs and why things were as they were. They were that way because they had always been so. His young wife giggled when she told him, in his ignorance, things she had always known. But she did not laugh when her brother's wife was taken by another warrior. She explained that solemnly with word and signs.

Yellow Robe belonged to a society called the Big Dogs. The wife stealer, Cut Neck, belonged to the Foxes. They were fellow tribesmen; they hunted together and fought side by side, but men of one society could take away wives from the other society if they wished, subject to certain limitations.

When Cut Neck rode up to the tepee, laughing and singing, and called to Yellow Robe's wife, "Come out! Come out!" she did as ordered, looking smug as usual, meek and entirely willing. Thereafter she rode beside him in ceremonial processions and carried his coup stick, while his other wife pretended not to care.

"But why?" the white man demanded of his wife, his Freedom. "Why did our brother let his woman go? He sits and smokes and does not speak."

Pretty Calf was shocked at the suggestion. Her brother could not possibly reclaim his woman, she explained. He could not even let her come back if she wanted to—and she probably would want to when Cut Neck tired of her. Yellow Robe could not even admit that his heart was sick. That was the way things were. Deviation meant dishonor.

The woman could have hidden from Cut Neck, she said. She could even have refused to go with him if she had been *ba-wurokee*—a really virtuous woman. But she had been his woman before, for a little while on a berrying expedition, and he had a right to claim her.

There was no sense in it, the white man insisted. He glared at his young wife. "If you go, I will bring you back!" he promised.

She laughed and buried her head against his shoulder. "I will not have to go," she said. "Horse is my first man. There is no hole in my moccasin."

He stroked her hair and said, *"Ba-wurokee."*

With great daring, she murmured, *"Hayha,"* and when he did not answer, because he did not know what she meant, she drew away, hurt.

"A woman calls her man that if she thinks he will not leave her. Am I wrong?"

The white man held her closer and lied, "Pretty Calf is not wrong. Horse will not leave her. Horse will not take another woman, either." No, he certainly would not. Parting from this one was going to be harder than getting her had been. *"Hayha,"* he murmured. "Freedom."

His conscience irked him, but not very much. Pretty Calf could get another man easily enough when he was gone, and a better provider. His hunting skill was improving, but he was still awkward.

There was no hurry about leaving. He was used to most of the Crow ways and could stand the rest. He was becoming prosperous. He owned five horses. His place in the life of the tribe was secure, such as it was. Three or four young women, including the one who had belonged to Yellow Robe, made advances to him. Pretty Calf took pride in the fact that her man was so attractive.

By the time he had what he needed for a secret journey, the grass grew yellow on the plains and the long cold was close. He was enslaved by the girl he called Freedom and, before the winter ended, by the knowledge that she was carrying his child . . .

The Big Dog society held a long ceremony in the spring. The white man strolled with his woman along the creek banks, thinking: When I get home I will tell them about the chants and the drumming. Sometime. Sometime.

Pretty Calf would not go to bed when they went back to the tepee.

"Wait and find out about my brother," she urged. "Something may happen."

So far as Horse could figure out, the Big Dogs were having some kind of election. He pampered his wife by staying up with her by the fire. Even the old woman, who was a great one for getting sleep when she was not working, prowled around restlessly.

The white man was yawning by the time the noise of the ceremony died down. When Yellow Robe strode in, garish and heathen in his paint and feathers and furs, the women cried out. There was conversation too fast for Horse to follow, and the old woman wailed once, but her son silenced her with a gruff command.

When the white man went to sleep, he thought his wife was weeping beside him.

The next morning she explained.

"He wears the bearskin belt. Now he can never retreat in battle. He will always be in danger. He will die."

Maybe he wouldn't, the white man tried to convince her. Pretty Calf recalled that some few men had been honored by the bearskin belt, vowed to the highest daring, and had not died. If they lived through the summer, then they were free of it.

"My brother wants to die," she mourned. "His heart is bitter."

Yellow Robe lived through half a dozen clashes with small parties of raiders from hostile tribes. His honors were many. He captured horses in an enemy camp, led two successful raids, counted first coup and snatched a gun from the hand of an enemy tribesman. He wore wolf tails on his moccasins and ermine skins on his shirt, and he fringed his leggings with scalps in token of his glory.

When his mother ventured to suggest, as she did many times, "My son should take a new wife, I need another woman to help me," he ignored her. He spent much time in prayer, alone in the hills or in conference with a medicine man. He fasted and made vows and kept them. And before he could be free of the heavy honor of the bearskin belt, he went on his last raid.

The warriors were returning from the north just as the white man and two other hunters approached from the south, with buffalo and elk meat dripping from the bloody hides tied on their restive ponies. One of the hunters grunted, and they stopped to watch a rider on the hill north of the tepee circle.

The rider dismounted, held up a blanket and dropped it. He repeated the gesture.

The hunters murmured in dismay. "Two! Two men dead!" They rode fast into the camp, where there was already wailing.

A messenger came down from the war party on the hill. The rest of the party delayed to paint their faces for mourning and for victory. One of the two dead men was Yellow Robe. They had put his body in a cave and walled it in with rocks. The other man died later, and his body was in a tree.

There was blood on the ground before the tepee to which Yellow Robe would return no more. His mother, with her hair chopped short, sat in the doorway, rocking back and forth on her haunches, wailing her heartbreak. She cradled one mutilated hand in the other. She had cut off another finger joint.

Pretty Calf had cut off chunks of her long hair and was crying as she gashed her arms with a knife. The white man tried to take the knife away, but she protested so piteously that he let her do as she wished. He was sickened with the lot of them.

Savages! he thought. Now I will go back! I'll go hunting alone, and I'll keep on going.

But he did not go just yet, because he was the only hunter in the lodge of the two grieving women, one of them old and the other pregnant with his child.

In their mourning, they made him a pauper again. Everything that meant comfort, wealth and safety they sacrificed to the spirits because of the death of Yellow Robe. The tepee, made of seventeen fine buffalo hides, the furs that should have kept them warm, the white deerskin dress, trimmed with elk teeth, that Pretty Calf loved so well, even their tools and Yellow Robe's weapons—everything but his sacred medicine objects—they left there on the prairie, and the whole camp moved away. Two of his best horses were killed as sacrifice, and the women gave away the rest.

They had no shelter. They would have no tepee of their own for two months at least of mourning, and then the women would have to tan hides to make it. Meanwhile they could live in temporary huts made of willows, covered with skins given them in pity by their friends. They could have lived with relatives, but Yellow Robe's women had no relatives.

The white man had not realized until then how terrible a thing it was for a Crow to have no kinfolk. No wonder old Greasy Hand had only stumps for fingers. She had mourned, from one year to the next, for everyone she had ever loved. She had no one left but her daughter, Pretty Calf.

Horse was furious at their foolishness. It had been bad enough for him, a captive, to be naked as a horse and poor as a slave, but that was because his captors had stripped him. These women had voluntarily given up everything they needed.

He was too angry at them to sleep in the willow hut. He lay under a sheltering tree. And on the third night of the mourning he made his plans. He had a knife and a bow. He would go after meat, taking two horses. And he would not come back. There were, he realized, many things he was not going to tell when he got back home.

In the willow hut, Pretty Calf cried out. He heard rustling there, and the old woman's querulous voice.

Some twenty hours later his son was born, two months early, in the tepee of a skilled medicine woman. The child was born without breath, and the mother died before the sun went down.

The white man was too shocked to think whether he should mourn, or how he should mourn. The old woman screamed until she was voiceless. Piteously she approached him, bent and trembling, blind with grief. She held out her knife and he took it.

She spread out her hands and shook her head. If she cut off any more finger joints, she could work no more. She could not afford any more lasting signs of grief.

The white man said, "All right! All right!" between his teeth. He hacked his arms with the knife and stood watching the blood run down. It was little enough to do for Pretty Calf, for little Freedom.

Now there is nothing to keep me, he realized. When I get home, I must not let them see the scars.

He looked at Greasy Hand, hideous in her grief-burdened age, and thought: I really am free now! When a wife dies, her husband has no more duty toward her family. Pretty Calf had told him so, long ago, when he wondered why a certain man moved out of one tepee and into another.

The old woman, of course, would be a scavenger. There was one other with the tribe, an ancient crone who had no relatives, towards whom no one felt any responsibility. She lived on food thrown away by the more fortunate. She slept in shelters that she built with her own knotted hands. She plodded wearily at the end of the procession when the camp moved. When she stumbled, nobody cared. When she died, nobody would miss her.

Tomorrow morning, the white man decided, I will go.

His mother-in-law's sunken mouth quivered. She said one word, questioningly. She said, *"Eero-oshay?"* She said, "Son?"

Blinking, he remembered. When a wife died, her husband was free. But her mother, who had ignored him with dignity, might if she wished ask him to stay. She invited him by calling him Son, and he accepted by answering Mother.

Greasy Hand stood before him, bowed with years, withered with unceasing labor, loveless and childless, scarred with grief. But with all her burdens, she still loved life enough to beg it from him, the only person she had any right to ask. She was stripping herself of all she had left, her pride.

He looked eastward across the prairie. Two thousand miles away was home. The old woman would not live forever. He could afford to wait, for he was young. He could afford to be magnanimous, for he knew he was a man. He gave her the answer. *"Eegya,"* he said. "Mother."

He went home three years later. He explained no more than to say, "I lived with the Crows for a while. It was some time before I could leave. They called me Horse."

He did not find it necessary either to apologize or to boast, because he was the equal of any man on earth.

This Is What It Means to Say Phoenix, Arizona

Sherman Alexie

Just after Victor lost his job at the BIA, he also found out that his father had died of a heart attack in Phoenix, Arizona. Victor hadn't seen his father in a few years, only talked to him on the telephone once or twice, but there still was a genetic pain, which was soon to be pain as real and immediate as a broken bone.

Victor didn't have any money. Who does have money on a reservation, except the cigarette and fireworks salespeople? His father had a savings account waiting to be claimed, but Victor needed to find a way to get to Phoenix. Victor's mother was just as poor as he was, and the rest of his family didn't have any use at all for him. So Victor called the Tribal Council.

"Listen," Victor said. "My father just died. I need some money to get to Phoenix to make arrangements."

"Now, Victor," the council said. "You know we're having a difficult time financially."

"But I thought the council had special funds set aside for stuff like this."

"Now, Victor, we do have some money available for the proper return of tribal members' bodies. But I don't think we have enough to bring your father all the way back from Phoenix."

"Well," Victor said. "It ain't going to cost all that much. He had to be cremated. Things were kind of ugly. He died of a heart attack in his trailer and nobody found him for a week. It was really hot, too. You get the picture."

"Now, Victor, we're sorry for your loss and the circumstances. But we can really only afford to give you one hundred dollars."

"That's not even enough for a plane ticket."

"Well, you might consider driving down to Phoenix."

"I don't have a car. Besides, I was going to drive my father's pickup back up here."

"Now, Victor," the council said. "We're sure there is somebody who could drive you to Phoenix. Or is there somebody who could lend you the rest of the money?"

"You know there ain't nobody around with that kind of money."

"Well, we're sorry, Victor, but that's the best we can do."

Victor accepted the Tribal Council's offer. What else could he do? So he signed the proper papers, picked up his check, and walked over to the Trading Post to cash it.

While Victor stood in line, he watched Thomas Builds-the-Fire standing near the magazine rack, talking to himself. Like he always did. Thomas was a storyteller that nobody wanted to listen to. That's like being a dentist in a town where everybody has false teeth.

Victor and Thomas Builds-the-Fire were the same age, had grown up and played in the dirt together. Ever since Victor could remember, it was Thomas who always had something to say.

Once, when they were seven years old, when Victor's father still lived with the family, Thomas closed his eyes and told Victor this story: "Your father's heart is weak. He is afraid of his own family. He is afraid of you. Late at night he sits in the dark. Watches the television until there's nothing but that white noise. Sometimes he feels like he wants to buy a motorcycle and ride away. He wants to run and hide. He doesn't want to be found."

Thomas Builds-the-Fire had known that Victor's father was going to leave, knew it before anyone. Now Victor stood in the Trading Post with a one-hundred-dollar check in his hand, wondering if Thomas knew that Victor's father was dead, if he knew what was going to happen next.

Just then Thomas looked at Victor, smiled, and walked over to him.

"Victor, I'm sorry about your father," Thomas said.

"How did you know about it?" Victor asked.

"I heard it on the wind. I heard it from the birds. I felt it in the sunlight. Also, your mother was just in here crying."

"Oh," Victor said and looked around the Trading Post. All the other Indians stared, surprised that Victor was even talking to Thomas. Nobody talked to Thomas anymore because he told the same damn stories over and over again. Victor was embarrassed, but he thought that Thomas might be able to help him. Victor felt a sudden need for tradition.

"I can lend you the money you need," Thomas said suddenly. "But you have to take me with you."

"I can't take your money," Victor said. "I mean, I haven't hardly talked to you in years. We're not really friends anymore."

"I didn't say we were friends. I said you had to take me with you."

"Let me think about it."

Victor went home with his one hundred dollars and sat at the kitchen table. He held his head in his hands and thought about Thomas Builds-the-Fire, remembered little details, tears and scars, the bicycle they shared for a summer, so many stories.

Thomas Builds-the-Fire sat on the bicycle, waited in Victor's yard. He was ten years old and skinny. His hair was dirty because it was the Fourth of July.

"Victor," Thomas yelled. "Hurry up. We're going to miss the fireworks."

After a few minutes, Victor ran out of his house, jumped the porch railing, and landed gracefully on the sidewalk.

"And the judges award him a 9.95, the highest score of the summer," Thomas said, clapped, laughed.

"That was perfect, cousin," Victor said. "And it's my turn to ride the bike."

Thomas gave up the bike and they headed for the fairgrounds. It was nearly dark and the fireworks were about to start.

"You know," Thomas said. "It's strange how us Indians celebrate the Fourth of July. It ain't like it was *our* independence everybody was fighting for."

"You think about things too much," Victor said. "It's just supposed to be fun. Maybe Junior will be there."

"Which Junior? Everybody on this reservation is named Junior."

And they both laughed.

The fireworks were small, hardly more than a few bottle rockets and a fountain. But it was enough for two Indian boys. Years later, they would need much more.

Afterwards, sitting in the dark, fighting off mosquitoes, Victor turned to Thomas Builds-the-Fire.

"Hey," Victor said. "Tell me a story."

Thomas closed his eyes and told this story: "There were these two Indian boys who wanted to be warriors. But it was too late to be warriors in the old way. All the horses were gone. So the two Indian boys stole a car and drove to the city. They parked the stolen car in front of the police station and then hitchhiked back home to the reservation. When they got back, all their friends cheered and their parents' eyes shone with pride. *You were very brave*, everybody said to the two Indian boys. *Very brave*."

"Ya-hey," Victor said. "That's a good one. I wish I could be a warrior."

"Me, too," Thomas said.

They went home together in the dark, Thomas on the bike now, Victor on foot. They walked through shadows and light from streetlamps.

"We've come a long ways," Thomas said. "We have outdoor lighting."

"All I need is the stars," Victor said. "And besides, you still think about things too much."

They separated then, each headed for home, both laughing all the way.

Victor sat at his kitchen table. He counted his one hundred dollars again and again. He knew he needed more to make it to Phoenix and back. He knew he needed Thomas Builds-the-Fire. So he put his money in his wallet and opened the front door to find Thomas on the porch.

"Ya-hey, Victor," Thomas said. "I knew you'd call me."

Thomas walked into the living room and sat down on Victor's favorite chair.

"I've got some money saved up," Thomas said. "It's enough to get us down there, but you have to get us back."

"I've got this hundred dollars," Victor said. "And my dad had a savings account I'm going to claim."

"How much in your dad's account?"

"Enough. A few hundred."

"Sounds good. When we leaving?"

When they were fifteen and had long since stopped being friends, Victor and Thomas got into a fistfight. That is, Victor was really drunk and beat Thomas up for no reason at all. All the other Indian boys stood around and watched it happen. Junior was there and so were Lester, Seymour, and a lot of others. The beating might have gone on until Thomas was dead if Norma Many Horses hadn't come along and stopped it.

"Hey, you boys," Norma yelled and jumped out of her car. "Leave him alone."

If it had been someone else, even another man, the Indian boys would've just ignored the warnings. But Norma was a warrior. She was powerful. She could have picked up any two of the boys and smashed their skulls together. But worse than that, she would have dragged them all over to some tipi and made them listen to some elder tell a dusty old story.

The Indian boys scattered, and Norma walked over to Thomas and picked him up.

"Hey, little man, are you okay?" she asked.

Thomas gave her a thumbs up.

"Why they always picking on you?"

Thomas shook his head, closed his eyes, but no stories came to him, no words or music. He just wanted to go home, to lie in his bed and let his dreams tell his stories for him.

• • •

Thomas Builds-the-Fire and Victor sat next to each other in the airplane, coach section. A tiny white woman had the window seat. She was busy twisting her body into pretzels. She was flexible.

"I have to ask," Thomas said, and Victor closed his eyes in embarrassment.

"Don't," Victor said.

"Excuse me, miss," Thomas asked. "Are you a gymnast or something?"

"There's no something about it," she said. "I was first alternate on the 1980 Olympic team."

"Really?" Thomas asked.

"Really."

"I mean, you used to be a world-class athlete?" Thomas asked.

"My husband still thinks I am."

Thomas Builds-the-Fire smiled. She was a mental gymnast, too. She pulled her leg straight up against her body so that she could've kissed her kneecap.

"I wish I could do that," Thomas said.

Victor was ready to jump out of the plane. Thomas, that crazy Indian storyteller with ratty old braids and broken teeth, was flirting with a beautiful Olympic gymnast. Nobody back home on the reservation would ever believe it.

"Well," the gymnast said. "It's easy. Try it."

Thomas grabbed at his leg and tried to pull it up into the same position as the gymnast. He couldn't even come close, which made Victor and the gymnast laugh.

"Hey," she asked. "You two are Indian, right?"

"Full-blood," Victor said.

"Not me," Thomas said. "I'm half magician on my mother's side and half clown on my father's."

They all laughed.

"What are your names?" she asked.

"Victor and Thomas."

"Mine is Cathy. Pleased to meet you all."

The three of them talked for the duration of the flight. Cathy the gymnast complained about the government, how they screwed the 1980 Olympic team by boycotting.

"Sounds like you all got a lot in common with Indians," Thomas said.

Nobody laughed.

After the plane landed in Phoenix and they had all found their way to the terminal, Cathy the gymnast smiled and waved good-bye.

"She was really nice," Thomas said.

"Yeah, but everybody talks to everybody on airplanes," Victor said. "It's too bad we can't always be that way."

"You always used to tell me I think too much," Thomas said. "Now it sounds like you do."

"Maybe I caught it from you."

"Yeah."

Thomas and Victor rode in a taxi to the trailer where Victor's father died.

"Listen," Victor said as they stopped in front of the trailer. "I never told you I was sorry for beating you up that time."

"Oh, it was nothing. We were just kids and you were drunk."

"Yeah, but I'm still sorry."

"That's all right."

Victor paid for the taxi and the two of them stood in the hot Phoenix summer. They could smell the trailer.

"This ain't going to be nice," Victor said. "You don't have to go in."

"You're going to need help."

Victor walked to the front door and opened it. The stink rolled out and made them both gag. Victor's father had lain in that trailer for a week in hundred-degree temperatures before anyone found him. And the only reason anyone found him was because of the smell. They needed dental records to identify him. That's exactly what the coroner said. They needed dental records.

"Oh, man," Victor said. "I don't know if I can do this."

"Well, then don't."

"But there might be something valuable in there."

"I thought his money was in the bank."

"It is. I was talking about pictures and letters and stuff like that."

"Oh," Thomas said as he held his breath and followed Victor into the trailer.

When Victor was twelve, he stepped into an underground wasp nest. His foot was caught in the hole, and no matter how hard he struggled, Victor couldn't pull free. He might have died there, stung a thousand times, if Thomas Builds-the-Fire had not come by.

"Run," Thomas yelled and pulled Victor's foot from the hole. They ran then, hard as they ever had, faster than Billy Mills, faster than Jim Thorpe, faster than the wasps could fly.

Victor and Thomas ran until they couldn't breathe, ran until it was cold and dark outside, ran until they were lost and it took hours to find their way home. All the way back, Victor counted his stings.

"Seven," Victor said. "My lucky number."

• • •

Victor didn't find much to keep in the trailer. Only a photo album and a stereo. Everything else had that smell stuck in it or was useless anyway.

"I guess this is all," Victor said. "It ain't much."

"Better than nothing," Thomas said.

"Yeah, and I do have the pickup."

"Yeah," Thomas said. "It's in good shape."

"Dad was good about that stuff."

"Yeah, I remember your dad."

"Really?" Victor asked. "What do you remember?"

Thomas Builds-the-Fire closed his eyes and told this story: "I remember when I had this dream that told me to go to Spokane, to stand by the Falls in the middle of the city and wait for a sign. I knew I had to go there but I didn't have a car. Didn't have a license. I was only thirteen. So I walked all the way, took me all day, and I finally made it to the Falls. I stood there for an hour waiting. Then your dad came walking up. *What the hell are you doing here?* he asked me. I said, *Waiting for a vision.* Then your father said, *All you're going to get here is mugged.* So he drove me over to Denny's, bought me dinner, and then drove me home to the reservation. For a long time I was mad because I thought my dreams had lied to me. But they didn't. Your dad was my vision. *Take care of each other* is what my dreams were saying. *Take care of each other.*"

Victor was quiet for a long time. He searched his mind for memories of his father, found the good ones, found a few bad ones, added it all up, and smiled.

"My father never told me about finding you in Spokane," Victor said.

"He said he wouldn't tell anybody. Didn't want me to get in trouble. But he said I had to watch out for you as part of the deal."

"Really?"

"Really. Your father said you would need the help. He was right."

"That's why you came down here with me, isn't it?" Victor asked.

"I came because of your father."

Victor and Thomas climbed into the pickup, drove over to the bank, and claimed the three hundred dollars in the savings account.

Thomas Builds-the-Fire could fly.

Once, he jumped off the roof of the tribal school and flapped his arms like a crazy eagle. And he flew. For a second, he hovered, suspended above all the other Indian boys who were too smart or too scared to jump.

"He's flying," Junior yelled, and Seymour was busy looking for the trick wires or mirrors. But it was real. As real as the dirt when Thomas lost altitude and crashed to the ground.

He broke his arm in two places.

"He broke his wing," Victor chanted, and the other Indian boys joined in, made it a tribal song.

"He broke his wing, he broke his wing, he broke his wing," all the Indian boys chanted as they ran off, flapping their wings, wishing they could fly, too. They hated Thomas for his courage, his brief moment as a bird. Everybody has dreams about flying. Thomas flew.

One of his dreams came true for just a second, just enough to make it real.

Victor's father, his ashes, fit in one wooden box with enough left over to fill a cardboard box.

"He always was a big man," Thomas said.

Victor carried part of his father and Thomas carried the rest out to the pickup. They set him down carefully behind the seats, put a cowboy hat on the wooden box and a Dodgers cap on the cardboard box. That's the way it was supposed to be.

"Ready to head back home," Victor asked.

"It's going to be a long drive."

"Yeah, take a couple days, maybe."

"We can take turns," Thomas said.

"Okay," Victor said, but they didn't take turns. Victor drove for sixteen hours straight north, made it halfway up Nevada toward home before he finally pulled over.

"Hey, Thomas," Victor said. "You got to drive for a while."

"Okay."

Thomas Builds-the-Fire slid behind the wheel and started off down the road. All through Nevada, Thomas and Victor had been amazed at the lack of animal life, at the absence of water, of movement.

"Where is everything?" Victor had asked more than once.

Now when Thomas was finally driving they saw the first animal, maybe the only animal in Nevada. It was a long-eared jackrabbit.

"Look," Victor yelled. "It's alive."

Thomas and Victor were busy congratulating themselves on their discovery when the jackrabbit darted out into the road and under the wheels of the pickup.

"Stop the goddamn car," Victor yelled, and Thomas did stop, backed the pickup to the dead jackrabbit.

"Oh, man, he's dead," Victor said as he looked at the squashed animal. "Really dead."

"The only thing alive in this whole state and we just killed it."

"I don't know," Thomas said. "I think it was suicide."

Victor looked around the desert, sniffed the air, felt the emptiness and loneliness, and nodded his head.

"Yeah," Victor said. "It had to be suicide."

"I can't believe this," Thomas said. "You drive for a thousand miles and there ain't even any bugs smashed on the windshield. I drive for ten seconds and kill the only living thing in Nevada."

"Yeah," Victor said. "Maybe I should drive."

"Maybe you should."

Thomas Builds-the-Fire walked through the corridors of the tribal school by himself. Nobody wanted to be anywhere near him because of all those stories. Story after story.

Thomas closed his eyes and this story came to him: "We are all given one thing by which our lives are measured, one determination. Mine are the stories which can change or not change the world. It doesn't matter which as long as I continue to tell the stories. My father, he died on Okinawa in World War II, died fighting for this country, which had tried to kill him for years. My mother, she died giving birth to me, died while I was still inside her. She pushed me out into the world with her last breath. I have no brothers or sisters. I have only my stories which came to me before I even had the words to speak. I learned a thousand stories before I took my first thousand steps. They are all I have. It's all I can do."

Thomas Builds-the-Fire told his stories to all those who would stop and listen. He kept telling them long after people had stopped listening.

Victor and Thomas made it back to the reservation just as the sun was rising. It was the beginning of a new day on earth, but the same old shit on the reservation.

"Good morning," Thomas said.

"Good morning."

The tribe was waking up, ready for work, eating breakfast, reading the newspaper, just like everybody else does. Willene LeBret was out in her garden wearing a bathrobe. She waved when Thomas and Victor drove by.

"Crazy Indians made it," she said to herself and went back to her roses.

Victor stopped the pickup in front of Thomas Builds-the-Fire's HUD house. They both yawned, stretched a little, shook dust from their bodies.

"I'm tired," Victor said.

"Of everything," Thomas added.

They both searched for words to end the journey. Victor needed to thank Thomas for his help, for the money, and make the promise to pay it all back.

"Don't worry about the money," Thomas said. "It don't make any difference anyhow."

"Probably not, enit?"

"Nope."

Victor knew that Thomas would remain the crazy storyteller who talked to dogs and cars, who listened to the wind and pine trees. Victor knew that he couldn't really be friends with Thomas, even after all that had happened. It was cruel but it was real. As real as the ashes, as Victor's father, sitting behind the seats.

"I know how it is," Thomas said. "I know you ain't going to treat me any better than you did before. I know your friends would give you too much shit about it."

Victor was ashamed of himself. Whatever happened to the tribal ties, the sense of community? The only real thing he shared with anybody was a bottle and broken dreams. He owed Thomas something, anything.

"Listen," Victor said and handed Thomas the cardboard box which contained half of his father. "I want you to have this."

Thomas took the ashes and smiled, closed his eyes, and told this story: "I'm going to travel to Spokane Falls one last time and toss these ashes into the water. And your father will rise like a salmon, leap over the bridge, over me, and find his way home. It will be beautiful. His teeth will shine like silver, like a rainbow. He will rise, Victor, he will rise."

Victor smiled.

"I was planning on doing the same thing with my half," Victor said. "But I didn't imagine my father looking anything like a salmon. I thought it'd be like cleaning the attic or something. Like letting things go after they've stopped having any use."

"Nothing stops, cousin," Thomas said. "Nothing stops."

Thomas Builds-the-Fire got out of the pickup and walked up his driveway. Victor started the pickup and began the drive home.

"Wait," Thomas yelled suddenly from his porch. "I just got to ask one favor."

Victor stopped the pickup, leaned out the window, and shouted back. "What do you want?"

"Just one time when I'm telling a story somewhere, why don't you stop and listen?" Thomas asked.

"Just once?"

"Just once."

Victor waved his arms to let Thomas know that the deal was good. It was a fair trade, and that was all Victor had ever wanted from his whole life. So Victor drove his father's pickup toward home while Thomas went into his house, closed the door behind him, and heard a new story come to him in the silence afterwards.

PART V

GRAPHIC STORIES:

FLYING UNDER THE RADAR

"The Harvey Pekar Name Story"
by Harvey Pekar

American Splendor, directed by Shari Springer Berman and Robert Pulcini, 2003

Ghost World—Chapter 5: "Hubba Hubba"
by Daniel Clowes

Ghost World, directed by Terry Zwigoff, 2001

Comics aren't called the "invisible art" for nothing. Adjectives like "underground," "marginalized," "bastard," "alternative," and "stepchild" are regularly used to describe today's adult comics industry. And yet some of today's most intriguing storytelling happens in the comics—maybe because few people are looking. Today, even successful comics appeal primarily to a niche audience. As Art Spiegelman, who won a Pulitzer Prize for his groundbreaking graphic novel *Maus*, has said, "Comics fly below the critical radar."

Mostly. Daniel Clowes doesn't fly undetected anymore, but reports of his celebrity are usually qualified. The word "famous" is often followed by "for a cartoonist." His work has been reviewed in the *New York Times* and *Time*. He's been profiled by *The New Yorker* and *Salon*. In 1998 *Newsweek* dubbed him "the country's premier underground cartoonist," and that same year his graphic story "Green Eyeliner" was included in *Esquire*'s fiction issue. Still, the adult audience for graphic stories remains relatively small. (Spiegelman once tried to narrow it down—he speculated his number of readers to be fewer than Danielle Steele's but more than those who read poetry.) In a story called "Message to the People of the Future," a nervously sweating character named Daniel Clowes worries about his artistic legacy, confessing to the reader, "An underground cartoonist is someone who creates pictographic scenarios, often wholly fictional, for the amusement of a small audience of marginal fringe-dwellers and drug addicts."

Maybe that's the beauty of it. Where else but in comics could you publish "Needledick the Bugfucker" (reads like it sounds) alongside a story which ends "and what's more, love does exist and is indeed a beautiful thing"? Where else would a publisher say, "It'll never sell, but go ahead," as Fantagraphics did with *Eightball*, the eclectic comic book Clowes puts out two or three times a year? Where else can you publish without an editor, as Clowes does at Fantagraphics? Scott McCloud, author of *Understanding Comics*, says, "Today comics is one of the very few forms of mass communication in which individual voices still have a chance to be heard." With a small but savvy audience primed for unusual and risky work, there's unprecedented freedom. And the form itself has barely been tapped. "Even in the face of utter indifference," Clowes has said, "there are those of us who will continue to create comics, if only because of the vast unexplored prairie between what has been done and the thrilling possibilities that lie around us in all directions."

"Hubba Hubba" is one of a set of graphic stories, collected under the title *Ghost World*, that feature Enid Coleslaw (an anagram of Daniel Clowes) and her friend Becky Doppelmeyer. Originally published in *Eightball*, the *Ghost World* series explores teenage ennui—with a satirical edge. Enid began as a drawing in Clowes's sketchbook with a matching voice inside his head. "When I started out I thought of her as this id creature—totally outgoing, follows her impulses. Then I realized halfway through that she was just more vocal than I was, but she has the same kind of confusion, self-doubts and identity issues that I still have. . . ." Enid is as complex as any character found in the best contemporary fiction, inviting the inevitable comparison to Holden Caulfield, literature's smartass-comes-of-age icon. Suprisingly, Enid can hold her own. "*Eightball* is the greatest comic book of the last two decades," says Clowes's friend and fellow comic artist Chris Ware, "and every issue is a huge step forward from the last—which always seems to be an impossibility. . . . His stuff makes the rest of us reconsider our own, and moves all sorts of subject matter that had seemed impossible before into approachable range."

It was director Terry Zwigoff's wife who convinced him that *Ghost World* should be a film. After making the Sundance award-winning documentary *Crumb*, about his underground cartoonist friend Robert Crumb, Zwigoff began looking around for a follow-up. He was familiar with the comics world, partly because his wife worked for a comic book distributor and partly because Crumb brought piles of comics with him when he stayed at Zwigoff's house. "I thought *Ghost World* was very strong, but I didn't find it as funny as Dan's other stuff. I didn't think it would make a good movie, but my wife kept telling me it would." Eventually he contacted Clowes and they hit it off. The screenplay was written collaboratively over a period of a year and a half; it then took another few years to get financing. "Unfortunately," Zwigoff says, "most people who are successful in Hollywood or any other business are not oddballs at all. They don't get the type of characters we have in the film—the misfits and the alienated." Fortunately, the two refused to compromise their eccentric vision, and Enid made the transition from page to screen without losing her edge. The *Washington Post* calls her "a character so real and poignant (yet hysterically funny) she'll linger for months or years."

Crumb was also instrumental in the making of Harvey Pekar's career. The two became friends in Cleveland, and it was Crumb who provided the first artwork for Pekar's meditation on ordinary life, the *American Splendor* comics series. (Pekar storyboards his comics, then enlists various artists to illustrate them.) His earliest work was published in the underground "comix," thanks to Crumb, but Pekar's work was never aimed at that audience. His comics are determinedly individual, constructing an autobiography "so staggeringly mundane as to border on the exotic," as Crumb puts it. *American Splendor* has never fit in any of the convenient categories. There's no superhero or big adventure. It doesn't lampoon or skewer anything or anyone (except maybe Pekar himself). And there's a marked lack of that alternative comics staple: smartass-ness. It is what it is: The Life and Times of Harvey Pekar. "The people who like my work most," Pekar says, "are readers of novels and short stories." His influences have been primarily literary, and he counts among them George Eliot and Balzac. "I want to write literature," Pekar told an interviewer, "that pushes people into their lives rather than helping them escape. . . . I think the so-called average person often exhibits a great deal of heroism getting through an ordinary day, and yet the reading public takes this heroism for granted."

Self-published for fourteen years, from 1976 until his bout with cancer made it impractical, *American Splendor* is the longest-running autobiographical series in comics. The artistic commitment and perseverance this represents can barely be overstated; it often involved lugging comic books from one location to another, dealing directly with distributors, and breaking even or sometimes even losing money. For some comics creators, self-publishing is a way to quickly respond to topical issues while avoiding any form of censorship. For Pekar, whose work didn't fit any existing niche, it was a necessity. But it has allowed him to say exactly what he wants to say the way he wants to say it. His honesty is brutal; his focus on the quotidian unrelenting. There is no visual consistency from one story to the next; he is slump-shouldered and hairy in Crumb's illustrations, cleft-chinned and sideburned in Gerry Shamray's. He eschews standard forms and narrative structures with a recognizable beginning, middle, and end. "I try to avoid pat endings," he has said. "Plot means nothing to me." He has a predilection for silent panels, which he uses to create a halting rhythm, "almost as if I'm an oral storyteller."

Shari Springer Berman and Robert Pulcini, the team who cowrote and codirected *American Splendor* (the film), were only vaguely familiar with Pekar's comics when they were approached about the project. When they settled down to read, the two became fascinated by the various artists' incarnations of Pekar and decided to use this shifting perspective as a device. The film intertwines Pekar as played by actor Paul Giamatti, Pekar as a cartoon, Pekar as seen on David Letterman's talk show, and Pekar as himself. "It felt appropriate to call attention to the artifice of the filmmaking in *American*

Splendor," Pulcini says, "because it . . . [is] in spirit with the character and the rebellious nature of the comic book." The screenplay is primarily based on Pekar's narrative comics, like "Our Cancer Year," but the filmmakers liked "The Harvey Pekar Name Story" so well that they decided to weave it in as an explanatory set piece.

Like Zwigoff, Berman and Pulcini had previously done only documentaries, but once they had an approach to the material they were able to write the screenplay in one month. It's a screenplay Pekar makes no bones about not having read. "He never tried to influence the movie," Berman says, "he never tried to tell us what to do. The only thing he asked us is to not whitewash him. . . . Harvey was like, 'Please don't make me into some perfect Hollywood guy with Tom Cruise playing me. I want something real.'" And that faithfulness to imperfection paid off. The film won the Sundance Grand Jury Prize and the Cannes Film Festival's Fipresci Prize. "In short," said Anthony Lane of *The New Yorker,* "*American Splendor* does what few movies of late have bothered, or dared, to do: it registers the beat of ordinary lives."

The relationship between comics and the movies is both illustrious and checkered. Superheroes, of course, have been fodder from the very beginning. But other, more obscure material has also been appropriated, with its creators given little or no credit. (In 1990, for example, the makers of the sci-fi film *Hardware* were sued—and settled out of court—for stealing their plot from a *2000AD* comics story.) It's the curse of the invisible. Perhaps, though, the success of *Ghost World* and *American Splendor* will help to change things for the better. "Comics is as wide an area as prose," Pekar once told an interviewer, ". . . and the fact that it's been used in such a limited way is totally crazy. What I hope people start to realize is that comics can be as versatile as any other medium. . . . When more people do that, and when more good work is produced [adult comics will take off]. Because nothing will attract people to comics like good work." But for now, you can still find his work in the back corner of the bookstore, shelved somewhere between Archie and Zippy the Pinhead.

THE HARVEY PEKAR NAME STORY

STORY BY HARVEY PEKAR   ART BY R. CRUMB

LATER SOME PEOPLE STARTED CALLING ME HARVEY "PECKER"...
I DIDN'T LIKE THAT...
THEN THERE WERE THOSE WHO REFERRED TO ME AS "HARVEY THE RABBIT"...
THEY THOUGHT THEY WERE BEING QUITE CLEVER...
BUT I WAS A PHYSICALLY STRONG AND DETERMINED YOUNG MAN.. AS TIME WENT ON I GAINED THE RESPECT OF MY PEERS...
... IN ONE WAY OR ANOTHER...
...THEY STOPPED MAKING NASTY REFERENCES TO MY NAME...
FOR AWHILE I FORGOT ABOUT IT...IT WAS AS IF I WAS NAMED...
....JOHN SMITH.
I MARRIED AT AN EARLY AGE.

MY WIFE, WHO WOULD ONE DAY BECOME MY EX-WIFE...
MY WIFE THOUGHT THAT I HAD AN EXCELLENT NAME. AND SHE CONVINCED ME THAT I DID.
IT WAS A UNIQUE NAME, A NAME WITH CHARACTER.
I WAS MARRIED IN THE SUMMER OF 1960 AND PROMPTLY GOT A TELEPHONE...
THE NEXT SPRING A NEW PHONE BOOK CAME OUT. IMAGINE MY SURPRISE WHEN I TURNED TO MY NAME AND SAW THAT, IN ADDITION TO ME, ANOTHER HARVEY PEKAR WAS LISTED!
I WAS LISTED AS HARVEY L. PEKAR... MY MIDDLE NAME IS LAWRENCE... HE WAS LISTED SIMPLY AS HARVEY PEKAR— NO MIDDLE INITIAL...
...THEREFORE, HIS WAS A PURER LISTING.
BUT I LEARNED TO ACCEPT IT. EACH YEAR I WOULD FEEL LESS STRONGLY AS I SAW THE OTHER HARVEY PEKAR'S NAME.
THEN, IN 1966, I NOTICED THAT A THIRD HARVEY PEKAR WAS LISTED IN THE PHONE BOOK!
THIS FILLED ME WITH CURIOSITY. HOW COULD THERE BE THREE PEOPLE WITH SUCH AN UNUSUAL NAME IN THE WORLD, LET ALONE IN ONE CITY!?
I ONCE GOT A LONG DISTANCE CALL AT MIDNIGHT FOR A HARVEY PEKAR. IT WAS A WOMAN CALLING FROM FLORIDA. I DIDN'T KNOW HER. SHE HAD MISTAKEN ME FOR ONE OF THE OTHER HARVEY PEKARS.

THE CALL CAUSED ME TO WONDER WHAT SORT OF PERSON HE WAS. OF COURSE I HAD NO WAY OF KNOWING...
THEN ONE DAY A PERSON I WORKED WITH EXPRESSED HER SYMPATHY TO ME CONCERNING WHAT SHE THOUGHT WAS THE DEATH OF MY FATHER. I KNEW MY FATHER TO BE ALIVE AND IN GOOD HEALTH AND ASKED HER WHERE SHE'D GOTTEN THE NOTION THAT HE'D DIED.
SHE POINTED OUT AN OBITUARY NOTICE IN THE NEWSPAPER FOR A MAN NAMED HARVEY PEKAR. ONE OF HIS SONS WAS NAMED HARVEY.
THESE WERE THE OTHER HARVEY PEKARS.
SIX MONTHS LATER HARVEY PEKAR JR. DIED.
ALTHOUGH I'D MET NEITHER MAN, I WAS FILLED WITH SADNESS. "WHAT WERE THEY LIKE" I THOUGHT. IT SEEMED THAT OUR LIVES HAD BEEN LINKED IN SOME INDEFINABLE WAY.
THE NEXT YEAR'S TELEPHONE DIRECTORY CONTAINED ONLY MY NAME.
BUT THE STORY DOES NOT END THERE, FOR TWO YEARS LATER ANOTHER HARVEY PEKAR APPEARED IN THE DIRECTORY!
WHAT KIND OF PEOPLE ARE THESE? WHERE DO THEY COME FROM, WHAT DO THEY DO? WHAT'S IN A NAME?
WHO IS HARVEY PEKAR?
END

...WHADDYA CALL A JAPANESE JEW?
I DON'T KNOW. WHERE ARE YOU TAKING ME?
SOSUMI!
GHOST WORLD
GET IT?

I'VE GONE BY THIS PLACE A MILLION TIMES BUT I CAN'T BELIEVE WE'RE FINALLY GOING IN!
YOU MADE ME RIDE TEN THOUSAND HOURS ON A BUS TO GO TO A STRIP MALL?
PET LAIR

YOU'LL THANK ME ONE DAY FOR INTRODUCING YOU TO... 'HUBBA HUBBA, THE ORIGINAL '50's DINER'!
ISN'T THIS PLACE THE GREATEST EVER!?
WATCH IT!
THE ORIGINAL '50's DINER

GOD, IT'S SO PATHETIC!
COULD THEY POSSIBLY BE MORE CLUELESS!? I'M SO HAPPY WE'RE HERE!

CHECK OUT THAT WAITER'S AWESOME "FIFTIES" HAIR-DO!
I FEEL AS THOUGH I'VE STEPPED DIRECTLY INTO 1954!

SAY! WHERE'S POTSIE AND RICHIE AND THE REST OF THE GANG?
AT THE SOCK HOP?
...OR THE CAR WASH...
THE CAR WASH?
WHATEVER!

HI! MY NAME IS ALLEN AND I'LL BE YOUR WAITER THIS AFTERNOON--
HI, AL!
OUR SPECIALS TODAY ARE--
CAN WE CALL YOU "WEIRD AL"?

HEH HEH ... OUR SPECIALS TODAY ARE: **PASTA VASILIO,** WHICH IS A PASTA SALAD WITH A LIGHT BASIL VINAIGRETTE --
THAT WAS A POPULAR DISH IN THE FIFTIES, HUH WEIRD AL?
I IMAGINE SO! ALSO, WE HAVE A SPINACH TORTELLINI IN A TOMATO PESTO SAUCE. BOTH OF THOSE ARE $6.95... SHALL I GIVE YOU A FEW MINUTES TO MULL IT OVER?
I JUST WANT AN ORDER OF ONION RINGS.
... I MIGHT ACTUALLY GET THE SPECIAL PASTA...
YOU **LOSER!**
♫ ...YOU'VE LOST THAT LO-VIN' FEELIN'... ♫
I HATE THIS SONG.
IT **SUCKS.**
WHAT DOES THAT EVEN MEAN?
IN BED WITH THE GOP: A LOBBYIST COMES CLEAN
WHO READS THOSE ARTICLES?
I **KNOW...**
OH **GOD,** I HATE THESE PEOPLE! PEOPLE WHO ARE **SUPER-SERIOUS** ABOUT POLITICS ALL THE TIME GIVE ME THE TOTAL CREEPS!
IT'S LIKE MY **DAD** ...I MEAN, WHO THE FUCK **CARES?!**
WOMEN!
SPERM DONOR WANTED
I KNOW, IT'S LIKE THAT GUY JASON-- IF YOU'RE NOT ALL **GUNG HO** ABOUT HIS SPECIFIC CAUSE, HE ACTS LIKE YOU'RE SOME TOTALLY SELF-OBSESSED **SNOB!**
LEATHER
"YEAH JASON, EVER SINCE YOU STOPPED EATING MEAT AND BATHING AND STARTED DOING GRAFITTI AND FUCKING UP ATM MACHINES, THE WORLD HAS BECOME A WAY BETTER PLACE!"
STILL, I THINK IT'S KIND OF COOL THAT YOUR DAD IS LIKE THAT...
IT'S DEFINITELY SOME PSYCHOLOG-ICAL THING... IT'S NOT LIKE THESE ARE JUST GROOVY, CONCERNED PEOPLE WHO ACTUALLY **CARE** ABOUT HUMANITY... IT'S LIKE THE SAME AS WHEN GUYS ARE REALLY INTO SPORTS!
I KNOW... OR COMPUTERS!
EXACTLY!

ALSO, MY DAD SAYS HE ONLY BELIEVES IN THE IDEA OF REVOLUTION ... HE SAYS IF THERE REALLY WAS A REVOLUTION, WE'D BE THE FIRST ONES THEY'D HAVE SHOT! ... I DON'T REALLY GET WHY WE'RE SUPPOSED TO WANT A REVOLUTION, ANYWAY...
I KNOW... CHECK OUT THE PERSONALS TO SEE IF ANY CUTE BOYS WROTE TO US...
FREE PAPER
IN BED WITH THE GOP

OKAY... EWW. DID YOU NOTICE ALL THE WEIRD STUFF IN THIS MENU? LIKE "THE GARDEN OF SALAD"...
I KNOW! AND INSTEAD OF "DESSERT" IT SAYS 'MIND-BENDERS'...
WHAT DOES THAT EVEN MEAN?

I WONDER IF WEIRD AL WROTE THIS.
♫ BI-16 GIRLS THEY DON'T CRY-YI-YI... ♫
THIS SONG SUCKS, TOO.

CAN I GET YOU LADIES ANYTHING ELSE, OR ARE YOU ALL SET?
LATER, I MIGHT BE INTERESTED IN ONE OF THOSE FAR-OUT "MIND-BENDERS."
=SNORT=

EWW! LISTEN TO THIS: "BOGEY SEEKS BACALL. I AM DWM 40-ISH SINGER-SONGWRITER, NON-SMOKER. YOU ARE FEM. 30-40, NON-JUDGE-MENTAL, LOVES: HONESTY, PILLOW-FIGHTS, MOONLIGHT SERENADES. BE MY MUSE."
I THINK THE KEY WORD IS "NON-JUDGEMENTAL."
THE

OH MY GOD! "BE THE OBJECT OF MY DESIRE. MARRIAGE-MINDED PROF SWM, 31 SEEKS PERFECT 10, 18-24. I WON'T TAKE NO FOR AN ANSWER."
GOD! THAT'S SO SCARY! MY GREATEST FEAR IS THAT SOME CREEP LIKE THAT WILL FALL IN LOVE WITH ME!
♂ SEEKING ♀

I KNOW. I'D WAY RATHER HAVE SOMEBODY HATE ME! OH MAN... "I SAW YOU AT CITIZEN KANE'S SUN. 21ST. YOU LOOKED OVER AND WE EXCHANGED BRIEF, UNFORGETTABLE SMILE. YOU: STUNNING REDHEAD, BLUE DRESS. ME: BEARDED WINDBREAKER. LET'S MEET FOR COFFEE/CONVERSATION."
'BEARDED WINDBREAKER'?

GOD, WHAT A PATHETIC FUCKING LOSER!
WE SHOULD CALL HIM AND PRETEND TO BE THE REDHEAD!
WE HAVE TO!

OH MY GOD, I FORGOT TO TELL YOU ABOUT THIS EPISODE OF "ORLANDO" I SAW YESTERDAY... THIS GIRL WENT OUT ON ONE DATE WITH SOME CREEP SHE BARELY KNEW, JUST TO BE NICE... NO BIG DEAL, RIGHT?

SO LIKE A WEEK LATER HE SHOWS UP AT HER WORK AND HE OPENS UP HIS SHIRT AND HE HAS THIS HUGE TATTOO WITH HER NAME AND LIKE HER YEARBOOK PICTURE ALL OVER HIS CHEST!
Kathy
SHE WOUND UP KILLING HIM AND NOW SHE'S IN PRISON!

THAT'S THE CREEPIEST THING I'VE EVER HEARD!
HOW ABOUT IT LADIES... DESSERT? COFFEE?

"DESSERT"?! BACK IN THE FIFTIES WE CALLED 'EM MINDBENDERS, DADDY-O!
LISTEN TO WHAT SONG THEY'RE PLAYING!

♫ ... WHO'S BENDIN' DOWN TO GIVE ME A RAINBOW? EVERYONE KNOWS IT'S WINDY... ♫
THIS PLACE IS GOD.

... I REMEMBER WHEN I FIRST STARTED READING THESE I THOUGHT "DWF" STOOD FOR "DWARF"... I COULD NEVER FIGURE OUT WHY SO MANY DWARVES WERE PLACING ADS...
LEAVE A MESSAGE THIS TIME!

GOD, HE SOUNDS SO GAY!
MAYBE THE REDHEAD IN THE BLUE DRESS IS A GUY!
SHH!

HI DAHLING, IT'S ME... YOUR REDHEAD FROM CITIZEN KANE'S! I WAS SIMPLY FLABBER-GASTED WHEN I SAW YOUR AD AND I'M DYING TO SEE YOU AGAIN! MEET ME AT A RESTAURANT CALLED HUBBA HUBBA IN THE VILLEVIEW PLAZA ON FRIDAY AT THREE O'CLOCK. I CAN'T WAIT TO SEE YOU, DAHLING... CIAO!

HA HA HA
HA HA HA HA
HA HA HA

HOW ARE WE GONNA GET THERE?
I KNOW... I'M NOT TAKING THE BUS AGAIN!

C'MON JOSH... PLEASE? I GUARANTEE YOU THIS PLACE IS A RIOT!
PLEASE JOSH?
I JUST THINK IT'S A REALLY FUCKED-UP TRICK TO PLAY ON SOMEBODY!
RECORDS

THE GUY PROBABLY WON'T EVEN SHOW UP! PLEASE JOSH?
PLEASE?
I DON'T WANT TO HAVE ANYTHING TO DO WITH IT!
COMEDY
FOLK

JESUS CHRIST JOSH, YOU DRIVE LIKE AN OLD MAN!
WHAT ARE YOU DOING?
COSMO

REALLY JOSH... DON'T YOU KNOW THAT'S A TOTAL SCAM?! THOSE GUYS MAKE LIKE TWO HUNDRED DOLLARS A DAY!
YOU DON'T KNOW WHAT YOU'RE TALKING ABOUT!
WON'T YOU PLEASE HELP
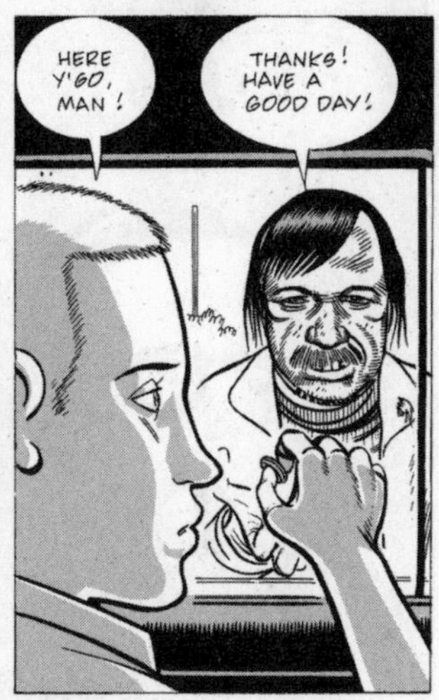
HERE Y'GO, MAN!
THANKS! HAVE A GOOD DAY!

HE JUST DOES THAT TO SHOW US WHAT A SUPERIOR HUMAN BEING HE IS!
YOU'RE THE TYPE OF GUY WHO ALWAYS SNAPS AT SOME POINT AND BECOMES A MASS MURDERER!

AREN'T THERE HUNDREDS OF PLACES LIKE THIS?
NOT HARDLY! THIS IS THE MONA LISA OF THE BAD, FAKE DINERS!
NICE!

SO WHERE'S "WEIRD AL"?
SHH! HE'S BACK THERE... I CAN SEE HIS HAIR!

I WANT TO "MAKE LOVE" TO HIM!
I'M GONNA TELL HIM YOU SAID THAT!

ARE YOU GUYS READY TO ORDER... OR DO YOU NEED A FEW MINUTES?
YES, WEIRD AL, BUT FIRST THERE'S SOMETHING I THINK YOU SHOULD KNOW--
SHUT UP!

MY FRIEND HERE SAYS SHE MMPPH

SO JOSH, TELL US ABOUT YOUR POLITICAL BELIEFS.
WHAT?
THE LAST TIME WE CAME HERE, BECKY AND I WERE DISCUSSING POLITICAL ISSUES...
I'M NOT SURE I BELIEVE YOU.

I'M SERIOUS. GIVE US YOUR WHOLE BASIC PHILOSOPHY IN A NUTSHELL.
I SUPPOSE I ENDORSE POLICIES THAT ARE OPPOSED TO STUPIDITY AND VIOLENCE... CRUELTY IN ANY FORM... CENSORSHIP...
I FIGURED SOMETHING LIKE THAT...
OH MY GOD, LOOK!

THAT'S OBVIOUSLY HIM!
I CAN'T BELIEVE HE SHOWED UP!

WHAT SHOULD WE DO?
ONE OF US SHOULD PRETEND TO BE THE GIRL!
HE OBVIOUSLY KNOWS WHAT SHE LOOKS LIKE.
OH DUH!

GOD, THIS IS SO UNBEARABLE!
I AGREE!

YOU GUYS CAN BRING THAT UP TO THE FRONT WHEN YOU'RE READY.
IS HE STILL STARING?
GO AHEAD AND LOOK, BUT DON'T MAKE IT TOO OBVIOUS.

HE DIDN'T STICK AROUND FOR VERY LONG... SHE'S ONLY TWENTY-FIVE MINUTES LATE...
HE FIGURED IT OUT.

WHAT DID HE SAY?
IT LOOKED LIKE "VERY FUNNY."
IT WAS SOMETHING FUCK!

HEY AL, DID THAT GUY SAY ANYTHING TO YOU BEFORE HE LEFT?
NOT A THING!

THANK YOU LADIES, AND COME AGAIN!

WHAT WERE YOU DOING?
LEAVING A TIP.
L 50'S DINER

CLICK CLI-CLICK

THAT WASN'T AS MUCH FUN AS LAST TIME.

♫ ... WHEN I WAS TWENTY-ONE ... IT WAS A VERY GOOD YEAR ... ♫
Clowes

PART VI

FIVE ALL-BUT-LOST STORIES

"The Wisdom of Eve"
by Mary Orr

All About Eve, directed by Joseph L. Mankiewicz, 1950

"A Reputation"
by Richard Edward Connell

Meet John Doe, directed by Frank Capra, 1941

"Mr. Blandings Builds His Castle"
by Eric Hodgins

Mr. Blandings Builds His Dream House, directed by H. C. Potter, 1948

"Cyclists' Raid"
by Frank Rooney

The Wild One, directed by Laslo Benedek, 1954

"Tomorrow"
by William Faulkner

Tomorrow, directed by Joseph Anthony, 1972

F. Scott Fitzgerald advised an author to "write for the youth of his own generation, the critics of the next, and the schoolmasters of ever afterwards"—but at the time of his death his most famous book, *The Great Gatsby*, was out of print. In fact, all of his books were out of print. John Cheever, on the other hand, professed not to care whether his work was read by future generations—and *his* most famous book, *The Stories of John Cheever*, has never gone out of print. So go figure. In *The Four Seasons of Success*, Budd Schulberg calls the literary world a "spectacular and cruel stock market," and so it is. Reputations inflate and deflate, books go in and out of print, legacies are won and lost based on literary awards and prizes. Often it all comes down to a combination of luck, talent, jungle warfare, and media savvy (Fitzgerald was notoriously careless with reporters). And it's never hurt to have a champion, preferably one in the academic community.

Today, all of Frank Rooney's work is out of print. A modestly successful novelist during the 1950s and '60s, he began writing after returning from duty in the South Pacific during World War II. "Cyclists' Raid," one of his first and most successful stories, was published in the January 1951 issue of *Harper's* and was subsequently included in both of the year's best-of volumes, *O. Henry Prize Stories* and *Best American Short Stories 1952*. Six years later Hollywood turned it into *The Wild One*, starring Marlon Brando. Herbert Gold considered the story so emblematic of the decade that he included it in *Fiction of the Fifties*, alongside James Baldwin's "Sonny's Blues," John Cheever's "The Country Husband," and Flannery O'Connor's "The Artificial Nigger." Rooney's novels, on the other hand, were enjoyed by some critics and not by others. One reviewer, likening him to an American Graham Greene, said, "Mr. Rooney is so adept at mixing violence with moral issues that one can be caught up in his itinerary without necessarily welcoming its destination."

"Cyclists' Raid" was inspired by a spurious incident reported in *Life*. According to the magazine, 4,000 members of a motorcycle club held the town of Hollister, California, under siege over the Fourth of July weekend,

1947. The story includes a photograph of a biker holding a bottle of beer and slouching insolently. Empty bottles litter the ground around him. The copy reads: "He and friends terrorize a town." Five months later, though, the bikers were back in Hollister with the town's blessing. "When the rodeo was in town, the cowboys were as bad," one resident recalls. And the photograph that inspired a story, that launched a movie, that spawned a genre of teenage rebellion films? It turns out it was staged. "I saw two guys scraping all these bottles together that had been lying in the street," Hollister resident August "Gus" Deserpa later said. "Then they positioned a motorcycle in the middle of the pile. After a while a drunk guy comes staggering out of the bar, and they got him to sit on the motorcycle, and started to take his picture."

Stanley Kramer, a producer/director known for his message films *(Guess Who's Coming to Dinner, On the Beach, Judgment at Nuremberg)*, found Rooney's story and decided it would make a good film. "It would be nice if I could say that it was all an original idea of mine," Kramer later said, "and that I had understood and captured a tear in the fabric of society before other producers, and then set out to make a film about it. The truth of the matter is that I read a story in *Harper's* called 'The Cyclists' [*sic*] about a group that ransacked a town. It touched my sense of social responsibility, and I thought it would make a good movie." Kramer, Brando, and writer Ben Maddow began the project by talking with a band of motorcyclists. "A lot of the dialogue is taken from our actual conversations with them. All the talk about 'We gotta go, that's all . . . just gotta move on' was something we heard over and over." The most famous line in the film came from one of these conversations. Kramer asked a biker, "What are you rebelling against?" and he answered "Whaddya got?" They put it in the film.

Maddow was replaced by John Paxton when Maddow was subpoenaed by the House Un-American Activities Committee. More trouble with the screenplay followed; the censors felt it was anti-American and Communist. According to Kramer, the original version "told the truth about the incident—that no charges were brought against the boys because they brought so much business to the town." Laslo Benedek was enlisted to direct, and changes to the script were made to please the censors. The resulting film upset both audiences and critics (although it pleased the makers of leather jackets and motorcycles*). Brando didn't like it either: "We started out to do something worthwhile, to explain the psychology of the hipster. But somewhere along the way we went off the track. The

* Tom Bolfert, head of archives for the Harley-Davidson Motor Company, told *Smithsonian* magazine: "Had Hollister not happened, had *Life* magazine not written their article, had Hollywood not glorified it, I don't know if we would be here today."

result was that instead of finding why young people tend to bunch into groups that seek expression, all that we did was show the violence." The British censors, feeling the film might be incendiary, banned it until 1968. There's no doubt it touched a nerve. As Robert Stone, speaking of Rooney's story and its adaptation, has put it: "America came to understand that some new rough beast had slouched out of California."

Like Rooney's, all of Richard Connell's work is out of print, too—except for one story. Which makes him one of the rare one-hit wonders in short-storydom. "The Most Dangerous Game," Connell's story of a literal manhunt, won the 1924 O. Henry Award and has been the subject of junior high term papers ever since. For a story to survive—and even thrive—for so long, distinct from its author's reputation, is extremely rare. But it's an irony Connell would have appreciated. As one of his other stories, "A Reputation," makes clear, Connell was quick to poke fun at the American notion of literary standing. The story's protagonist, Saunders Rook, is a second-rate writer whose minor essays are rejected by minor editors of minor magazines until he declares, somewhat accidentally, that he will commit suicide on the Fourth of July in protest against the state of American civilization. Suddenly, he's hot.* His essays are in vogue, people know his name, he's courted by the "celebrities" of the Authors' Club. (If this story line sounds familiar, it's because it later became the basis for Frank Capra's *Meet John Doe.* For the film the literary references were dropped and the social implications enhanced.) Connell's reputation was not dissimilar to Rook's. When his third story collection was published, a reviewer remarked that it "ranks, though high, in the great army of the second-rate." A hardworking writer who didn't take himself too seriously, Connell published over three hundred stories and contributed to dozens of screenplays. His story collection, *Apes and Angels,* is dedicated:

TO THE EARNEST AND PURPOSEFUL MEN AND WOMEN OF THE WORLD, WHO HAVE MADE IT WHAT IT IS TODAY— . . .

TO ARTISTS WHO THINK AN IMPORTANT MANNER MAKES MATTER IMPORTANT— . . .

TO REVILERS OF PUBLIC TASTE WHO FORGET THAT CLARITY BEGINS AT HOME—

* Connell's story still seems surprisingly relevant (or prescient). It was written sixty-five years before writer Tama Janowitz made a "literary video" for MTV; seventy-five years before author Leslie Epstein spent nearly $10,000 of his own money on the tiny classifieds at the bottom of the *New York Times* front page, attempting to woo critic Michiko Kakutani into reviewing his book (whose protagonist, incidentally, has a crush on Kakutani); and eighty years before Jonathan Yardley of the *Washington Post* observed that "It is necessary from time to time for someone to point out that most of the persons occupying the palace of literary reputation are wearing surprisingly few—if any—clothes."

TO CRITICS WHOSE MOST LETHAL EPITHET IS "LIGHT," WHO DEEM TEARS MORE CIVILIZED THAN LAUGHTER, AND THE CAUSING OF PAIN A HIGHER ART THAN THE GIVING OF PLEASURE—

. . . FOR THE JOY THEY HAVE GIVEN ME.

The irony, of course, is that Connell has faded into obscurity—sans stunts—just as he must have known he would.

Connell's story came to director Frank Capra through screenwriter Robert Presnell, who had collaborated with Connell on its film treatment (retitled *The Life and Death of John Doe*). Capra and screenwriter Robert Riskin, enabled by a string of audience-pleasing films *(It Happened One Night, Mr. Deeds Goes to Town, Mr. Smith Goes to Washington)*, had just formed their own independent production company and were looking for a property that would satisfy both public and critics. (Capra later admitted that the "Capra-corn" barbs had "pierced the outer blubber.") Of the Connell-Presnell treatment, he said, "I read it. A bell rang. Riskin read it. A carillon chimed. We bought it before Presnell left the office." The story was unusually cynical for a Capra film, but that was the attraction. He and Riskin wanted to "astonish the critics with contemporary realities: the ugly face of hate; the power of uniformed bigots in red, white, and blue shirts; the agony of disillusionment, and the wild dark passions of mobs. We would give them a brutal story. . . ." Neither Connell nor Presnell worked on the Capra screenplay, but Riskin did name a character after Connell in sly tribute. (There is also a character named Budington in *Mr. Deeds Goes to Town*, based on a story by Clarence Budington Kelland.)

The problem from the beginning was the ending. The suicide of John Doe, played by Gary Cooper, didn't seem to be an option. (At least not in a Capra film.) But neither Capra nor Riskin could come up with a suitable alternative. Calling it "The Mystery of the Unsolved Ending," they brought in script doctors Myles Connolly and Jules Furthman. Neither of them had a solution either. Capra later said: "Making a film out of *Meet John Doe* proved to be as full of surprises as breaking a half-rogue wild stallion to the saddle. . . . It was still untamed when, with blinkers on it, we shoved the maverick into a theater for its opening night."

Capra claims there were five endings for the film; three of them showed in New York in the spring of 1941. The first ending was chosen in desperation the night before the movie opened. The *New York Times* called this version "the hardest-hitting and most trenchant picture on the theme of democracy that Messrs. Capra and Riskin have yet made," but admitted the ending was "obviously a sop." Audiences didn't like it, and within days that ending was removed and another substituted. That didn't play well either. Finally a viewer calling himself John Doe wrote to Capra and suggested that the "only thing that can keep John Doe from jumping is the John Does themselves."* Capra liked the idea and recalled the cast to shoot this new ending. He and Riskin told the *New York Times* that they didn't know whether this version would work either, but they felt it might be an improvement. The movie's multiple endings were widely publicized, and despite its generally genial critical reception *John Doe* has subsequently carried with it a tinge of failure. Capra himself felt he made seven-eighths of a good film, but "was an acceptable ending ever possible for *John Doe*? I still don't know."

John Doe and all of the Capra-Riskin films bear an additional weight: the mysterious disintegration of the Capra-Riskin relationship. In 1950, Riskin suffered a major stroke and for the last five years of his life he was severely disabled. Capra called only once during Riskin's long illness and did not attend the funeral. According to Pat McGilligan, who has collected and edited Riskin's screenplays, Riskin's wife, Fay Wray, was baffled. "She tried to rationalize it as Capra caring too much about Riskin to see him in such a sorry state. But she grew to believe that, as Capra's career began to lull, it became vital for him to usurp Riskin." Then came "The Capra Contention." In 1977, Capra wrote a letter to the *Los Angeles Times* that began: "Oh my! 'Tis that season again. The season when some Hollywood writer beats his breast, hoping to keep alive the 30-year-old myth that Robert Riskin's scriptwriting was responsible for the success of Frank Capra's films." Capra went on to say that Riskin was one of his "dearest friends" and that "yes, Robert Riskin was a giant among scriptwriters—at least when he worked with me."† Letters both for and against Capra and Riskin poured into the *Los Angeles Times.* Rintels wrote an official reply, which ends with the following few lines: "What concerns me more than Capra's place in history is his dear friend's. I don't know what that will be, but I do know that it would have been far greater if only his director had been a bigger man, and I begrudge Capra that." And so it all comes around—or back—to "A Reputation."

Working in Hollywood wasn't the only way for a writer's reputation to suffer. Writing commercial fiction was another. Edward J. O'Brien, the first editor of the highly influential *Best American Short Stories* series—and a man deeply opposed to commercial fiction—said this about his selections: "I am looking for the man and woman who has something to say. . . . I want to feel that the storyteller . . . is as much in earnest as a sincere

* This version comes from Capra's autobiography, but according to Joseph McBride, author of *Frank Capra: The Catastrophe of Success,* Capra's letters contain only one letter with this suggestion. It was signed "EGF" and was sent to Riskin.

† This was in response to an essay the week before in which David W. Rintels, president of Writers' Guild West, suggested, "Capra did not do all he might have done to enlighten the world that what so often passed for 'Capra touches' had in fact been written by Riskin."

clergyman, an unselfish physician, or an idealistic lawyer. I want to feel that he belongs to a profession that is a sort of priesthood, and not that he is holding down a job or running a bucket shop." Easy for him to say. Money has always been the bane of nearly every writer's existence, and even luminaries like William Faulkner have been caught on the wrong side of the commercial tracks.

In 1940, Faulkner published "Tomorrow" in *The Saturday Evening Post* for $1,000. In letters to various friends, he mentioned his attempts to write potboilers, particularly for the *Post*, as, he told one correspondent, "the most I could hope for a good story is three or four hundred." Despite early echoes of his classic novel *Intruder in the Dust*, which also features a murder trial and characters Chick and Uncle Gavin, "Tomorrow" is not included in Faulkner's collected stories and has been largely overlooked. So is the story second-rate? Or has it been tainted by the *Post*'s reputation for purely commercial fiction, as has been suggested by Faulkner scholars David Yellin and Marie Connors? In defense of the story, Yellin and Connors state, "Regardless of the neglect the story has suffered because of its association with Faulkner's lesser works, or of his purpose in writing it, 'Tomorrow' does capture that sense of a profound, complex, and intense existence of southern life identified with the best of Faulkner's fiction."

What little attention and legitimacy "Tomorrow" has received is a direct result of Horton Foote's screenplay for the 1972 adaptation, and the live teleplay that preceded it. Judith Crist, an admirer of the film, placed it on the year's top-ten list and later wrote, "Through the years I have spread the gospel of *Tomorrow*, offering it in 'critic's choice' series, urging it on college film society programs, using it as a lecture supplement, showing it again—and again. . . . Why the passion for the film *Tomorrow*? It stems primarily from its being the first, and probably the only film to re-create the world of William Faulkner in both the letter and spirit."

Mary Orr, author of "The Wisdom of Eve," upon which the film *All About Eve* is based, didn't even receive screen credit for her story. Orr was first an actress, then a writer, and her reputation as the latter has always been overshadowed by her participation in the *Eve* franchise, in which she and Joseph Mankiewicz—although they never met—were uneasy partners. "The Wisdom of Eve" was based on a story she'd heard from Elisabeth Bergner (the star of a play her husband was directing) while making Wiener schnitzel in a farmhouse kitchen. Orr sold it to *Cosmopolitan* and later adapted it into a stage play, *The Wisdom of Eve*. At the time it was routine for studio story departments to circulate promising stories, and when Joseph Mankiewicz read "Eve" he saw it as the backbone for the show-business film he wanted to write and direct. The studio purchased the story for him for $5,000 (a lot at the time), but screen credit for Orr wasn't written into the contract. As a result, her name does not appear anywhere in the credits. Mankiewicz, for his part, was angry about the money, later saying she "made a fortune," while he received only his salary. (The other bitter party was Bergner, who also felt financially slighted.) Orr may have had the last laugh, though. She retained the rights to her play, and when that was adapted into the stage musical *Applause*, sole credit went to Orr, and Mankiewicz's name was left off the playbill.

Money aside, *All About Eve* was Mankiewicz's career film. He stuffed his screenplay with observations about a subject he had been studying for years: women. "I'm well-nigh besotted by them. Writing about men is so damned . . . limited," he said. "Women are, by comparison, as if assembled by the wind." The unique problems of women performers particularly fascinated him: "Forty years of age. Four O. Give or take a year, the single most critical chronological milestone in the life of an actress. Look, I knew these women. I'd been in love with some—I'd worked with many of them." His dialogue on the topic—and he wasn't dubbed "The Talk Man" for nothing—is witty, catty, improbably clever, and heartbreakingly true. Forty-something actress Margo Channing contemplates her younger lover: "Bill's thirty-two. He looks thirty-two. He looked it five years ago, he'll look it twenty years from now. I hate men." Age was also an issue for Margola, Margo's short-story counterpart: "If Margola ever sees forty-five again, I'll have my eyes lifted." But if Orr's "The Wisdom of Eve" lacks the bitter irony of Mankiewicz's screenplay, well, remember it was written by a *twenty-six-year-old* actress.

Eric Hodgins, author of "Mr. Blandings Builds His Castle," was a journalist with a waspish wit whose reputation as a writer has been obscured by his long tenure at *Fortune.* For years he was the magazine's managing editor, working alongside (and managing) its stable of top-rate talent, including Archibald MacLeish and James Agee. His friend John Kenneth Galbraith called Hodgins "one of the best writers of his time," saying, "Too few knew Eric Hodgins . . . because during his great writing years he was at Time, Inc., and the organization always stood between its people and the world. No matter how brilliant the writer, his reputation rarely got beyond the corporate shell. Inside, it was a wonderful story by Hodgins. Outside it was an interesting story in *Fortune.*" Among Hodgins's many books—all out of print except for *Mr. Blandings Builds His Dream House,* which was reissued in 1999—is *Episode: Report on the Accident Inside My Skull.** In it, he describes the stroke he suffered at the age of sixty and his efforts to recover physically, emotionally, and financially. With humor and honesty he tells of "The Tremendous Trifles" that now

* This is a special book, and if the world were a better, fairer, place it would still be in print.

filled his life ("That my left hand could not distinguish between an old bottle cap and electric light bulb"), his thoughts of suicide ("I was not Half in Love with Easeful Death; I was wholly in love with it"), and his feelings about the obligatory gift of flowers ("I am sorry to have to cross pistils with the nation's florists, but unless flowers are quite inexpensive and casually arranged, they are an insult"). "Life ain't neat," Hodgins wrote in the foreword to his unfinished autobiography. "My life has been a testament to this vast truth. It has been a testament to very little else. Professionally, the profession being journalism, it has been a mild success; emotionally, it has been a disaster almost from beginning to end."

"Mr. Blandings Builds His Castle" first appeared in April 1946, in a special architectural issue of *Fortune.* When it was a hit, Hodgins expanded it into a novel, which quickly became a Book-of-the-Month selection (as did its sequel, *Blandings' Way*). RKO snapped up the movie rights for $200,000, prompting Hodgins to say later, "Everything pleasant happened to that effort; this has caused me many times to reflect on the total disrelation between struggle and reward. The book almost wrote itself. . . . After all, I *was* Mr. Blandings and I *had* built a dream house." Unfortunately, the money didn't begin rolling in until after Hodgins was forced to sell said dream house. He later tried but was unable to buy it back. In 1975, the owner of Hodgins's home told the *New York Times*, "It's the most functional house I've ever seen. It's about zero maintenance." Apparently Mr. Blandings spoke for Hodgins when he said, "When we build, let us build forever."

The film was directed by H. C. Potter, whose personal style the *New York Times* has called "elusive." A popular director of comedies, he also codirected Disney's World War II animated/live action propaganda film *Victory Through Air Power*, which is credited with being the impetus for the U.S. Air Corps Long Range Bombing efforts. In *Mr. Blandings,* Potter and screenwriters Norman Panama and Melvin Frank retained Hodgins's tone of gentle satire and the film was a hit. Bosley Crowther of the *Times* wrote, "The business, as here represented, of a man putting a roof over his family's head is so harmlessly entertaining and so conducive to a feeling of good-will that, made the experience of a nation, it could change the destiny of the world." In fact, the film was so popular it generated a spin-off radio series starring Cary Grant and his future wife, Betsy Drake. The faintest praise may have come from James Agee, Hodgins's former colleague and critic for the *Nation*, when he called it: "A bulls-eye for middle-class middle-brows. For the low and the high not hard to take and just as easy to let alone."

And so it goes. As time passes, books necessarily go out of print. And with the exception of Faulkner, it's been a bearish market lately for these authors of all-but-lost stories. They may not have gotten the credit they wanted (or deserved) or the money they wanted (or deserved), but here's the good news: As long as the movies that were adapted from their work are remembered, there will be those who care enough to find and read the original stories. As W. H. Auden once said, "Some books are undeservedly forgotten, none are undeservedly remembered."

The Wisdom of Eve

Mary Orr

A young girl is on her way to Hollywood with a contract for one thousand dollars a week from a major film company in her pocketbook. I shall call her Eve Harrington because that is not her name, though the Eve part of the alias is not unapt, considering the original's snaky activities in a once-peaceful garden. In a year or two, I am sure Miss Harrington will be as much a household word to you as Ingrid Bergman or Joan Fontaine. When she is a star, I am equally positive that the slick publicity agents of Hollywood who surround these celestial beings with glamour will give you their version of her success. But no matter what they concoct, it will not be as interesting or ironic as her real story. It would never occur to them to tell you the truth. Stars must be presented to their public in a warm, sympathetic light, and one could scratch a long time before kindling any such spark from the personality of Eve Harrington.

I first saw her on a cold, snowy night in January. I was sitting snugly under a fur rug in the back seat of Margola Cranston's town car. We were parked at the stage entrance of Margola's theater, waiting for her to come out. By we, I mean her chauffeur Henry and I. Henry sat patiently in front of me, displaying the proper fortitude of one whose chief occupation in life was to wait. But marking time is not my long suit, and my gloved fingers played an irritated tattoo on Margola's polychrome upholstery. I am an actress myself and am able to get in and out of my makeup with the same speed that I duck in and out of a cold shower. Not so Margola. Rarely did she leave the theater before a quarter to twelve. What went on in her dressing room for three quarters of an hour was a mystery known only to her maid, Alice, and herself. Consequently, if one wanted to see Margola after the theater one waited. However, it was not a lone vigil.

There was a crowd at the stage door. They were the usual autograph fans, all with little books open and fountain pens dripping ink. Some appeared to be intelligent theatergoers; they carried programs for Margola to sign and had obviously seen the play that evening. I could hear their enthusiastic comments through the tiny opening where I had lowered the car window to let my cigarette smoke escape. A few were boys in uniform with dreams of dating Margola—dreams that would not come true. There was only one person standing there I could not catalogue. She stood nearest the car, and I could see her face clearly in the light of the streetlamp.

It was a young, unusual face, but not in the least pretty. Because she was rather plain, the amount of makeup she was wearing seemed to me very odd. What I mean is, false eyelashes can look very much at home on Lana Turner, but the same pair could be incongruous on a schoolteacher. This girl had a serious, prim expression. She was dressed in a warm, practical red coat. On her head she wore a small dark tam-o'-shanter which didn't seem to agree with the coat. She also wore high-heeled, open-toed shoes, and standing there in the slush her feet must have been cold. Her hands were thrust into her coat pockets and a shabby purse dangled from her left arm. Her manner was shy and reticent. Under their long lashes, her eyes stared at the ground. She stood first on one foot and then on the other to keep warm, but displayed no fatigue at the long wait.

I continued to wonder who she was and why she was there until Margola finally appeared at the stage entrance. I had seen her come out many times. It was a superb act. I knew perfectly well she was not in the least surprised to see the crowd gathered there, but her expression was one of delighted amazement. So many people gathered there to see her! It could not be! She smiled and signed the autograph books and spoke first to one and then to another. She radiated graciousness. Everyone would go away exclaiming, "What charm!" "So modest!" "How kind!"

Margola would then climb into the car and apologize for keeping me waiting by saying, "Those tiresome people! Such bores! What fools!"

I was one of Margola's few women friends. My husband, Lloyd Richards, had written the play in which she was then appearing with great success. Lloyd had also written another one of her most popular vehicles. No one knew better than he that a large part of their success was due to Margola's performance. Without her, they might have run five, six, or seven weeks. With her, the first play had lasted two years, and the current smash hit showed stubborn signs of outdoing it. For there was no doubt that Margola was a truly great actress.

Watching her sign the autographs, I wondered for the thousandth time what made her so great. Nobody would guess it to see her out of the theater. She was tiny, with the childish figure of a Botticelli angel. On stage, her clothes were done by Carnegie, Valentia, and Mainbocher. Offstage, they were done by Cranston. They consisted generally of old sweaters and tweed skirts. I had once peeked into her closet and discovered a dozen gowns utterly unworn. I have known her six years and seen her twice in a decent dress. Once was at a funeral of a big producer for whom she had no respect and once when she had to receive a Critics Award she didn't want.

Her hair was another cross her friends had to bear. When she was not on stage, it was generally piled on the top of her head as if she had just fallen out of the bath. Even on stage it could sometimes be said to resemble a theater cleaner's mop. That night it was tucked beneath a hand-painted handkerchief which she had tied under her chin, peasant fashion. She wore a mink coat, true enough, but on her it might have been an old muskrat. It was down to her ankles and six years out of style. Nobody but a genius could dress as she did and get away with it.

Lloyd has always said that for him she is utterly devoid of sex appeal. To me she is tremendously attractive. He gives her one asset in the way of beauty—a very obvious one—a pair of enormous eyes, which behind the footlights can betray every thought in a character's mind with crystal clarity. Also, she seems to have the secret of eternal youth. I have seen her in the bright sunshine with no makeup on and she doesn't look a day over twenty-nine or thirty. If Margola ever sees forty-five again, I'll have my eyes lifted.

We got along together from the first day we met. I often disagreed with her, argued with her, and wisecracked at her expense. Sometimes Lloyd would look worried and tell me not to go too far, to remember that I owed my penthouse and sables largely to her. However, in spite of my acid tongue, to this day she has preferred my company to most other women's.

Being Margola's best friend is in many ways a bit of a bore. I'm the type of female who only feels at home dressed in a Daché hat at the Stork Club or El Morocco. As Margola always looks like a tourist, it is well nigh impossible to persuade her to have supper at any café-society haunt. She favors a bar behind some delicatessen shop, Sardi's, or her own home.

On the night in question it was home—and home to Margola is a nest of forty rooms at Great Neck, Long Island, called Capulet's Cottage. That meant I had to stay all night, for first there would be a huge supper, and then conversation until three or four in the morning, as Margola loves to talk by the light of the moon. Consequently, my overnight bag rested uncomfortably on my feet. Lloyd had kissed me good-bye when I'd left for the theater and gone off with a gleam in his eye to a stag poker session.

"Have a nice cat party" had been his parting words, and I knew that he was privately relieved we were not having a foursome with Margola's husband, Clement Howell. Clement is a clever enough director and producer but very English and pompous. Lloyd can take only a certain number of broad A's.

Margola was close to the car when the shabby little girl with the red coat suddenly stepped into her line of vision. I saw Margola's eyes cloud up and her expression change to one of annoyance. The girl spoke a few words and looked at her in the most supplicating way, her large eyes filled with tears. But she didn't succeed in melting the star's icy attitude. I couldn't hear what Margola said to her exactly, but I knew it wasn't nice, and I did catch the last phrase, which was, "I don't want you pestering me every night." With that, she climbed into the car and slammed the door. "Get going, Henry," she commanded the chauffeur and sank back into the corner of the seat like a sulky child.

"Well," I said in my most sarcastic tone, "I thought you were always so charming to your public. What's the matter with little Miss Redcoat? Is she selling something?"

Margola glared at me. "You don't know what I've been through with that girl. You can't imagine what she's said and done to me. How she lied to me and made a fool of me."

"Now, Margola," I said, "don't act. Don't be so dramatic. What could a poor girl like that do to you?"

"It's too long a story," she said. "Besides, I get in a rage every time I think about it."

I lighted a cigarette and handed it to her. "Come on," I said. "You'll have to tell me now. We've got a long drive ahead and nothing to do but talk."

She inhaled deeply. "Her name's Eve Harrington," she said. "Translated, it spells—well, she is the most awful girl I've ever met. There are no lengths to which she won't go."

"Start at the beginning," I urged. "Not with the third act. How did you happen to meet this paragon of all the virtues?"

"It was Clement's fault," Margola sighed after a moment's pause. "He first drew my attention to her. He asked me if I'd ever noticed the girl who stood at the stage entrance and simply watched me come out. She didn't ask for an autograph or a picture or try to speak to me—just stood there and looked.

"I said that I hadn't.

"He said she always wore a red coat and to be sure to give a look next time."

"She was wearing a red coat tonight," I interrupted.

"I know." She flicked my remark aside impatiently. "Well, the next time I went into the theater—for a matinee it was—I saw her. She was there when the afternoon performance was over. I saw her again when I came back after dinner, and when the evening performance was over she was still there.

"This time, when I got rid of the crowd, I spoke to her. I asked her if there was anything I could do for her, and she said no. I said I had noticed her at the matinee and that my husband had seen her before. She said she stood there every night. I couldn't believe my ears. I said, 'Well, what do you want?' She said, 'Nothing.' I said, 'There must be something,' and finally she said that she knew if she stood there long enough eventually I would speak to her. I asked if that was all she wanted and she said yes, that she had first seen me in San Francisco when I toured in *Have a Heart."* That was my husband's first play in which Margola had appeared. "She said she had followed me to Los Angeles and eventually come on to New York."

"Just to stand at your stage door?" I asked, amazed.

"She went to the play," Margola added, "as often as she could afford to."

"What devotion," I said.

"That," said Margola sadly, "is what I assumed. I was most impressed. I thought: This is my most ardent fan. She follows me clear across the Great Divide. She sees my plays constantly when she obviously has very little money. She stands night after night at my stage door just to see me come out and finally have me speak to her. I was moved."

"So what went on?" I urged.

"Well," Margola answered, "I felt that I had to do something to repay this child for her admiration. She was only twenty-two. I thought: I'll give her an evening she'll always remember. So I invited her to come home with me. She acted as if she were in a seventh heaven. She had a slight accent which she told me was Norwegian.

"She said that her people had come over here six or seven years before and had finally left her with an aunt and gone back to Norway on a trip. Of course, because of the war they hadn't been able to return, and she hadn't heard from them in months. In the meantime, she had married a young American flier and had been living in San Francisco because he had gone to the Pacific from there. I asked her how she got along and she said that at first she had had her husband's allotment, but then he had been killed over Bougainville and since then she had lived very meagerly on his insurance."

"How sad."

"Exactly what I thought," Margola said. "She told me that seeing me act and watching my plays had been her only happiness since she had had the wire about her husband. It seemed to me that I must do something for her. I found out that she could type and do shorthand. She'd worked as a secretary in San Francisco. It suddenly came to me that this girl might make just the secretary for me. You know I'm hard to please, but here was someone who adored me, who would be loyal, who was quiet and at the same time well bred. She spoke English beautifully and seemed intelligent.

"So I asked her if she'd like to work for me. You've never seen such a response. She burst into tears and kissed my hand. I generally hate that sort of thing because I know it's insincere, but this time I was sure it was genuine. She was so naive, so unsubtle."

"The way you read that line suggests she wasn't."

"Don't jump cues," Margola snapped. And for my impatience, I had to wait until she had drawn three or four puffs on her cigarette.

"Well, I gave the wretched girl clothes to wear. I gave her twenty-five dollars a week. All she had to do was tend to my correspondence, send out pictures, and so forth. Some letters she was to answer without bothering me, but anything that she felt needed my particular attention she was to show to me. At first she was ideal. Then after a month or so she began to annoy me."

"How?" I couldn't help asking.

"By staring at me. She stared at me all the time. I would turn around suddenly and catch her eyes on me. It gave me the creeps. Finally, I couldn't stand it any longer. I suddenly realized that she was studying me, imitating my gestures, my ways of speech, almost doing the same things. It was like having a living shadow. At last I told Clement that he should use the girl at the office, that she could attend to my mail there instead of at home. I wanted to get her out of the house, and at the same time I didn't want to fire her. I still felt sorry for her. Besides, her work was very satisfactory.

"Clement was delighted with her," Margola continued, a little thin-lipped. "His own secretary had just left to be married and this girl fitted right into her place. She began to read plays for us and made some quite intelligent observations. Then one day we had a rehearsal—it was when we were putting Miss Caswell into the sister part—and I had a toothache and didn't go.

"My understudy hadn't been called. She was out, and the stage manager wasn't able to get in touch with her. Eve had gone to the rehearsal with Clement to take his notes, and when there wasn't anybody to do my part, she volunteered. Clement told the stage manager to give her the script so that she could read it, and to his amazement she said, 'Oh, I don't need that.' Well, my dear"—Margola leaned closer to me as the car spun around a corner—"would you believe it, she knew every line of my part? Not only every line but every *inflection*, every *gesture.* Clement was there to watch Miss Caswell and he said he forgot all about her, he was so fascinated by Eve's unexpected performance."

"Was she really good?"

"Good?" Margola raised a penciled eyebrow. "Good? She was marvelous! Clement even hinted she was slightly better than I am. He didn't dare say so, of course, but he teased me that she was. He said if he'd closed his eyes he wouldn't have known the difference."

"What about the Norwegian accent?"

"Apparently"—Margola shrugged—"that just went. I understand why now."

"I don't," I said.

"You will," Margola stated bluntly. "Anyway, Clement was so amazed at the girl's exhibition that he took her out to tea afterward. She confessed to him that she had always wanted to be an actress and asked him to help her. Asked *him*—not me! Don't you think that was hatefully deceitful?"

I admitted that it was, but I thought privately that the girl had been rather smart. Great actresses are not noted for encouraging brilliant ingenues.

"She told him that she'd only stood around my stage door because she wanted to meet *him*, that she considered him the most brilliant director and producer in New York. He didn't tell me that. I found it out later. But Clem was very flattered. After all, he's only a man, and I get more than my share of attention. He's always introduced as Miss Cranston's husband—it probably irritates him more than he admits. But here was somebody looking up at him with saucer eyes, telling him he was wonderful, and he fell for it. He told me she was the most talented young girl he had seen in years, that we must help her. I said nothing. I knew I had to handle this very carefully. I asked Eve why she hadn't told *me* she wanted to be an actress and asked *me* to help her. She had the nerve"—Margola paused for effect—"to tell me she knew I wouldn't like the competition."

I laughed out loud. It was ridiculous. Even the best actors in her supporting casts have a tendency to melt into the scenery when Margola gets into her stride. "She doesn't lack ego," I chuckled.

"Ego!" Margola stubbed out her cigarette in the ashtray. "Wait till I tell you about the letter! It arrived several days after this rehearsal. Eve came to my dressing room before the performance with four or five letters. This particular one was among them. She told me that she thought I ought to give them my personal attention. I put them into my purse, took them home, and forgot about them.

"Several days later, Eve asked me if I had read them, and I said that I hadn't. She particularly urged me to do so. I promised to, but I still put it off. I hate reading mail. In a few days, she was nagging me again to know if I had read the letters. I still hadn't. That night Alice told me that Miss Harrington had come to my dressing room while I was on stage and had gone through my pockets and my purse looking for something.

"I didn't like that, and after the show I called Eve down for it. She said she was looking for those letters, that there was one that, on second thought, she felt I ought not to see. I said that as she had given me the letter in the first place it was a little absurd to decide now that I shouldn't see it. But whether I read the letters or not, she was never again to go through my things.

"She burst into tears and cried that she only wanted to spare me pain. I had been so kind to her, she didn't want my feelings hurt. She had only given me the letter because when she had first read it she had been so thrilled that she wanted me to see it; thinking it over, she realized that it might hurt me.

"I remarked that after the things critics had written about me, nothing in any letter could possibly faze me.

"I realize now that this entire performance was to get me to read that letter without any more delay, and I'm sorry to say it worked. That night when I got home it was the first thing I did. It was very easy to pick out the one she was referring to. It went something like this—

"Dear Miss Cranston,

"Today I was buying a ticket to see a performance of your play. The door to the theater was open, and as I could hear voices and no one was watching the door I wandered inside to see what was going on. It seemed to be a rehearsal. A young girl was playing the part that I recognized, when I saw the actual performance, as your role—I presume she was your understudy. I know that stars of your caliber are always jealous of the ability of young people, but my dear Miss Cranston, I put you above such petty feelings. I am sure that loving the theater as you do, you will wish to enrich it. In your company, hidden backstage, is the most brilliant young performer I have ever seen. I was spellbound. She brought all your ability plus youth to the part. I waited outside for this young girl and asked her name. It was Harrington. Do help her to get the break she so richly deserves.

"It was signed 'One of your devoted followers.' "

"Of course she wrote it herself," I gasped.

"I think so," Margola said. "I was positive, but it was typewritten, so I couldn't prove it. The next day I merely said to Eve that it was quite a coincidence that the theater door was ajar when she happened to be rehearsing my part. We never mentioned it again."

I resisted comment. I could sense Margola was working up to a big scene.

"Not long after this, the John Bishop auditions came up."

I nodded. John Bishop is one of Broadway's better producers. Every season he holds auditions where talented unknowns can come and do a scene of their own choosing on the stage of his theater. The judges are other producers, talent scouts from film companies, and agents. Mr. Bishop's official reason for this competition is his altruistic desire to give embryonic thespians a chance to be seen—the winner often steps right into a Broadway show.

"Well, darling," Margola went on, "Eve was crazy to participate in Johnny's auditions. She went to Clem and pleaded with him to give her an introduction to Johnny. He said it wasn't necessary, that she merely had to fill in the application blank in Johnny's office and when her turn came she would be called. She found that to be true, and from then on she was no use as a secretary at all. She was in a complete dither about what scene to do and wanted Clement to advise her and coach her. I told her to do a scene from *A Kiss for Cinderella* as I felt she was rather the pathetic, wistful type, but Clem picked out a bit of Ibsen—Hilda in *The Master Builder*—because it would suit her Scandinavian accent.

"She naturally took Clement's advice—not mine. She studied the scene, and when she had memorized it Clement heard her go through it. He came home enthralled. Again, he thought she was marvelous. He insisted that I come down to the theater and give her some suggestions. By this time I was so curious to see the future Jeanne Eagels that I consented. One day before the matinee, I went to the theater early and she did the scene for me."

"Was she really terrific?" I asked.

"I was impressed," Margola admitted reluctantly. "She was talented, there was no question about that. She had a marvelous voice and she read the lines with great sincerity, though this didn't disguise the fact that she was utterly inexperienced and awkward. I suppose that didn't show up when she was copying me in my part because she had me for a model. I did what I could to help her to hide these defects and showed her a few other little tricks, and she picked them up quickly enough. I wasn't as excited as Clement, but I could see that there was something to his statements.

"The auditions took place in a few days. She got down to the finals, and then, on the big day, won them. Everybody was terribly excited about her. Movie scouts knocked themselves out to make tests of her, agents wanted to put her on their files. She thought she was made. She was a star overnight, so now the story could come out."

"What story?"

"Her story. Her true story. Pathetic, wistful, naive Eve Harrington gave out an interview to the newspapers on how she had fooled the finest actress in the theater for several months!"

"Fooled you? How?"

"In every way. Her entire story was a piece of fiction. She'd never been any closer to San Francisco than Milwaukee, where she was born. She was Norwegian by descent, but had picked up her accent from a waitress in her father's restaurant. Her parents were safely in Wisconsin."

"Why did she want an accent?"

"Glamour, my dear. So many foreign actresses are successful here. She thought an accent would make her."

"But the parents being trapped by the war in Norway. What was the point of that?" I asked.

"Sympathy. The husband was a plea in the same direction."

"You mean she wasn't a widow?"

"She'd never been married."

"My God!" I said.

"The entire plot was a masterpiece of detail," Margola went on, enjoying my amazement. "In Milwaukee she had been a secretary with stage ambitions. She saved enough money to come to New York and live for six months. Once here, she laid a careful campaign to get ahead in the theater. She made up her mind to become acquainted with Clem and me. I think her ideas went even further. I believe she planned to break up our marriage.

"Being married to a big producer-director would just suit Eve. She once made a remark to me that every important actress in the theater had a successful man behind her. That part hadn't jelled, but the rest had worked pretty well. As Clem's secretary she had met most of the big agents, playwrights, and important actors. Now, in addition to these contacts, she'd received a chance to show her ability and had come off the winner.

"It looked very amusing in print that director Clement Howell had had a genius right in his own office and that it had remained for another producer to discover her. Poor Clem took a lot of kidding on that score. That interview was the loudest crowing I ever read. The funniest part was how I had fallen for that stuff about her being my great fan. It made her out an even greater actress—that she had played a role in real life so convincingly that we had both been taken completely for a ride. I could have strangled her. Naturally, she didn't wait to be fired. She resigned as Clem's secretary—told him she couldn't be tied down to an office any longer.

"She began to dress in clothes and costumes that would be noticed. And she began to wear makeup in quantity because the report on most of her screen tests was 'no sex appeal.' "

"Why is she still standing at your stage door?" I asked. "I don't understand."

"That's where we had the last laugh," said Margola brightly. "The only thing happened that she hadn't bargained for. You know what Broadway is like. One day you're the toast of the town and the next you're forgotten. She was too inexperienced to have learned that real and lasting success is built only on a long-term foundation. She thought she was all set, and it went to her head. She took a few more screen tests but didn't photograph well enough to be sensational, and Hollywood doesn't bother to experiment with lights and makeup unless you have a real hit behind you. She was an odd type—certainly not the conventional ingenue—and no part turned up for her. Pretty soon the agents and producers just forgot about her. She couldn't even get in to see John Bishop himself, and she was his official protegee.

"That's when she came crying back to Clem and me. She says she'll stand at the stage door every night until I forgive her, that she was a silly fool when she gave out that interview. That she really did adore me and at first her only thought had been to get to know me. That she'll be everlastingly grateful if we will only help her to get a part. But I don't fall into the same trap twice," said Margola determinedly. "So far as I'm concerned she can stand at that entrance until she turns into a statue. I shan't lift a finger to help her."

"It's rather a pity," I said, "since you say she really is talented."

"So what?" Margola said. "Lots of girls are talented and never get a chance to show it. She had a chance, and she muffed it by her own conceit. She'll never get another opportunity."

"Probably not." I sighed and stared through the car window at the reflected stars twinkling like footlights in Little Neck Bay. No, I thought to myself, the little girl with the red coat will probably spend the rest of her life in obscurity.

But I was wrong. So was Margola. Eve Harrington had that rare second chance. I curse the day that she got it. For Margola was right. Eve was a bitch. I know, for it was through me that opportunity knocked twice on her door.

Several weeks after Margola told me this story, Lloyd finished his new play and a prominent manager made immediate plans to produce it. It was a strange play, different from anything Lloyd had written before and very hard to cast. There was one part which presented a real dilemma. It required a young emotional actress of great strength and power. At the same time, it wasn't large enough for a star, having only three scenes.

Lloyd and the manager tried actress after actress, and no one was right. He wanted a certain timid quality that was apparently unobtainable from the synthetic blondes of Broadway. I knew where he could find it. I knew the perfect girl was standing at Margola's stage door. I had never forgotten the shy expression in Eve Harrington's wide eyes. Finally, when in desperation the manager was about to call the production off, I suggested her to Lloyd.

"Go around there," I suggested. "She always wears a red coat. You can't miss her. If you wash the makeup off her face, you'll have exactly the right type. Furthermore, I hear she really can act."

Lloyd thought I was kidding, but finally he did as I told him. Eve read the part the next day, and they gave it to her. The search was over.

All through rehearsals, Lloyd and the director carefully coached Eve to hide her awkwardness. Lloyd began taking her out to lunch to talk about the part. On the opening night, she walked off with the show. It was a hit, and I had to admit it was partly her performance.

Her notices were amazing. The movies got excited about her all over again. This time, with her success behind her, her tests were a different story. What had once struck Hollywood as a lack of sex appeal now was called "a rare quality." So Eve is on the train with her contract in her pocket.

I'm going on a trip, also. I'm heading for Reno to get a divorce. For in spite of her success, Eve had found the time to get engaged to a famous playwright. She's going to marry my husband, Lloyd Richards.

A Reputation

Richard Edward Connell

Smoke and talk filled the dining-room of the Heterogeneous Club, one of those small, intimate clubs of reasonably liberal professional men and women one finds here and there in New York City. Alone, in his accustomed corner, Saunders Rook alternately sipped black coffee and fingered a wan mustache. He was on the fringe of an animated group, in it without being of it, and on this, as on other evenings, was taking an inconspicuous, nodding part in the conversation, sometimes going so far as to say, "Not really?" to which the speaker would reply perfunctorily, "Yes, really," and go on as before.

Nobody knew much about Saunders Rook, and he aroused little, if any, curiosity. It was assumed by the other members, on what grounds no one could say, that he was an artist of some kind; perhaps he wrote music criticism for one of the more pallid of the weeklies; maybe he contributed notes on birds to an ornithological review; again, it might be that he was an architect, specializing in designing ornamental drinking-fountains; perhaps he gave lessons on the flute. His pepper-and-salt suits, his silent neckties, his manner gave no hint. Yet he was not an enigma; he'd gladly have told all about himself had anyone cared to ask him.

The members must have seen Saunders Rook scores of times before that fateful evening, but had you asked any of them to describe him, the reply doubtless would have been:

"Oh, yes, Saunders Rook. I believe there is such a fellow around the club. Let me see. No, I don't think he's very tall or very short or very dark or very light. In fact, I don't believe he's very anything."

How and when he became a member of the club no one knew, and presumably no one had ever been concerned about knowing. Perhaps he was a friend of a friend of a member now deceased. He dined at the club four or five times a week and paid his bills. No one remembered having seen his face anywhere else. The Heterogeneous Club is proud of the range and brilliance of its talk but until this night it had never discussed Saunders Rook. After this night it could talk of little else.

Saunders Rook was not a glum, sullen, aloof soul; he was not unnoticed by choice; evening after evening he was on the edge of the circle of talk, listening as politely attentive as a well-trained collie. He may even have ventured on one or two occasions to come out with something positive; but if he ever did so, it made no impression on the members of the club, and they were a not unimpressionable lot.

On this night, as he sat over his coffee, Saunders Rook from time to time moistened his lips with his tongue and cleared his throat as if he were making ready to say something important, and then compressed his lips as if he had decided that it was not worth saying.

The truth was that Saunders Rook was afflicted with "cab-wit," that he was one of those unfortunates who think of the bright things they might have said only while on their way home in a taxicab. He was oppressed by the knowledge that if he did say anything, it would probably be as colorless and unoriginal as he suspected himself to be. He was oppressed mildly, for he was mild in all things, by the certainty that he could not compete with the witty Max Skye or the sparkling Lucile Davega, who could always quote something arresting from Krafft-Ebing. He did not enjoy being ignored any more than any other man does, and he had his full share of man's natural desire for a beam of lime-light. A craving for attention had of late been growing more insistent within him. His mind began to play with ideas, which, he reasoned, if uttered in a loud enough voice, might bring his hearers to their, and his, feet. He wanted just for once to cause a stir. Just once, he told himself, would appease him.

Then came the lull that always comes from time to time when groups are talking, and Saunders Rook found himself saying distinctly:

"On the Fourth of July I shall commit suicide."

Just why he said that he did not know. It must have been sheer inspiration. As a matter of fact, he had never contemplated doing anything of the kind. He had never demanded much of life; his existence was not rigorous, but placid. He was a sub-editor on a woman's magazine—he conducted the etiquette page—and this brought him twelve hundred dollars a year. He had inherited an income of twelve hundred more. He was able to live in modest comfort, for he was an orphan and a bachelor; he had a season ticket at the opera; his health was good. If he had a cross, it was a light one: minor editors of minor magazines usually rejected his minor essays, imitations of Charles Lamb, hymning the joys of pipe-smoking and pork-chops. So it startled him not a little to hear himself announcing his imminent self-destruction.

But it produced the desired effect with an electrical suddenness. The lull became a hush; not only the group at his own long table, but other groups had heard, and the eyes of the entire room were directed to the man with the wan mustache.

"But, my dear fellow," cried Max Skye, "you don't really mean that."

Saunders Rook curbed an exigent impulse to recant on the spot, and replied firmly:

"But I do mean it."

A woman member in a far corner called:

"Would you mind repeating what you said? I'm not sure I heard you correctly."

Saunders Rook cleared his throat and said again,

"On the Fourth of July I shall commit suicide."

The members began to shift their chairs so that they could more plainly see and hear him.

"But why?" asked Lucile Davega.

"Yes, why?" came from other members. Some were a little excited.

Saunders Rook had not thought that far ahead, and the question confused him. He wanted very much to say, "Of course, I was only jesting." No, he couldn't do that. What a dolt they'd think him! Hastily he ransacked his brain, cleared his throat to gain time, and declared:

"As a protest against the state of civilization in America."

Again sheer inspiration. The state of civilization, up to that moment, had never worried him. He heard an interested ripple run round the room.

"But what do you consider the state of civilization to be?" asked Max Skye, bending toward him.

"Rotten," said Saunders Rook, emphatically. Now that he was in for it, there was no sense in halfway expressions. "Rotten," if not elegant, was strong, he decided.

He heard someone in a corner whisper:

"I say, who is that fellow?"

"Why, his name is Book or Cook or something," was the whispered answer.

He smiled. He hoped they would think it the quiet, resolute smile of martyrdom.

"But Mr.—er—Rook," said Lucile Davega, "have you made all your plans?"

Here was another contingency for which he had not prepared. He slowly cleared his throat.

"I have," he said gravely. Then, with a touch of mystery, added, "And I haven't." He hoped they would probe no further. But the Heterogeneous Club is composed of inveterate probers.

"Oh, won't you tell us all about them?" As Lucile Davega said this she clasped her hands. Mr. Rook frowned ever so slightly. They acted as if he were planning a trip to Bermuda. He'd have to show them how deadly in earnest he was.

"If you insist," he said, his mind groping wildly for plans. Unanimously, they insisted.

"Mind you it must go no further than this room," he said. They all said that of course it wouldn't.

"Well," said Saunders Rook, speaking very deliberately, "of course, you see, since it is to be a protest, it must have a certain amount of publicity."

Everyone nodded approvingly.

"So I thought," he felt his way along, "that I should do it in some rather public place."

"Central Park?" suggested Max Skye.

"Exactly," replied Saunders Rook, grasping at the idea. "The very place I had in mind."

There were murmurs of "Splendid!" "A big thought!" "There's a lot more to these quiet chaps than meets the eye."

Saunders Rook, hearing, glowed.

Just then Oscar Findlater made one of his infrequent appearances at the club. The members were proud of belonging to the same club as Oscar Findlater, who was editor of *The Liberal Voice*, most advanced and oracular of weeklies. He was a vastly serious person of Jovian demeanor. Usually the members flocked about him to catch the pronouncements that dropped from his lips, but on this evening they only nodded toward him and continued to gaze expectantly at Saunders Rook. To Saunders Rook, Oscar Findlater had always seemed a god, despite the fact that *The Liberal Voice* had rejected numerous choice essays on pipe-smoking by the fireplace and kindred topics over which Saunders Rook had toiled. He had mildly envied the attention paid to the editorial Olympian. Now he, Saunders Rook, was actually stealing the spot-light from the great man. It was most pleasant.

"Good evening, Findlater," said Max Skye. "You know Saunders Rook, don't you?"

The editor murmured something about never having had that pleasure.

"Rook," announced Max Skye, impressively, "is going to commit suicide."

"On the Fourth of July," added Judy Atwater.

"As a protest," contributed Rogers Joyce.

"Against the rotten condition of civilization in America," finished Lucile Davega.

Oscar Findlater gazed at the wan mustache with sharpened interest.

"Not really?" he exclaimed.

"Yes," said Saunders Rook, in the voice of a man whose mind is irrevocably made up, "really."

"By Jove!" cried Oscar Findlater, and sat down. He was plainly stirred. "Do you mind talking to me about it?"

"Not at all," said Saunders Rook, trying to inject casualness into his tone, "if you think it all interesting."

"Interesting?" Oscar Findlater excitedly stroked the black ribbon that streamed from his nose-glasses. "Why, man alive, it's overpowering. Biggest idea I've struck all year."

He studied Saunders Rook.

"Your mind is made up?" the great man asked.

"Absolutely."

"Nothing can change it?"

"Nothing."

"Well," said Findlater, with a sigh, "then I suppose we must make the best of it."

He sank his head on his bosom, the usual attitude by which his disciples knew he was submerged in thought. Then he said:

"Rook, would you consider doing a series of essays for *The Liberal Voice*?

Would he? What a question! Saunders Rook could only nod.

"Let's say six essays tracing the genesis of the idea, you know, and arraigning civilization."

But Saunders Rook merely nodded.

"Of course," went on Oscar Findlater, "there are only three weeks between now—" he paused, embarrassed—"and then."

Saunders Rook murmured:

"Of course."

"Still," exclaimed Oscar Findlater, struck by a happy thought, "we could bring out the last three posthumously."

"Posthumously," echoed Saunders Rook, sepulchrally. At that second came again the impulse to say, "But, of course, this is all in fun." He stifled it. After all, it was something to have essays in *The Liberal Voice*, even posthumously. "How long should they be?" Saunders Rook found himself asking carelessly.

"Oh, about three thousand words; more if necessary. Not too heavy in tone, of course, or morbid. Readable, you know, almost chatty; but with an underlying strain of philosophy."

"Precisely," said Saunders Rook.

"We'll want the first one immediately," said the editor.

"You shall have it," promised Saunders Rook.

He could not but note the admiration, almost awe, in the circle of eyes. He was wise enough to depart before the spell was broken.

"Well," he said, rising, "I think I'll run along to bed now. Can't be too careful of my health, you know." He tossed this last sentence off with a grim smile. He was full of inspiration tonight.

The members crowded around him.

"Will you come to my studio for tea tomorrow?" asked Lucile Davega.

"And dine with me afterward at the Author's Club," insisted Max Skye. "Some fellows I want you to meet."

"We'd love to have you come up to Crofton for a weekend," said Rogers Joyce. "The crowd up there would like to know you. Jolly lot. Keen on new ideas like yours."

For the first time in his thirty-three years Saunders Rook had the gratifying sensation of being inundated with invitations, of being sought after. He consulted a datebook, appeared surprised to find that it so happened that he was not booked up to any extent in the near future, and accepted sundry invitations.

As he strolled to his snug two rooms and bath in Grove Street, Saunders Rook could not but congratulate himself on being a singularly fortunate fellow.

At the tea given by Lucile Davega Saunders Rook experienced a new and not unwelcome sensation: he was lionized. He found it extremely pleasant to play the lion to a studio of pretty women. He noted how the tea went cold and the toast untasted as they flocked around him. Also, each one found an opportunity to take him aside and say:

"Of course you don't really mean it."

"But I do," he would reply almost severely.

"But what have you got against civilization?"

"It's rotten," he would growl. He was getting better and better in the rôle.

"Oh Mr. Rook!"

He enjoyed the sensation he was creating.

One girl, Margery Storey, who was young and had red hair, a combination that sometimes appeared in Saunders Rook's dreams and private yearnings, whispered to him that she was sure he was disappointed in love; but, she added archly, there were plenty of uncaught fish in the sea.

He said sternly that love or lack of it did not enter into his plan at all. The act he was to perform was to be a perfectly calm, philosophic protest against the state of civilization in America.

"You will remember," he told her, "how the early Christians walked naked into the arenas as a protest against the brutality of the gladiatorial combats. My motive, I hope, is equally untinged by any selfish emotion."

His heart was accelerated by her glance, so full of compassion. She said a little diffidently that she was a painter, and would he sit for his portrait? She'd love to do it; her studio was Number 148—

No, he interrupted, he could not. Actually he wanted to very much. He was busy, he explained, on a series of essays for *The Liberal Voice.*

"After that, then?" she suggested.

"For me," said Saunders Rook, "there will be no 'after that.' "

Her blue eyes were full of sympathy.

"It seems too bad," she said. "You are still so young."

He smiled a smile of practiced cynicism.

"In years, perhaps," he said.

He saw that he had moved her.

Decidedly, this new rôle of his was worth playing, said Saunders Rook to himself as he donned his dinner-jacket that night in preparation for his dinner with Max Skye at the Author's Club. He was pleased with himself. In retrospect were the sympathetic blue eyes of Margery Storey; in prospect, a dinner among the celebrities of the Author's Club, into which sacred premises he had never gone physically, but solely in his most roseate imaginings.

Max Skye, who was a poet of no mean repute, introduced Saunders Rook to a group of notable men.

"This," said Max Skye, with the air of a showman, "is Mr. Saunders Rook, who is going to commit suicide on the Fourth of July."

Saunders Rook bowed to them; gravely they bowed back and stared at him, fascinated.

"In Central Park," continued Max Skye.

Saunders Rook bowed deeply.

"As a protest against the rotten state of our civilization," added Max Skye.

Saunders Rook again bowed.

They returned his bows with marked deference, he noted delightedly. He managed, however, to maintain an air of great world-weariness as he said:

"When one feels as I do about it, what else can one do?"

He had rehearsed this coming up in the taxicab.

"Mr. Rook is writing a series of six essays for *The Liberal Voice,*" announced Max Skye, plainly proud to be the discoverer and friend of so remarkable a man.

"But," objected Deline, the novelist, a man Saunders Rook had long admired from afar, "how can you publish six essays? It's June now. When could the other three be published?"

"Posthumously," said Saunders Rook, with a touch of pride.

"Posthumously?"

They all repeated the word as if there was a magic in it.

"But why do you feel that the state of civilization requires so drastic a protest?"

Deline asked this question as Saunders Rook was enjoying the third course, tender roast young guinea-fowl with mushrooms; Rook loved good food.

"Because," said Saunders Rook, with fork poised, "it's rotten."

Around the table went murmurs of approbation and interest.

"But, my dear fellow," exclaimed Deline, warmly laying his hand on Saunders Rook's arm, "we need men like you."

"Yes, yes," cried others about the table. "America needs men with the courage of their convictions."

"You see," said Deline, with a wave of his hand. "You're needed."

No one had ever before intimated to Saunders Rook that he was in the least needed. The happy thought occurred to him to rise and say, "In that case, gentlemen, I shall stay with you." But he didn't say that. Going home in a taxicab, he wished that he had. What he actually did was to sit with folded arms, a picture of determination, and say:

"When one feels as I do about it, what else can one do?"

Perhaps, after all, he mused, it was just as well he had not recanted. It was something to be told by a great novelist that you are needed. Perhaps, if he recanted, they might discover that they did not need him so much after all.

A few days later as he sat at his desk among the other sub-editors—beauty editors, household editors, baby-care and feeding editors, kiddie page editors, cooking editors—he was summoned, just as he'd finished writing a letter to a lady in Waterloo, Iowa, to tell her that engraved invitations are not required for a straw-ride, into the sanctum and presence of the publisher and owner of the magazine, Keable Gowler, a man of terrifying importance in Saunders Rook's eyes. Until that moment it had not occurred to Saunders Rook that he was anything more to Mr. Gowler than a name on the payroll and rather far down on the payroll at that. Yet Mr. Gowler greeted him with a fatherly affability, and offered him a chair.

"Well, Rook, tell me all about it," said Mr. Gowler, with heavy geniality.

"About what, Mr. Gowler?"

"This story I've been hearing about you and the Fourth of July."

"Really now—" began Saunders Rook.

"Is it true, or is it not true that you are going to commit suicide in Madison Square?" demanded Mr. Gowler.

"Central Park," corrected Saunders Rook, mildly.

"It is true, then?"

"Yes."

Mr. Gowler made tutting noises with his lips.

"Oh, come now, Rook," he said, "you're not serious."

"I am," said Saunders Rook. He was pleased to know that he was more than a mere name to his employer, and he wished to remain a personage.

"But, my dear young man," cried Mr. Gowler, distressed, "I ask you, would that be fair to the magazine? People might hold us responsible, you know."

"No, they won't."

"How can we be sure?"

"I have made it plain," said Saunders Rook, "that no petty, personal motives are behind my act. It is to be purely a protest against the state of civilization in America."

"America seems pretty civilized to me," observed Mr. Gowler. "What's wrong with it?"

"It's rotten," said Saunders Rook.

Mr. Gowler looked horrified, but he surveyed Mr. Rook with a strong, new interest.

"Come, now," said Mr. Gowler, soothingly. "Let's see if we can't settle this thing. We'd miss you, Rook. The interior decoration page would miss you."

"I do the etiquette page, Mr. Gowler," said Saunders Rook, gently.

"Yes, yes. I meant that; why, of course," said Mr. Gowler, hastily. He decapitated a cigar and faced Saunders Rook. "Look here, Rook," he said, "I'm afraid we've been hiding your light under a bushel around here. To be frank with you, I didn't realize the stuff you were made of—until a few days ago." Mr. Gowler paused significantly.

"Now, what this magazine needs," he went on, "is a live young man of forceful character, who has modern ideas and isn't afraid to back them up. Roscoe Quimper is getting old; been an editor too long; we need a man with spirit for his position. Will you take it?"

Saunders Rook moistened dry lips; speech failed him; it was a post he had long coveted. He affected to consider.

"It pays fifteen thousand," said Mr. Gowler. His tone was actually persuasive.

Saunders Rook thought swiftly.

"I'll take charge, Mr. Gowler."

"Good!" cried Mr. Gowler. "Good!"

"Until the Fourth of July," added Saunders Rook.

Mr. Gowler evinced his concern by a sharp elevation of his shrubbery of eyebrows.

"Then you are in earnest?"

"Absolutely."

"Of course"—this was said almost cajolingly—"if fifteen thousand seems too little, I might be willing to—"

Saunders Rook held up his hand.

"Thanks," he said, "but it's not a question of money."

Mr. Gowler shook his head dejectedly.

"Then I guess there's nothing I can say. Still"—he brightened—"even if your mind is made up, you could take charge until the Fourth of July and outline a policy and get things started, couldn't you?"

"If you wish," said Saunders Rook, handsomely.

"Good!" ejaculated Mr. Gowler. "Good!"

Saunders Rook, somewhat in a daze, started for the door.

"Oh, by the way, Rook," said Mr. Gowler, "couldn't you take dinner with us next Thursday? The governor of the State, two United States senators, a few congressmen, and a professor will be there. They'd like to know you."

Saunders Rook riffled through his date-book and said he might be late, as he had two teas and a talk before a Brooklyn club scheduled for that day, but that he would try to get to the dinner in time for the dessert. Mr. Gowler was greatly obliged to him.

At the dinner at Keable Gowler's Fifth Avenue house the attention paid to Saunders Rook by the governor, the senators, the assorted congressmen, the professor, and their wives would have flattered a person even less susceptible than he. In trumpet tones Mr. Gowler announced him:

"This is Mr. Saunders Rook, one of my most valued associates. On the Fourth of July, as a protest against our civilization, he will commit suicide in Washington Square."

"Central Park," said Saunders Rook, bowing modestly.

"Not really?" they all said in breathless chorus.

"Yes, really," said Saunders Rook.

He talked, and they listened. He had been expanding the idea, and had worked up an indictment or two against civilization.

Over his after-dinner liqueur the governor declared that, if necessary, he would do the only thing he could think of to prevent Saunders Rook from robbing the State of so valued a citizen, and that was to call out the militia. He was not prepared to say, he remarked darkly, how he should employ it, for he was fresh in the gubernatorial chair. However, he knew that a governor has the power to call out the militia, and he was interested to learn what would happen if he did call it out. Surely the case of Saunders Rook, he maintained, warranted that step.

The senator from Alabama promised that he would see the President at once, and volunteered to get the cooperation of Federal troops to help the governor's militia. Saunders Rook listened, sphinx-like, outwardly impassive, inwardly agog. The senator from North Dakota said that it had not before been called to his attention that the state of civilization in these United States was sufficiently rotten to cause a man of his good friend Rook's high type to plan so violent a protest, but now that it had been called to his attention, something should be done about it by the Senate. Political considerations, he said, prevented him from committing himself to any definite program, but this he would do: he would rush back to Washington on the morrow and start a senatorial investigation into civilization at which Saunders Rook would be the chief witness.

One of the congressmen present said that for his part he was prepared to introduce a resolution in the House of Representatives calling for the immediate appropriation of three hundred thousand dollars for the establishing of a congressional commission of seven on civilization, and that, obviously, the only person for the chairmanship was Mr. Rook. Another congressman said he was in hearty agreement with his honorable colleague in principle, but would like to amend the bill, so that it would call for eight hundred thousand dollars and a commission of twenty-one. While they were debating this point, Saunders Rook forced himself to depart. He had to look over the proofs of his article in *The Liberal Voice*, he said. Keable Gowler himself helped Saunders Rook on with his coat and urged him to come again.

The appearance of the first Rook article brought him a tidal wave of letters. Scores of persons in all parts of the globe begged him for various reasons not to do it; two elderly ladies offered to adopt him and leave him their not inconsiderable estates; a group of young Russian radicals by cable offered to jump into the Volga on the Fourth of July to show they were in sympathy with him; eleven clergymen asked permission to call; a publishing house offered him a handsome figure for his diary, novel, or what had he? Fourteen ladies of different ages offered to marry him, and of these seven sent photographs, of which two were quite personable; three motion picture companies asked him to name his own price for the exclusive rights; a vaudeville syndicate offered him two thousand a week for a ten-minute monolog twice daily until the Fourth of July; the police commissioner wrote to warn him that suicide is an offense amounting to disorderly conduct, and is punishable by fine or imprisonment, or both. A procession of reporters, photographers, feature-story writers, and interviewers invaded his apartment. In newspapers and magazines his wan features began to appear, accompanied by stories of varying degrees of accuracy. He began to be pointed out on the street; ribs were nudged as he passed. He loved it.

Crowded days passed, days full of pleasurable excitement and intense living for Saunders Rook. So swiftly did they speed by that it was a distinct shock for him, one morning, to be awakened by a boy with a tall stack of telegrams. The messages were from many people and many places; some urged, begged, and a few even conjured him not to do it today; many said simply, "Farewell." Today? Saunders Rook glanced at the date on the telegrams—"July Fourth."

He dressed himself with care in his new gray suit and lavender tie, took his bamboo stick, and sauntered up Fifth Avenue. It was a delicious, sunlit day; the avenue was bright with flags; somewhere a parade was forming, and he heard the gay sounds of distant bands. Life had never seemed quite so fair to Saunders Rook, but, and he stopped abruptly, what of tomorrow?

Today, on the Fourth of July, the eyes of a nation were on him. He bought a morning paper. Yes, there he was on the front page, a picture, smudged, but resolute-looking, and a two-column headline, "Saunders, Self-Slain Today for Civilization's Sake."

He wiped his brow with his silk handkerchief. It was impossible for him not to think of himself on July fifth; also July sixth, seventh, eighth.

"What a lot of dynamite there is in one little word!" he muttered to himself. "What a difference there is between, 'Saunders Rook, the man who *is* going to commit suicide on the Fourth of July,' and 'Saunders Rook, the man who *was* going to commit suicide on the Fourth of July.' One is romantic, promising, glorious; the other,—ugh!—the other is the epitaph of a weakling, a turncoat, a failure."

He stopped before a picture-store and moodily gazed at a seascape in the window. He recalled that some sage had said, "Any man can make a reputation; it takes a real man to keep one." He had a reputation, he reflected. He derived pleasure from that fact even now. It was more than he had dared hope for. Three weeks before it had seemed that he had been cast for a minor rôle in life, the voice of the mob offstage; almost overnight he had attained stardom. He, who had never expected to have a line to speak, had strutted and postured and declaimed in the center of the stage and heard the sweet music of applause. Today he was a hero; tomorrow he would be a joke. The day was warm, but he shuddered.

A holiday crowd in summer colors was passing. There was laughter in the air. How intelligent the people looked, he mused, and how civilized! A graceful, powerful motorcar purred by.

He paused before a window full of books, and saw many that interested him. He glanced up at the spired heights of a church, and his gaze traveled onward to a new building, towering, shapely, beautiful; men, he reflected, had made it, had shaped the steel and stone to their will. The paper dropped from his fingers, and a passing stranger courteously picked it up, and handed it to Saunders Rook with a friendly smile. Saunders Rook felt an impulse to cry aloud, "This land, these times aren't so rotten, after all."

The words died still-born. Down Fifty-Second Street he heard the shrill cry of a newsboy, "all about Saunders Rook, the martyr."

He hurried on toward Central Park. The governor had kept his word; he had called out the militia; alert soldiers with fixed bayonets patrolled the paths and scrutinized the picnickers from under their hat-brims. The green lawns were dotted with blue policemen. They, too, were watchful. Indeed, as Saunders Rook slipped into the park, unrecognized, he saw a burly officer collar a mild, blond little man, and heard the man protesting loudly that he was not Saunders Rook, but only Ole Svenson, a pastry-cook, and that the thing he had just eaten was not poison, but a banana. As he left the man struggling in the hands of the law, Saunders Rook shrugged his shoulders, smiled a pale smile, and penetrated deeper into the park.

"They've gone to a lot of trouble on my account," he said to himself, almost proudly. "It wasn't always like that. Funny how little interest people took in me when I only wanted to live."

He picked a flower and stuck it in his buttonhole.

"It's great to have a reputation," he remarked. Then, as he paced along, added, "But it's tough to have to live up to it."

He had reached the sequestered end of the reservoir, and, glancing about, saw neither soldier nor policeman in sight.

"Stupid, incompetent fools!" he muttered.

He stood looking down into the cool, clear water. Then he raised his head and drew the fresh air into his lungs, and expelled it with a sigh. How well he felt! Slowly from an inside pocket he took his little red date-book, and with his fountain-pen wrote in his round, precise hand:

"I do this as a protest against the rotten state of civilization. Saunders Rook." He blotted it neatly with a pocket blotter. He looked up at the smiling sky and sighed deeply.

"Still, after all, a reputation is a reputation," he said.

Then he jumped.

Mr. Blandings Builds His Castle

Eric Hodgins

The sweet old farmhouse burrowed into the upward slope of the land so that you could enter either its bottom or middle floor at ground level. Its window trim was delicate and the lights in its sash were a bubbly amethyst. Its rooftree seemed to sway a little against the sky, and the massive chimney that rose out of it tilted a little to the south. Where the white paint was flecking off on the siding, there showed the blush of what must once have been a coat of rich, dense red.

In front of it, rising and spreading along the whole length of the house, was the vastest lilac tree that Mr. and Mrs. Blandings had ever seen. When the house was new, the lilac must have been a shrub planted in the dooryard—and house and shrub had gone on together, side by side, since then. That was a hundred and seventy years ago this April.

Using a penknife as a key, the real estate man unlocked a lower door. As it swung back, the top hinge gave way and splashed in a red powder on the floor. The door lurched against Mr. Blandings and gave him a sharp crack on the forehead, but the damage was repaired in an instant and Mr. Blandings, a handkerchief at his temple and his wife by his side, stood looking through one of the misty amethyst window-lights at an arc of beauty that made them both cry out. The land rushed downward to the river valley a mile away; then it rose again, layer after layer, plane after plane of hills and higher hills lighter beyond them. The air was luminous and there were twenty shades of browns and greens in the plowed and wooded and folded earth.

"On a clear day you can see the Catskills," said the real estate man.

Mr. and Mrs. Blandings were not such fools as to exclaim at this revelation. Mrs. Blandings flicked a glove in which a cobweb and spider had become entangled; Mr. Blandings, his lips pursed and his eyes half-closed, was a picture of controlled reserve. By the way the two of them said "Uh-hum?" with a rising inflection in perfect unison, the real estate man knew that his sale was made. Not today, of course; the offer might not come for a fortnight. But it would come; it would come with all the certainty of the equinox. He computed five per cent of $10,275 rapidly in his head and turned to the chimney footing.

"You'd have to do a little pointing up here," he said, indicating a compact but disorderly pile of stone, in which a blackened hollow suggested a fireplace that had been in good working order at the time of the Treaty of Ghent. Mrs. Blandings, looking at the rubble, saw instead the kitchen of the Wayside Inn: a distaff plump with flax lying idly on the polished hearth; a tempered scale of copper pans and skillets near the oven wall; a bootjack in the corner; a shoat glistening on the spit.

What Mr. Blandings saw broke through into speech: "With a flagstone floor in here it would be a nice place for a beer party on a Saturday night. You'd put the keg right in that corner."

"You could at that," said the real estate man, as if he had just heard a brilliant revision of atomic theory. He quickly did five per cent of $11,550 in his head; aloud, he said: "Let's go upstairs and then take a look at your orchard. There's a very interesting story connected with . . ."

The effect of the plural possessive pronoun was as a fiery liquor in Mr. and Mrs. Blandings's veins.

Thus it came about that Mr. and Mrs. Blandings bought—for $11,550—the old Halleck place, the old house and the gorgeous acres surrounding it. But it would be a year, at least, before the Blandingses would "build." Mr. Blandings had stated, unequivocally, that you wouldn't catch him building until prices were "right." The forces that were to make prices right in the residential-construction industry were not known to Mr. Blandings, but he did not know that he did not know them. Mr. Blandings's eventual cost of building when prices were right was somewhat in excess, by a percentage only an astrologer could calculate, of what it would have been had he built when they were not so right. But the excess percentage was removed from Mr. Blandings at a later time, when he was numb from shock and scarcely felt a thing.

"Let's say your land'll cost you $10,000, round numbers," the real estate man had said in the days before it had actually cost $11,550. "And let's say it'll cost you $10,000 to restore that farmhouse. So you've made a $20,000 investment that'll stand you all the rest of your life, to say nothing of having a home to live in, and the benefit of what your friend Mr. Grover calls 'the indescribable charm' of the place." This lyric passage had served the Blandingses in lieu of thought for several months until, one evening, Mrs. Blandings had looked up from her mending.

"Do you suppose it's worth our while to remodel that old house?" she had asked in a faraway voice.

If she had flatly announced the illegitimacy of the two Blandings children she could scarcely have had a more thunderous effect upon her husband.

"I only mean," she went on in an effort to silence him, "that maybe someone should look at it besides Mr. Funkhauser."

Mr. Funkhauser was a young architect to whom Mr. Blandings had taken a shine. Working mostly from photographs, plus some measurements taken one rainy day on Bald Mountain, he had been covering reams of sketch tissue with the graceful swashes of a 6-B pencil, and making of the old Halleck farmhouse something quite else again. The Blandingses had found the results enchanting.

"What's the matter with Funkhauser?" asked Mr. Blandings.

"I only mean," said Mrs. Blandings, "that he's so enthusiastic about everything that sometimes I think he gets carried away. I'd like to have some other sort of person look at the old house before we get too far along—an engineer, or somebody."

Eventually Mr. Blandings came to believe that he himself had had this prudent idea. He asked his lawyer friend Bill Cole to dig him up an engineer—a good practical fellow who wouldn't be carried away by *anything*. As a result, Mr. Giobatta Appolonio, engineer, did indeed visit the old Halleck place with Mr. and Mrs. Blandings some days later. In his black shoes, dark business suit, and derby he made an odd picture among the roaming hills, particularly compared with Mr. Blandings in his slightly aggressive rural tweeds.

Mrs. Blandings had expected Mr. Appolonio to bring a bag of instruments along like a physician, and perhaps to practice the physician's rites of auscultation or palpation on her dwelling. But Mr. Appolonio's only instrument was a foot rule, and far from palpating her house, he did not even seem to want to go near it. He merely stood looking at it for five minutes from about a hundred feet away. He then went up to it and kicked it on one corner. Mr. and Mrs. Blandings winced in unison when something unidentified fell off. Mr. Appolonio returned to his clients and spoke to them in a soft voice.

"You should ought to tear it down," said he.

"That stinking roughneck has simply no feeling for antiquity," said Mr. Blandings, taking a spastic gulp out of his glass.

"I wish you wouldn't drink when you're upset," said Mrs. Blandings. She and her husband were back in their city apartment. The train trip home with Mr. Appolonio had been very trying. Once home, Mr. Blandings had written out a check for his $50 fee and mailed it to him instantly with a curt, correct note. But now Mr. Blandings was alone with God and Mrs. Blandings, and there was no concealing from either one that Mr. Blandings had paid a considerable sum, above land cost alone, for a structure that he had now been advised (for $50 more) to destroy. In Mr. Blandings's view, his wife was an accessory before the fact, and God stood convicted of the grossest sort of contributory negligence—but condemn them as he might, he could see no recourse from either of them, or from the real estate man, or from Ephemus W. Halleck.

There remained, however, the luckless Mr. Funkhauser, still doodling happily on his sketch tissue, dreaming towers and battlements, spires and turrets, onto a lousy old wreck of a farmhouse that had neither sills nor chimney to support its present crumbling weight. Him Mr. Blandings fired with a vicious suddenness that left, as one residue, a folder in the files of the American Institute of Architects labeled "Funkhauser-Blandings Grievance Case." After an eventual chilly interchange, Mr. Blandings paid Mr. Funkhauser's bill of $635 for "Preliminary Plans of Restored Blandings Residence," and received the blueprints thereof. They were cold comfort. So was the report of Mr. Joe Perlasky, a local house wrecker and junkyard proprietor. Mr. Blandings had consulted him on the sly, in the hope of presenting to Mrs. Blandings the happy news that they could realize perhaps $2,000 out of the materials salvaged from the razing of the structure that was to have been the home of their children's children. Mr. Perlasky had figured for fifteen minutes and then announced that he would take the house down, leave everything neat and clean around the foundation, and not charge Mr. Blandings a penny more than $850. *"Charge?"* cried Mr. Blandings. "Atsa right," said Mr. Perlasky, explaining his modest figure by saying that he might just possibly be able to use some of the beams on another job.

It was at this point that Mr. Blandings's stout heart failed him. After a painful discussion, the entire Blandings Building Project was put by to await a new and happier time. In calculation one evening, Mr. Blandings came face to face with the figure that in land cost, surveys, Mr. Appolonio's fee, legal expenses (so far), Mr. Funkhauser's blueprints, demolition estimates, and a dozen other items all small in themselves, he had so far spent or obligated himself to a total of $13,881.34, and not the rasp of one saw or the blow of one hammer had yet been heard on Bald Mountain.

"Don't act surprised when the children grow up to be guttersnipes, hearing words like that in their own living room," said Mrs. Blandings.

"We can fix up that old house," said Mr. Simms, the new architect. "Of course we can. But it'll cost you as much as building a new house, or more, and you won't have what you want. My advice, if you'll let me be frank, is to start afresh."

Starting afresh sounded to Mr. and Mrs. Blandings like what they wanted most in all the world to do.

The Blandingses had begun their home-building career with the assumption that they had $20,000 to spend. When the real estate man had pointed out to them that $10,000 for land and the old house, plus $10,000 for "restoration" came to this precise figure, the logic and arithmetic had seemed very simple indeed. It was somewhat more clouded now, but not hopelessly so—not hopelessly so by a long shot, Mr. Blandings kept saying to himself. Manifestly, with some $14,000 invested so far, you couldn't skimp on the building by putting up a mere $6,000 bungalow. No—the house the Blandings would have to build was that $10,000 house they had in mind from the beginning. Prices were somewhat higher now, of course, so an adjusted figure would probably be something nearer $12,500. That was the figure to shoot at anyway; it might come out a little on the high side, but still . . . And suppose it even turned out to be $15,000, when you included everything, as of course it wouldn't. . . .

The Blandingses began to spend their weekends in a rented cottage not far from their mountaintop, and Mr. Simms used to drop in on them almost every Saturday or Sunday afternoon. He developed a really charming habit of bringing his drawing board, T square, and triangles along with him, and in the sweet vernal afternoons he and the Blandingses would confer and plan together. Things went swimmingly. Mr. Blandings had only one complaint. "Simms makes things too small," he said. "I think he's got wonderfully ingenious ideas, but my God, if there's one thing I don't want in the country, it's to feel *cramped*."

To this criticism Mr. Simms replied that he was watching the cubage. The Blandingses had never heard of cubage before; it was, Mr. Simms explained, merely the over-all cubic contents that the walls and roof enclosed, and a rough rule of thumb was to figure that the sort of house the Blandingses wanted would cost about 45 to 50 cents a cubic foot. This sounded dirt cheap to Mr. and Mrs. Blandings, neither of whom were conscious of the traps held for the unwary by an exponential equation of no higher than the third power. Mr. Simms, they felt (and told him), was holding a little too tight a rein on the cubage, good fault though it was. Mr. Simms sighed a little. "It's getting to look more like an $18,000 house every day," he said to the Blandingses, who made noises of mild deprecation but did not pause for long.

What the Blandingses wanted was simple enough: a two-story house in quiet, modern good taste; frame and whitewashed brick veneer, to blend with the older architectural examples that dotted the hills about them. They wanted a good-sized living room, a dining room, and kitchen on the first floor; four bedrooms and accompanying baths on the second;

a roomy cellar, a good attic, plenty of closets, and a couple of nice porches. And that was all.

The Blandingses soon discovered they had overlooked the servant problem. With thirty-one acres to look after, they'd have to have "a couple"—he to do the outdoor work, she to cook. To get them space for a small living room, bedroom, and bath off the kitchen called for some ingenuity, but Mr. Simms supplied it after adding twelve more feet to the house's long dimension. Mrs. Blandings's closet proposal (on which she would not retreat one inch) called for two per bedroom, one in every hallway, plus one broom closet, three kitchen closets, one closet for outdoor clothes, one linen closet, one storage closet for wood, one storage closet for card tables, etc. Mr. Blandings specified a liquor closet, with spring lock. It all added up to twenty-four closets, and Mrs. Blandings would brook no counterproposals. (The closets alone were to account for just a little under 2,000 cubic feet on Mr. Simms's conscientious plans.)

The Blandingses watched their house grow on the drawing board with warmth and pride. A study for Mr. Blandings became necessary the instant an opportunity for it opened up. Mrs. Blandings put in for a small cubicle, off the master bedroom, which she referred to as a "sulking room"—something that could serve her either as a dressing room or tiny study. And it would be awfully nice to have a little place with a sink and shelves for vases to do her flower arranging, she thought. Mr. Blandings got the notion that a built-in bar off the living room hall, scarcely larger than a closet and piped for cold water only, would add immeasurably to the house's whole feeling of hospitality—and who was Mr. Simms, who liked a snort himself now and again, to dispute him? One day Mr. Simms said, "It's beginning to look more like a $22,000 house than anything else," and for the first time the word "mansion" was used in conversation—facetiously, of course. The plans progressed; the house grew.

Mr. John Tesavis, well driller, appeared one summer day on the Blandings acres with his rig, under contract to drill a deep ("artesian," in the usage of the community) well at $4 per foot for the first three hundred feet, and $6 a foot thereafter, if necessary. Mr. Blandings was momentarily dismayed by the empiricism of selecting a well site ("I sinks she might as good go here as anywhere," Mr. Tesavis had said, indicating a wide area that seemed no different from any other half acre on Bald Mountain), but once the work was in progress he would sit on the bank for hours in fascination as the rig lifted the five hundred-pound steel drill-bit up three feet, let it down with a shattering slam, and instantly repeated its cycle. By the time Mr. Tesavis was down thirty feet the Blandingses could tell when the rig was working even when they were three miles away: a faint concussion would shake the ground under their feet every time the drill took its pulverizing bite. Mr. Tesavis was drilling through elemental rock.

"There ought to be some better way," Mr. Blandings moaned one night after Mr. Tesavis had announced that he was down 201 feet and his "string" was stuck. Mrs. Blandings voiced regret that her husband had refused the services of a neighborhood dowser who had offered to pick an infallible well site by means of his forked applewood stick, on payment of $25. Mr. Blandings had summarily rejected this suggestion and was now wondering if it might not have been worth $25 merely to have Mrs. Blandings on the defensive instead of, as was again the miserable case, vice versa. But his spirits rebounded next day on the news that Mr. Tesavis had been able to free his string and had also encountered liquids: somewhere in the bowels of geology the drill had struck a fissure through which one-half gallon of water per minute was now flowing into the Blandings's bore. This was far from the twenty gallons a minute that Mr. Blandings had always thought of as a desirable supply, but at least it kept down the cloud of pulverized rock in which Mr. Tesavis, unshakable as the Duke of Wellington at his nerve-racking task, had hitherto been working.

It was apparent at last that the plans would soon be finished. Mr. Blandings, having missed several sessions between his wife and Mr. Simms, had fallen seriously behind the procession and had the uneasy feeling that his house was now beyond his control. He would discover his wife and his architect discussing in familiar terms the breezeway, of which he had never heard. Matters of cabinets, shelving, random-width floor boards, gutters, dry wells, olive-knuckle butts, flues, muntins, mullions, tiles, shakes, ranges, pitches, and reveals came at him in unexpected ways and from unanticipated angles.

There was a bathroom on the second floor right above the front entrance to the house, and although Mr. Blandings was willing to accept this as part of the same cosmic plan that had put the rock under Mr. Tesavis, Mrs. Blandings fought it like a tigress, and more than once embarrassed Mr. Blandings by the vividness with which she embodied her objections. Eventually, Mr. Simms got the bathroom established in the rear, but if Mrs. Blandings had won a battle, history might still assess that here she had lost the war: the house length grew by four feet.

"I sometimes wonder if you people know what you're heading into," Mr. Simms said one night as he packed up to go home, but he and the Blandingses were in a relaxed mood, with highballs in their hands. It was a bad evening for warnings, anyway: a littler earlier, Mr. Tesavis had run crash into eight gallons of water at 297 feet and had telephoned the joyful news.

"When we build, let us think that we build for ever," John Ruskin once wrote. Mr. Blandings held a similar view. The curse of America was jerry-building, he was eloquent in saying, and the Blandings house bore out the philosophies of quality and permanence. The floors were to be oak, the waterlines red brass; the plumbing fixtures did not bear the tradename Sphinx for nothing; the incombustible shingles were the same as those developed to meet Mr. Rockefeller's wishes for the restoration of Williamsburg; the hardware was to be supplied by the nearest thing to Benvenuto Cellini in Connecticut.

When Mr. Simms, after going into a monastic seclusion for three weeks, emerged again, it was with a set of drawings and specifications that floored the Blandings's flat: the simple plans and elevations that they had seen grow on the drafting board were superseded now by section drawings, framing plans, wiring diagrams, and detail sheets; everything had become so dense with dimensions as to be undecipherable except to experts. There was also a set of specifications the thickness of a Chicago telephone directory. It was time to ask for bids.

Mr. Blandings now felt it appropriate to consult Mr. Anson Dolliver, the president of the local First National Bank, about borrowing some money. Mr. Blandings had had the foresight, a year earlier, to open a checking account in Mr. Dolliver's bank and to keep his balance at a level he was sure a country bank would consider opulent. Mr. Dolliver had been cordiality itself. "If we can ever help you out, up there on the hill," he had said, "just let us know." Now that at last Mr. Blandings was ready to apply for some mortgage money at Mr. Dolliver's bank, he envisioned cordiality in the extreme, the proffer of a fine cigar, the suggestion of a leisurely lunch at the tavern on the green, and an open line of credit at a nominal rate.

What he encountered was nothing like that at all. As Mr. Blandings stated his readiness to contract a loan, Mr. Dolliver bit off the end of a cigar for himself and spat daintily in Mr. Blandings's direction but proffered nothing. "Why, great grief," he said, as if he had been asked to do somebody's laundry, "we're loaned full up to our legal limit right now. Love to help you out, but . . ." He left the sentence unfinished. Then he added, listlessly, "My brother's the president of the savings bank across the hall. He might be able to do something for you, although of course I couldn't know for sure. . . ."

Mr. Blandings had three separate conversations with the savings bank brother, at the end of which the second-string Dolliver admitted that there might be circumstances under which he would make Mr. Blandings a $10,000 mortgage loan at 6 per cent. Feeling like Lord Keynes at the end of a tough mission, Mr. Blandings said that he had hoped for more money at less rate, and Mr. Dolliver responded with a concise lecture on the risks of rural real estate that Mr. Blandings wished he had been able to think up by himself a year ago. So Mr. Blandings contented himself by wondering aloud how soon he might have Mr. Dolliver's accommodation, since his bids were almost due and he hoped to begin breaking ground very soon.

Mr. Dolliver snapped forward in his chair. "You want this money for *construction*?" he asked, in a tone that made Mr. Blandings feel that he had sought a criminal abortion from an archbishop. Mr. Blandings said he did. He tried to make his voice firm, but in spite of his strongest efforts a tremulous harmonic crept into it.

"You've had me at a misapprehension," said Mr. Dolliver. "This bank never makes construction loans. If that's your situation and you have some government bonds, I think my brother in the commercial bank across the hall could work out something very satisfactory for you."

Mr. Blandings at this point discontinued negotiations with both Dolliver brothers and closed out his checking account. It had not been pleasant to deal with the Dollivers and their banks, but Mr. Blandings was at least able to congratulate himself that here was one episode in his building experience that had not cost him any money. He merely did not have his loan.

Mr. Simms arrived on a Saturday morning, looking a little constricted about the mouth, but brisk. "We've got all our bids," he said. "I've summarized them on the top sheet."

Mr. Blandings opened the manila folder, and leaped upward as from a bayonet thrust through the chair bottom.

"Jesus H. Mahogany Christ!" cried Mr. Blandings, and let the folder slip from his grasp. Mrs. Blandings, who had had her second child without anesthesia on the grounds that she did not wish to miss the experience, picked up the sheets as they slithered on the floor. She bent a level gaze on them and read:

ESTIMATES	BLANDINGS JOB	BALD MOUNTAIN
Antonio Doloroso, Builders		$32,117.00
Caries & Plumline		34,265.00
Julius Akimbo & Co.		37,500.00
Zack, Tophet & Payne		28,920.50
John Retch & Sons		30,852.00

"There are a couple of things to be noted from this," said Mr. Simms, speaking in an even, level, slightly rapid voice. "In the first place, Julius

Akimbo obviously doesn't want the job or he wouldn't have put in any round-figure bid that size. As for that bid from Zack, Tophet & Payne I wouldn't touch it with a ten-foot pole. They have a reputation for bidding low and then loading on the extras. That sort of gives us three to choose between. They're all good builders; John Retch is as good as any, and with that low figure I don't think you'll go wrong on him. Even so, we'll have to cut some costs."

This, Mr. Blandings thought in a blurred way, was putting it mildly. The cost-cutting job began then and there. What Mr. Blandings now discovered was that you could cut the cost of a $31,000 house somewhat, but there is no way on earth of cutting a $31,000 house to $21,000, to say nothing of anything lower. There were some things that were irremediable; it was no longer possible to shrink the house even by the process of restoring the fatal bathroom to its flaunting position over the front door. Too much else had altered in the meanwhile, and you could no more reverse the growth process of the house than you could shrink an adolescent back into last year's clothes by denying him food.

But there were, of course, some things to be done. The house could not be abandoned. Although Mr. Simms had never spoken of money and seemed wholly content to go on helping the Blandingses build their house forever, Mr. Blandings was aware that the standard architect's fee, according to the procedures of the American Institute of Architects, to which Mr. Simms belonged, was 10 per cent of the cost of the house—and God knows that if anyone had ever earned $3,100, it was Mr. Simms. With that obligation outstanding there was simply no turning back: the house must be built. As the deflation progressed, bronze casement windows changed to steel of the lightest cross section made. Red brass piping became galvanized iron. A whole flagged terrace disappeared. The roofing specifications came down in the world. The house would now be insulated only to the eaves—and to hell with having a cool attic in summer. The plumbing fixtures became notably less Pompeian.

Even so, it was slow, dispiriting work. It depressed Mr. Blandings deeply to observe that the elimination of the big flagged terrace, on which he had already, in anticipation, had a few delicious drinks, saved him, on Mr. Retch's figures, only $172.50. "If I was *adding* the terrace it wouldn't cost me a cent less than $700," said Mr. Blandings savagely. But he said it to himself, for he no longer had anyone to talk to. He was being cheated, he was being bilked, he was being made a fool of, but he could not find the villain because everyone was a villain—his wife, Mr. Simms, the local bank, John Retch and his burly, ugly, insolent sons, Mr. Funkhauser, Mr. Appolonio, Ephemus Halleck, and the real estate man—all, all had made him the butt and victim of a huge conspiracy, clever and cruel.

"There!" he heard Mrs. Blandings saying to Mr. Simms a fortnight later. "We've got Mr. Retch's figures down to $26,991.17. That's more like it."

"What's more like *what*?" snarled Mr. Blandings.

"I think we've pared it down as far as it will go," said Mr. Simms tactfully. "It's more money than you started out to spend, but you're getting a fine house. Retch is an honest builder, and that's about what your house will cost you *if* you don't start getting into extras with him."

With one voice Mr. and Mrs. Blandings assured Mr. Simms that there would be *no* extras. Far, far off in outer space, the Gods of Residential Construction offered a chirruping laugh.

Mr. Blandings's ego, scarred by forces too vast to identify, was powerfully restored a week later on his visit to the big, impressive savings bank in the industrial city of Seagate. Thither Mr. Blandings and his friend and attorney Bill Cole had gone to seek the mortgage that had come to naught with the local banks. In no more than an hour's conversation the bank agreed to advance Mr. Blandings $18,000 at 5 per cent, the loan to be amortized over twenty years, anticipation of repayments permitted. (That left plenty for Mr. Blandings to raise by other means, but he knew where he could hock the stock he held in his own company.) And, *of course*, it would be a construction loan; Mr. Blandings could have a wad of cash as soon as the bank's title attorneys completed their search on the old Halleck property.

This last puzzled Mr. Blandings but did not disturb him. "I thought we'd done that," he said to Bill Cole as they left the bank together. "What did I pay old Judge Quondam $125 for when I bought the property from Halleck originally?"

Bill Cole explained that that had been a title search, all right. "It would have satisfied the local bank if you'd been able to do business with them," he said. "But Seagate-Proletarian has five million dollars out in mortgages in a hundred communities besides yours, and they have to have their own guarantees and satisfactions, naturally. It won't amount to much. Their title attorneys are Barratry, Lynch & Replevin; they'll soak you $200 but it'll be worth it to have their stamp of approval. Mostly they'll just send a man up to check old Judge Quondam and his county records."

"Old Judge Quondam died last spring," said Mr. Blandings. "The whole town closed down the afternoon of his funeral."

"Oh," said Bill, and then, after a pause, "Well, he didn't take his records with him, I guess."

On a crisp autumn morning the steam shovel arrived. Mr. and Mrs. Blandings, Mr. Simms, and John Retch himself were present for the ground breaking, and Mrs. Blandings was delighted with the rugged honesty and great good humor of Mr. Retch—"A rough diamond with a heart of gold," she said afterward. Mrs. Blandings was also happy that Mr. Blandings seemed himself again, as indeed he was. Any man who can raise $18,000 in an hour's conversation with one of the biggest savings banks in the East has certainly no call to be so jumpy about finances as Mr. Blandings could now see, looking back on it all, he had permitted himself to become. The $10,000-odd he would have to borrow on his company stock was just about the net of his burden—that was one way of looking at it. Everything else had been cash he would have spent on something else if it hadn't been for the house: something silly, probably, and certainly not with all the solid permanence of a home for his wife and children, forever. As for the mortgage, that was the bank's worry, not his; they were going to get 5 per cent for their worrying, and if they were satisfied, so was he. Interest would be $900 the first year, but it would go down as he amortized his loan, and that was pretty piffling when you considered it as the rent on a twelve-room house. . . .

"I wonder why the steam shovel isn't working," said Mrs. Blandings. It had been over an hour now since they had last heard its snortings come drifting down the hill.

"He's been at it five hours," said Mr. Blandings, speaking of the villainous-looking man who had turned out to be the excavating subcontractor. "Let's see what things look like."

Hand in hand, the Blandingses, like happy children, climbed the hill—*their* hill, as Mrs. Blandings put it. On the summit Mr. Attilio Campobasso's steam shovel rested unevenly on its treads. From the south portion of the staked-out ground it had dug a hole, gratifyingly sharp, that went down six feet at the edges. Toward the north end the excavation was ragged and uneven, and while the shovel operator sat in his cab and smoked, three men with hand shovels were at work with the earth. The noise that came forth from their instruments was the same sort of noise you heard in the morning when a light fall of snow was being scraped from the city pavement. As they worked, Mr. and Mrs. Blandings could see growing the outlines of what appeared to be a mammoth, ossified whale.

"Looka that," said Mr. Campobasso, in disgusted elation.

"Boulder?" asked Mr. Blandings.

"Boulder!" said Mr. Campobasso, uttering an unmusical laugh. "Atsa no boulder. Atsa *ledge.* We go home now, come back next week, start blasting, keep on blasting plenty, yes *sir.* One thing you never got to worry your house settle any, sitting on granite, no *sir.*"

When he got back to his fireside, Mr. Blandings looked up Mr. Retch's estimates on excavation. The job was to be done for $500 flat, except for the proviso, "If rock is encountered, removal by blasting at $0.24 per cubic foot." It had not seemed much, but the nature of cubic equations had once before eluded Mr. Blandings. This time he put pencil to paper to discover that an excavation sixty feet long, twenty-eight feet wide, and six feet deep contains 10,080 cubic feet.

Mr. Blandings was just beginning to wonder what sizable fraction of this figure should be multiplied by $0.24 when the phone rang. With a leaden hand, Mr. Blandings placed the receiver at an ear that did not wish to hear. Bill Cole's voice greeted him with what Mr. Blandings instantly knew to be false cheer.

"I don't want you to fly off the handle, Jim," Bill's voice said, "but there's a little hitch."

"What kind of a hitch?" Mr. Blandings heard himself ask.

"I've just been talking to Barratry, Lynch's man, Joe Pugh, who's doing your legal job for the bank," said Bill Cole, becoming almost aggressively hearty.

"And so what?" said Mr. Blandings.

"There's a flaw in the title," said Mr. Blandings' attorney.

Excerpts from Mrs. Blandings's diary:

OCTOBER 7

Jim's cold not any better. He has spent a miserable three days in bed, with more hot toddies than I think warranted. Mr. Campobasso's blasting foreman wanted to know if we had liability insurance: a sharp piece of rock apparently fell on one of old Mr. Lange's chickens half a mile down the road, and he was very nasty about it. Blasting probably to go on another two weeks, at least. Mr. C's foreman says the way the ledge is tilted (right?) almost straight up makes it impossible to get rock out even with picks and shovels even after the blast has gone off. Nervous headache.

OCTOBER 10

I don't understand trouble over the title, and I don't think Bill Cole does either. The title lawyers say they have nothing to show them that Mr. Halleck was entitled to act as the administrator of *his father's estate*, from which it seems we bought, not from Mr. Halleck himself. Mr. Dolliver at First National Bank was *gleeful* when he bumped into me this morning, said anybody but a dumb city bank would know that of course Ephemus was his father's administrator, and had always "been so accepted" since the old man died in 1922. It would all never have happened if we'd done business with him, he said. Blatherskite! The law firm wants Mr. Halleck to post a $10,000 bond to guarantee his "performance as administrator," before we get our loan, but he won't. He doesn't speak to us anymore when we meet him, I don't know why.

OCTOBER 22

Mr. Retch asked for some money today, and I guess he's entitled to it. He got Campobasso to compromise his blasting bill at a flat $1,900! A nasty man, if I ever saw one. Jim put up most of his Amalgamated stock to borrow $15,000 to tide us over until the bank loan comes through. We have to get something called a "waiver of lien" from every one of Mr. Retch's subcontractors before the bank gives us a penny, and there must be at least twenty of them! The subcontractors have to promise the bank they won't sue us if we don't pay their bills. Silly! Why shouldn't they?

NOVEMBER 4

It *would* freeze in November so hard the concrete man can't pour any forms for the cellar walls! No work on the house for the last eight days at all, but a man came around and wanted to sell us a tennis court this afternoon. There were also three tree salesmen on the premises. I didn't know trees *had* salesmen.

NOVEMBER 9

The men started pouring concrete for the cellar walls today, but when Mr. Simms saw what they were doing he stopped them and tried to get Mr. Retch on the phone. They were putting hardly any cement in with the sand and gravel at all—a fine situation! Suppose Mr. Simms hadn't just happened to come around. Mr. Retch was in Maryland on another job. A load of shingles came today but they're not the right kind. We won't need any shingles until spring, anyway at this rate, if then.

NOVEMBER 15

What are we going to do with all the rock that Campobasso man excavated for the cellar? Nobody will take any responsibility for it;

even Mr. Simms just shrugs his shoulders and changes the subject. But there it is, a mountain of it, right in front of where the front door is supposed to be. I *insist* it be carted away. Mr. Retch says there is nothing about it in the contract, and I must say I couldn't find anything myself.

NOVEMBER 20

The woodwork is going up! I guess that's the wrong word for it, but there are a lot of square poles sticking up in the air from the concrete, and I never heard so much sawing and hammering. There must have been ten men working all around everything today.

NOVEMBER 25

I'm just sick about the whole house! The framing (right word!) is finished for the wing and it is all *miles too high*! I thought we were getting a sweet modest house that hugged the hills close in its arms, and here instead is something that looks like a skyscraper! It just goes up and up. Mr. Simms was very short when I telephoned him about it and ended up by suggesting that I "take a pill or something." I just know that *somebody* is making a *terrible* mistake. Jim very sullen.

NOVEMBER 27

Glory be! Bill Cole says the bank and its lawyers are ready for "the closing." This means now we get our money at last. All Jim has to do is give the law firm $500 "in escrow" in case anything should go wrong with those wretched "waivers of lien" from those filthy subcontractors. Jim turned purple at the idea of giving Barratry, Lynch another $500, but he wrote out a check just the same. Five toilets arrived today and they're lying all around the field. It looked *unspeakably* vulgar!

NOVEMBER 28

I must admit I was wrong about the wing framing being too high. Now that all the framing is up, it all looks very nice. Mr. Retch was a changed man today, after he got a check. He swears he will get the house "closed in" before the snow flies, and that everything is going to go "like clockwork" from now on.

The men nailed a little tree to the top of the roof this noon. Then they knocked off and came down to our cottage and stood around until one of them hinted that when the evergreen went up on the ridgepole, it was up to the owner to stand a round of drinks for all the workmen. Jim didn't seem to think much of this idea at first, but it's remarkable how well he fell in with it after the first twenty minutes. To bed very late.

The winter was slowly closing in on Bald Mountain. The house as it stood now reminded Mr. Blandings of a flayed elephant: the brick veneer ended in different courses at different places; above it, the diagonal sheathing of yellow pine, crusty with resin and punctured with knotholes, rose to the eaves. The roof was a wavy expanse of tar paper, dotted with shiny metal disks. The house's appearance was the nakedness of muscle, stripped of skin and fat.

Mr. Blandings did not like the looks of the sheathing lumber; he felt that he could either speak of it and make a fool of himself or stay silent and be bilked. He chose the latter of course, not as the least painful but merely as the least conspicuous. He was dismayed by the ragged lopsidedness of the holes where someday windows were supposed to be. But the worst thing, the thing so bad that neither Mr. nor Mrs. Blandings dared speak of such a matter as blame, was the microscopic size of the rooms—of the spaces, that is, where studding indicated some sort of partition in the future. There were five times as many spaces as the Blandingses could in any way account for, but even the largest, in the Blandings's eyes, was a cubicle. "Is this the *living* room?" Mrs. Blandings had wailed from amidst a rectangular grove of two-by-fours. Mr. Blandings merely sat down on a nail keg and stared through a hole in the wall. He no longer had enough energy to appear dejected. "I guess so," he said. "Mr. Simms says a room always looks like this before the partitions go up and the furniture goes in."

"Where would we have space for any furniture?" sobbed Mrs. Blandings.

"Where would we have money for any furniture?" asked Mr. Blandings.

All work on the house had now come to a stop. The window casements had not come.

The truck had left the factory and would be on the site tomorrow. No, the truck had not left, but that was immaterial: the windows had been shipped by freight, and the car must have been lost by some negligent waybill clerk. No, the windows would be shipped by truck *when* they were ready, which would not be for another three weeks. No, the windows must be there and mislaid by the contractor. No, an order for the windows had never been received, but "we would give your valued customer promptest attention should we be so favored."

Mr. Blandings actually felt a sense of triumph when, after a while, roughly half of the windows arrived and the truckmen dumped them in a disorderly pile in the roadway. Several days later two window installers arrived, very drunk, looked at the windows, and roamed away again, never to return. Mr. Blandings ventured to inquire of Mr. Retch why some work could not go forward, even in the absence of the remaining windows or any crew to install them. This inquiry struck Mr. Retch as in the most flagrant bad taste. Mr. Retch was himself in a pet. The window company, as the price of signing its waiver of lien, had stuck Mr. Retch for cash on the barrelhead and was now letting him whistle. In coarse tones he explained to Mr. Blandings that *(a)* the mason subcontractor was stalled since he could not complete his brick courses around the missing frames, all of which were for the first floor; *(b)* the heating subcontractor could make no further progress until the house was closed in; *(c)* the tiler hired for the bathrooms could affix no tile; *(d)* not even the subfloors could be laid when the house was still open to rain and snow; *(e)* it was manifest that plastering could never be started now until spring, if at all, and *(f)* the electrical subcontractor's workmen refused to run any more BX cable around wet joists and columns. He ended by confidently predicting that the whole house would shortly burn down from one of the half-dozen temporary oilstoves the workmen insisted on using to keep their hands warm enough to hold a hammer, and whose fault would the whole blinking business be then?

Suddenly, enough windows arrived to build a biscuit factory.

Out of an infinite variety of rectangular steel shapes Mr. Retch selected those frames that seemed to accord roughly with the dimensions on Mr. Simms's plans, and sought to get the window company to send back a crew of window installers, preferably sober enough to put the windows into the sheathing holes right side up. The window company called Mr. Blandings to say that his contractor had been grossly abusive over the telephone, that in twenty years' experience they had never been treated with such inhumanity by such a tin-pot contractor, and that Mr. Blandings would be held responsible for the fact that the contractor had given the window company a bad check for $1,407.56. When Mr. Blandings relayed this intelligence to Mr. Retch, Mr. Retch produced a canceled check to the order of the window company and told Mr. Blandings that in thirty years' experience in the construction trades this was the first time an owner had ever accused him of fraud, and if he'd like to take his glasses off they could settle it outside, and if Mr. Retch lost he would build the rest of Mr. Blandings's house at his own expense. Mrs. Blandings's diary for the year ended with a notation, dated December 27, that she was taking the children to Sarasota for the winter, and did not mention the house at all. Of Mr. Blandings she merely recorded that he was "better."

Letter from Mr. J. H. Blandings to Mr. John Retch:

FEBRUARY 5

Dear Retch:

It is some time since my wife or I have visited the house, and I can only hope that the work is progressing as fast as the receipt of money requisitions from you seems to indicate. We will hope to see things again as soon as the weather moderates.

Meanwhile, I am considerably disturbed by the number of "extras" that are accumulating on your bills. So far as my wife and I are aware, we have authorized only two changes from the original plans: the depth of the reveal at the front door was altered by Mr. Simms with our approval, and we also authorized relocation and redesign of the concrete cellar steps after Mrs. Blandings fell down them. Except for these items, which seem to total $577.60, God knows why, I am at a loss to understand the multitude of other matters being billed to me, or in most cases what the items specified refer to at all. I herewith quote and comment on the following from your latest requisition:

"Redesign of doors No. 102, 107, 108, 112 . . . . $120.00"
(Mr. Simms tells me that there was no redesign on any doors on the job whatsoever.)

"New installation of well casing. . . . . $96.50"
(If, according to your own explanation, the well casing installed by Mr. John Tesavis on his contract with me was cracked by the blasting done by your excavating subcontractor, I fail to see why I should bear replacement cost.)

"Substitution of 220-volt main switch panel in cellar . . . . $139.89"
(What is the meaning of this? It is the eighth major extra so far on the electrical subcontract. Why was a 220-volt switch panel "substituted" for something else?)

"Furring down ceiling for kitchen cabinets. . . . . $102.00"
(Insofar as I understand this charge, I consider it outrageous. You must have known the dimensions of the kitchen cabinets from the

beginning; if you did not, then either you or Mr. Simms appear guilty of negligence. But you bill *me* just the same.)

"Mortising five butts . . . . *$1.68"*
(This refers to something I do not understand and the charge is small—but apparently whenever a carpenter picks up an extra chisel it costs me extra money.)

"Furnishing and installing one Zuz-Zuz Water Soft-N-R . . . . . *$365.50"*
(I will not have any such piece of equipment in my house. Who authorized it? I will not pay this charge, nor any subsequent extra for "Removal of Zuz-Zuz Water Soft-N-R.")

"Time and overtime relocating oil burner . . . . *$215.00"*
(The oil burner was never relocated; it is supposed to be where it is marked on the plans. If your heating contractor thought it would be a good idea to relocate it in the living room, I have no doubt I will have to endure it there, but the cost of this change should be borne by whomever it gave pleasure to make it.)

All this totals to $1,040.57—a not inconsiderable expenditure. I shall expect to hear from you directly.

From Mr. John Retch to Mr. J. H. Blandings:

". . . only time in our experience when an owner has taken any such position. We have passed up many extra items without bill, because we have wanted you to be satisfied all along the line. Pardon our suggestion that you and Mrs. Blandings ought to get together, but furring of kitchen ceiling was discussed with her and she said cabinets must fit exactly 'at all costs.' We could have left in the smaller electrical switch panel specified by the architect against advice of electrician and leave resulting fire hazard up to you, but preferred to take the honest course and bill you in the open. The Zuz-Zuz people make a fine water softener, and we were looking out for your interests in not letting the unusually corrosive water from your well ruin your fine boilers and water lines. We discussed this with Mr. Simms when we could not get ahold of you and he said he would explain, which it appears he has not. As to the oil burner . . ."

From Mr. J. H. Blandings to Mr. John Retch:

". . . and I enclose a check for $1,040.57 but will positively not be responsible for any further . . ."

• • •

When Mr. and Mrs. Blandings resumed their visits to Bald Mountain it was in the flowering spring. They saw the house, and a cry escaped them. It was a cry of joy. There it stood in its gleaming whiteness, more lovely than the fairest drawings that ever Mr. Simms had drawn. The house seemed to wait them as a girl would wait with downcast eyes for her lover's first shy kiss.

The entrance to the citadel was not accomplished with ease; the house appeared, on closer examination, to be more like a full-rigged ship floating placidly on a sea of mud where the new grading had been liquefied by the warm rains. But once across this ten-foot moat, the Blandingses removed their ruined shoes and stood with reverence upon their gleaming oaken floors . . .

Of course, there were little misfortunes here and there. The fireplace molding was nothing like what Mrs. Blandings had had in her mind's eye all along, from somewhere. The elaborate and "very advanced" fluorescent lighting in the dining room was later discovered to turn a healthy roast of beef into a purple mass of putrescence on the dining table, and the hum of the ballasts hidden in the lighting cove was so distracting to conversation that the whole installation was eventually removed and replaced by the more conventional type of lamp invented by Thomas Alva Edison in 1879. "We have never recommended fluorescent equipment for rooms of low noise-level," the Nadir Electric Supply Co. wrote tartly in answer to Mr. Blandings's protest. For the thousandth time Mr. Blandings moaned his refrain: "Why didn't anybody tell me?"

One major boner by the otherwise flawless Mr. Simms was also upsetting: in changing the location of the electric hot-water heater on the plans one hot summer night he had relocated the waterlines but forgotten to specify electrical connections to the new position, and neither owner, architect, builder, plumber, electrical subcontractor, nor any other mortal soul, had discovered the oversight until the day the Blandingses moved in and turned on their first tap. Most of the cellar wiring had to be ripped out to permit the new stretch of heavy power cable to run from the main busses to the heater, and Mr. Simms had insisted on paying the $275 for this item himself. There was, too, the window hardware, which would not work, and one bathroom floor to which the linoleum would not adhere even under Gestapo-like methods of attack. All the doors stuck except those that would not latch at all.

But the Blandingses had built a good house—a very fine house indeed. Its process of morphology might, for a moment, be noted. The ovum had been the farmhouse on which $10,000 was to be spent for "restoration."

The larva was the $15,000 house that Mr. Simms began to design. The pupal stage was reached when Mr. Retch began to build something for a contract price of $26,991.17. The eventually emerged home, in full adult form, bore (as in all organic processes) little resemblance to its embryo, either to the aesthete's or to the cost accountant's eye. Only Mr. Blandings *really* knows how much he spent on Bald Mountain, compared with the $20,000 concept for land and building with which he began, but no one would go wrong if he took something like $51,000 as a basic figure.

The Christmas House Number of *House & Home (Combined with The Home Lovely)* lay before Mr. Savington Funkhauser, A.I.A., who was wondering why, at the end of a hard day at the drafting board, he had opened it at all. "Our problem was to create a modern home in a community dominated by fine old colonial farmhouses that had stood the test of revolutionary days and before," he read, "and to achieve a youthful spirit without doing violence to the tradition of those stout forebears of ours whose indomitable strivings have been the heritage of . . ."

"Spittle," said Mr. Funkhauser in a toneless voice, aloud. He looked for a title at the top of the page to tell him what he was reading. In thin swash lettering he saw *"Home Lovely's* December House-of-the-Month is Tribute to Taste and Ingenuity with Materials Old and New." There seemed here no conveyance of information whatsoever, and Mr. Funkhauser would have tossed the magazine aside but could not rouse himself enough.

"It was a challenge to our ingenuity," he read on in a sort of mild hypnosis, "but my husband and I tackled the difficulties with a will, and out of a combination of budgeted planning, a determination to keep our primary objectives ever before us, and the closest and most friendly three-way cooperation between architect, owner, and builder, we were able to achieve our aims with a minimum of misunderstandings and additional items of expense that occasionally mar the joys of building that *sine qua non* of all normal couples' ambitions, the Home of One's Own."

"Whose bilge *is* this?" Mr. Funkhauser asked of the fireplace. On the instant, a picture caption answered him: "Mrs. J. Holocoup Blandings, whose delightful mountain dwelling is this month's *Home Lovely* choice as . . ."

Mr. Funkhauser's right arm moved suddenly, and the Christmas House Number described a graceful arc, disappearing into the chromium-bound cylinder of Nutasote that served Mr. Funkhauser as a waste receiver. A moment later the young architect fished it out again, and turned back to the assistant editor's interview with "the chic and attractive Mrs. Blandings, mistress of 'Surrogate Acres.'" For some five wordless minutes he studied the dim halftones and spidery line cuts arranged ingeniously askew on the chalky paper. Suddenly he came on something familiar, and a flush darkened his face. He muttered for a moment and then, taking pen and paper, he commenced a letter:

"Dear Mr. Blandings," he wrote. "In the December issue of *House & Home* I notice, in the midst of the display of your new residence and in an interview that purports to be with your wife, a reference that says, 'Once the impracticalities of an earlier designer had been discarded as wholly unsuitable . . .' I would scarcely have credited this to be a reference to myself and some work I did for you from which I later withdrew, were it not that on the following page an illustration labeled 'Discarded Study' is a manifest caricature of a rendering I submitted to you on June 3, 1938. Taken in conjunction, the sentence and drawing offer to my professional standing an affront and damage that I cannot afford to let pass unnoticed. I am instructing my attorneys, Messrs. Barratry, Lynch & Replevin, to communicate with you regarding possible steps toward redress which . . ."

Miles away, on Bald Mountain, in the midst of Surrogate Acres, beneath an uninsulated composition roof that creaked slightly under the growing snow load of an early winter storm, Mr. Blandings stirred uneasily in his sleep. He was dreaming that his house was on fire.

Cyclists' Raid

Frank Rooney

Joel Bleeker, owner and operator of the Pendelton Hotel, was adjusting the old redwood clock in the lobby when he heard the sound of the motors. At first he thought it might be one of those four-engine planes on the flights from Los Angeles to San Francisco which occasionally got far enough off course to be heard in the valley. And for a moment, braced against the steadily approaching vibrations of the sound, he had the fantastic notion that the plane was going to strike the hotel. He even glanced at his daughter, Cathy, standing a few feet to his right and staring curiously at the street.

Then, with his fingers still on the hour hand of the clock, he realized that the sound was not something coming down from the air but the high, sputtering racket of many vehicles moving along the ground. Cathy, and Bert Timmons, who owned one of the two drugstores in the town, went out onto the veranda, but Bleeker stayed by the clock, consulting the railroad watch he pulled from his vest pocket and moving the hour hand on the clock forward a minute and a half. He stepped back deliberately, shut the glass case, and looked at the huge brass numbers and the two ornate brass pointers. It was eight minutes after seven, approximately twenty-two minutes until sundown. He put the railroad watch back in his pocket and walked slowly and incuriously through the open doors of the lobby. He was methodical and orderly, and the small things he did every day—like setting the clock—were important to him. He was not to be hurried—especially by something as elusively irritating as a sound, however unusual.

There were only three people on the veranda when Bleeker came out of the lobby—his daughter Cathy, Timmons, and Francis LaSalle, co-owner of LaSalle and Fleet, Hardware. They stood together quietly, looking, without appearing to stare, at a long stern column of red motorcycles coming from the south, filling the single main street of the town with the noise of a multitude of pistons and the crackling of exhaust pipes. They could see now that the column was led by a single white motorcycle which, when it came abreast of the hotel, turned abruptly right and stopped. They saw, too, that the column, without seeming to slow down or to execute any elaborate movement, had divided itself into two single files. At the approximate second, having received a signal from their leader, they also turned right and stopped.

The whole flanking action, singularly neat and quite like the various vehicular formations he remembered in the army, was distasteful to Bleeker. It recalled a little too readily his tenure as a lieutenant colonel overseas in England, France, and finally Germany.

"Mr. Bleeker?"

Bleeker realized the whole troop—no one in the town either then or after that night was ever agreed on the exact number of men in the troop—had dismounted and that the leader was addressing him.

"I'm Bleeker." Although he hadn't intended to, he stepped forward when he spoke, much as he had stepped forward in the years when he commanded a battalion.

"I'm Gar Simpson and this is Troop B of the Angeleno Motorcycle Club," the leader said. He was a tall, spare man, and his voice was coldly courteous to the point of mockery. "We expect to bivouac outside your town tonight and we wondered if we might use the facilities of your hotel. Of course, sir, we'll pay."

"There's a washroom downstairs. If you can put up with that—"

"That will be fine, sir. Is the dining room still open?"

"It is."

"Could you take care of twenty men?"

"What about the others?"

"They can be accommodated elsewhere, sir."

Simpson saluted casually and, turning to the men assembled stiffly in front of the hotel, issued a few quiet orders. Quickly and efficiently, the men in the troop parked their motorcycles at the curb. About a third of the group detached itself and came deferentially but steadily up the hotel steps. They passed Bleeker who found himself maneuvered aside and went into the lobby. As they passed him, Bleeker could see the slight covert movement of their faces—though not their eyes, which were covered by large green goggles—toward his daughter Cathy. Bleeker frowned after them but before he could think of anything to say, Simpson, standing at his left, touched his arm.

"I've divided the others into two groups," he said quietly. "One group will eat at the diner and the other at the Desert Hotel."

"Very good," Bleeker said. "You evidently know the town like a book. The people, too. Have you ever been here before?"

"We have a map of all the towns in this part of California, sir. And of course we know the names of all the principal hotels and their proprietors. Personally, I could use a drink. Would you join me?"

"After you," Bleeker said.

He stood watching Simpson stride into the lobby and without any hesitation go directly to the bar. Then he turned to Cathy, seeing Timmons and LaSalle lounging on the railing behind her, their faces already indistinct in the plummeting California twilight.

"You go help in the kitchen, Cathy," Bleeker said. "I think it'd be better if you didn't wait on tables."

"I wonder what they look like behind those goggles," Cathy said.

"Like anybody else," Timmons said. He was about thirty, somewhat coarse and intolerant and a little embarrassed at being in love with a girl as young as Cathy. "Where did you think they came from? Mars?"

"What did they say the name of their club was?" Cathy said.

"Angeleno," LaSalle said.

"They must be from Los Angeles. Heigh-ho. Shall I wear my very best gingham, citizen colonel?"

"Remember now—you stay in the kitchen," Bleeker said.

He watched her walk into the lobby, a tall slender girl of seventeen, pretty and enigmatic, with something of the brittle independence of her mother. Bleeker remembered suddenly, although he tried not to, the way her mother had walked away from him that frosty January morning two years ago saying, "I'm going for a ride." And then the two-day search in the mountains after the horse had come back alone and the finding of her body—the neck broken—in the stream at the foot of the cliff. During the war he had never really believed that he would live to get back to Cathy's mother, and after the war he hadn't really believed he would be separated from her—not again—not twice in so short a time.

Shaking his head—as if by that motion he could shed his memories as easily as a dog sheds water—Bleeker went in to join Gar Simpson who was sitting at a table in the barroom. Simpson stood politely when Bleeker took the opposite chair.

"How long do you fellows plan to stay?" Bleeker asked. He took the first sip of his drink, looked up, and stared at Simpson.

"Tonight and tomorrow morning," Simpson said.

Like all the others, he was dressed in a brown windbreaker, khaki shirt, khaki pants, and, as Bleeker had previously observed, wore dark calf-length boots. A cloth and leather helmet lay on the table beside Simpson's drink, but he hadn't removed his flat green goggles, an accouterment giving him and the men in his troop the appearance of some tropical tribe with enormous semiprecious eyes, lidless and immovable. That was Bleeker's first impression and, absurd as it was, it didn't seem an exaggeration of fancy but of truth.

"Where do you go after this?"

"North." Simpson took a rolled map from a binocular case slung over his shoulder and spread it on the table. "Roughly we're following the arc of an ellipse with its southern tip based on Los Angeles and its northern end touching Fresno."

"Pretty ambitious for a motorcycle club."

"We have a month," Simpson said. "This is our first week, but we're in no hurry and we're out to see plenty of country."

"What are you interested in mainly?"

"Roads. Naturally, being a motorcycle club—you'd be surprised at the rate we're expanding—we'd like to have as much of California as possible opened up to us."

"I see."

"Keeps the boys fit, too. The youth of America. Our hope for the future." Simpson pulled sternly at his drink, and Bleeker had the impression that Simpson was repressing, openly, and with pride, a vast sparkling ecstasy.

Bleeker sat and watched the young men in the troop file upstairs from the public washroom and stroll casually but nevertheless with discipline into the dining room. They had removed their helmets and strapped them to their belts, each helmet in a prescribed position to the left of the belt-buckle, but—like Simpson—they had retained their goggles. Bleeker wondered if they ever removed the goggles long enough to wash under them and, if they did, what the flesh under them looked like.

"I think I'd better help out at the tables," Bleeker said. He stood up, and Simpson stood with him. "You say you're from Troop B? Is that right?"

"Correct. We're forming Troop G now. Someday—"

"You'll be up to Z," Bleeker said.

"And not only in California."

"Where else for instance?"

"Nevada—Arizona—Colorado—Wyoming."

Simpson smiled, and Bleeker, turning away from him abruptly, went into the dining room where he began to help the two waitresses at the tables. He filled water glasses, set out extra forks, and brought steins of beer from the bar. As he served the troop, their polite thank you's, ornate and insincere, irritated him. It reminded him of tricks taught to animals, the animals only being allowed to perform under certain obvious conditions of security. And he didn't like the cool way they stared at the two waitresses, both older women and fixtures in the town, and then leaned their heads together as if every individual thought had to be pooled and divided equally among them. He admitted, after some covert study, that the twenty men were really only variations of one, the variations, with few exceptions, being too subtle for him to recognize and differentiate. It was the goggles, he decided, covering that part of the face which is most noteworthy and most needful for identification—the eyes and the mask around the eyes.

Bleeker went into the kitchen, pretending to help but really to be near Cathy. The protective father, he thought ironically, watching his daughter cut pie and lay the various colored wedges on the white blue-bordered plates.

"Well, Daddy, what's the verdict?" Cathy looked extremely grave, but he could see that she was amused.

"They're a fine body of men."

"Uh-huh. Have you called the police yet?"

He laughed. "It's a good thing you don't play poker."

"Child's play." She slid the last piece of blueberry pie on a plate. "I saw you through the door. You looked like you were ready to crack the Siegfried line—singlehanded."

"That man Simpson."

"What about him?"

"Why don't you go upstairs and read a book or something?"

"Now, Daddy—you're the only professional here. They're just acting like little tin soldiers out on a spree."

"I wish to God they were made of tin."

"All right. I'll keep away from them. I promise." She made a gesture of crossing her throat with the thin edge of a knife. He leaned over and kissed her forehead, his hand feeling awkward and stern on her back.

After dinner the troop went into the bar, moving with a strange co-ordinated fluency that was both casual and military, and sat jealously together in one corner of the room. Bleeker served them pitchers of beer, and for the most part they talked quietly together, Simpson at their center, their voices guarded and urgent as if they possessed information which couldn't be disseminated safely among the public.

Bleeker left them after a while and went upstairs to his daughter's room. He wasn't used to being severe with Cathy and he was a little embarrassed by what he had said to her in the kitchen. She was turning the collars of some of his old shirts, using a portable sewing machine he had bought her as a present on her last birthday. As he came in, she held one of the shirts comically to the floor lamp, and he could see how thin and transparent the material was. Her mother's economy in small things, almost absurd when compared to her limitless generosity in matters of importance, had been one of the family jokes. It gave him an extraordinary sense of pleasure, so pure it was like a sudden inhalation of oxygen, to see that his daughter had not only inherited this tradition but had considered it meaningful enough to carry on. He went down the hall to his own room without saying anything further to her. Cathy was what he himself was in terms which could mean absolutely nothing to anyone else.

He had been in his room for perhaps an hour, working on the hotel accounts and thinking obliquely of the man Simpson, when he heard, faintly and apparently coming from no one direction, the sound of singing. He got up and walked to the windows overlooking the street. Standing there, he thought he could fix the sound farther up the block toward Cunningham's bar. Except for something harsh and mature in the voices, it was the kind of singing that might be heard around a Boy Scout campfire, more rhythmic than melodic and more stirring than tuneful. And then he could hear it almost under his feet, coming out of the hotel lobby and making three or four people on the street turn and smile foolishly toward the doors of the veranda.

Oppressed by something sternly joyous in the voices, Bleeker went downstairs to the bar, hearing, as he approached, the singing become louder and fuller. Outside of Simpson and the twenty men in the troop there were only three townsmen—including LaSalle—in the bar. Simpson, seeing Bleeker in the door, got up and walked over to him, moving him out into the lobby where they could talk.

"I hope the boys aren't disturbing you," he said.

"It's early," Bleeker said.

"In an organization as large and selective as ours it's absolutely necessary to insist on a measure of discipline. And it's equally necessary to allow a certain amount of relaxation."

"The key word is selective, I suppose."

"We have our standards," Simpson said primly.

"May I ask you what the hell your standards are?"

Simpson smiled. "I don't quite understand your irritation, Mr. Bleeker."

"This is an all-year-round thing, isn't it? This club of yours?"

"Yes."

"And you have an all-year-round job with the club?"

"Of course."

"That's my objection, Simpson. Briefly and simply stated, what you're running is a private army." Bleeker tapped the case slung over Simpson's shoulder. "Complete with maps, all sorts of local information, and of course a lobby in Sacramento."

"For a man who has traveled as widely as you have, Mr. Bleeker, you display an uncommon talent for exaggeration."

"As long as you behave yourselves I don't care what you do. This is a small town and we don't have many means of entertainment. We go to bed at a decent hour and I suggest you take that into consideration. However, have your fun. Nobody here has any objections to that."

"And of course we spend our money."

"Yes," Bleeker said. "You spend your money."

He walked away from Simpson and went out onto the veranda. The singing was now both in front and in back of him. Bleeker stood for a moment on the top steps of the veranda looking at the moon, hung like a slightly soiled but luminous pennant in the sky. He was embarrassed by his outburst to Simpson and he couldn't think why he had said such things. Private army. Perhaps, as Simpson had said, he was exaggerating. He was a small-town man and he had always hated the way men surrendered their individuality to attain perfection as a unit. It had been necessary during the war but it wasn't necessary now. Kid stuff—with an element of growing pains.

He walked down the steps and went up the sidewalk toward Cunningham's bar. They were singing there, too, and he stood outside the big plate-glass window peering in at them and listening to the harsh, pounding voices colored here and there with the sentimentalism of strong beer. Without thinking further he went into the bar. It was dim and cool and alien to his eyes, and at first he didn't notice the boy sitting by himself in a booth near the front. When he did, he was surprised—more than surprised, shocked—to see that the boy wasn't wearing his goggles but had placed them on the table by a bottle of Coca-Cola. Impulsively, he walked over to the booth and sat across from the boy.

"This seat taken?"

He had to shout over the noise of the singing. The boy leaned forward over the table and smiled.

"Hope we're not disturbing you."

Bleeker caught the word "disturbing" and shook his head negatively. He pointed to his mouth, then to the boy and to the rest of the group. The boy, too, shook his head. Bleeker could see that he was young, possibly twenty-five, and that he had dark straight hair cut short and parted neatly at the side. The face was square but delicate, the nose short, the mouth wide. The best thing about the boy, Bleeker decided, were his eyes, brown, perhaps, or dark gray, set in two distorted ovals of white flesh which contrasted sharply with the heavily tanned skin on the cheeks, forehead and jaws. With his goggles on he would have looked like the rest. Without them he was a pleasant young man, altogether human and approachable.

Bleeker pointed to the Coca-Cola bottle. "You're not drinking."

"Beer makes me sick."

Bleeker got the word "beer" and the humorous ulping motion the boy made. They sat exchanging words and sometimes phrases, illustrated always with a series of clumsy, groping gestures until the singing became less coherent and spirited and ended finally in a few isolated coughs. The men in the troop were moving about individually now, some leaning over the bar and talking in hoarse whispers to the bartender, others walking unsteadily from group to group and detaching themselves immediately to go over to another group, the groups, usually two or three men, constantly edging away from themselves and colliding with and being held briefly by others. Some simply stood in the center of the room and brayed dolorously at the ceiling.

Several of the troop walked out of the bar, and Bleeker could see them standing on the wide sidewalk looking up and down the street—as contemptuous of one another's company as they had been glad of it earlier. Or not so much contemptuous as unwilling to be coerced too easily by any authority outside themselves. Bleeker smiled as he thought of Simpson and the man's talk of discipline.

"They're looking for women," the boy said.

Bleeker had forgotten the boy temporarily, and the sudden words spoken in a normal voice startled and confused him. He thought quickly of Cathy—but then Cathy was safe in her room—probably in bed. He took the watch from his vest pocket and looked at it carefully.

"Five minutes after ten," he said.

"Why do they do that?" the boy demanded. "Why do they have to be so damned indecent about things like that? They haven't got the nerve to do anything but stare at waitresses. And then they get a few beers in them and go around pinching and slapping—they—"

Bleeker shivered with embarrassment. He was looking directly into the boy's eyes and seeing the color run under the tears and the jerky pinching movement of the lids as against something injurious and baleful. It was an emotion too rawly infantile to be seen without being hurt by it, and he felt both pity and contempt for a man who would allow himself to display such a feeling—without any provocation—so nakedly to a stranger.

"Sorry," the boy said.

He picked up the green goggles and fitted them awkwardly over his eyes. Bleeker stood up and looked toward the center of the room. Several of the men turned their eyes and then moved their heads away without seeming to notice the boy in the booth. Bleeker understood them. This was the one who could be approached. The reason for that was clear, too. He didn't belong. Why and wherefore he would probably never know.

He walked out of the bar and started down the street toward the hotel.

The night was clear and cool and smelled faintly of the desert, of sand, of heated rock, of the sweetly-sour plants growing without water and even of the sun which burned itself into the earth and never completely withdrew. There were only a few townsmen on the sidewalk wandering up and down, lured by the presence of something unusual in the town and masking, Bleeker thought, a ruthless and menacing curiosity behind a tolerant grin. He shrugged his shoulders distastefully. He was like a cat staring into a shadow the shape of its fears.

He was no more than a hundred feet from the hotel when he heard—or thought he heard—the sound of automatic firing. It was a well-remembered sound but always new and frightening.

Then he saw the motorcycle moving down the middle of the street, the exhaust sputtering loudly against the human resonance of laughter, catcalls, and epithets. He exhaled gently, the pain in his lungs subsiding with his breath. Another motorcycle speeded after the first, and he could see four or five machines being wheeled out and the figures of their riders leaping into the air and bringing their weight down on the starting pedals. He was aware, too, that the lead motorcycles, having traversed the length of the street, had turned and were speeding back to the hotel. He had the sensation of moving—even when he stood still—in relation to the objects heading toward each other. He heard the high unendurable sound of metal squeezing metal and saw the front wheel of a motorcycle twist and wobble and its rider roll along the asphalt toward the gutter where he sat up finally and moved his goggled head feebly from side to side.

As Bleeker looked around him, he saw the third group of men which had divided earlier from the other two coming out of the bar across the street from Cunningham's, waving their arms in recognizable motions of cheering. The boy who had been thrown from the motorcycle vomited quietly into the gutter. Bleeker walked very fast toward the hotel. When he reached the top step of the veranda, he was caught and jostled by some five or six cyclists running out of the lobby, one of whom fell and was kicked rudely down the steps. Bleeker staggered against one of the pillars and broke a fingernail catching it. He stood there for a moment, fighting his temper, and then went into the lobby.

A table had been overthrown and lay on its top, its wooden legs stiffly and foolishly exposed, its magazines scattered around it, some with their pages spread face down so that the bindings rose along the back. He stepped on glass and realized one of the panels in the lobby door had been smashed. One of the troop walked stupidly out of the bar, his body sagging against the impetus propelling him forward until without actually falling he lay stretched on the floor, beer gushing from his mouth and nose and making a green and yellow pool before it sank into the carpet.

As Bleeker walked toward the bar, thinking of Simpson and of what he could say to him, he saw two men going up the stairs toward the second floor. He ran over to intercept them. Recognizing the authority in his voice, they came obediently down the stairs and walked across the lobby to the veranda, one of them saying over his shoulder, "Okay, Pop, okay—keep your lid on." The smiles they exchanged enraged him. After they were out of sight, he ran swiftly up the stairs, panting a little, and along the hall to his daughter's room.

It was quiet and there was no strip of light beneath the door. He stood listening for a moment with his ear to the panels and then turned back toward the stairs.

A man or boy, any of twenty or forty or sixty identical figures, goggled and in khaki, came around the corner of the second-floor corridor and put his hand on the knob of the door nearest the stairs. He squeezed the knob gently and then moved on to the next door, apparently unaware of Bleeker. Bleeker, remembering not to run or shout or knock the man down, walked over to him, took his arm and led him down the stairs, the arm unresisting, even flaccid, in his grip.

Bleeker stood indecisively at the foot of the stairs, watching the man walk automatically away from him. He thought he should go back upstairs and search the hall. And he thought, too, he had to reach Simpson. Over the noise of the motorcycles moving rapidly up and down the street, he heard a crash in the bar, a series of drunken elongated curses, ending abruptly in a small sound like a man's hand laid flatly and sharply on a table.

His head was beginning to ache badly and his stomach to sour under the impact of a slow and steady anger. He walked into the bar and stood staring at Francis LaSalle—LaSalle and Fleet, Hardware—who lay sprawled on the floor, his shoulders touching the brass rail under the bar and his head turned so that his cheek rubbed the black polished wood above the rail. The bartender had his hands below the top of the bar and he was watching Simpson and a half a dozen men arranged in a loose semicircle above and beyond LaSalle.

Bleeker lifted LaSalle, who was a little dazed but not really hurt, and set him on a chair. After he was sure LaSalle was all right, he walked up to Simpson.

"Get your men together," he said. "And get them out of here."

Simpson took a long yellow wallet folded like a book and laid some money on the bar.

"That should take care of the damages," he said. His tongue was a little thick, and his mouth didn't quite shut after the words were spoken, but Bleeker didn't think he was drunk. Bleeker saw, too—or thought he saw—

the little cold eyes behind the glasses as bright and as sterile as a painted floor. Bleeker raised his arm slightly and lifted his heels off the floor, but Simpson turned abruptly and walked away from him, the men in the troop swaying at his heels like a pack of lolling hounds. Bleeker stood looking foolishly after them. He had expected a fight, and his body was still poised for one. He grunted heavily.

"Who hit him?" Bleeker motioned toward LaSalle.

"Damned if I know," the bartender said. "They all look alike to me."

That was true, of course. He went back into the lobby, hearing LaSalle say, weakly and tearfully, "Goddamn them—the bastards." He met Campbell, the deputy sheriff, a tall man with the arms and shoulders of a child beneath a foggy, bloated face.

"Can you do anything?" Bleeker asked. The motorcycles were racing up and down the street, alternately whining and backfiring, and one had jumped the curb and was cruising on the sidewalk.

"What do you want me to do?" Campbell demanded. "Put 'em all in jail?"

The motorcycle on the sidewalk speeded up and skidded obliquely into a plate-glass window, the front wheel bucking and climbing the brick base beneath the window. A single large section of glass slipped edge-down to the sidewalk and fell slowly toward the cyclist who, with his feet spread and kicking at the cement, backed clumsily away from it. Bleeker could feel the crash in his teeth.

Now there were other motorcycles on the sidewalk. One of them hit a parked car at the edge of the walk. The rider standing astride his machine beat the window out of the car with his gloved fists. Campbell started down the steps toward him but was driven back by a motorcycle coming from his left. Bleeker could hear the squeal of the tires against the wooden riser at the base of the steps. Campbell's hand was on his gun when Bleeker reached him.

"That's no good," he yelled. "Get the state police. Ask for a half dozen squad cars."

Campbell, angry but somewhat relieved, went up the steps and into the lobby. Bleeker couldn't know how long he stood on the veranda watching the mounting devastation on the street—the cyclist racing past store windows and hurling, presumably, beer bottles at the glass fronts; the two, working as a team, knocking down weighing machines and the signs in front of the motion-picture theater; the innumerable mounted men running the angry townspeople, alerted and aroused by the awful sounds of damage to their property, back into their suddenly lighted homes again or up the steps of his hotel or into niches along the main street, into doorways, and occasionally into the ledges and bays of glassless windows.

He saw Simpson—or rather a figure on the white motorcycle, helmeted and goggled—stationed calmly in the middle of the street under a hanging lamp. Presumably, he had been there for some time but Bleeker hadn't seen him, the many rapid movements on the street making any static object unimportant and even, in a sense, invisible. Bleeker saw him now and he felt again that spasm of anger which was like another life inside his body. He could have strangled Simpson then, slowly and with infinite pride. He knew without any effort of reason that Simpson was making no attempt to control his men but waiting rather for that moment when their minds, subdued but never actually helpless, would again take possession of their bodies.

Bleeker turned suddenly and went back into the lobby as if by that gesture of moving away he could pin his thoughts to Simpson, who, hereafter, would be responsible for them. He walked over to the desk where Timmons and Campbell, the deputy, were talking.

"You've got the authority," Timmons was saying angrily. "Fire over their heads. And if that doesn't stop them—"

Campbell looked uneasily at Bleeker. "Maybe if we could get their leader—"

"Did you get the police?" Bleeker asked.

"They're on their way," Campbell said. He avoided looking at Timmons and continued to stare hopefully and miserably at Bleeker.

"You've had your say," Timmons said abruptly. "Now I'll have mine."

He started for the lobby doors, but Campbell, suddenly incensed, grabbed his arm.

"You leave this to me," he said. "You start firing a gun—"

Campbell's mouth dropped, and Bleeker, turning his head, saw the two motorcycles coming through the lobby doors. They circled leisurely around for a moment and then one of them shot suddenly toward them, the goggled rider looming enormously above the wide handlebars. They scattered, Bleeker diving behind a pillar, and Campbell and Timmons jumping behind the desk. The noise of the two machines assaulted them with as much effect as the sight of the speeding metal itself.

Bleeker didn't know why, in course of watching the two riders, he looked into the hall toward the foot of the stairway. Nor did it seem at all unreasonable that when he looked he should see Cathy standing there. Deeply, underneath the outward preoccupation of his mind, he must have been thinking of her. Now there she was. She wore the familiar green robe, belted and pulled in at the waist, and beneath its hem he could see the white slippers and the pink edge of her nightgown. Her hair was down, and he had the impression her eyes were not quite open, although, obviously, they were. She looked, he thought, as if she had waked, frowned at the clock, and come downstairs to scold him for staying up too late. He had no idea what time it was.

He saw—and of course Cathy saw—the motorcycle speeding toward her. He was aware that he screamed at her, too. She did take a slight backward step and raise her arms in a pathetic warding gesture toward the inhuman figure on the motorcycle, but neither could have changed—in that dwarfed period of time and in that short, unmaneuverable space—the course of their actions.

She lay finally across the lower steps, her body clinging to and equally arching away from the base of the newel post. And there was the sudden, shocking exposure of her flesh, the robe and the gown torn away from the leg as if pushed aside by the blood welling from her thigh. When he reached her, there was blood in her hair, too, and someone—not Cathy—was screaming into his ears.

After a while the doctor came, and Cathy, her head bandaged and her leg in splints, could be carried into his office and laid on the couch. Bleeker sat on the edge of the couch, his hand over Cathy's, watching the still white face whose eyes were closed and would not, he knew, open again. The doctor, after his first examination, had looked up quickly, and since Bleeker, too, had been bent over Cathy, their heads had been very close together for a moment. The doctor had assumed, almost immediately, his expression of professional austerity, but Bleeker had seen him in that moment when he had been thinking as a man, fortified of course by a doctor's knowledge, and Bleeker had known then that Cathy would die but that there would be also this interval of time.

Bleeker turned from watching Cathy and saw Timmons standing across the room. The man was—or had been—crying, but his face wasn't set for it, and the tears, points of colorless, sparkling water on his jaws, were unexpectedly delicate against the coarse texture of his skin. Timmons waved a bandaged hand awkwardly, and Bleeker remembered, abruptly and jarringly, seeing Timmons diving for the motorcycle which had reversed itself, along with the other, and raced out of the lobby.

There was no sound now either from the street or the lobby. It was incredible, thinking of the racket a moment ago, that there should be this utter quietude, not only the lack of noise but the lack of the vibration of movement. The doctor came and went, coming to bend over Cathy and then going away again. Timmons stayed. Beyond shifting his feet occasionally, he didn't move at all but stood patiently across the room, his face toward Cathy and Bleeker but not, Bleeker thought once when he looked up, actually seeing them.

"The police," Bleeker said sometime later.

"They're gone," Timmons said in a hoarse whisper. And then after a while, "They'll get 'em—don't worry."

Bleeker saw that the man blushed helplessly and looked away from him. The police were no good. They would catch Simpson. Simpson would pay damages. And that would be the end of it. Who could identify Cathy's assailant? Not himself, certainly—not Timmons nor Campbell. They were all alike. They were standardized figurines, seeking in each other a willful loss of identity, dividing themselves equally among one another until there was only a single mythical figure, unspeakably sterile and furnishing the norm for hundreds of others. He could not accuse something which didn't actually exist.

He wasn't sure of the exact moment when Cathy died. It might have been when he heard the motorcycle, unbelievably solitary in the quiet night, approaching the town. He knew only that the doctor came for the last time and that there was now a coarse, heavy blanket laid mercifully over Cathy. He stood looking down at the blanket for a moment, whatever he was feeling repressed and delayed inside him, and then went back to the lobby and out onto the veranda. There were a dozen men standing there looking up the street toward the sound of the motorcycle, steadily but slowly coming nearer. He saw that when they glanced at each other their faces were hard and angry but when they looked at him they were respectful and a little abashed.

Bleeker could see from the veranda a number of people moving among the smashed store-fronts, moving, stopping, bending over and then straightening up to move somewhere else, all dressed somewhat extemporaneously and therefore seeming without purpose. What they picked up they put down. What they put down they stared at grimly and then picked up again. They were like a dispossessed minority brutally but lawfully discriminated against. When the motorcycle appeared at the north end of the street, they looked at it and then looked away again, dully and seemingly without resentment.

It was only after some moments that they looked up again, this time purposefully, and began to move slowly toward the hotel where the motorcycle had now stopped, the rider standing on the sidewalk, his face raised to the veranda.

No one on the veranda moved until Bleeker, after a visible effort, walked down the steps and stood facing the rider. It was the boy Bleeker had talked to in the bar. The goggles and helmet were hanging at his belt.

"I couldn't stand it any longer," the boy said. "I had to come back."

He looked at Bleeker as if he didn't dare look anywhere else. His face was adolescently shiny and damp, the marks, Bleeker thought, of a proud and articulate fear. He should have been heroic in his willingness to come back to the town after what had been done to it, but to Bleeker he was only a dirty little boy returning to a back fence his friends had defaced with pornographic writing and calling attention to the fact that he was afraid to erase the writing but was determined nevertheless to do it. Bleeker was revolted. He hated the boy far more than he could have hated Simpson for bringing this to his attention when he did not want to think of anything or anyone but Cathy.

"I wasn't one of them," the boy said. "You remember, Mr. Bleeker. I wasn't drinking."

This declaration of innocence—this willingness to take blame for acts which he hadn't committed—enraged Bleeker.

"You were one of them," he said.

"Yes. But after tonight—"

"Why didn't you stop them?" Bleeker demanded loudly. He felt the murmur of the townspeople at his back and someone breathed harshly on his neck. "You were one of them. You could have done something. Why in God's name didn't you do it?"

"What could I do?" the boy said. He spread his hands and stepped back as if to appeal to the men beyond Bleeker.

Bleeker couldn't remember, either shortly after or much later, exactly what he did then. If the boy hadn't stepped back like that—if he hadn't raised his hand. . . . Bleeker was in the middle of a group of bodies and he was striking with his fists and being struck. And then he was kneeling on the sidewalk, holding the boy's head in his lap and trying to protect him from the heavy shoes of the men around him. He was crying out, protesting, exhorting, and after a time the men moved away from him and someone helped him carry the boy up the steps and lay him on the veranda. When he looked up finally, only Timmons and the doctor were there. Up and down the street there were now only shadows and the diminishing sounds of invisible bodies. The night was still again as abruptly as it had been confounded with noise.

Some time later Timmons and the doctor carried the boy, alive but terribly hurt, into the hotel. Bleeker sat on the top step of the veranda, staring at the moon which had shifted in the sky and was now nearer the mountains in the west. It was not in any sense romantic or inflamed but coldly clear and sane. And the light it sent was cold and sane and lit in himself what he could have liked to hide.

He could have said that having lost Cathy he was not afraid any longer of losing himself. No one would blame him. Cathy's death was his excuse for striking the boy, hammering him to the sidewalk, and stamping on him as he had never believed he could have stamped on any living thing. No one would say he should have lost Cathy lightly—without anger and without that appalling desire to avenge her. It was utterly natural—as natural as a man drinking a few beers and riding a motorcycle insanely through a town like this. Bleeker shuddered. It might have been all right for a man like Timmons who was and would always be incapable of thinking what he—Joel Bleeker—was thinking. It was not—and would never be—all right for him.

Bleeker got up and stood for a moment on the top step of the veranda. He wanted, abruptly and madly, to scream his agony into the night with no more restraint than that of an animal seeing his guts beneath him on the ground. He wanted to smash something—anything—glass, wood, stone—his own body. He could feel his fists going into the boy's flesh. And there was that bloody but living thing on the sidewalk and himself stooping over to shield it.

After a while, aware that he was leaning against one of the wooden pillars supporting the porch and aware, too, that his flesh was numb from being pressed against it, he straightened up slowly and turned to go back into the hotel.

There would always be time to make his peace with the dead. There was little if any time to make his peace with the living.

Tomorrow

William Faulkner

Uncle Gavin had not always been county attorney. But the time when he had not been was more than twenty years ago and it had lasted for such a short period that only the old men remembered it, and even some of them did not. Because in that time he had had but one case.

He was a young man then, twenty-eight, only a year out of the state-university law school where, at grandfather's instigation, he had gone after his return from Harvard and Heidelberg; and he had taken the case voluntarily, persuaded grandfather to let him handle it alone, which grandfather did, because everyone believed the trial would be a mere formality.

So he tried the case. Years afterward he still said it was the only case, either as a private defender or a public prosecutor, in which he was convinced that right and justice were on his side, that he ever lost. Actually he did not lose it—a mistrial in the fall court term, an acquittal in the following spring term—the defendant a solid, well-to-do farmer, husband and father, too, named Bookwright, from a section called Frenchman's Bend in the remote southeastern corner of the county; the victim a swaggering bravo calling himself Buck Thorpe and called Bucksnort by the other young men whom he had subjugated with his fists during the three years he had been in Frenchman's Bend; kinless, who had appeared overnight from nowhere, a brawler, a gambler, known to be a distiller of illicit whiskey and caught once on the road to Memphis with a small drove of stolen cattle, which the owner promptly identified. He had a bill of sale for them, but none in the county knew the name signed to it.

And the story itself was old and unoriginal enough: The country girl of seventeen, her imagination fired by the swagger and the prowess and the daring and the glib tongue; the father who tried to reason with her and got exactly as far as parents usually do in such cases; then the interdiction, the forbidden door, the inevitable elopement at midnight; and at four o'clock the next morning Bookwright waked Will Varner, the justice of the peace and the chief officer of the district, and handed Varner his pistol and said, "I have come to surrender. I killed Thorpe two hours ago." And a neighbor named Quick, who was first on the scene, found the half-drawn pistol in Thorpe's hand; and a week after the brief account was printed in the Memphis papers, a woman appeared in Frenchman's Bend who claimed to be Thorpe's wife, and with a wedding license to prove it, trying to claim what money or property he might have left.

I can remember the surprise that the grand jury even found a true bill; when the clerk read the indictment, the betting was twenty to one that the jury would not be out ten minutes. The district attorney even conducted the case through an assistant, and it did not take an hour to submit all the evidence. Then Uncle Gavin rose, and I remember how he looked at the jury—the eleven farmers and storekeepers and the twelfth man, who was to ruin his case—a farmer, too, a thin man, small, with thin gray hair and that appearance of hill farmers—at once frail and work-worn, yet curiously imperishable—who seem to become old men at fifty and then become invincible to time. Uncle Gavin's voice was quiet, almost monotonous, not ranting as criminal-court trials had taught us to expect; only the words were a little different from the ones he would use in later years. But even then, although he had been talking to them for only a year, he could already talk so that all the people in our country—the Negroes, the hill people, the rich flatland plantation owners—understood what he said.

"All of us in this country, the South, have been taught from birth a few things which we hold to above all else. One of the first of these—not the best; just one of the first—is that only a life can pay for the life it takes; that the one death is only half complete. If that is so, then we could have saved both these lives by stopping this defendant before he left his house that night; we could have saved at least one of them, even if we had had to take this defendant's life from him in order to stop him. Only we didn't know in time. And that's what I am talking about—not about the dead man and his character and the morality of the act he was engaged in; not about self-defense, whether or not this defendant was justified in forcing the issue to the point of taking life, but about us who are not dead and what we don't know—about all of us, human beings who at bottom want to do right, want not to harm others; human beings with all the complexity of human passions and feelings and beliefs, in the accepting or rejecting of which we had no choice, trying to do the best we can with them or despite them—this defendant, another human being with that same complexity of passions and instincts and beliefs, faced by a problem—the inevitable misery of his child who, with the headstrong folly of youth—again that same old complexity which she, too, did not ask to inherit—was incapable of her own preservation—and solved that problem to the best of his ability and beliefs, asking help of no one, and then abode by his decision and his act."

He sat down. The district attorney's assistant merely rose and bowed to the court and sat down again. The jury went out and we didn't even leave the room. Even the judge didn't retire. And I remember the long breath, something, which went through the room when the clock hand above the bench passed the ten-minute mark and then passed the half-hour mark, and the judge beckoned a bailiff and whispered to him, and the bailiff went out and returned and whispered to the judge, and the judge rose and banged his gavel and recessed the court.

I hurried home and ate my dinner and hurried back to town. The office was empty. Even grandfather, who took his nap after dinner, regardless of who hung and who didn't, returned first; after three o'clock then, and the whole town knew now that Uncle Gavin's jury was hung by one man, eleven to one for acquittal; then Uncle Gavin came in fast, and grandfather said, "Well, Gavin, at least you stopped talking in time to hang just your jury and not your client."

"That's right, sir," Uncle Gavin said. Because he was looking at me with his bright eyes, his thin, quick face, his wild hair already beginning to turn white. "Come here, Chick," he said. "I need you for a minute."

"Ask Judge Frazier to allow you to retract your oration, then let Charley sum up for you," grandfather said. But we were outside then, on the stairs, Uncle Gavin stopping halfway down, so that we stood exactly halfway from anywhere, his hand on my shoulder, his eyes brighter and intenter than ever.

"This is not cricket," he said. "But justice is accomplished lots of times by methods that won't bear looking at. They have moved the jury to the back room in Mrs. Rouncewell's boardinghouse. The room right opposite that mulberry tree. If you could get into the back yard without anybody seeing you, and be careful when you climb the tree—"

Nobody saw me. But I could look through the windy mulberry leaves into the room, and see and hear, both—the nine angry and disgusted men sprawled in chairs at the far end of the room; Mr. Holland, the foreman, and another man standing in front of the chair in which the little, worn, dried-out hill man sat. His name was Fentry. I remembered all their names, because Uncle Gavin said that to be a successful lawyer and politician in our country you did not need a silver tongue nor even an intelligence; you needed only an infallible memory for names. But I would have remembered his name anyway, because it was Stonewall Jackson—Stonewall Jackson Fentry.

"Don't you admit that he was running off with Bookwright's seventeen-year-old daughter?" Mr. Holland said. "Don't you admit that he had a pistol in his hand when they found him? Don't you admit that he wasn't hardly buried before that woman turned up and proved she was already his wife? Don't you admit that he was not only no-good but dangerous, and that if it hadn't been Bookwright, sooner or later somebody else would have had to, and that Bookwright was just unlucky?"

"Yes," Fentry said.

"Then what do you want?" Mr. Holland said. "What do you want?"

"I can't help it," Fentry said. "I ain't going to vote Mr. Bookwright free."

And he didn't. And that afternoon Judge Frazier discharged the jury and set the case for retrial in the next term of court; and the next morning Uncle Gavin came for me before I had finished breakfast.

"Tell your mother we might be gone overnight," he said. "Tell her I promise not to let you get either shot, snake-bit or surfeited with soda pop. . . . Because I've got to know," he said. We were driving fast now, out the northeast road, and his eyes were bright, not baffled, just intent and eager. "He was born and raised and lived all his life out here at the very other end of the county, thirty miles from Frenchman's Bend. He said under oath that he had never even seen Bookwright before, and you can look at him and see that he never had enough time off from hard work to learn how to lie in. I doubt if he ever even heard Bookwright's name before."

We drove until almost noon. We were in the hills now, out of the rich flat land, among the pine and bracken, the poor soil, the little tilted and barren patches of gaunt corn and cotton which somehow endured, as the people they clothed and fed somehow endured; the roads we followed less than lanes, winding and narrow, rutted and dust choked, the car in second gear half the time. Then we saw the mailbox, the crude lettering: G. A. FENTRY; beyond it, the two-room log house with an open hall, and even I, a boy of twelve, could see that no woman's hand had touched it in a lot of years. We entered the gate.

Then a voice said, "Stop! Stop where you are!" And we hadn't even seen him—an old man, barefoot, with a fierce white bristle of mustache, in patched denim faded almost to the color of skim milk, smaller, thinner even than the son, standing at the edge of the worn gallery, holding a shotgun across his middle and shaking with fury or perhaps with the palsy of age.

"Mr Fentry—" Uncle Gavin said.

"You've badgered and harried him enough!" the old man said. It was fury; the voice seemed to rise suddenly with a fiercer, an uncontrollable blaze of it: "Get out of here! Get off my land! Go!"

"Come," Uncle Gavin said quietly. And still his eyes were only bright, eager, intent and grave. We did not drive fast now. The next mailbox was within the mile, and this time the house was even painted, with beds of petunias beside the steps, and the land about it was better, and this time the man rose from the gallery and came down to the gate.

"Howdy, Mr. Stevens," he said. "So Jackson Fentry hung your jury for you."

"Howdy, Mr. Pruitt," Uncle Gavin said. "It looks like he did. Tell me."

And Pruitt told him, even though at that time Uncle Gavin would forget now and then and his language would slip back to Harvard and even to Heidelberg. It was as if people looked at his face and knew that what he asked was not just for his own curiosity or his own selfish using.

"Only ma knows more about it than I do," Pruitt said. "Come up to the gallery."

We followed him to the gallery, where a plump, white-haired old lady in a clean gingham sunbonnet and dress and a clean white apron sat in a low rocking chair, shelling field peas into a wooden bowl. "This is Lawyer Stevens," Pruitt said. "Captain Stevens' son, from town. He wants to know about Jackson Fentry."

So we sat, too, while they told it, the son and the mother talking in rotation.

"That place of theirs," Pruitt said. "You seen some of it from the road. And what you didn't see don't look no better. But his pa and his grandpa worked it, made a living for themselves and raised families and paid their taxes and owed no man. I don't know how they done it, but they did. And Jackson was helping from the time he got big enough to reach up to the plow handles. He never got much bigger than that neither. None of them ever did. I reckon that was why. And Jackson worked it, too, in his time, until he was about twenty-five and already looking forty, asking no odds of nobody, not married and not nothing, him and his pa living alone and doing their own washing and cooking, because how can a man afford to marry when him and his pa have just one pair of shoes between them. If it had been worth while getting a wife a-tall, since that place had already killed his ma and his grandma both before they were forty years old. Until one night—"

"Nonsense," Mrs. Pruitt said. "When your pa and me married, we didn't even own a roof over our heads. We moved into a rented house, on rented land—"

"All right," Pruitt said. "Until one night he come to me and said how he had got him a sawmilling job down at Frenchman's Bend."

"Frenchman's Bend?" Uncle Gavin said, and now his eyes were much brighter and quicker than just intent. "Yes," he said.

"A day-wage job," Pruitt said. "Not to get rich; just to earn a little extra money maybe, risking a year or two to earn a little extra money, against the life his grandpa led until he died between the plow handles one day, and that his pa would lead until he died in a corn furrow, and then it would be his turn, and not even no son to come and pick him up out of the dirt. And that he had traded with a nigger to help his pa work their place while he was gone, and would I kind of go up there now and then and see that his pa was all right."

"Which you did," Mrs. Pruitt said.

"I went close enough," Pruitt said. "I would get close enough to the field to hear him cussing at the nigger for not moving fast enough and to watch the nigger trying to keep up with him, and to think what a good thing it was Jackson hadn't got two niggers to work the place while he was gone, because if that old man—and he was close to sixty then—had had to spend one full day sitting in a chair in the shade with nothing in his hands to chop or hoe with, he would have died before sundown. So Jackson left. He walked. They didn't have but one mule. They ain't never had but one mule. But it ain't but about thirty miles. He was gone about two and a half years. Then one day—"

"He come home that first Christmas," Mrs. Pruitt said.

"That's right," Pruitt said. "He walked them thirty miles home and spent Christmas Day, and walked them other thirty miles back to the sawmill."

"Whose sawmill?" Uncle Gavin said.

"Quick's," Pruitt said. "Old Man Ben Quick's. It was the second Christmas he never come home. Then, about the beginning of March, about when the river bottom at Frenchman's Bend would be starting to dry out to where you could skid logs through it and you would have thought he would be settled down good to his third year of sawmilling, he come home to stay. He didn't walk this time. He come in a hired buggy. Because he had the goat and the baby."

"Wait," Uncle Gavin said.

"We never knew how he got home," Mrs. Pruitt said. "Because he had been home over a week before we even found out he had the baby."

"Wait," Uncle Gavin said.

They waited, looking at him, Pruitt sitting on the gallery railing and Mrs. Pruitt's fingers still shelling the peas out of the long brittle hulls, looking at Uncle Gavin. His eyes were not exultant now any more than they had been baffled or even very speculative before; they had just got brighter, as if whatever it was behind them had flared up, steady and fiercer, yet still quiet, as if it were going faster than the telling was going.

"Yes," he said. "Tell me."

"And when I finally heard about it and went up there," Mrs. Pruitt said, "that baby wasn't two weeks old. And how he had kept it alive, and just on goat's milk—"

"I don't know if you know it," Pruitt said. "A goat ain't like a cow. You milk a goat every two hours or so. That means all night too."

"Yes," Mrs. Pruitt said. "He didn't even have diaper cloths. He had some split floursacks the midwife had showed him how to put on. So I made some cloths and I would go up there; he had kept the nigger on to help his pa in the field and he was doing the cooking and washing and nursing that baby, milking the goat to feed it; and I would say, 'Let me take it. At least until he can be weaned. You come stay at my house, too, if you want,' and him just looking at me—little, thin, already wore-out something that never in his whole life had ever set down to a table and et all he could hold—saying, 'I thank you, ma'am. I can make out.' "

"Which was correct," Pruitt said. "I don't know how he was at sawmilling, and he never had no farm to find out what kind of a farmer he was. But he raised that boy."

"Yes," Mrs. Pruitt said. "And I kept on after him: 'We hadn't even heard you was married,' I said. 'Yessum,' he said. 'We was married last year. When the baby come, she died.' 'Who was she?' I said. 'Was she a Frenchman Bend girl?' 'No'm,' he said. 'She come from downstate.' 'What was her name?' I said. 'Miss Smith,' he said."

"He hadn't even had enough time off from hard work to learn how to lie either," Pruitt said. "But he raised that boy. After their crops were in in the fall, he let the nigger go, and next spring him and the old man done the work like they use to. He had made a kind of satchel, like they say Indians does, to carry the boy in. I would go up there now and then while the ground was still cold and see Jackson and his pa plowing and chopping brush, and that satchel hanging on a fence post and that boy asleep bolt upright in it like it was a feather bed. He learned to walk that spring, and I would stand there at the fence and watch that durn little critter out there in the middle of the furrow, trying his best to keep up with Jackson, until Jackson would stop the plow at the turn row and go back and get him and set him straddle of his neck and take up the plow and go on. In the late summer he could walk pretty good. Jackson made him a little hoe out of a stick and a scrap of shingle, and you could see Jackson chopping in the middle-thigh cotton, but you couldn't see the boy at all; you could just see the cotton shaking where he was."

"Jackson made his clothes," Mrs. Pruitt said. "Stitched them himself, by hand. I made a few garments and took them up there. I never done it but once though. He took them and he thanked me. But you could see it. It was like he even begrudged the earth itself for what that child had to eat to keep alive. And I tried to persuade Jackson to take him to church, have him baptized. 'He's already named,' he said. 'His name is Jackson and Longstreet Fentry. Pa fit under both of them.' "

"He never went nowhere," Pruitt said. "Because where you saw Jackson, you saw that boy. If he had had to steal that boy down there at Frenchman's Bend, he couldn't 'a' hid no closer. It was even the old man that would ride over to Haven Hill store to buy their supplies, and the only time Jackson and that boy was separated as much as one full breath was once a year when Jackson would ride in to Jefferson to pay their taxes, and when I first seen the boy I thought of a setter puppy, until one day I knowed Jackson had gone to pay their taxes and I went up there and the boy was under the bed, not making any fuss, just backed up into the corner, looking out at me. He didn't blink once. He was exactly like a fox or a wolf cub somebody had caught just last night."

We watched him take from his pocket a tin of snuff and tilt a measure of it into the lid and then into his lower lip, tapping the final grain from the lid with delicate deliberation.

"All right," Uncle Gavin said. "Then what?"

"That's all," Pruitt said. "In the next summer him and the boy disappeared."

"Disappeared?" Uncle Gavin said.

"That's right. They were just gone one morning. I didn't know when. And one day I couldn't stand it no longer, I went up there and the house was empty, and I went on to the field where the old man was plowing, and at first I thought the spreader between his plow handles had broke and he had tied a sapling across the handles, until he seen me and snatched the sapling off, and it was that shotgun, and I reckon what he said to me was about what he said to you this morning when you stopped there. Next year he had the nigger helping him again. Then, about five years later, Jackson come back. I don't know when. He was just there one morning. And the nigger was gone again, and him and his pa worked the place like they use to. And one day I couldn't stand it no longer, I went up there and I stood at the fence where he was plowing, until after a while the land he was breaking brought him up to the fence, and still he hadn't never looked at me; he plowed right by me, not ten feet away, still without looking at me, and he turned and come back, and I said, 'Did he die, Jackson?' and then he looked at me. 'The boy,' I said. And he said, 'What boy?' "

They invited us to stay for dinner.

Uncle Gavin thanked them. "We brought a snack with us," he said. "And it's thirty miles to Varner's store, and twenty-two from there to Jefferson. And our roads ain't quite used to automobiles yet."

So it was just sundown when we drove up to Varner's store in Frenchman's Bend Village; again a man rose from the deserted gallery and came down the steps to the car.

It was Isham Quick, the witness who had first reached Thorpe's body—a tall, gangling man in the middle forties, with a dreamy kind of face and near-sighted eyes, until you saw there was something shrewd behind them, even a little quizzical.

"I been waiting for you," he said. "Looks like you made a water haul." He blinked at Uncle Gavin. "That Fentry."

"Yes," Uncle Gavin said. "Why didn't you tell me?"

"I didn't recognize it myself," Quick said. "It wasn't until I heard your jury was hung, and by one man, that I associated them names."

"Names?" Uncle Gavin said. "What na— Never mind. Just tell it."

So we sat on the gallery of the locked and deserted store while the cicadas shrilled and rattled in the trees and the lightning bugs blinked and drifted above the dusty road, and Quick told it, sprawled on the bench beyond Uncle Gavin, loose-jointed, like he would come all to pieces the first time he moved, talking in a lazy sardonic voice, like he had all night to tell it in and it would take all night to tell it. But it wasn't that long. It wasn't long enough for what was in it. But Uncle Gavin says it don't take many words to tell the sum of any human experience; that somebody has already done it in eight: He was born, he suffered and he died.

"It was pap that hired him. But when I found out where he had come from, I knowed he would work, because folks in that country hadn't never had time to learn nothing but hard work. And I knowed he would be honest for the same reason: that there wasn't nothing in his country a man could want bad enough to learn how to steal it. What I seem to have underestimated was his capacity for love. I reckon I figured that, coming from where he come from, he never had none a-tall, and for that same previous reason—that even the comprehension of love had done been lost out of him back down the generations where the first one of them had had to take his final choice between the pursuit of love and the pursuit of keeping on breathing.

"So he come to work, doing the same work and drawing the same pay as the niggers done. Until in the late fall, when the bottom got wet and we got ready to shut down for the winter, I found out he had made a trade with pap to stay on until spring as watchman and caretaker, with three days out to go home Christmas. And he did, and the next year when we started up, he had done learned so much about it and he stuck to it so, that by the middle of summer he was running the whole mill hisself, and by the end of summer pap never went out there no more a-tall and I just went when I felt like it, maybe once a week or so; and by fall pap was even talking about building him a shack to live in in place of that shuck mattress and a old broke-down cookstove in the boiler shed. And he stayed through that winter too. When he went home that Christmas we never even knowed it, when he went or when he come back, because even I hadn't been out there since fall.

"Then one afternoon in February—there had been a mild spell and I reckon I was restless—I rode out there. The first thing I seen was her, and it was the first time I had ever done that—a woman, young, and maybe when she was in her normal health she might have been pretty, too; I don't know. Because she wasn't just thin, she was gaunted. She was sick, more than just starved-looking, even if she was still on her feet, and it wasn't just because she was going to have that baby in a considerable less than another month. And I says, 'Who is that?' and he looked at me and says, 'That's my wife,' and I says, 'Since when? You never had no wife last fall. And that child ain't a month off.' And he says, 'Do you want us to leave?' and I says, 'What do I want you to leave for?' I'm going to tell this from what I know now, what I found out after them two brothers showed up here three years later with their court paper, not from what he ever told me, because he never told nobody nothing."

"All right," Uncle Gavin said. "Tell."

"I don't know where he found her. I don't know if he found her somewhere, or if she just walked into the mill one day or one night and he looked up and seen her, and it was like the fellow says—nobody knows where or when love or lightning either is going to strike, except that it ain't going to strike there twice, because it don't have to. And I don't believe she was hunting for the husband that had deserted her—likely he cut and run soon as she told him about the baby—and I don't believe she was scared or ashamed to go back home just because her brothers and father had tried to keep her from marrying the husband, in the first place. I believe it was just some more of that same kind of black-complected and not extra-intelligent and pretty durn ruthless blood pride that them brothers themselves was waving around here for about a hour that day.

"Anyway, there she was, and I reckon she knowed her time was going to be short, and him saying to her, 'Let's get married,' and her saying, 'I can't marry you. I've already got a husband.' And her time come and she was down then, on that shuck mattress, and him feeding her with a spoon, likely, and I reckon she knowed she wouldn't get up from it, and he got the midwife, and the baby was born, and likely her and the midwife both knowed by then she would never get up from that mattress and maybe they even convinced him at last, or maybe she knowed it wouldn't make no difference nohow and said yes, and he taken the mule pap let him keep at the mill and rid seven miles to Preacher Whitfield's and brung Whitfield back about daylight, and Whitfield married them and she died, and him and Whitfield buried her. And that night he come to the house and told pap he was quitting, and left the mule, and I went out to the mill a few days later and he was gone—just the shuck mattress and the stove, and the dishes and skillet mammy let him have, all washed and clean and set on the shelf. And in the third summer from then, them two brothers, them Thorpes—"

"Thorpes," Uncle Gavin said. It wasn't loud. It was getting dark fast now, as it does in our country, and I couldn't see his face at all any more. "Tell," he said.

"Black-complected like she was—the youngest one looked a heap like her—coming up in the surrey, with the deputy or bailiff or whatever he was, and the paper all wrote out and stamped and sealed all regular, and I says, 'You can't do this. She come here of her own accord, sick and with nothing, and he taken her in and fed her and nursed her and got help to born that child and a preacher to bury her; they was even married before she died. The preacher and the midwife both will prove it.' And the oldest brother says, 'He couldn't marry her. She already had a husband. We done already attended to him.' And I says, 'All right. He taken that boy when nobody come to claim him. He has raised that boy and clothed and fed him for two years and better.' And the oldest one drawed a money purse half outen his pocket and let it drop back again. 'We aim to do right about that, too—when we have seen the boy,' he says. 'He is our kin. We want him and we aim to have him.' And that wasn't the first time it ever occurred to me that this world ain't run like it ought to be run a heap of more times than what it is, and I says, 'It's thirty miles up there. I reckon you all will want to lay over here tonight and rest your horses.' And the oldest one looked at me and says, 'The team ain't tired. We won't stop.' 'Then I'm going with you,' I says. 'You are welcome to come,' he says.

"We drove until midnight. So I thought I would have a chance then, even if I never had nothing to ride. But when we unhitched and laid down on the ground, the oldest brother never laid down. 'I ain't sleepy,' he says. 'I'll set up a while.' So it wasn't no use, and I went to sleep and then the sun was up and it was too late then, and about middle morning we come to that mailbox with the name on it you couldn't miss, and the empty house with nobody in sight or hearing neither, until we heard the ax and went around to the back, and he looked up from the woodpile and seen what I reckon he had been expecting to see every time the sun rose for going on three years now. Because he never even stopped. He said to the little boy, 'Run. Run to the field to grandpap. Run,' and come straight at the oldest brother with the ax already raised and the down-stroke already started, until I managed to catch it by the haft just as the oldest brother grabbed him and we lifted him clean off the ground, holding him, or trying to. 'Stop it, Jackson!' I says. 'Stop it! They got the law!'

"Then a puny something was kicking and clawing me about the legs; it was the little boy, not making a sound, just swarming around me and the brother both, hitting at us as high as he could reach with a piece of wood Fentry had been chopping. 'Catch him and take him on to the surrey,' the oldest one says. So the youngest one caught him; he was almost as hard to hold as Fentry, kicking and plunging even after the youngest one had picked him up, and still not making a sound, and Fentry jerking and lunging like two men until the youngest one and the boy was out of sight. Then he collapsed. It was like all his bones had turned to water, so that me and the oldest brother lowered him down to the chopping block like he never had no bones a-tall, laying back against the wood he had cut, panting, with a little froth of spit at each corner of his mouth. 'It's the law, Jackson,' I says. 'Her husband is still alive.'

" 'I know it,' he says. It wasn't much more than whispering. 'I been expecting it. I reckon that's why it taken me so by surprise. I'm all right now.'

" 'I'm sorry for it,' the brother says. 'We never found out about none of it until last week. But he is our kin. We want him home. You done well by him. We thank you. His mother thanks you. Here,' he says. He taken the money purse outen his pocket and puts it into Fentry's hand. Then he turned and went away. After a while I heard the carriage turn and go back down the hill. Then I couldn't hear it any more. I don't know whether Fentry ever heard it or not.

" 'It's the law, Jackson,' I says. 'But there's two sides to the law. We'll go to town and talk to Captain Stevens. I'll go with you.'

"Then he set up on the chopping block, setting up slow and stiff. He wasn't panting so hard now and he looked better now, except for his eyes, and they was mostly just dazed looking. Then he raised the hand that had the money purse in it and started to mop his face with the money purse, like it was a handkerchief; I don't believe he even knowed there was anything in his hand until then, because he taken his hand down and looked at the money purse for maybe five seconds, and then he tossed it—he didn't fling it; he just tossed it like you would a handful of dirt you had been examining to see what it would make—over behind the chopping block and got up and walked across the yard toward the woods, walking straight and not fast, and not looking much bigger than that little boy, and into the woods. 'Jackson,' I says. But he never looked back.

"And I stayed that night at Rufus Pruitt's and borrowed a mule from him; I said I was just looking around, because I didn't feel much like talking to nobody, and the next morning I hitched the mule at that gate and started up the path, and I didn't see old man Fentry on the gallery a-tall at first.

"When I did see him he was moving so fast I didn't even know what he had in his hands until it went 'boom!' and I heard the shot rattling in the leaves overhead and Rufus Pruitt's mule trying his durn best either to break the hitch rein or hang hisself from the gatepost.

"And one day about six months after he had located here to do the balance of his drinking and fighting and sleight-of-hand with other folks' cattle, Bucksnort was on the gallery here, drunk still and running his mouth, and about a half dozen of the ones he had beat unconscious from time to time by foul means and even by fair on occasion, as such emergencies arose, laughing every time he stopped to draw a fresh breath. And I happened to look up, and Fentry was setting on his mule out there in the road.

"He was just setting there, with the dust of them thirty miles caking into the mule's sweat, looking at Thorpe. I don't know how long he had been there, not saying nothing, just setting there and looking at Thorpe; then he turned the mule and rid back up the road toward them hills he hadn't ought to never have left. Except maybe it's like the fellow says, and there ain't nowhere you can hide from either lightning or love. And I didn't know why then. I hadn't associated them names. I knowed that Thorpe was familiar to me, but that other business had been twenty years ago and I had forgotten it until I heard about that hung jury of yourn. Of course he wasn't going to vote Bookwright free. . . . It's dark. Let's go to supper."

But it was only twenty-two miles to town now, and we were on the highway now, the gravel; we would be home in an hour and a half, because sometimes we could make thirty and thirty-five miles an hour, and Uncle Gavin said that someday all the main roads in Mississippi would be paved like the streets in Memphis and every family in America would own a car. We were going fast now.

"Of course he wasn't," Uncle Gavin said. "The lowly and invincible of the earth—to endure and endure and then endure, tomorrow and tomorrow and tomorrow. Of course he wasn't going to vote Bookwright free."

"I would have," I said. "I would have freed him. Because Buck Thorpe was bad. He—"

"No, you wouldn't," Uncle Gavin said. He gripped my knee with one hand even though we were going fast, the yellow light beam level on the yellow road, the bugs swirling down into the light beam and ballooning away. "It wasn't Buck Thorpe, the adult, the man. He would have shot that man as quick as Bookwright did, if he had been in Bookwright's place. It was because somewhere in that debased and brutalized flesh which Bookwright slew there still remained, not the spirit maybe, but at least the memory, of that little boy, that Jackson and Longstreet Fentry, even though the man the boy had become didn't know it, and only Fentry did. And you wouldn't have freed him either. Don't ever forget that. Never."

PART VII

THE GOOD, THE BAD, AND THE UNADAPTABLE

"Bringing Up Baby"
by Hagar Wilde

Bringing Up Baby, directed by Howard Hawks, 1938

"Babylon Revisited"
by F. Scott Fitzgerald

The Last Time I Saw Paris, directed by Richard Brooks, 1954

"The Swimmer"
by John Cheever

The Swimmer, directed by Frank Perry, 1968

The paradox is this: Great stories often make poor movies and vice versa. Lawrence Kasdan *(Silverado, The Big Chill)* has said that he finds this idea both liberating and inspiring: "My experience is that high art often starts in low places." And in fact, some of the most successful movies of all time have come from "low places." In the early days of cinema, potboilers were everywhere and so were their film adaptations. Classic films like *Stagecoach, All About Eve,* and *Bringing Up Baby* were all adapted from fiction found in mass-market magazines. (In fact, "Stage to Lordsburg," the basis for *Stagecoach,* and Hagar Wilde's "Bringing Up Baby" were published in the same issue of *Collier's.*) Stories like these were routinely snatched up by the studios on the off chance that they might make a good film. And if the quality of writing was mediocre, it didn't matter. What mattered was the story.

Howard Hawks was more candid about it than most directors. "Above all in a motion picture is the story," he said over and over, and it was this single-minded focus on storytelling over what he called "camera trick-work" that allowed him to move effortlessly across film genres. No director, before or since, has amassed as many classics in as many different styles: from gangster films (*Scarface,* 1932), to film noir (*The Big Sleep,* 1946), to Westerns (*Red River,* 1948), to horror (*The Thing,* 1951), to musicals (*Gentlemen Prefer Blondes,* 1953) to war dramas (*Sergeant York,* 1941)—and, of course, to the definitive screwball comedy, *Bringing Up Baby,* starring Katharine Hepburn and Cary Grant.

Hawks often let his movies form organically, filming sequentially and rewriting the script every day to incorporate new interactions between story, actors, and characters. The *Bringing Up Baby* set was an unusually happy one, with much on-set improvising and censor-baiting. (All of the "bone" double entendres managed to survive the Hays Office.) According to Fritz Feld, who played the psychiatrist in the supper club, "Hawks would come in and say, 'It's a nice day today. Let's go to the races.' And we'd pack up and *go* to the races. Kate continued her custom of serving tea on the set. We all laughed and laughed, and were very happy." Not surprisingly, the picture went wildly over budget, but Hawks's easy, relaxed manner was the incubator that created a classic. "The difficult work," Hawks once said, "is the preparation: finding the story, deciding how to tell it, what to show and what not to show."

Wilde's story was recommended to Hawks by the RKO story department because the dialogue was "hilariously funny and the possibilities for further complication are limitless." The story was purchased for $1,004 and Wilde was persuaded, despite her initial reluctance, to come to Hollywood to work on the screenplay. A novelist, playwright, and short-story writer in her early thirties, Wilde had already done a four-week stint in Hollywood working for Howard Hughes, but the experience had not been pleasant. In fact, her 1933 O. Henry Prize–winning story, "The Brat," was a caustic send-up of movie-style manipulation, which one of the judges said "shed an entirely new light on Hollywood theatrics." Although Dudley Nichols was the seasoned screenwriter on *Bringing Up Baby*, Wilde was retained to create additional situations and ensure the comic tone and characters remained consistent with her story. Her experience on the film must have been a positive one—*everyone* had fun—because afterward she continued to work in films, most notably with Hawks again on *I Was a Male War Bride* and with Raymond Chandler on *The Unseen.*

Despite her work on both coasts—she also wrote several successful Broadway plays—Wilde is a forgotten writer. There are scores of books on the comedies of the thirties with long discussions about the genius of *Bringing Up Baby*, but only a few of them even mention Hagar Wilde's name. She died in 1971, penniless and bitter, at the Motion Picture Country Home.* A number of years later one of her friends wrote a letter to the *New York Times* under the title "When Film Directors Get Credit for What Screenwriters Do": "All these years," Wilde's friend wrote, "I have marveled at the way critics gasp with awe at the genius of a film director for qualities created by the writer. . . . Only the imagination of Hagar Wilde could have produced that hunt through a Connecticut night in pursuit of a leopard named Baby. . . . At the time she died . . . her film was being enjoyed by millions on late night television. None of these showings added a penny . . . [to what she received for] the rights."

Still, Wilde almost surely never meant her story to be considered great literature: It's a typical situation comedy that emphasizes zany plot over depth of characterization or insight. So how did an average commercially intended story become a movie hailed by the National Society of Film Critics as one of the 100 Essential Films? First off, it was a collaborative

* When I called the Motion Picture Country Home to confirm the date of her death, their public relations official (after asking me who he was) said, "*Bringing Up Baby*? Are you *sure* there's so little information? She was a *major* screenwriter."

effort with Hawks providing an environment flexible enough to take advantage of the happy accident. When Hepburn broke the heel off her shoe during filming, Grant whispered to her the ad-lib line "I was born on the side of a hill" and they kept on going. In her autobiography, Hepburn recalled, "Everyone contributed anything and everything they could to that script." And because RKO was in receivership at the time, the filmmakers were unusually free of interference. The executives may have suspected Hawks of going over budget, but they simply had bigger problems to deal with. And, perhaps most important, there was Hawks's preference for using "personalities" instead of "actors." Both Hepburn and Grant played a variation of themselves in the film, shrugging into Wilde's two-dimensional characters as if they were off-the-rack suits, then tailoring them to fit perfectly. Which was exactly what Hawks wanted. Of Hepburn he said, "She played perfectly—not trying to be funny, but being very, very natural and *herself.*"

If "Bringing Up Baby" went from B-list story to A-list movie, F. Scott Fitzgerald's "Babylon Revisited" did just the opposite—and theories as to why abound. A muddle from the beginning, it began when independent producer Lester Cowan started looking for a story in which to star Shirley Temple. Settling on "Babylon Revisited," Cowan paid Fitzgerald $900 for the rights to his story, and then a few thousand* more for a screenplay, with some promise of more money on the back end. Fitzgerald wrote his wife, Zelda: "So then in a beautifully avaricious way, knowing I'd been sick and was probably hard up, Mr. Cowan hired me to do the script on a percentage basis. He gives me—or *gave* me—what worked out to a few hundred a week to do a quick script. . . . I'm supposed to be grateful because since I haven't done a movie for so long the conclusion is easy for this scum that I can't write." In a later letter to Zelda, though, his talk of the screenplay was more upbeat: "I think I've written a really brilliant continuity. It had better be for it seems to be a last life line that Hollywood has thrown me. It is a strong life line—to write as I please upon a piece of my own."

Written nearly ten years before Fitzgerald began his screenplay, "Babylon Revisited" is generally considered one of Fitzgerald's finest, most mature stories. John Chamberlain singled it out in his 1935 review of *Taps at Reveille,* the collection in which it is included, as evidence of Fitzgerald's "significance" (which was very much in question at the time). "Charlie's

* Sources vary, but Fitzgerald received somewhere between $2,300 and $5,000 for the story *and* screenplay. Ironically, this is approximately one-tenth to one-fifth of what up-and-comer Hagar Wilde received for her story and screenplay ($22,500).

[the protagonist's] repentance," Chamberlain wrote, "his ghost-ridden feeling, is a commentary on the life of 1929 that is comparable to Proust's commentary on the Parisian society of *Remembrance of Things Past.* The implications of 'Babylon Revisited' are as obvious as the implications, say, of *An American Tragedy.*" Fitzgerald's own screenplay, though, is a much different thing. Because of the Shirley Temple attachment, the child Honoria (renamed Victoria) became the focus of the story. Then entirely new plotlines—including murder and insurance fraud—were introduced, with it all concluding in a happy Hollywood way. The film was never made. Author/screenwriter Budd Schulberg, who received the screenplay from Fitzgerald as a gift when his daughter Victoria was born (the reason for the name change), came across it many years later while going through a box labeled "other people's manuscripts." When it was published, he wrote in the introduction: "We move this 'lost' manuscript from the shelf to publication with the admission that the piece is flawed. Most authors who adapt their own literary work are stubbornly faithful to their original creations. Fitzgerald, perhaps because he had become so immersed in screen technique, takes enormous liberties with his story.... In his zeal to 'make a movie' rather than attempt to retell his short story in cinematic form, he has stood it on its head...."

Fitzgerald died shortly after completing the screenplay, so we'll never have an adequate answer to the pressing question: What was he thinking? Subsequently, Cowan tried to enlist other people to rewrite his script, including Schulberg and Irwin Shaw, to no avail. James Thurber often told the tale of how one writer who was approached by Cowan said, "This is the most perfect motion-picture scenario I've ever read. I don't see why you want to revise it." To which Cowan replied, "You're absolutely right. I'll pay you two thousand dollars a week to stay out here and keep me from changing one word of it." Cowan's persistence paid off, though—he wound up selling Fitzgerald's screenplay to MGM for $100,000. It was a bad investment for MGM, though. When the project was again greenlighted in the early fifties, an entirely new script was written by the Epstein brothers *(Casablanca)* using the title of the Kern-Hammerstein song "The Last Time I Saw Paris." Bosley Crowther, presumably unaware of Fitzgerald's own perfidy, reviewed the film for the *New York Times*: "Where Fitzgerald did it in a few words—in a few subtle phrases that evoked a reckless era of golden dissipation toward the end of the Twenties' boom—[director] Richard Brooks... has done it in a nigh two-hour assembly of bistro balderdash and lush, romantic scenes.... The story is trite. The motivations are thin. The writing is gloss and pedestrian. The acting is pretty much forced."

Perhaps the film was doomed from the start. There are those like Kurt Vonnegut who claim it *couldn't* have worked: "When a movie company buys a [work] they're shortchanged, because often one character is missing—the author. I think that is one reason there have been no good films of Hemingway or Fitzgerald stories or novels. . . ." Hollywood scholar Tom Dardis thinks it shouldn't have even been attempted: "It is not at all clear why either Cowan or Fitzgerald ever thought a story like 'Babylon Revisited' could be transformed into a feature-length film script." And there are, in hindsight, a litany of reasons it *didn't* work. Certainly the filmmakers were careless with the original story—much more careless than Hawks was with Wilde's "Bringing Up Baby." But because Fitzgerald's work is so firmly anchored to the zeitgeist of the twenties and thirties, their most crippling change may have been the transposition to a post–World War II time frame. As John Cheever once observed, "One always knows reading Fitzgerald what time it is, precisely where you are, the kind of country. No writer has ever been so true in placing the scene." Of course this is a problem only for those familiar with Fitzgerald's original work—provenance in this case is a heavy burden.

If works by Hemingway and Fitzgerald always prove to be difficult adaptations, then there are also seemingly *impossible* ones. Long before Charlie Kaufman's struggles with Susan Orlean's nearly unadaptable book resulted in a movie-about-not-being-able-to-make-a-movie (*Adaptation*, 2002), screenwriter Eleanor Perry wrestled with John Cheever's squirrelly story "The Swimmer." And it's probably no accident that Cheever watched it all from the sidelines. He once admitted the story was "terribly difficult to write." While he was often able to finish a story in days, "The Swimmer" took him months: "I couldn't ever show my hand. Night was falling, the year was dying. It wasn't a question of technical problems, but one of imponderables. When he [protagonist Neddy Merrill] finds it's dark and cold, it has to have happened. And, by God, it did happen. I felt the dark and cold for some time after I finished that story." Cheever didn't elaborate on the "imponderables" but presumably his own alcoholism at the time played a part.

Although he downplayed it, "The Swimmer" is, in fact, a technical feat, a trickster's triumph, a high-wire balancing act worthy of a Wallenda. The tone, as in many of Cheever's stories, teeters on a narrow edge between fantasy and realism. It's a fantastic premise, a man swimming home using a string of neighborhood pools, and yet it's *just* within the realm of possibility. And then there's the task of using water and weather—almost all of Cheever's stories contain a telling description of the sky—without leaving the reader feeling as if she or he has been draped in heavy-handed metaphor. "The trick," Cheever confided, "was to get the winter constellations in the midsummer sky without anyone knowing about it." To do this his narrative had to be deliberately cagey. "It seems to me," Cheever once said, "that falsehood is a critical element in fiction. Part of the thrill of being told a story is the chance of being hoodwinked or taken. . . . The telling of lies is a sort of sleight-of-hand that displays our deepest feelings about life." And with "The Swimmer" Cheever has told a whopper—but somehow he gets away with it.

Moviemakers, with their habit of rushing into things that make angels tremble, often overlook the potential difficulties of adapting a literary work, but everyone involved with *The Swimmer* understood the dangers. Cheever himself, who claimed Hollywood made him suicidal—"The stores were selling yarmulkes for dogs. . . . My God!"—awarded the project to husband-and-wife team Frank and Eleanor Perry over several better-heeled offers. Pre-Sundance independent filmmakers, the Perrys demonstrated a regard for literary material and had already made a successful small film, *David and Lisa,* about two mentally ill teenagers who fall in love. Eleanor Perry (the screenwriter) had long been a Cheever fan, and when she read "The Swimmer" in *The New Yorker* she "saw it as a film right away, but *no* one else did." Her husband, Frank Perry (the director), was skeptical: "That I felt it would be difficult to adapt is putting it mildly. I thought Eleanor was crazy." Even the star, Burt Lancaster, was worried: "At best it is tricky. Ned's predicament is real and serious, but he avoids direct comment on it. . . . One wrong note and it will seem phony. I'm scared to death. . . ."*

Given the potential pitfalls, the results are admirable. Vincent Canby of the *New York Times* gave everyone involved with the film kudos for just making the attempt: "It's . . . an uneven, patchy kind of movie, occasionally gross and mawkish, and one I liked very much. I like the Perrys for having liked it, and I like Burt Lancaster, who is essentially miscast in the title role, for having wanted to do it." Over the years the film has grown in stature, and the unfavorable comparisons to the story have become less frequent. Instead, the film is often likened to a really, really good episode of *The Twilight Zone.*

It's a paradox (or a curse, depending on your point of view): Great stories almost always make less-than-great movies. But the why is elusive. When an adaptation goes well it's easy to point to a felicitous mixture of people, talent, and circumstances, but when one doesn't go well . . . In the

* Recently there has been talk of a remake (with Alec Baldwin in the role of Neddy Merrill), but no words of trepidation yet.

same lecture in which Lawrence Kasdan said he reveled in the "low places," he quoted something screenwriter Abraham Polonsky once said: "For me, movies are irrevocably rooted in kitsch, in childhood, in storytelling, in the rubbish of paperbacks and sitting under streetlights. . . ." And it is comforting to know that the process is still a little sexy, still a little magical.

Bringing Up Baby

Hagar Wilde

David was surprised when Suzan's call was announced. They'd had a row the night before and it was Suzan's custom to punish the people who quarreled with her by making them call first, thereby placing them at a disadvantage. David reflected that Suzan must want something. For a brief moment he considered having Ching tell her that he had gone out with a "velly plitty lady" but Suzan was smart and she'd know that he was skulking there listening to every word. No, the thing to do was take this call and make Suzan feel that she'd been something of a weakling to ring him up.

He said, "Hello, Suzan." In brighter moments she was Suzy.

Suzan's voice was vague and far away as though she were lighting a cigarette, which she was. "Do you want a panther?"

"Do I want a panther?" David said. He untwisted the telephone cord, a futile gesture, but instinctive. "I can't hear you very well. Come closer to the transmitter."

Her voice came, cupped and resounding, even scratching a little along the sides of the wires. "I said, do you want a panther?"

"No," David said. "Why should I?"

"Well, for that matter," Suzan said peevishly, "why should I? But I've got one."

"Where would you get a panther?"

"Mark."

Mark was her brother. He'd been away for two months, nobody knew quite where except that he was below the equator. An important point presented itself to David. "How big?" he said.

"Big," said Suzan. "He just fits into the bathroom. Aunt Elizabeth is coming and I have to farm the beast out somewhere."

"Suzan Vance, you get right out of that apartment."

"Nonsense," said Suzan. "I have a lease. Maybe Tommy—"

"Tommy's out of town."

"Rats," Suzan said.

Suzan's maid had taken her stand in the corridor but she had retained a key. This she delivered to David, who arrived breathless, with an oration. "It's not me that's putting any wild beast into any bathroom. If she wants it in the bathroom she can put it in the bathroom and I wish her good luck."

At this point, Suzan, a bit disheveled, popped her head out at them. "You can come in now, lionheart. I've stowed him away. Oh, hello, David."

David followed her inside. His hands were a bit clammy and perspiration was starting around his hairline. "Suzan," he said, "I will not allow—"

"Don't stand there yapping about what you'll allow. Try to think of some nice, responsible person you know who likes panthers."

"No responsible person likes panthers!" David yelled.

A familiar gleam entered Suzan's eyes. "My brother Mark likes panthers and you wouldn't tell Mark to his face that he wasn't responsible."

David kept his temper because losing it never got him anywhere. "Darling—"

She said sharply, "Don't wheedle. If you're going to try and get your own way come out in the open and fight like a man."

"I was about to say, we'll get somebody from a zoo to—"

Suzan said stubbornly, "Mark says I'm to keep him, so I'm going to keep him." It had a note of finality. "I've other things on my mind. Listen." Producing two documents from a pile of mail on the table, she waved them at him and then read the first, prefacing the reading by saying, "From Mark. From Brazil":

Dear Suzy:

I'm sending you Baby, a panther I picked up. He's three years old, gentle as a kitten and he likes dogs.

Suzan paused, frowned a little and then smiled apologetically. "I don't know whether Mark means he eats dogs or is fond of them," she said. "Mark's so vague at times." She continued reading:

He also likes music, particularly that song "I Can't Give You Anything but Love, Baby." It may be because his name is in the lyric but, anyway, it enchants him. Try getting records with the word baby in them. That shouldn't be hard if music is what it was when I left. Guard him with

> your life. I am leaving Brazil tomorrow. Will communicate with you from the next port. Don't feed Baby potatoes. He gets sick as a dog.

"I wish he'd get sick as a panther and die," said David.

"Don't interrupt. Mark adds a postscript. Wouldn't Mark put a thing like this in a postscript! 'Aunt Elizabeth's changed her will in our favor again. Give the old girl my love when she arrives.' " Suzan put the letter down and stared at it angrily. "When she arrives! As though he didn't know that I never open Aunt Elizabeth's letters except on the first of the month!"

"I don't follow you," David said.

"Mark's probably known for weeks that she was coming, but I didn't. She writes four times a month, once with a check and three times with lectures, so naturally I skip the lectures. Fortunately I save them in neat little piles. Here's her last. I opened it after I read Mark's. Aunt Elizabeth says in it that she is arriving in America on the twelfth."

"That's tomorrow," said David.

"I know it," Suzan said, glaring. She went on reading:

> Why have you not replied to my last letter? I intend leaving my erstwhile friend Drusilla Maretti for good this time. Nobody could get on with her, what with her overweening conceit about a voice that might have been good once but certainly is nothing to listen to now and that moth-eaten cheetah she's always lugging about. I am thoroughly out of patience.
>
> I will expect you to move out to the Connecticut house for the length of my stay.
>
> I understand that you are engaged. You might have apprised me of this fact but I suppose I can expect very little from you and Mark in the way of acting like human beings. However, I want your fiancé to come to Connecticut with us. It's a good idea, in the country, to have a man in the house.
>
> Drusilla and I, at the moment, are not speaking. It makes things very difficult, living in the same house. I look forward, in America, to peace and quiet.
>
> *Your affectionate aunt,*
> *Elizabeth Reardon*

Suzan stared into space, two frown wrinkles deeply embedded over her nose.

"So she comes to America to get away from a cheetah," she said, "and runs smack into a panther. Just after she's changed her will. It doesn't make sense."

"Drusilla Maretti's the opera singer, isn't she?"

"The ex-opera singer. They've lived together for years. They should both be packed away in woollies, knitting. But, no, they give the most ghastly dinner parties and wear feathers in their hair and serve champagne and Drusilla sings after dinner and Aunt Elizabeth sits in the corner and sneers."

"I've always wanted to make faces back at singers, too," said David.

"Then one of them packs up in a huff and makes a dramatic exit, saying she hopes she'll never set eyes on the other again. Two months later they're back together again, thick as thieves. Well, anyway—" Suzan sat briskly erect. This meant that she was now prepared to deal with the matter in hand. "Aunt Elizabeth can't know that we have Baby."

"Can Baby know that we have Aunt Elizabeth?"

"Don't be tiresome. We'll take him up to Connecticut in the station wagon. Two of the tenant houses are empty. We'll tie him in one and sneak food out to him nights."

"You mean I'll sneak food out to him nights," said David.

"Well, what do you think of it?"

"I think it's lousy," David said, his head in his hands, "but I don't suppose that makes any difference."

"How would you like me not to have any money if I ever decide to marry you?" Suzan demanded.

"I shouldn't like it. I've only got just enough to live on in luxury and entertain you. I certainly can't keep you."

"Precisely. So you help or I won't marry you."

"You broke our engagement last night," David said.

"Oh, that," said Suzan airily.

Hauling a panther seventy miles in a station wagon without bars between you and the panther is no joke. Suzan kept referring to Baby as a lamb, because he was quiet but David was aware at all moments during the drive that Baby was no lamb. Those few hours marked a turning point in David's life. He realized that life was not all fun and that it might end in death by drowning or perhaps, through no fault of your own, by having a panther who was in a position of advantage take a dislike to you. He marveled at Suzan, who seemed perfectly cool and unaware of the fact that chance plays such an important part in whether one lives or dies and the manner of the latter.

He was still regarding Suzan with wonder at three o'clock the following afternoon. They sat in the drawing room of the Connecticut house. Suzan was pensively staring at the arrangement of a bowl of heather as though she hadn't another care in the world. She in no way resembled the girl who had pushed Baby into a deserted house a stone's throw away and secured him with what she optimistically called a sailor's knot.

She looked like a normal, exceptionally pretty girl of twenty-two, wearing a most attractive print dress and awaiting an aunt who was, if not beloved, at least highly respected. But there was an expression about her mouth that David had come to know. She wore it when she'd outwitted somebody.

Elizabeth Reardon was the biggest woman David had ever seen outside of a circus tent. She was accompanied by a personal maid named Marie, a chauffeur named Anthony and a fox terrier named George.

When Suzan said, "I'm glad to see you, Aunt Elizabeth," she replied, "I've always said you'd grow up to be an accomplished liar." Then she looked at David. "Is this the man you're going to marry?" She implied that if Suzan had been a better specimen she might have expected better luck.

George, the fox terrier, and Aunt Elizabeth had lived together so long that each knew, without consulting the other, what had to be done first. Their first duty was an inspection of the premises.

An awkward moment arose when Aunt Elizabeth came face to face with Baby's rations. As David pointed out later, one look at Elizabeth should have told them that she'd go straight as a homing pigeon to the source of life. She yanked open the refrigerator door and there reposed what in its most elegant terminology could only be called a hunk of meat.

"What," said Aunt Elizabeth with loathing, "is that?"

Suzan stammered, "Meat."

"For what?" said her aunt.

David jumped into the breach with, "For George."

"George doesn't eat muck like that. Throw it away."

Under her and George's eagle eyes they chucked it into a garbage receptacle.

Then Aunt Elizabeth unpacked.

The day wore on. It wore on everybody. When Aunt Elizabeth retired at nine o'clock Suzan and David dived quietly out the back door and rummaged for Baby's supper. "Got it," said Suzan finally and inelegantly.

Baby was pathetically glad to see them. Not only had he been feeling the pangs of inner panther but he'd been lonely. He rolled over on his back and Suzan scratched his stomach. "Cute," Suzan said.

"Very cute," said David at a safe distance.

Suddenly Suzan jumped, listened and came over to clutch his arm, hissing, "What was that?" Baby had pricked up his ears and abandoned his supper momentarily.

What she'd heard was a sniffing sound. It grew in volume. It finally stood in the doorway. It was George, spying as usual.

"Grab him," said Suzan.

"You grab him," said David. "You know him better."

"That's why I won't grab him," Suzan said, dancing agitatedly.

David advanced, saying, "Nice George." George growled.

"He knows better than that," Suzan said, still dancing.

She panted, as they plunged toward the house with George in David's arms. "He must like you. He hasn't growled once since you picked him up."

"He can't," David said bitterly. "His mouth is full of my hand."

They persuaded George to relinquish David's hand and shut him up in Suzan's bedroom.

The following morning at ten o'clock a great uproar started, made its way down the corridor and turned out to be Aunt Elizabeth rousing the house. She stood in Suzan's doorway and said, "Get up."

Suzan stirred sleepily and sat up. She hadn't had much sleep.

"What's George doing under your bed?"

"Growling the first part of the night and snoring the last," said Suzan.

"Well, get up. Get that young man—what's his name?—David. Get him up, too."

Suzan sighed.

Suzan's devotion to George that day was a thing of beauty. The fact that it awoke in George no answering loyalty proved rather conclusively that he had a nasty character.

Suzan took him into the kitchen and gave him his breakfast with her own hands, standing guard while he ate it. When he went outside for his morning constitutional, Suzan was at his heels. George was all for heading straight toward the tenant cottage but at the risk of life and limb Suzan carried him in the other direction. She did everything but follow him into a hollow tree. After maneuvering him back into the house she sank exhausted upon the divan, her eyes glued upon his hideous form.

George stretched out on the drawing room threshold and snoozed peacefully, his snore mounting in volume as he drew farther and farther away from a waking world. Suzan began to understand the principle of hypnotism. The object held in front of the eyes needn't be bright. It can be just a dog who is intent upon visiting a panther against your wishes.

David came in and found her, fast asleep, her arm tucked under her head. He joined Aunt Elizabeth in a game of double solitaire in the sunroom.

At three o'clock Suzan started up like a frightened doe. Asleep at the switch. Asleep on sentry duty. George was gone. Suzan started a systematic search of the house. She ended up in the sunroom gesturing wildly behind her aunt's back, making a pretense of barking and pointing toward the tenant cottage. David stared. "George is such a nice dog," Suzan said desperately.

"Nonsense," Aunt Elizabeth said, without turning, "George is a fiend and you very well know it."

"He's gone for a walk *all by himself*," said Suzan.

"That's because nobody with any sense would go with him," her aunt said.

David said, rising, "Excuse me, I just thought of something."

"Finish the hand," barked Aunt Elizabeth.

Suzan snatched David's cards. "I'll finish it."

She finished it and then she, too, bolted. Aunt Elizabeth could hear her little rubber heels thudding down the front steps at a terrific rate.

"Mad," said the old lady. "Balmy, the lot of them." She went on playing.

Suzan lunged around the corner of the tenant cottage. David was sitting on the top step. Suzan stood, quivering like an anguished pointer. "Were you in time?"

"Oh, plenty," said David. He displayed a frayed end of rope.

Suzan gaped and sank weakly beside him. "What do we do now?"

"I wonder," David said, "how one goes about telling people there's a panther at large without telling how he got at large."

"They j-just say they s-saw a panther."

"We might try it," David said.

Suzan didn't reply.

David made his plan on the way back. "I'll just call a zoo and tell them I've seen a panther. Then they'll come and catch him."

"It's too simple," said Suzan.

Aunt Elizabeth was still engrossed in her solitaire when Suzan came in. She slipped a ten into a king space and said, "Where's David?"

"Telephoning a friend," said Suzan.

David's opponent on the telephone was saying, "Yeah, I heard you. You saw a panther. In Connecticut."

"Well, aren't you going to do something about it?"

"You do something about it. You had the fun. Go to bed and sleep it off."

David clutched the instrument desperately and sank his mouth into the transmitter. "I tell you this is a bona fide *panther*!"

"Listen, I know every species of panther and this isn't one of them."

"He must be having a fight with his friend," said Aunt Elizabeth, slipping a queen into a king space.

The doorbell rang. Suzan went to answer it. Aunt Elizabeth took advantage of her absence to cheat on a large scale. She'd practically run her cards out when Suzan returned, flourishing a cablegram.

Aunt Elizabeth opened it, saying, "It's from Mark," and then, sharply, "Don't play until I've read it. It's not fair."

Upstairs, David was saying despairingly, "Let me talk to the man in charge. The man in charge of *everything*."

Aunt Elizabeth adjusted her spectacles and read in a monotone, "Welcome America are you pleased with Baby Love Mark."

She put the cablegram down and stared at it. "Baby?"

"He means me," Suzan bleated.

"You're no baby," said Aunt Elizabeth, "and he doesn't say a word about my panther. You might know. Mark's always been highly unreliable. Cable him at once and say I want to know whether he's going to keep his promise."

Suzan had risen, disarranging her cards by clutching motions. "Panther?" said Suzan. "Promise?"

"Mark promised me a panther and I mean to get it. I'm not going to have Drusilla Maretti lording it over me any longer with her cheetah. I've given that young scoundrel enough money to run the White House—I've changed my will in his favor—and yours, I might add, though why I don't know—and all I asked was a panther. Then he cables me asking if I'm pleased with you. That's the way Mark does things."

"Excuse me," Suzan said faintly.

As she staggered from the room she heard her aunt booming, "I'll get a panther if I have to rob a zoo! Why I should have to pay a stranger to go out and hunt for me when I have a nephew—"

Suzan skidded across the waxed floors of the bedroom and landed at David's feet, saying, "Don't call the zoo! That Mark! He couldn't tell me! Don't call the zoo, David!"

David hung up. "I've called the zoo. It's all fixed."

"Call them back and unfix it. Don't ask questions. Call them back."

"I will not," David said indignantly. "I offered the man two hundred dollars and the panther, if he'd come over. And he's coming, with some helpers."

"You gave him Baby!" she raged. "You gave away my life's happiness, my brother's trust in me, my brother's inheritance—"

"Stop flinging your arms about," said David. "Explain."

Suzan explained but when David called back the zoo somebody said that everybody except himself and the night watchman had gone hunting a panther that was loose.

Suzan drew a deep, determined breath. "Then there's only one hope left. We must find him before they do. Have you any idea how to catch a panther?"

"No," said David simply.

"Start thinking about it," said Suzan. "If those men from the zoo ring the doorbell one of us must answer it and get rid of them."

"How?" David said, but she was already on her way downstairs. He followed.

While they were at dinner there was a loud and insistent pealing of the doorbell.

Suzan drifted from the room and flew down the corridor. Opening the door a crack she slid out, closing it behind her. The man who stood outside was rubbing his chin as though by so doing he could free it of a two days' growth of beard. "You the party that called us about a panther?"

"Oh, no, indeed," said Suzan.

"Man live around here by the name of Melton?"

"Never heard of him," said Suzan.

"I've asked everybody on this road so far."

"Well, there are still five miles of this road. If you're going west, that is. Seven, if you're going east."

He hesitated, looking east. "Better lock up your chickens tonight, lady. There's a panther loose around somewhere."

"Haven't got any chickens," Suzan said, as though she'd just played an ace on his king. She went back to her dinner.

Seeing the expression around her mouth, David knew that she had been successful. He envisioned all the men from the zoo locked in the back of their truck with the ignition out.

Aunt Elizabeth, as was her custom, retired at nine. Suzan and David crept down the back stairs to confer in the basement. "Now," Suzan said in a hoarse whisper, "we must be methodical about this. Before we act we must think."

"You think," said David. "I'll just sit here and recover from the thinking I was doing at dinner."

"What would be the most logical thing to take on a panther hunt?"

"A bigger panther," David said.

"If you were a panther," said Suzan, "where would you go?"

"I'd come home to Aunt Elizabeth."

They set out finally with a length of rope and a landing net which Suzan insisted upon taking despite the fact that it was for fish. She said that it might come in handy and that it would be no trouble to carry it. It was no trouble for anyone but David, who carried it.

They saw the panther only once, and briefly. He was with George, and seemed willing enough to come home, but when Suzan bent down and temptingly held out a bit of Baby's dinner meat, George growled insinuatingly and walked away. Baby, stretching luxuriously, hesitated only a moment between love and duty. He followed the dog, disappearing into the woods in three leaps. They started after him. It kept growing darker.

The quarrel started at twelve o'clock. It was born when Suzan tripped and fell over a log. She lay there, flat on her face, until David picked her up. He made the mistake of saying, "Watch where you're going."

They'd been walking since nine-thirty. Suzan had torn her frock. Privately, she had despaired of finding Baby and that made matters worse. Her voice trembled. She said, "Watch where I'm going yourself, smart aleck—I mean watch where—" and then she began crying.

"Now, look," David said. "I'd suggest that we go home."

Suzan stamped her wrath out on innocent shrubs. "Go home and tuck yourself into bed, quitter! Go on home. I'm going to find that beast if it—t-takes me the rest of my natural life! The idea, turning a wild animal loose on an innocent countryside and then g-going home and sleeping—with lives in danger—all over—"

David said, "Oh, Suzan, do stop making an ass of yourself."

"So," said Suzan. She jumped back hastily into her dignity. "So," she said, and stalked off. David followed. Suzan stopped. "Please, David," she said, "I'd rather you didn't."

"Didn't what?"

"Didn't come with me," said Suzan frigidly. "This time, David, I am through. The other times have been silly quarrels, but this time I am thoroughly, quite thoroughly, through."

"Oh, very well," David said. He sat down on a log.

He could hear Suzan crashing away from him. Then she crashed back toward him after a bit. Presently, in a quavering voice quite near him she said, "David?"

David kept quiet.

"Oooh!" said Suzan, and headed straight for the main road. Establishing your independence is one thing and mucking about in the woods alone at twelve o'clock at night is another.

David followed at a reasonable distance. He threw away the landing net but retained the rope, mindful of the fact that it was a clothesline and useful in its way.

The moon was up. Ahead, he could see Suzan looking from side to side but she wasn't looking for Baby. She was looking for something to jump out at her from behind a tree. David was resigned to the fact that the most baleful and horrible revenge that has ever been perpetrated on a man by a woman was being cooked up but it didn't seem to matter. The only thing of importance in the whole world was a bed. A wide, comfortable bed with big, soft pillows. A bed that was sturdy. A bed where a man could sink back, close his eyes and just ache in peace until he fell asleep.

As Suzan came abreast of a large, white house, she stopped suddenly. She dropped to her hands and knees and started crawling. David thought, "The little beast has sprained her ankle," but after a moment he realized that she was crawling toward an objective. The objective was a monotonous, low growling sound. George. Suzan disappeared behind a largish clump of hydrangeas. David advanced. After looking a moment he could distinguish a big, cat-like form outlined against the sky, comfortably ensconced on the veranda roof of the white house.

Suzan was saying, "Good Baby. Nice Baby, come down."

David gave up and sat down in a clump of sumac.

Suzan was waxing indignant. Knowing Suzan, David knew that she was stamping her foot. "Come down at *once*!" George growled louder.

There was a short silence. Suzan was thinking. David hoped she wouldn't decide to climb the trellis and come to grips with her problem.

The fruit of her thought came, after a long moment. She lifted her voice in song.

"I can't give you anything but love, ba-by,
That's the only thing I've plenty o-of, ba-by . . ."

A window was flung up and a pajama-clad man appeared in the aperture. Obviously, he was at a loss to know where to start. He said finally, "What are you doing, may I ask?"

"Singing," Suzan said.

"If you're paying a bet there must be someplace else you can pay it," the man said. By this time his wife had joined him at the window. Clearly, she didn't like Suzan's looks.

"I'm not paying a bet," Suzan said distinctly. "There's a panther on your roof."

"I'm not going to bandy words with you at this time of night." He, too, was beginning not to like Suzan.

"There's a panther on your roof and it's my panther," Suzan said stubbornly, "and I'm going to get him. To get him, I have to sing."

"There is nothing on my roof," he said.

"There is! Come out and look!"

The woman's face softened. She said something to her husband. He drew back from the opening like a turtle whose shell had been tapped. The woman leaned farther out and said, "Sing if you like, dear."

Suzan started. "I can't give you anything but love, baby . . ."

The woman regarded her pityingly, shaking her head a little.

A door banged. The man had put on his pants hurriedly. Baby, alarmed, disappeared over the edge of the roof.

Suzan was yelling, "He went that way!"

She struggled in the gentle but firm grip of a man who knew his duty. He kept saying, "Hush, hush. It's all right."

"You've frightened him away," Suzan wailed furiously, "and now I'll never find him again."

"See, he's still there," her captor said soothingly. "See him?"

"He's not!" Suzan yelled. "Let go of my arm! Let go!"

"He'll come back, don't worry. Now you tell me where you live. Do you know?"

"Of course I know," Suzan said indignantly, "but that's not the point. I have to get my panther." She appealed desperately to him. "Won't you help me?"

"I certainly will," he said.

With a sigh of relief, David pushed his way through the sumac thicket. Suzan was safe. Of course, when she discovered that the man thought her batty, the man wasn't safe, but that was his responsibility, not David's.

It was dark among the trees. David stumbled around looking up into them for Baby and under them for George. Now and then he called, hoping that George would growl in reply.

He came upon them in a small clearing. Baby was lying in a wagon track and George was standing beside him. David had an unpleasant feeling that they'd been watching him all the time. He tried to remember all the things he'd ever heard about dealing with animals. Looking Baby straight in the eyes was a bit difficult in the dark and from a distance. He tried cooing at them and making wild promises about steak at home, but George only growled.

Only the picture of sitting all night in that clearing, watching Baby, drove him to unwind the rope and walk toward them. Baby rolled over on his back to have his stomach scratched. David scratched it and put the rope around his neck. From there on it was simple. He merely walked home. Baby padded along at his side and George followed at his heels, growling.

Every light in the house was on and Aunt Elizabeth, in a fury, was on the telephone. David went in, towing Baby.

Aunt Elizabeth was shouting, "Of course I have a niece but she's decently in bed, not singing around under windows! Why should I come to the police station and identify her? It's no responsibility of mine or my niece's if you've picked up a feeble-minded female! Don't take any checks from her, mind."

David grinned, feeling a twinge of sympathy for the local police force.

"I tell you," Aunt Elizabeth shouted, "that the girl's an imposter! My niece is a sober, self-respecting citizen!" Then she looked up and saw David. She stared at Baby. She looked back at David. She turned to the telephone. "Wait a minute, my good man," she said. "I might be wrong."

David handed Elizabeth the end of the clothesline. He took the telephone from her unresisting hand. "Put your prisoner on the wire, Sergeant," he said. "If it's Miss Vance we'll be able to identify her by her voice."

A furious squeaking sailed into the room from the receiver.

"Don't take that tone," David said warningly.

"Da-*vid*!" said Suzan.

"Am I marvelous?"

"You're anything you said," wailed Suzan.

"Are we engaged or aren't we?"

"All right," Suzan said sulkily.

"I'll be right over," David said. He hung up.

After he'd gone Aunt Elizabeth stood staring at Baby, who was rolling over to have his stomach scratched. "Imagine," she said into space, "Mark can't send me a panther from the wilds of Brazil but these two can scare one up in Connecticut woods. That's rather sweet. I've misjudged Suzan. I think—yes, I think I'll cut Mark off and give Suzan all the money."

Babylon Revisited

F. Scott Fitzgerald

I

"And where's Mr. Campbell?" Charlie asked.

"Gone to Switzerland. Mr. Campbell's a pretty sick man, Mr. Wales."

"I'm sorry to hear that. And George Hardt?" Charlie inquired.

"Back in America, gone to work."

"And where is the Snow Bird?"

"He was in here last week. Anyway, his friend, Mr. Schaeffer, is in Paris."

Two familiar names from the long list of a year and a half ago. Charlie scribbled an address in his notebook and tore out the page.

"If you see Mr. Schaeffer, give him this," he said. "It's my brother-in-law's address. I haven't settled on a hotel yet."

He was not really disappointed to find Paris was so empty. But the stillness in the Ritz bar was strange and portentous. It was not an American bar anymore—he felt polite in it, and not as if he owned it. It had gone back into France. He felt the stillness from the moment he got out of the taxi and saw the doorman, usually a frenzy of activity at this hour, gossiping with a *chasseur* by the servants' entrance.

Passing through the corridor, he heard only a single, bored voice in the once-clamorous women's room. When he turned into the bar he traveled the twenty feet of green carpet with his eyes fixed straight ahead by old habit; and then, with his foot firmly on the rail, he turned and surveyed the room, encountering only a single pair of eyes that fluttered up from a newspaper in the corner. Charlie asked for the head barman, Paul, who in the latter days of the bull market had come to work in his own custom-built car—disembarking, however, with due nicety at the nearest corner. But Paul was at his country house today and Alix giving him information.

"No, no more," Charlie said, "I'm going slow these days."

Alix congratulated him: "You were going pretty strong a couple of years ago."

"I'll stick to it all right," Charlie assured him. "I've stuck to it for over a year and a half now."

"How do you find conditions in America?"

"I haven't been to America for months. I'm in business in Prague, representing a couple of concerns there. They don't know about me down there."

Alix smiled.

"Remember the night of George Hardt's bachelor dinner here?" said Charlie. "By the way, what's become of Claude Fessenden?"

Alix lowered his voice confidentially: "He's in Paris, but he doesn't come here anymore. Paul doesn't allow it. He ran up a bill of thirty thousand francs, charging all his drinks and his lunches, and usually his dinner, for more than a year. And when Paul finally told him he had to pay, he gave him a bad check."

Alix shook his head sadly.

"I don't understand it, such a dandy fellow. Now he's all bloated up—" He made a plump apple of his hands.

Charlie watched a group of strident queens installing themselves in a corner.

"Nothing affects them," he thought. "Stocks rise and fall, people loaf or work, but they go on forever." The place oppressed him. He called for the dice and shook with Alix for a drink.

"Here for long, Mr. Wales?"

"I'm here for four or five days to see my little girl."

"Oh-h! You have a little girl?"

Outside, the fire-red, gas-blue, ghost-green signs shone smokily through the tranquil rain. It was late afternoon and the streets were in movement; the *bistros* gleamed. At the corner of the Boulevard des Capucines he took a taxi. The Place de la Concorde moved by in pink majesty; they crossed the logical Seine, and Charlie felt the sudden provincial quality of the Left Bank.

Charlie directed his taxi to the Avenue de l'Opera, which was out of his way. But he wanted to see the blue hour spread over the magnificent façade, and imagine that the cab horns, playing endlessly the first few bars of *La Plus que Lente,* were the trumpets of the Second Empire. They were closing the iron grill in front of Brentano's Bookstore and people were already at dinner behind the trim little bourgeois hedge of Duval's. He had never eaten at a really cheap restaurant in Paris. Five-course dinner, four francs fifty, eighteen cents, wine included. For some odd reason he wished that he had.

As they rolled on to the Left Bank and he felt its sudden provincialism, he thought, "I spoiled this city for myself. I didn't realize it, but the days came along one after another, and then two years were gone, and everything was gone, and I was gone."

He was thirty-five, and good to look at. The Irish mobility of his face was sobered by a deep wrinkle between his eyes. As he rang his brother-in-law's bell in the Rue Palatine, the wrinkle deepened till it pulled down his brows; he felt a cramping sensation in his belly. From behind the maid who opened the door darted a lovely little girl of nine who shrieked "Daddy!" and flew up, struggling like a fish, into his arms. She pulled his head around by one ear and set her cheek against his.

"My old pie," he said.

"Oh, daddy, daddy, daddy, daddy, dads, dads, dads!"

She drew him into the salon, where the family waited, a boy and a girl his daughter's age, his sister-in-law and her husband. He greeted Marion with his voice pitched carefully to avoid either feigned enthusiasm or dislike, but her response was more frankly tepid, though she minimized her expression of unalterable distrust by directing her regard toward his child. The two men clasped hands in a friendly way and Lincoln Peters rested his for a moment on Charlie's shoulder.

The room was warm and comfortably American. The three children moved intimately about, playing through the yellow oblongs that led to other rooms; the cheer of six o'clock spoke in the eager smacks of the fire and the sounds of French activity in the kitchen. But Charlie did not relax; his heart sat up rigidly in his body and he drew confidence from his daughter, who from time to time came close to him, holding in her arms the doll he had brought.

"Really extremely well," he declared in answer to Lincoln's question. "There's a lot of business there that isn't moving at all, but we're doing even better than ever. In fact, damn well. I'm bringing my sister over from America next month to keep house for me. My income last year was bigger than it was when I had money. You see, the Czechs—"

His boasting was for a specific purpose; but after a moment, seeing a faint restiveness in Lincoln's eye, he changed the subject:

"Those are fine children of yours, well brought up, good manners."

"We think Honoria's a great little girl too."

Marion Peters came back from the kitchen. She was a tall woman with worried eyes, who had once possessed a fresh American loveliness. Charlie had never been sensitive to it and was always surprised when people spoke of how pretty she had been. From the first there had been an instinctive antipathy between them.

"Well, how do you find Honoria?" she asked.

"Wonderful. I was astonished how much she's grown in ten months. All the children are looking well."

"We haven't had a doctor for a year. How do you like being back in Paris?"

"It seems very funny to see so few Americans around."

"I'm delighted," Marion said vehemently. "Now at least you can go into a store without their assuming you're a millionaire. We've suffered like everybody, but on the whole it's a good deal pleasanter."

"But it was nice while it lasted," Charlie said. "We were sort of royalty, almost infallible, with a sort of magic around us. In the bar this afternoon"—he stumbled, seeing his mistake—"there wasn't a man I knew."

She looked at him keenly. "I should think you've had enough of bars."

"I only stayed a minute. I take one drink every afternoon and no more."

"Don't you want a cocktail before dinner?" Lincoln asked.

"I take only one drink every afternoon, and I've had that."

"I hope you keep to it," said Marion.

Her dislike was evident in the coldness with which she spoke, but Charlie only smiled; he had larger plans. Her very aggressiveness gave him an advantage, and he knew enough to wait. He wanted them to initiate the discussion of what they knew had brought him to Paris.

At dinner he couldn't decide whether Honoria was most like him or her mother. Fortunate if she didn't combine the traits of both that had brought them to disaster. A great wave of protectiveness went over him. He thought he knew what to do for her. He believed in character; he wanted to jump back a whole generation and trust in character again as the eternally valuable element. Everything else wore out.

He left soon after dinner, but not to go home. He was curious to see Paris by night with clearer and more judicious eyes than those of other days. He bought a *stapontin* for the Casino and watched Josephine Baker go through her chocolate arabesques.

After an hour he left and strolled toward Montmartre, up the Rue Pigalle into the Place Blanche. The rain had stopped and there were a few people in evening clothes disembarking from taxis in front of cabarets, and *cocottes* prowling singly or in pairs, and many Negroes. He passed a lighted door from which issued music, and stopped with the sense of familiarity; it was Bricktop's, where he had parted with so many hours and so much money. A few doors farther on he found another ancient rendezvous and incautiously put his head inside. Immediately an eager orchestra burst into sound, a pair of professional dancers leaped to their feet and a maitre d'hôtel swooped toward him, crying, "Crowd just arriving, sir!" But he withdrew quickly.

"You have to be damn drunk," he thought.

Zelli's was closed, the bleak and sinister cheap hotels surrounding it were dark; up in the Rue Blanche there was more light and a local, colloquial French crowd. The Poet's Cave had disappeared, but the two great mouths of the Café of Heaven and the Café of Hell still yawned—even devoured, as he watched, the meager contents of a tourist bus—a German, a Japanese, and an American couple who glanced at him with frightened eyes.

So much for the effort and ingenuity of Montmartre. All the catering to vice and waste was on an utterly childish scale, and he suddenly realized the meaning of the word "dissipate"—to dissipate into thin air; to make nothing out of something. In the little hours of the night every move from place to place was an enormous human jump, an increase of paying for the privilege of slower and slower motion.

He remembered thousand-franc notes given to an orchestra for playing a single number, hundred-franc notes tossed to a doorman for calling a cab.

But it hadn't been given for nothing.

It had been given, even the most wildly squandered sum, as an offering to destiny that he might not remember the things most worth remembering, the things that now he would always remember—his child taken from his control, his wife escaped to a grave in Vermont.

In the glare of a *brasserie* a woman spoke to him. He bought her some eggs and coffee, and then, eluding her encouraging stare, gave her a twenty-franc note and took a taxi to his hotel.

II

He woke upon a fine fall day—football weather. The depression of yesterday was gone and he liked the people on the streets. At noon he sat opposite Honoria at Le Grand Vatel, the only restaurant he could think of not reminiscent of champagne dinners and long luncheons that began at two and ended in a blurred and vague twilight.

"Now, how about vegetables? Oughtn't you to have some vegetables?"

"Well, yes."

"Here's *épinards* and *chou-fleur* and carrots and *haricots*."

"I'd like *chou-fleur*."

"Wouldn't you like to have two vegetables?"

"I usually only have one at lunch."

The waiter was pretending to be inordinately fond of children. *"Qu'elle est mignonne la petite! Elle parle exactement comme une Française."*

"How about dessert? Shall we wait and see?"

The waiter disappeared. Honoria looked at her father expectantly.

"What are we going to do?"

"First, we're going to that toy store in the Rue Saint-Honoré and buy you anything you like. And then we're going to the vaudeville at the Empire."

She hesitated. "I like it about the vaudeville, but not the toy store."

"Why not?"

"Well, you brought me this doll." She had it with her. "And I've got lots of things. And we're not rich anymore, are we?"

"We never were. But today you are to have anything you want."

"All right," she agreed resignedly.

When there had been her mother and a French nurse he had been inclined to be strict; now he extended himself, reached out for a new tolerance; he must be both parents to her and not shut any of her out of communication.

"I want to get to know you," he said gravely. "First let me introduce myself. My name is Charles J. Wales, of Prague."

"Oh, daddy!" her voice cracked with laughter.

"And who are you, please?" he persisted, and she accepted a rôle immediately. "Honoria Wales, Rue Palatine, Paris."

"Married or single?"

"No, not married. Single."

He indicated the doll. "But I see you have a child, madame."

Unwilling to disinherit it, she took it to her heart and thought quickly: "Yes, I've been married, but I'm not married now. My husband is dead."

He went on quickly, "And the child's name?"

"Simone. That's after my best friend at school."

"I'm very pleased that you're doing so well at school."

"I'm third this month," she boasted. "Elsie"—that was her cousin—"is only about eighteenth, and Richard is at the bottom."

"You like Richard and Elsie, don't you?"

"Oh, yes, I like Richard quite well and I like her all right."

Cautiously and casually he asked: "And Aunt Marion and Uncle Lincoln—which do you like best?"

"Oh, Uncle Lincoln, I guess."

He was increasingly aware of her presence. As they came in, a murmur of ". . . adorable" followed them, and now the people at the next table bent all their silences upon her, staring as if she were something no more conscious than a flower.

"Why don't I live with you?" she asked suddenly. "Because mamma's dead?"

"You must stay here and learn more French. It would have been hard for daddy to take care of you so well."

"I don't really need much taking care of anymore. I do everything for myself."

Going out of the restaurant, a man and a woman unexpectedly hailed him.

"Well, the old Wales!"

"Hello there, Lorraine. . . . Dunc."

Sudden ghosts out of the past: Duncan Schaeffer, a friend from college, Lorraine Quarrles, a lovely, pale blonde of thirty-one; one of a crowd who had helped them make months into days in the lavish times of three years ago.

"My husband couldn't come this year," she said, in answer to his question. "We're poor as hell. So he gave me two hundred a month and told me I could do my worst on that. . . . This is your little girl?"

"What about coming back and sitting down?" Duncan asked.

"Can't do it." He was glad for an excuse. As always, he felt Lorraine's passionate, provocative attraction, but his own rhythm was different now.

"Well, how about dinner?" she asked.

"I'm not free. Give me your address and let me call you."

"Charlie, I believe you're sober," she said judicially. "I honestly believe he's sober, Dunc. Pinch him and see if he's sober."

Charlie indicated Honoria with his head. They both laughed.

"What's your address?" said Duncan skeptically.

He hesitated, unwilling to give the name of his hotel.

"I'm not settled yet. I'd better call you. We're going to see the vaudeville at the Empire."

"There! That's what I want to do," Lorraine said. "I want to see some clowns and acrobats and jugglers. That's just what we'll do, Dunc."

"We've got to do an errand first," said Charlie. "Perhaps we'll see you there."

"All right, you snob. . . . Good-by, beautiful little girl."

"Good-by."

Honoria bobbed politely.

Somehow, an unwelcome encounter. They liked him because he was functioning, because he was serious; they wanted to see him, because he was stronger than they were now, because they wanted to draw a certain sustenance from his strength.

At the Empire, Honoria proudly refused to sit upon her father's folded coat. She was already an individual with a code of her own, and Charlie was more and more absorbed by the desire of putting a little of himself into her before she crystallized utterly. It was hopeless to try to know her in so short a time.

Between the acts they came upon Duncan and Lorraine in the lobby where the band was playing.

"Have a drink?"

"All right, but not up at the bar. We'll take a table."

"The perfect father."

Listening abstractedly to Lorraine, Charlie watched Honoria's eyes leave their table, and he followed them wistfully about the room, wondering what they saw. He met her glance and she smiled.

"I liked that lemonade," she said.

What had she said? What had he expected? Going home in a taxi afterward, he pulled her over until her head rested against his chest.

"Darling, do you ever think of your mother?"

"Yes, sometimes," she answered vaguely.

"I don't want you to forget her. Have you got a picture of her?"

"Yes, I think so. Anyhow, Aunt Marion has. Why don't you want me to forget her?"

"She loved you very much."

"I loved her too."

They were silent for a moment.

"Daddy, I want to come and live with you," she said suddenly.

His heart leaped; he had wanted it to come like this.

"Aren't you perfectly happy?"

"Yes, but I love you better than anybody. And you love me better than anybody, don't you, now that mummy's dead?"

"Of course I do. But you won't always like me best, honey. You'll grow up and meet somebody your own age and go marry him and forget you ever had a daddy."

"Yes, that's true," she agreed tranquilly.

He didn't go in. He was coming back at nine o'clock and he wanted to keep himself fresh and new for the thing he must say then.

"When you're safe inside, just show yourself in that window."

"All right. Good-by, dads, dads, dads, dads."

He waited in the dark street until she appeared, all warm and glowing in the window above and kissed her fingers out into the night.

III

They were waiting. Marion sat behind the coffee service in a dignified black dinner dress that just faintly suggested mourning. Lincoln was walking up and down with the animation of one who had already been talking. They were as anxious as he was to get into the question. He opened it almost immediately:

"I suppose you know what I want to see you about—why I really came to Paris."

Marion played with the black stars on her necklace and frowned.

"I'm awfully anxious to have a home," he continued. "And I'm awfully anxious to have Honoria in it. I appreciate your taking Honoria for her mother's sake, but things have changed now"—he hesitated and then continued more forcibly—"changed radically with me, and I want to ask you to reconsider the matter. It would be silly for me to deny that about three years ago I was acting badly—"

Marion looked up at him with hard eyes.

"—but all that's over. As I told you, I haven't had more than a drink a day for over a year, and I take that drink deliberately, so that the idea of alcohol won't get too big in my imagination. You see the idea?"

"No," said Marion succinctly.

"It's a sort of stunt I set myself. It keeps the matter in proportion."

"I get you," said Lincoln. "You don't want to admit it's got any attraction for you."

"Something like that. Sometimes I forget and don't take it. But I try to take it. Anyhow, I couldn't afford to drink in my position. The people I represent are more than satisfied with what I've done, and I'm bringing my sister over from Burlington to keep house for me, and I want awfully to have Honoria too. You know that even when her mother and I weren't getting along well we never let anything that happened touch Honoria. I know she's fond of me and I know I'm able to take care of her and—well, there you are. How do you feel about it?"

He knew that now he would have to take a beating. It would last an hour or two hours, and it would be difficult, but if he modulated his inevitable resentment to the chastened attitude of the reformed sinner, he might win his point in the end.

Keep your temper, he told himself. You don't want to be justified. You want Honoria.

Lincoln spoke first: "We've been talking it over ever since we got your letter last month. We're happy to have Honoria here. She's a dear little thing, and we're glad to be able to help her, but of course this isn't the question—"

Marion interrupted suddenly. "How long are you going to stay sober, Charlie?" she asked.

"Permanently, I hope."

"How can anybody count on that?"

"You know I never did drink heavily until I gave up business and came over here with nothing to do. Then Helen and I began to run around with—"

"Please leave Helen out of it. I can't bear to hear you talk about her like that."

He stared at her grimly; he had never been certain how fond of each other the sisters were in life.

"My drinking only lasted about a year and a half—from the time we came over until I—collapsed."

"It was time enough."

"It was time enough," he agreed.

"My duty is entirely to Helen," she said. "I try to think what she would have wanted me to do. Frankly, from the night you did that terrible thing you haven't really existed for me. I can't help that. She was my sister."

"Yes."

"When she was dying she asked me to look out for Honoria. If you hadn't been in a sanitarium then, it might have helped matters."

He had no answer.

"I'll never in my life be able to forget the morning when Helen knocked at my door, soaked to the skin and shivering and said you'd locked her out."

Charlie gripped the sides of the chair. This was more difficult than he expected; he wanted to launch out into a long expostulation and explanation, but he only said: "The night I locked her out—" and she interrupted, "I don't feel up to going over that again."

After a moment's silence, Lincoln said: "We're getting off the subject. You want Marion to set aside her legal guardianship and give you Honoria. I think the main point for her is whether she has confidence in you or not."

"I don't blame Marion," Charlie said slowly, "but I think she can have entire confidence in me. I had a good record up to three years ago. Of course, it's within human possibilities I might go wrong anytime. But if we wait much longer I'll lose Honoria's childhood and my chance for a home." He shook his head, "I'll simply lose her, don't you see?"

"Yes, I see," said Lincoln.

"Why didn't you think of all this before?" Marion asked.

"I suppose I did, from time to time, but Helen and I were getting along badly. When I consented to the guardianship, I was flat on my back in a sanitarium and the market had cleaned me out. I knew I'd acted badly, and I thought if it would bring any peace to Helen, I'd agree to anything. But now it's different. I'm functioning, I'm behaving damn well, so far as—"

"Please don't swear at me," Marion said.

He looked at her, startled. With each remark the force of her dislike became more and more apparent. She had built up all her fear of life into one wall and faced it toward him. This trivial reproof was possibly the result of some trouble with the cook several hours before. Charlie became increasingly alarmed at leaving Honoria in this atmosphere of hostility against himself; sooner or later it would come out, in a word here, a shake of the head there, and some of that distrust would be irrevocably implanted in Honoria. But he pulled his temper down out of his face and shut it up inside him; he had won a point, for Lincoln realized the absurdity of Marion's remark and asked her lightly since when she had objected to the word "damn."

"Another thing," Charlie said: "I'm able to give her certain advantages now. I'm going to take a French governess to Prague with me. I've got a lease on a new apartment—"

He stopped, realizing that he was blundering. They couldn't be expected to accept with equanimity the fact that his income was again twice as large as their own.

"I suppose you can give her more luxuries than we can," said Marion. "When you were throwing away money we were living along watching every ten francs. . . . I suppose you'll start doing it again."

"Oh, no," he said. "I've learned. I worked hard for ten years, you know—until I got lucky in the market, like so many people. Terribly lucky. It won't happen again."

There was a long silence. All of them felt their nerves straining, and for the first time in a year Charlie wanted a drink. He was sure now that Lincoln Peters wanted him to have his child.

Marion shuddered suddenly; part of her saw that Charlie's feet were planted on the earth now, and her own maternal feeling recognized the naturalness of his desire; but she had lived for a long time with a prejudice—a prejudice founded on a curious disbelief in her sister's happiness, and which, in the shock of one terrible night, had turned to hatred for him. It had all happened at a point in her life where the discouragement of ill health and adverse circumstances made it necessary for her to believe in tangible villainy and a tangible villain.

"I can't help what I think!" she cried out suddenly. "How much you were responsible for Helen's death, I don't know. It's something you'll have to square with your own conscience."

An electric current of agony surged through him; for a moment he was almost on his feet, an unuttered sound echoing in his throat. He hung on to himself for a moment, another moment.

"Hold on there," said Lincoln uncomfortably. "I never thought you were responsible for that."

"Helen died of heart trouble," Charlie said dully.

"Yes, heart trouble." Marion spoke as if the phrase had another meaning for her.

Then, in the flatness that followed her outburst, she saw him plainly and she knew he had somehow arrived at control over the situation. Glancing at her husband, she found no help from him, and as abruptly as if it were a matter of no importance, she threw up the sponge.

"Do what you like!" she cried, springing up from her chair. "She's your child. I'm not the person to stand in your way. I think if it were my child I'd rather see her—" She managed to check herself. "You two decide it. I can't stand this. I'm sick. I'm going to bed."

She hurried from the room; after a moment Lincoln said:

"This has been a hard day for her. You know how strongly she feels—" His voice was almost apologetic: "When a woman gets an idea in her head."

"Of course."

"It's going to be all right. I think she sees now that you—can provide for the child, and so we can't very well stand in your way or Honoria's way."

"Thank you, Lincoln."

"I'd better go along and see how she is."

"I'm going."

He was still trembling when he reached the street, but a walk down the Rue Bonaparte to the *quais* set him up, and as he crossed the Seine, fresh and new by the *quai* lamps, he felt exultant. But back in his room he couldn't sleep. The image of Helen haunted him. Helen whom he had loved so until they had senselessly begun to abuse each other's love, to tear it into shreds. On that terrible February night that Marion remembered so vividly, a slow quarrel had gone on for hours. There was a scene at the Florida, and then he attempted to take her home, and then she kissed young Webb at a table; after that there was what she had hysterically said. When he arrived home alone he turned the key in the lock in wild anger. How could he know she would arrive an hour later alone, that there would be a snowstorm in which she had wandered about in slippers, too confused to find a taxi? Then the aftermath, her escaping pneumonia by a miracle, and all the attendant horror. They were "reconciled," but that was the beginning of the end, and Marion, who had seen with her own eyes and who imagined it to be one of many scenes from her sister's martyrdom, never forgot.

Going over it again brought Helen nearer, and in the white, soft light that steals upon half sleep near morning he found himself talking to her again. She said that he was perfectly right about Honoria and that she wanted Honoria to be with him. She said she was glad he was being good and doing better. She said a lot of other things—very friendly things—but she was in a swing in a white dress, and swinging faster and faster all the time, so that at the end he could not hear clearly all that she said.

IV

He woke up feeling happy. The door of the world was open again. He made plans, vistas, futures for Honoria and himself, but suddenly he grew sad, remembering all the plans he and Helen had made. She had not planned to die. The present was the thing—work to do and someone to love. But not to love too much, for he knew the injury that a father can do to a daughter or a mother to a son by attaching them too closely: afterward, out in the world, the child would seek in the marriage partner the same blind tenderness and, failing probably to find it, turn against love and life.

It was another bright, crisp day. He called Lincoln Peters at the bank where he worked and asked if he could count on taking Honoria when he left for Prague. Lincoln agreed that there was no reason for delay. One thing—the legal guardianship. Marion wanted to retain that a while longer. She was upset by the whole matter, and it would oil things if she felt that the situation was still in her control for another year. Charlie agreed, wanting only the tangible, visible child.

Then the question of a governess. Charles sat in a gloomy agency and talked to a cross Béarnaise and to a buxom Breton peasant, neither of whom he could have endured. There were others whom he would see tomorrow.

He lunched with Lincoln Peters at Griffons, trying to keep down his exultation.

"There's nothing quite like your own child," Lincoln said. "But you understand how Marion feels too."

"She's forgotten how hard I worked for seven years there," Charlie said. "She just remembers one night."

"There's another thing." Lincoln hesitated. "While you and Helen were tearing around Europe and throwing money away, we were just getting along. I didn't touch any of the prosperity because I never got ahead enough to carry anything but my insurance. I think Marion felt there was some kind of injustice in it—you not even working toward the end, and getting richer and richer."

"It went just as quick as it came," said Charlie.

"Yes, a lot of it stayed in the hands of *chasseurs* and saxophone players and maîtres d'hôtel—well, the big party's over now, I just said that to explain Marion's feeling about those crazy years. If you drop in about six o'clock tonight before Marion's too tired, we'll settle the details on the spot."

Back at his hotel, Charlie found a *pneumatique* that had been redirected from the Ritz bar where Charlie had left his address for the purpose of finding a certain man.

Dear Charlie

You were so strange when we saw you the other day that I wondered if I did something to offend you. If so, I'm not conscious of it. In fact, I have thought about you too much for the last year, and it's always been in the back of my mind that I might see you if I came over here. We *did* have such good times that crazy spring, like the night you and I stole the butcher's tricycle, and the time we tried to call on the president and you had the old derby rim and the wire cane. Everybody seems so old lately, but I don't feel old a bit. Couldn't we get together some time today for old time's sake? I've got a vile hangover for the moment, but will be feeling better this afternoon and will look for you about five in the sweatshop at the Ritz.

Always devotedly,
Lorraine

His first feeling was one of awe that he had actually, in his mature years, stolen a tricycle and pedaled Lorraine all over the *étoile* between the small hours and dawn. In retrospect it was a nightmare. Locking out Helen didn't fit in with any other act of his life, but the tricycle incident did—it was one of many. How many weeks or months of dissipation to arrive at that condition of utter irresponsibility?

He tried to picture how Lorraine had appeared to him then—very attractive; Helen was unhappy about it, although she said nothing. Yesterday, in the restaurant, Lorraine had seemed trite, blurred, worn away. He emphatically did not want to see her, and he was glad Alix had not given away his hotel address. It was a relief to think, instead, of Honoria, to think of Sundays spent with her and of saying good morning to her and of knowing she was there in his house at night, drawing her breath in the darkness.

At five he took a taxi and bought presents for all the Peters—a piquant cloth doll, a box of Roman soldiers, flowers for Marion, big linen handkerchiefs for Lincoln.

He saw, when he arrived in the apartment, that Marion had accepted the inevitable. She greeted him as though he were a recalcitrant member of the family, rather than a menacing outsider. Honoria had been told she was going; Charlie was glad to see that her tact made her conceal her excessive happiness. Only on his lap did she whisper her delight and the question "When?" before she slipped away with the other children.

He and Marion were alone for a minute in the room, and on an impulse he spoke out boldly:

"Family quarrels are bitter things. They don't go according to any rules. They're not like aches or wounds; they're more like splits in the skin that won't heal because there's not enough material. I wish you and I could be on better terms."

"Some things are hard to forget," she answered. "It's a question of confidence." There was no answer to this and presently she asked, "When do you propose to take her?"

"As soon as I can get a governess. I hoped the day after tomorrow."

"That's impossible. I've got to get her things in shape. Not before Saturday."

He yielded. Coming back into the room, Lincoln offered him a drink.

"I'll take my daily whisky," he said.

It was warm here, it was a home, people together by a fire. The children felt very safe and important; the mother and father were serious, watchful. They had things to do for the children more important than his visit here. A spoonful of medicine was, after all, more important than the strained relations between Marion and himself. They were not dull people, but they were very much in the grip of life and circumstances. He wondered if he couldn't do something to get Lincoln out of his rut at the bank.

A long peal at the doorbell; the *bonne à tout faire* passed through and went down the corridor. The door opened upon another long ring, and then voices and the three in the salon looked up expectantly. Richard moved to bring the corridor within his range of vision, and Marion rose. Then the maid came back along the corridor, closely followed by the voices, which developed under the light into Duncan Schaeffer and Lorraine Quarrles.

They were gay, they were hilarious, they were roaring with laughter. For a moment Charlie was astounded; unable to understand how they ferreted out the Peters' address.

"Ah-h-h!" Duncan wagged his finger roguishly at Charlie. "Ah-h-h!"

They both slid down another cascade of laughter. Anxious and at a loss, Charlie shook hands with them quickly and presented them to Lincoln and Marion. Marion nodded, scarcely speaking. She had drawn back a step toward the fire; her little girl stood beside her, and Marion put an arm about her shoulder.

With growing annoyance at the intrusion, Charlie waited for them to explain themselves. After some concentration Duncan said:

"We came to invite you out to dinner. Lorraine and I insist that all this shishi, cagey business 'bout your address got to stop."

Charlie came closer to them, as if to force them backward down the corridor.

"Sorry, but I can't. Tell me where you'll be and I'll phone you in half an hour."

This made no impression. Lorraine sat down suddenly on the side of a chair, and focusing her eyes on Richard, cried, "Oh, what a nice little boy! Come here, little boy." Richard glanced at his mother, but did not move. With a perceptible shrug of her shoulders, Lorraine turned back to Charlie:

"Come and dine. Sure your cousins won' mine. See you so sel'om. Or solemn."

"I can't," said Charlie sharply. "You two have dinner and I'll phone you."

Her voice became suddenly unpleasant. "All right, we'll go. But I remember once when you hammered on my door at four A.M. I was enough of a good sport to give you a drink. Come on, Dunc."

Still in slow motion, with blurred, angry faces, with uncertain feet, they retired along the corridor.

"Good night," Charlie said.

"Good night!" responded Lorraine emphatically.

When he went back into the salon Marion had not moved, only now her son was standing in the circle of her other arm. Lincoln was still swinging Honoria back and forth like a pendulum from side to side.

"What an outrage!" Charlie broke out. "What an absolute outrage!"

Neither of them answered. Charlie dropped into an armchair, picked up his drink, set it down again and said:

"People I haven't seen for two years having the colossal nerve—"

He broke off. Marion had made the sound "Oh!" in one swift, furious breath, turned her body from him with a jerk and left the room.

Lincoln set down Honoria carefully.

"You children go in and start your soup," he said, and when they obeyed, he said to Charlie:

"Marion's not well and she can't stand shocks. That kind of people make her really physically sick."

"I didn't tell them to come here. They wormed your name out of somebody. They deliberately—"

"Well, it's too bad. It doesn't help matters. Excuse me a minute."

Left alone, Charlie sat tense in his chair. In the next room he could hear the children eating, talking in monosyllables, already oblivious to the scene between their elders. He heard a murmur of conversation from a farther room and then the ticking bell of a telephone receiver picked up, and in a panic he moved to the other side of the room and out of earshot.

In a minute, Lincoln came back. "Look here, Charlie. I think we'd better call off dinner for tonight. Marion's in bad shape."

"Is she angry with me?"

"Sort of," he said, almost roughly. "She's not strong and—"

"You mean she's changed her mind about Honoria?"

"She's pretty bitter right now. I don't know. You phone me at the bank tomorrow."

"I wish you'd explain to her I never dreamed these people would come here. I'm just as sore as you are."

"I couldn't explain anything to her now."

Charlie got up. He took his coat and hat and started down the corridor.

Then he opened the door of the dining room and said in a strange voice, "Good night, children."

Honoria rose and ran around the table to hug him.

"Good night, sweetheart," he said vaguely, and then trying to make his voice more tender, trying to conciliate something, "Good night, dear children."

V

Charlie went directly to the Ritz bar with the furious idea of finding Lorraine and Duncan, but they were not there, and he realized that in any case there was nothing he could do. He had not touched his drink at the Peters', and now he ordered a whisky-and-soda. Paul came over to say hello.

"It's a great change," he said sadly. "We do about half the business we did. So many fellows I hear about back in the States lost everything, maybe not in the first crash, but then in the second. Your friend George Hardt lost every cent, I hear. Are you back in the States?"

"No, I'm in business in Prague."

"I heard that you lost a lot in the crash."

"I did," and he added grimly, "but I lost everything I wanted in the boom."

"Selling short."

"Something like that."

Again the memory of those days swept over him like a nightmare—the people they had met traveling; then people who couldn't add a row of figures or speak a coherent sentence. The little man Helen had consented to dance with at the ship's party, who had insulted her ten feet from the table; the women and girls carried screaming with drink or drugs out of public places—

—The men who locked their wives out in the snow, because the snow of twenty-nine wasn't real snow. If you didn't want it to be snow, you just paid some money.

He went to the phone and called the Peters' apartment; Lincoln answered.

"I called up because this thing is on my mind. Has Marion said anything definite?"

"Marion's sick," Lincoln answered shortly. "I know this thing isn't altogether your fault, but I can't have her go to pieces about it. I'm afraid we'll have to let it slide for six months; I can't take the chance of working her up to this state again."

"I see."

"I'm sorry, Charlie."

He went back to his table. His whisky glass was empty, but he shook his head when Alix looked at it questioningly. There wasn't much he could do now except send Honoria some things; he would send her a lot of things tomorrow. He thought rather angrily that this was just money—he had given so many people money. . . .

"No, no more," he said to the waiter. "What do I owe you?"

He would come back someday; they couldn't make him pay forever. But he wanted his child, and nothing was much good now, beside that fact. He wasn't young anymore, with a lot of nice thoughts and dreams to have by himself. He was absolutely sure Helen wouldn't have wanted him to be so alone.

The Swimmer

John Cheever

It was one of those midsummer Sundays when everyone sits around saying, "I *drank* too much last night." You might have heard it whispered by the parishioners leaving church, heard it from the lips of the priest himself, struggling with his cassock in the vestiarium, heard it from the golf links and the tennis courts, heard it from the wildlife preserve where the leader of the Audubon group was suffering from a terrible hangover. "I *drank* too much," said Donald Westerhazy. "We all *drank* too much," said Lucinda Merrill. "It must have been the wine," said Helen Westerhazy. "I *drank* too much of that claret."

This was the edge of the Westerhazys' pool. The pool, fed by an artesian well with a high iron content, was a pale shade of green. It was a fine day. In the west there was a massive stand of cumulus cloud so like a city seen from a distance—from the bow of an approaching ship—that it might have had a name. Lisbon. Hackensack. The sun was hot. Neddy Merrill sat by the green water, one hand in it, one around a glass of gin. He was a slender man—he seemed to have the especial slenderness of youth—and while he was far from young he had slid down his banister that morning and given the bronze backside of Aphrodite on the hall table a smack, as he jogged toward the smell of coffee in his dining room. He might have been compared to a summer's day, particularly the hours of one, and while he lacked a tennis racket or a sail bag the impression was definitely one of youth, sport, and clement weather. He had been swimming and now he was breathing deeply, stertorously as if he could gulp into his lungs the components of that moment, the heat of the sun, the intenseness of his pleasure. It all seemed to flow into his chest. His own house stood in Bullet Park, eight miles to the south, where his four beautiful daughters would have had their lunch and might be playing tennis. Then it occurred to him that by taking a dogleg to the southwest he could reach his home by water.

His life was not confining and the delight he took in this observation could not be explained by its suggestion of escape. He seemed to see, with a cartographer's eye, that string of swimming pools, that quasi-subterranean stream that curved across the county. He had made a discovery, a contribution to modern geography; he would name the stream Lucinda after his wife. He was not a practical joker nor was he a fool but he was determinedly original and had a vague and modest idea of himself as a legendary figure. The day was beautiful and it seemed to him that a long swim might enlarge and celebrate its beauty.

He took off a sweater that was hung over his shoulders and dove in. He had an inexplicable contempt for men who did not hurl themselves into pools. He swam a choppy crawl, breathing either with every stroke or every fourth stroke and counting somewhere well in the back of his mind the one-two one-two of a flutter kick. It was not a serviceable stroke for long distances but the domestication of swimming had saddled the sport with some customs and in his part of the world a crawl was customary. To be embraced and sustained by the light green water was less a pleasure, it seemed, than the resumption of a natural condition, and he would have liked to swim without trunks, but this was not possible, considering his project. He hoisted himself up on the far curb—he never used the ladder—and started across the lawn. When Lucinda asked where he was going he said he was going to swim home.

The only maps and charts he had to go by were remembered or imaginary but these were clear enough. First there were the Grahams, the Hammers, the Lears, the Howlands, and the Crosscups. He would cross Ditmar Street to the Bunkers and come, after a short portage, to the Levys, the Welchers, and the public pool in Lancaster. Then there were the Hallorans, the Sachses, the Biswangers, Shirley Adams, the Gilmartins, and the Clydes. The day was lovely, and that he lived in a world so generously supplied with water seemed like a clemency, a beneficence. His heart was high and he ran across the grass. Making his way home by an uncommon route gave him the feeling that he was a pilgrim, an explorer, a man with a destiny, and he knew that he would find friends all along the way; friends would line the banks of the Lucinda River.

He went through a hedge that separated the Westerhazys' land from the Grahams', walked under some flowering apple trees, passed the shed that housed their pump and filter, and came out at the Grahams' pool. "Why Neddy," Mrs. Graham said, "what a marvelous surprise. I've been trying to get you on the phone all morning. Here, let me get you a drink." He saw then, like any explorer, that the hospitable customs and traditions of the natives would have to be handled with diplomacy if he was ever going to reach his destination. He did not want to mystify or seem rude to the Grahams nor did he have the time to linger there. He swam the length of their pool and joined them in the sun and was rescued, a few minutes later, by the arrival of two carloads of friends from Connecticut. During the uproarious reunions he was able to slip away. He went down by the front of the Grahams' house, stepped over the thorny hedge, and crossed a vacant lot to the Hammers'. Mrs. Hammer, looking up from her roses, saw him swim by although she wasn't quite sure who it was. The Lears heard him splashing past the open windows of their living room. The Howlands and the Crosscups were away. After leaving the Howlands' he crossed Ditmar Street and started for the Bunkers', where he could hear, even at that distance, the noise of a party.

The water refracted the sound of voices and laughter and seemed to suspend it in midair. The Bunkers' pool was on a rise and he climbed some stairs to a terrace where twenty-five or thirty men and women were drinking. The only person in the water was Rusty Towers, who floated there on a rubber raft. Oh, how bonny and lush were the banks of the Lucinda River! Prosperous men and women gathered by the sapphire-colored waters while caterer's men in white coats passed them cold gin. Overhead a red de Haviland trainer was circling around and around and around in the sky with something like the glee of a child in a swing. Ned felt a passing affection for the scene, a tenderness for the gathering, as if it was something he might touch. In the distance he heard thunder. As soon as Enid Bunker saw him she began to scream: "Oh, look who's here! What a marvelous surprise! When Lucinda said you couldn't come I thought I'd *die*." She made her way to him through the crowd, and when they had finished kissing she led him to the bar, a progress that was slowed by the fact that he stopped to kiss eight or ten other women and shake the hands of as many men. A smiling bartender he had seen at a hundred parties gave him a gin and tonic and he stood by the bar for a moment, anxious not to get stuck in any conversation that would delay his voyage. When he seemed about to be surrounded he dove in and swam close to the side to avoid colliding with Rusty's raft. At the far end of the pool he bypassed the Tomlinsons with a broad smile and jogged up the garden path. The gravel cut his feet but this was only unpleasantness. The party was confined to the pool, and as he went toward the house he heard the brilliant, watery sound of voices fade, heard the noise of a radio from the Bunkers' kitchen, where someone was listening to a ball game. Sunday afternoon. He made his way through the parked cars and down the grassy border of their driveway to Alewives Lane. He did not want to be seen on the road in his bathing trunks, but there was no traffic and he made the short distance to the Levys' driveway, marked with a PRIVATE PROPERTY sign and a green tube for the *New York Times*. All the doors and windows of the big house were open but there were no signs of life; not even a dog barked. He went around the side of the house to the pool and saw that the Levys had only recently left. Glasses and bottles and dishes of nuts were on a table at the deep end, where there was a bathhouse or gazebo, hung with Japanese lanterns. After swimming the pool he got himself a glass and poured a drink. It was his fourth or fifth drink and he had swum nearly half the length of the Lucinda River. He felt tired, clean, and pleased at that moment to be alone; pleased with everything.

It would storm. The stand of cumulus cloud—that city—had risen and darkened, and while he sat there he heard the percussiveness of thunder again. The de Haviland trainer was still circling overhead and it seemed to Ned that he could almost hear the pilot laugh with pleasure in the afternoon; but when there was another peal of thunder he took off for home. A train whistle blew and he wondered what time it had gotten to be. Four? Five? He thought of the provincial station at that hour, where a waiter, his tuxedo concealed by a raincoat, a dwarf with some flowers wrapped in newspaper, and a woman who had been crying would be waiting for the local. It was suddenly growing dark; it was that moment when the pinheaded birds seemed to organize their song into some acute and knowledgeable recognition of the storm's approach. Then there was a fine noise of rushing water from the crown of an oak at his back, as if a spigot there had been turned. Then the noise of the fountains came from the crowns of all the tall trees. Why did he love storms, what was the meaning of his excitement when the door sprang open and the rain wind fled rudely up the stairs, why had the simple task of shutting the widows of an old house seemed fitting and urgent, why did the first watery notes of a storm wind have for him the unmistakable sound of good news, cheer, glad tidings? Then there was an explosion, a smell of cordite, and rain lashed the Japanese lanterns that Mrs. Levy had bought in Kyoto the year before last, or was it the year before that?

He stayed in the Levys' gazebo until the storm had passed. The rain had cooled the air and he shivered. The force of the wind had stripped a maple of its red and yellow leaves and scattered them over the grass and the water. Since it was midsummer the tree must be blighted, and yet he felt a peculiar sadness at this sign of autumn. He braced his shoulders, emptied his glass, and started for the Welchers' pool. This meant crossing the Lindleys' riding ring and he was surprised to find it overgrown with grass and all the jumps dismantled. He wondered if the Lindleys had sold their horses or gone away for the summer and put them out to board. He seemed to remember having heard something about the Lindleys and their horses but the memory was unclear. On he went, barefoot through the wet grass, to the Welchers', where he found their pool was dry.

This breach in his chain of water disappointed him absurdly, and he felt like some explorer who seeks a torrential headwater and finds a dead stream. He was disappointed and mystified. It was common enough to go away for the summer but no one ever drained his pool. The Welchers had definitely gone away. The pool furniture was folded, stacked, and covered with a tarpaulin. The bathhouse was locked. All the windows of the house were shut, and when he went around to the driveway in front he saw a FOR SALE sign nailed to a tree. When had he last heard from the Welchers—when, that is, had he and Lucinda last regretted to dine with them? It seemed only a week or so ago. Was his memory failing or had he so disciplined it in the repression of unpleasant facts that he had damaged his sense of truth? Then in the distance he heard the sound of a tennis game. This cheered him, cleared away all his apprehensions and let him regard the overcast sky and the cold air with indifference. This was the day that Neddy Merrill swam across the country. This was the day! He started off then for his most difficult portage.

Had you gone for a Sunday afternoon ride that day you might have seen him, close to naked, standing on the shoulders of Route 424, waiting for a chance to cross. You might have wondered if he was the victim of foul play, had his car broken down, or was he merely a fool. Standing barefoot in the deposits of the highway—beer cans, rags, and blowout patches—exposed to all kinds of ridicule, he seemed pitiful. He had known when he started that this was a part of his journey—it had been on his maps—but confronted with the lines of traffic, worming through the summery light, he found himself unprepared. He was laughed at, jeered at, a beer can was thrown at him, and he had no dignity or humor to bring to the situation. He could have gone back, back to the Westerhazys', where Lucinda would still be sitting in the sun. He had signed nothing, vowed nothing, pledged nothing, not even to himself. Why, believing as he did, that all human obduracy was susceptible to common sense, was he unable to turn back? Why was he determined to complete his journey even if it meant putting his life in danger? At what point had this prank, this joke, this piece of horseplay become serious? He could not go back, he could not even recall with any clearness the green water at the Westerhazys', the sense of inhaling the day's components, the friendly and relaxed voices saying that they had all drunk too much. In the space of an hour, more or less, he had covered a distance that made his return impossible.

An old man, tooling down the highway at fifteen miles an hour, let him get to the middle of the road, where there was a grass divider. Here he was exposed to the ridicule of the northbound traffic, but after ten or fifteen minutes he was able to cross. From here he had only a short walk to the Recreation Center at the edge of the village of Lancaster, where there were some handball courts and a public pool.

The effect of the water on voices, the illusion of brilliance and suspense, was the same here as it had been at the Bunkers' but the sounds here were louder, harsher, and more shrill, and as soon as he entered the crowded enclosure he was confronted with regimentation. "ALL SWIMMERS MUST TAKE A SHOWER BEFORE USING THE POOL. ALL SWIMMERS MUST USE THE FOOTBATH. ALL SWIMMERS MUST WEAR THEIR IDENTIFICATION DISKS." He took a shower, washed his feet in a cloudy and bitter solution, and made his way to the edge of the water. It stank of chlorine and looked to him like a sink. A pair of lifeguards in a pair of towers blew police whistles at what seemed to be regular intervals and abused the swimmers through a public address system. Neddy remembered the sapphire water at the Bunkers' with longing and thought that he might contaminate himself—damage his own prosperousness and charm—by swimming in this murk, but he reminded himself that he was an explorer, a pilgrim, and that this was merely a stagnant bend in the Lucinda River. He dove, scowling with distaste, into the chlorine and had to swim with his head above water to avoid collisions, but even so he was bumped into, splashed, and jostled. When he got to the shallow end both lifeguards were shouting at him: "Hey, you, you without the identification disk, get outa the water." He did, but they had no way of pursuing him and he went through the reek of suntan oil and chlorine out through the hurricane fence and passed the handball courts. By crossing the road he entered the wooded part of the Halloran estate. The woods were not cleared and the footing was treacherous and difficult until he reached the lawn and the clipped beech hedge that encircled their pool.

The Hallorans were friends, an elderly couple of enormous wealth who seemed to bask in the suspicion that they might be Communists. They were zealous reformers but they were not Communists, and yet when they were accused, as they sometimes were, of subversion, it seemed to gratify and excite them. Their beech hedge was yellow and he guessed this had been blighted like the Levys' maple. He called hullo, hullo, to warn the Hallorans of his approach, to palliate his invasion of their privacy. The Hallorans, for reasons that had never been explained to him, did not wear bathing suits. No explanations were in order, really. Their nakedness was a detail in their uncompromising zeal for reform and he stepped politely out of his trunks before he went through the opening in the hedge.

Mrs. Halloran, a stout woman with white hair and a serene face, was reading the *Times*. Mr. Halloran was taking beech leaves out of the water with a scoop. They seemed not surprised or displeased to see him. Their pool was perhaps the oldest in the country, a fieldstone rectangle, fed by a brook. It had no filter or pump and its waters were the opaque gold of the stream.

"I'm swimming across the county," Ned said.

"Why, I didn't know one could," exclaimed Mrs. Halloran.

"Well, I've made it from the Westerhazys'," Ned said. "That must be about four miles."

He left his trunks at the deep end, walked to the shallow end, and swam this stretch. As he was pulling himself out of the water he heard Mrs. Halloran say, "We've been *terribly* sorry to hear about all your misfortunes, Neddy."

"My misfortunes?" Ned asked. "I don't know what you mean."

"Why we heard that you'd sold the house and that your poor children . . ."

"I don't recall having sold the house," Ned said, "and the girls are at home."

"Yes," Mrs. Halloran sighed. "Yes. . . ." Her voice filled the air with an unseasonable melancholy and Ned spoke briskly. "Thank you for the swim."

"Well, have a nice trip," said Mrs. Halloran.

Beyond the hedge he pulled on his trunks and fastened them. They were loose and he wondered if, during the space of an afternoon, he could have lost some weight. He was cold and he was tired and the naked Hallorans and their dark water had depressed him. The swim was too much for his strength but how could he have guessed this, sliding down the banister that morning and sitting in the Westerhazys' sun? His arms were lame. His legs felt rubbery and ached at the joints. The worst of it was the cold in his bones and the feeling that he might never be warm again. Leaves were falling down around him and he smelled wood smoke on the wind. Who would be burning wood at this time of year?

He needed a drink. Whiskey would warm him, pick him up, carry him through the last of his journey, refresh his feeling that it was original and valorous to swim across the county. Channel swimmers took brandy. He needed a stimulant. He crossed the lawns in front of the Hallorans' house and went down a little path to where they had built a house for their only daughter, Helen, and her husband, Eric Sachs. The Sachses' pool was small and he found Helen and her husband there.

"Oh, *Neddy*," Helen said. "Did you lunch at Mother's?"

"Not *really*," Ned said. "I *did* stop to see your parents." This seemed to be explanation enough. "I'm terribly sorry to break in on you like this but I've taken a chill and I wonder if you'd give me a drink."

"Why, I'd *love* to," Helen said, "but there hasn't been anything in this house to drink since Eric's operation. That was three years ago."

Was he losing his memory, had his gift for concealing painful facts let him forget that he had sold his house, that his children were in trouble, and that his friend had been ill? His eyes slipped from Eric's face to his abdomen, where he saw three pale, sutured scars, two of them at least a foot long. Gone was his navel, and what, Neddy thought, would the roving hand, bed-checking one's gifts at 3 A.M., make of a belly with no navel, no link to birth, this breach in the succession?

"I'm sure you can get a drink at the Biswangers'," Helen said. "They're having an enormous do. You can hear it from here. Listen!"

She raised her head and from across the road, the lawns, the gardens, the woods, the fields, he heard again the brilliant noise of voices over water. "Well, I'll get wet," he said, still feeling that he had no freedom of choice about his means of travel. He dove into the Sachses' cold water, and gasping, close to drowning, made his way from one end of the pool to the other. "Lucinda and I want *terribly* to see you," he said over his shoulder, his face set toward the Biswangers'. "We're sorry it's been so long and we'll call you *very* soon."

He crossed some fields to the Biswangers' and the sounds of revelry there. They would be honored to give him a drink, they would be happy to give him a drink. The Biswangers invited him and Lucinda for dinner four times a year, six weeks in advance. They were always rebuffed and yet they continued to send out their invitations, unwilling to comprehend the rigid and undemocratic realities of their society. They were the sort of people who discussed the price of things at cocktails, exchanged market tips during dinner, and after dinner told dirty stories to mixed company. They did not belong to Neddy's set—they were not even on Lucinda's Christmas card list. He went toward their pool with feelings of indifference, charity, and some unease, since it seemed to be getting dark and these were the longest days of the year. The party when he joined it was noisy and large. Grace Biswanger was the kind of hostess who asked the optometrist, the veterinarian, the real-estate dealer, and the dentist. No one was swimming and the twilight, reflected on the water of the pool, had a wintry gleam. There was a bar and he started for this. When Grace Biswanger saw him she came toward him, not affectionately as he had every right to expect, but bellicosely.

"Why this party has everything," she said loudly, "including a gate crasher."

She could not deal him a social blow—there was no question about this and he did not flinch. "As a gate crasher," he asked politely, "do I rate a drink?"

"Suit yourself," she said. "You don't seem to pay much attention to invitations."

She turned her back on him and joined some guests, and he went to the bar and ordered a whiskey. The bartender served him but he served him rudely. His was a world in which the caterer's men kept the social score, and to be rebuffed by a part-time barkeep meant that he had suffered some loss of social esteem. Or perhaps the man was new and uninformed. Then he heard Grace at his back say: "They went for broke overnight—nothing but income—and he showed up drunk one Sunday and asked us to loan him five thousand dollars. . . ." She was always talking about money. It was worse than eating your peas off a knife. He dove into the pool, swam its length, and went away.

The next pool on his list, the last but two, belonged to his old mistress, Shirley Adams. If he had suffered any injuries at the Biswangers' they would be cured here. Love—sexual roughhouse in fact—was the supreme elixir, the pain killer, the brightly colored pill that would put the spring back into his step, the joy of life in his heart. They had had an affair last week, last month, last year. He couldn't remember. It was he who had broken it off, his was the upper hand, and he stepped through the gate of the wall that surrounded her pool with nothing so considered as self-confidence. It seemed in a way to be his pool, as the lover, particularly the illicit lover, enjoys the possessions of his mistress with an authority unknown to holy matrimony. She was there, her hair the color of brass, but her figure, at the edge of the lighted, cerulean water, excited in him no profound memories. It had been, he thought, a lighthearted affair, although she had wept when he broke it off. She seemed confused to see him and he wondered if she was still wounded. Would she, God forbid, weep again?

"What do you want?" she asked.

"I'm swimming across the county."

"Good Christ. Will you ever grow up."

"What's the matter?"

"If you've come here for my money," she said, "I won't give you another cent."

"You could give me a drink."

"I could but I won't. I'm not alone."

"Well, I'm on my way."

He dove in and swam the pool, but when he tried to haul himself up onto the curb he found that the strength in his arms and shoulders had gone, and he paddled to the ladder and climbed out. Looking over his shoulder he saw, in the lighted bathhouse, a young man. Going out onto the dark lawn he smelled chrysanthemums or marigolds—some stubborn autumnal fragrance—on the night air, strong as gas. Looking overhead he saw that the stars had come out, but why should he seem to see

Andromeda, Cepheus and Cassiopeia? What had become of the constellations of midsummer? He began to cry.

It was probably the first time in his adult life that he had ever cried, certainly the first time in his life that he had ever felt so miserable, cold, tired, and bewildered. He could not understand the rudeness of the caterer's barkeep or the rudeness of a mistress who had come to him on her knees and showered his trousers with tears. He had swum too long, he had been immersed too long, and his nose and his throat were sore from the water. What he needed then was a drink, some company, and some clean, dry clothes, and while he could have cut directly across the road to his home he went on to the Gilmartins' pool. Here, for the first time in his life, he did not dive but went down the steps into the icy water and swam a hobbled sidestroke that he might have learned as a youth. He staggered with fatigue on his way to the Clydes' and paddled the length of their pool, stopping again and again with his hand on the curb to rest. He climbed up the ladder and wondered if he had the strength to get home. He had done what he wanted, he had swum the county, but he was so stupefied with exhaustion that his triumph seemed vague. Stooped, holding on to the gateposts for support, he turned up the driveway of his own house.

The place was dark. Was it so late that they had all gone to bed? Had Lucinda stayed at the Westerhazys' for supper? Had the girls joined her there or gone someplace else? Hadn't they agreed, as they usually did on Sunday, to regret all their invitations and stay at home? He tried the garage doors to see what cars were in but the doors were locked and rust came off the handles onto his hands. Going toward the house, he saw the force of the thunderstorm had knocked one of the rain gutters loose. It hung down over the front door like an umbrella rib, but it could be fixed in the morning. The house was locked, and he thought that the stupid cook or the stupid maid must have locked the place up until he remembered that it had been some time since they had employed a maid or a cook. He shouted, pounded on the door, tried to force it with his shoulder, and then, looking in at the windows, saw the place was empty.

PART VIII

SUSPENSE = STYLE?

"The Killers"
by Ernest Hemingway

 The Killers, directed by Robert Siodmak, 1946

"The Basement Room"
by Graham Greene

 The Fallen Idol, directed by Carol Reed, 1948

"Memento Mori"
by Jonathan Nolan

 Memento, directed by Christopher Nolan, 2000

"The son-of-a-bitch writes on water," screenwriter Ben Hecht said of master stylist Ernest Hemingway after attempting to adapt his novel *A Farewell to Arms.* Prose style, as Hecht found out the hard way, is one of those things that doesn't translate. It's barely even definable. Robert Frost once called style "that which indicates how the writer takes himself and what he is saying. . . . It is the mind skating circles around itself as it moves forward." (Whatever that means.) A highly stylized story doesn't necessarily make a bad adaptation, though—as another Hemingway adaptation, *The Killers,* proves—and it often makes an interesting one. And it's particularly interesting when story style meets movie style, as in the case of these three pairs.

As the quintessential tough-guy author, Ernest Hemingway inspired the hardboiled school of writing (James M. Cain, Dashiell Hammett) that film noir mined in movie after movie. So it's fitting that one of the classic noirs, *The Killers,* was adapted from the toughest of the Tough Guy's work. "The Killers," which first appeared in *Scribner's* in March 1927, was originally titled "The Matadors," which can probably be explained by the fact that Hemingway was living in Madrid at the time—"Always," he said, "a good place for working." In an interview with George Plimpton, he described the day (May 16, 1926) when the San Isidro bullfights were snowed out and he wrote "The Killers" and two other stories: "First I wrote 'The Killers' which I'd tried to write before and failed. Then after lunch I got into bed to keep warm and wrote 'Today is Friday.' I had so much juice I thought maybe I was going crazy and I had about six other stories to write. So I got dressed and walked to Fornos, the old bull fighters' café, and drank more coffee and then came back and wrote 'Ten Indians.' This made me very sad and I drank some brandy and went to sleep."

Hemingway's spare, precise style and "iceberg" principle of writing—"There is seven-eighths . . . underwater for every part that shows"—is well suited to the short story, and "The Killers" is one of his best. (John

Updike included it in *The Best American Short Stories of the Century.*) Often called cinematic, Hemingway's style has turned out to be a siren's song for many would-be adapters. On the face of it, his reliance on dialogue and action should transfer well to the screen. But the effect Hemingway achieves in his fiction is through absence, not presence. As Gabriel García Márquez states, "his stories . . . give the impression something is missing, and this is precisely what confers their mystery and their beauty." Or, as film critic Peter Walsh has observed, "The things that matter to Hemingway, love, sex, death, and courage, are seldom expressed but always understood."

Hemingway liked *The Killers*, unlike many of the films adapted from his work. (After Universal gave him a copy, he held frequent screenings for guests visiting his home in Cuba, although he sometimes fell asleep after the first reel.) But, if *The Killers* is arguably the best adaptation of Hemingway's work, it is ultimately not the most faithful. Screenwriters Anthony Veiller and John Huston (uncredited because he was under contract with Warner Bros.) let Hemingway's story unfold almost as written over the first ten minutes of the film. Of course, the problem they must have had then was: Now what? The backstory they devised is pretty standard melodrama involving an insurance investigation, robbery, double crosses, and a femme fatale. Somewhere along the way, Hemingway's "matadors" are lost in the shuffle: Courage is no longer the theme. That the film is now considered a classic is due far less to the screenwriter's adaptation than it is to director Robert Siodmak's visual style.

Film noir is almost always better than it has a right to be. Or, as Paul Schrader puts it, noir is a "triumph of style over substance." Siodmak, who was fluent in the German expressionism that so infuses film noir, was a perfect fit for this type of film. He began his career in Germany with the state-funded film company Universum Film A.G, supported by the Third Reich, but he fled to Paris in 1933 when he was attacked in the press by Nazi propaganda chief Josef Goebbels. In 1939, he sailed to the United States one day before war was declared in France and found work in Hollywood, directing a string of B films before he made his mark with *Phantom Lady* (1944), an adaptation of a pulpy Cornell Woolrich novel. There, Siodmak's visual sense helped overcome a mediocre story, and several years later it served *The Killers* just as well. When it was released, Bosley Crowther of the *New York Times* called the story "mere movie melodrama" that "does not enhance the literary distinction of Hemingway's classic a bit." That the film has had staying power has little to do with Hemingway, though, and much to do with Siodmak. It's the glow of the diner against the backdrop of a dimly lit street. It's the play of shadow across the Swede's (Burt Lancaster's) face as he waits for death. It's the confusion of the heist scene as viewed from above. Unlike other adaptations of Hemingway's almost-unadaptable work, Siodmak's film noir framework allowed him a safety net. Style substitutes: It doesn't help make the point, it becomes the point.

These days Siodmak's name is usually preceded by the words "neglected," "underrated," or "misunderstood." Pauline Kael noted that his work is "often mistakenly attributed to other directors or to highly publicized producers." Even during his successful studio days, he was apparently unable to count on everyone knowing his name. He often wore a blue blazer with the phonetic pronunciation of his name—SEE-ODD-MACK—on the back. As early as 1946, after the successes of *The Spiral Staircase* (1946) and *The Killers,* Siodmak expressed concern about references to him as "a second Alfred Hitchcock." Universal responded by announcing that he would do two films "sans mystery, creeps or chills" (as the *New York Times* put it). But the projects he had been promised fell through for one reason or another, and he was asked to step in to relieve director Frank Tuttle on *The Swell Guy** (1946), twenty-six days into production. After that came *Time Out of Mind* (1947), which he called "that preposterous film." In 1948 he returned to the dark side with *Cry of the City* and followed it with his best work, *Criss Cross* (1949).

In 1953, after ten years in Hollywood as one of the most prominent directors of film noir, Siodmak returned to Europe. "No, Hollywood did not give me up," he said. "I gave it up. I saw what was coming. I did not want to be caught in the transition that is going on there now. What is going on is a sort of anarchy.... Most of the big studios are little more than leasing organizations. The stars are in charge. These egomaniacs who want to direct and write and produce." One of the egomaniacs he was talking about was Burt Lancaster, who starred in and coproduced Siodmak's final Hollywood film, *The Crimson Pirate* (1952). Of the Lancaster–Harold Hecht production, Siodmak complained, "I was not taken into their confidence, didn't know about changes until the last minute, and was kept out of any discussions regarding script, characters or casting." (And he had given Lancaster his big break in *The Killers.*) The real problems were larger than Lancaster's ego, though. The studio system, in which Siodmak was very comfortable, was breaking up. And film noir was on its way out. (Purists bookend the period with *The Maltese Falcon* [1941] on one end and *Touch of Evil* [1958] on the other.) Siodmak started over in Europe, living

* He went uncredited.

in Switzerland and making films, with mixed success, in West Germany, France, Great Britain, Spain, and Romania.*

British director Carol Reed is another neglected filmmaker with a string of back-to-back classics—*Odd Man Out* (1947), *The Fallen Idol* (1948), *The Third Man* (1949)—who imploded in the latter half of his career. There were many factors. Like Siodmak, he was caught in the middle of the drastically changing film environment of the 1950s.† Then Alexander Korda, his friend, patron, and head of London Films—the man behind most of his big successes—died in 1956. And finally, like all directors who don't write, he was forced to continually search for good material. He was well aware of the type of stories he did well, but he struggled to find them. The search was particularly difficult for him, as he was not a reader. He depended upon his second wife Pempy to read extensively and make recommendations. He also leaned on a reader employed by Korda's outfit, Baroness Moura Budberg, a Russion émigré (and former mistress of Maxim Gorky and H. G. Wells, both of whom died in her arms). According to Robert F. Moss, author of *The Films of Carol Reed,* both Reed's son and his nephew, screenwriter Andrew Birkin, believe that Reed's biggest problem as a director was his own inability to find suitable stories.

His most successful pairing was with author and screenwriter Graham Greene, who wrote three of his films (*The Fallen Idol, The Third Man,* and *Our Man in Havana* [1959]). The two became close friends. They enjoyed the same type of story, they had a similar sense of humor, and they both had "a passionate need to be English gentlemen in the most theatrical sense of the word," as one observer described it. But after they made three films together, Reed's career was in a steep decline and Greene had retreated from the film business. "I've made films in the forties, fifties, and sixties," Greene later said. "But the time comes when one's enthusiasm begins to slacken. One's left with only enough enthusiasm for one's own work, which is writing novels." But there was almost a fourth collaboration, which might have given Reed a personal and professional boost. The two men met on the French Riviera in the early 1970s. Greene had an idea for a story, a period piece set in Spain during the Napoleonic War. Reed was enthusiastic and talked to a number of studios about the project, but couldn't get a definite commitment. And, ever the English gentleman, he

* In 1957 his *Nachts, wenn der Teufel kam,* was nominated for (but didn't win) an Oscar in the Best Foreign Film category. It is the true story of Bruno Ludke, a serial killer who strangled eight women in Nazi Germany during World War II.

† British cinema in the fifties struggled financially, politically, and technically. Competition with television and American films contributed to its decline. Audiences dropped from over 30 million a week to about 8 million a week by the 1960s.

felt it would be disrespectful to ask Greene to work on spec. So the project died, and Reed died shortly thereafter. Reed's directions for the burial of his body are indicative of his humility—or his sense of humor. He is buried in a noisy cemetery along the M4, a highway leading to Heathrow airport, so that, as his nephew Birkin puts it, "people could remember him vaguely on their way to the airport or on their way back."

Reed is, in fact, remembered only vaguely. *The Fallen Idol*, the second of his triumvirate, won the British Academy Award for Best Picture, and made numerous ten-best lists. Now, however, it is a difficult film to find, though well worth the search. Reed's choice of material was daring; even Greene was unsure of his story's adaptability. "I was surprised when Carol Reed suggested that I should collaborate with him on a film of 'The Basement Room' because it seemed to me that the subject was unfilmable—a murder committed by the most sympathetic character and an unhappy ending which would certainly have imperiled the £250,000 that films nowadays cost." "A Basement Room," about a boy who witnesses a fatal accident, is told primarily from a child's point of view. Greene's story isn't cloying, though—as child narratives often are—because Philip is not innocent, even at age seven. (Greene's characters are rarely, if ever, innocent. George Orwell once said of him: "He appears to share the idea, which has been floating around ever since Baudelaire, that there is something rather *distingué* in being damned; Hell is a sort of high-class nightclub . . .") There is a shifting, uncertain quality to Greene's prose in this story. Time moves back and forth, sometimes within a single sentence, while perspectives shift unexpectedly from character to character. Although Reed couldn't replicate these shifts or Greene's long, fluid sentences, he managed to convey much the same idea by using many noirish visual elements: strange camera angles, haunting shadows, dark and glistening streets, a leitmotif of vertical "prison" bars. Although he does not have the access to Philip's thoughts that Greene has in the story, his camera captures the sense of a child being locked out of an adult world. Ultimately, though—despite all the noirish touches—in Reed's hands, the story is more loving than dark.

Greene approved of Reed's changes, in part because he was aware of the necessities of the film medium. In 1939, he wrote, "A film with a severely limited appeal must be—to that extent—a bad film." And it is almost certainly true that audiences would not have enjoyed or accepted a film as downbeat and hopeless as Greene's story. Reed was equally respectful of Greene's contribution, as he was of authors and stories in general. Whenever possible, he tried to adapt material with the original author—even if he was inexperienced—instead of hiring screenwriters. "It's talent that counts," he said, "not technique." In fact, Greene and Reed seem to have been members of a mutual admiration society. In his foreword to a volume containing "A Basement Room" and the treatment for *The Third Man*, Greene wrote, "Of one thing about both these films [*Fallen Idol* and *The Third Man*] I have complete certainty, that their success is due to Carol Reed, the only director I know with that particular warmth of human sympathy, the extraordinary feeling for the right face for the right part, the exactitude of cutting, and not least important the power of sympathizing with an author's worries and an ability to guide him."

Few writers have embraced film in the way that Greene did, or have been involved in as many aspects of the filmmaking process, from critic to screenwriter to coproducer to performer. As a critic he developed the concept of "poetic cinema," where film is (or should be) "poetry expressed in images, which let in a little more of the common life than is in the story." From there it was a short leap to writing screenplays, although even he called his first attempt—an adaptation of a John Galsworthy short story—"disastrous." But by the time he met Carol Reed, he had written a successful screenplay for *Brighton Rock*, based on his own novel. His preference, though, was to adapt short stories. "A short story makes a much better film than a novel. A novel is too long. . . . There have to be too many compromises. The cuts made may seem unimportant but you suddenly find that an unimportant cut has changed the whole character of a character. Short stories make far better films . . . three or four [of the Thames series*] are among the best films that have been made out of my work. It's difficult to judge whether the film or the story came first."

In the case of Jonathan Nolan's story "Memento Mori" and Christopher Nolan's film *Memento*, it really is a chicken/egg question. Technically, though, the story precedes the movie—by a hair. Jonathan Nolan got the idea for a story while doing the "standard traveling student routine." He'd taken time off from college, but was intrigued by the discussions of anterograde amnesia—a condition caused by anything from venereal disease to alcoholism to a blow in the head—he recalled from his Psych 101 class. "It is," Jonathan admits, "quite rare in its chronic form. But if you went by the number of pages devoted to it in psych books, you'd think it was an epidemic." After returning from New Zealand and Europe, he helped his brother, filmmaker Christopher Nolan, drive their father's car from Chicago to Los Angeles. "By Wyoming we'd run out of conversation topics," Jonathan says, "so I told him about the story I was working on. Suddenly he had a bunch of ideas about how he could work it into a movie. When I got back to school I sent him my notes and we parted company—

* A 1975–1976 British television series in which eighteen of Greene's stories were adapted under the title *Shades of Greene*.

he went off to write it into a film, and I went off to write it into a story." Both brothers were intrigued by the irony of a man tormented by a past he can't remember.

"Memento Mori" shifts between what Jonathan calls "a series of Dear John letters" and an uncertain but objective narration of events. ("Earl looks at the picture for a long time. Maybe he begins to cry. Maybe he just stares silently at the picture.") Nolan's purpose was to intentionally confront the reader with the protagonist's disjointed and disoriented state of mind. "At first I wanted to try and present it as a series of fragments . . . in the form of a deck of cards," Jonathan says. "The reader would be encouraged to shuffle the deck before reading it, and then forced to assemble a bigger picture from the pieces just like the protagonist. That approach proved unworkable for the story itself, but returned in the guise of a promotional website for the film (otnemem.com) [designed by Jonathan] and then in the menus for the special edition DVD." The story's solution is far less confusing than the special-edition DVD menu (designed by the Nolans), which can be very frustrating.* "It's a DVD that isn't comfortable," Jonathan admits. "Yes, you can have all these materials, but we're not going to put them together for you in a fashion that kind of lays down and plays dead."

Rarely, if ever, has a film been as holistically stylish as *Memento.* From the special-edition DVD ("with attitude," says Jonathan), designed to look like a psychiatric file, to the promotional website (again, with attitude): "You just kind of wander through it," Jonathan says. "People got interested in the website itself as its own piece, its own work of art." To the structure and style of the film itself: a noirish thriller told backwards.

Newsweek hailed *Memento* as "a gripping, utterly unexpected noir, glinting with bits of poetry and a hard, deadpan humor," and in 2002, *Premiere* magazine named Christopher Nolan one of "25 under 35: The Next Generation of Hollywood's Power Elite." He may be young, but he's been directing a long time. His first film (made when he was seven) was a no-budget short starring his action figures that he shot with his father's 8mm camera. His first feature film, *Following* (1998), was a no-budget thriller starring his friends that he shot in 16mm black and white. "We figured out that . . . we could shoot fifteen minutes of footage every week, and pay for that, and keep going one day a week as we earned money through our various jobs." *Following,* which also features a nonlinear narrative, did well at film festivals, but it was *Memento* that got people talking.

* A hint: To get to the Supplemental Menu, select the clock from the main menu. Then answer "C" on the next two questions. After that, you'll be asked to respond to the statement "The best jigsaw puzzles are the ones missing a couple pieces." Select "E" . . . strongly agree. Now you're at the Supplemental Menu.

Christopher, who has a degree in literature, has often remarked on how reading has influenced his work, particularly in regard to his experimentations with chronology. "I started thinking about the narrative freedoms that authors had enjoyed for centuries and it seemed to me that filmmakers should enjoy those freedoms as well." Christopher cites Graham Swift's *Waterland* as a particular influence, but there have been a number of prominent novels with fractured narratives and a few that have been told backward, like Martin Amis's *Time's Arrow.* (Jonathan's story would not have been called innovative, as the film was, if it had been told backward.) Christopher is interested in innovation, in escaping boundaries and dodging dimensions. With *Memento,* he says he wanted to "create an experience that doesn't feed into your head, that bleeds around the edges. I was going for something that lived in its own shape." It makes you wonder . . . If, as André Maurois has said, "style is the hallmark of a temperament stamped upon the material at hand," then what must the holidays be like when the Nolan clan gets together? Do they ever find their Easter eggs?

The Killers

Ernest Hemingway

The door of Henry's lunch-room opened and two men came in. They sat down at the counter.

"What's yours?" George asked them.

"I don't know," one of the men said. "What do you want to eat, Al?"

"I don't know," said Al. "I don't know what I want to eat."

Outside it was getting dark. The street-light came on outside the window. The two men at the counter read the menu. From the other end of the counter Nick Adams watched them. He had been talking to George when they came in.

"I'll have a roast pork tenderloin with apple sauce and mashed potato," the first man said.

"It isn't ready yet."

"What the hell do you put it on the card for?"

"That's the dinner," George explained. "You can get that at six o'clock."

George looked at the clock on the wall behind the counter.

"It's five o'clock."

"The clock says twenty minutes past five," the second man said.

"It's twenty minutes fast."

"Oh, to hell with the clock," the first man said. "What have you got to eat?"

"I can give you any kind of sandwiches," George said. "You can have ham and eggs, bacon and eggs, liver and bacon, or a steak."

"Give me chicken croquettes with green peas and cream sauce and mashed potatoes."

"That's the dinner."

"Everything we want's the dinner, eh? That's the way you work it."

"I can give you ham and eggs, bacon and eggs, liver—"

"I'll take ham and eggs," the man called Al said. He wore a derby hat and a black overcoat buttoned across the chest. His face was small and white and he had tight lips. He wore a silk muffler and gloves.

"Give me bacon and eggs," said the other man. He was about the same size as Al. Their faces were different, but they were dressed like twins. Both wore overcoats too tight for them. They sat leaning forward, their elbows on the counter.

"Got anything to drink?" Al asked.

"Silver beer, Bevo, ginger ale," George said.

"I mean you got anything to drink?"

"Just those I said."

"This is a hot town," said the other. "What do they call it?"

"Summit."

"Ever hear of it?" Al asked his friend.

"No," said the friend.

"What do you do here nights?" Al asked.

"They eat the dinner," his friend said. "They all come here and eat the big dinner."

"That's right," George said.

"So you think that's right?" Al asked George.

"Sure."

"You're a pretty bright boy, aren't you?"

"Sure," said George.

"Well, you're not," said the other little man. "Is he, Al?"

"He's dumb," said Al. He turned to Nick. "What's your name?"

"Adams."

"Another bright boy," Al said. "Ain't he a bright boy, Max?"

"The town's full of bright boys," Max said.

George put the two platters, one of ham and eggs, the other of bacon and eggs, on the counter. He set down two side-dishes of fried potatoes and closed the wicket into the kitchen.

"Which is yours?" he asked Al.

"Don't you remember?"

"Ham and eggs."

"Just a bright boy," Max said. He leaned forward and took the ham and eggs. Both men ate with their gloves on. George watched them eat.

"What are *you* looking at?" Max looked at George.

"Nothing."

"The hell you were. You were looking at me."

"Maybe the boy meant it for a joke, Max," Al said.

George laughed.

"*You* don't have to laugh," Max said to him. "*You* don't have to laugh at all, see?"

"All right," said George.

"So he thinks it's all right." Max turned to Al. "He thinks it's all right. That's a good one."

"Oh, he's a thinker," Al said. They went on eating.

"What's the bright boy's name down the counter?" Al asked Max.

"Hey, bright boy," Max said to Nick. "You go around on the other side of the counter with your boy friend."

"What's the idea?" Nick asked.

"There isn't any idea."

"You better go around, bright boy," Al said. Nick went around behind the counter.

"What's the idea?" George asked.

"None of your damn business," Al said. "Who's out in the kitchen?"

"The nigger."

"What do you mean the nigger?"

"The nigger that cooks."

"Tell him to come in."

"What's the idea?"

"Tell him to come in."

"Where do you think you are?"

"We know damn well where we are," the man called Max said. "Do we look silly?"

"You talk silly," Al said to him. "What the hell do you argue with this kid for? Listen," he said to George, "tell the nigger to come out here."

"What are you going to do to him?"

"Nothing. Use your head, bright boy. What would we do to a nigger?"

George opened the slit that opened back into the kitchen. "Sam," he called. "Come in here a minute."

The door to the kitchen opened and the nigger came in. "What was it?" he asked. The two men at the counter took a look at him.

"All right, nigger. You stand right there," Al said.

Sam, the nigger, standing in his apron, looked at the two men sitting at the counter. "Yes, sir," he said. Al got down from his stool.

"I'm going back to the kitchen with the nigger and bright boy," he said. "Go on back to the kitchen, nigger. You go with him, bright boy." The little man walked after Nick and Sam, the cook, back into the kitchen. The door shut after them. The man called Max sat at the counter opposite George. He didn't look at George but looked in the mirror that ran along back of the counter. Henry's had been made over from a saloon into a lunch-counter.

"Well, bright boy," Max said, looking into the mirror, "why don't you say something?"

"What's it all about?"

"Hey, Al," Max called, "bright boy wants to know what it's all about."

"Why don't you tell him?" Al's voice came from the kitchen.

"What do you think it's all about?"

"I don't know."

"What do you think?"

Max looked into the mirror all the time he was talking.

"I wouldn't say."

"Hey, Al, bright boy says he wouldn't say what he thinks it's all about."

"I can hear you, all right," Al said from the kitchen. He had propped open the slit that dishes passed through into the kitchen with a catsup bottle. "Listen, bright boy," he said from the kitchen to George. "Stand a little further along the bar. You move a little to the left, Max." He was like a photographer arranging for a group picture.

"Talk to me, bright boy," Max said. "What do you think's going to happen?"

George did not say anything.

"I'll tell you," Max said. "We're going to kill a Swede. Do you know a big Swede named Ole Andreson?"

"Yes."

"He comes here to eat every night, don't he?"

"Sometimes he comes here."

"He comes here at six o'clock, don't he?"

"If he comes."

"We know all that, bright boy," Max said. "Talk about something else. Ever go to the movies?"

"Once in a while."

"You ought to go to the movies more. The movies are fine for a bright boy like you."

"What are you going to kill Ole Andreson for? What did he ever do to you?"

"He never had a chance to do anything to us. He never even seen us."

"And he's only going to see us once," Al said from the kitchen.

"What are you going to kill him for, then?" George asked.

"We're killing him for a friend. Just to oblige a friend, bright boy."

"Shut up," said Al from the kitchen. "You talk too goddam much."

"Well, I got to keep bright boy amused. Don't I, bright boy?"

"You talk too damn much," Al said. "The nigger and my bright boy are amused by themselves. I got them tied up like a couple of girl friends in the convent."

"I suppose you were in a convent."

"You never know."

"You were in a kosher convent. That's where you were."

George looked up at the clock.

"If anybody comes in you tell them the cook is off, and if they keep after it, you tell them you'll go back and cook yourself. Do you get that bright boy?"

"All right," George said. "What you going to do with us afterward?"

"That'll depend," Max said. "That's one of those things you never know at the time."

George looked up at the clock. It was a quarter past six. The door from the street opened. A street-car motorman came in.

"Hello, George," he said. "Can I get supper?"

"Sam's gone out," George said. "He'll be back in about half an hour."

"I'd better go up the street," the motorman said. George looked at the clock. It was twenty minutes past six.

"That was nice, bright boy," Max said. "You're a regular little gentleman."

"He knew I'd blow his head off," Al said from the kitchen.

"No," said Max. "It ain't that. Bright boy is nice. He's a nice boy. I like him."

At six-fifty-five George said: "He's not coming."

Two other people had been in the lunch-room. Once George had gone out to the kitchen and made a ham-and-egg sandwich "to go" that a man wanted to take with him. Inside the kitchen he saw Al, his derby hat tipped back, sitting on a stool beside the wicket with the muzzle of a sawed-off shotgun resting on the ledge. Nick and the cook were back to back in the corner, a towel tied in each of their mouths. George had cooked the sandwich, wrapped it up in oiled paper, put it in a bag, brought it in, and the man had paid for it and gone out.

"Bright boy can do everything," Max said. "He can cook and everything. You'd make some girl a nice wife, bright boy."

"Yes?" George said. "Your friend, Ole Andreson, isn't going to come."

"We'll give him ten minutes," Max said.

Max watched the mirror and the clock. The hands of the clock marked seven o'clock, and then five minutes past seven.

"Come on, Al," said Max. "We better go. He's not coming."

"Better give him five minutes," Al said from the kitchen.

In the five minutes a man came in, and George explained that the cook was sick. "Why the hell don't you get another cook?" the man asked. "Aren't you running a lunch-counter?" He went out.

"Come on, Al," Max said.

"What about the two bright boys and the nigger?"

"They're all right."

"You think so?"

"Sure. We're through with it."

"I don't like it," said Al. "It's sloppy. You talk too much."

"Oh, what the hell," said Max. "We got to keep amused, haven't we?"

"You talk too much, all the same," Al said. He came out from the kitchen. The cut-off barrels of the shotgun made a slight bulge under the waist of his too tight-fitting overcoat. He straightened his coat with his gloved hands.

"So long, bright boy," he said to George. "You got a lot of luck."

"That's the truth," Max said. "You ought to play the races, bright boy."

The two of them went out the door. George watched them through the window pass under the arc-light and cross the street. In their tight overcoats and derby hats they looked like a vaudeville team. George went back through the swinging door into the kitchen and untied Nick and the cook.

"I don't want any more of that," said Sam, the cook. "I don't want any more of that."

Nick stood up. He had never had a towel in his mouth before.

"Say," he said. "What the hell?" He was trying to swagger it off.

"They were going to kill Ole Andreson," George said. "They were going to shoot him when he came in to eat."

"Ole Andreson?"

"Sure."

The cook felt the corners of his mouth with his thumbs.

"They all gone?" he asked.

"Yeah," said George. "They're gone now."

"I don't like it," said the cook. "I don't like any of it at all."

"Listen," George said to Nick. "You'd better go see Ole Andreson."

"All right."

"You better not have anything to do with it at all," Sam, the cook, said. "You better stay way out of it."

"Don't go if you don't want to," George said.

"Mixing up in this ain't going to get you anywhere," the cook said. "You stay out of it."

"I'll go see him," Nick said to George. "Where does he live?"

The cook turned away.

"Little boys always know what they want to do," he said.

"He lives up at Hirsch's rooming-house," George said to Nick.

"I'll go up there."

Outside the arc-light shone through the bare branches of a tree. Nick walked up the street beside the car-tracks and turned at the next arc-light down a side street. Three houses up the street was Hirsch's rooming-house. Nick walked up the two steps and pushed the bell. A woman came to the door.

"Is Ole Andreson here?"

"Do you want to see him?"

"Yes, if he's in."

Nick followed the woman up a flight of stairs and back to the end of a corridor. She knocked on the door.

"Who is it?"

"It's somebody to see you, Mr. Andreson," the woman said.

"It's Nick Adams."

"Come in."

Nick opened the door and went into the room. Ole Andreson was lying on the bed with all his clothes on. He had been a heavyweight prizefighter and he was too long for the bed. He lay with his head on two pillows. He did not look at Nick.

"What was it?" he asked.

"I was up at Henry's," Nick said, "and two fellows came in and tied up me and the cook, and they said they were going to kill you."

It sounded silly when he said it. Ole Andreson said nothing.

"They put us out in the kitchen," Nick went on. "They were going to shoot you when you came in to supper."

Ole Andreson looked at the wall and did not say anything.

"George thought I better come and tell you about it."

"There isn't anything I can do about it," Ole Andreson said.

"I'll tell you what they were like."

"I don't want to know what they were like," Ole Andreson said. He looked at the wall. "Thanks for coming to tell me about it."

"That's all right."

Nick looked at the big man lying on the bed.

"Don't you want me to go and see the police?"

"No," Ole Andreson said. "That wouldn't do any good."

"Isn't there something I could do?"

"No. There ain't anything to do."

"Maybe it was just a bluff."

"No. It ain't just a bluff."

Ole Andreson rolled over toward the wall.

"The only thing is," he said, talking toward the wall, "I just can't make up my mind to go out. I been in here all day."

"Couldn't you get out of town?"

"No," Ole Andreson said. "I'm through with all that running around."

He looked at the wall.

"There ain't anything to do now."

"Couldn't you fix it up some way?"

"No. I got in wrong." He talked in the same flat voice. "There ain't anything to do. After a while I'll make up my mind to go out."

"I better go back and see George," Nick said.

"So long," said Ole Andreson. He did not look toward Nick. "Thanks for coming around."

Nick went out. As he shut the door he saw Ole Andreson with all his clothes on, lying on the bed looking at the wall.

"He's been in his room all day," the landlady said downstairs. "I guess he don't feel well. I said to him: 'Mr. Andreson, you ought to go out and take a walk on a nice fall day like this,' but he didn't feel like it."

"He doesn't want to go out."

"I'm sorry he don't feel well," the woman said. "He's an awfully nice man. He was in the ring, you know."

"I know it."

"You'd never know it except from the way his face is," the woman said. They stood talking just inside the street door. "He's just as gentle."

"Well, good night, Mrs. Hirsch," Nick said.

"I'm not Mrs. Hirsch," the woman said. "She owns the place. I just look after it for her. I'm Mrs. Bell."

"Well, good night, Mrs. Bell," Nick said.

"Good night," the woman said.

Nick walked up the dark street to the corner under the arc-light, and then along the car-tracks to Henry's eating-house. George was inside, back of the counter.

"Did you see Ole?"

"Yes," said Nick. "He's in his room and he won't go out."

The cook opened the door from the kitchen when he heard Nick's voice.

"I don't even listen to it," he said, and shut the door.

"Did you tell him about it?" George asked.

"Sure. I told him but he knows what it's all about."

"What's he going to do?"

"Nothing."

"They'll kill him."

"I guess they will."

"He must have got mixed up in something in Chicago."

"I guess so," said Nick.

"It's a hell of a thing."

"It's an awful thing," Nick said.

They did not say anything. George reached down for a towel and wiped the counter.

"I wonder what he did?" Nick said.

"Double-crossed somebody. That's what they kill them for."

"I'm going to get out of this town," Nick said.

"Yes," said George. "That's a good thing to do."

"I can't stand to think about him waiting in the room and knowing he's going to get it. It's too damned awful."

"Well," said George, "you better not think about it."

The Basement Room

Graham Greene

1

When the front door had shut them out and the butler Baines had turned back into the dark heavy hall, Philip began to live. He stood in front of the nursery door, listening until he heard the engine of the taxi die out along the street. His parents were gone for a fortnight's holiday; he was "between nurses," one dismissed and the other not arrived; he was alone in the great Belgravia house with Baines and Mrs. Baines.

He could go anywhere, even through the green baize door to the pantry or down the stairs to the basement living-room. He felt a stranger in his home because he could go into any room and all the rooms were empty.

You could only guess who had once occupied them: the rack of pipes in the smoking-room beside the elephant tusks, the carved wood tobacco jar; in the bedroom the pink hangings and pale perfumes and the three-quarter-finished jars of cream which Mrs. Baines had not yet cleared away; the high glaze on the never-opened piano in the drawing-room, the china clock, the silly little tables and the silver: but here Mrs. Baines was already busy, pulling down the curtains, covering the chairs in dust-sheets.

"Be off out of here, Master Philip," and she looked at him with her hateful peevish eyes, while she moved round, getting everything in order, meticulous and loveless and doing her duty.

Philip Lane went downstairs and pushed at the baize door; he looked into the pantry, but Baines was not there; then he set foot for the first time on the stairs to the basement. Again he had the sense: this is life. All his seven nursery years vibrated with the strange, the new experience. His crowded busy brain was like a city which feels the earth tremble at a distant earthquake shock. He was apprehensive, but he was happier than he had ever been. Everything was more important than before.

Baines was reading a newspaper in his shirtsleeves. He said, "Come in,

Phil, and make yourself at home. Wait a moment and I'll do the honours," and going to a white cleaned cupboard he brought out a bottle of ginger-beer and half a Dundee cake. "Half-past eleven in the morning," Baines said. "It's opening time, my boy," and he cut the cake and poured out the ginger-beer. He was more genial than Philip had ever known him, more at his ease, a man in his own home.

"Shall I call Mrs. Baines?" Philip asked, and he was glad when Baines said no. She was busy. She liked to be busy, so why interfere with her pleasure?

"A spot of drink at half-past eleven," Baines said, pouring himself out a glass of ginger-beer, "gives an appetite for chop and does no man any harm."

"A chop?" Philip asked.

"Old Coasters," Baines said, "call all food chop."

"But it's not a chop?"

"Well, it might be, you know, cooked with palm oil. And then some paw-paw to follow."

Philip looked out of the basement window at the dry stone yard, the ash-can and the legs going up and down beyond the railings.

"Was it hot there?"

"Ah, you never felt such heat. Not a nice heat, mind, like you get in the park on a day like this. Wet," Baines said, "corruption." He cut himself a slice of cake. "Smelling of rot," Baines said, rolling his eyes round the small basement room, from clean cupboard to clean cupboard, the sense of bareness, of nowhere to hide a man's secrets. With an air of regret for something lost he took a long draught of ginger-beer.

"Why did father live out there?"

"It was his job," Baines said, "same as this is mine now. And it was mine then too. It was a man's job. You wouldn't believe it now, but I've had forty niggers under me, doing what I told them to."

"Why did you leave?"

"I married Mrs. Baines."

Philip took the slice of Dundee cake in his hand and munched it round the room. He felt very old, independent and judicial; he was aware that Baines was talking to him as man to man. He never called him Master Philip as Mrs. Baines did, who was servile when she was not authoritative.

Baines had seen the world; he had seen beyond the railings, beyond the tired legs of typists, the Pimlico parade to and from Victoria. He sat there over his ginger pop with the resigned dignity of an exile; Baines didn't complain; he had chosen his fate; and if his fate was Mrs. Baines he had only himself to blame.

But to-day, because the house was almost empty and Mrs. Baines was upstairs and there was nothing to do, he allowed himself a little acidity.

"I'd go back to-morrow if I had the chance."

"Did you ever shoot a nigger?"

"I never had any call to shoot," Baines said. "Of course I carried a gun. But you didn't need to treat them bad. That just made them stupid. Why," Baines said, bowing his thin grey hair with embarrassment over the ginger pop, "I loved some of those damned niggers. I couldn't help loving them. There they'd be laughing, holding hands; they liked to touch each other; it made them feel fine to know the other fellow was round. It didn't mean anything we could understand; two of them would go about all day without losing hold, grown men; but it wasn't love; it didn't mean anything we could understand."

"Eating between meals," Mrs. Baines said. "What would your mother say, Master Philip?"

She came down the steep stairs to the basement, her hands full of pots of cream and salve, tubes of grease and paste. "You oughtn't to encourage him, Baines," she said, sitting down in a wicker armchair and screwing up her small ill-humoured eyes at the Coty lipstick, Pond's cream, the Leichner rouge and Cyclax powder and Elizabeth Arden astringent.

She threw them one by one into the wastepaper basket. She saved only the cold cream. "Telling the boy stories," she said. "Go along to the nursery, Master Philip, while I get lunch."

Philip climbed the stairs to the baize door. He heard Mrs. Baines's voice like the voice in a nightmare when the small Price light has guttered in the saucer and the curtains move; it was sharp and shrill and full of malice, louder than people ought to speak, exposed.

"Sick to death of your ways, Baines, spoiling the boy. Time you did some work about the house," but he couldn't hear what Baines said in reply. He pushed open the baize door, came up like a small earth animal in his grey flannel shorts into a wash of sunlight on a parquet floor, the gleam of mirrors dusted and polished and beautified by Mrs. Baines.

Something broke downstairs, and Philip sadly mounted the stairs to the nursery. He pitied Baines; it occurred to him how happily they could live together in the empty house if Mrs. Baines were called away. He didn't want to play with his Meccano sets; he wouldn't take out his train or his soldiers; he sat at the table with his chin on his hands: this is life; and suddenly he felt responsible for Baines, as if he were the master of the house and Baines an ageing servant who deserved to be cared for. There was not much one could do; he decided at least to be good.

He was not surprised when Mrs. Baines was agreeable at lunch; he was used to her changes. Now it was "another helping of meat, Master Philip," or "Master Philip, a little more of this nice pudding." It was a pudding he liked, Queen's pudding with a perfect meringue, but he wouldn't eat a second helping lest she might count that a victory. She was the kind of woman who thought that any injustice could be counterbalanced by something good to eat.

She was sour, but she liked making sweet things; one never had to complain of a lack of jam or plums; she ate well herself and added soft sugar to the meringue and the strawberry jam. The half light through the basement window set the motes moving above her pale hair like dust as she sifted the sugar, and Baines crouched over his plate saying nothing.

Again Philip felt responsibility. Baines had looked forward to this, and Baines was disappointed: everything was being spoilt. The sensation of disappointment was one which Philip could share; knowing nothing of love or jealousy or passion he could understand better than anyone this grief, something hoped for not happening, something promised not fulfilled, something exciting turning dull. "Baines," he said, "will you take me for a walk this afternoon?"

"No," Mrs. Baines said, "no. That he won't. Not with all the silver to clean."

"There's a fortnight to do it in," Baines said.

"Work first, pleasure afterwards." Mrs. Baines helped herself to some more meringue.

Baines suddenly put down his spoon and fork and pushed his plate away. "Blast," he said.

"Temper," Mrs. Baines said softly, "temper. Don't you go breaking any more things, Baines, and I won't have you swearing in front of the boy. Master Philip, if you've finished you can get down." She skinned the rest of the meringue off the pudding.

"I want to go for a walk," Philip said.

"You'll go and have a rest."

"I will go for a walk."

"Master Philip," Mrs. Baines said. She got up from the table leaving her meringue unfinished, and came towards him, thin, menacing, dusty in the basement room. "Master Philip, you do as you're told." She took him by the arm and squeezed it gently; she watched him with a joyless passionate glitter and above her head the feet of the typists trudged back to the Victoria offices after the lunch interval.

"Why shouldn't I go for a walk?" But he weakened; he was scared and ashamed of being scared. This was life; a strange passion he couldn't understand moving in the basement room. He saw a small pile of broken glass swept into a corner by a waste-paper basket. He looked to Baines for help and only intercepted hate; the sad hopeless hate of something behind bars.

"Why shouldn't I?" he repeated.

"Master Philip," Mrs. Baines said, "you've got to do as you're told. You mustn't think just because your father's away, there's nobody here to—"

"You wouldn't dare," Philip cried, and was startled by Baines's low interjection:

"There's nothing she wouldn't dare."

"I hate you," Philip said to Mrs. Baines. He pulled away from her and ran to the door, but she was there before him; she was old, but she was quick.

"Master Philip," she said, "you'll say you're sorry." She stood in front of the door quivering with excitement. "What would your father do if he heard you say that?"

She put a hand out to seize him, dry and white with constant soda, the nails cut to the quick, but he backed away and put the table between them, and suddenly to his surprise she smiled; she became again as servile as she had been arrogant. "Get along with you, Master Philip," she said with glee, "I see I'm going to have my hands full till your father and mother come back."

She left the door unguarded and when he passed her she slapped him playfully. "I've got too much to do to-day to trouble about you. I haven't covered half the chairs," and suddenly even the upper part of the house became unbearable to him as he thought of Mrs. Baines moving about shrouding the sofas, laying out the dust-sheets.

So he wouldn't go upstairs to get his cap but walked straight out across the shining hall into the street, and again, as he looked this way and that way, it was life he was in the middle of.

2

It was the pink sugar cakes in the window on a paper doily, the ham, the slab of mauve sausage, the wasps driving like small torpedoes across the pane that caught Philip's attention. His feet were tired by pavements; he had been afraid to cross the road, had simply walked first in one direction, then in the other. He was nearly home now; the square was at the end of the street; this was a shabby outpost of Pimlico, and he smudged the pane with his nose looking for sweets, and saw between the cakes and ham a different Baines. He hardly recognised the bulbous eyes, the bald forehead. It was a happy, bold and buccaneering Baines, even though it was, when you looked closer, a desperate Baines.

Philip had never seen the girl. He remembered Baines had a niece and he thought that this might be her. She was thin and drawn, and she wore a white mackintosh; she meant nothing to Philip; she belonged to a world about which he knew nothing at all. He couldn't make up stories about her, as he could make them up about withered Sir Hubert Reed, the Permanent Secretary, about Mrs. Wince-Dudley who came up once a year from Penstanley in Suffolk with a green umbrella and an enormous black handbag, as he could make them up about the upper servants in all the houses where he went to tea and games. She just didn't belong; he thought of mermaids and Undine; but she didn't belong there either, nor to the adventures of Emil, nor to the Bastables. She sat there looking at an iced pink cake in the detachment and mystery of the completely disinherited, looking at the half-used pots of powder which Baines had set out on the marble-topped table between them.

Baines was urging, hoping, entreating, commanding, and the girl looked at the tea and the china pots and cried. Baines passed his handkerchief across the table, but she wouldn't wipe her eyes; she screwed it in her palm and let the tears run down, wouldn't do anything, wouldn't speak, would only put up a silent despairing resistance to what she dreaded and wanted and refused to listen to at any price. The two brains battled over the tea-cups loving each other, and there came to Philip outside, beyond the ham and wasps and dusty Pimlico pane, a confused indication of the struggle.

He was inquisitive and he did not understand and he wanted to know. He went and stood in the doorway to see better; he was less sheltered than he had ever been; other people's lives for the first time touched and pressed and moulded. He would never escape that scene. In a week he had forgotten it; but it conditioned his career, the long austerity of his life; when he was dying he said: "Who is she?"

Baines had won; he was cocky and the girl was happy. She wiped her face, she opened a pot of powder, and their fingers touched across the table. It occurred to Philip that it would be amusing to imitate Mrs. Baines's voice and call "Baines" to him from the door.

It shrivelled them; you couldn't describe it in any other way; it made them smaller, they weren't happy any more and they weren't bold. Baines was the first to recover and trace the voice, but that didn't make things as they were. The sawdust was spilled out of the afternoon; nothing you did could mend it, and Philip was scared. "I didn't mean . . ." He wanted to say that he loved Baines, that he had only wanted to laugh at Mrs. Baines. But he had discovered that you couldn't laugh at Mrs. Baines. She wasn't Sir Hubert Reed, who used steel nibs and carried a pen-wiper in his pocket; she wasn't Mrs. Wince-Dudley; she was darkness when the night-light went out in a draught; she was the frozen blocks of earth he had seen one winter in a graveyard when someone said, "They need an electric drill"; she was the flowers gone bad and smelling in the little closet room at Penstanley. There was nothing to laugh about. You had to endure her when she was there and forget about her quickly when she was away, suppress the thought of her, ram it down deep.

Baines said, "It's only Phil," beckoned him in and gave him the pink iced cake the girl hadn't eaten, but the afternoon was broken, the cake was like dry bread in the throat. The girl left them at once; she even forgot to take the powder; like a small blunt icicle in her white mackintosh she stood in the doorway with her back to them, then melted into the afternoon.

"Who is she?" Philip asked. "Is she your niece?"

"Oh, yes," Baines said, "that's who she is; she's my niece," and poured the last drops of water on to the coarse black leaves in the teapot.

"May as well have another cup," Baines said.

"The cup that cheers," he said hopelessly, watching the bitter black fluid drain out of the spout.

"Have a glass of ginger pop, Phil?"

"I'm sorry. I'm sorry, Baines."

"It's not your fault, Phil. Why, I could believe it wasn't you at all, but her. She creeps in everywhere." He fished two leaves out of his cup and laid them on the back of his hand, a thin soft flake, and a hard stalk. He beat them with his hand: "To-day," and the stalk detached itself, "to-morrow, Wednesday, Thursday, Friday, Saturday, Sunday," but the flake wouldn't come, stayed where it was, drying under his blows, with a resistance you wouldn't believe it to possess. "The tough one wins," Baines said.

He got up and paid the bill and out they went into the street. Baines said, "I don't ask you to say what isn't true. But you needn't mention to Mrs. Baines you met us here."

"Of course not," Philip said, catching something of Sir Hubert Reed's manner, "I understand, Baines." But he didn't understand a thing; he was caught up in other people's darkness.

"It was stupid," Baines said. "So near home, but I hadn't got time to think, you see. I'd got to see her."

"Of course, Baines."

"I haven't time to spare," Baines said. "I'm not young. I've got to see that she's all right."

"Of course you have, Baines."

"Mrs. Baines will get it out of you if she can."

"You can trust me, Baines," Philip said in a dry important Reed voice; and then, "Look out. She's at the window watching." And there indeed she was, looking up at them, between the lace curtains, from the basement room, speculating. "Need we go in, Baines?" Philip asked, cold lying heavy on his stomach like too much pudding; he clutched Baines's arm.

"Careful," Baines said softly, "careful."

"But need we go in, Baines? It's early. Take me for a walk in the park."

"Better not."

"But I'm frightened, Baines."

"You haven't any cause," Baines said. "Nothing's going to hurt you. You just run along upstairs to the nursery. I'll go down by the area and talk to Mrs. Baines." But even he stood hesitating at the top of the stone steps pretending not to see her, where she watched between the curtains. "In at the front door, Phil, and up the stairs."

Philip didn't linger in the hall; he ran, slithering on the parquet Mrs. Baines had polished, to the stairs. Through the drawing-room doorway on the first floor he saw the draped chairs; even the china clock on the mantel was covered like a canary's cage; as he passed it, it chimed the hour, muffled and secret under the duster. On the nursery table he found his supper laid out: a glass of milk and a piece of bread and butter, a sweet biscuit, and a little cold Queen's pudding without the meringue. He had no appetite; he strained his ears for Mrs. Baines's coming, for the sound of voices, but the basement held its secrets; the green baize door shut off that world. He drank the milk and ate the biscuit, but he didn't touch the rest, and presently he could hear the soft precise footfalls of Mrs. Baines on the stairs: she was a good servant, she walked softly; she was a determined woman, she walked precisely.

But she wasn't angry when she came in; she was ingratiating as she opened the night-nursery door—"Did you have a good walk, Master Philip?"—pulled down the blinds, laid out his pyjamas, came back to clear his supper. "I'm glad Baines found you. Your mother wouldn't like you being out alone." She examined the tray. "Not much appetite, have you, Master Philip? Why don't you try a little of this nice pudding? I'll bring you up some more jam for it."

"No, no, thank you, Mrs. Baines," Philip said.

"You ought to eat more," Mrs. Baines said. She sniffed round the room like a dog. "You didn't take any pots out of the waste-paper basket in the kitchen, did you, Master Philip?"

"No," Philip said.

"Of course you wouldn't. I just wanted to make sure." She patted his shoulder and her fingers flashed to his lapel; she picked off a tiny crumb of pink sugar. "Oh, Master Philip," she said, "that's why you haven't any appetite. You've been buying sweet cakes. That's not what your pocket money's for."

"But I didn't," Philip said. "I didn't."

She tasted the sugar with the tip of her tongue.

"Don't tell lies to me, Master Philip. I won't stand for it any more than your father would."

"I didn't, I didn't," Philip said. "They gave it me. I mean Baines," but she had pounced on the word "they." She had got what she wanted; there was no doubt about that, even when you didn't know what it was she wanted. Philip was angry and miserable and disappointed because he hadn't kept Baines's secret. Baines oughtn't to have trusted him; grown-up people should keep their own secrets, and yet here was Mrs. Baines immediately entrusting him with another.

"Let me tickle your palm and see if you can keep a secret." But he put his hand behind him; he wouldn't be touched. "It's a secret between us, Master Philip, that I know all about them. I suppose she was having tea with him," she speculated.

"Why shouldn't she?" he said, the responsibility for Baines weighing on his spirit, the idea that he had got to keep her secret when he hadn't kept Baines's making him miserable with the unfairness of life. "She was nice."

"She was nice, was she?" Mrs. Baines said in a bitter voice he wasn't used to.

"And she's his niece."

"So that's what he said," Mrs. Baines struck softly back at him like the clock under the duster. She tried to be jocular. "The old scoundrel. Don't tell him I know, Master Philip." She stood very still between the table and the door, thinking very hard, planning something. "Promise you won't tell. I'll give you that Meccano set, Master Philip. . . ."

He turned his back on her; he wouldn't promise, but he wouldn't tell. He would have nothing to do with their secrets, the responsibilities they were determined to lay on him. He was only anxious to forget. He had received already a larger dose of life than he had bargained for, and he was scared. "A 2A Meccano set, Master Philip." He never opened his Meccano set again, never built anything, never created anything, died, the old dilettante, sixty years later with nothing to show rather than preserve the memory of Mrs. Baines's malicious voice saying good night, her soft determined footfalls on the stairs to the basement, going down, going down.

3

The sun poured in between the curtains and Baines was beating a tattoo on the water-can. "Glory, glory," Baines said. He sat down on the end of the bed and said, "I beg to announce that Mrs. Baines has been called away. Her mother's dying. She won't be back till to-morrow."

"Why did you wake me up so early?" Philip said. He watched Baines with uneasiness; he wasn't going to be drawn in; he'd learnt his lesson. It wasn't right for a man of Baines's age to be so merry. It made a grown person human in the same way that you were human. For if a grown-up could behave so childishly, you were liable too to find yourself in their world. It was enough that it came at you in dreams: the witch at the corner, the man with a knife. So "It's very early," he complained, even though he loved Baines, even though he couldn't help being glad that Baines was happy. He was divided by the fear and the attraction of life.

"I want to make this a long day," Baines said. "This is the best time." He pulled the curtains back. "It's a bit misty. The cat's been out all night. There she is, sniffing round the area. They haven't taken in any milk at 59. Emma's shaking out the mats at 63." He said, "This was what I used to think about on the Coast: somebody shaking mats and the cat coming home. I can see it to-day," Baines said, "just as if I was still in Africa. Most days you don't notice what you've got. It's a good life if you don't weaken." He put a penny on the washstand. "When you've dressed, Phil, run and get a *Mail* from the barrow at the corner. I'll be cooking the sausages."

"Sausages?"

"Sausages," Baines said. "We're going to celebrate to-day. A fair bust." He celebrated at breakfast, restless, cracking jokes, unaccountably merry and nervous. It was going to be a long long day, he kept on coming back to that: for years he had waited for a long day, he had sweated in the damp Coast heat, changed shirts, gone down with fever, lain between the blankets and sweated, all in the hope of this long day, that cat sniffing round the area, a bit of mist, the mats beaten at 63. He propped the *Mail* in front of the coffee-pot and read pieces aloud. He said, "Cora Down's been married for the fourth time." He was amused, but it wasn't his idea of a long day. His long day was the Park, watching the riders in the Row, seeing Sir Arthur Stillwater pass beyond the rails ("He dined with us once in Bo; up from Freetown; he was governor there"), lunch at the Corner House for Philip's sake (he'd have preferred himself a glass of stout and some oysters at the York bar), the Zoo, the long bus ride home in the last summer light: the leaves in the Green Park were beginning to turn and the motors nuzzled out of Berkeley Street with the low sun gently glowing on their windscreens. Baines envied no one, not Cora Down, or Sir Arthur Stillwater, or Lord Sandale, who came out on to the steps of the Naval and Military and then went back again because he hadn't got anything to do and might as well look at another paper. "I said don't let me see you touch that black again." Baines had led a man's life; everyone on top of the bus pricked their ears when he told Philip all about it.

"Would you have shot him?" Philip asked, and Baines put his head back and tilted his dark respectable manservant's hat to a better angle as the bus swerved round the Artillery Memorial.

"I wouldn't have thought twice about it. I'd have shot to kill," he boasted, and the bowed figure went by, steel helmet, the heavy cloak, the downturned rifle and the folded hands.

"Have you got the revolver?"

"Of course I've got it," Baines said. "Don't I need it with all the burglaries there've been?" This was the Baines whom Philip loved: not Baines singing and carefree, but Baines responsible, Baines behind barriers, living this man's life.

All the buses streamed out from Victoria like a convoy of aeroplanes to bring Baines home with honour. "Forty blacks under me," and there waiting near the area steps was the proper conventional reward, love at lighting-up time.

"It's your niece," Philip said, recognising the white mackintosh, but not the happy sleepy face. She frightened him like an unlucky number; he nearly told Baines what Mrs. Baines had said; but he didn't want to bother, he wanted to leave things alone.

"Why, so it is," Baines said. "I shouldn't wonder if she was going to have a bite of supper with us." But he said they'd play a game, pretend they didn't know her, slip down the area steps, "and here," Baines said, "we are," lay the table, put out the cold sausages, a bottle of beer, a bottle of ginger pop, a flagon of harvest burgundy. "Everyone his own drink," Baines said. "Run upstairs, Phil, and see if there's been a post."

Philip didn't like the empty house at dusk before the lights went on. He hurried. He wanted to be back with Baines. The hall lay there in quiet and shadow prepared to show him something he didn't want to see. Some letters rustled down, and someone knocked. "Open in the name of the Republic." The tumbrils rolled, the head bobbed in the bloody basket. Knock, knock, and the postman's footsteps going away. Philip gathered the letters. The slit in the door was like the grating in a jeweller's window. He remembered the policeman he had seen peer through. He had said to his nurse, "What's he doing?" and when she said, "He's seeing if everything's all right," his brain immediately filled with images of all that might be wrong. He ran to the baize door and the stairs. The girl was already there and Baines was kissing her. She leant breathless against the dresser. "This is Emmy, Phil."

"There's a letter for you, Baines."

"Emmy," Baines said, "it's from her." But he wouldn't open it. "You bet she's coming back."

"We'll have supper, anyway," Emmy said. "She can't harm that."

"You don't know her," Baines said. "Nothing's safe. Damn it," he said, "I was a man once," and he opened the letter.

"Can I start?" Philip asked, but Baines didn't hear; he presented in his stillness and attention an example of the importance grown-up people attached to the written word: you had to write your thanks, not wait and speak them, as if letters couldn't lie. But Philip knew better than that, sprawling his thanks across a page to Aunt Alice who had given him a doll he was too old for. Letters could lie all right, but they made the lie permanent: they lay as evidence against you; they made you meaner than the spoken word.

"She's not coming back till to-morrow night," Baines said. He opened the bottles, he pulled up the chairs, he kissed Emmy again against the dresser.

"You oughtn't to," Emmy said, "with the boy here."

"He's got to learn," Baines said, "like the rest of us," and he helped Philip to three sausages. He only took one for himself; he said he wasn't hungry; but when Emmy said she wasn't hungry either he stood over her and made her eat. He was timid and rough with her; he made her drink the Harvest Burgundy because he said she needed building up; he wouldn't take no for an answer, but when he touched her his hands were light and clumsy too, as if he were afraid to damage something delicate and didn't know how to handle anything so light.

"This is better than milk and biscuits, eh?"

"Yes," Philip said, but he was scared, scared for Baines as much as for himself. He couldn't help wondering at every bite, at every draught of the ginger pop, what Mrs. Baines would say if she ever learnt of this meal; he couldn't imagine it, there was a depth of bitterness and rage in Mrs. Baines you couldn't sound. He said, "She won't be coming back to-night?" but you could tell by the way they immediately understood him that she wasn't really away at all; she was there in the basement with them, driving them to longer drinks and louder talk, biding her time for the right cutting word. Baines wasn't really happy; he was only watching happiness from close to instead of from far away.

"No," he said, "she'll not be back till late to-morrow." He couldn't keep his eyes off happiness; he'd played around as much as other men, he kept on reverting to the Coast as if to excuse himself for his innocence; he wouldn't have been so innocent if he'd lived his life in London, so innocent when it came to tenderness. "If it was you, Emmy," he said, looking at the white dresser, the scrubbed chairs, "this'd be like a home." Already the room was not quite so harsh; there was a little dust in corners, the silver needed a final polish, the morning's paper lay untidily on a chair. "You'd better go to bed, Phil; it's been a long day."

They didn't leave him to find his own way up through the dark shrouded house; they went with him, turning on lights, touching each other's fingers on the switches; floor after floor they drove the night back;

they spoke softly among the covered chairs; they watched him undress, they didn't make him wash or clean his teeth, they saw him into bed and lit the night-light and left his door ajar. He could hear their voices on the stairs, friendly like the guests he heard at dinner-parties when they moved down to the hall, saying good night. They belonged; wherever they were they made a home. He heard a door open and a clock strike, he heard their voices for a long while, so that he felt they were not far away and he was safe. The voices didn't dwindle, they simply went out, and he could be sure that they were still somewhere not far from him, silent together in one of the many empty rooms, growing sleepy together as he grew sleepy after the long day.

He just had time to sigh faintly with satisfaction, because this too perhaps had been life, before he slept and the inevitable terrors of sleep came round him: a man with a tricolour hat beat at the door on His Majesty's service, a bleeding head lay on the kitchen table in a basket, and the Siberian wolves crept closer. He was bound hand and foot and couldn't move; they leapt around him breathing heavily; he opened his eyes and saw Mrs. Baines was there, her grey untidy hair in threads over his face, her black hat askew. A loose hairpin fell on the pillow and one musty thread brushed his mouth. "Where are they?" she whispered. "Where are they?"

4

Philip watched her in terror. Mrs. Baines was out of breath as if she had been searching all the empty rooms, looking under loose covers.

With her untidy grey hair and her black dress buttoned to her throat, her gloves of black cotton, she was so like the witches of his dreams that he didn't dare to speak. There was a stale smell in her breath.

"She's here," Mrs. Baines said, "you can't deny she's here." Her face was simultaneously marked with cruelty and misery; she wanted to "do things" to people, but she suffered all the time. It would have done her good to scream, but she daren't do that: it would warn them. She came ingratiatingly back to the bed where Philip lay rigid on his back and whispered, "I haven't forgotten the Meccano set. You shall have it to-morrow, Master Philip. We've got secrets together, haven't we? Just tell me where they are."

He couldn't speak. Fear held him as firmly as any nightmare. She said, "Tell Mrs. Baines, Master Philip. You love your Mrs. Baines, don't you?" That was too much; he couldn't speak, but he could move his mouth in terrified denial, wince away from her dusty image.

She whispered, coming closer to him, "Such deceit. I'll tell your father. I'll settle with you myself when I've found them. You'll smart; I'll see you smart." Then immediately she was still, listening. A board had creaked on the floor below, and a moment later, while she stooped listening above his bed, there came the whispers of two people who were happy and sleepy together after a long day. The night-light stood beside the mirror and Mrs. Baines could see bitterly there her own reflection, misery and cruelty wavering in the glass, age and dust and nothing to hope for. She sobbed without tears, a dry, breathless sound; but her cruelty was a kind of pride which kept her going; it was her best quality, she would have been merely pitiable without it. She went out of the door on tiptoe, feeling her way across the landing, going so softly down the stairs that no one behind a shut door could hear her. Then there was complete silence again; Philip could move; he raised his knees; he sat up in bed; he wanted to die. It wasn't fair, the walls were down again between his world and theirs; but this time it was something worse than merriment that the grown people made him share; a passion moved in the house he recognised but could not understand.

It wasn't fair, but he owed Baines everything: the Zoo, the ginger pop, the bus ride home. Even the supper called on his loyalty. But he was frightened; he was touching something he touched in dreams: the bleeding head, the wolves, the knock, knock, knock. Life fell on him with savagery: you couldn't blame him if he never faced it again in sixty years. He got out of bed, carefully from habit put on his bedroom slippers, and tiptoed to the door: it wasn't quite dark on the landing below because the curtains had been taken down for the cleaners and the light from the street came in through the tall windows. Mrs. Baines had her hand on the glass door-knob; she was carefully turning it; he screamed, "Baines, Baines."

Mrs. Baines turned and saw him cowering in his pyjamas by the banisters; he was helpless, more helpless even than Baines, and cruelty grew at the sight of him and drove her up the stairs. The nightmare was on him again and he couldn't move; he hadn't any more courage left for ever; he'd spent it all, had been allowed no time to let it grow, no years of gradual hardening; he couldn't even scream.

But the first cry had brought Baines out of the best spare bedroom and he moved quicker than Mrs. Baines. She hadn't reached the top of the stairs before he'd caught her round the waist. She drove her black cotton gloves at his face and he bit her hand. He hadn't time to think, he fought her savagely like a stranger, but she fought back with knowledgeable hate. She was going to teach them all and it didn't really matter whom she began with; they had all deceived her; but the old image in the glass was by her side, telling her she must be dignified, she wasn't young enough to yield her dignity; she could beat his face, but she mustn't bite; she could push, but she mustn't kick.

Age and dust and nothing to hope for were her handicaps. She went over the banisters in a flurry of black clothes and fell into the hall; she lay before the front door like a sack of coals which should have gone down the area into the basement. Philip saw; Emmy saw; she sat down suddenly in the doorway of the best spare bedroom with her eyes open as if she were too tired to stand any longer. Baines went slowly down into the hall.

It wasn't hard for Philip to escape; they'd forgotten him completely; he went down the back, the servants' stairs, because Mrs. Baines was in the hall; he didn't understand what she was doing lying there; like the startling pictures in a book no one had read to him, the things he didn't understand terrified him. The whole house had been turned over to the grown-up world; he wasn't safe in the night-nursery; their passions had flooded it. The only thing he could do was to get away, by the back stairs, and up through the area, and never come back. You didn't think of the cold, of the need of food and sleep; for an hour it would seem quite possible to escape from people for ever.

He was wearing pyjamas and bedroom slippers when he came up into the square, but there was no one to see him. It was that hour of the evening in a residential district when everyone is at the theatre or at home. He climbed over the iron railings into the little garden: the plane-trees spread their large pale palms between him and the sky. It might have been an illimitable forest into which he had escaped. He crouched behind a trunk and the wolves retreated; it seemed to him between the little iron seat and the tree-trunk that no one would ever find him again. A kind of embittered happiness and self-pity made him cry; he was lost; there wouldn't be any more secrets to keep; he surrendered responsibility once and for all. Let grown-up people keep to their world and he would keep to his, safe in the small garden between the plane-trees. "In the lost childhood of Judas Christ was betrayed"; you could almost see the small unformed face hardening into the deep dilettante selfishness of age.

Presently the door of 48 opened and Baines looked this way and that; then he signalled with his hand and Emmy came; it was as if they were only just in time for a train, they hadn't a chance of saying good-bye; she went quickly by like a face at a window swept past the platform, pale and unhappy and not wanting to go. Baines went in again and shut the door; the light was lit in the basement, and a policeman walked round the square, looking into the areas. You could tell how many families were at home by the lights behind the first-floor curtains.

Philip explored the garden: it didn't take long: a twenty-yard square of bushes and plane-trees, two iron seats and a gravel path, a padlocked gate at either end, a scuffle of old leaves. But he couldn't stay: something stirred in the bushes and two illuminated eyes peered out at him like a

Siberian wolf, and he thought how terrible it would be if Mrs. Baines found him there. He'd have no time to climb the railings; she'd seize him from behind.

He left the square at the unfashionable end and was immediately among the fish-and-chip shops, the little stationers selling Bagatelle, among the accommodation addresses and the dingy hotels with open doors. There were few people about because the pubs were open, but a blowsy woman carrying a parcel called out to him across the street and the commissionaire outside a cinema would have stopped him if he hadn't crossed the road. He went deeper: you could go farther and lose yourself more completely here than among the plane-trees. On the fringe of the square he was in danger of being stopped and taken back: it was obvious where he belonged: but as he went deeper he lost the marks of his origin. It was a warm night: any child in those free-living parts might be expected to play truant from bed. He found a kind of camaraderie even among grown-up people; he might have been a neighbour's child as he went quickly by, but they weren't going to tell on him, they'd been young once themselves. He picked up a protective coating of dust from the pavements, of smuts from the trains which passed along the backs in a spray of fire. Once he was caught in a knot of children running away from something or somebody, laughing as they ran; he was whirled with them round a turning and abandoned, with a sticky fruit-drop in his hand.

He couldn't have been more lost; but he hadn't the stamina to keep on. At first he feared that someone would stop him; after an hour he hoped that someone would. He couldn't find his way back, and in any case he was afraid of arriving home alone; he was afraid of Mrs. Baines, more afraid than he had ever been. Baines was his friend, but something had happened which gave Mrs. Baines all the power. He began to loiter on purpose to be noticed, but no one noticed him. Families were having a last breather on the doorsteps, the refuse bins had been put out and bits of cabbage stalks soiled his slippers. The air was full of voices, but he was cut off; these people were strangers and would always now be strangers; they were marked by Mrs. Baines and he shied away from them into a deep class-consciousness. He had been afraid of policemen, but now he wanted one to take him home; even Mrs. Baines could do nothing against a policeman. He sidled past a constable who was directing traffic, but he was too busy to pay him any attention. Philip sat down against a wall and cried.

It hadn't occurred to him that was the easiest way, that all you had to do was to surrender, to show you were beaten and accept kindness. . . . It was lavished on him at once by two women and a pawnbroker. Another policeman appeared, a young man with a sharp incredulous face. He looked as if he noted everything he saw in pocket-books and drew conclusions.

A woman offered to see Philip home, but he didn't trust her: she wasn't a match for Mrs. Baines immobile in the hall. He wouldn't give his address; he said he was afraid to go home. He had his way; he got his protection. "I'll take him to the station," the policeman said, and holding him awkwardly by the hand (he wasn't married; he had his career to make) he led him round the corner up the stone stairs into the little bare over-heated room where Justice waited.

5

Justice waited behind a wooden counter on a high stool; it wore a heavy moustache; it was kindly and had six children ("three of them nippers like yourself"); it wasn't really interested in Philip, but it pretended to be, it wrote the address down and sent a constable to fetch a glass of milk. But the young constable was interested; he had a nose for things.

"Your home's on the telephone, I suppose," Justice said. "We'll ring them up and say you are safe. They'll fetch you very soon. What's your name, sonny?"

"Philip."

"Your other name."

"I haven't got another name." He didn't want to be fetched; he wanted to be taken home by someone who would impress even Mrs. Baines. The constable watched him, watched the way he drank the milk, watched him when he winced away from questions.

"What made you run away? Playing truant, eh?"

"I don't know."

"You oughtn't to do it, young fellow. Think how anxious your father and mother will be."

"They are away."

"Well, your nurse."

"I haven't got one."

"Who looks after you, then?" That question went home. Philip saw Mrs. Baines coming up the stairs at him, the heap of black cotton in the hall. He began to cry.

"Now, now, now," the sergeant said. He didn't know what to do; he wished his wife were with him; even a policewoman might have been useful.

"Don't you think it's funny," the constable said, "that there hasn't been an inquiry?"

"They think he's tucked up in bed."

"You are scared, aren't you?" the constable said. "What scared you?"

"I don't know."

"Somebody hurt you?"

"No."

"He's had bad dreams," the sergeant said. "Thought the house was on fire, I expect. I've brought up six of them. Rose is due back. She'll take him home."

"I want to go home with you," Philip said; he tried to smile at the constable, but the deceit was immature and unsuccessful.

"I'd better go," the constable said. "There may be something wrong."

"Nonsense," the sergeant said. "It's a woman's job. Tact is what you need. Here's Rose. Pull up your stockings, Rose. You're a disgrace to the Force. I've got a job of work for you." Rose shambled in: black cotton stockings drooping over her boots, a gawky Girl Guide manner, a hoarse hostile voice. "More tarts, I suppose."

"No, you've got to see this young man home." She looked at him owlishly.

"I won't go with her," Philip said. He began to cry again. "I don't like her."

"More of that womanly charm, Rose," the sergeant said. The telephone rang on his desk. He lifted the receiver. "What? What's that?" he said. "Number 48? You've got a doctor?" He put his hand over the telephone mouth. "No wonder this nipper wasn't reported," he said. "They've been too busy. An accident. Woman slipped on the area stairs."

"Serious?" the constable asked. The sergeant mouthed at him; you didn't mention the word death before a child (didn't he know? he had six of them), you made noises in the throat, you grimaced, a complicated shorthand for a word of only five letters anyway.

"You'd better go, after all," he said, "and make a report. The doctor's there."

Rose shambled from the stove; pink apply-dapply cheeks, loose stockings. She stuck her hands behind her. Her large morgue-like mouth was full of blackened teeth. "You told me to take him and now just because something interesting . . . I don't expect justice from a man . . ."

"Who's at the house?" the constable asked.

"The butler."

"You don't think," the constable said, "he saw . . ."

"Trust me," the sergeant said. "I've brought up six. I know 'em through and through. You can't teach me anything about children."

"He seemed scared about something."

"Dreams," the sergeant said.

"What name?"

"Baines."

"This Mr. Baines," the constable said to Philip, "you like him, eh? He's good to you?" They were trying to get something out of him; he was suspicious of the whole roomful of them; he said "yes" without conviction because he was afraid at any moment of more responsibilities, more secrets.

"And Mrs. Baines?"

"Yes."

They consulted together by the desk. Rose was hoarsely aggrieved; she was like a female impersonator, she bore her womanhood with an unnatural emphasis even while she scorned it in her creased stockings and her weather-exposed face. The charcoal shifted in the stove; the room was over-heated in the mild late summer evening. A notice on the wall described a body found in the Thames, or rather the body's clothes: wool vest, wool pants, wool shirt with blue stripes, size ten boots, blue serge suit worn at the elbows, fifteen-and-a-half celluloid collar. They couldn't find anything to say about the body, except its measurements, it was just an ordinary body.

"Come along," the constable said. He was interested, he was glad to be going, but he couldn't help being embarrassed by his company, a small boy in pyjamas. His nose smelt something, he didn't know what, but he smarted at the sight of the amusement they caused: the pubs had closed and the streets were full again of men making as long a day of it as they could. He hurried through the less frequented streets, chose the darker pavements, wouldn't loiter, and Philip wanted more and more to loiter, pulling at his hand, dragging with his feet. He dreaded the sight of Mrs. Baines waiting in the hall: he knew now that she was dead. The sergeant's mouthings had conveyed that; but she wasn't buried; she wasn't out of sight; he was going to see a dead person in the hall when the door opened.

The light was on in the basement, and to his relief the constable made for the area steps. Perhaps he wouldn't have to see Mrs. Baines at all. The constable knocked on the door because it was too dark to see the bell, and Baines answered. He stood there in the doorway of the neat bright basement room and you could see the sad complacent plausible sentence he had prepared wither at the sight of Philip; he hadn't expected Philip to return like that in the policeman's company. He had to begin thinking all over again; he wasn't a deceptive man; if it hadn't been for Emmy he would have been quite ready to let the truth lead him where it would.

"Mr. Baines?" the constable asked.

He nodded; he hadn't found the right words; he was daunted by the shrewd knowing face, the sudden appearance of Philip there.

"This little boy from here?"

"Yes," Baines said. Philip could tell that there was a message he was trying to convey, but he shut his mind to it. He loved Baines, but Baines had involved him in secrets, in fears he didn't understand. The glowing morning thought "This is life" had become under Baines's tuition the repugnant memory "That was life": the musty hair across the mouth, the breathless cruel tortured inquiry "Where are they?", the heap of black cotton tipped into the hall. That was what happened when you loved: you got involved; and Philip extricated himself from life, from love, from Baines with a merciless egotism.

There had been things between them, but he laid them low, as a retreating army cuts the wires, destroys the bridges. In the abandoned country you may leave much that is dear—a morning in the Park, an ice at a Corner House, sausages for supper—but more is concerned in the retreat than temporary losses. There are old people who, as the tractors wheel away, implore to be taken, but you can't risk the rearguard for their sake: a whole prolonged retreat from life, from care, from human relationship is involved.

"The doctor's here," Baines said. He nodded at the door, moistened his mouth, kept his eyes on Philip, begging for something like a dog you can't understand. "There's nothing to be done. She slipped on those stone basement stairs. I was in here. I heard her fall." He wouldn't look at the constable's spidery writing which got a terrible lot on one page.

"Did the boy see anything?"

"He can't have done. I thought he was in bed. Hadn't we better go up? It's a shocking thing. Oh," Baines said, losing control, "it's a shocking thing for a child."

"She's through here?" the constable asked.

"I haven't moved her an inch," Baines said.

"He'd better then—"

"Go up the area and through the hall," Baines said and again he begged dumbly like a dog: one more secret, keep this secret, do this for old Baines, he won't ask another.

"Come along," the constable said. "I'll see you up to bed. You're a gentleman; you must come in the proper way through the front door like the master should. Or will you go along with him, Mr. Baines, while I see the doctor?"

"Yes," Baines said, "I'll go." He came across the room to Philip, begging, begging, all the way with his soft old stupid expression: this is Baines, the old Coaster; what about a palm-oil chop, eh? a man's life; forty niggers; never used a gun; I tell you I couldn't help loving them: it wasn't what we call love, nothing we could understand. The messages flickered out from the last posts at the border, imploring, beseeching, reminding: this is your old friend Baines; what about an elevens; a glass of ginger pop won't do you any harm; sausages; a long day. But the wires were cut, the messages just faded out into the enormous vacancy of the neat scrubbed room in which there had never been a place where a man could hide his secrets.

"Come along, Phil, it's bedtime. We'll just go up the steps . . ." Tap, tap, tap, at the telegraph; you may get through, you can't tell, somebody may mend the right wire. "And in at the front door."

"No," Philip said, "no. I won't go. You can't make me go. I'll fight. I won't see her."

The constable turned on them quickly. "What's that? Why won't you go?"

"She's in the hall," Philip said. "I know she's in the hall. And she's dead. I won't see her."

"You moved her then?" the constable said to Baines. "All the way down here? You've been lying, eh? That means you had to tidy up. . . . Were you alone?"

"Emmy," Philip said, "Emmy." He wasn't going to keep any more secrets: he was going to finish once and for all with everything, with Baines and Mrs. Baines and the grown-up life beyond him; it wasn't his business and never, never again, he decided, would he share their confidences and companionship. "It was all Emmy's fault," he protested with a quaver which reminded Baines that after all he was only a child; it had been hopeless to expect help there; he was a child; he didn't understand what it all meant; he couldn't read this shorthand of terror; he'd had a long day and he was tired out. You could see him dropping asleep where he stood against the dresser, dropping back into the comfortable nursery peace. You couldn't blame him. When he woke in the morning, he'd hardly remember a thing.

"Out with it," the constable said, addressing Baines with professional ferocity, "who is she?" just as the old man sixty years later startled his secretary, his only watcher, asking, "Who is she? Who is she?" dropping lower and lower into death, passing on the way perhaps the image of Baines: Baines hopeless, Baines letting his head drop, Baines "coming clean."

Memento Mori

Jonathan Nolan

> "What like a bullet can undeceive!"
>
> —HERMAN MELVILLE

Your wife always used to say you'd be late for your own funeral. Remember that? Her little joke because you were such a slob—always late, always forgetting stuff, even before the incident.

Right about now you're probably wondering if you were late for hers.

You were there, you can be sure of that. That's what the picture's for—the one tacked to the wall by the door. It's not customary to take pictures at a funeral, but somebody, your doctors, I guess, knew you wouldn't remember. They had it blown up nice and big and stuck it right there, next to the door, so you couldn't help but see it every time you got up to find out where she was.

The guy in the picture, the one with the flowers? That's you. And what are you doing? You're reading the headstone, trying to figure out whose funeral you're at, same as you're reading it now, trying to figure why someone stuck that picture next to your door. But why bother reading something that you won't remember?

She's gone, gone for good, and you must be hurting right now, hearing the news. Believe me, I know how you feel. You're probably a wreck. But give it five minutes, maybe ten. Maybe you can even go a whole half hour before you forget.

But you will forget—I guarantee it. A few more minutes and you'll be heading for the door, looking for her all over again, breaking down when you find the picture. How many times do you have to hear the news before some other part of your body, other than that busted brain of yours, starts to remember?

Never-ending grief, never-ending anger. Useless without direction. Maybe you can't understand what's happened. Can't say I really understand, either. Backwards amnesia. That's what the sign says. CRS disease. Your guess is as good as mine.

Maybe you can't understand what happened to you. But you do remember what happened to HER, don't you? The doctors don't want to talk about it. They won't answer my questions. They don't think it's right for a man in your condition to hear about those things. But you remember enough, don't you? You remember his face.

This is why I'm writing to you. Futile, maybe. I don't know how many times you'll have to read this before you listen to me. I don't even know how long you've been locked up in this room already. Neither do you. But your advantage in forgetting is that you'll forget to write yourself off as a lost cause.

Sooner or later you'll want to do something about it. And when you do, you'll just have to trust me, because I'm the only one who can help you.

Earl opens one eye after another to a stretch of white ceiling tiles interrupted by a hand-printed sign taped right above his head, large enough for him to read from the bed. An alarm clock is ringing somewhere. He reads the sign, blinks, reads it again, then takes a look at the room.

It's a white room, overwhelmingly white, from the walls and the curtains to the institutional furniture and the bedspread.

The alarm clock is ringing from the white desk under the window with the white curtains. At this point Earl probably notices that he is lying on top of his white comforter. He is already wearing a dressing gown and slippers.

He lies back and reads the sign taped to the ceiling again. It says, in crude block capitals, THIS IS YOUR ROOM. THIS IS A ROOM IN A HOSPITAL. THIS IS WHERE YOU LIVE NOW.

Earl rises and takes a look around. The room is large for a hospital—empty linoleum stretches out from the bed in three directions. Two doors and a window. The view isn't very helpful, either—a close of trees in the center of a carefully manicured piece of turf that terminates in a sliver of two-lane blacktop. The trees, except for the evergreens, are bare—early spring or late fall, one or the other.

Every inch of the desk is covered with Post-it notes, legal pads, neatly printed lists, psychological textbooks, framed pictures. On top of the mess is a half-completed crossword puzzle. The alarm clock is riding a pile of folded newspapers. Earl slaps the snooze button and takes a cigarette from the pack taped to the sleeve of his dressing gown. He pats the empty pockets of his pajamas for a light. He rifles the papers on the desk, looks quickly through the drawers. Eventually he finds a box of kitchen matches taped to the wall next to the window. Another sign is taped just above the box. It says in loud yellow letters, CIGARETTE? CHECK FOR LIT ONES FIRST, STUPID.

Earl laughs at the sign, lights his cigarette, and takes a long draw. Taped to the window in front of him is another piece of loose-leaf paper headed YOUR SCHEDULE.

It charts off the hours, every hour, in blocks: 10:00 P.M. to 8:00 A.M. is labeled GO BACK TO SLEEP. Earl consults the alarm clock: 8:15. Given the light outside, it must be morning. He checks his watch: 10:30. He presses the watch to his ear and listens. He gives the watch a wind or two and sets it to match the alarm clock.

According to the schedule, the entire block from 8:00 to 8:30 has been labeled BRUSH YOUR TEETH. Earl laughs again and walks over to the bathroom.

The bathroom window is open. As he flaps his arms to keep warm, he notices the ashtray on the windowsill. A cigarette is perched on the ashtray, burning steadily through a long finger of ash. He frowns, extinguishes the old butt, and replaces it with the new one.

The toothbrush has already been treated to a smudge of white paste. The tap is of the push-button variety—a dose of water with each nudge. Earl pushes the brush into his cheek and fiddles it back and forth while he opens the medicine cabinet. The shelves are stocked with single-serving packages of vitamins, aspirin, antidiuretics. The mouthwash is also single-serving, about a shot-glass-worth of blue liquid in a sealed plastic bottle. Only the toothpaste is regular-sized. Earl spits the paste out of his mouth and replaces it with the mouthwash. As he lays the toothbrush next to the toothpaste, he notices a tiny wedge of paper pinched between the glass shelf and the steel backing of the medicine cabinet. He spits the frothy blue fluid into the sink and nudges for some more water to rinse it down. He closes the medicine cabinet and smiles at his reflection in the mirror.

"Who needs half an hour to brush their teeth?"

The paper has been folded down to a minuscule size with all the precision of a sixth-grader's love note. Earl unfolds it and smooths it against the mirror. It reads

IF YOU CAN STILL READ THIS, THEN YOU'RE A FUCKING COWARD.

Earl stares blankly at the paper, then reads it again. He turns it over. On the back it reads

P.S.: AFTER YOU'VE READ THIS, HIDE IT AGAIN.

Earl reads both sides again, then folds the note back down to its original size and tucks it underneath the toothpaste.

Maybe then he notices the scar. It begins just beneath the ear, jagged and thick, and disappears abruptly into his hairline. Earl turns his head and stares out of the corner of his eye to follow the scar's progress. He traces it with a fingertip, then looks back down at the cigarette burning in the ashtray. A thought seizes him and he spins out of the bathroom.

He is caught at the door to his room, one hand on the knob. Two pictures are taped to the wall by the door. Earl's attention is caught first by the MRI, a shiny black frame for four windows into someone's skull. In marker, the picture is labeled YOUR BRAIN. Earl stares at it. Concentric circles in different colors. He can make out the big orbs of his eyes and, behind these, the twin lobes of his brain. Smooth wrinkles, circles, semicircles. But right there in the middle of his head, circled in marker, tunneled in from the back of his neck like a maggot into an apricot, is something different. Deformed, broken, but unmistakable. A dark smudge, the shape of a flower, right there in the middle of his brain.

He bends to look at the other picture. It is a photograph of a man holding flowers, standing over a fresh grave. The man is bent over, reading the headstone. For a moment this looks like a hall of mirrors or the beginnings of a sketch of infinity: the one man bent over, looking at the smaller man, bent over, reading the headstone. Earl looks at the picture for a long time. Maybe he begins to cry. Maybe he just stares silently at the picture. Eventually, he makes his way back to the bed, flops down, seals his eyes shut, tries to sleep.

The cigarette burns steadily away in the bathroom. A circuit in the alarm clock counts down from ten, and it starts ringing again.

Earl opens one eye after another to a stretch of white ceiling tiles, interrupted by a hand-printed sign taped right above his head, large enough for him to read from the bed.

You can't have a normal life anymore. You must know that. How can you have a girlfriend if you can't remember her name? Can't have kids, not unless you want them to grow up with a dad who doesn't recognize them. Sure as hell can't hold down a job. Not too many professions out there that value forgetfulness. Prostitution, maybe. Politics, of course.

No. Your life is over. You're a dead man. The only thing the doctors are hoping to do is teach you to be less of a burden to the orderlies. And they'll probably never let you go home, wherever that would be.

So the question is not "to be or not to be," because you aren't. The question is whether you want to do something about it. Whether revenge matters to you.

It does to most people. For a few weeks, they plot, they scheme, they take measures to get even. But the passage of time is all it takes to erode that initial impulse. Time is theft, isn't that what they say? And time eventually convinces most of us that forgiveness is a virtue. Conveniently, cowardice and forgiveness look identical at a certain distance. Time steals your nerve.

If time and fear aren't enough to dissuade people from their revenge, then there's always authority, softly shaking its head and saying, We understand, but you're the better man for letting it go. For rising above it. For not sinking to their level. And besides, says authority, if you try anything stupid, we'll lock you up in a little room.

But they already put you in a little room, didn't they? Only they don't really lock it or even guard it too carefully because you're a cripple. A corpse. A vegetable who probably wouldn't remember to eat or take a shit if someone wasn't there to remind you.

And as for the passage of time, well, that doesn't really apply to you anymore, does it? Just the same ten minutes, over and over again. So how can you forgive if you can't remember to forget?

You probably were the type to let it go, weren't you? Before. But you're not the man you used to be. Not even half. You're a fraction; you're the ten-minute man.

Of course, weakness is strong. It's the primary impulse. You'd probably prefer to sit in your little room and cry. Live in your finite collection of memories, carefully polishing each one. Half a life set behind glass and pinned to cardboard like a collection of exotic insects. You'd like to live behind that glass, wouldn't you? Preserved in aspic.

You'd like to but you can't, can you? You can't because of the last addition to your collection. The last thing you remember. His face. His face and your wife, looking to you for help.

And maybe this is where you can retire to when it's over. Your little collection. They can lock you back up in another little room and you can live the rest of your life in the past. But only if you've got a little piece of paper in your hand that says you got him.

You know I'm right. You know there's a lot of work to do. It may seem impossible, but I'm sure if we all do our part, we'll figure something out. But you don't have much time. You've only got about ten minutes, in fact. Then it starts all over again. So do something with the time you've got.

Earl opens his eyes and blinks into the darkness. The alarm clock is ringing. It says 3:20, and the moonlight streaming through the window means it must be the early morning. Earl fumbles for the lamp, almost knocking it over in the process. Incandescent light fills the room, painting the metal furniture yellow, the walls yellow, the bedspread, too. He lies back and looks up at the stretch of yellow ceiling tiles above him, interrupted by a handwritten sign taped to the ceiling. He reads the sign two, maybe three times, then blinks at the room around him.

It is a bare room. Institutional, maybe. There is a desk over by the window. The desk is bare except for the blaring alarm clock. Earl probably notices, at this point, that he is fully clothed. He even has his shoes on under the sheets. He extracts himself from the bed and crosses to the desk. Nothing in the room would suggest that anyone lived there, or ever had, except for the odd scrap of tape stuck here and there to the wall. No pictures, no books, nothing. Through the window, he can see a full moon shining on carefully manicured grass.

Earl slaps the snooze button on the alarm clock and stares a moment at the two keys taped to the back of his hand. He picks at the tape while he searches through the empty drawers. In the left pocket of his jacket, he finds a roll of hundred-dollar bills and a letter sealed in an envelope. He checks the rest of the main room and the bathroom. Bits of tape, cigarette butts. Nothing else.

Earl absentmindedly plays with the lump of scar tissue on his neck and moves back toward the bed. He lies back down and stares up at the ceiling and the sign taped to it. The sign reads, GET UP, GET OUT RIGHT NOW. THESE PEOPLE ARE TRYING TO KILL YOU.

Earl closes his eyes.

They tried to teach you to make lists in grade school, remember? Back when your day planner was the back of your hand. And if your assignments came off in the shower, well, then they didn't get done. No direction, they said. No discipline. So they tried to get you to write it all down somewhere more permanent.

Of course, your grade-school teachers would be laughing their pants wet if they could see you now. Because you've become the exact product of their organizational lessons. Because you can't even take a piss without consulting one of your lists.

They were right. Lists are the only way out of this mess.

Here's the truth: People, even regular people, are never just any one person with one set of attributes. It's not that simple. We're all at the mercy of the limbic system, clouds of electricity drifting through the brain. Every man is broken into twenty-four-hour fractions, and then again within those twenty-four hours. It's a daily pantomime, one man yielding control to the next: a backstage crowded with old hacks clamoring for their turn in the spotlight. Every week, every day. The angry man hands the baton over to the sulking man, and in turn to the sex addict, the introvert, the conversationalist. Every man is a mob, a chain gang of idiots.

This is the tragedy of life. Because for a few minutes of every day, every man becomes a genius. Moments of clarity, insight, whatever you want to call them. The clouds part, the planets get in a neat little line, and everything becomes obvious. I should quit smoking, maybe, or here's how I could make a fast million, or such and such is the key to eternal happiness. That's the miserable truth. For a few moments, the secrets of the universe are opened to us. Life is a cheap parlor trick.

But then the genius, the savant, has to hand over the controls to the next guy down the pike, most likely the guy who just wants to eat potato chips, and insight and brilliance and salvation are all entrusted to a moron or a hedonist or a narcoleptic.

The only way out of this mess, of course, is to take steps to ensure that you control the idiots that you become. To take your chain gang, hand in hand, and lead them. The best way to do this is with a list.

It's like a letter you write to yourself. A master plan, drafted by the guy who can see the light, made with steps simple enough for the rest of the idiots to understand. Follow steps one through one hundred. Repeat as necessary.

Your problem is a little more acute, maybe, but fundamentally the same thing.

It's like that computer thing, the Chinese room. You remember that? One guy sits in a little room, laying down cards with letters written on them in a language he doesn't understand, laying them down one letter at a time in a sequence according to someone else's instructions. The cards are supposed to spell out a joke in Chinese. The guy doesn't speak Chinese, of course. He just follows his instructions.

There are some obvious differences in your situation, of course: You broke out of the room they had you in, so the whole enterprise has to be portable. And the guy giving the instructions—that's you, too, just an earlier version of you. And the joke you're telling, well, it's got a punch line. I just don't think anyone's going to find it very funny.

So that's the idea. All you have to do is follow your instructions. Like climbing a ladder or descending a staircase. One step at a time. Right down the list. Simple.

And the secret, of course, to any list is to keep it in a place where you're bound to see it.

He can hear the buzzing through his eyelids. Insistent. He reaches out for the alarm clock, but he can't move his arm.

Earl opens his eyes to see a large man bent double over him. The man looks up at him, annoyed, then resumes his work. Earl looks around him. Too dark for a doctor's office.

Then the pain floods his brain, blocking out the other questions. He squirms again, trying to yank his forearm away, the one that feels like it's burning. The arm doesn't move, but the man shoots him another scowl. Earl adjusts himself in the chair to see over the top of the man's head.

The noise and the pain are both coming from a gun in the man's hand—a gun with a needle where the barrel should be. The needle is digging into the fleshy underside of Earl's forearm, leaving a trail of puffy letters behind it.

Earl tries to rearrange himself to get a better view, to read the letters on his arm, but he can't. He lies back and stares at the ceiling.

Eventually the tattoo artist turns off the noise, wipes Earl's forearm with a piece of gauze, and wanders over to the back to dig up a pamphlet describing how to deal with a possible infection. Maybe later he'll tell his wife about this guy and his little note. Maybe his wife will convince him to call the police.

Earl looks down at the arm. The letters are rising up from the skin, weeping a little. They run from just behind the strap of Earl's watch all the way to the inside of his elbow. Earl blinks at the message and reads it again. It says, in careful little capitals, I RAPED AND KILLED YOUR WIFE.

• • •

It's your birthday today, so I got you a little present. I would have just bought you a beer, but who knows where that would have ended?

So instead, I got you a bell. I think I may have had to pawn your watch to buy it, but what the hell did you need a watch for, anyway?

You're probably asking yourself, Why a bell. In fact, I'm guessing you're going to be asking yourself that question every time you find it in your pocket. Too many of these letters now. Too many for you to dig back into every time you want to know the answer to some little question.

It's a joke, actually. A practical joke. But think of it this way: I'm not really laughing at you so much as with you.

I'd like to think that every time you take it out of your pocket and wonder, Why do I have this bell? a little part of you, a little piece of your broken brain, will remember and laugh, like I'm laughing now.

Besides, you do know the answer. It was something you learned before. So if you think about it, you'll know.

Back in the old days, people were obsessed with the fear of being buried alive. You remember now? Medical science not being quite what it is today, it wasn't uncommon for people to suddenly wake up in a casket. So rich folks had their coffins outfitted with breathing tubes. Little tubes running up to the mud above so that if someone woke up when they weren't supposed to, they wouldn't run out of oxygen. Now, they must have tested this out and realized that you could shout yourself hoarse through the tube, but it was too narrow to carry much noise. Not enough to attract attention, at least. So a string was run up the tube to a little bell attached to the headstone. If a dead person came back to life, all he had to do was ring his little bell till someone came and dug him up again.

I'm laughing now, picturing you on a bus or maybe in a fast-food restaurant, reaching into your pocket and finding your little bell and wondering to yourself where it came from, why you have it. Maybe you'll even ring it.

Happy birthday, buddy.

I don't know who figured out the solution to our mutual problem, so I don't know whether to congratulate you or me. A bit of a lifestyle change, admittedly, but an elegant solution, nonetheless.

Look to yourself for the answer.

That sounds like something out of a Hallmark card. I don't know when you thought it up, but my hat's off to you. Not that you know what the hell I'm talking about. But, honestly, a real brainstorm. After all, everybody else needs mirrors to remind themselves who they are. You're no different.

The little mechanical voice pauses, then repeats itself. It says, "The time is 8:00 A.M. This is a courtesy call." Earl opens his eyes and replaces the receiver. The phone is perched on a cheap veneer headboard that stretches behind the bed, curves to meet the corner, and ends at the minibar. The TV is still on, blobs of flesh color nattering away at each other. Earl lies back down and is surprised to see himself, older now, tanned, the hair pulling away from his head like solar flares. The mirror on the ceiling is cracked, the silver fading in creases. Earl continues to stare at himself, astonished by what he sees. He is fully dressed, but the clothes are old, threadbare in places.

Earl feels the familiar spot on his left wrist for his watch, but it's gone. He looks down from the mirror to his arm. It is bare and the skin has changed to an even tan, as if he never owned a watch in the first place. The skin is even in color except for the solid black arrow on the inside of Earl's wrist, pointing up his shirtsleeve. He stares at the arrow for a moment. Perhaps he doesn't try to rub it off anymore. He rolls up his sleeve.

The arrow points to a sentence tattooed along Earl's inner arm. Earl reads the sentence once, maybe twice. Another arrow picks up at the beginning of the sentence, points farther up Earl's arm, disappearing under the rolled-up shirtsleeve. He unbuttons his shirt.

Looking down on his chest, he can make out the shapes but cannot bring them into focus, so he looks up at the mirror above him.

The arrow leads up Earl's arm, crosses at the shoulder, and descends onto his upper torso, terminating at a picture of a man's face that occupies most of his chest. The face is that of a large man, balding, with a mustache and a goatee. It is a particular face, but like a police sketch it has a certain unreal quality.

The rest of his upper torso is covered in words, phrases, bits of information, and instructions, all of them written backward on Earl, forward in the mirror.

Eventually Earl sits up, buttons his shirt, and crosses to the desk. He takes out a pen and a piece of notepaper from the desk drawer, sits, and begins to write.

I don't know where you'll be when you read this. I'm not even sure if you'll bother to read this. I guess you don't need to.

It's a shame, really, that you and I will never meet. But, like the song says, "By the time you read this note, I'll be gone."

We're so close now. That's the way it feels. So many pieces put together, spelled out. I guess it's just a matter of time until you find him.

Who knows what we've done to get here? Must be a hell of a story, if only you could remember any of it. I guess it's better that you can't.

I had a thought just now. Maybe you'll find it useful.

Everybody is waiting for the end to come, but what if it already passed us by? What if the final joke of Judgment Day was that it had already come and gone and we were none the wiser? Apocalypse arrives quietly; the chosen are herded off to heaven, and the rest of us, the ones who failed the test, just keep on going, oblivious. Dead already, wandering around long after the gods have stopped keeping score, still optimistic about the future.

I guess if that's true, then it doesn't matter what you do. No expectations. If you can't find him, then it doesn't matter, because nothing matters. And if you do find him, then you can kill him without worrying about the consequences. Because there are no consequences.

That's what I'm thinking about right now, in this crappy little room. Framed pictures of ships on the wall. I don't know, obviously, but if I had to guess, I'd say we're somewhere up the coast. If you're wondering why your left arm is five shades browner than your right, I don't know what to tell you. I guess we must have been driving for a while. And, no, I don't know what happened to your watch.

And all these keys: I have no idea. Not a one that I recognize. Car keys and house keys and the little fiddly keys for padlocks. What have we been up to?

I wonder if he'll feel stupid when you find him. Tracked down by the ten-minute man. Assassinated by a vegetable.

I'll be gone in a moment. I'll put down the pen, close my eyes, and then you can read this through if you want.

I just wanted you to know that I'm proud of you. No one who matters is left to say it. No one left is going to want to.

Earl's eye's are wide open, staring through the window of the car. Smiling eyes. Smiling through the window at the crowd gathering across the street. The crowd gathering around the body in the doorway. The body emptying slowly across the sidewalk and into the storm drain.

A stocky guy, facedown, eyes open. Balding head, goatee. In death, as in police sketches, faces tend to look the same. This is definitely somebody in particular. But really, it could be anybody.

Earl is still smiling at the body as the car pulls away from the curb. The car? Who's to say? Maybe it's a police cruiser. Maybe it's just a taxi.

As the car is swallowed into traffic, Earl's eyes continue to shine out into the night, watching the body until it disappears into a circle of concerned pedestrians. He chuckles to himself as the car continues to make distance between him and the growing crowd.

Earl's smile fades a little. Something has occurred to him. He begins to pat down his pockets; leisurely at first, like a man looking for his keys, then a little more desperately. Maybe his progress is impeded by a set of handcuffs. He begins to empty the contents of his pockets out onto the seat next to him. Some money. A bunch of keys. Scraps of paper.

A round metal lump rolls out of his pocket and slides across the vinyl seat. Earl is frantic now. He hammers at the plastic divider between him and the driver, begging the man for a pen. Perhaps the cabbie doesn't speak much English. Perhaps the cop isn't in the habit of talking to suspects. Either way, the divider between the man in front and the man behind remains closed. A pen is not forthcoming.

The car hits a pothole, and Earl blinks at his reflection in the rearview mirror. He is calm now. The driver makes another corner, and the metal lump slides back over to rest against Earl's leg with a little jingle. He picks it up and looks at it, curious now. It is a little bell. A little metal bell. Inscribed on it are his name and a set of dates. He recognizes the first one: the year in which he was born. But the second date means nothing to him. Nothing at all.

As he turns the bell over in his hands, he notices the empty space on his wrist where his watch used to sit. There is a little arrow there, pointing up his arm. Earl looks at the arrow, then begins to roll up his sleeve.

"You'd be late for your own funeral," she'd say. Remember? The more I think about it, the more trite that seems. What kind of idiot, after all, is in any kind of rush to get to the end of his own story?

And how would I know if I were late, anyway? I don't have a watch anymore. I don't know what we did with it.

What the hell do you need a watch for, anyway? It was an antique. Deadweight tugging at your wrist. Symbol of the old you. The you that believed in time.

No. Scratch that. It's not so much that you've lost your faith in time as that time has lost its faith in you. And who needs it, anyway? Who wants to be one of those saps living in the safety of the future, in the safety of the moment after the moment in which they felt something powerful? Living in the next moment, in which they feel nothing. Crawling down the hands of the clock, away from the people who did unspeakable things to them. Believing the lie that time will heal all wounds—which is just a nice way of saying that time deadens us.

But you're different. You're more perfect. Time is three things for most people, but for you, for us, just one. A singularity. One moment. This moment. Like you're the center of the clock, the axis on which the hands turn. Time moves about you but never moves you. It has lost its ability to affect you. What is it they say? That time is theft? But not for you. Close your eyes and you can start all over again. Conjure up that necessary emotion, fresh as roses.

Time is an absurdity. An abstraction. The only thing that matters is this moment. This moment a million times over. You have to trust me. If this moment is repeated enough, if you keep trying—and you have to keep trying—eventually you will come across the next item on your list.

PART IX

FAMILY FILM:

NOSTALGIA FOR AN UNLIVED PAST

"Red Ryder Nails the Hammond Kid"
by Jean Shepherd

A Christmas Story, directed by Bob Clark, 1983

"My Friend Flicka"
by Mary O'Hara

My Friend Flicka, directed by Harold D. Schuster, 1943

"Shoeless Joe Jackson Comes to Iowa"
by W. P. Kinsella

Field of Dreams, directed by Phil Alden Robinson, 1989

Family films are big business. So is nostalgia. But combining the two to make films that potentially appeal to both children and adults is the biggest business of all. One recent study of films made between 1988 and 1997 indicates that G-rated films are, on average, eight to nine times more profitable than R-rated films. And nostalgia really sells: Witness the return of Burma Shave, the redesigned Coke bottles, and the retro architecture of baseball parks like Cleveland's Jacobs Field and Oriole Park at Camden Yards. The following three stories (and their film adaptations)—all wildly successful in their time—combine family and nostalgia in different ways, from Jean Shepherd's steel-town nostalgia to Mary O'Hara's wartime nostalgia to W. P. Kinsella's baseball nostalgia. And there's one more thread running through each of these stories and movies: a unique sort of "daddy nostalgia."

From 1956 to 1977, radio entertainer Jean Shepherd, author of "Red Ryder Nails the Hammond Kid," broadcast from New York station WOR. His Depression-era childhood was a frequent subject of his nightly monologue, and many of his stories featured the "Old Man," a character roughly based on Shepherd's own father, who left home when Shepherd was sixteen. When Shepherd wasn't talking about "the festering years of his childhood" in his fictional hometown of Hohman, Indiana—he really grew up in Hammond, Indiana—he was remarking on the absurdities of modern life, like the names of magazines: "What we need is *Insight* and we get *Look*!" Or the names of cars: "Name them the truth! Can't you imagine the Cadillac Narcissus? Or the Dodge Oedipus? How about the Plymouth Son-of-a-Bitch?" And when he wasn't doing that, he was berating his listeners, calling them "fatheads out there in the darkness, losers in the Sargasso Sea of existence." Or encouraging them to put their radios in their open windows with the volume all the way up while he screamed epithets over the airwaves. No homespun, fire-in-the-hearth storyteller was he. Media guru Marshall McLuhan claimed that Shepherd reinvented both radio and literature through "a new kind of novel that he writes nightly." "I think," Shepherd once said, "that there is a whole area of the wild, swinging anthill that we're all a part of that goes almost completely unreported and unnoticed by the vast body of the press and literature. It's a kind of recording of the daily frustration and the momentary exaltation of the fact of living itself."

Shepherd's audience—he called them his Night People (and was credited by *The American Dictionary of Slang and Usage* for this neologism)—did more than listen. They *followed.* And together, they and Shepherd perpetrated the *I, Libertine* hoax, Shepherd's first foray into the publishing world. It began when Shepherd asked a bookstore clerk for a volume containing reprinted scripts of an old radio serial, "Vic and Sade." When the clerk told him it was unavailable—and in fact, didn't exist because it wasn't on any publisher's list—Shepherd mobilized his Night People. "What better way to restore the status quo," he asked them, "than to shake the Day People's faith in their organization. And what better place to start than with bookshop clerks whose lists make them the most organized of all?" He solicited suggestions for a fictitious book and author with which to confound the system. Thousands responded; he picked *I, Libertine* by Frederick Ewing. The fabricated Ewing had an impressive résumé. He was an Oxford graduate and retired Royal Navy Commander, as well as a scholar "well remembered" for his BBC talks on "erotica of the eighteenth century."

Shepherd's listeners bombarded libraries and bookstores with requests for Ewing's "classic work." Within weeks, publisher Ian Ballantine was trying desperately to obtain the paperback rights to the mysteriously unavailable novel. Eventually he learned of the hoax, but made an unusual suggestion: that they really publish such a book. Shepherd and science fiction writer Ted Sturgeon* quickly knocked out a bawdy tale based on the life and times of Elizabeth Chudleigh, Duchess of Kingston. (A description of the duchess's unacknowledged heir stated, "His teeth were excellent, especially the upper right incisor.") Across a cover illustration by *Mad* magazine artist Kelly Freas sprawled the words *Turbulent! Turgid! Tempestuous!* It became a bestseller. (All proceeds, incidentally, went to charity.) "Few touched on the real point of the story," Shepherd said later. "Most papers got it wrong, and said things like 'Disk jockey sells non-existent book to listeners.' It was the *listeners* who sold a non-existent book to the *world*! Only the *Wall Street Journal*† and the overseas press

* Sturgeon was no hack. An extremely influential SF author, his short story "Microcosmic God" is considered one of the five best SF stories of all time. He also wrote several episodes of *Star Trek,* and developed the concept of the "Prime Directive" (that no Star Fleet personnel may interfere with the healthy development of alien life or culture).

† The *Wall Street Journal* may have gotten the facts right, but they did spell Shepherd's name wrong.

got it right." Eleven years later Shepherd published (for real this time) *In God We Trust: All Others Pay Cash*, the book of stories containing "Red Ryder Nails the Hammond Kid."

Oral storytelling like Shepherd's is to the modern short story as wisteria is to an orchid. No delicately balanced perfection here. Shepherd's stories wind; they meander; in written form they break most of the principles of short-story writing—most notably concision. "Red Ryder" follows the method Shepherd developed while on the radio, a circling around and into a subject, sometimes beginning with an observation about American life, sometimes tuning up with an extemporaneous web of words. "But here it is on a quiet February night . . ." one broadcast began, "time to listen and time to sit, time to wait for the next channel cat to make the bend, time to wait for the next starfish to reproduce its kind, almost impossible to kill a starfish, you know, almost impossible even to understand a starfish. I once knew a starfish in Hamilton, Ontario . . ." While jazz played in the background, Shepherd told tales with detours, chuckles, repetitions, pauses, riffs, and stories embedded within stories. Pieces like "Red Ryder," developed and honed nightly, found their way into his stand-up routine and later into his books. In all, Shepherd penned five volumes, thereby preserving many of his best stories, but it was his narration—the voice, the chuckle, the bemused pauses—that charmed and mobilized two generations of nocturnal listeners.

Which is why tapes of Shepherd's broadcasts are still sold over the Internet by a fervently devoted cult following, and why Bob Clark, director of *A Christmas Story*, insisted on using Shepherd's voiceover. Clark became one of Shepherd's fans in the late sixties, while driving to his girlfriend's house one night. He tuned in to Shepherd's show, was immediately hooked, and ended up driving around his girlfriend's block until Shepherd finished his forty-five-minute yarn. It took Clark fourteen years to convince a studio to finance a film based on Shepherd's stories. Meanwhile Clark directed low-budget horror films like *Deathdream* (1974) and *Black Christmas* (1974), and wrote for the *Dukes of Hazzard* television show. It was the financial success of the raunchy sex comedy *Porky's* (1982), which he wrote and directed, that paved the way for *A Christmas Story*.

Clark cowrote *A Christmas Story* with Shepherd and his wife, Leigh Brown—a task that couldn't have been easy, as Shepherd was well into his curmudgeonly years.* Reportedly, Shepherd disliked the softness Clark brought to the project; his own vision was more like "Dickens's *Christmas*

* Shepherd became bitter and reclusive after he was dropped from WOR. He was belligerent in public appearances and ultimately even disowned his children; when he died in 1999, his will stated that he had no issue.

Carol as retold by Scrooge." It was, however, a serendipitous pairing: Shepherd brought sophistication to Clark's work, and Clark brought accessibility to Shepherd's. Whatever the behind-the-scenes tussles may have been, they were worthwhile. *A Christmas Story* now ranks with *It's a Wonderful Life* in the pantheon of holiday classics.

Mary O'Hara's was a different kind of nostalgia. Her story "My Friend Flicka," published a few months before Pearl Harbor, tapped into a wartime longing for a simpler, disappearing life. O'Hara came late to the writing of prose. She began her first career in Hollywood as a reader who summarized and recommended stories for possible adaptation, then quickly graduated to screenwriting.* In the 1920s she worked as a writer on dozens of silent films, including *The Prisoner of Zenda* (1922) and *Braveheart* (1925), produced by Cecil de Mille. When de Mille asked her how she learned her trade so quickly, she attributed it to an ability to synopsize that she'd learned as a preacher's daughter: "At the dinner table after [the service], each of us would be asked to prove that we had listened, and not daydreamed." De Mille liked her answer and had his publicity manager release this sentence to the newspapers: "Mary O'Hara learned to write for the screen by listening to her father's sermons." Eventually, though, she became disillusioned with the moviemaking process, saying, "Screenwriters are cursed with amateur criticism. They are obliged to submit their copy to the examination of so many people, most of them ignorant, and all with different ideas . . . this precluded any possibility of doing my best work." In 1930, O'Hara moved to Wyoming with her second husband, Helge Sture-Vasa, and began a new career as a short-story writer and novelist (her third career would be as a musical composer).

In Wyoming, O'Hara began writing stories inspired by ranch life. Then, ever the professional, she enrolled in a summer extension course at Columbia in order to polish her work. Her instructor was Whit Burnett, publisher of *Story*. He and her classmates particularly admired "My Friend Flicka," one of the stories she had brought with her. (Their one quibble was with the ending: They didn't believe the horse would get well. O'Hara was forced to confess that the story was based on a real filly who, unlike Flicka, didn't recover. "But I always believed she would have got well," she told her class, "if only I had known and could have got down there to the stream to hold on to her.") Burnett not only published "Flicka" in *Story*, he encouraged her to expand it into a novel, and he remained her mentor

* Hollywood was an easier place for women to work during the teens, 1920s, and early 1930s. According to Cari Beauchamp, biographer of early screenwriter Frances Marion, almost one-quarter of the screenwriters in Hollywood during the 1920s were women, and half of all the films copyrighted between 1911 and 1925 were written by women.

for many years. Later O'Hara said, "Everyone tells you [screenwriting] does not teach you how to write, it teaches you how not to. I do not agree. You can learn character, plot, dramatic construction, editing, visualization." O'Hara always had very strong ideas about what a story should and shouldn't be. "Love is the theme of all of my books," she said, "because it is the theme of my own life and of human life as I see it. I abhor sentimentality, but I never cease to marvel at the miracles love can perform." This might lead one to believe that she lived the contented Wyoming home life of her characters, the McLaughlins. In fact, her second husband turned out to be a scoundrel and a bigamist,* who even hinted at one point that he had written *Flicka* and O'Hara had stolen it from him.

"My Friend Flicka" was an immediate success. The story was included in both best-of collections (*Best American Short Stories* and *O. Henry Prize Stories*), and the novel that quickly followed was named one of the ten best of 1941 by the *New York Times.* Although O'Hara didn't write "Flicka" for (only) young adult readers, over the years it has been pigeonholed as a children's book. (Ironically, though, it is still occasionally banned from schools, along with *Catcher in the Rye*, presumably because the word *abortion* is used.) This could be because the story (and novel) are so closely associated with the film adaptation starring Roddy McDowall—now widely considered a children's film.

In 1943, when *My Friend Flicka* was released, audiences were attending movies—pretty much *any* movie—in record numbers, something they would continue to do throughout the war years. (A front-page story in the *Hollywood Reporter* proclaimed in 1942: "The sale of tickets at the nation's box office is unbelievable. Nothing approximating the amounts now being sold ever hit this business before. Good and bad pictures seemingly get the same audience draw.") *Flicka* was a Technicolor postcard of American pastoral life, an idyll of wartime escapism that told the world "why we fight." In fact, *Flicka* was one of forty films selected by the Motion Picture Bureau of the Overseas Branch of the Office of War Information to follow Allied troops into countries liberated from Germany. The selections were based on a film's ability to provide entertainment, build morale, and depict authentic American life. (Even O'Hara's story was singled out as an antidote to fascist evil. In her introduction to *Best American Short Stories 1942,* in which "My Friend Flicka" appeared, Martha Foley wrote: "In its short stories, America can hear something being said that can be

* O'Hara's biographer, Sharon Whitehill, says Sture-Vasa "falsified virtually everything about himself—his name, his ancestry, his date and place of birth, his upbringing, his schooling, his military service and rank—not to mention the existence of a first wife and son and four grandchildren!"

heard even above the crashing of bombs and the march of Panzer divisions. That is the fact that America is aware of human values as never before, posed as they are against a Nazi conception of a world dead to such values. The majority of the stories in this volume are not war stories. But in all of them, I believe, is implicit a new recognition of certain fundamental principles without which no nation can survive as a civilized state.")

Flicka was assembled by studio veterans who clearly understood their wartime mission. Director Harold D. Schuster had moved up the Fox ladder from small-part actor to assistant cameraman to film editor to director, accomplishing the first three rungs in one year. Screenwriters Lillie Hayward and Francis E. Faragoh had both been around, too. Hayward had over forty screen credits before *Flicka*, and Faragoh had scripted both *Little Caesar* (1931) and *Frankenstein* (1931). The changes they made to O'Hara's book were small and telling, exemplified by "Flicka's Lesson," a sentimental ending O'Hara would probably have had trouble writing herself. "She's [Flicka's] taught us a few things . . ." Ken's father (who might be headed for the war) tells him. "Important things. You: responsibility. Me: that there is such a thing as hope beyond hope. Sometimes when things are at their lowest ebb all we need to do is have a little more love, a little more patience, and a little more faith."* According to *Showman's Trade Review*, *Flicka* was a hit with its wartime audience: It was the fifth most popular film of the year (*Casablanca* was twenty-third). O'Hara was "delighted": "It could have been so bad. I was sitting there, all keyed up, waiting for the inevitable shocks, as every author does. But no shocks!" (She did, however, think that McDowall was miscast, and Preston Foster, who played his father, was "awful.")

Although outwardly they have little in common, W. P. Kinsella's message is not dissimilar to O'Hara's. He wrote "Shoeless Joe Jackson Comes to Iowa" as a love letter. To Iowa, where he studied at the Iowa Writers Workshop and fell in love with cornfields and fireflies. To baseball, his muse for sixty-odd years. And to his father, a former semi-professional baseball player who instilled in him a love of the game. "I began thinking," Kinsella says, "about some of the stories my dad had told me about Shoeless Joe Jackson and what had happened to him after he was wrongly banned from baseball; they were good stories but not necessarily true. Then I thought, What would happen if . . . ?" In Kinsella's world, the answer to "What if?" could be anything. "I like to keep attempting the

* Although *Flicka* was written before the Hollywood Writers Mobilization congress of 1943, of which Faragoh was chair, the minutes of the congress indicate the state of mind among screenwriters during that period. Proving that they were an organization firmly behind the war effort, Robert Rossen (who later adapted and directed *All the King's Men* and *The Hustler*) articulated the screenwriters' mission: to write about "people who were going to win, despite any condition."

impossible," he says. "I like to do audacious things. I like to weave fact and fantasy. I like to alter history." "Shoeless Joe" takes place in a dream world, where skies are robin's-egg blue and the air smells like syrup; it's an intentionally benign and optimistic vision from a man who doesn't believe, but hopes, at least on the page. "There are no gods," Kinsella has said, "there is no magic. I may be a wizard, though, for it takes a wizard to know there are none." But as long as he's dreaming about an alternate universe, "it *has* to involve baseball, because baseball would have a part to play in a perfect world."

Kinsella, a Canadian, has written about baseball early and often. An eighth-grade effort titled "Diamond Doom" mixed death with double plays: "The right fielder did it while no one was looking, and hid the gun under a piece of turf." Written decades later, "Shoeless Joe Jackson Comes to Iowa" caught the eye of an editor, who suggested that Kinsella expand it into a novel. The story became the first chapter of *Shoeless Joe.* "I discovered with *Shoeless Joe* that there were a whole lot of fans who were readers and were dying to read good fiction about baseball. I said, 'Boy, I can keep writing them as long as they can keep buying them.' " George Plimpton used Kinsella's baseball stories as partial proof of his "Small Ball Theory," which posited that the smaller the ball, the better the fiction. (Only fiction about golf exceeds that of baseball in both quantity and quality. Baseball's problem is its lack of international appeal, Plimpton surmised.) And *Sports Illustrated* ranked *Shoeless Joe* forty-seventh of the top hundred sports books of all time. Unfortunately, Kinsella hasn't been able to continue cranking them out. In 1997, he was struck by a car while walking in his neighborhood. He now suffers from lateral movement vertigo and has lost his ability to write fiction. Before his accident, Kinsella was involved in other potential movie projects, but now he has to be content with the success of *Field of Dreams.* "I loved the finished movie," he says. "Most writers are unhappy with film adaptations of their work and rightly so. *Field of Dreams,* however, caught the spirit and essence of *Shoeless Joe* while making the necessary changes to make the work more visual."

Phil Alden Robinson, writer and director of *Field of Dreams,* has admitted a fondness for adaptations: "I have very few original ideas and I so admire people who come up with ideas for movies. Someone else does the heavy lifting—you obviously have to do a lot of work to make something work for the screen, but it's wonderful to have that as a grounding." But at first, Robinson didn't even want to read *Shoeless Joe.* He was given the book by a friend, but the idea of a farmer who hears voices didn't interest him. "I took it home, grumbling, and I started it and literally couldn't put it down until I finished it." In the case of *Field,* the heavy lifting may not have been the story—Robinson stuck fairly close to the book—but the process of realizing it in other forms. It took five years to get the film off the ground, and then filming was murderous. The corn wouldn't grow. Temperatures were in the hundreds. The shooting schedule was tight. In interviews that he gave shortly after the film wrapped, Robinson used phrases like "never again" and "long break." "I was just really overwhelmed by the difficulty of the job," Robinson said. "You're just constantly surrounded by doubt, mostly your own."

Though it is now considered a classic, when the film was released critical reaction was polarized. Roger Ebert called it a "delicate movie, a fragile construction of one goofy fantasy after another." Richard Corliss of *Time* called it a "male weepie at its wussiest." Despite its sentimentality, *Field* ranks thirty-eighth on *Sports Illustrated*'s list of the fifty greatest sports movies. But, like Kinsella's accident, there is a sad footnote to the film as well. The two families who own the property on which the film's baseball field was built have been involved in ongoing disputes over zoning and commercialism. Now there are two separate entrances to the field and two separate gift shops. The admission—to put the battle in perspective—is free on both sides. "It's too bad they can't get along," Kinsella says. "If I owned the property I'd be charging $20. After all, this is America."

We may be jaded, but we're not stupid: We know nostalgia is inherently disingenuous. We know that Ray Kinsella's baseball field is a fantasy. We know that in the real world Flicka would probably die and Ralphie's parents divorce. But so what? "We tell ourselves stories in order to live," Joan Didion wrote. "We interpret what we see, select the most workable of multiple choices." It's what we want for ourselves, but even more, it's what we want for our children. A world in which fathers are gruff but still loving; absent but all-knowing. Where our relationships with them can be repaired, even from beyond the grave. And what's wrong with a little hope, a few dreams? Even Shepherd, that pessimistic purveyor of recooked history, had a phrase for it. He called it "nostalgia for an unlived past."

Red Ryder Nails the Hammond Kid

Jean Shepherd

"DISARM THE TOY INDUSTRY"

Printed in angry block red letters the slogan gleamed out from the large white button like a neon sign. I carefully reread it to make sure that I had not made a mistake.

"DISARM THE TOY INDUSTRY"

That's what it said. There was no question about it.

The button was worn by a tiny Indignant-type little old lady wearing what looked like an upturned flowerpot on her head and, I suspect (viewing it from this later date), a pair of Keds tennis shoes on her feet, which were primly hidden by the Automat table at which we both sat.

I, toying moodily with my chicken pot pie, which of course is a specialty of the house, surreptitiously examined my fellow citizen and patron of the Automat. Wiry, lightly powdered, tough as spring steel, the old doll dug with Old Lady gusto into her meal. Succotash, baked beans, creamed corn, side order of Harvard beets. Bad news—a Vegetarian type. No doubt also a dedicated Cat Fancier.

Silently we shared our tiny Automat table as the great throng of pre-Christmas quick-lunchers eddied and surged in restless excitement all around us. Of course there were the usual H & H club members spotted here and there in the mob; out-of-work seal trainers, borderline bookies, ex-Opera divas, and panhandlers trying hard to look like Madison Avenue account men just getting out of the cold for a few minutes. It is an Art, the ability to nurse a single cup of coffee through an entire ten-hour day of sitting out of the biting cold of mid-December Manhattan.

And so we sat, wordlessly as is the New York custom, for long moments until I could not contain myself any longer.

"Disarm the Toy Industry?" I tried for openers.

She sat unmoved, her bright pink and ivory dental plates working over a mouthful of Harvard beets, attacking them with a venom usually associated with the larger carnivores. The red juice ran down over her powdered chin and stained her white lace bodice. I tried again:

"Pardon me, Madam, you're dripping."

"Eh?"

Her ice-blue eyes flickered angrily for a moment and then glowed as a mother hen's looking upon a stunted, dwarfed offspring. Love shone forth.

"Thank you, sonny."

She dabbed at her chin with a paper napkin and I knew that contact had been made. Her uppers clattered momentarily and in an unmistakably friendly manner.

"Disarm the Toy Industry?" I asked.

"It's an outrage!" she barked, causing two elderly gentlemen at the next table to spill soup on their vests. Loud voices are not often heard in the cloistered confines of the H & H.

"It's an outrage the way the toymakers are forcing the implements of blasphemous War on the innocent children, the Pure in Spirit, the tiny babes who are helpless and know no better!"

Her voice at this point rising to an Evangelical quaver, ringing from change booth to coffee urn and back again. Four gnarled atheists three tables over automatically, by reflex action alone, hurled four "Amen's" into the unanswering air. She continued:

"It's all a Government plot to prepare the Innocent for evil, Godless War! I know what they're up to! Our Committee is on to them, and we intend to expose this decadent Capitalistic evil!"

She spoke in the ringing, anvil-like tones of a True Believer, her whole life obviously an unending fight against They, the plotters. She clawed through her enormous burlap handbag, worn paperback volumes of Dogma spilling out upon the floor as she rummaged frantically until she found what she was searching for.

"Here, sonny. Read this. You'll see what I mean." She handed me a smudgy pamphlet from some embattled group of Right Thinkers, based—of course—in California, denouncing the U.S. as a citadel of Warmongers, profit-greedy despoilers of the young and promoters of world-wide Capitalistic decadence, all through plastic popguns and Sears Roebuck fatigue suits for tots.

She stood hurriedly, scooping her dog-eared library back into her enormous rucksack and hurled her parting shot:

"Those who eat meat, the flesh of our fellow creatures, the innocent slaughtered lamb of the field, are doing the work of the Devil!" Her gimlet eyes spitted the remains of my chicken pot pie with naked malevolence.

She spun on her left Ked and strode militantly out into the crisp, brilliant Christmas air and back into the fray.

I sat rocking slightly in her wake for a few moments, stirring my lukewarm coffee meditatively, thinking over her angry, militant slogan.

"DISARM THE TOY INDUSTRY"

A single word floated into my mind's arena for just an instant—"Canal water!"—and then disappeared. I thought on: As if the Toy industry has any control over the insatiable desire of the human spawn to own Weaponry, armaments, and the implements of Warfare. It's the same kind of mind that thought if making whiskey were prohibited people would stop drinking.

I began to mull over my own youth, and, of course, its unceasing quest for roscoes, six-shooters and any sort of blue hardware—simulated or otherwise—that I could lay my hands on. It is no coincidence that the Zip Green was invented by kids. The adolescent human carnivore is infinitely ingenious when confronted with a Peace movement.

Outside in the spanking December breeze a Salvation Army Santa Claus listlessly tolled his bell, huddled in a doorway to avoid the direct blast of the wind. I sipped my coffee and remembered another Christmas, in another time, in another place, and a gun.

I remember clearly, itchingly, nervously, maddeningly the first time I laid eyes on it, pictured in a three-color, smeared illustration in a full-page back cover ad in *Open Road for Boys*, a publication which at the time had an iron grip on my aesthetic sensibilities, and the dime that I had to scratch up every month to stay with it. It was actually an early *Playboy.* It sold dreams, fantasies, incredible adventures and a way of life. Its center foldouts consisted of gigantic Kodiak bears charging out of the page at the reader, to be gunned down in single hand-to-hand combat by the eleven-year-old Killers armed only with hunting knife and fantastic bravery.

Its Christmas issue weighed over seven pounds, its pages crammed with the effluvia of the Good Life of male Juvenalia, until the senses reeled and Avariciousness, the growing desire to own Everything, was almost unbearable. Today there must be millions of ex-subscribers who still can't pass Abercrombie & Fitch without a faint, keening note of desire and the unrequited urge to glom on to all of it. Just to have it, to feel it.

Early in the Fall the ad first appeared. It was a magnificent thing of balanced copy and pictures, superb artwork and subtly contrived catch phrases. I was among the very first hooked, I freely admit it.

BOYS! AT LAST YOU CAN OWN AN OFFICIAL RED RYDER CARBINE ACTION TWO-HUNDRED SHOT RANGE MODEL AIR RIFLE!

This in block red and black letters surrounded by a large balloon coming out of Red Ryder's own mouth, wearing his enormous ten-gallon Stetson, his jaw squared, staring out at me manfully and speaking directly to me, eye to eye. In his hand was the knurled stock of as beautiful, as coolly deadly-looking a piece of weaponry as I'd ever laid eyes on.

YES, FELLOWS . . .

Red Ryder continued under the gun:

YES, FELLOWS, THIS TWO-HUNDRED-SHOT CARBINE ACTION AIR RIFLE, JUST LIKE THE ONE I USE IN ALL MY RANGE WARS CHASIN' THEM RUSTLERS AND BAD GUYS CAN BE YOUR VERY OWN! IT HAS A SPECIAL BUILT-IN SECRET COMPASS IN THE STOCK FOR TELLING THE DIRECTION IF YOU'RE LOST ON THE TRAIL, AND ALSO AN OFFICIAL RED RYDER SUNDIAL FOR TELLING TIME OUT IN THE WILDS. YOU JUST LAY YOUR CHEEK 'GAINST THIS STOCK, SIGHT OVER MY OWN SPECIAL DESIGN CLOVERLEAF SIGHT, AND YOU JUST CAN'T MISS. TELL DAD IT'S GREAT FOR TARGET SHOOTING AND VARMINTS, AND IT WILL MAKE A SWELL CHRISTMAS GIFT!

The next issue arrived and Red Ryder was even more insistent, now implying that the supply of Red Ryder BB guns was limited and to order now or See Your Dealer Before It's Too Late!

It was the second ad that actually did the trick on me. It was late November and the Christmas fever was well upon me. I thought about a Red Ryder air rifle in all my waking hours, seven days a week, in school and out. I drew pictures of it in my Reader, in my Arithmetic book, on my hand in indelible ink, on Helen Weathers' dress in front of me, in crayon. For the first time in my life the initial symptoms of genuine lunacy, of Mania, set in.

I imagined innumerable situations calling for the instant and irrevocable need for a BB gun, great fantasies where I fended off creeping marauders burrowing through the snow toward the kitchen, where only I and I alone stood between our tiny huddled family and insensate Evil. Masked bandits attacking my father, to be mowed down by my trusted cloverleaf-sighted deadly weapon. I seriously mulled over the possibility of an invasion of raccoons, of which there were several in the county. Acts of selfless Chivalry defending Esther Jane Alberry from escaped circus tigers. Time and time again I saw myself a miraculous crack shot, picking off sparrows on the wing to the gasps of admiring girls and envious rivals on Cleveland Street. There was one dream that involved my entire class getting lost on a field trip in the swamps, wherein I led the tired, hungry band back to civilization, using only my Red Ryder compass and sundial. There was no question about it. Not only should I have such a gun, it was an absolute necessity!

Early December saw the first of the great blizzards of that year. The wind howling down out of the Canadian wilds a few hundred miles to the north had screamed over frozen Lake Michigan and hit Hohman, laying on the town great drifts of snow and long, story-high icicles and sub-zero temperatures where the air cracked and sang. Streetcar wires creaked under caked ice and kids plodded to school through forty-five-mile-an-hour gales, tilting forward like tiny furred radiator ornaments, moving stiffly over the barren, clattering ground.

Preparing to go to school was about like getting ready for extended Deep-Sea Diving. Longjohns, corduroy knickers, checkered flannel Lumberjack shirt, four sweaters, fleece-lined leatherette sheepskin, helmet, goggles, mittens with leatherette gauntlets and a large red star with an Indian Chief's face in the middle, three pair of sox, high-tops, overshoes and a sixteen-foot scarf wound spirally from left to right until only the faint glint of two eyes peering out of a mound of moving clothing told you that a kid was in the neighborhood.

There was no question of staying home. It never entered anyone's mind. It was a hardier time, and Miss Bodkin was a hardier teacher than the present breed. Cold was something that was accepted, like air, clouds and parents; a fact of Nature, and as such could not be used in any fraudulent scheme to stay out of school.

My mother would simply throw her shoulder against the front door, pushing back the advancing drifts and stone ice, the wind raking the living-room rug with angry fury for an instant, and we would be launched, one after the other, my brother and I, like astronauts into unfriendly Arctic space. The door clanged shut behind us and that was it. It was make school or die!

Scattered out over the icy waste around us could be seen other tiny befurred jots of wind-driven humanity. All painfully toiling toward the Warren G. Harding School, miles away over the tundra, waddling under the weight of frost-covered clothing like tiny frozen bowling balls with feet. An occasional piteous whimper would be heard faintly, but lost instantly in the sigh of the eternal wind. All of us were bound for geography lessons involving the exports of Peru, reading lessons dealing with fat cats and dogs named Jack. But over it all like a faint, thin, offstage chorus was the building excitement. Christmas was on its way. Each day was more exciting than the last, because Christmas was one day closer. Lovely, beautiful, glorious Christmas, around which the entire year revolved.

Off on the far horizon, beyond the railroad yards and the great refinery tanks, lay our own private mountain range. Dark and mysterious, cold and uninhabited, outlined against the steel-gray skies of Indiana winter, the Mills. It was the Depression, and the natives had been idle so long that they no longer even considered themselves out of work. Work had ceased to exist, so how could you be out of it? A few here and there picked up a day or so a month at the Roundhouse or the Freight yards or the slag heaps at the Mill, but mostly they just spent their time clipping out coupons from the back pages of *True Romances* magazine, coupons that promised virgin territories for distributing ready-made suits door to door or offering untold riches repairing radios through correspondence courses.

Downtown Hohman was prepared for its yearly bacchanalia of peace on earth and good will to men. Across Hohman Avenue and State Street, the gloomy main thoroughfares—drifted with snow that had lain for months and would remain until well into Spring, ice encrusted, frozen drifts along the curbs—were strung strands of green and red Christmas bulbs, and banners that snapped and cracked in the gale. From the streetlights hung plastic ivy wreaths surrounding three-dimensional Santa Claus faces.

For several days the windows of Goldblatt's department store had been curtained and dark. Their corner window was traditionally a major high-water mark of the pre-Christmas season. It set the tone, the motif of their giant Yuletide Jubilee. Kids were brought in from miles around just to see the window. Old codgers would recall vintage years when the window had flowered more fulsomely than in ordinary times. This was one of those years. The magnificent display was officially unveiled on a crowded Saturday night. It was an instant smash hit. First Nighters packed earmuff to earmuff, their steamy breath clouding up the sparkling plate glass, jostled in rapt admiration before a golden, tinkling panoply of mechanized, electronic Joy.

This was the heyday of the Seven Dwarfs and their virginal den mother, Snow White. Walt Disney's seven cutie-pies hammered and sawed, chiseled and painted while Santa, bouncing Snow White on his mechanical knee, ho-ho-ho'd through eight strategically placed loudspeakers—interspersed by choruses of "Heigh ho, heigh ho, it's off to work we go." Grumpy sat at the controls of a miniature eight-wheel Rock Island Road steam engine and Sleepy played a marimba, while in the background, inexplicably, Mrs. Claus ceaselessly ironed a red shirt. Sparkling artificial snow drifted down on Shirley Temple dolls, Flexible Flyers and Tinker

Toy sets glowing in the golden spotlight. In the foreground a frontier stockade built of Lincoln Logs was manned by a company of kilted lead Highlanders who were doughtily fending off an attack by six U.S. Army medium tanks. (History has always been vague in Indiana.) A few feet away stood an Arthurian cardboard castle with Raggedy Andy sitting on the drawbridge, his feet in the moat, through which a Lionel freight train burping real smoke went round and round. Dopey sat in Amos and Andy's pedal-operated Fresh Air Taxicab beside a stuffed panda holding a lollipop in his paw, bearing the heart-tugging legend, "Hug me." From fluffy cotton clouds above, Dionne quintuplet dolls wearing plaid golf knickers hung from billowing parachutes, having just bailed out of a high-flying balsawood Fokker triplane. All in all, Santa's workshop made Salvador Dali look like Norman Rockwell. It was a good year. Maybe even a great one. Like a swelling Christmas balloon, the excitement mounted until the whole town tossed restlessly in bed—and made plans for the big day. Already my own scheme was well under way, my personal dream. Casually, carefully, calculatingly, I had booby-trapped the house with copies of *Open Road for Boys*, all opened to Red Ryder's slit-eyed face. My father, a great john reader, found himself for the first time in his life in alien literary waters. My mother, grabbing for her copy of *Screen Romances*, found herself cleverly euchred into reading a Red Ryder sales pitch; I had stuck a copy of *ORFB* inside the cover showing Clark Gable clasping Loretta Young to his heaving breast.

At breakfast I hinted that there was a rumor of loose bears in the neighborhood, and that I was ready to deal with them if I had the proper equipment. At first my mother and the Old Man did not rise to the bait, and I began to push, grow anxious, and, of course, inevitably overplayed my hand. Christmas was only weeks away, and I could not waste time with subtlety or droll innuendo.

My brother, occasionally emerging from under the daybed during this critical period, was already well involved in some private Little Brother persiflage of his own involving an Erector Set with motor, capable of constructing drawbridges, Eiffel towers, Ferris wheels, and operating guillotines. I knew that if he got wind of *my* scheme, all was lost. He would then begin wheedling and whining for what I wanted, which would result in nobody scoring, since he was obviously too young for deadly weapons. So I cleverly pretended that I wanted nothing more than a simple, utilitarian, unpretentious Sandy Andy, a highly symbolic educational toy popular at the time, consisting of a kind of funnel under which was mounted a tiny conveyer belt of scooplike gondolas. It came equipped with a bag of white sand that was poured into the funnel. The sand trickling out of the bottom into the gondolas set the belt in motion. As each gondola was filled, it moved down the track to be replaced by another, which, when filled, moved down another notch. And endlessly they went, dumping sand out at the bottom of the track and starting up the back loop to be refilled again—on and on until all the sand was deposited in the red cup at the bottom of the track. The kid then emptied the cup into the funnel and it started all over again—ceaselessly, senselessly, round and round. How like Life itself; it was the perfect toy for the Depression. Other kids in the neighborhood were embarked on grandiose, pie-in-the-sky dreams of Lionel electric trains, gigantic Gilbert chemistry sets, and other totally unimaginable impossibilities.

Through my brain nightly danced visions of six-guns snapped from the hip and shattering bottles—and a gnawing nameless frenzy of impending ecstasy. Then came my first disastrous mistake. In a moment of unguarded rashness I brought the whole plot out into the open. I was caught by surprise while pulling on my high-tops in the kitchen, huddled next to the stove, the only source of heat in the house at that hour of the morning. My mother, leaning over a pot of simmering oatmeal, suddenly asked out of the blue:

"What would you like for Christmas?"

Horrified, I heard myself blurt: "A Red Ryder BB gun!"

Without pausing or even missing a stroke with her tablespoon, she shot back: "Oh no. You'll shoot out one of your eyes."

It was the classic Mother BB Gun Block! I was sunk! That deadly phrase, used many times before by hundreds of mothers, was not surmountable by any means known to Kid-dom. I had really booted it, but such was my mania, my desire for a Red Ryder carbine, that I immediately began to rebuild the dike.

"I was just kidding. Even though Flick is getting one." (A lie.) "I guess . . . I guess . . . I sure would like a Sandy Andy, I guess."

I watched the back of her Chinese red chenille bathrobe anxiously, looking for any sign that my shaft had struck home.

"They're dangerous. I don't want anybody shooting their eyes out."

The boom had been lowered and I was under it. With leaden heart and frozen feet I waddled to school, bereft but undaunted.

At Recess time little knots of kids huddled together for warmth amid the gray craggy snowbanks and the howling gale. The telephone wires overhead whistled like banshees while the trapeze rings on the swings clanked hollowly as Schwartz and Flick and Bruner and I discussed the most important thing next to What I'm Going to Get For Christmas, which was What I'm Getting My Mother and Father for Christmas. We talked in hushed, hoarse whispers to guard against Security leaks. The selection of a present was always done with greater secrecy than that which usually surrounds a State Department White Paper on Underground Subversive Operations in a Foreign Country. Schwartz, his eyes darting over his shoulder as he spoke, leaned into the wind and hissed:

"I'm getting my father . . ."

He paused dramatically, hunching forward to exclude unfriendly ears, his voice dropping even lower. We listened intently for his punchline.

". . . a new Flit gun!"

The sheer creative brilliance of it staggered us for a moment. Schwartz smiled smugly, his earmuffs bobbing jauntily as he leaned back into the wind, knowing he had scored. Flick, looking suspiciously at a passing female first grader who could be a spy for his mother, waited until the coast was clear and then launched his entry into the icy air.

"For my father I'm getting . . ."

Again we waited, Schwartz with a superior smirk playing faintly on his chapped lips.

". . . a rose that *squirts*!"

We had all seen these magnificent appliances at George's Candy Store, and instantly we saw that this was a gift *anyone* would want. They were bright-red celluloid, with a white rubber bulb for pocket use. At this point, luckily, the bell rang, calling us back to our labors before I had to divulge my own gifts, which I knew did not come up to these magnificent strokes of genius.

I had not made an irrevocable choice for my mother, but I had narrowed the field down to two spectacular items I had been stealthily eyeing at Woolworth's for several weeks. The first was a tasteful string of beads about the size of small walnuts, brilliant ruby in color with tiny yellow flowers embedded in the glass. The other and more expensive gift—$1.98—was a pearl-colored perfume atomizer, urn-shaped, with golden lion's feet and matching gold top and squeeze bulb. It was not an easy choice. It was the age-old conflict between the Classic and the Sybaritic, and that is never easily resolved.

For my father, I had already made the down payment on a family-size can of Simoniz. One of my father's favorite proverbs, one he never tired of quoting, was:

"Motorists wise, Simoniz."

He was as dedicated a hood-shiner as ever bought a fourth-hand Graham Paige, with soaring hopes and bad valves. I could hardly wait to see him unwrap the Simoniz on Christmas Eve, with the light of the red, yellow, green, and blue bulbs on the tree making that magnificent can glow like the deep flush of myrrh and frankincense. It was all I could do, a constant tortured battle, to keep myself from spilling the beans and thus destroying the magnificent moment of stunned surprise, the disbelieving delight which I knew would fell him like a thunderclap when he saw that I had gone all out.

In fact, several times over the supper table I had meaningfully asked: "I'll bet you can't guess what I got you for Christmas, Dad."

Once, instead of saying: "Hmmmmm," he answered by saying: "Hmmm. Let's see. Is it a new furnace?"

My kid brother fell over sideways in nutty little-kid laughter and knocked over his milk, because my father was one of the most feared Furnace Fighters in Northern Indiana.

"That clanky old son of a bitch," he called it, and many's the night with the snow drifting in through the Venetian blinds and the windows rattling like frozen tom-toms he would roar down the basement steps, knocking over Ball jars and kicking roller skates out of the way, bellowing:

"THAT SON OF A BITCH HAS GONE OUT AGAIN! THAT GODDAMN CLANKY SON OF A BITCH!!"

The hot-air registers breathed into the clammy air the whistling breath of the Antarctic. A moment of silence. The stillness of the tundra gripped the living room; the hoarfrost sparkled like jewels in the moonlight on my mother's Brillo pad in the kitchen sink.

CLANK! K-BOOM! CLANK! K-BOOM! *CLANK*!

"SONOFABITCH!"

CLANK! K-BOOM! K-BOOM! CLANKCLANK!

He would be operating something called The Shaker, a long iron handle that stuck out of the bottom of that zinc and tin monster called The Furnace.

"For Chrissake, open up the goddamn damper, willya! How the hell did it get turned all the way down again!? GODDAMMIT!"

My mother would leap out of bed and rush into the kitchen in the dark to pull a chain behind the broom closet door marked "Draft."

"FOR CHRISSAKE, STUPID, I SAID THE GODDAMN *DAMPER*!"

My kid brother and I would huddle under our baseball quilt in our Dr. Denton sleepers, waiting for the uproar to strike us. That's why my brother knocked over the milk when my Old Man said the thing about a new furnace. Indiana wit is always pungent and to the point.

My father was also an expert Clinker Fisher. The furnace was always producing something called "clinkers" which got stuck in the grates, causing faint puffs of blue smoke to come out from under the daybed.

"Sonofabitch clinker!"

The Old Man would jump up at the first whiff and rush down into the basement for a happy night at the old iron fishing hole with his trusty poker. People in Northern Indiana fought Winter tooth and claw; bodily, and there was never a letup.

I had not yet decided on what to get my kid brother for Christmas. It was going to be either a rubber dagger or a Dick Tracy Junior Crimefighter Disguise Kit, containing three false noses and a book of instructions on how to trap crooks. Picking something for your kid brother is never easy, particularly if what you get him is something you yourself have always wanted. This can lead to nothing but bad blood, smoldering rivalries, and scuffling in the bathroom. I myself was lukewarm on rubber daggers at this point in the game, so I was inclined to figure that a good big one with a painted silver blade might do the trick. I was a little doubtful about the Dick Tracy Kit, since I sensed vaguely that there might be trouble over one of the noses, a large orange job with plastic horn-rimmed glasses attached. A dark-horse possibility was a tin zeppelin with red propellers and blue fins. I figured this was something you could really get your teeth into, and it was what I eventually decided on, not realizing that one of the hardest things to wrap in green tissue paper with Santa Claus stickers and red string is a silver zeppelin. Zeppelins are not easy to disguise.

It was now the second week of December and all the stores in town stayed open nights, which meant that things were really getting serious. Every evening immediately after supper we would pile into the car and drive downtown for that great annual folk rite, that most ecstatic, golden, tinseled, quivering time of all kidhood: Christmas shopping. Milling crowds of blue-jowled, agate-eyed foundry workers, gray-faced refinery men, and motley hordes of open-hearth, slag-heap, Bessemer-converter, tin-mill, coke-plant, and welding-shop fugitives trudged through the wildly pulsing department stores, through floor after floor of shiny, beautiful, unattainable treasures, trailed by millions of leatherette-jacketed, high-topped, mufflered kids, each with a gnawing hunger to Get It All. Worried-looking, flush-faced mothers wearing frayed cloth coats with ratty fox-fur collars, their hands chapped and raw from years of dishwater therapy, rode herd on the surging mob, ranging far and wide into the aisles and under the counters, cuffing, slapping, dragging, whiners of all sizes from department to department.

At the far end of Toyland in Goldblatt's, on a snowy throne framed with red-and-white candy canes under a suspended squadron of plastic angels blowing silver trumpets in a glowing golden grotto, sat the Man, the Connection: Santa Claus himself. In Northern Indiana Santa Claus is a big man, both spiritually and physically, and the Santa Claus at Goldblatt's was officially recognized among the kids as being unquestionably THE Santa Claus. In person. Eight feet tall, shiny high black patent-leather boots, a nimbus cloud of snowy-white beard, and a real, thrumming, belt-creaking stomach. No pillows or stuffing. I mean a real *stomach*!

A long line of nervous, fidgeting, greedy urchins wound in and out of the aisles, shoving, sniffling, and above all waiting, waiting to tell HIM what they wanted. In those days it was not easy to disbelieve fully in Santa Claus, because there wasn't much else to believe in, and there were many theological arguments over the nature of, the existence of, the affirmation and denial of his existence. However, ten days before zero hour, the air pulsing to the strains of "We Three Kings of Orient Are," the store windows garlanded with green-and-red wreaths, and the toy department bristling with shiny Flexible Flyers, there were few who *dared* to disbelieve. As each day crept on to the next like some arthritic glacier, the atheists among us grew moodier and less and less sure of ourselves, until finally in each scoffing heart was the floating, drifting, nagging suspicion:

"Well, you never can tell."

It did not pay to take chances, and so we waited in line for our turn. Behind me a skinny seven-year-old girl wearing a brown stocking cap and gold-rimmed glasses hit her little brother steadily to keep him in line. She had green teeth. He was wearing an aviator's helmet with the goggles pulled down over his eyes. His galoshes were open and his maroon corduroy knickers were damp. Behind them a fat boy in a huge sheepskin coat stood numbly, his eyes watering in vague fear, his nose red and running. Ahead of my brother and me, a long, uneven procession of stocking caps, mufflers, mittens, and earmuffs inched painfully forward, while in the hazy distance, in his magic glowing cave, Mister Claus sat each in turn on his broad red knee and listened to exultant dream after exultant dream was whispered, squeaked, shouted, or sobbed into his shell-like, whisker-encased ear.

Closer and closer we crept. My mother and father had stashed us in line and disappeared. We were alone. Nothing stood between us and our confessor, our benefactor, our patron saint, our dispenser of BB guns, but 297 other beseechers at the throne. I have always felt that later generations of tots, products of less romantic upbringing, cynical nonbelievers in Santa Claus from birth, can never know the nature of the true dream. I was well into my twenties before I finally gave up on the Easter bunny, and I am not convinced that I am the richer for it. Even now there are times when I'm not so sure about the stork.

Over the serpentine line roared a great sea of sound: tinkling bells, recorded carols, the hum and clatter of electric trains, whistles tooting, mechanical cows mooing, cash registers dinging, and from far off in the faint distance the "Ho-ho-ho-ing" of jolly old Saint Nick.

One moment my brother and I were safely back in the Tricycle and Irish Mail department and the next instant we stood at the foot of Mount

Olympus itself. Santa's enormous gleaming white snowdrift of a throne soared ten or fifteen feet above our heads on a mountain of red and green tinsel carpeted with flashing Christmas-tree bulbs and gleaming ornaments. Each kid in turn was prodded up a tiny staircase at the side of the mountain on Santa's left as he passed his customer on to his right and down a red chute—back into oblivion for another year.

Pretty ladies dressed in Snow White costumes, gauzy gowns glittering with sequins, and tiaras clipped to their golden, artificial hair, presided at the head of the line, directing traffic and keeping order. As we drew nearer, Santa seemed to loom larger and larger. The tension mounted. My brother was now whimpering steadily. I herded him ahead of me while, behind, the girl in the glasses did the same with her kid brother. Suddenly there was no one left ahead of us in line. Snow White grabbed my brother's shoulder with an iron grip and he was on his way up the slope.

"Quit dragging your feet. Get moving," she barked at the toiling little figure climbing the stairs.

The music from above was deafening:

JINGLE BELLS, JINGLE BELLS, JINGLE ALL THE WAY . . . sung by 10,000 echo-chambered, reverberating chipmunks. . . .

High above me in the sparkling gloom I could see my brother's yellow-and-brown stocking cap as he squatted briefly on Santa's gigantic knee. I heard a booming "Ho-ho-ho," then a high, thin, familiar, trailing wail, one that I had heard billions of times before, as my brother broke into his Primal cry. A claw dug into my elbow and I was launched upward toward the mountaintop.

I had long before decided to level with Santa, to really lay it on the line. No Sandy Andy, no kid stuff. If I was going to ride the range with Red Ryder, Santa Claus was going to have to get the straight poop.

"AND WHAT'S YOUR NAME, LITTLE BOY?"

His booming baritone crashed out over the chipmunks. He reached down and neatly hooked my sheepskin collar, swooping me upward, and there I sat on the biggest knee in creation, looking down and out over the endless expanse of Toyland and down to the tiny figures that wound off into the distance.

"Uhh . . . uhhh . . . uhhh . . ."

"THAT'S A FINE NAME, LITTLE BOY! HO-HO-HO!"

Santa's warm, moist breath poured down over me as though from some cosmic steam radiator. Santa smoked Camels, like my Uncle Charles.

My mind had gone blank! Frantically I tried to remember what it was I wanted. I was blowing it! There was no one else in the world except me and Santa now. And the chipmunks.

"Uhhh . . . ahhhh . . ."

"WOULDN'T YOU LIKE A NICE FOOTBALL?"

My mind groped. Football, football. Without conscious will, my voice squeaked out:

"Yeah."

My God, a football! My mind slammed into gear. Already Santa was sliding me off his knee toward the red chute, and I could see behind me another white-faced kid bobbing upward.

"I want a Red Ryder BB gun with a special Red Ryder sight and a compass in the stock with a sundial!" I shouted.

"HO-HO-HO! YOU'LL SHOOT YOUR EYE OUT, KID. HO-HO-HO! MERRY CHRISTMAS!"

Down the chute I went.

I have never been struck by a bolt of lightning, but I know how it must feel. The back of my head was numb. My feet clanked leadenly beneath me as I returned to earth at the bottom of the chute. Another Snow White shoved the famous free gift into my mitten—a barely recognizable plastic Kris Kringle stamped with bold red letters: MERRY XMAS. SHOP AT GOLDBLATT'S FREE PARKING—and spun me back out into Toyland. My brother stood sniveling under a counter piled high with Raggedy Ann dolls, from nowhere my mother and father appeared.

"Did you tell Santa what you wanted?" the Old Man asked.

"Yeah. . . ."

"Did he ask you if you had been a good boy?"

"No."

"Ha! Don't worry. He knows anyway. I'll bet he knows about the basement window. Don't worry. He knows."

Maybe *that* was it! My mind reeled with the realization that maybe Santa *did* know how rotten I had been and that the football was not only a threat but a punishment. There had been for generations on Cleveland Street a theory that if you were not "a good boy" you would reap your just deserts under the Christmas tree. This idea had been largely discounted by the more confirmed evildoers in the neighborhood, but now I could not escape the distinct possibility that there was something to it. Usually for a full month or so before the big day most kids walked the straight and narrow, but I had made a drastic slip from the paths of righteousness by knocking out a basement window with a sled runner and then compounding the idiocy by denying it when all the evidence was incontrovertible. This caused an uproar which had finally resulted in my getting my mouth washed out with Lux and a drastic curtailment of allowance to pay for the glass. I could see that either my father or Santa, or perhaps both, were not content to let bygones be bygones. Were they in league with each other? Or was Santa actually a mother in disguise?

The next few days groaned by. Now only three more school days remained before Christmas vacation, that greatest time of all the year. As it drew closer, Miss Iona Pearl Bodkin, my homeroom teacher, became more and more manic, whipping the class into a veritable frenzy of Yuletide joy. We belted out carol after carol. We built our own paper Christmas tree with cut-out ornaments. We strung long strings of popcorn chains. Crayon Santas and silver-paper wreaths poured out of our assembly line.

In the corner of the room, atop a desk decorated with crepe-paper rosettes, sat our Christmas grab bag. Every kid in the class had bought a gift for the grab bag with someone's name—drawn from a hat—attached. I had bought for Helen Weathers a large, amazingly life-like, jet-black rubber tarantula. I cackled fiendishly as I wrapped it, and even now its beady green eyes glared from somewhere in the depths of the Christmas grab bag. I knew she'd like it.

Miss Bodkin, after recess, addressed us:

"I want all of you to write a theme . . ."

A theme! A rotten theme before Christmas! There must be kids somewhere who love writing themes, but to a normal airbreathing human kid, writing themes is like torture that ranks only with the dreaded medieval chin-breaker of Inquisitional fame. A theme!

". . . entitled 'What I want for Christmas,' " she concluded.

The clouds lifted. I saw a faint gleam of light at the other end of the black cave of gloom which had enveloped me since my visit to Santa. Rarely had the words poured from my penny pencil with such feverish fluidity. Here was a theme on a subject that needed talking about if ever one did! I remember to this day its glorious winged phrases and concise imagery:

> What I want for Christmas is a Red Ryder BB gun with a compass in the stock and this thing that tells time. I think everybody should have a Red Ryder BB gun. They are very good for Christmas. I don't think a football is a very good Christmas present.

I wrote it on blue-lined paper from my Indian Chief tablet, being very careful about the margins. Miss Bodkin was very snippy about uneven margins. The themes were handed in and I felt somehow that when Miss Bodkin read mine she would sympathize with my plight and make an appeal on my behalf to the powers that be, and that everything would work out, somehow. She was my last hope.

The final day before vacation dawned dank and misty, with swirling eddies of icy wind that rattled the porch swing. Warren G. Harding School glowed like a jeweled oasis amid the sooty snowbanks of the playground. Lights blazed from all the windows, and in every room the Christmas party spirit had kids writhing in their seats. The morning winged by, and after lunch Miss Bodkin announced that the rest of the afternoon would be party time. She handed out our graded themes, folded, with our names scrawled on the outside. A big red *B* in Miss Bodkin's direct hand glowed on my literary effort. I opened it, expecting Miss Bodkin's usual penciled corrections, which ran along the lines of "Watch margins" or "Check sp." But this time a personal note leaped up, flew around the room, and fastened itself leech-like on the back of my neck:

"You'll shoot your eye out. Merry Christmas."

I sat in my seat, shipping water from every seam. Was there no end to this conspiracy of irrational prejudice against Red Ryder and his peacemaker? Nervously I pulled out of my desk the dog-eared back page of *Open Road for Boys*, which I had carried with me everywhere, waking and sleeping, for the past few weeks. Red Ryder's handsome orange face with the big balloon coming out of his mouth did not look discouraged or defeated. Red must have been a kid once himself, and they must have told him the same thing when he asked for his first Colt .44 for Christmas.

I stuffed my tattered dreams back into my geography book and gloomily watched the other, happier, carefree, singing kids who were going to *get* what they wanted for Christmas as Miss Bodkin distributed little green baskets filled with hard candy. Somewhere off down the hall the sixth-grade glee club was singing "Oh little town of Bethlehem, how still we see thee lie. . . ."

Mechanically my jaws crunched on the concrete-hard rock candy and I stared hopelessly out of the window, past cut-out Santas and garlands of red and green chains. It was already getting dark. Night falls fast in Northern Indiana at that time of year. Snow was beginning to fall, drifting softly through the feeble yellow glow of the distant street lamps while around me unbridled merriment raged higher and higher.

By suppertime that night I had begun to resign myself to my fate. After all, I told myself, you can always use another football, and, anyway, there will be other Christmases.

The day before, I had gone with my father and mother to the frozen parking lot next to the Esso station where, after long and soul-searching discussion, we had picked out our tree.

"There's a bare spot on the back."

"It'll fluff out, lady, when it gets hot."

"Is this the kind the needles fall out?"

"Nah, that's them balsams."

"Oh."

Now it stood in the living room, fragrantly, toweringly, teeteringly. Already my mother had begun the trimming operations. The lights were lit, and the living room was transformed into a small, warm paradise.

From the kitchen intoxicating smells were beginning to fill the house. Every year my mother baked two pumpkin pies, spicy and immobilizingly rich. Up through the hot-air registers echoed the boom and bellow of my father fighting The Furnace. I was locked in my bedroom in a fever of excitement. Before me on the bed were sheets of green and yellow paper, balls of colored string, and cellophane envelopes of stickers showing sleighing scenes, wreaths, and angels blowing trumpets. The zeppelin was already lumpily done—it had taken me forty-five minutes—and now I struggled with the big one, the magnificent gleaming gold and pearl perfume atomizer, knowing full well that I was wrapping what would undoubtedly become a treasured family heirloom. I checked the lock on the door, and for double safety hollered:

"DON'T ANYONE OPEN THIS DOOR!"

I turned back to my labors until finally there they were—my masterworks of creative giving piled in a neat pyramid on the quilt. My brother was locked in the bathroom, wrapping the fly swatter he had bought for the Old Man.

Our family always had its Christmas on Christmas Eve. Other less fortunate people, I had heard, opened their presents in the chill clammy light of dawn. Far more civilized, *our* Santa Claus recognized that barbaric practice for what it was. Around midnight great heaps of tissuey, crinkly, sparkly, enigmatic packages appeared among the lower branches of the tree and half hidden among the folds of the white bedsheet that looked in the soft light like some magic snowbank.

Earlier, just after the tree had been finished, my father had taken me and my brother out in the Graham-Paige to "pick up a bottle of wine." When we returned, Santa had been there and gone! On the end table and the bookcase were bowls of English walnuts, cashews, and almonds and petrified hard candy. My brother circled around the tree, moaning softly, while I, cooler and more controlled, quickly eyed the mountain of revealingly wrapped largess—and knew the worst.

Out of the kitchen came my mother, flushed and sparkly-eyed, bearing two wineglasses filled with special Walgreen drugstore vintage that my Old Man especially favored. Christmas had officially begun. As they sipped their wine we plunged into the cornucopia, quivering with desire and the ecstasy of unbridled avarice. In the background, on the radio, Lionel Barrymore's wheezy, friendly old voice spoke kindly of Bob Cratchit and Tiny Tim and the ghost of Old Marley.

The first package I grabbed was tagged "To Randy from Santa." I feverishly passed it over to my brother, who always was a slow reader, and returned to work. Aha!

"To Ralphie from Aunt Clara"—on a largish, lumpy, red-wrapped gift that I suspected to be the crummy football. Frantically I tore off the wrappings. Oh no! OH NO! A pair of fuzzy, pink, idiotic, cross-eyed, lop-eared, bunny slippers! Aunt Clara had for years labored under the delusion that I was not only perpetually four years old but also a girl. My mother instantly added oil to the flames by saying:

"Oh, aren't they sweet! Aunt Clara always gives you the nicest presents. Put 'em on; see if they fit."

They did. Immediately my feet began to sweat as those two fluffy little bunnies with blue button eyes stared sappily up at me, and I knew that for at least two years I would have to wear them every time Aunt Clara visited us. I just hoped that Flick would never spot them, as the word of this humiliation could easily make life at Warren G. Harding School a veritable hell.

Next to me in harness my kid brother silently, doggedly stripped package after package until he hit the zeppelin. It was the jackpot!

"WOW! A ZEPPELIN! WHOOPEE! WOW!"

Falling over sideways with an ear-splitting yell, he launched it upward into the middle branches of the tree. Two glass angels and a golden bugle crashed to the floor, and a string of lights winked out.

"It's not supposed to fly, you nut," I said.

"AHH, WHAT GOOD IS A ZEPPELIN THAT DON'T FLY!?"

"It rolls. And beeps."

Instantly he was on his knees pushing the Graf Zeppelin, beeping fiendishly, propellers clacking, across the living room rug. It was a sound that was to become sickeningly familiar in the months ahead. I suspect even at that moment my mother knew that one day the zeppelin would mysteriously disappear, never to beep again.

My father was on his feet with the first blink of the dying tree lights. He loved nothing better than to track down the continual short circuits and burned-out bulbs of Christmas tree light strings. Oblivious, I continued to ravage my gifts, feigning unalloyed joy at each lousy Sandy Andy, dump truck, and Monopoly game. My brother's gift to me was the only bright spot in an otherwise remarkably mediocre haul: a rubber Frankenstein face which I knew would come in handy. I immediately put it on and, peering through the slit eyes, continued to open my booty.

"Oh, how terrible!" my mother said. "Take it off and put it away."

"I think it looks good on him," my father said. I stood up and did my already famous Frankenstein walk, clumping stiff-legged around the living room and back to the tree.

Finally it was all over. There were no more mysterious packages under the tree, only a great pile of crumpled tissue paper, string, and empty boxes. In the excitement I had forgotten Red Ryder and the BB gun, but now it all came back. Skunked! Well, at least I had a Frankenstein face. And there was no denying that I had scored heavily with the Simoniz and the atomizer, as well as the zeppelin. The joy of giving can uplift the saddened heart.

My brother lay dozing amid the rubble, the zeppelin clasped in one hand and his new fire truck in the other. My father bent over from his easy chair, his eighth glass of wine in his hand.

"Say, don't I see something over there stuck behind the drapes? Why, I think there *is* something over there behind the drapes."

He was right! There *was* a tiny flash of red under the ecru curtains. Like a shot I was off, and milliseconds later I knew that old Santa had come through! A long, heavy, red-wrapped package marked "To Ralphie from Santa" had been left somehow behind the curtains. In an instant the wrappings were off, and there it was again! A Red Ryder carbine-action range-model BB gun lay in its crinkly white packing, blue-steel barrel graceful and taut, its dark, polished stock gleaming like all the treasures of the Western world. And there, burned into the walnut, his level gaze unmistakable, his jaw clean and hard, was Red Ryder himself coolly watching my every move. His face was even more beautiful and malevolent than the pictures in the advertisements showed.

Over the radio thundered a thousand-voiced heavenly choir: "JOY TO THE WORLD, THE LORD HAS COME . . ."

My mother sat and smiled a weak, doubtful smile while my Old Man grinned broadly from behind his wineglass.

The magnificent weapon came equipped with two heavy tubes of beautiful Copproteck BBs, gleaming gold and as hard as sin itself. Covered with a thin film of oil they poured with a "ssshhhing" sound into the 200-shot magazine through a BB-size hole in the side of that long blue-steel tube. They added weight and a feeling of danger to the gun. There was also printed targets, twenty-five of them, with a large bull's-eye inside concentric rings marked "One-Two-Three-Four," and the bull's-eye was printed right in the middle of a portrait of Red Ryder himself.

I could hardly wait to try it out, but the instruction booklet said, in Red Ryder's own words:

Kids, never fire a BB gun in the house. They can really shoot. And don't ever shoot at other kids. I never shoot anybody but bad guys, and I don't want any of my friends hurt.

It was well past midnight anyway and, excitement or no, I was getting sleepy. Tomorrow was Christmas Day, and the relatives were coming over to visit. That would mean even more loot of one kind or another.

In my warm bed in the cold still air I could hear the falling snow brushing softly against the dark window. Next to me in the blackness lay my oiled blue-steel beauty, the greatest Christmas gift I had ever received. Gradually I drifted off to sleep—pranging ducks on the wing, and getting off spectacular hip-shots as I dissolved into nothingness.

Dawn came. As the gray light crept around the shades and over the quilt, I was suddenly and tinglingly awake. Stealthily I dressed in my icy maroon corduroy knickers, my sheepskin coat, and my plaid sweater. I pulled on my high-tops and found my mittens, crept through the dark living room, fragrant with Christmas tree, and out onto the porch. Inside the house the family slept the sleep of the just and the fulfilled.

During the night a great snow had fallen, covering the gritty remains of past snowfalls. The trees hung rich and heavy with fluffy down. The sun, soaring bright and brilliantly sharp over Pulaski's Candy Store, lit up the soft, rolling moonscape of snow with orange and gold splashes of color. Overnight the temperature had dropped thirty degrees or more, and the brittle, crackling air was still and clean, and it hurt the lungs to breathe it. The temperature stood at perhaps fifteen to twenty below zero, cold enough to make the telephone wires creak and groan in agony. From the eaves of the front porch gnarled crystal icicles stretched all the way to the drifts on the buried lawn.

I trudged down the steps, barely discernible in the soft fluff, and now I stood in the clean air, ready to consummate my great, long, painful, ecstatic love affair. Brushing the snow off the third step, I propped up a gleaming Red Ryder target, the black rings and bull's-eye standing out starkly against the snowy whiteness. Above the bull's-eye Red Ryder watched me, his eyes following my every move. I backed off into the snow a good twenty feet, slammed the stock down onto my left kneecap, holding the barrel with my mittened left hand, flipped the mitten off my right and, hooking my finger in the icy carbine lever, cocked my blue-steel buddy for the first time. I heard the BB click down into the chamber; the spring inside twanged sharply, and with a clunk she rested taut, hard, and loaded in my chapped, rapidly blueing hands.

For the first time I sighted down over that cold barrel, the heart-shaped rear sight almost brushing my nose and the blade of the front sight wavering back and forth, up and down, and finally coming to rest sharply, cutting the heart and laying dead on the innermost ring. Red Ryder didn't move a muscle, his Stetson flaring out above the target as he waited.

Slowly I squeezed the frosty trigger. Back . . . back . . . back. For one instant I thought wildly: It doesn't work! We'll have to send it back! And then:

CRRAAACK!

The gun jerked upward and for a brief instant everything stood still. The target twitched a tiny tick—and then a massive wallop, a gigantic, slashing impact crashed across the left side of my face. My horn-rimmed glasses spun from my head into a snowbank. For several seconds I stood, not knowing what had happened, warm blood trailing down over my cheek and onto the walnut stock of my Red Ryder 200-shot range-model BB gun.

I lowered the barrel convulsively. The target still stood; Red Ryder was unscratched. A ragged, uncontrolled tidal wave of pain, throbbing and singing, rocked my head. The ricocheting BB had missed my eye by perhaps a half inch, and a long, angry, bloody welt extended from my cheekbone almost to my ear. It was divine retribution! Red Ryder had struck again! Another bad guy had been gunned down!

Frantically I scrambled for my glasses. And then the most catastrophic blow of all—they were pulverized! Few things brought such swift and terrible retribution on a kid during the Depression as a pair of busted glasses. The left lens was out as clean as a whistle, and for a moment I thought: I'll fake it! They'll never know the lens is gone! But then, gingerly fingering my rapidly swelling black eye, I realized that here was a shiner on the way that would top even the one I got the time I fought Grover Dill.

As I put the cold horn-rim back on my nose, the front door creaked open just a crack and I could make out the blur of my mother's Chinese-red chenille bathrobe.

"Be careful. Don't shoot out your eye! Just be careful now."

She hadn't seen! Rapidly my mind evolved a spectacular fantasy involving a falling icicle and how it had hit the gun barrel which caused the stock to bounce up and cut my cheek and break my glasses and I tried to get out of the way but the icicle fell off the roof and hit the gun and it bounced up and hit me and . . . I began to cry uproariously, faking it at first, but then the shock and fear took over and it was the real thing—heaving, sobbing, retching.

I was now in the bathroom, my mother bending over me, telling me:

"There now, see, it's a little bump. You're lucky you didn't cut your eye.

Those icicles sometimes even kill people. You're really lucky. Here, hold this rag on it, and don't wake your brother."

I HAD PULLED IT OFF!

I sipped the bitter dregs of coffee that remained in my cup, suddenly catapulted by a falling tray back into the cheerful, impersonal, brightly lit clatter of Horn & Hardart. I wondered whether Red Ryder was still dispensing retribution and frontier justice as of old. Considering the number of kids I see with broken glasses, I suspect he is.

My Friend Flicka

Mary O'Hara

Report cards for the second semester were sent out soon after school closed in mid-June.

Kennie's was a shock to the whole family.

"If I could have a colt all for my own," said Kennie, "I might do better."

Rob McLaughlin glared at his son. "Just as a matter of curiosity," he said, "how do you go about it to get a *zero* in an examination? Forty in arithmetic; seventeen in history! But a zero? Just as one man to another, what goes on in your head?"

"Yes, tell us how you do it, Ken," chirped Howard.

"Eat your breakfast, Howard," snapped his mother.

Kennie's blond head bent over his plate until his face was almost hidden. His cheeks burned.

McLaughlin finished his coffee and pushed his chair back. "You'll do an hour a day on your lessons all through the summer."

Nell McLaughlin saw Kennie wince as if something had actually hurt him.

Lessons and study in the summertime, when the long winter was just over and there weren't hours enough in the day for all the things to do!

Kennie took things hard. His eyes turned to the wide-open window with a look almost of despair.

The hill opposite the house, covered with arrow-straight jack pines, was sharply etched in the thin air of the eight-thousand-foot altitude. Where it fell away, vivid green grass ran up to meet it; and over range and upland poured the strong Wyoming sunlight that stung everything into burning color. A big jack rabbit sat under one of the pines, waving his long ears back and forth.

Ken had to look at his plate and blink back tears before he could turn to his father and say carelessly, "Can I help you in the corral with the horses this morning, Dad?"

"You'll do your study every morning before you do anything else." And McLaughlin's scarred boots and heavy spurs clattered across the kitchen floor. "I'm disgusted with you. Come, Howard."

Howard strode after his father, nobly refraining from looking at Kennie.

"Help me with the dishes, Kennie," said Nell McLaughlin as she rose, tied on a big apron, and began to clear the table.

Kennie looked at her in despair. She poured steaming water into the dishpan and sent him for the soap powder.

"If I could have a colt," he muttered again.

"Now get busy with that dish towel, Ken. It's eight o'clock. You can study till nine and then go up to the corral. They'll still be there."

At supper that night, Kennie said, "But Dad, Howard had a colt all of his own when he was only eight. And he trained it and schooled it all himself; and now he's eleven and Highboy is three, and he's riding him. I'm nine now, and even if you did give me a colt now, I couldn't catch up to Howard because I couldn't ride it till it was a three-year-old and then I'd be twelve."

Nell laughed. "Nothing wrong with that arithmetic."

But Rob said, "Howard never gets less than seventy-five average at school; and hasn't disgraced himself and his family by getting more demerits than any other boy in his class."

Kennie didn't answer. He couldn't figure it out. He tried hard, he spent hours poring over his books. That was supposed to get you good marks, but it never did. Everyone said he was bright, why was it that when he studied he didn't learn? He had a vague feeling that perhaps he looked out the window too much; or looked through the walls to see clouds and sky and hills, and wonder what was happening out there. Sometimes it wasn't even a wonder, but just a pleasant drifting feeling of nothing at all, as if nothing mattered, as if there was always plenty of time, as if the lessons would get done of themselves. And then the bell would ring and study period was over.

If he had a colt—

When the boys had gone to bed that night Nell McLaughlin sat down with her overflowing mending-basket and glanced at her husband.

He was at his desk as usual, working on account books and inventories.

Nell threaded a darning needle and thought, "It's either that whacking big bill from the vet for the mare that died, or the last half of the tax bill."

It didn't seem just the auspicious moment to plead Kennie's cause. But then, these days, there was always a line between Rob's eyes and a harsh note in his voice.

"Rob," she began.

He flung down his pencil and turned around.

"Damn that law!" he exclaimed.

"What law?"

"The state law that puts high taxes on pedigreed stock. I'll have to do as the rest of 'em do—drop the papers."

"Drop the papers! But you'll never get decent prices if you don't have registered horses."

"I don't get decent prices now."

"But you will some day, if you don't drop the papers."

"Maybe." He bent again over the desk.

Rob, thought Nell, was a lot like Kennie himself. He set his heart. Oh, how stubbornly he set his heart on just some one thing he wanted above everything else. He had set his heart on horses and ranching way back when he had been a crack rider at West Point; and he had resigned and thrown away his army career just for the horses. Well, he'd got what he wanted—

She drew a deep breath, snipped her thread, laid down the sock, and again looked across at her husband as she unrolled another length of darning cotton.

To get what you want is one thing, she was thinking. The three-thousand-acre ranch and the hundred head of horses. But to make it pay—for a dozen or more years they had been trying to make it pay. People said ranching hadn't paid since the beef barons ran their herds on public land; people said the only prosperous ranchers in Wyoming were the dude ranchers; people said—

But suddenly she gave her head a little rebellious, gallant shake. Rob would always be fighting and struggling against something, like Kennie; perhaps like herself too. Even those first years when there was no water piped into the house, when every day brought a new difficulty or danger, how she had loved it! How she still loved it!

She ran the darning ball into the toe of a sock, Kennie's sock. The length of it gave her a shock. Yes, the boys were growing up fast, and now Kennie—Kennie and the colt—

After a while she said, "Give Kennie a colt, Rob."

"He doesn't deserve it." The answer was short. Rob pushed away his papers and took out his pipe.

"Howard's too far ahead of him; older and bigger and quicker and his wits about him, and—"

"Ken doesn't half try; doesn't stick at anything."

She put down her sewing. "He's crazy for a colt of his own. He hasn't had another idea in his head since you gave Highboy to Howard."

"I don't believe in bribing children to do their duty."

"Not a bribe." She hesitated.

"No? What would you call it?"

She tried to think it out. "I just have the feeling Ken isn't going to pull anything off, and"—her eyes sought Rob's—"it's time he did. It isn't the school marks alone, but I just don't want things to go on any longer with Ken never coming out at the right end of anything."

"I'm beginning to think he's just dumb."

"He's not dumb. Maybe a little thing like this—if he had a colt of his own, trained him, rode him—"

Rob interrupted. "But it isn't a little thing, nor an easy thing to break and school a colt the way Howard has schooled Highboy. I'm not going to have a good horse spoiled by Ken's careless ways. He goes woolgathering. He never knows what he's doing."

"But he'd *love* a colt of his own, Rob. If he could do it, it might make a big difference in him."

"*If* he could do it! But that's a big if."

At breakfast next morning Kennie's father said to him, "When you've done your study come out to the barn. I'm going in the car up to section twenty-one this morning to look over the brood mares. You can go with me."

"Can I go too, Dad?" cried Howard.

McLaughlin frowned at Howard. "You turned Highboy out last evening with dirty legs."

Howard wriggled. "I groomed him—"

"Yes, down to his knees."

"He kicks."

"And whose fault is that? You don't get on his back again until I see his legs clean."

The two boys eyed each other, Kennie secretly triumphant and Howard chagrined. McLaughlin turned at the door. "And, Ken, a week from today I'll give you a colt. Between now and then you can decide what one you want."

Kennie shot out of his chair and stared at his father. "A—a-spring colt, Dad, or a yearling?"

McLaughlin was somewhat taken aback, but his wife concealed a smile. If Kennie got a yearling colt, he would be even up with Howard.

"A yearling colt, your father means, Ken," she said smoothly. "Now hurry with your lessons. Howard will wipe."

Kennie found himself the most important personage on the ranch. Prestige lifted his head, gave him an inch more of height and a bold stare, and made him feel different all the way through. Even Gus and Tim Murphy, the ranch hands, were more interested in Kennie's choice of a colt than anything else.

Howard was fidgety with suspense. "Who'll you pick, Ken? Say—pick Doughboy, why don't you? Then when he grows up he'll be sort of twins with mine, in his name anyway. Doughboy, Highboy, see?"

The boys were sitting on the worn wooden step of the door which led from the tack room into the corral, busy with rags and polish, shining their bridles.

Ken looked at his brother with scorn. Doughboy would never have half of Highboy's speed.

"Lassie, then," suggested Howard. "She's black as ink, like mine. And she'll be fast—"

"Dad says Lassie'll never go over fifteen hands."

Nell McLaughlin saw the change in Kennie and her hopes rose. He went to his books in the morning with determination and really studied. A new alertness took the place of the day-dreaming. Examples in arithmetic were neatly written out and, as she passed his door before breakfast, she often heard the monotonous drone of his voice as he read his American history aloud.

Each night, when he kissed her, he flung his arms around her and held her fiercely for a moment, then, with a winsome and blissful smile into her eyes, turned away to bed.

He spent days inspecting the different bands of horses and colts. He sat for hours on the corral fence, very important, chewing straws. He rode off on one of the ponies for half the day, wandering through the mile-square pastures that ran down toward the Colorado border.

And when the week was up, he announced his decision. "I'll take that yearling filly of Rocket's. The sorrel with the cream tail and mane."

His father looked at him in surprise. "The one that got tangled in the barbed wire? That's never been named?"

In a second all Kennie's new pride was gone. He hung his head defensively. "Yes."

"You've made a bad choice, son. You couldn't have picked a worse."

"She's fast, Dad. And Rocket's fast—"

"It's the worst line of horses I've got. There's never one amongst them with real sense. The mares are hellions and the stallions outlaws; they're untamable."

"I'll tame her."

Rob guffawed. "Not I, nor anyone, has ever been able to really tame any one of them."

Kennie's chest heaved.

"Better change your mind, Ken. You want a horse that'll be a real friend to you, don't you?"

"Yes"—Kennie's voice was unsteady.

"Well, you'll never make a friend of that filly. She's all cut and scarred up already with tearing through barbed wire after that bitch of a mother of hers. No fence'll hold 'em—"

"I know," said Kennie, still more faintly.

"Change your mind?" asked Howard briskly.

"No."

Rob was grim and put out. He couldn't go back on his word. The boy had to have a reasonable amount of help in breaking and taming the filly, and he could envision precious hours, whole days, wasted in the struggle.

Nell McLaughlin despaired. Once again Ken seemed to have taken the wrong turn and was back where he had begun; stoical, silent, defensive.

But there was a difference that only Ken could know. The way he felt about his colt. The way his heart sang. The pride and joy that filled him so full that sometimes he hung his head so they wouldn't see it shining out of his eyes.

He had known from the very first that he would choose that particular yearling because he was in love with her.

The year before, he had been out working with Gus, the big Swedish ranch hand, on the irrigation ditch, when they had noticed Rocket standing in a gully on the hillside, quiet for once, and eyeing them cautiously.

"Ay bet she got a colt," said Gus, and they walked carefully up the draw. Rocket gave a wild snort, thrust her feet out, shook her head wickedly, then fled away. And as they reached the spot, they saw standing there the wavering, pinkish colt, barely able to keep its feet. It gave a little squeak and started after its mother on crooked, wobbling legs.

"Yee whiz! Luk at de little *flicka*!" said Gus.

"What does *flicka* mean, Gus?"

"Swedish for little gurl, Ken—"

Ken announced at supper, "You said she'd never been named. I've named her. Her name is Flicka."

The first thing to do was to get her in. She was running with a band of yearlings on the saddleback, cut with ravines and gullies, on section twenty.

They all went out after her, Ken, as owner, on old Rob Roy, the wisest horse on the ranch.

Ken was entranced to watch Flicka when the wild band of youngsters discovered that they were being pursued and took off across the mountain. Footing made no difference to her. She floated across ravines, always two lengths ahead of the others. Her pink mane and tail whipped in the wind. Her long delicate legs had only to aim, it seemed, at a particular spot, for her to reach it and sail on. She seemed to Ken a fairy horse.

He sat motionless, just watching and holding Rob Roy in, when his father thundered past on Sultan and shouted, "Well, what's the matter? Why didn't you turn 'em?"

Kennie woke up and galloped after.

Rob Roy brought in the whole band. The corral gates were closed, and an hour was spent shunting the ponies in and out and through the chutes, until Flicka was left alone in the small round corral in which the baby colts were branded. Gus drove the others away, out the gate, and up the saddleback.

But Flicka did not intend to be left. She hurled herself against the poles which walled the corral. She tried to jump them. They were seven feet high. She caught her front feet over the top rung, clung, scrambled, while Kennie held his breath for fear the slender legs would be caught between the bars and snapped. Her hold broke, she fell over backward, rolled, screamed, tore around the corral. Kennie had a sick feeling in the pit of his stomach and his father looked disgusted.

One of the bars broke. She hurled herself again. Another went. She saw the opening and as neatly as a dog crawls through a fence, inserted her head and forefeet, scrambled through and fled away, bleeding in a dozen places.

As Gus was coming back, just about to close the gate to the upper range, the sorrel whipped through it, sailed across the road and ditch with her inimitable floating leap, and went up the side of the saddleback like a jack rabbit.

From way up the mountain, Gus heard excited whinnies, as she joined the band he had just driven up, and the last he saw of them they were strung out along the crest running like deer.

"Yee whiz!" said Gus, and stood motionless and staring until the ponies had disappeared over the ridge. Then he closed the gate, remounted Rob Roy, and rode back to the corral.

Rob McLaughlin gave Kennie one more chance to change his mind. "Last chance, son. Better pick a horse that you have some hope of riding one day. I'd have got rid of this whole line of stock if they weren't so damned fast that I've had the fool idea that some day there might turn out one gentle one in the lot—and I'd have a racehorse. But there's never been one so far, and it's not going to be Flicka."

"It's not going to be Flicka," chanted Howard.

"Perhaps she might be gentled," said Kennie; and Nell, watching, saw that although his lips quivered, there was fanatical determination in his eye.

"Ken," said Rob, "it's up to you. If you say you want her, we'll get her. But she wouldn't be the first of that line to die rather than give in. They're beautiful and they're fast, but let me tell you this, young man, they're *loco*!"

Kennie flinched under his father's direct glance.

"If I go after her again, I'll not give up whatever comes, understand what I mean by that?"

"Yes."

"What do you say?"

"I want her."

They brought her in again. They had better luck this time. She jumped over the Dutch half-door of the stable and crashed inside. The men slammed the upper half of the door shut and she was caught.

The rest of the band were driven away, and Kennie stood outside of the stable, listening to the wild hoofs beating, the screams, the crashes. His Flicka inside there! He was drenched with perspiration.

"We'll leave her to think it over," said Rob, when dinnertime came. "Afterward, we'll go up and feed and water her."

But when they went up afterward, there was no Flicka in the barn. One of the windows, higher than the mangers, was broken.

The window opened into a pasture an eighth of a mile square, fenced in barbed wire six feet high. Near the stable stood a wagon load of hay. When they went around the back of the stable to see where Flicka had hidden herself, they found her between the stable and the hay wagon, eating.

At their approach she leaped away, then headed east across the pasture.

"If she's like her mother," said Rob, "she'll go right through the wire."

"Ay bet she'll go over," said Gus. "She yumps like a deer."

"No horse can jump that," said McLaughlin.

Kennie said nothing because he could not speak. It was, perhaps, the most terrible moment of his life. He watched Flicka racing toward the eastern wire.

A few yards from it, she swerved, turned, and raced diagonally south.

"It turned her! It turned her!" cried Kennie, almost sobbing. It was the first sign of hope for Flicka. "Oh, Dad! She has got sense. She has! She has!"

Flicka turned again as she met the southern boundary of the pasture; again at the northern; she avoided the barn. Without abating anything of her whirlwind speed, following a precise, accurate calculation and turning each time on a dime, she investigated every possibility. Then, seeing that there was no hope, she raced south toward the range where she had spent her life, gathered herself, and shot into the air.

Each of the three men watching had the impulse to cover his eyes, and Kennie gave a sort of howl of despair.

Twenty yards of fence came down with her as she hurled herself through. Caught on the upper strands, she turned a complete somersault, landing on her back, her four legs dragging the wires down on top of her, and tangling herself in them beyond hope of escape.

"Damn the wire!" cursed McLaughlin. "If I could afford decent fences—"

Kennie followed the men miserably as they walked to the filly. They stood in a circle watching, while she kicked and fought and thrashed until the wire was tightly wound and knotted about her, cutting, piercing and tearing great three-cornered pieces of flesh and hide. At last she was unconscious, streams of blood running on her golden coat, and pools of crimson widening and spreading on the grass beneath her.

With the wire-cutter which Gus always carried in the hip pocket of his overalls, he cut all the wire away, and they drew her into the pasture, repaired the fence, placed hay, a box of oats and a tub of water near her, and called it a day.

"I don't think she'll pull out of it," said McLaughlin.

Next morning Kennie was up at five, doing his lessons. At six he went out to Flicka.

She had not moved. Food and water were untouched. She was no longer bleeding, but the wounds were swollen and caked over.

Kennie got a bucket of fresh water and poured it over her mouth. Then he leaped away, for Flicka came to life, scrambled up, got her balance, and stood swaying.

Kennie went a few feet away and sat down to watch her. When he went in to breakfast, she had drunk deeply of the water and was mouthing the oats.

There began then, a sort of recovery. She ate, drank, limped about the pasture; stood for hours with hanging head and weakly splayed out legs, under the clump of cottonwood trees. The swollen wounds scabbed and began to heal.

Kennie lived in the pasture too. He followed her around, he talked to her. He too lay snoozing or sat under the cottonwoods; and often, coaxing her with hand outstretched, he walked very quietly toward her. But she would not let him come near her.

Often she stood with her head at the south fence, looking off to the mountain. It made the tears come to Kennie's eyes to see the way she longed to get away.

Still Rob said she wouldn't pull out of it. There was no use putting a halter on her. She had no strength.

One morning, as Ken came out of the house, Gus met him and said, "De filly's down."

Kennie ran to the pasture, Howard close behind him. The right hind leg which had been badly swollen at the knee joint had opened in a festering wound, and Flicka lay flat and motionless, with staring eyes.

"Don't you wish now you'd chosen Doughboy?" asked Howard.

"Go away!" shouted Ken.

Howard stood watching while Kennie sat down on the ground and took Flicka's head on his lap. Though she was conscious and moved a little, she did not struggle nor seem frightened. Tears rolled down Kennie's cheeks as he talked to her and petted her. After a few moments, Howard walked away.

"Mother what do you do for an infection when it's a horse?" asked Kennie.

"Just what you'd do if it was a person. Wet dressings. I'll help you Ken. We mustn't let those wounds close or scab over until they're clean. I'll make a poultice for that hind leg, and help you put it on. Now that she'll let us get close to her, we can help her a lot."

"The thing to do is see that she eats," said Rob. "Keep up her strength."

But he himself would not go near her. "She won't pull out of it," he said. "I don't want to see her or think about her."

Kennie and his mother nursed the filly. The big poultice was bandaged on the hind leg. It drew out much poisoned matter and Flicka felt better and was able to stand again.

She watched for Kennie now, and followed him like a dog, hopping on three legs, holding up the right hind leg with its huge knob of a bandage in comical fashion.

"Dad, Flicka's my friend now; she likes me," said Ken.

His father looked at him. "I'm glad of that, son. It's a fine thing to have a horse for a friend."

Kennie found a nicer place for her. In the lower pasture the brook ran over cool stones. There was a grassy bank, the size of a corral, almost on a level with the water. Here she could lie softly, eat grass, drink fresh running water. From the grass, a twenty-foot hill sloped up, crested with overhanging trees. She was enclosed, as it were, in a green, open-air nursery.

Kennie carried her oats morning and evening. She would watch for him to come, eyes and ears pointed to the hill. And one evening Ken, still some distance off, came to a stop and a wide grin spread over his face. He had heard her nicker. She had caught sight of him coming and was calling to him!

He placed the box of oats under her nose and she ate while he stood beside her, his hand smoothing the satin-soft skin under her mane. It had a nap as deep as plush. He played with her long, cream-colored tresses; arranged her forelock neatly between her eyes. She was a bit dish-faced, like an Arab, with eyes set far apart. He lightly groomed and brushed her while she stood turning her head to him whichever way he went.

He spoiled her. Soon she would not step to the stream to drink but he must hold a bucket for her. And she would drink, then lift her dripping muzzle, rest it on the shoulder of his blue chambray shirt, her golden eyes dreaming off into the distance; then daintily dip her mouth to drink again.

When she turned her head to the south, and pricked her ears, and stood tense and listening, Ken knew she heard the other colts galloping on the upland.

"You'll go back there some day, Flicka," he whispered. "You'll be three and I'll be eleven. You'll be so strong you won't know I'm on your back, and we'll fly like the wind. We'll stand on the very top where we can look over the whole world, and smell the snow from Neversummer Range. Maybe we'll see antelope—"

This was the happiest month of Kennie's life.

With the morning, Flicka always had new strength and would hop three-legged up the hill to stand broadside to the early sun, as horses love to do.

The moment Ken woke, he'd go to the window, and see her there; and when he was dressed and at his table studying, he sat so that he could raise his head and see Flicka.

After breakfast, she would be waiting for him and the box of oats at the gate; and for Nell McLaughlin with fresh bandages and buckets of disinfectant; and all three would go together to the brook, Flicka hopping along ahead of them, as if she was leading the way.

But Rob McLaughlin would not look at her.

One day all the wounds were swollen again. Presently they opened, one by one; and Kennie and his mother made more poultices.

Still the little filly climbed the hill in the early morning and ran about on three legs. Then she began to go down in flesh and almost overnight wasted away to nothing. Every rib showed; the glossy hide was dull and brittle, and was pulled over the skeleton as if she were a dead horse.

Gus said, "It's de fever. It burns up her flesh. If you could stop de fever she might get vell."

McLaughlin was standing in his window one morning and saw the little skeleton hopping about three-legged in the sunshine, and he said, "That's the end. I won't have a thing like that on my place."

Kennie had to understand that Flicka had not been getting well all this time; she had been slowly dying.

"She still eats her oats," he said mechanically.

They were all sorry for Ken. Nell McLaughlin stopped disinfecting and dressing the wounds. "It's no use, Ken," she said gently. "You know Flicka's going to die, don't you?"

"Yes, Mother."

Ken stopped eating. Howard said, "Ken doesn't eat anything any more. Don't he have to eat his dinner, Mother?"

But Nell answered, "Leave him alone."

Because the shooting of wounded animals is all in the day's work on the western plains, and sickening to everyone, Rob's voice, when he gave the order to have Flicka shot, was as flat as if he had been telling Gus to kill a chicken for dinner.

"Here's the Marlin, Gus. Pick out a time when Ken's not around and put the filly out of her misery."

Gus took the rifle. "*Ja*, Boss—"

Ever since Ken had known that Flicka was to be shot, he had kept his eye on the rack which held the firearms. His father allowed no firearms in the bunkhouse. The gun rack was in the dining-room of the ranch house; and, going through it to the kitchen three times a day for meals, Ken's eye scanned the weapons to make sure that they were all there.

That night they were not all there. The Marlin rifle was missing.

When Kennie saw that, he stopped walking. He felt dizzy. He kept staring at the gun rack, telling himself that it surely was there—he counted again and again—he couldn't see clearly—

Then he felt an arm across his shoulders and heard his father's voice.

"I know, son. Some things are awful hard to take. We just have to take 'em. I have to, too."

Kennie got hold of his father's hand and held on. It helped steady him.

Finally he looked up. Rob looked down and smiled at him and gave him a little shake and squeeze. Ken managed a smile too.

"All right now?"

"All right, Dad."

They walked in to supper together.

Ken even ate a little. But Nell looked thoughtfully at the ashen color of his face; and at the little pulse that was beating in the side of his neck.

After supper he carried Flicka her oats, but he had to coax her and she would only eat a little. She stood with her head hanging, but when he stroked it and talked to her, she pressed her face into his chest and was content. He could feel the burning heat of her body. It didn't seem possible that anything so thin could be alive.

Presently Kennie saw Gus come into the pasture carrying the Marlin. When he saw Ken, he changed his direction and sauntered along as if he was out to shoot some cottontails.

Ken ran to him. "When are you going to do it, Gus?"

"Ay was goin' down soon now, before it got dark—"

"Gus, don't do it tonight. Wait till morning. Just one more night, Gus."

"Vell, in de morning, den, but it got to be done, Ken. Yer fader gives de order."

"I know. I won't say anything more."

An hour after the family had gone to bed, Ken got up and put on his clothes. It was a warm moonlit night. He ran down to the brook, calling softly, "Flicka! Flicka!"

But Flicka did not answer with a little nicker; and she was not in the nursery, nor hopping about the pasture. Ken hunted for an hour.

At last he found her down the creek, lying in the water. Her head had been on the bank, but as she lay there, the current of the stream had sucked and pulled at her, and she had had no strength to resist; and little by little her head had slipped down until when Ken got there only the muzzle was resting on the bank, and the body and legs were swinging in the stream.

Kennie slid into the water, sitting on the bank, and he hauled at her head. But she was heavy and the current dragged like a weight; and he began to sob because he had no strength to draw her out.

Then he found a leverage for his heels against some rocks in the bed of the stream, and he braced himself against these, and pulled with all his might; and her head came up onto his knees, and he held it cradled in his arms.

He was glad that she had died of her own accord, in the cool water, under the moon, instead of being shot by Gus. Then, putting his face close to hers, and looking searchingly into her eyes, he saw that she was alive and looking back at him.

And then he burst out crying, and hugged her, and said, "Oh, my little Flicka, my little Flicka."

The long night passed.

The moon slid slowly across the heavens.

The water rippled over Kennie's legs, and over Flicka's body. And gradually the heat and fever went out of her. And the cool running water washed and washed her wounds.

When Gus went down in the morning with the rifle, they hadn't moved. There they were, Kennie sitting in water over his thighs and hips, with Flicka's head in his arms.

Gus seized Flicka by the head, and hauled her out on the grassy bank, and then, seeing that Kennie couldn't move, cold and stiff and half-paralyzed as he was, lifted him in his arms and carried him to the house.

"Gus," said Ken through chattering teeth, "don't shoot her, Gus."

"It ain't fur me to say, Ken. You know dat."

"But the fever's left her, Gus."

"Ay wait a little, Ken—"

Rob McLaughlin drove to Laramie to get the doctor, for Ken was in violent chills that would not stop. His mother had him in bed wrapped in hot blankets when they got back.

He looked at his father imploringly as the doctor shook down the thermometer.

"She might get well now, Dad. The fever's left her. It went out of her when the moon went down."

"All right, son. Don't worry. Gus'll feed her, morning and night, as long as she's—"

"As long as I can't do it," finished Kennie happily.

The doctor put the thermometer in his mouth and told him to keep it shut.

All day Gus went about his work, thinking of Flicka. He had not been back to look at her. He had been given no more orders. If she was alive, the order to shoot her was still in effect. But Kennie was ill, McLaughlin making his second trip to town taking the doctor home, and would not be back till long after dark.

After their supper in the bunkhouse, Gus and Tim walked down to the brook. They did not speak as they approached the filly, lying stretched out flat on the grassy bank, but their eyes were straining at her to see if she was dead or alive.

She raised her head as they reached her.

"By the powers!" exclaimed Tim, "there she is!"

She dropped her head, raised it again, and moved her legs and became tense as if struggling to rise. But to do so she must use her right hind leg to brace herself against the earth. That was the damaged leg, and at the first bit of pressure with it, she gave up and fell back.

"We'll swing her on to the other side," said Tim. "Then she can help herself."

"Ja—"

Standing behind her, they leaned over, grabbed hold of her left legs, front and back, and gently hauled her over. Flicka was as lax and willing as a puppy. But the moment she found herself lying on her right side, she began to scramble, braced herself with her good left leg, and tried to rise.

"Yee whiz!" said Gus. "She got plenty strength yet."

"Hi!" cheered Tim. "She's up!"

But Flicka wavered, slid down again, and lay flat. This time she gave notice that she would not try again by heaving a deep sigh and closing her eyes.

Gus took his pipe out of his mouth and thought it over. Orders or no orders, he would try to save the filly. Ken had gone too far to be let down.

"Ay'm goin' to rig a blanket sling fur her, Tim, and get her on her feet and keep her up."

There was a bright moonlight to work by. They brought down the post-hole digger and set two aspen poles deep into the ground either side of the filly, then, with ropes attached to the blanket, hoisted her by a pulley.

Not at all disconcerted, she rested comfortably in the blanket under her belly, touched her feet on the ground, and reached for the bucket of water Gus held for her.

Kennie was sick a long time. He nearly died. But Flicka picked up. Every day Gus passed the word to Nell, who carried it to Ken. "She's cleaning up her oats." . . . "She's out of the sling." . . . "She bears a little weight on the bad leg."

Tim declared it was a real miracle. They argued about it, eating their supper.

"Na," said Gus. "It was de cold water, washin' de fever outa her. And more dan dot—it was Ken—you tink it don't count? All night dot boy sits dere, and says, 'Hold on, Flicka, Ay'm here wid you. Ay'm standin' by,' two of us togedder—"

Tim stared at Gus without answering, while he thought it over. In the silence, a coyote yapped far off on the plains, and the wind made a rushing sound high up in the jack pines on the hill.

Gus filled his pipe.

"Sure," said Tim finally. "Sure, that's it."

Then came the day when Rob McLaughlin stood smiling at the foot of Kennie's bed and said, "Listen! Hear your friend?"

Ken listened and heard Flicka's high, eager whinny.

"She don't spend much time by the brook any more. She's up at the gate of the corral half the time, nickering for you."

"For me!"

Rob wrapped a blanket around the boy and carried him out to the corral gate.

Kennie gazed at Flicka. There was a look of marveling in his eyes. He felt as if he had been living in a world where everything was dreadful and hurting but awfully real; and *this* couldn't be real; this was all soft and happy, nothing to struggle over or worry about or fight for any more. Even his father was proud of him! He could feel it in the way Rob's big arms held him. It was all like a dream and far away. He couldn't, yet, get close to anything.

But Flicka—Flicka—alive, well, pressing up to him, recognizing him, nickering—

Kennie put out a hand—weak and white—and laid it on her face. His thin little fingers straightened her forelock the way he used to do, while Rob looked at the two with a strange expression about his mouth, and a glow in his eyes that was not often there.

"She's still poor, Dad, but she's on four legs now."

"She's picking up."

Ken turned his face up, suddenly remembering. "Dad! She did get gentled, didn't she?"

"Gentle—as—a kitten—"

They put a cot down by the brook for Ken, and boy and filly got well together.

Shoeless Joe Jackson Comes to Iowa

W. P. Kinsella

My father said he saw him years later playing in a tenth-rate commercial league in a textile town in Carolina, wearing shoes and an assumed name. "He'd put on fifty pounds and the spring was gone from his step in the outfield, but he could still hit. Oh, how that man could hit. No one has ever been able to hit like Shoeless Joe."

Two years ago at dusk on a spring evening, when the sky was a robin's egg blue and the wind as soft as a day-old chick, as I was sitting on the verandah of my farm home in eastern Iowa, a voice very clearly said to me, "If you build it, he will come."

The voice was that of a ballpark announcer. As he spoke, I instantly envisioned the finished product I knew I was being asked to conceive. I could see the dark, squarish speakers, like ancient sailors' hats, attached to aluminum-painted light standards that glowed down into a baseball field, my present position being directly behind home plate.

In reality, all anyone else could see out there in front of me was a tattered lawn of mostly dandelions and quack grass that petered out at the edge of a cornfield perhaps fifty yards from the house.

Anyone else was my wife Annie, my daughter Karin, a corn-colored collie named Carmeletia Pope, and a cinnamon and white guinea pig named Junior who ate spaghetti and sang each time the fridge door opened. Karin and the dog were not quite two years old.

"If you build it, he will come," the announcer repeated in scratchy Middle American, as if his voice had been recorded on an old 78-rpm record.

A three-hour lecture or a five-hundred-page guidebook could not have given me clearer directions: dimensions of ballparks jumped over and around me like fleas, cost figures for light standards and floodlights whirled around my head like the moths that dusted against the porch light above me.

That was all the instruction I ever received: two announcements and a vision of a baseball field. I sat on the verandah until the satiny dark was complete. A few curdly clouds striped the moon and it became so silent I could hear my eyes blink.

Our house is one of those massive old farm homes, square as a biscuit box with a sagging verandah on three sides. The floor of the verandah slopes so that marbles, baseballs, tennis balls and ball bearings all accumulate in a corner like a herd of cattle clustered with their backs to a storm. On the north verandah is a wooden porch swing where Annie and I sit on humid August nights, sip lemonade from teary glasses, and dream.

When I finally went to bed, and after Annie inched into my arms in that way she has, like a cat that you suddenly find sound asleep on your lap, I told her about the voice and I told her that I knew what it wanted me to do.

"Oh love," she said, "if it makes you happy you should do it," and she found my lips with hers, and I shivered involuntarily as her tongue touched mine.

Annie: she has never once called me crazy. Just before I started the first landscape work, as I stood looking out at the lawn and the cornfield wondering how it could look so different in daylight, considering the notion of accepting it all as a dream and abandoning it, Annie appeared at my side and her arm circled my waist. She leaned against me and looked up, cocking her head like one of the red squirrels that scamper along the power lines from the highway to the house. "Do it, love," she said, as I looked down at her, that slip of a girl with hair the color of cayenne pepper and at least a million freckles on her face and arms, that girl who lives in blue jeans and T-shirts and at twenty-four could pass for sixteen.

I thought back to when I first knew her. I came to Iowa to study. She was the child of my landlady. I heard her one afternoon outside my window as she told her girlfriends, "When I grow up I'm going to marry . . ." and she named me. The others were going to be nurses, teachers, pilots or movie stars, but Annie chose me as her occupation. She was ten. Eight years later we were married. I chose willingly, lovingly to stay in Iowa, eventually rented this farm, bought this farm, operating it one inch from bankruptcy. I don't seem meant to farm, but I want to be close to this precious land, for Annie and me to be able to say, "This is ours."

Now I stand ready to cut into the cornfield, to chisel away a piece of our livelihood to use as dream currency, and Annie says, "Oh, love, if it makes you happy you should do it." I carry her words in the back of my mind, stored the way a maiden aunt might wrap a brooch, a remembrance of a long-lost love. I understand how hard that was for her to say and how it got harder as the project advanced. How she must have told her family not to ask me about the baseball field I was building, because they stared at me dumb-eyed, a row of silent, thick-set peasants with red faces. Not an imagination among them except to forecast the wrath of God that will fall on the heads of pagans such as I.

He, of course, was Shoeless Joe Jackson.

JOSEPH JEFFERSON (SHOELESS JOE) JACKSON
BORN: BRANDON MILLS, S.C., JULY 16, 1887
DIED: GREENVILLE, S.C., DECEMBER 5, 1951

In April, 1945, Ty Cobb picked Shoeless Joe as the best left fielder of all time.

He never learned to read or write. He created legends with a bat and a glove. He wrote records with base hits, his pen a bat, his book History.

Was it really a voice I heard? Or was it perhaps something inside me making a statement that I did not hear with my ears but with my heart? Why should I want to follow this command? But as I ask, I already know the answer. I count the loves in my life: Annie, Karin, Iowa, Baseball. The great god Baseball.

My birthstone is a diamond. When asked, I say my astrological sign is "hit and run," which draws a lot of blank stares here in Iowa, where thirty thousand people go to see the University of Iowa Hawkeyes football team while thirty regulars, including me, watch the baseball team perform.

My father, I've been told, talked baseball statistics to my mother's belly while waiting for me to be born.

My father: born, Glen Ullin, N.D., April 14, 1896. Another diamond birthstone. Never saw a professional baseball game until 1919 when he came back from World War I where he was gassed at Passchendaele. He settled in Chicago, where he inhabited a room above a bar across from Comiskey Park and quickly learned to live and die with the White Sox. Died a little when, as prohibitive favorites, they lost the 1919 World Series to Cincinnati, died a lot the next summer when eight members of the team were accused of throwing that World Series.

Before I knew what baseball was, I knew of Connie Mack, John McGraw, Grover Cleveland Alexander, Ty Cobb, Babe Ruth, Tris Speaker, Tinker-to-Evers-to-Chance, and, of course, Shoeless Joe Jackson. My father loved underdogs, cheered for the Brooklyn Dodgers and the hapless St. Louis Browns, loathed the Yankees, which I believe was an inherited trait, and insisted that Shoeless Joe was innocent, a victim of big business and crooked gamblers.

That first night, immediately after the voice and the vision, I did nothing except sip my lemonade a little faster and rattle the ice cubes in my glass. The vision of the baseball park lingered—swimming, swaying—

seeming to be made of red steam, though perhaps it was only the sunset. There was a vision within the vision: one of Shoeless Joe Jackson playing left field. Shoeless Joe Jackson who last played major league baseball in 1920 and was suspended for life, along with seven of his compatriots by Commissioner Keneshaw Mountain Landis, for his part in throwing the 1919 World Series.

"He hit .375 against the Reds in the 1919 World Series and played errorless ball," my father would say, scratching his head in wonder.

Instead of nursery rhymes, I was raised on the story of the Black Sox scandal, and instead of Tom Thumb or Rumpelstiltskin, I grew up hearing of the eight disgraced ballplayers: Weaver, Cicotte, Risberg, Felsch, Gandil, Williams, McMullin, and always, Shoeless Joe Jackson.

"Twelve hits in an eight-game series. And *they* suspended *him*," father would cry, and Shoeless Joe became the symbol of the tyranny of the powerful over the powerless. The name Keneshaw Mountain Landis became synonymous with the Devil.

It is more work than you might imagine to build a baseball field. I laid out a whole field, but it was there in spirit only. It was really only left field that concerned me. Home plate was made from pieces of cracked two-by-four embedded in the earth. The pitcher's mound rocked like a cradle when I stood on it. The bases were stray blocks of wood, unanchored. There was no backstop or grandstand, only one shaky bleacher beyond the left-field wall. There was a left-field wall, but only about fifty feet of it, twelve feet high, stained dark green and braced from the rear. And the left-field grass. My intuition told me that it was the grass that was important. It took me three seasons to hone that grass to its proper texture, to its proper color. I made trips to Minneapolis and one or two other cities where the stadiums still have natural grass infields and outfields. I would arrive hours before a game and watch the groundskeepers groom the field like a prize animal, then stay after the game when in the cool of the night the same groundsmen appeared with hoses, rakes, and patched the grass like medics attending wounded soldiers.

I pretended to be building a Little League ballfield and asked their secrets and sometimes was told. I took interest in their total operation; they wouldn't understand if I told them I was building only a left field.

Three seasons I've spent seeding, watering, fussing, praying, coddling that field like a sick child until it glows parrot-green, cool as mint, soft as moss, lying there like a cashmere blanket. I began watching it in the evenings, sitting on the rickety bleacher just beyond the fence. A bleacher I had constructed for an audience of one.

My father played some baseball, Class B teams in Florida and California. I found his statistics in a dusty minor league record book. In Florida, he played for a team called the Angels and, by his records, was a better-than-average catcher. He claimed to have visited all forty-eight states and every major league ballpark before, at forty, he married and settled down a two-day drive from the nearest major league team. I tried to play, but ground balls bounced off my chest and fly balls dropped between my hands. I might have been a fair designated hitter, but the rule was too late in coming.

There is a story of the urchin who, tugging at Shoeless Joe Jackson's sleeve as he emerged from a Chicago courthouse, said, "Say it ain't so, Joe."

Jackson's reply reportedly was, "I'm afraid it is, kid."

When he comes, I won't put him on the spot by asking. The less said the better. It is likely that he did accept some money from gamblers. But throw the Series? Never! Shoeless Joe led both teams in hitting in that 1919 Series. It was the circumstances. The circumstances. The players were paid peasant salaries while the owners became rich. The infamous Ten Day Clause, which voided contracts, could end any player's career without compensation, pension, or even a ticket home.

The second sprint, on a toothachy May evening, a covering of black clouds lumbered off westward like ghosts of buffalo and the sky became the cold color of a silver coin. The forecast was for frost.

The left-field grass was like green angora, soft as a baby's cheek. In my mind I could see it dull and crisp, bleached by frost, and my chest tightened.

Then I used a trick a groundskeeper in Minneapolis taught me, saying it was taught to him by grape farmers in California. I carried out a hose and making the spray so fine it was scarcely more than a fog, I sprayed the soft, shaggy spring grass all that chilled night. My hands ached and my own face became wet and cold, but as I watched, the spray froze on the grass, enclosing each blade in a gossamer-crystal coating of ice. A covering that served like a coat of armor to dispel the real frost that was set like a weasel upon killing in the night. I seemed to stand taller than ever before as the sun rose, turning the ice to eye-dazzling droplets, each a prism, making the field an orgy of rainbows.

Annie and Karin were at breakfast when I came in, the bacon and coffee smells and their laughter pulling me like a magnet.

"Did it work, love?" Annie asked, and I knew she knew by the look on my face that it did. And Karin, clapping her hands and complaining of how cold my face was when she kissed me, loved every second of it.

"And how did he get a name like Shoeless Joe?" I would ask my father, knowing full well the story but wanting to hear it again. And no matter how many times I heard it, I would still picture a lithe ballplayer, his great bare feet, white as baseballs, sinking into the outfield grass as he sprinted for a line drive. Then, after the catch, his toes gripping the grass like claws, he would brace and throw to the infield.

"It wasn't the least bit romantic," my dad would say. "When he was still in the minor leagues he bought a new pair of spikes and they hurt his feet; about the sixth inning he took them off and played the outfield in just his socks. The other players kidded him, called him Shoeless Joe, and the name stuck for all time."

It was hard for me to imagine that a sore-footed young outfielder taking off his shoes one afternoon not long after the turn of the century could generate a legend.

I came to Iowa to study, one of the thousands of faceless students who pass through large universities, but I fell in love with Iowa. Fell in love with the land, the people, with the sky, the cornfields and Annie. Couldn't find work in my field, took what I could get. For years, each morning I bathed and frosted my cheeks with Aqua Velva, donned a three-piece suit and snap-brim hat, and, feeling like Superman emerging from a telephone booth, set forth to save the world from a lack of life insurance. I loathed the job so much that I did it quickly, urgently, almost violently. It was Annie who got me to rent the farm. It was Annie who got me to buy it. I operate it the way a child fits together his first puzzle, awkwardly, slowly, but when a piece slips into the proper slot, with pride and relief and joy.

I built the field and waited, and waited, and waited.

"It will happen, honey," Annie would say when I stood shaking my head at my folly. People look at me. I must have a nickname in town. But I could feel the magic building like a storm gathering. It felt as if small animals were scurrying through my veins. I knew it was going to happen soon.

"There's someone on your lawn," Annie says to me, staring into the orange-tinted dusk. "I can't see him clearly, but I can tell someone is there." She was quite right, at least about it being *my* lawn, although it is not in the strictest sense of the word a lawn, it is a *left field.*

I watch Annie looking out. She is soft as a butterfly, Annie is, with an evil grin and a tongue that travels at the speed of light. Her jeans are painted to her body and her pointy little nipples poke at the front of a black T-shirt with the single word RAH! emblazoned in waspish yellow capitals. Her red hair is short and curly. She has the green eyes of a cat.

Annie understands, though it is me she understands and not always what is happening. She attends ballgames with me and squeezes my arm when there's a hit, but her heart isn't in it and she would just as soon be at home. She loses interest if the score isn't too close or the weather warm, or the pace fast enough. To me it is baseball and that is all that matters. It is the game that is important—the tension, the strategy, the ballet of the fielders, the angle of the bat.

I have been more restless than usual this night. I have sensed the magic drawing closer, hovering somewhere out in the night like a zeppelin, silky and silent, floating like the moon until the time is right.

Annie peeks through the drapes. "There *is* a man out there; I can see his silhouette. He's wearing a baseball uniform, an old-fashioned one."

"It's Shoeless Joe Jackson," I say. My heart sounds like someone flicking a balloon with their index finger.

"Oh," she says. Annie stays very calm in emergencies. She Band-Aids bleeding fingers and toes, and patches the plumbing with gum and good wishes. Staying calm makes her able to live with me. The French have the right words for Annie—she has a good heart.

"Is he the Jackson on TV? The one you yell, 'Drop it, Jackson,' at?"

Annie's sense of baseball history is not highly developed.

"No, that's Reggie. This is Shoeless Joe Jackson. He hasn't played major league baseball since 1920."

"Well, aren't you going to go out and chase him off your lawn, or something?"

Yes. What am I going to do? I wish someone else understood. My daughter has the evil grin and bewitching eyes. She climbs into my lap and watches television baseball with me. There is magic about her.

"I think I'll go upstairs and read for a while," Annie says. "Why don't you invite Shoeless Jack in for coffee?" I feel the greatest tenderness toward her then, something akin to the rush of love I felt the first time I held my daughter in my arms. Annie senses that magic is about to happen. She knows that she is not part of it. My impulse is to pull her to me as she walks by, the denim of her thighs making a tiny music. But I don't. She will be waiting for me and she will twine her body about me and find my mouth with hers.

As I step out on the verandah, I can hear the steady drone of the crowd, like bees humming on a white afternoon, and the voices of the vendors, like crows cawing.

A little ground mist, like wisps of gauze, snakes in slow circular motions just above the grass.

"The grass is soft as a child's breath," I say to the moonlight. On the porch wall I find the switch, and the single battery of floodlights I have erected behind the left-field fence sputters to life. "I've shaved it like a golf green, tended it like I would my own baby. It has been powdered and lotioned and loved. It is ready."

Moonlight butters the whole Iowa night. Clover and corn smells are thick as syrup. I experience a tingling like the tiniest of electric wires touching the back of my neck, sending warm sensations through me like the feeling of love. Then, as the lights flare, a scar against the blue-black sky, I see Shoeless Joe Jackson standing out in left field. His feet spread wide, body bent forward from the waist, hands on hips, he waits. There is the sharp crack of the bat and Shoeless Joe drifts effortlessly a few steps to his left, raises his right hand to signal for the ball, camps under it for a second or two, catches the ball, at the same time transferring it to his throwing hand, and fires it into the infield.

I make my way to left field, walking in the darkness far outside the third-base line, behind where the third-base stands would be. I climb up on the wobbly bleacher behind the fence. I can look right down on Shoeless Joe. He fields a single on one hop and pegs the ball to third.

"How does it play?" I holler down.

"The ball bounces true," he replies.

"I know." I am smiling with pride and my heart thumps mightily against my ribs. "I've hit a thousand line drives and as many grounders. It's true as a felt-top table."

"It is," says Shoeless Joe. "It is true."

I lean back and watch the game. From where I sit the scene is as complete as in any of the major league baseball parks I have ever attended: the two teams, the stands, the fans, the lights, the vendors, the scoreboard. The only difference is that I sit alone in the left-field bleacher and the only player who seems to have substance is Shoeless Joe Jackson. When Joe's team is at bat, the left fielder below me is transparent as if he were made of vapor. He performs mechanically, but seems not to have facial features. We do not converse.

A great amphitheater of grandstand looms dark against the sky, the park is surrounded by decks of floodlights making it brighter than day, the crowd buzzes, the vendors hawk their wares, and I cannot keep the promise I made myself not to ask Shoeless Joe Jackson about his suspension and what it means to him.

While the pitcher warms up for the third inning we talk.

"It must have been . . . it must have been like . . ." but I can't find the words.

"Like having a part of me amputated, slick and smooth and painless, like having an arm or a leg taken off with one swipe of a scalpel, big and blue as a sword," and Joe looks up at me and his dark eyes seem about to burst with the pain of it. "A friend of mine used to tell about the war, how him and a buddy was running across a field when a piece of shrapnel took his friend's head off, and how the friend ran, headless, for several strides before he fell. I'm told that old men wake in the night and scratch itchy legs that have been dust for fifty years. That was me. Years and years later, I'd wake in the night with the smell of the ballpark in my nostrils and the cool of the grass on my feet. The thrill of the grass . . ."

How I wish my father could be here with me. He died before we had television in our part of the country. The very next year he could have watched in grainy black and white as Don Larsen pitched a no-hitter in the World Series. He would have loved hating the Yankees as they won that game. We were always going to go to a major league baseball game, he and I. But the time was never right, the money always needed for something else. One of the last days of his life, late in the night while I sat with him because the pain wouldn't let him sleep, the radio dragged in a staticky station broadcasting a White Sox game. We hunched over the radio and cheered them on, but they lost. Dad told the story of the Black Sox Scandal for the last time. Told of seeing two of those World Series games, told of the way Shoeless Joe Jackson hit, told the dimensions of Comiskey Park, and how during the series the mobsters in striped suits sat in the box seats with their colorful women, watching the game and perhaps making plans to go out later and kill a rival.

"You must go," he said. "I've been in all sixteen major league parks. I want you to do it too. The summers belong to somebody else now, have for a long time." I nodded agreement.

"Hell, you know what I mean," he said, shaking his head. I did indeed.

"I loved the game," Shoeless Joe went on. "I'd have played for food money. I'd have played for free and worked for food. It was the game, the parks, the smells, the sounds. Have you ever held a bat or a baseball to your face? The varnish, the leather. And it was the crowd, the excitement of them rising as one when the ball was hit deep. The sound was like a chorus. Then there was the chug-a-lug of the tin lizzies in the parking lots and the hotels with their brass spittoons in the lobbies and brass beds in the rooms. It makes me tingle all over like a kid on his way to his first doubleheader, just to talk about it."

The year after Annie and I were married, the year we first rented this farm, I dug Annie's garden for her; dug it by hand, stepping a spade into the soft black soil, ruining my salesman's hands. After I finished it rained, an Iowa spring rain as soft as spray from a warm hose. The clods of earth I had dug seemed to melt until the garden leveled out, looking like a patch of black ocean. It was near noon on a gentle Sunday when I walked out to that garden. The soil was soft and my shoes disappeared as I plodded until I was near the center. There I knelt, the soil cool on my knees. I looked up at the low gray sky; the rain had stopped and the only sound was the surrounding trees dripping fragrantly. Suddenly I thrust my hands wrist-deep into the snuffy-black earth. The air was pure. All around me the clean smell of earth and water. Keeping my hands buried I stirred the earth with my fingers and I knew I loved Iowa as much as a man could love a piece of earth.

When I came back to the house Annie stopped me at the door, made me wait on the verandah, then hosed me down as if I were a door with too many handprints on it, while I tried to explain my epiphany. It is very difficult to describe an experience of religious significance while you are being sprayed with a garden hose by a laughing, loving woman.

"What happened to the sun?" Shoeless Joe says to me, waving his hand toward the banks of floodlights that surround the park.

"Only stadium in the big leagues that doesn't have them is Wrigley Field," I say. "The owners found that more people could attend night games. They even play the World Series at night now."

Joe purses his lips, considering.

"It's harder to see the ball, especially at the plate."

"When there are breaks they usually go against the ballplayers, right? But I notice you're three for three so far," I add, looking down at his uniform, the only identifying marks a large S with an O in the top crook, an X in the bottom, and an American flag with forty-eight stars on his left sleeve near the elbow.

Joe grins. "I'd play for the Devil's own team just for the touch of a baseball. Hell, I'd play in the dark if I had to."

I want to ask about that day in December, 1951. If he'd lasted another few years things might have been different. There was a move afoot to have his record cleared, but it died with him. I wanted to ask, but my instincts told me not to. There are things it is better not to know.

It is one of those nights when the sky is close enough to touch, so close that looking up is like seeing my own eyes reflected in a rain barrel. I sit in the bleacher just outside the left-field fence. I clutch in my hand a hot dog with mustard, onions and green relish. The voice of the crowd roars in my ears like the sea. Chords of "The Star-Spangled Banner" and "Take Me Out to the Ballgame" float across the field. A Coke bottle is propped against my thigh, squat, greenish, the ice-cream-haired elf grinning conspiratorially from the cap.

Below me in left field, Shoeless Joe Jackson glides over the plush velvet grass, silent as a jungle cat. He prowls and paces, crouches ready to spring as, nearly three hundred feet away, the ball is pitched. At the sound of the bat he wafts in whatever direction is required as if he were on ball bearings.

Then the intrusive sound of a screen door slamming reaches me, and I blink and start. I recognize it as the sound of the door to my house and looking into the distance, I can see a shape that I know is my daughter toddling down the back steps. Perhaps the lights or the crowd has awakened her and she has somehow eluded Annie. I judge the distance to the steps. I am just to the inside of the foul pole, which is exactly 330 feet from home plate. I tense. Karin will surely be drawn to the lights and the emerald dazzle of the infield. If she touches anything, I fear it will all disappear, perhaps forever. Then as if she senses my discomfort she stumbles away from the lights, walking in the ragged fringe of darkness well outside the third-base line. She trails a blanket behind her, one tiny fist rubbing a sleepy eye. She is barefoot and wears a white flannelette nightgown covered in an explosion of daisies.

She climbs up the bleacher, alternating a knee and a foot on each step, and crawls into my lap, silently, like a kitten. I hold her close and wrap the blanket around her feet. The play goes on; her innocence has not disturbed the balance.

"What is it?" she says shyly, her eyes indicating that she means all that she sees.

"Just watch the left fielder," I say. "He'll tell you all you ever need to know about a baseball game. Watch his feet as the pitcher accepts the sign and gets ready to pitch. A good left fielder knows what pitch is coming and he can tell from the angle of the bat where the ball is going to be hit and, if he's good, how hard."

I look down at Karin. She cocks one sky-blue eye at me, wrinkling her nose, then snuggles into my chest, the index finger of her right hand tracing tiny circles around her nose.

The crack of the bat is sharp as the yelp of a kicked cur. Shoeless Joe whirls, takes five loping strides directly toward us, turns again, reaches up, and the ball smacks into his glove. The final batter dawdles in the on-deck circle.

"Can I come back again?" Joe asks.

"I built this left field for you. It's yours any time you want to use it. They play 162 games a season now."

"There are others," he says. "If you were to finish the infield, why, old Chick Gandil could play first base, and we'd have the Swede at shortstop and Buck Weaver at third." I can feel his excitement rising. "We could stick McMullin in at second, and Cicotte and Lefty Williams would like to pitch again. Do you think you could finish the center field? It would mean a lot to Happy Felsch."

"Consider it done," I say, hardly thinking of the time, the money, the backbreaking labor it entails. "Consider it done," I say again, then stop suddenly as an idea creeps into my brain like a runner inching off first base.

"I know a catcher," I say. "He never made the majors, but in his prime he was good. Really good. Played Class B ball in Florida and California . . ."

"We could give him a try," says Shoeless Joe. "You give us a place to play and we'll look at your catcher."

I swear the stars have moved in close enough to eavesdrop as I sit in this single rickety bleacher that I built with my unskilled hands, looking down at Shoeless Joe Jackson. A breath of clover travels on the summer wind. Behind me, just yards away, brook water plashes softly in the darkness, a frog shrills, fireflies dazzle the night like red pepper. A petal falls.

"God, what an outfield," he says. "What a left field." He looks up at me and I look down at him. "This must be heaven," he says.

"No. It's Iowa," I reply automatically. But then I feel the night rubbing softly against my face like cherry blossoms; look at the sleeping girl-child in my arms, her small hand curled around one of my fingers; think of the fierce warmth of the woman waiting for me in the house; inhale the fresh-cut grass smell that seems locked in the air like permanent incense, and listen to the drone of the crowd, as below me Shoeless Joe Jackson tenses, watching the angle of the distant bat for a clue as to where the ball will be hit.

"I think you're right, Joe," I say, but softly enough not to disturb his concentration.

PART X

WORLD FILMS:

NOW YOU

SEE THEM,

NOW YOU DON'T

"In a Grove"
by Ryunosuke Akutagawa

 Rashomon, directed by Akira Kurosawa, 1951

"The Lady with the Pet Dog"
by Anton Chekhov

 The Lady with the Dog, directed by Josef Heifitz, 1960

 Dark Eyes, directed by Nikita Mikhalkov, 1987

It's become a chicken/egg thing: We don't watch international films because they aren't available, and they aren't available because we don't watch them. In 2004 there were a record fifty-six entries into the Best Foreign Language Film category of the Academy Awards; five were subsequently nominated. Of those five, only *one* had been released in the United States prior to its nomination (*The Barbarian Invasions* from Canada). The barriers, of course, are both cultural and financial. If an international film grosses $5 million in the United States, it's doing well—and anyone who reads *Entertainment Weekly* knows how *that* rates. Of the three films discussed here, all were well received in the United States—even the Soviet films. But only *Rashomon* is widely available in video stores—and even that had a tough go of it at first.

The story of multiple and conflicting accounts of a rape and murder, *Rashomon* has become one of the most famous and critically lauded films of all time, but it almost didn't leave Japan. According to movie legend, when the Japanese were invited to submit an entry to the Venice Film Festival in 1951, they didn't even consider *Rashomon*—the film's producers hadn't liked it, nor did anyone think it would be intelligible to a Western audience. But Guilliana Stramigioli, then head of Italiafilm in Japan, had seen and admired the film and recommended it to the Venice contingent. When *Rashomon* won the Grand Prix, everyone was shocked, including its director, Akira Kurosawa, who didn't even know it had been entered. Then it went on to win the American Academy Award for Best Foreign Language Film. No one at the time thought a Japanese film could capture the imagination of the world, particularly less than a decade after the end of World War II. But its few minutes of fame have stretched into a half-century. In America it's even managed to burrow far enough into popular consciousness to serve as a punch line in a *Simpsons* episode:

MARGE: Come on Homer, Japan will be fun. You liked *Rashomon*.

HOMER: That's not how I remember it.

Even before all the prizes, Kurosawa had a lot of directorial clout. "Many of my friends sought to dissuade me from making *Rashomon*," Kurosawa recalled. "They thought the picture's theme too unusual and wondered why I should take such a risk while free to take my pick of other types of stories." *Rashomon* is based on Ryunosuke Akutagawa's cryptic story "In a Grove." Even now, it seems a strange and daring choice of material—the story makes no effort to reconcile facts or elucidate theme—but apparently Kurosawa was intrigued by its possibilities. While casting about for a story to film, he recalled reading a script by an apprentice filmmaker, Shinobu Hashimoto. "The script I remembered was his Akutagawa adaptation [of "In a Grove"] called 'Male-Female.' Probably my subconscious told me it was not right to have put that script aside; probably I was—without being aware of it—wondering all the while if I couldn't do something with it." Hashimoto's script was too short, Kurosawa thought, so he added a number of elements, including an additional conflicting account (the woodcutter's), another Akutagawa story, "Rashomon" (primarily for atmosphere), and the rescue of an abandoned baby (primarily for closure). Still, the day before shooting started, his three assistant directors came to him, complaining that they didn't understand the script. Kurosawa says he explained it to them like this: "Human beings are unable to be honest with themselves about themselves. They cannot talk about themselves without embellishing. This script portrays such human beings—the kind who cannot survive without lies to make them feel they are better people than they really are."

Who could have predicted the success of a film shot in just a few weeks by a crew who only vaguely understood the story? When *Rashomon* premiered, audiences were stunned by its visual style. Bosley Crowther of the *New York Times* wrote: "The photography is excellent and the flow of images is expressive beyond words." What Kurosawa had done was both new and retro; he went back to silent movies to rediscover the power of images. "I sensed a need," he said, "to go back to the origins of the motion picture to find this particular beauty again." It was a visual experiment by a man who loved the medium. "Take 'myself,' " he once said, "subtract 'movies,' and the result is zero."

Akutagawa's story is far more inscrutable than Kurosawa's movie. It offers neither explanation nor redemption, and the question of truth (or lies) is not directly posed. This bleak and intellectual outlook characterizes Akutagawa, who committed suicide at the age of thirty-five. His career, though short, was intense; he produced around 150 stories, as well as poems, diaries, travelogues, and literary criticism. His work—eclectic, stylistically experimental, and carefully sculpted—has always been difficult to categorize. He was the product of a very particular time, the intense westernization that began with Japan's Meiji period (1868–1912). In school he was taught English and Chinese as well as the classics of Eastern and Western literature. On his own he devoured nearly everything in his local library. After his death, Japanese author Kikuchi Kan wrote, "No one in the future can emulate his lofty culture, exquisite taste, and Oriental and Western learning. As an embodiment of the ancient tradition and taste of the Orient and the knowledge and taste of the Occident he will remain a representative writer of Japan."

"In a Grove" illustrates this cultural blend of East and West. The episode is borrowed from the *Konjaku Monogatari* (medieval Japanese tales, circa 1120), but the narrative form is similar to Robert Browning's *The Ring and the Book.** The story's theme of relative truth is often described as un-Japanese, but it was apparently a philosophy Akutagawa adhered to. "Unfortunately," he once wrote, "I know that some truths cannot be told save through lies." This, of course, is the foundation of Western fictional literature, but in Akutagawa's day, *shishosetsu* (personal confession based on the author's life) was the most popular form of Japanese literature. Near the end of his life, Akutagawa's work leaned more in this direction, but still he questioned its validity. "No one," he wrote, "can confess completely; at the same time no one can express anything without confessing." "Cogwheels," a story written shortly before his death, clearly contains autobiographical material as it describes the narrator's descent into a state bordering on schizophrenia. Shortly after it was completed Akutagawa took an overdose of drugs.

Ever inscrutable and wary of easy answers, he began his open suicide letter entitled "A Note to a Certain Old Friend" with a refusal to explain his death: "Probably no one who attempts suicide . . . is fully aware of all of his motives, which are usually too complex. At least in my case it is prompted by a vague sense of anxiety, a vague sense of anxiety about my own future." He did not elucidate any further. His writings indicate that he was unhappy and beset by personal and financial problems. And, as "Cogwheels" makes clear, he was gradually descending into a state of unreality; the story ends with the horrible question "Isn't there anyone to come and strangle me quietly in my sleep?" (He also mentioned in that work his worry that madness was an inherited trait; his mother became mentally unstable when he was just a year old.) Some attribute his suicide to outside factors, including his concerns about the changing political

* Akutagawa's uncertain reputation in Japan is often attributed to his tendency to "borrow." Robert Browning's poem, which also contains multiple conflicting testimonies, is based on a Roman murder (circa 1698) that Browning read about in what is referred to as the *Old Yellow Book*, a volume he bought from a market stall for one lira.

climate. The Taisho period, Japan's experiment in democracy, ended in 1926, a year before his death, and within a few years the military would have almost complete control of the government. Of course any and all of these speculations may be true (how *Rashomon*esque). Those who knew him best, though, claimed Akutagawa's suicide always seemed inevitable.

If Akutagawa's stories are filled with "horror and extravagance," as Jorge Luis Borges once put it, Russian author Anton Chekhov's are filled with anything but. Still, circumstantially, there are a number of similarities between the two men. They both had short, productive careers plagued by ill health (Chekhov died from tuberculosis at the age of forty-four); both lived and wrote during a time of political twilight ("The Lady with the Pet Dog" was written less than twenty years before the October Revolution and Lenin's rise to power); and both worked outside of the accepted literary traditions of their place and time (Chekhov was often criticized for not tackling big themes).

In fact, Chekhov's stories are often about small things and silly people. Rejecting the prevalent Russian notion that literature must bear a clear social or moral message, he instead tried to describe ordinary people as truthfully as possible. Perhaps, having trained as a medical doctor, Chekhov had a natural inclination toward objectivity. Or maybe it began with indecision, as he wrote in a letter to Dmitri Grigorovich, the writer who first recognized Chekhov's talent: "I still lack a political, religious and philosophical world view. I change it every month—and so I'll have to limit myself to descriptions of how my heroes love, marry, give birth, die, and how they speak." In any case, "absence of lengthy verbiage of a political-social-economic nature" became his first of six principles for a good story.* With these principles he created something new, a story without judgments . . . or answers. Often his stories end by simply stopping. In a letter to Alexei Suvorin, his friend and (highly political) editor, he clarified his position. "You are confusing two concepts: *answering the questions* and *formulating them correctly*. Only the latter is required of an author."

Considered by many to be one of the greatest stories ever written, "The Lady with the Pet Dog" was completed in 1899, less than five years before Chekhov's death. Because of his poor health, he had begun spending winters in Yalta, the resort town on the Black Sea that serves as the setting for his story. At the time of its writing he had met, but not yet married, Olga Knipper, an actress with the Moscow Art Theater. (Many see her as the prototype for Anna, as apparently she did herself.) "The Lady" is one of Chekhov's final three stories—after this he would concentrate

* The second principle was objectivity; the third, truthfulness; the fourth, brevity; the fifth, originality; the sixth, compassion.

exclusively on plays—and in it, his style and themes are refined to an almost pure state. There is the seemingly unbridgeable emotional distance between men and women. (Ironically, though one of Chekhov's favorite fictional subjects was marriage, he wrote all of his stories while still a bachelor.) There is the Chekhovian question—will they or won't they?—posed but not answered. And there is the prerevolutionary Russian intellectual: depicted but not condemned.

When Josef Heifitz adapted Chekhov's story for film sixty years later, it received a great deal of critical praise, including a Special Jury Prize at the Cannes Film Festival. But the extent of *The Lady with the Dog*'s success is not immediately apparent. It is, in fact, a hat trick. At once literal in its translation of Chekhov's story, mesmerizing as a film experience in its own right, and deftly PC in its role as a state-sanctioned tribute to Chekhov (in honor of the Chekhov Centenary), *The Lady* is also a testament to the ingenuity of Soviet filmmakers. Even in the "thaw" following Joseph Stalin's death in 1953, the stated aim of Soviet film was still to educate and disseminate Soviet philosophy. Russian film expert Louis Menashe warns, "It has always been difficult to judge Soviet cinema by ordinary and universal standards. . . . [Their] films reveal and, being Soviet, made under the censor's eye, they also conceal; thus we have to watch them cautiously, alert to omission or hidden meaning." In other words, when watching Soviet films—even adaptations of prerevolutionary works like Heifitz's *The Lady with the Dog*—it doesn't hurt to have a decoder ring nearby.

Heifitz's directorial career was a long and varied one. He began his lifelong affiliation with Lenfilm Studios in 1928, and he and his long-time collaborator screenwriter/director Alexander Zarkhi were a prominent team working there during the Stalin years. Up through World War II they appear to have been "true believers," and their films reflect the glorification of state ideals. But, as both men were Jewish, they were forced to step out of the public eye in the late forties in order to avoid being targeted by Stalin's anti-cosmopolitan campaign (a movement aimed at forcing all "foreigners"—with a special emphasis on Jews—out of the Soviet Union).* After Stalin's death Heifitz returned to directing (solo now). His later work contains more liberal elements than his previous films. *Rumyantsev's Case* (1956), which depicted a captain in the militia in an unfavorable light (gasp!), caused a sensation when it was released. Heifitz continued

* The main targets of the anti-cosmopolitan campaign were Jewish people working in theater and film, as well as writers and scholars. In *Soviet Cinematography 1918–1991*, Dmitry and Vladimir Shlapentokh speculate that it was Stalin's genuine passion for film that was responsible for keeping all directors from being sent to the Gulag (unlike other film personnel).

directing until 1980, but his best-known work is probably *The Lady with the Dog*. Swedish director Ingmar Bergman praised it lavishly: "[It] balances at one and the same time the tragedy and comedy that one always finds in Chekhov. This is one film that I shall want to see many times."

It helps to understand the context in which *The Lady* was made. Soviet adaptations are unique in the history of film; nowhere else—and perhaps never again—have filmmakers worked under (and against) such specific constraints. Adaptations were expected to be literal; their purpose was to bring literature to the masses. But at the same time they had to pass political muster. Balancing aesthetic and state concerns became a highly specialized skill among film directors. According to Russian cinema expert David Gillespie, "In adapting literary works for the screen, especially those from the pre-revolutionary past, directors were encouraged, indeed required, to add an ideological gloss to the finished cinematic product. Literature, even the classics, had to bear a clear political message." (Things relaxed slightly after the death of Stalin, but the political parameters still remained in place.) An author like Chekhov, prerevolutionary and largely apolitical, was in obvious need of "gloss," and Heifitz's film makes an interesting case study. Many scenes are lifted from the story verbatim; the dialogue is almost exact, even the props are just as they are described in the story. What is instructive is what has been added. For example, the scene in which a man tries to sell Gurov a dog that looks just like Anna's (poverty/despair of the working class). Or the scene where Gurov's acquaintance at the club pays people to perform humiliating acts (the moral corruption of the upper class). Heifitz's real triumph—albeit a transparent one—is that these scenes are so in keeping with the rest of the film that they're barely noticeable as ideological additions.

Nearly thirty years later Nikita Mikhalkov gave Chekhov's story a completely different spin in his 1987 adaptation, *Dark Eyes*. Charismatic, compelling, and controversial, Mikhalkov is one of the most famous and influential Russian directors working today. Certainly he is one of the most well known outside of Russia. (His *Burnt by the Sun*, which he wrote, directed, and starred in, won the Academy Award for Best Foreign Film in 1995.) His pedigrees are both Soviet and Russian: His father wrote the lyrics to the Soviet national anthem (and was recently asked to do the same for the new Russian anthem set to the same music); his great-grandfather and grandfather were successful Russian painters; and his older brother is film director Andrei Konchalovsky. Mikhalkov established an international reputation with *A Slave of Love* (1976) and *An Unfinished Piece for Player Piano* (1977). Italian actor Marcello Mastroianni saw those films and was so impressed he sought out Mikhalkov and proposed they work together (even though Mastroianni does not speak Russian and

Mikhalkov does not speak Italian). *Dark Eyes*, a joint Soviet-Italian enterprise, became one of the earliest, most prominent, and most successful examples of coproduction.*

Mikhalkov wrote the screenplay with his longtime partner Alexander Adabashyan and Italian writer Suso Cecchi D'Amico. No longer compelled to be literally faithful, Mikhalkov took a number of liberties, beginning with casting the Italian Mastroianni in the Gurov-ish role (now called Romano). " 'The Lady with the Little Dog' was sort of a pretext for the film," Mikhalkov said, "not the subject. It's a movie that takes its motifs from Chekhov. . . . There is a particular atmosphere, like a musical tune, which is special to Chekhov. We decided to make a movie about the tuning of Chekhov." Several other Chekhov stories were woven into the piece, including "The Name Day Party" and "Anna Around the Neck," but it was the liberties taken with "The Lady with the Pet Dog" that annoyed many reviewers. Stanley Kauffmann of *The New Republic* wrote, "Those who know the story, or the lovely Soviet film of it by Josef Heifitz, will wonder why it was substantively altered. . . . Some of the alterations don't much hurt the Chekhov story, but the ending reduces tragedy to pathos—or would do so if it succeeded. The film's last moments consist of two twists that I mustn't reveal; the mere fact that there are twists is proof of debasement." Julie Salmon of the *Wall Street Journal* disagreed: "The rueful, ironic roots of this gorgeous movie are as Russian as the Chekhov stories on which it is based." Pauline Kael of *The New Yorker* was scathing, calling the film a "massive hunk of Italo-Russian kitsch."

Mikhalkov is a love-him-or-hate-him kind of guy—and to a great extent it's because he is unabashedly, unapologetically Russian. He is also powerful, perhaps the only director able to make the Russian equivalent of a blockbuster. (His *Barber of Siberia* [1998] cost $45 million, about $44 million more than the average Russian film.) In 1998 he was elected head of the Russian Filmmakers Union, a not inconsiderable role in a country where cinema and politics have always been blatant bedfellows. Since the end of the Soviet Union the Russian film industry has suffered greatly, and many believe Mikhalkov is the strong leader required to pull it—and maybe even the country—out of trouble.† Its problems have been

* Gorbachev's glasnost opened the country to the outside and, as a result, filmmaking in the Soviet Union changed drastically. State funding continued, but the movement was toward "self-financing," using independent production companies and foreign investments. Coproductions, which gave the Soviets access to newer film technologies and a bigger audience base, flourished during this time.

† Proving how tightly wed Russian cinema and politics still are, there was even talk in June 2000 of Mikhalkov running in the country's presidential election—a rumor he did not immediately squelch.

extensive: When the major film studios collapsed financially, production slowed to a trickle; dismantling the distribution system led to the unavailability of domestic films in many cities; equipment in theaters fell into disrepair; and, perhaps most important, the Russian audience—which in the 1980s was more avid than audiences anywhere else in the world—lost interest. In response, Mikhalkov has become the leading proponent of patriotic *(otechestvenny)* cinema, and surprisingly, the example he points to is Depression-era America. "America walked out of its crisis thanks to its cinema," he says. And recently things have been looking better: In the last year, more than four hundred theaters have been upgraded; production and distribution are improving; and, best of all, Russian audiences appear to be returning.

There's no consensus on the state of world cinema today. The half-full people will point to the international success of recent films like *Crouching Tiger, Hidden Dragon* and *Amelie.* The half-empty people will argue that those are the exceptions that prove the rule, and that there is still great resistance to subtitles and dubbing, for example. There is one sad fact, though, that may make the argument moot: Film everywhere is decomposing at an astonishing rate, and world film is particularly vulnerable. Kurosawa's stature ensures that his films will continue to be well taken care of, but the Russian archives are much more vulnerable. But there is hope. In the last several years, the Russian Cinema Council (RusCiCo) has undertaken to restore and reissue 120 Russian films, including *Dark Eyes* and *Lady with the Dog.* Neither is fully available yet, but they should be soon. So chalk one up for the half-full people.

In a Grove

Ryunosuke Akutagawa
Translated by Takashi Kojima

The Testimony of a Woodcutter Questioned by a High Police Commissioner

Yes, sir. Certainly, it was I who found the body. This morning, as usual, I went to cut my daily quota of cedars, when I found the body in a grove in a hollow in the mountains. The exact location? About 150 meters off the Yamashina stage road. It's an out-of-the-way grove of bamboo and cedars.

The body was lying flat on its back dressed in a bluish silk kimono and a wrinkled head-dress of the Kyoto style. A single sword-stroke had pierced the breast. The fallen bamboo-blades around it were stained with bloody blossoms. No, the blood was no longer running. The wound had dried up, I believe. And also, a gad-fly was stuck fast there, hardly noticing my footsteps.

You ask me if I saw a sword or any such thing?

No, nothing, sir. I found only a rope at the root of a cedar near by. And . . . well, in addition to a rope, I found a comb. That was all. Apparently he must have made a battle of it before he was murdered, because the grass and fallen bamboo-blades had been trampled down all around.

"A horse was near by?"

No, sir. It's hard enough for a man to enter, let alone a horse.

The Testimony of a Traveling Buddhist Priest Questioned by a High Police Commissioner

The time? Certainly, it was about noon yesterday, sir. The unfortunate man was on the road from Sekiyama to Yamashina. He was walking toward Sekiyama with a woman accompanying him on horseback, who I have since learned was his wife. A scarf hanging from her head hid her face from view. All I saw was the color of her clothes, a lilac-colored suit. Her horse was a sorrel with a fine mane. The lady's height? Oh, about four feet five inches. Since I am a Buddhist priest, I took little notice about her details. Well, the man was armed with a sword as well as a bow and arrows. And I remember that he carried some twenty odd arrows in his quiver.

Little did I expect that he would meet such a fate. Truly human life is as evanescent as the morning dew or a flash of lightning. My words are inadequate to express my sympathy for him.

The Testimony of a Policeman Questioned by a High Police Commissioner

The man that I arrested? He is a notorious brigand called Tajomaru. When I arrested him, he had fallen off his horse. He was groaning on the bridge at Awataguchi. The time? It was in the early hours of last night. For the record, I might say that the other day I tried to arrest him, but unfortunately he escaped. He was wearing a dark blue silk kimono and a large plain sword. And, as you see, he got a bow and arrows somewhere. You say that this bow and these arrows look like the ones owned by the dead man? Then Tajomaru must be the murderer. The bow wound with leather strips, the black lacquered quiver, the seventeen arrows with hawk feathers—these were all in his possession I believe. Yes, sir, the horse is, as you say, a sorrel with a fine mane. A little beyond the stone bridge I found the horse grazing by the roadside, with his long rein dangling. Surely there is some providence in his having been thrown by the horse.

Of all the robbers prowling around Kyoto, this Tajomaru has given the most grief to the women in the town. Last autumn a wife who came to the mountain back of the Pindora of the Toribe Temple, presumably to pay a visit, was murdered, along with a girl. It has been suspected that it was his doing. If this criminal murdered the man, you cannot tell what he may have done with the man's wife. May it please your honor to look into this problem as well.

The Testimony of an Old Woman Questioned by a High Police Commissioner

Yes, sir, that corpse is the man who married my daughter. He does not come from Kyoto. He was a samurai in the town of Kokufu in the province of Wakasa. His name was Kanazawa no Takehiko, and his age was twenty-six. He was of a gentle disposition, so I am sure he did nothing to provoke the anger of others.

My daughter? Her name is Masago, and her age is nineteen. She is a spirited, fun-loving girl, but I am sure she has never known any man except Takehiko. She has a small, oval, dark-complected face with a mole at the corner of her left eye.

Yesterday Takehiko left for Wakasa with my daughter. What bad luck it is that things should have come to such a sad end! What has become of my daughter? I am resigned to giving up my son-in-law as lost, but the fate of my daughter worries me sick. For heaven's sake leave no stone unturned to find her. I hate that robber Tajomaru, or whatever his name is. Not only my son-in-law, but my daughter . . . (Her later words were drowned in tears.)

Tajomaru's Confession

I killed him, but not her. Where's she gone? I can't tell. Oh, wait a minute. No torture can make me confess what I don't know. Now things have come to such a head, I won't keep anything from you.

Yesterday a little past noon I met that couple. Just then a puff of wind blew, and raised her hanging scarf, so that I caught a glimpse of her face. Instantly it was again covered from my view. That may have been one reason; she looked like a Bodhisattva. At that moment I made up my mind to capture her even if I had to kill her man.

Why? To me killing isn't a matter of such great consequence as you might think. When a woman is captured, her man has to be killed anyway. In killing, I use the sword I wear at my side. Am I the only one who kills people? You, you don't use your swords. You kill people with your power, with your money. Sometimes you kill them on the pretext of working for their good. It's true they don't bleed. They are in the best of health, but all the same you've killed them. It's hard to say who is a greater sinner, you or me. (An ironical smile.)

But it would be good if I could capture a woman without killing her man. So, I made up my mind to capture her, and do my best not to kill him. But it's out of the question on the Yamashina stage road. So I managed to lure the couple into the mountains.

It was quite easy. I became their traveling companion, and I told them there was an old mound in the mountain over there, and that I had dug it open and found many mirrors and swords. I went on to tell them I'd buried the things in a grove behind the mountain, and that I'd like to sell them at a low price to anyone who would care to have them. Then . . . you see, isn't greed terrible? He was beginning to be moved by my talk before he knew it. In less than half an hour they were driving their horse toward the mountain with me.

When he came in front of the grove, I told them that the treasures were buried in it, and I asked them to come and see. The man had no objection—he was blinded by greed. The woman said she would wait on horseback. It was natural for her to say so, at the sight of a thick grove. To tell you the truth, my plan worked just as I wished, so I went into the grove with him, leaving her behind alone.

The grove is only bamboo for some distance. About fifty yards ahead there's a rather open clump of cedars. It was a convenient spot for my purpose. Pushing my way through the grove, I told him a plausible lie that the treasures were buried under the cedars. When I told him this, he pushed his laborious way toward the slender cedar visible through the grove. After a while the bamboo thinned out, and we came to where a number of cedars grew in a row. As soon as we got there, I seized him from behind. Because he was a trained, sword-bearing warrior, he was quite strong, but he was taken by surprise, so there was no help for him. I soon tied him up to the root of a cedar. Where did I get a rope? Thank heaven, being a robber, I had a rope with me, since I might have to scale a wall at any moment. Of course it was easy to stop him from calling out by gagging his mouth with fallen bamboo leaves.

When I disposed of him, I went to his woman and asked her to come and see him, because he seemed to have been suddenly taken sick. It's needless to say that this plan also worked well. The woman, her sedge hat off, came into the depths of the grove, where I led her by the hand. The instant she caught sight of her husband, she drew a small sword. I've never seen a woman of such violent temper. If I'd been off guard, I'd have got a thrust in my side. I dodged, but she kept on slashing at me. She might have wounded me deeply or killed me. But I'm Tajomaru. I managed to strike down her small sword without drawing my own. The most spirited woman is defenseless without a weapon. At last I could satisfy my desire for her without taking her husband's life.

Yes . . . without taking his life. I had no wish to kill him. I was about to run away from the grove, leaving the woman behind in tears, when she frantically clung to my arm. In broken fragments of words, she asked that either her husband or I die. She said it was more trying than death to have her shame known to two men. She gasped out that she wanted to be the wife of whichever survived. Then a furious desire to kill him seized me. (Gloomy excitement.)

Telling you in this way, no doubt I seem a crueler man than you. But that's because you didn't see her face. Especially her burning eyes at that moment. As I saw her eye to eye, I wanted to make her my wife even if I were to be struck by lightning. I wanted to make her my wife . . . this single desire filled my mind. This was not only lust, as you might think. At that time if I'd had no other desire than lust, I'd surely not have minded knocking her down and running away. Then I wouldn't have stained my sword with his blood. But the moment I gazed at her face in the dark grove, I decided not to leave there without killing him.

But I didn't like to resort to unfair means to kill him. I untied him and told him to cross swords with me. (The rope that was found at the root of the cedar is the rope I dropped at the time.) Furious with anger, he drew his thick sword. And quick as thought, he sprang at me ferociously, without speaking a word. I needn't tell you how our fight turned out. The twenty-third stroke . . . please remember this. I'm impressed with this fact still. Nobody under the sun has ever clashed swords with me twenty strokes. (A cheerful smile.)

When he fell, I turned toward her, lowering my blood-stained sword. But to my great astonishment she was gone. I wondered to where she had run away. I looked for her in the clump of cedars. I listened, but heard only a groaning sound from the throat of the dying man.

As soon as we started to cross swords, she may have run away through the grove to call for help. When I thought of that, I decided it was a matter of life and death to me. So, robbing him of his sword and bow and arrows, I ran out to the mountain road. There I found her horse still grazing quietly. It would be a mere waste of words to tell you the later details, but before I entered town I had already parted with the sword. That's all my confession. I know that my head will be hung in chains anyway, so put me down for the maximum penalty. (A defiant attitude.)

The Confession of a Woman Who Had Come to the *Shimizu* Temple

That man in the blue silk kimono, after forcing me to yield to him, laughed mockingly as he looked at my bound husband. How horrified my husband must have been! But no matter how hard he struggled in agony, the rope cut into him all the more tightly. In spite of myself I ran stumblingly toward his side. Or rather I tried to run toward him, but the man instantly knocked me down. Just at that moment I saw an indescribable light in my husband's eyes. Something beyond expression . . . his eyes make me shudder even now. That instantaneous look of my husband, who couldn't speak a word, told me all his heart. The flash in his eyes was neither anger nor sorrow . . . only a cold light, a look of loathing. More struck by the look in his eyes than by the blow of the thief, I called out in spite of myself and fell unconscious.

In the course of time I came to, and found that the man in blue silk was gone. I saw only my husband still bound to the root of the cedar. I raised myself from the bamboo-blades with difficulty, and looked into his face; but the expression in his eyes was just the same as before.

Beneath the cold contempt in his eyes, there was hatred. Shame, grief, and anger . . . I don't know how to express my heart at that time. Reeling to my feet, I went up to my husband.

"Takejiro," I said to him, "since things have come to this pass, I cannot live with you. I'm determined to die . . . but you must die, too. You saw my shame. I can't leave you alive as you are."

This was all I could say. Still he went on gazing at me with loathing and contempt. My heart breaking, I looked for his sword. It must have been taken by the robber. Neither his sword nor his bow and arrows were to be seen in the grove. But fortunately my small sword was lying at my feet. Raising it over head, once more I said, "Now give me your life. I'll follow you right away."

When he heard those words, he moved his lips with difficulty. Since his mouth was stuffed with leaves, of course his voice could not be heard at all. But at a glance I understood his words. Despising me, his look said only, "Kill me." Neither conscious nor unconscious, I stabbed the small sword through the lilac-colored kimono into his breast.

Again at this time I must have fainted. By the time I managed to look up, he had already breathed his last—still in bonds. A streak of sinking sunlight streamed through the clump of cedars and bamboos, and shone on his pale face. Gulping down my sobs, I untied the rope from his dead body. And . . . and what has become of me since I have no more strength to tell you. Anyway I hadn't the strength to die. I stabbed my own throat with the small sword, I threw myself into a pond at the foot of the mountain, and I tried to kill myself in many ways. Unable to end my life, I am still living in dishonor. (A lonely smile.) Worthless as I am, I must have been forsaken even by the most merciful Kwannon. I killed my own husband. I was violated by the robber. Whatever can I do? Whatever can I . . . I . . . (Gradually, violent sobbing.)

The Story of the Murdered Man, as Told Through a Medium

After violating my wife, the robber, sitting there, began to speak comforting words to her. Of course I couldn't speak. My whole body was tied fast to the root of a cedar. But meanwhile I winked at her many times, as much as to say "Don't believe the robber." I wanted to convey some such meaning to her. But my wife, sitting dejectedly on the bamboo leaves, was looking hard at her lap. To all appearance, she was listening to his words. I was agonized by jealousy. In the meantime the robber went on with his clever talk, from one subject to another. The robber finally made his bold, brazen proposal. "Once your virtue is stained, you won't get along well with your husband, so won't you be my wife instead? It's my love for you that made me be violent toward you."

While the criminal talked, my wife raised her face as if in a trance. She had never looked so beautiful as at that moment. What did my beautiful wife say in answer to him while I was sitting bound there? I am lost in space, but I have never thought of her answer without burning with anger and jealousy. Truly she said, . . . "Then take me away with you wherever you go."

This is not the whole of her sin. If that were all, I would not be tormented so much in the dark. When she was going out of the grove as if in a dream, her hand in the robber's, she suddenly turned pale, and pointed at me tied to the root of the cedar, and said, "Kill him! I cannot marry you as long as he lives." "Kill him!" she cried many times, as if she had gone crazy. Even now these words threaten to blow me headlong into the bottomless abyss of darkness. Has such a hateful thing come out of a human mouth ever before? Have such cursed words ever struck a human ear, even once? Even once such a . . . (A sudden cry of scorn.) At these words the robber himself turned pale. "Kill him," she cried, clinging to his arms. Looking hard at her, he answered neither yes nor no. . . . but hardly had I thought about his answer before she had been knocked down into the bamboo leaves. (Again a cry of scorn.) Quietly folding his arms, he looked at me and said, "What will you do with her? Kill her or save her? You have only to nod. Kill her?" For these words alone I would like to pardon his crime.

While I hesitated, she shrieked and ran into the depths of the grove. The robber instantly snatched at her, but he failed even to grasp her sleeve.

After she ran away, he took up my sword, and my bow and arrows. With a single stroke he cut one of my bonds. I remember his mumbling, "My fate is next." Then he disappeared from the grove. All was silent after that. No, I heard someone crying. Untying the rest of my bonds, I listened carefully, and I noticed that it was my own crying. (Long silence.)

I raised my exhausted body from the root of the cedar. In front of me there was shining the small sword which my wife had dropped. I took it up and stabbed it into my breast. A bloody lump rose to my mouth, but I didn't feel any pain. When my breast grew cold, everything was as silent as the dead in their graves. What profound silence! Not a single bird-note was heard in the sky over this grave in the hollow of the mountains. Only a lonely light lingered on the cedars and mountain. By and by the light gradually grew fainter, till the cedars and bamboo were lost to view. Lying there, I was enveloped in deep silence.

Then someone crept up to me. I tried to see who it was. But darkness had already been gathering round me. Someone . . . that someone drew the small sword softly out of my breast in its invisible hand. At the same time once more blood flowed into my mouth. And once and for all I sank down into the darkness of space.

The Lady with the Pet Dog

Anton Chekhov
Translated by Avrahm Yarmolinsky

I

A new person, it was said, had appeared on the esplanade: a lady with a pet dog. Dmitry Dmitrich Gurov, who had spent a fortnight at Yalta and had got used to the place, had also begun to take an interest in new arrivals. As he sat in Vernet's confectionary shop, he saw, walking on the esplanade, a fair-haired young woman of medium height, wearing a beret; a white Pomeranian was trotting behind her.

And afterwards he met her in the public garden and in the square several times a day. She walked alone, always wearing the same beret and always with the white dog; no one knew who she was and everyone called her simply "the lady with the pet dog."

"If she is here alone without husband or friends," Gurov reflected, "it wouldn't be a bad thing to make her acquaintance."

He was under forty, but he already had a daughter twelve years old, and two sons at school. They had found a wife for him when he was very young, a student in his second year, and by now she seemed half as old again as he. She was a tall, erect woman with dark eyebrows, stately and dignified and, as she said of herself, intellectual. She read a great deal, used simplified spelling in her letters, called her husband, not Dmitry, but Dimitry, while he privately considered her of limited intelligence, narrow-minded, dowdy, was afraid of her, and did not like to be at home. He had begun being unfaithful to her long ago—had been unfaithful to her often and, probably for that reason, almost always spoke ill of women, and when they were talked of in his presence used to call them "the inferior race."

It seemed to him that he had been sufficiently tutored by bitter experience to call them what he pleased, and yet he could not have lived without "the inferior race" for two days together. In the company of men he was bored and ill at ease, he was chilly and uncommunicative with them;

but when he was among women he felt free, and knew what to speak to them about and how to comport himself; and even to be silent with them was no strain on him. In his appearance, in his character, in his whole make-up there was something attractive and elusive that disposed women in his favor and allured them. He knew that, and some force seemed to draw him to them, too.

Oft-repeated and really bitter experience had taught him long ago that with decent people—particularly Moscow people—who are irresolute and slow to move, every affair which at first seems a light and charming adventure inevitably grows into a whole problem of extreme complexity, and in the end a painful situation is created. But at every new meeting with an interesting woman this lesson of experience seemed to slip from his memory, and he was eager for life, and everything seemed so simple and diverting.

One evening while he was dining in the public garden the lady in the beret walked up without haste to take the next table. Her expression, her gait, her dress, and the way she did her hair told him that she belonged to the upper class, that she was married, that she was in Yalta for the first time and alone, and that she was bored there. The stories told of the immorality in Yalta are to a great extent untrue; he despised them, and knew that such stories were made up for the most part by persons who would have been glad to sin themselves if they had had the chance; but when the lady sat down at the next table three paces from him, he recalled these stories of easy conquests, of trips to the mountains, and the tempting thought of a swift, fleeting liaison, a romance with an unknown woman of whose very name he was ignorant, suddenly took hold of him.

He beckoned invitingly to the Pomeranian, and when the dog approached him, shook his finger at it. The Pomeranian growled; Gurov threatened it again.

The lady glanced at him and at once dropped her eyes.

"He doesn't bite," she said and blushed.

"May I give him a bone?" he asked; and when she nodded he inquired affably, "Have you been in Yalta long?"

"About five days."

"And I am dragging out the second week here."

There was a short silence.

"Time passes quickly, and yet it is so dull here!" she said, not looking at him.

"It's only the fashion to say it's dull here. A provincial will live in Belyov or Zhizdra and not be bored, but when he comes here it's 'Oh, the dullness! Oh, the dust!' One would think he came from Granada."

She laughed. Then both continued eating in silence, like strangers, but after dinner they walked together and there sprang up between them the light banter of people who are free and contented, to whom it does not matter where they go or what they talk about. They walked and talked of the strange light on the sea: the water was a soft, warm, lilac color, and there was a golden band of moonlight upon it. They talked of how sultry it was after the hot day. Gurov told her that he was a native of Moscow, that he had studied languages and literature at the university, but had a post in a bank; that at one time he had trained to become an opera singer but had given it up, that he owned two houses in Moscow. And he learned from her that she had grown up in Petersburg, but had lived in S— since her marriage two years previously, that she was going to stay in Yalta for about another month, and that her husband, who needed a rest, too, might perhaps come to fetch her. She was not certain whether her husband was a member of a Government Board or served on a Zemstvo* Council, and this amused her. And Gurov learned too that her name was Anna Sergeyevna.

Afterwards in his room at the hotel he thought about her—and was certain that he would meet her the next day. It was bound to happen. Getting into bed he recalled that she had been a schoolgirl only recently, doing lessons like his own daughter; he thought how much timidity and angularity there was still in her laugh and her manner of talking with a stranger. It must have been the first time in her life that she was alone in a setting in which she was followed, looked at, and spoken to for one secret purpose alone, which she could hardly fail to guess at. He thought of her slim, delicate throat, her lovely gray eyes.

"There's something pathetic about her, though," he thought, and dropped off.

II

A week passed since they had struck up an acquaintance. It was a holiday. It was close indoors, while in the street the wind whirled the dust about and blew people's hats off. One was thirsty all day, and Gurov often went into the restaurant and offered Anna Sergeyevna a soft drink or ice cream. One did not know what to do with oneself.

In the evening when the wind had abated they went out on the pier to watch the steamer come in. There were a great many people walking about the dock; they had come to welcome someone and they were carrying bunches of flowers. And two peculiarities of a festive Yalta crowd stood out: the elderly ladies were dressed like young ones and there were many generals.

Owing to the choppy sea, the steamer arrived late, after sunset, and it was a long time tacking about before it put in at the pier. Anna Sergeyevna

* County council.

peered at the steamer and the passengers through her lorgnette as though looking for acquaintances, and whenever she turned to Gurov her eyes were shining. She talked a great deal and asked questions jerkily, forgetting the next moment what she had asked; then she lost her lorgnette in the crush.

The festive crowd began to disperse; it was now too dark to see people's faces; there was no wind any more, but Gurov and Anna Sergeyevna still stood as though waiting to see someone else come off the steamer. Anna Sergeyevna was silent now, and sniffed her flowers without looking at Gurov.

"The weather has improved this evening," he said. "Where shall we go now? Shall we drive somewhere?"

She did not reply.

Then he looked at her intently, and suddenly embraced her and kissed her on the lips, and the moist fragrance of her flowers enveloped him; and at once he looked round him anxiously, wondering if anyone had seen them.

"Let us go to your place," he said softly. And they walked off together rapidly.

The air in her room was close and there was the smell of the perfume she had bought at the Japanese shop. Looking at her, Gurov thought: "What encounters life offers!" From the past he preserved the memory of carefree, good-natured women whom love had made gay and who were grateful to him for the happiness he gave them, however brief it might be; and of women like his wife who lived without sincerity, with too many words, affectedly, hysterically, with an expression that it was not love or passion that engaged them but something more significant; and of two or three others, very beautiful frigid women, across whose faces would suddenly flit a rapacious expression—an obstinate desire to take from life more than it could give, and these were women no longer young, capricious, unreflecting, domineering, unintelligent, and when Gurov grew cold to them their beauty aroused his hatred, and the lace on their lingerie seemed to him to resemble scales.

But here there was the timidity, the angularity of inexperienced youth, a feeling of awkwardness; and there was a sense of embarrassment, as though someone had suddenly knocked at the door. Anna Sergeyevna, "the lady with the pet dog," treated what had happened in a peculiar way, very seriously, as though it were her fall—so it seemed, and this was odd and inappropriate. Her features drooped and faded, and her long hair hung down sadly on either side of her face; she grew pensive and her dejected pose was that of a Magdalene in a picture by an old master.

"It's not right," she said. "You don't respect me now, you first of all."

There was a watermelon on the side table. Gurov cut himself a slice and began eating it without haste. They were silent for at least half an hour.

There was something touching about Anna Sergeyevna; she had the purity of a well-bred, naïve woman who has seen little of life. The single candle burning on the table barely illumined her face, yet it was clear that she was unhappy.

"Why should I stop respecting you, darling?" asked Gurov. "You don't know what you're saying."

"God forgive me," she said, and her eyes filled with tears. "It's terrible."

"It's as though you were trying to exonerate yourself."

"How can I exonerate myself? No. I am a bad, low woman; I despise myself and I have no thought of exonerating myself. It's not my husband but myself I have deceived. And not only just now; I have been deceiving myself for a long time. My husband may be a good, honest man, but he is a flunkey! I don't know what he does, what his work is, but I know he is a flunkey! I was twenty when I married him. I was tormented by curiosity; I wanted something better. 'There must be a different sort of life,' I said to myself. I wanted to live! To live, to live! Curiosity kept eating at me—you don't understand it, but I swear to God I could no longer control myself; something was going on in me; I could not be held back. I told my husband I was ill, and came here. And here I have been walking about as though in a daze, as though I were mad; and now I have become a vulgar, vile woman whom anyone may despise."

Gurov was already bored with her; he was irritated by her naïve tone, by her repentance, so unexpected and so out of place, but for the tears in her eyes he might have thought she was joking or play-acting.

"I don't understand, my dear," he said softly. "What do you want?"

She hid her face on his breast and pressed close to him.

"Believe me, believe me, I beg you," she said, "I love honesty and purity, and sin is loathsome to me; I don't know what I'm doing. Simple people say, 'The Evil One has led me astray.' And I may say of myself now that the Evil One has led me astray."

"Quiet, quiet," he murmured.

He looked into her fixed, frightened eyes, kissed her, spoke to her softly and affectionately, and by degrees she calmed down, and her gaiety returned; both began laughing.

Afterwards when they went out there was not a soul on the esplanade. The town with its cypresses looked quite dead, but the sea was still sounding as it broke upon the beach; a single launch was rocking on the waves and on it a lantern was blinking sleepily.

They found a cab and drove to Oreanda.

"I found out your surname in the hall just now: it was written on the board—von Dideritz," said Gurov. "Is your husband German?"

"No; I believe his grandfather was German, but he is Greek Orthodox himself."

At Oreanda they sat on a bench not far from the church, looked down at the sea, and were silent. Yalta was barely visible through the morning mist; white clouds rested motionlessly on the mountaintops. The leaves did not stir on the trees, cicadas twanged, and the monotonous muffled sound of the sea that rose from below spoke of the peace, the eternal sleep awaiting us. So it rumbled below when there was no Yalta, no Oreanda here; so it rumbles now, and it will rumble as indifferently and as hollowly when we are no more. And in this constancy, in this complete indifference to the life and death of each of us, there lies, perhaps, a pledge of our eternal salvation, of the unceasing advance of life upon earth, of unceasing movement towards perfection. Sitting beside a young woman who in the dawn seemed so lovely, Gurov, soothed and spellbound by these magical surroundings—the sea, the mountains, the clouds, the wide sky—thought how everything is really beautiful in this world when one reflects: everything except what we think or do ourselves when we forget the higher aims of life and our own human dignity.

A man strolled up to them—probably a guard—looked at them, and walked away. And this detail, too, seemed so mysterious and beautiful. They saw a steamer arrive from Feodosia, its lights extinguished in the glow of dawn.

"There is dew on the grass," said Anna Sergeyevna, after a silence.

"Yes, it's time to go home."

They returned to the city.

Then they met every day at twelve o'clock on the esplanade, lunched and dined together, took walks, admired the sea. She complained that she slept badly, that she had palpitations, asked the same questions, troubled now by jealousy and now by the fear that he did not respect her sufficiently. And often in the square or the public garden, when there was no one near them, he suddenly drew her to him and kissed her passionately. Complete idleness, these kisses in broad daylight exchanged furtively in dread of someone's seeing them, the heat, the smell of the sea, and the continual flitting before his eyes of idle, well-dressed, well-fed people, worked a complete change in him; he kept telling Anna Sergeyevna how beautiful she was, how seductive, was urgently passionate; he would not move a step away from her, while she was often pensive and continually pressed him to confess that he did not respect her, did not love her in the least, and saw in her nothing but a common woman. Almost every evening rather late they drove somewhere out of town, to Oreanda or to the waterfall; and the excursion was always a success, the scenery invariably impressed them as beautiful and magnificent.

They were expecting her husband, but a letter came from him saying that he had eye-trouble, and begging his wife to return home as soon as possible. Anna Sergeyevna made haste to go.

"It's a good thing I am leaving," she said to Gurov. "It's the hand of Fate!"

She took a carriage to the railway station, and he went with her. They were driving the whole day. When she had taken her place in the express, and when the second bell had rung, she said, "Let me look at you once more—let me look at you again. Like this."

She was not crying but was so sad that she seemed ill and her face was quivering.

"I shall be thinking of you—remembering you," she said. "God bless you; be happy. Don't remember evil against me. We are parting forever—it has to be, for we ought never to have met. Well, God bless you."

The train moved off rapidly, its lights soon vanished, and a minute later there was no sound of it, as though everything had conspired to end as quickly as possible that sweet trance, that madness. Left alone on the platform, and gazing into the dark distance, Gurov listened to the twang of the grasshoppers and the hum of the telegraph wires, feeling as though he had just waked up. And he reflected, musing, that there had now been another episode or adventure in his life, and it, too, was at an end, and nothing was left of it but a memory. He was moved, sad, and slightly remorseful: this young woman whom he would never meet again had not been happy with him; he had been warm and affectionate with her, but yet in his manner, his tone, and his caresses there had been a shade of light irony, the slightly coarse arrogance of a happy male who was, besides, almost twice her age. She had constantly called him kind, exceptional, high-minded; obviously he had seemed to her different from what he really was, so he had involuntarily deceived her.

Here at the station there was already a scent of autumn in the air; it was a chilly evening.

"It is time for me to go north, too," thought Gurov as he left the platform. "High time!"

III

At home in Moscow the winter routine was already established; the stoves were heated, and in the morning it was still dark when the children were having breakfast and getting ready for school, and the nurse would light the lamp for a short time. There were frosts already. When the first snow falls, on the first day the sleighs are out, it is pleasant to see the white earth, the white roofs; one draws easy, delicious breaths, and the season brings back the days of one's youth. The old limes and birches, white with hoar-frost, have a good-natured look; they are closer to one's heart than cypresses and palms, and near them one no longer wants to think of mountains and the sea.

Gurov, a native of Moscow, arrived there on a fine frosty day, and when he put on his fur coat and warm gloves and took a walk along Petrovka, and when on Saturday night he heard the bells ringing, his recent trip and the places he had visited lost all charm for him. Little by little he became immersed in Moscow life, greedily read three newspapers a day, and declared that he did not read the Moscow papers on principle. He already felt a longing for restaurants, clubs, formal dinners, anniversary celebrations, and it flattered him to entertain distinguished lawyers and actors, and to play cards with a professor at the physicians' club. He could eat a whole portion of meat stewed with pickled cabbage and served in a pan, Moscow style.

A month or so would pass and the image of Anna Sergeyevna, it seemed to him, would become misty in his memory, and only from time to time he would dream of her with her touching smile as he dreamed of others. But more than a month went by, winter came into its own, and everything was still clear in his memory as though he had parted from Anna Sergeyevna only yesterday. And his memories glowed more and more vividly. When in the evening stillness the voices of his children preparing their lessons reached his study, or when he listened to a song or to an organ playing in a restaurant, or when the storm howled in the chimney, suddenly everything would rise up in his memory; what had happened on the pier and the early morning with the mist on the mountains, and the steamer coming from Feodosia, and the kisses. He would pace about his room a long time, remembering and smiling; then his memories passed into reveries, and in his imagination the past would mingle with what was about to come. He did not dream of Anna Sergeyevna, but she followed him about everywhere and watched him. When he shut his eyes he saw her before him as though she were there in the flesh, and she seemed to him lovelier, younger, tenderer than she had been, and he imagined himself a finer man than he had been in Yalta. Of evenings she peered out at him from the bookcase, from the fireplace, from the corner—he heard her breathing, the caressing rustle of her clothes. In the street he followed women with his eyes, looking for someone who resembled her.

Already he was tormented by a strong desire to share his memories with someone. But in his home it was impossible to talk of his love, and he had no one to talk to outside; certainly he could not confide in his tenants or in anyone at the bank. And what was there to talk about? He hadn't loved her then, had he? Had there been anything beautiful, poetical, edifying, or simply interesting in his relations with Anna Sergeyevna? And he was forced to talk vaguely of love, of women, and no one guessed what he meant; only his wife would twitch her black eyebrows and say, "The part of the philanderer does not suit you at all, Dimitry."

One evening, coming out of the physicians' club with an official with whom he had been playing cards, he could not resist saying:

"If you only knew what a fascinating woman I became acquainted with at Yalta!"

The official got into his sledge and was driving away, but he turned suddenly and shouted:

"Dmitry Dmitrich!"

"What is it?"

"You were right this evening: the sturgeon was a bit high."

These words, so commonplace, for some reason moved Gurov to indignation, and struck him as degrading and unclean. What savage manners, what mugs! What stupid nights, what dull, humdrum days! Frenzied gambling, gluttony, drunkenness, continual talk always about the same thing! Futile pursuits and conversations always about the same topics take up the better part of one's time, the better part of one's strength, and in the end there is left a life clipped and wingless, an absurd mess, and there is no escaping or getting away from it—just as though one were in a madhouse or a prison.

Gurov, boiling with indignation, did not sleep all night. And he had a headache all the next day. And the following nights too he slept badly; he sat up in bed, thinking, or paced up and down his room. He was fed up with his children, fed up with the bank; he had no desire to go anywhere or to talk of anything.

In December during the holidays he prepared to take a trip and told his wife he was going to Petersburg to do what he could for a young friend—and he set off for S—. What for? He did not know himself. He wanted to see Anna Sergeyevna and talk with her, to arrange a rendezvous if possible.

He arrived at S— in the morning, and at the hotel took the best room, in which the floor was covered with gray army cloth, and on the table there was an inkstand, gray with dust and topped by a figure on horseback, its hat in its raised hand and its head broken off. The porter gave him the necessary information: von Dideritz lived in a house of his own on Staro-Goncharnaya Street, not far from the hotel: he was rich and lived well and kept his own horses; everyone in the town knew him. The porter pronounced the name: "Dridiritz."

Without haste Gurov made his way to Staro-Goncharnaya Street and found the house. Directly opposite the house stretched a long gray fence studded with nails.

"A fence like that would make one run away," thought Gurov, looking now at the fence, now at the windows of the house.

He reflected: this was a holiday, and the husband was apt to be at home. And in any case, it would be tactless to go into the house and disturb her. If he were to send her a note, it might fall into her husband's hands, and that might spoil everything. The best thing was to rely on chance. And he kept walking up and down the street and along the fence, waiting for the chance. He saw a beggar go in at the gate and heard the dogs attack him; then an hour later he heard a piano, and the sound came to him faintly and indistinctly. Probably it was Anna Sergeyevna playing. The front door opened suddenly, and an old woman came out, followed by the familiar white Pomeranian. Gurov was on the point of calling to the dog, but his heart began beating violently, and in his excitement he could not remember the Pomeranian's name.

He kept walking up and down, and hated the gray fence more and more, and by now he thought irritably that Anna Sergeyevna had forgotten him, and was perhaps already diverting herself with another man, and that that was very natural in a young woman who from morning till night had to look at that damn fence. He went back to his hotel room and sat on the couch for a long while, not knowing what to do, then he had dinner and a long nap.

"How stupid and annoying this all is!" he thought when he woke and looked at the dark windows: it was already evening. "Here I've had a good sleep for some reason. What am I going to do at night?"

He sat on the bed, which was covered with a cheap gray blanket of the kind seen in hospitals, and he twitted himself in his vexation:

"So there's your lady with the pet dog. There's your adventure. A nice place to cool your heels in."

That morning at the station a playbill in large letters had caught his eye. *The Geisha* was to be given for the first time. He thought of this and drove to the theater.

"It's quite possible that she goes to first nights," he thought.

The theater was full. As in all provincial theaters, there was a haze above the chandelier, the gallery was noisy and restless; in the front row, before the beginning of the performance the local dandies were standing with their hands clasped behind their backs; in the Governor's box the Governor's daughter, wearing a boa, occupied the front seat, while the Governor himself hid modestly behind the portiere and only his hands were visible; the curtain swayed; the orchestra was a long time tuning up.

While the audience was coming in and taking their seats, Gurov scanned the faces eagerly.

Anna Sergeyevna, too, came in. She sat down in the third row, and when Gurov looked at her his heart contracted, and he understood clearly that in the whole world there was no human being so near, so precious, and so important to him; she, this little, undistinguished woman, lost in a provincial crowd, with a vulgar lorgnette in her hand, filled his whole life now, was his sorrow and his joy, the only happiness that he now desired for himself, and to the sounds of the bad orchestra, of the miserable local violins, he thought how lovely she was. He thought and dreamed.

A young man with small side-whiskers, very tall and stooped, came in with Anna Sergeyevna and sat down beside her; he nodded his head at every step and seemed to be bowing continually. Probably this was the husband whom at Yalta, in an excess of bitter feeling, she had called a flunkey. And there really was in his lanky figure, his side-whiskers, his small bald patch, something of a flunkey's retiring manner, his smile was mawkish, and in his buttonhole there was an academic badge like a waiter's number.

During the first intermission, the husband went out to have a smoke; she remained in her seat. Gurov, who was also sitting in the orchestra, went up to her and said in a shaky voice, with a forced smile:

"Good evening!"

She glanced at him and turned pale, then looked at him again in horror, unable to believe her eyes, and gripped the fan and the lorgnette tightly together in her hands, evidently trying to keep herself from fainting. Both were silent. She was sitting, he was standing, frightened by her distress and not daring to take a seat beside her. The violins and the flute that were being tuned up sang out. He suddenly felt frightened: it seemed as if all the people in the boxes were looking at them. She got up and went hurriedly to the exit; he followed her, and both of them walked blindly along the corridors and up and down stairs, and figures in the uniforms prescribed for magistrates, teachers, and officials of the Department of Crown Lands, all wearing badges, flitted before their eyes, as did also ladies, and fur coats on hangers; they were conscious of drafts and the smell of stale tobacco. And Gurov, whose heart was beating violently, thought:

"Oh, Lord! Why are these people here and this orchestra!"

And at this instant he suddenly recalled how when he had seen Anna Sergeyevna off at the station he had said to himself that all was over between them and that they would never meet again. But how distant the end still was!

On the narrow, gloomy staircase over which it said, "To the Ampitheatre," she stopped.

"How you frightened me!" she said, breathing hard, still pale and stunned. "Oh, how you frightened me! I am barely alive. Why did you come? Why?"

"But do understand, Anna, do understand—" he said hurriedly, under his breath. "I implore you, do understand—"

She looked at him with fear, with entreaty, with love; she looked at him intently, to keep his features more distinctly in her memory.

"I suffer so," she went on, not listening to him. "All this time I have been thinking of nothing but you; I live only by the thought of you. And I wanted to forget, to forget; but why, oh, why have you come?"

On the landing above them two high school boys were looking down and smoking, but it was all the same to Gurov; he drew Anna Sergeyevna to him and began kissing her face and hands.

"What are you doing, what are you doing!" she was saying in horror, pushing him away. "We have lost our senses. Go away today; go away at once—I conjure you by all that is sacred, I implore you— People are coming this way!"

Someone was walking up the stairs.

"You must leave," Anna Sergeyevna went on in a whisper. "Do you hear, Dmitry Dmitrich? I will come and see you in Moscow. I have never been happy; I am unhappy now, and I never, never shall be happy, never! So don't make me suffer still more! I swear I'll come to Moscow. But now let us part. My dear, good, precious one, let us part!"

She pressed his hand and walked rapidly downstairs, turning to look round at him, and from her eyes he could see that she really was unhappy. Gurov stood for a while, listening, then when all grew quiet, he found his coat and left the theater.

IV

And Anna Sergeyevna began coming to see him in Moscow. Once every two or three months she left S— telling her husband that she was going to consult a doctor about a woman's ailment from which she was suffering—and her husband did and did not believe her. When she arrived in Moscow she would stop at the Slavyansky Bazar Hotel, and at once send a man in a red cap to Gurov. Gurov came to see her, and no one in Moscow knew of it.

Once he was going to see her in this way on a winter morning (the messenger had come the evening before and not found him in). With him walked his daughter, whom he wanted to take to school; it was on the way. Snow was coming down in big wet flakes.

"It's three degrees above zero,* and yet it's snowing," Gurov was saying to his daughter. "But this temperature prevails only on the surface of the earth; in the upper layers of the atmosphere there is quite a different temperature."

"And why doesn't it thunder in winter, papa?"

He explained that, too. He talked, thinking all the while that he was on his way to a rendezvous, and no living soul knew of it, and probably no one would ever know. He had two lives, an open one, seen and known by all who needed to know it, full of conventional truth and conventional falsehood, exactly like the lives of his friends and acquaintances; and another life that went on in secret. And through some strange, perhaps accidental, combination of circumstances, everything that was of interest and importance to him, everything that was essential to him, everything about which he felt sincerely and did not deceive himself, everything that constituted the core of his life, was going on concealed from others; while all that was false, the shell in which he hid to cover the truth—his work at the bank, for instance, his discussions at the club, his references to the "inferior race," his appearances at anniversary celebrations with his wife—all that went on in the open. Judging others by himself, he did not believe what he saw, and always fancied that every man led his real, most interesting life under cover of secrecy as under cover of light. The personal life of every individual is based on secrecy, and perhaps it is partly for that reason that civilized man is so nervously anxious that personal privacy should be respected.

Having taken his daughter to school, Gurov went on to the Slavyansky Bazar Hotel. He took off his fur coat in the lobby, went upstairs, and knocked gently at the door. Anna Sergeyevna, wearing his favorite gray dress, exhausted by the journey and by waiting, had been expecting him since the previous evening. She was pale, and looked at him without a smile, and he had hardly entered when she flung herself on his breast. That kiss was a long, lingering one, as though they had not seen one another for two years.

"Well, darling, how are you getting on there?" he asked. "What news?"

"Wait; I'll tell you in a moment—I can't speak."

She could not speak; she was crying. She turned away from him, and pressed her handkerchief to her eyes.

"Let her have her cry; meanwhile I'll sit down," he thought, and he seated himself in an armchair.

Then he rang and ordered tea, and while he was having his tea she

* On the Celsius scale—about thirty-seven degrees Fahrenheit.

remained standing at the window with her back to him. She was crying out of sheer agitation, in the sorrowful consciousness that their life was so sad; that they could only see each other in secret and had to hide from people like thieves! Was it not a broken life?

"Come, stop now, dear!" he said.

It was plain to him that this love of theirs would not be over soon, that the end of it was not in sight. Anna Sergeyevna was growing more and more attached to him. She adored him, and it was unthinkable to tell her that their love was bound to come to an end some day; besides, she would not have believed it!

He went up to her and took her by the shoulders, to fondle her and say something diverting, and at that moment he caught sight of himself in the mirror.

His hair was already beginning to turn gray. And it seemed to him that he had grown so much older in the last few years, and lost his looks. The shoulders on which his hands rested were warm and heaving. He felt compassion for this life, still so warm and lovely, but probably already about to begin to fade and wither like his own. Why did she love him so much? He always seemed to women different from what he was, and they loved in him not himself, but the man whom their imagination created and whom they had been eagerly seeking all their lives; and afterwards, when they saw their mistake, they loved him nevertheless. And not one of them had been happy with him. In the past he had met women, come together with them, parted from them, but he had never once loved; it was anything you please, but not love. And only now when his head was gray he had fallen in love, really, truly—for the first time in his life.

Anna Sergeyevna and he loved each other as people do who are very close and intimate, like man and wife, like tender friends; it seemed to them that Fate itself had meant them for one another, and they could not understand why he had a wife and she a husband; and it was as though they were a pair of migratory birds, male and female, caught and forced to live in different cages. They forgave each other what they were ashamed of in their past, they forgave everything in the present, and felt that this love of theirs had altered them both.

Formerly in moments of sadness he had soothed himself with whatever logical arguments came into his head, but now he no longer cared for logic; he felt profound compassion, he wanted to be sincere and tender.

"Give it up now, my darling," he said. "You've had your cry; that's enough. Let us have a talk now, we'll think of something."

Then they spent a long time taking counsel together, they talked of how to avoid the necessity for secrecy, for deception, for living in different cities, and not seeing one another for long stretches of time. How could they free themselves from these intolerable fetters?

"How? How?" he asked, clutching his head. "How?"

And it seemed as though in a little while the solution would be found, and then a new and glorious life would begin; and it was clear to both of them that the end was still far off, and that what was to be most complicated and difficult for them was only just beginning.

PART XI

THE INDEPENDENTS:

MONEY CHANGES EVERYTHING

"Where Are You Going, Where Have You Been?"
by Joyce Carol Oates

Smooth Talk, directed by Joyce Chopra, 1985

"Auggie Wren's Christmas Story"
by Paul Auster

Smoke, directed by Wayne Wang, 1995

"Emergency"
by Denis Johnson

Jesus' Son, directed by Alison Maclean, 1999

"Killings"
by Andre Dubus

In the Bedroom, directed by Todd Field, 2001

Compromise. It's a word most literary authors can't abide . . . followed pretty closely by the other C word, collaboration.

So that makes Hollywood a scary place for writers, as it has been since the beginning. In his 1936 essay "The Crack-Up," F. Scott Fitzgerald partially blamed film's "mechanical and communal art" for his mental disintegration: "As long past as 1930, I had a hunch that the talkies would make even the best selling novelist as archaic as silent pictures. People still read . . . but there was a rankling indignity, that to me had become almost an obsession, in seeing the power of the written word subordinated to another power, a more glittering, a grosser power. . . ." Recently, director Lawrence Kasdan *(The Big Chill, Body Heat)* put it a slightly different way: "Sometimes Hollywood movies seem stupidly resistant to the fascinating unpredictability of human beings. A writer I know was in a meeting once with a studio executive who said with exasperation, 'These characters are way too complicated for a movie this expensive.' " Paul Schrader, who directed the low-budget independent film *Affliction*, adapted from a novel by Russell Banks, has even put a dollar figure on this threshold for complicated characters: He likes to say that somewhere around $14 million you have to put white hats on the good guys and black hats on the bad guys.

And for a literary writer, them's fightin' words.

One of the most stubborn, uncompromising authors working today is Denis Johnson. Poet, novelist, essayist, and playwright, he chronicles life in the drugged-out, dog-eared corners of society. And he speaks from experience. In the 1970s, while in his twenties, Johnson struggled with drug addiction and eventually landed in rehab. His story collection, *Jesus' Son* (the title is from Lou Reed's song "Heroin"), is a semi-autobiographical chronicle of that time and includes the story "Emergency" (chosen by Robert Stone as one of the twenty best stories of 1992). As a collection, it seems unlikely film material, with its elliptical structure and wandering addict/alcoholic main character, known only as Fuckhead (or FH). But, as with all of Johnson's work, there is a preoccupation with redemption that sets his work apart from other drug tales. "To go on living and to understand the past," he has said, "is like taking up another life. It is like waking up after your death and being able to look back and understand."

Alison Maclean, who directed the film adaptation of *Jesus' Son* ($2.5 million), had already read Johnson's collection when she was approached to do the movie. "I was quite stunned by it and went on to read many of his other books and had a bit of an obsession with him after that. But I never thought of it as a film because it's a book of short stories and they are not particularly connected apart from the main character." Throughout the adaptation process she was keenly aware of the difficulties. "People were nervous about the structure, about the drugs. Nervous that Fuckhead was unlikable, that he was *called* Fuckhead." As a result, the film was made completely outside of Hollywood, using independent funds. Maclean's (and the screenwriter's) respect for the material is obvious. She employed frequent voiceovers to retain the lush, language-filled, hallucinatory nature of Johnson's stories. She also retained the episodic structure, complete with story titles. Roger Ebert, who included the film in his annual Overlooked Film Festival, applauded its "wry humor, poignancy, sorrow and wildness," concluding, "like all good films it isn't for everybody (only bad films are for everybody)."

And that's the nice compatibility between independent films and literary fiction: Neither tries to be all things to all people. This is, almost by definition, not true for the big-budget Hollywood film. In his essay "Director's Problems," Alfred Hitchcock, one of the most commercially successful directors of all time, states, "The cost of making a picture is so great, and there are so many aspects of the business—world markets, American markets, and so on—that we find it difficult to get our money back, even for a successful film with a universal appeal, let alone in films that have experimented with the story or the artist. That is the thing that has long kept the cinema back. I should say it has pretty well gone a long way to destroy the art."

If the spectre of cost is destructive, another kiss of death—in adaptations, anyway—is remaining too close to the source. But at least in today's environment most authors understand this. In 1985, while pointing out the progress of literary adaptations, Joy Gould Boyum observed: "The literary establishment seems not to have noticed . . . that so many of the arguments it puts forth against adaptation . . . are really about film-as-it-was, rather than about film-as-it-is; about film when it was synonymous with Hollywood and had to submit to the taste of moguls, the structures of the star system, and the censoring eye of the Hays Office; about film when it was more of a mass medium than it is today and, consequently, operated with very different notions as to the nature of its audience."

But lately the literary establishment *has* begun to notice the change, and some authors are even willing—happily—to jump into the fray.

Paul Auster did just that when he wrote the screenplay for Wayne Wang's *Smoke* ($7 million), based on his own "Auggie Wren's Christmas Story," commissioned by the *New York Times.* When Wang read the story, he was impressed by its inherent questioning of reality and fiction, truth and lies. A few weeks later he called Auster and suggested that it would make a good premise for a movie. It took four years, and as Wang puts it, "a lot of economic, emotional, and creative twists and turns and ups and downs," but eventually the movie was made and presented as a "film by Wayne Wang and Paul Auster." Many of Auster's narrative tics are present in his screenplay, including his fascination with coincidence, his fondness for digression, and what he has called the "force of contradiction." Prone to self-consciousness—poet W. S. Merwin calls it "self-consciously tracing a self-consciousness"—Auster transformed the story's "Paul" into "Paul Benjamin," the pseudonym he used for his baseball detective novel *Squeeze Play.* In typically self-reflexive fashion, "Auggie Wren's Christmas Story" appears at the end of the film as a reverberating set piece, a story-within-a-story and a movie-within-a-movie. As Peter Travers observed in *Rolling Stone,* "Those immune to the film's sly strategy will think the story comes from nowhere. Others will revel in the ending's emotional resonance. There's magic in it."

Thus began Auster's foray into film. He and Wang went on to film an un-sequel, *Blue in the Face*, conceived as a six-day improvisation using *Smoke*'s cigar store as a setting. The idea grew out of the rehearsals for *Smoke*, which were so funny and inventive that Wang and Auster decided to attempt a follow-up. Auster wrote notes for each of the actors, roughing out each situation, and ended up getting credit as codirector when Wang fell ill on the second day of the shoot. Three years later, Auster wrote and directed his own film, *Lulu on the Bridge*, about a jazz saxophonist whose life is permanently changed after being hit by a stray bullet in a New York nightclub. (Between *Blue in the Face* and *Lulu on the Bridge*, Auster found time to serve as a judge at the Cannes Film Festival, an experience he recalls fondly. "All I had to do was flash it [the red juror's badge] and every door opened. . . . When my wife and I got home to Brooklyn after the festival, we kept talking about how we wanted our red badge back, how we wanted a red badge for New York.")

Born after World War II, and raised on film and television, Auster represents a new breed of writers whose work reacts, implicitly and explicitly, to media's overwhelming centrifugal force. These are writers actively trying to resolve the intersection between fiction and film, who are trying to develop—each on his or her own terms—a workable, interesting, mutually beneficial relationship with the film community. Who understand, much better than their predecessors, the power of the medium and the shape-shifting nature of stories (Auster has even allowed one of his novels to be adapted into a comic book). And who are, nevertheless, filled with ambivalence about the nature of film: its two-dimensionality and the way it encourages passive involvement. "Needless to say," Auster admits, "I'm always going to come down on the side of books. But that doesn't mean movies can't be wonderful. It's another way of telling stories, that's all, and I suppose its important to remember what each medium can and can't do. . . ."

Although she is a generation older than Auster, Joyce Carol Oates agrees. Unlike many of her contemporaries—Philip Roth, William Styron, John Updike, to name a few—she is willing to believe that "almost any novel of any substance" can be made into an interesting movie with the right screenplay and the right director. "Certain things one does in prose can't be translated . . . but directors can do other things to make up for that." Even so, she declined involvement in Joyce Chopra's adaptation of her story "Where Are You Going, Where Have You Been?" Oates publicly praised *Smooth Talk* ($1 million) for its "visual freshness, its sense of motion and life; the attentive intelligence the director has brought to the semi-secret world of the American adolescent." Even though the ending—every author's nightmare!—was changed to something more upbeat. "I assume they are professionals to their fingertips. . . . I would fiercely defend the placement of a semicolon in one of my novels but I would probably have deferred in the end to Joyce Chopra's decision to reverse the story's conclusion. . . ." Generously, she admits her ending, allegorical and ambiguous, is probably "impossible to transfigure into film."

Oates has written more than seventy-five books in nearly every genre, including popular suspense (under the pseudonym Rosamond Smith) and sportswriting (her book of essays *On Boxing* was well reviewed). Once called "the dark lady of American letters," she has always been fascinated by the macabre underbelly of American life and her short stories are among her best work. Early drafts of "Where Are You Going, Where Have You Been?" were based on accounts of a tabloid psychopath known as the Pied Piper of Tucson, who seduced and occasionally murdered teenage girls. The identity of the charismatic Pied Piper was known to a circle of teenagers in the area, but they kept his identity a secret. It was this fact that intrigued Oates. Over the course of many drafts, the character based on the murderer dropped into the background, and one of his innocent victims became the center of the story. The resulting story,

"Where Are You Going, Where Have You Been?" was chosen by John Updike as one of the best stories of the century.

The *other* Joyce's career serves as something of a cautionary tale. Chopra began as a documentary filmmaker and gained notoriety with her short film, *Joyce at 34*, about the impact her pregnancy had on her film career. *Smooth Talk* was her first fiction feature film, a result of reading Oates's story. "It just stayed in my brain. I knew that if I ever did a dramatic film, this was what I'd like to do." The *New York Times* praised her direction, saying it showed "the kind of discipline very rare in movies" and dubbed *Smooth Talk* "a small, exceptionally successful movie." It went on to win Best Dramatic Feature at the U.S. Film Festival and the Grand Jury Prize at the Sundance Film Festival. Then disaster struck. Chopra's next film was the ill-fated big-budget adaptation of Jay McInerney's *Bright Lights, Big City*, a semi-autobiographical novel of a young writer who drifts through a world of clubs and cocaine. From the beginning the subject matter was problematic, considered by studio execs to be both subversive and unconventional. Several screenwriters cranked out unusable scripts, while studio execs worried about how to make the main character likeable. Eventually the studio fired Chopra for "indecision," citing their "strong financial interest in the film." Although she continues to work in both television and films (and recently directed the TV adaptation of Oates's novel *Blonde*), Chopra's reputation never quite recovered.

With Hollywood films becoming more and more safe and predictable, restless and thoughtful filmmakers are exploring independent avenues and using contemporary fiction as their muse. But with the minuscule budgets they face, even the movie rights to a *literary* novel may be prohibitive. (E. Annie Proulx recently netted $500,000 for movie rights to *The Shipping News*, and Charles Frazier's *Cold Mountain* went for $1.3 million.) Still, if small independent filmmakers can't afford to purchase the rights to prize-winning novels, they *can* usually afford the rights to prize-winning stories—and a lot of fine stories, with film potential, are being written today.

Rob Festinger spotted Andre Dubus's "Killings" while working as a reader for HBO. HBO passed on the story, but Festinger was so enamored of it that he wrote a script himself (his first). Separately, Todd Field, who had already directed a short based on a Dubus story, became interested in adapting "Killings." When Field tracked down the movie rights, he found Festinger. "I liken it to running a marathon," Festinger says, "I ran the first leg, then we worked in tandem, and the handover is where Todd took it." During the process, the two became friends with Dubus, and ultimately dedicated *In the Bedroom* ($1.7 million) to him.

The movie—nominated for five Academy Awards, including Best Picture—expanded on Dubus's story but remained tied to his themes, particularly his ongoing concern with violence. A retired Marine Corps captain, Dubus was comfortable with firearms: "I love the relaxed concentration of aiming a gun and squeezing its trigger." His first published story was about a boy who shoots his sister's boyfriend under ambiguous circumstances. Subsequently, he published scores of stories dealing with variations on the theme: racial violence, family violence, sexual violence, violence against or by children, murder, homicidal revenge, suicide. "Killings" is one in a chain of stories that culminated in Dubus's "giving up the gun," as he titled his 1990 essay describing his decision. Field expounded on this in an interview with *The Guardian*: "I see Andre's story, 'Killings,' as a reflection of American consciousness. . . . It's about a sense of values, of morality, in terms of the nature of violence and how it's dealt with. Andre's characters are very complicated, they're flawed, they have a sense of right and wrong that's not always very clear, and the actions they take are often violent."

So maybe the new C word—at least among independent filmmakers and literary authors—is cooperation. Writers today are willing to forge a more complex relationship, based on mutual respect, one that bears little resemblance to the old-school reaction of Fitzgerald and Hemingway (fear and loathing, respectively). Authors like Auster aren't scared: "You see, the interesting thing about books, as opposed, say, to films, is that it's always just one person encountering the book, it's not an audience, it's one to one. It's me the writer and you the reader, and we're together on that page, and I think it's probably about the most intimate place where human consciousnesses meet. And that's why books are never going to die. It's impossible."

Where Are You Going, Where Have You Been?

Joyce Carol Oates

TO BOB DYLAN

Her name was Connie. She was fifteen and she had a quick nervous giggling habit of craning her neck to glance into mirrors, or checking other people's faces to make sure her own was all right. Her mother, who noticed everything and knew everything and who hadn't much reason any longer to look at her own face, always scolded Connie about it. "Stop gawking at yourself, who are you? You think you're so pretty?" she would say. Connie would raise her eyebrows at these familiar complaints and look right through her mother, into a shadowy vision of herself as she was right at that moment: she knew she was pretty and that was everything. Her mother had been pretty once too, if you could believe those old snapshots in the album, but now her looks were gone and that was why she was always after Connie.

"Why don't you keep your room clean like your sister? How've you got your hair fixed—what the hell stinks? Hair spray? You don't see your sister using that junk."

Her sister June was twenty-four and still lived at home. She was a secretary in the high school Connie attended, and if that wasn't bad enough—with her in the same building—she was so plain and chunky and steady that Connie had to hear her praised all the time by her mother and her mother's sisters. June did this, June did that, she saved money and helped clean the house and cooked and Connie couldn't do a thing, her mind was all filled with trashy daydreams. Their father was away at work most of the time and when he came home he wanted supper and he read the newspaper at supper and after supper he went to bed. He didn't bother talking much to them, but around his bent head Connie's mother kept picking at her until Connie wished her mother were dead and she herself were dead and it were all over. "She makes me want to throw up sometimes," she complained to her friends. She had a high, breathless, amused voice which made everything she said sound a little forced, whether it was sincere or not.

There was one good thing: June went places with girlfriends of hers, girls who were just as plain and steady as she, and so when Connie wanted to do that her mother had no objections. The father of Connie's best girlfriend drove the girls the three miles to town and left them off at a shopping plaza, so that they could talk through the stores or go to a movie, and when he came to pick them up again at eleven he never bothered to ask what they had done.

They must have been familiar sights, walking around that shopping plaza in their shorts and flat ballerina slippers that always scuffed the sidewalk, with charm bracelets jingling on their thin wrists; they would lean together to whisper and laugh secretly if someone passed by who amused or interested them. Connie had long dark blond hair that drew anyone's eye to it, and she wore part of it pulled up on her head and puffed out and the rest of it she let fall down her back. She wore a pullover jersey blouse that looked one way when she was at home and another way when she was away from home. Everything about her had two sides to it, one for home and one for anywhere that was not home: her walk that could be childlike and bobbing, or languid enough to make anyone think she was hearing music in her head, her mouth which was pale and smirking most of the time, but bright and pink on these evenings out, her laugh which was cynical and drawling at home—"Ha, ha, very funny"—but high-pitched and nervous anywhere else, like the jingling of the charms on her bracelet.

Sometimes they did go shopping or to a movie, but sometimes they went across the highway, ducking fast across the busy road, to a drive-in restaurant where older kids hung out. The restaurant was shaped like a big bottle, though squatter than a real bottle, and on its cap was a revolving figure of a grinning boy who held a hamburger aloft. One night in midsummer they ran across, breathless with daring, and right away someone leaned out a car window and invited them over, but it was just a boy from high school they didn't like. It made them feel good to be able to ignore him. They went up through the maze of parked and cruising cars to the bright-lit, fly-infested restaurant, their faces pleased and expectant as if they were entering a sacred building that loomed out of the night to give them what haven and what blessing they yearned for. They sat at the counter and crossed their legs at the ankles, their thin shoulders rigid with excitement, and listened to the music that made everything so good: the music was always in the background like music at a church service, it was something to depend upon.

A boy named Eddie came in to talk with them. He sat backward on his stool, turning himself jerkily around in semicircles and then stopping and turning again, and after a while he asked Connie if she would like something to eat. She said she did and so she tapped her friend's arm on her way out—her friend pulled her face up into a brave droll look—and Connie said she would meet her at eleven, across the way. "I just hate to leave her like that," Connie said earnestly, but the boy said that she wouldn't be alone for long. So they went out to his car and on the way Connie couldn't help but let her eyes wander over the windshields and faces all around her, her face gleaming with a joy that had nothing to do with Eddie or even this place; it might have been the music. She drew her shoulders up and sucked in her breath with the pure pleasure of being alive, and just at that moment she happened to glance at a face just a few feet from hers. It was a boy with shaggy black hair, in a convertible jalopy painted gold. He stared at her and then his lips widened into a grin. Connie slit her eyes at him and turned away, but she couldn't help glancing back and there he was still watching her. He wagged a finger and laughed and said, "Gonna get you, baby," and Connie turned away again without Eddie noticing anything.

She spent three hours with him, at the restaurant where they ate hamburgers and drank Cokes in wax cups that were always sweating, and then down an alley a mile or so away, and when he left her off at five to eleven only the movie house was still open at the plaza. Her girlfriend was there, talking with a boy. When Connie came up the two girls smiled at each other and Connie said, "How was the movie?" and the girl said, "*You* should know." They rode off with the girl's father, sleepy and pleased, and Connie couldn't help but look at the darkened shopping plaza with its big empty parking lot and its signs that were faded and ghostly now, and over at the drive-in restaurant where cars were still circling tirelessly. She couldn't hear the music at this distance.

Next morning June asked her how the movie was and Connie said, "So-so."

She and that girl and occasionally another girl went out several times a week that way, and the rest of the time Connie spent around the house—it was summer vacation—getting in her mother's way and thinking, dreaming, about the boys she met. But all the boys fell back and dissolved into a single face that was not even a face, but an idea, a feeling, mixed up with the urgent insistent pounding of the music and the humid night air of July. Connie's mother kept dragging her back to the daylight by finding things for her to do or saying, suddenly, "What's this about the Pettinger girl?"

And Connie would say nervously, "Oh, her. That dope." She always drew thick clear lines between herself and such girls, and her mother was simple and kindly enough to believe her. Her mother was so simple,

Connie thought, that it was maybe cruel to fool her so much. Her mother went scuffling around the house in old bedroom slippers and complained over the telephone to one sister about the other, then the other called up and the two of them complained about the third one. If June's name was mentioned her mother's tone was approving, and if Connie's name was mentioned it was disapproving. This did not really mean she disliked Connie and actually Connie thought that her mother preferred her to June because she was prettier, but the two of them kept up a pretense of exasperation, a sense that they were tugging and struggling over something of little value to either of them. Sometimes, over coffee, they were almost friends, but something would come up—some vexation that was like a fly buzzing suddenly around their heads—and their faces went hard with contempt.

One Sunday Connie got up at eleven—none of them bothered with church—and washed her hair so that it could dry all day long, in the sun. Her parents and sister were going to a barbecue at an aunt's house and Connie said no, she wasn't interested, rolling her eyes to let her mother know just what she thought of it. "Stay home alone then," her mother said sharply. Connie sat out back in a lawn chair and watched them drive away, her father quiet and bald, hunched around so that he could back the car out, her mother with a look that was still angry and not at all softened through the windshield, and in the back seat poor old June all dressed up as if she didn't know what a barbecue was, with all the running yelling kids and the flies. Connie sat with her eyes closed in the sun, dreaming and dazed with the warmth about her as if this were a kind of love, the caresses of love, and her mind slipped over onto thoughts of the boy she had been with the night before and how nice he had been, how sweet it always was, not the way someone like June would suppose but sweet, gentle, the way it was in movies and promised in songs; and when she opened her eyes she hardly knew where she was, the back yard ran off into weeds and a fence-line of trees and behind it the sky was perfectly blue and still. The asbestos "ranch house" that was now three years old startled her—it looked small. She shook her head as if to get awake.

It was too hot. She went inside the house and turned on the radio to drown out the quiet. She sat on the edge of her bed, barefoot, and listened for an hour and a half to a program called XYZ Sunday Jamboree, record after record of hard, fast, shrieking songs she sang along with, interspersed by exclamations from "Bobby King": "An' look here you girls at Napoleon's—Son and Charley want you to pay real close attention to this song coming up!"

And Connie paid close attention herself, bathed in a glow of slow-pulsed joy that seemed to rise mysteriously out of the music itself and lay languidly about the airless little room, breathed in and breathed out with each gentle rise and fall of her chest.

After a while she heard a car coming up the drive. She sat up at once, startled, because it couldn't be her father so soon. The gravel kept crunching all the way in from the road—the driveway was long—and Connie ran to the window. It was a car she didn't know. It was an open jalopy, painted a bright gold that caught the sunlight opaquely. Her heart began to pound and her fingers snatched at her hair, checking it, and she whispered "Christ. Christ," wondering how bad she looked. The car came to a stop at the side door and the horn sounded four short taps as if this were a signal Connie knew.

She went into the kitchen and approached the door slowly, then hung out the screen door, her bare toes curling down off the step. There were two boys in the car and now she recognized the driver: he had shaggy, shabby black hair that looked crazy as a wig and he was grinning at her.

"I ain't late, am I?" he said.

"Who the hell do you think you are?" Connie said.

"Toldja I'd be out, didn't I?"

"I don't even know who you are."

She spoke sullenly, careful to show no interest or pleasure, and he spoke in a fast bright monotone. Connie looked past him to the other boy, taking her time. He had fair brown hair, with a lock that fell onto his forehead. His sideburns gave him a fierce, embarrassed look, but so far he hadn't even bothered to glance at her. Both boys wore sunglasses. The driver's glasses were metallic and mirrored everything in miniature.

"You wanta come for a ride?" he said.

Connie smirked and let her hair fall loose over one shoulder.

"Don'tcha like my car? New paint job," he said. "Hey."

"What?"

"You're cute."

She pretended to fidget, chasing flies away from the door.

"Don'tcha believe me, or what?" he said.

"Look, I don't even know who you are," Connie said in disgust.

"Hey, Ellie's got a radio, see. Mine's broke down." He lifted his friend's arm and showed her the little transistor the boy was holding, and now Connie began to hear the music. It was the same program that was playing inside the house.

"Bobby King?" she said.

"I listen to him all the time. I think he's great."

"He's kind of great," Connie said reluctantly.

"Listen, that guy's *great.* He knows where the action is."

Connie blushed a little, because the glasses made it impossible for her to see just what this boy was looking at. She couldn't decide if she liked him or if he was just a jerk, and so she dawdled in the doorway and wouldn't come down or go back inside. She said, "What's all that stuff painted on your car?"

"Can'tcha read it?" He opened the door very carefully, as if he was afraid it might fall off. He slid out just as carefully, planting his feet firmly on the ground, the tiny metallic world in his glasses slowing down like gelatine hardening and in the midst of it Connie's bright green blouse. "This here is my name, to begin with," he said. ARNOLD FRIEND was written in tarlike black letters on the side, with a drawing of a round grinning face that reminded Connie of a pumpkin, except it wore sunglasses. "I wanta introduce myself, I'm Arnold Friend and that's my real name and I'm gonna be your friend, honey, and inside the car's Ellie Oscar, he's kinda shy." Ellie brought his transistor radio up to his shoulder and balanced it there. "Now these numbers are a secret code, honey," Arnold Friend explained. He read off the numbers 33, 19, 17 and raised his eyebrows at her to see what she thought of that, but she didn't think much of it. The left rear fender had been smashed and around it was written, on the gleaming gold background: DONE BY CRAZY WOMAN DRIVER. Connie had to laugh at that. Arnold Friend was pleased at her laughter and looked up at her. "Around the other side's a lot more—you wanta come and see them."

"No."

"Why not?"

"Why should I?"

"Don'tcha wanta see what's on the car? Don'tcha wanta go for a ride?"

"I don't know."

"Why not?"

"I've got things to do."

"Like what?"

"Things."

He laughed as if she had said something funny. He slapped his thighs. He was standing in a strange way, leaning back against the car as if he were balancing himself. He wasn't tall, only an inch or so taller than she would be if she came down to him. Connie liked the way he was dressed, which was the way all of them dressed: tight faded jeans stuffed into black, scuffed boots, a belt that pulled his waist in and showed how tan he was, and a white pullover shirt that was a little soiled and showed the hard small muscles of his arms and shoulders. He looked as if he probably did hard work, lifting and carrying things. Even his neck looked muscular. And his face was a familiar face, somehow: the jaw and chin and cheeks slightly darkened, because he hadn't shaved for a day or two, and the nose long and hawklike, sniffing as if she were a treat he was going to gobble up and it was all a joke.

"Connie, you ain't telling the truth. This is your day set aside for a ride with me and you know it," he said, still laughing. The way he straightened and recovered from his fit of laughing showed that it had been all fake.

"How do you know what my name is?" she said suspiciously.

"It's Connie."

"Maybe and maybe not."

"I know my Connie," he said, wagging his finger. Now she remembered him even better, back at the restaurant, and her cheeks warmed at the thought of how she sucked in her breath just at the moment she passed him—how she must have looked to him. And he had remembered her. "Ellie and I come out here especially for you," he said. "Ellie can sit in back. How about it?"

"Where?"

"Where what?"

"Where're we going?"

He looked at her. He took off the sunglasses and she saw how pale the skin around his eyes was, like holes that were not in shadow but instead in light. His eyes were like chips of broken glass that catch the light in an amiable way. He smiled. It was as if the idea of going for a ride somewhere, to some place, was a new idea to him.

"Just for a ride, Connie sweetheart."

"I never said my name was Connie," she said.

"But I know what it is. I know your name and all about you, lots of things," Arnold Friend said. He had not moved yet but stood still leaning back against the side of his jalopy. "I took a special interest in you, such a pretty girl, and found out all about you like I know your parents and sister are gone somewheres and I know where and how long they're going to be gone, and I know who you were with last night, and your best girlfriend's name is Betty. Right?"

He spoke in a simple lilting voice, exactly as if he were reciting the words to a song. His smile assured her that everything was fine. In the car Ellie turned up the volume on his radio and did not bother to look around at them.

"Ellie can sit in the back seat," Arnold Friend said. He indicated his friend with a casual jerk of his chin, as if Ellie did not count and she should not bother with him.

"How'd you find out all that stuff?" Connie said.

"Listen: Betty Schultz and Tony Fitch and Jimmy Pettinger and Nancy Pettinger," he said, in a chant. "Raymond Stanley and Bob Hutter—"

"Do you know all those kids?"

"I know everybody."

"Look, you're kidding. You're not from around here."

"Sure."

"But—how come we never saw you before?"

"Sure you saw me before," he said. He looked down at his boots, as if he were a little offended. "You just don't remember."

"I guess I'd remember you," Connie said.

"Yeah?" He looked up at this, beaming. He was pleased. He began to mark time with the music from Ellie's radio, tapping his fists lightly together. Connie looked away from his smile to the car, which was painted so bright it almost hurt her eyes to look at it. She looked at that name, ARNOLD FRIEND. And up at the front fender was an expression that was familiar—MAN THE FLYING SAUCERS. It was an expression kids had used the year before, but didn't use this year. She looked at it for a while as if the words meant something to her that she did not yet know.

"What're you thinking about? Huh?" Arnold Friend demanded. "Not worried about your hair blowing around in the car, are you?"

"No."

"Think I maybe can't drive good?"

"How do I know?"

"You're a hard girl to handle. How come?" he said. "Don't you know I'm your friend? Didn't you see me put my sign in the air when you walked by?"

"What sign?"

"My sign." And he drew an X in the air, leaning out toward her. They were maybe ten feet apart. After his hand fell back to his side the X was still in the air, almost visible. Connie let the screen door close and stood perfectly still inside it, listening to the music from her radio and the boy's blend together. She stared at Arnold Friend. He stood there so stiffly relaxed, pretending to be relaxed, with one hand idly on the door handle as if he were keeping himself up that way and had no intention of ever moving again. She recognized most things about him, the tight jeans that showed his thighs and buttocks and the greasy leather boots and the tight shirt, and even that slippery friendly smile of his, that sleepy dreamy smile that all the boys used to get across ideas they didn't want to put into words. She recognized all this and also the singsong way he talked, slightly mocking, kidding, but serious and a little melancholy, and she recognized the way he tapped one fist against the other in homage to the perpetual music behind him. But all these things did not come together.

She said suddenly, "Hey, how old are you?"

His smile faded. She could see then that he wasn't a kid, he was much older—thirty, maybe more. At this knowledge her heart began to pound faster.

"That's a crazy thing to ask. Can'tcha see I'm your own age?"

"Like hell you are."

"Or maybe a coupla years older, I'm eighteen."

"Eighteen?" she said doubtfully.

He grinned to reassure her and lines appeared at the corners of his mouth. His teeth were big and white. He grinned so broadly his eyes became slits and she saw how thick the lashes were, thick and black as if painted with a black tarlike material. Then he seemed to become embarrassed, abruptly, and looked over his shoulder at Ellie. "*Him*, he's crazy," he said. "Ain't he a riot, he's a nut, a real character." Ellie was still listening to the music. His sunglasses told nothing about what he was thinking. He wore a bright orange shirt unbuttoned halfway to show his chest, which was a pale, bluish chest and not muscular like Arnold Friend's. His shirt collar was turned up all around and the very tips of the collar pointed out past his chin as if they were protecting him. He was pressing the transistor radio up against his ear and sat there in a kind of daze, right in the sun.

"He's kinda strange," Connie said.

"Hey, she says you're kinda strange! Kinda strange!" Arnold Friend cried. He pounded on the car to get Ellie's attention. Ellie turned for the first time and Connie saw with shock that he wasn't a kid either—he had a fair, hairless face, cheeks reddened slightly as if the veins grew too close to the surface of his skin, the face of a forty-year-old baby. Connie felt a wave of dizziness rise in her at this sight and she stared at him as if waiting for something to change the shock of the moment, make it all right again. Ellie's lips kept shaping words, mumbling along with the words blasting in his ear.

"Maybe you two better go away," Connie said faintly.

"What? How come?" Arnold Friend cried. "We come out here to take you for a ride. It's Sunday." He had the voice of the man on the radio now. It was the same voice, Connie thought. "Don'tcha know it's Sunday all day and honey, no matter who you were with last night today you're with Arnold Friend and don't you forget it!—Maybe you better step out here," he said, and this last was in a different voice. It was a little flatter, as if the heat was finally getting to him.

"No. I got things to do."

"Hey."

"You two better leave."

"We ain't leaving until you come with us."

"Like hell I am—"

"Connie, don't fool around with me. I mean, I mean, don't fool *around*," he said, shaking his head. He laughed incredulously. He placed his sunglasses on top of his head, carefully, as if he were indeed wearing a wig, and brought the stems down behind his ears. Connie stared at him, another wave of dizziness and fear rising in her so that for a moment he wasn't even in focus but was just a blur, standing there against his gold car, and she had the idea that he had driven up the driveway all right but had come from nowhere before that and belonged nowhere and that everything about him and even about the music that was so familiar to her was only half real.

"If my father comes and sees you—"

"He ain't coming. He's at a barbecue."

"How do you know that?"

"Aunt Tillie's. Right now they're—uh—they're drinking. Sitting around," he said vaguely, squinting as if he were staring all the way to town and over to Aunt Tillie's back yard. Then the vision seemed to get clear and he nodded energetically. "Yeah. Sitting around. There's your sister in a blue dress, huh? And high heels, the poor sad bitch—nothing like you, sweetheart! And your mother's helping some fat woman with the corn, they're cleaning the corn—husking the corn—"

"What fat woman?" Connie cried.

"How do I know what fat woman, I don't know every goddam fat woman in the world!" Arnold Friend laughed.

"Oh, that's Mrs. Hornby . . . Who invited her?" Connie said. She felt a little light-headed. Her breath was coming quickly.

"She's too fat. I don't like them fat. I like them the way you are, honey," he said, smiling sleepily at her. They stared at each other for a while, through the screen door. He said softly, "Now what you're going to do is this: you're going to come out that door. You're going to sit up front with me and Ellie's going to sit in the back, the hell with Ellie, right? This isn't Ellie's date. You're my date. I'm your lover, honey."

"What? You're crazy—"

"Yes, I'm your lover. You don't know what that is but you will," he said. "I know that too. I know all about you. But look: it's real nice and you couldn't ask for nobody better than me, or more polite. I always keep my word. I'll tell you how it is, I'm always nice at first, the first time. I'll hold you so tight you won't think you have to try to get away or pretend anything because you'll know you can't. And I'll come inside you where it's all secret and you'll give in to me and you'll love me—"

"Shut up! You're crazy!" Connie said. She backed away from the door. She put her hands against her ears as if she'd heard something terrible, something not meant for her. "People don't talk like that, you're crazy," she muttered. Her heart was almost too big now for her chest and its pumping made sweat break out all over her. She looked out to see Arnold Friend pause and then take a step toward the porch lurching. He almost fell. But, like a clever drunken man, he managed to catch his balance. He wobbled in his high boots and grabbed hold of one of the porch posts.

"Honey?" he said. "You still listening?"

"Get the hell out of here!"

"Be nice, honey. Listen."

"I'm going to call the police—"

He wobbled again and out of the side of his mouth came a fast spat curse, an aside not meant for her to hear. But even this "Christ!" sounded forced. Then he began to smile again. She watched this smile come, awkward as if he were smiling from inside a mask. His whole face was a mask, she thought wildly, tanned down onto his throat but then running out as if he had plastered makeup on his face but had forgotten about his throat.

"Honey—? Listen, here's how it is. I always tell the truth and I promise you this: I ain't coming in that house after you."

"You better not! I'm going to call the police if you—if you don't—"

"Honey," he said, talking right through her voice, "honey, I'm not coming in there but you are coming out here. You know why?"

She was panting. The kitchen looked like a place she had never seen before, some room she had run inside but which wasn't good enough, wasn't going to help her. The kitchen window had never had a curtain, after three years, and there were dishes in the sink for her to do—probably—and if you ran your hand across the table you'd probably feel something sticky there.

"You listening, honey? Hey?"

"—going to call the police—"

"Soon as you touch the phone I don't need to keep my promise and can come inside. You won't want that."

She rushed forward and tried to lock the door. Her fingers were shaking. "But why lock it," Arnold Friend said gently, talking right into her face. "It's just a screen door. It's just nothing." One of his boots was at a strange angle, as if his foot wasn't in it. It pointed out to the left, bent at the ankle. "I mean, anybody can break through a screen door and glass and wood and iron or anything else if he needs to, anybody at all and specially Arnold Friend. If the place got lit up with a fire honey you'd come runnin' out into my arms, right into my arms an' safe at home—like you knew I was your lover and'd stopped fooling around. I don't mind a nice shy girl but I don't like no fooling around." Part of those words were spoken with a slight rhythmic lilt, and Connie somehow recognized them—the echo of a song from last year, about a girl rushing into her boyfriend's arms and coming home again—

Connie stood barefoot on the linoleum floor, staring at him. "What do you want?" she whispered.

"I want you," he said.

"What?"

"Seen you that night and thought, that's the one, yes sir. I never needed to look any more."

"But my father's coming back. He's coming to get me. I had to wash my hair first—" She spoke in a dry, rapid voice, hardly raising it for him to hear.

"No, your Daddy is not coming and yes, you had to wash your hair and you washed it for me. It's nice and shining and all for me, I thank you, sweetheart," he said, with a mock bow, but again he almost lost his balance. He had to bend and adjust his boots. Evidently his feet did not go all the way down; the boots must have been stuffed with something so that he would seem taller. Connie stared out at him and behind him Ellie in the car, who seemed to be looking off toward Connie's right, into nothing. This Ellie said, pulling the words out of the air one after another as if he were just discovering them, "You want me to pull out the phone?"

"Shut your mouth and keep it shut," Arnold Friend said, his face red from bending over or maybe from embarrassment because Connie had seen his boots. "This ain't none of your business."

"What—what are you doing? What do you want?" Connie said. "If I call the police they'll get you, they'll arrest you—"

"Promise was not to come in unless you touch that phone, and I'll keep that promise," he said. He resumed his erect position and tried to force his shoulders back. He sounded like a hero in a movie, declaring something important. He spoke too loudly and it was as if he were speaking to someone behind Connie. "I ain't made plans for coming in that house where I don't belong but just for you to come out to me, the way you should. Don't you know who I am?"

"You're crazy," she whispered. She backed away from the door but did not want to go into another part of the house, as if this would give him permission to come through the door. "What do you . . . You're crazy, you . . ."

"Huh? What're you saying, honey?"

Her eyes darted everywhere in the kitchen. She could not remember what it was, this room.

"This is how it is, honey: you come out and we'll drive away, have a nice ride. But if you don't come out we're gonna wait till your people come home and then they're all going to get it."

"You want that telephone pulled out?" Ellie said. He held the radio away from his ear and grimaced, as if without the radio the air was too much for him.

"I toldja shut up, Ellie," Arnold Friend said, "you're deaf, get a hearing aid, right? Fix yourself up. This little girl's no trouble and's gonna be nice to me, so Ellie keep to yourself, this ain't your date—right? Don't hem in on me. Don't hog. Don't crush. Don't bird dog. Don't trail me," he said in a rapid meaningless voice, as if he were running through all the expressions he'd learned but was no longer sure which one of them was in style, then rushing on to new ones, making them up with his eyes closed, "Don't crawl under my fence, don't squeeze in my chipmunk hole, don't sniff my glue, suck my popsicle, keep your own greasy fingers on yourself!" He shaded his eyes and peered in at Connie, who was backed against the kitchen table. "Don't mind him honey he's just a creep. He's a dope. Right? I'm the boy for you and like I said you come out here nice like a lady and give me your hand, and nobody else gets hurt, I mean, your nice old bald-headed daddy and your mummy and your sister in her high heels. Because listen: why bring them in this?"

"Leave me alone," Connie whispered.

"Hey, you know that old woman down the road, the one with the chickens and stuff—you know her?"

"She's dead!"

"Dead? What? You know her?" Arnold Friend said.

"She's dead—"

"Don't you like her?"

"She's dead—she's—she isn't here any more—"

"But don't you like her, I mean, you got something against her? Some grudge or something?" Then his voice dipped as if he were conscious of a rudeness. He touched the sunglasses perched on top of his head as if to make sure they were still there. "Now you be a good girl."

"What are you going to do?"

"Just two things, or maybe three," Arnold Friend said. "But I promise it won't last long and you'll like me the way you get to like people you're close to. You will. It's all over for you here, so come on out. You don't want your people in any trouble, do you?"

She turned and bumped against a chair or something, hurting her leg, but she ran into the back room and picked up the telephone. Something roared in her ear, a tiny roaring, and she was so sick with fear that she could do nothing but listen to it—the telephone was clammy and very heavy and her fingers groped down to the dial but were too weak to touch it. She began to scream into the phone, into the roaring. She cried out, she cried for her mother, she felt her breath start jerking back and forth in her lungs as if it were something Arnold Friend were stabbing her with again and again with no tenderness. A noisy sorrowful wailing rose all about her and she was locked inside it the way she was locked inside this house.

After a while she could hear again. She was sitting on the floor with her wet back against the wall.

Arnold Friend was saying from the door, "That's a good girl. Put the phone back."

She kicked the phone away from her.

"No, honey. Pick it up. Put it back right."

She picked it up and put it back. The dial tone stopped.

"That's a good girl. Now you come outside."

She was hollow with what had been fear, but what was now just an emptiness. All that screaming had blasted it out of her. She sat, one leg cramped under her, and deep inside her brain was something like a pinpoint of light that kept going and would not let her relax. She thought, I'm not going to see my mother again. She thought, I'm not going to sleep in my bed again. Her bright green blouse was all wet.

Arnold Friend said, in a gentle-loud voice that was like a stage voice, "The place where you came from ain't there any more, and where you had in mind to go is canceled out. This place you are now—inside your daddy's house—is nothing but a cardboard box I can knock down any time. You know that and always did know it. You hear me?"

She thought, I have got to think. I have to know what to do.

"We'll go out to a nice field, out in the country here where it smells so nice and it's sunny," Arnold Friend said. "I'll have my arms tight around you so you won't need to try to get away and I'll show you what love is like, what it does. The hell with this house! It looks solid all right," he said. He ran a fingernail down the screen and the noise did not make Connie shiver, as it would have the day before. "Now put your hand on your heart, honey. Feel that? That feels solid too but we know better, be nice to me, be sweet like you can because what else is there for a girl like you but to be sweet and pretty and give in?—and get away before her people come back?"

She felt her pounding heart. Her hand seemed to enclose it. She thought for the first time in her life that it was nothing that was hers, that belonged to her, but just a pounding, living thing inside this body that wasn't really hers either.

"You don't want them to get hurt," Arnold Friend went on. "Now get up, honey. Get up all by yourself."

She stood.

"Now turn this way. That's right. Come over here to me—Ellie, put that away, didn't I tell you? You dope. You miserable creepy dope," Arnold

Friend said. His words were not angry but only part of an incantation. The incantation was kindly. "Now come out through the kitchen to me honey and let's see a smile, try it, you're a brave sweet little girl and now they're eating corn and hot dogs cooked to bursting over an outdoor fire, and they don't know one thing about you and never did and honey you're better than them because not a one of them would have done this for you."

Connie felt the linoleum under her feet; it was cool. She brushed her hair back out of her eyes. Arnold Friend let go of the post tentatively and opened his arms for her, his elbows pointing in toward each other and his wrists limp, to show that this was an embarrassed embrace and a little mocking, he didn't want to make her self-conscious.

She put out her hand against the screen. She watched herself push the door slowly open as if she were safe back somewhere in the other doorway, watching this body and this head of long hair moving out into the sunlight where Arnold Friend waited.

"My sweet little blue-eyed girl," he said, in a half-sung sigh that had nothing to do with her brown eyes but was taken up just the same by the vast sunlit reaches of the land behind him and on all sides of him, so much land that Connie had never seen before and did not recognize except to know that she was going to it.

Auggie Wren's Christmas Story

Paul Auster

I heard this story from Auggie Wren. Since Auggie doesn't come off too well in it, at least not as well as he'd like to, he's asked me not to use his real name. Other than that, the whole business about the lost wallet and the blind woman and the Christmas dinner is just as he told it to me.

Auggie and I have known each other for close to eleven years now. He works behind the counter of a cigar store on Court Street in downtown Brooklyn, and since it's the only store that carries the little Dutch cigars I like to smoke, I go in there fairly often. For a long time, I didn't give much thought to Auggie Wren. He was a strange little man who wore a hooded blue sweatshirt and sold me cigars and magazines, the impish, wisecracking character who always had something funny to say about the weather or the Mets or the politicians in Washington, and that was the extent of it.

But then one day several years ago he happened to be looking through a magazine in the store, and he stumbled across a review of one of my books. He knew it was me because a photograph accompanied the review, and after that things changed between us. I was no longer just another customer to Auggie, I had become a distinguished person. Most people couldn't care less about books and writers, but it turned out that Auggie considered himself an artist. Now that he had cracked the secret of who I was, he embraced me as an ally, a confidant, a brother-in-arms. To tell the truth, I found it rather embarrassing. Then, almost inevitably, a moment came when he asked if I would be willing to look at his photographs. Given his enthusiasm and goodwill, there didn't seem to be any way I could turn him down.

God knows what I was expecting. At the very least, it wasn't what Auggie showed me the next day. In a small, windowless room at the back of the store, he opened a cardboard box and pulled out twelve identical black photo albums. This was his life's work, he said, and it didn't take him more than five minutes a day to do it. Every morning for the past twelve years, he had stood at the corner of Atlantic Avenue and Clinton Street at precisely seven o'clock and had taken a single color photograph of precisely the same view. The project now ran to more than four thousand photographs. Each album represented a different year, and all the pictures were laid out in sequence, from January 1 to December 31, with the dates carefully recorded under each one.

As I flipped through the albums and began to study Auggie's work, I didn't know what to think. My first impression was that it was the oddest, most bewildering thing I had ever seen. All the pictures were the same. The whole project was a numbing onslaught of repetition, the same street and the same buildings over and over again, an unrelenting delirium of redundant images. I couldn't think of anything to say to Auggie, so I continued turning pages, nodding my head in feigned appreciation. Auggie himself seemed unperturbed, watching me with a broad smile on his face, but after I'd been at it for several minutes, he suddenly interrupted me and said, "You're going too fast. You'll never get it if you don't slow down."

He was right, of course. If you don't take the time to look, you'll never manage to see anything. I picked up another album and forced myself to go more deliberately. I paid closer attention to details, took note of shifts in the weather, watched for the changing angles of light as the seasons advanced. Eventually, I was able to detect subtle differences in the traffic flow, to anticipate the rhythm of different days (the commotion of workday mornings, the relative stillness of weekends, the contrast between Saturdays and Sundays). And then, little by little, I began to recognize the faces of the people in the background, the passers-by on their way to work, the same people in the same spot every morning, living an instant of their lives in the field of Auggie's camera.

Once I got to know them, I began to study their postures, the way they carried themselves from one morning to the next, trying to discover their moods from these surface indications, as if I could imagine stories for them, as if I could penetrate the invisible dramas locked inside their bodies. I picked up another album. I was no longer bored, no longer puzzled as I had been at first. Auggie was photographing time, I realized, both natural time and human time, and he was doing it by planting himself in one tiny corner of the world and willing it to be his own, by standing guard in the space he had chosen for himself. As he watched me pore over his work, Auggie continued to smile with pleasure. Then, almost as if he had been reading my thoughts, he began to recite a line from Shakespeare. "Tomorrow and tomorrow and tomorrow," he muttered under his breath, "time creeps on its petty pace." I understood then that he knew exactly what he was doing.

That was more than two thousand pictures ago. Since that day, Auggie and I have discussed his work many times, but it was only last week that I learned how he acquired his camera and started taking pictures in the first place. That was the subject of the story he told me, and I'm still struggling to make sense of it.

Earlier the same week, a man from the *New York Times* called me and asked if I would be willing to write a short story that would appear in the paper on Christmas morning. My first impulse was to say no, but the man was very charming and persistent, and by the end of the conversation I told him I would give it a try. The moment I hung up the phone, however, I fell into a deep panic. What did I know about Christmas? I asked myself. What did I know about writing short stories on commission?

I spent the next several days in despair, warring with the ghosts of Dickens, O. Henry and other masters of the Yuletide spirit. The very phrase "Christmas story" had unpleasant associations for me, evoking dreadful outpourings of hypocritical mush and treacle. Even at their best, Christmas stories were no more than wish-fulfillment dreams, fairy tales for adults, and I'd be damned if I'd ever allowed myself to write something like that. And yet, how could anyone propose to write an unsentimental Christmas story? It was a contradiction in terms, an impossibility, an out-and-out conundrum. One might just as well try to imagine a racehorse without legs, or a sparrow without wings.

I got nowhere. On Thursday I went out for a long walk, hoping the air would clear my head. Just past noon, I stopped in at the cigar store to replenish my supply, and there was Auggie, standing behind the counter as always. He asked me how I was. Without really meaning to, I found myself unburdening my troubles to him. "A Christmas story?" he said after I had finished. "Is that all? If you buy me lunch, my friend, I'll tell you the best Christmas story you ever heard. And I guarantee that every word of it is true."

We walked down the block to Jack's, a cramped and boisterous delicatessen with good pastrami sandwiches and photographs of old Dodgers teams hanging on the walls. We found a table at the back, ordered our food, and then Auggie launched into his story.

"It was the summer of seventy-two," he said. "A kid came in one morning and started stealing things from the store. He must have been about nineteen or twenty, and I didn't think I'd ever seen a more pathetic shoplifter in my life. He's standing by the rack of paperbacks along the far wall and stuffing books into the pockets of his raincoat. It was crowded around the counter just then, so I didn't see him at first. But once I noticed what he was up to, I started to shout. He took off like a jackrabbit, and by the time I managed to get out from behind the counter, he was already tearing down Atlantic Avenue. I chased after him for about half a block, and then I gave up. He'd dropped something along the way, and since I didn't feel like running anymore, I bent down to see what it was.

"It turned out to be his wallet. There wasn't any money inside, but his driver's license was there along with three or four snapshots. I suppose I could have called the cops and had him arrested. I had his name and address from the license, but I felt kind of sorry for him. He was a measly little punk, and once I looked at those pictures in his wallet, I couldn't bring myself to feel very angry at him. Robert Goodwin. That was his name. In one of the pictures, I remember, he was standing with his arms around his mother or grandmother. In another one, he was sitting there at age nine or ten dressed in a baseball uniform with a big smile on his face. I just didn't have the heart. He was probably on dope now, I figured. A poor kid from Brooklyn without much going for him, and who cared about a couple of trashy paperbacks anyway?

"So I held onto the wallet. Every once in awhile I'd get a little urge to send it back to him, but I kept delaying and never did anything about it. Then Christmas rolls around and I'm stuck with nothing to do. The boss usually invites me over to his house to spend the day, but that year he and his family were down in Florida visiting relatives. So I'm sitting in my apartment that morning feeling a little sorry for myself, and then I see Robert Goodwin's wallet lying on a shelf in the kitchen. I figure what the hell, why not do something nice for once, and I put on my coat and go out to return the wallet in person.

"The address was over in Boerum Hill, somewhere in the projects. It was freezing out that day, and I remember getting lost a few times trying to find the right building. Everything looks the same in that place, and you keep going over the same ground thinking you're somewhere else. Anyway, I finally get to the apartment I'm looking for and ring the bell. Nothing happens. I assume no one's there, but I try again just to make sure. I wait a little longer, and just when I'm about to give up, I hear someone shuffling to the door. An old woman's voice asks who's there, and I say I'm looking for Robert Goodwin. 'Is that you, Robert?' the old woman says, and then she undoes about fifteen locks and opens the door.

"She has to be at least eighty, maybe ninety years old, and the first thing I notice about her is that she's blind. 'I knew you'd come, Robert,' she says. 'I knew you wouldn't forget your Granny Ethel on Christmas.' And then she opens her arms as if she's about to hug me.

"I didn't have much time to think, you understand. I had to say something real fast, and before I knew what was happening, I could hear the words coming out of my mouth. 'That's right, Granny Ethel,' I said. 'I came back to see you on Christmas.' Don't ask me why I did it. I don't have any idea. Maybe I didn't want to disappoint her or something, I don't know. It just came out that way, and then this old woman was suddenly hugging me there in front of the door, and I was hugging her back.

"I didn't exactly say that I was her grandson. Not in so many words, at least, but that was the implication. I wasn't trying to trick her, though. It was like a game we'd both decided to play—without having to discuss the rules. I mean, that woman *knew* I wasn't her grandson Robert. She was old and dotty, but she wasn't so far gone that she couldn't tell the difference between a stranger and her own flesh and blood. But it made her happy to pretend, and since I had nothing better to do anyway, I was happy to go along with her.

"So we went into the apartment and spent the day together. The place was a real dump, I might add, but what else can you expect from a blind woman who does her own housekeeping? Every time she asked me a question about how I was, I would lie to her. I told her I'd found a good job working in a cigar store, I told her I was about to get married, I told her a hundred pretty stories, and she made like she believed every one of them. 'That's fine, Robert,' she would say, nodding her head and smiling. 'I always knew things would work out for you.'

"After a while, I started getting pretty hungry. There didn't seem to be much food in the house, so I went out to a store in the neighborhood and brought back a mess of stuff. A precooked chicken, vegetable soup, a bucket of potato salad, a chocolate cake, all kinds of things. Ethel had a couple of bottles of wine stashed in her bedroom, and so between us we managed to put together a fairly decent Christmas dinner. We both got a little tipsy from the wine, I remember, and after the meal was over we went out to sit in the living room, where the chairs were more comfortable. I had to take a pee, so I excused myself and went to the bathroom down the hall. That's where things took yet another turn. It was ditsy enough doing my little jig as Ethel's grandson, but what I did next was positively crazy, and I've never forgiven myself for it.

"I go into the bathroom, and stacked up against the wall next to the shower, I see a pile of six or seven cameras. Brand-new thirty-five-millimeter cameras, still in their boxes, top-quality merchandise. I figure this is the work of the real Robert, a storage place for one of his recent hauls. I've never taken a picture in my life, and I've certainly never stolen anything, but the moment I see those cameras sitting in the bathroom, I decide I want one of them for myself. Just like that. And without even stopping to think about it, I tuck one of the boxes under my arm and go back to the living room.

"I couldn't have been gone for more than a few minutes, but in that time Granny Ethel had fallen asleep in her chair. Too much Chianti, I suppose. I went into the kitchen to wash the dishes, and she slept through the whole racket, snoring like a baby. There didn't seem to be any point in disturbing her, so I decided to leave. I couldn't even write a note to say good-bye, seeing that she was blind and all, and so I just left. I put her grandson's wallet on the table, picked up the camera again, and walked out of the apartment. And that's the end of the story."

"Did you ever go back to see her?" I asked.

"Once," he said. "About three or four months later, I felt bad about stealing the camera. I hadn't even used it yet. I finally made up my mind to return it, but Ethel wasn't there anymore. I don't know what happened to her, but someone else had moved into the apartment, and he couldn't tell me where she was."

"She probably died."

"Yeah, probably."

"Which means that she spent her last Christmas with you."

"I guess so. I never thought of it that way."

"It was a good deed, Auggie. It was a nice thing you did for her."

"I lied to her, and then I stole from her. I don't see how you can call that a good deed."

"You made her happy. And the camera was stolen anyway. It's not as if the person you took it from really owned it."

"Anything for art, eh, Paul?"

"I wouldn't say that. But at least you've put the camera to good use."

"And now you've got your Christmas story, don't you?"

"Yes," I said. "I suppose I do."

I paused for a moment, studying Auggie as a wicked grin spread across his face. I couldn't be sure, but the look in his eyes at that moment was so mysterious, so fraught with the glow of some inner delight, that it suddenly occurred to me that he had made the whole thing up. I was about to ask him if he'd been putting me on, but then I realized he would never tell. I had been tricked into believing him, and that was the only thing that mattered. As long as there's one person to believe it, there's no story that can't be true.

"You're an ace, Auggie," I said. "Thanks for being so helpful."

"Any time," he answered, still looking at me with that maniacal light in his eyes. "After all, if you can't share your secrets with your friends, what kind of friend are you?"

"I guess I owe you one."

"No you don't. Just put it down the way I told it to you, and you don't owe me a thing."

"Except lunch."

"That's right. Except the lunch."

I returned Auggie's smile with a smile of my own, and then I called out to the waiter and asked for the check.

Emergency

Denis Johnson

I'd been working in the emergency room for about three weeks, I guess. This was in 1973, before the summer ended. With nothing to do on the overnight shift but batch the insurance reports from the daytime shifts, I just started wandering around, over to the coronary-care unit, down to the cafeteria, et cetera, looking for Georgie, the orderly, a pretty good friend of mine. He often stole pills from the cabinets.

He was running over the tiled floor of the operating room with a mop. "Are you still doing that?" I said.

"Jesus, there's a lot of blood here," he complained.

"Where?" The floor looked clean enough to me.

"What the hell were they doing in here?" he asked me.

"They were performing surgery, Georgie," I told him.

"There's so much goop inside of us, man," he said, "and it all wants to get out." He leaned his mop against a cabinet.

"What are you crying for?" I didn't understand.

He stood still, raised both arms slowly behind his head, and tightened his ponytail. Then he grabbed the mop and started making broad random arcs with it, trembling and weeping and moving all around the place really fast. "What am I *crying* for?" he said. "Jesus. Wow, oh boy, perfect."

I was hanging out in the E.R. with fat, quivering Nurse. One of the Family Service doctors that nobody liked came in looking for Georgie to wipe up after him. "Where's Georgie?" this guy asked.

"Georgie's in O.R.," Nurse said.

"Again?"

"No," Nurse said. "Still."

"Still? Doing what?"

"Cleaning the floor."

"Again?"

"No," Nurse said again. "Still."

Back in O.R., Georgie dropped his mop and bent over in the posture of a child soiling its diapers. He stared down with his mouth open in terror.

He said, "What am I going to do about these fucking *shoes*, man?"

"Whatever you stole," I said, "I guess you already ate it all, right?"

"Listen to how they squish," he said, walking around carefully on his heels.

"Let me check your pockets, man."

He stood still a minute, and I found his stash. I left him two of each, whatever they were. "Shift is about half over," I told him.

"Good. Because I really, really, really need a drink," he said. "Will you please help me get this blood mopped up?"

Around 3:30 A.M. a guy with a knife in his eye came in, led by Georgie.

"I hope *you* didn't do that to him," Nurse said.

"Me?" Georgie said. "No. He was like this."

"My wife did it," the man said. The blade was buried to the hilt in the outside corner of his left eye. It was a hunting knife kind of thing.

"Who brought you in?" Nurse said.

"Nobody. I just walked down. It's only three blocks," the man said.

Nurse peered at him. "We'd better get you lying down."

"Okay, I'm certainly ready for something like that," the man said.

She peered a bit longer into his face.

"Is your other eye," she said, "a glass eye?"

"It's plastic, or something artificial like that," he said.

"And you can see out of *this* eye?" she asked, meaning the wounded one.

"I can see. But I can't make a fist out of my left hand because this knife is doing something to my brain."

"My God," Nurse said.

"I guess I'd better get the doctor," I said.

"There you go," Nurse agreed.

They got him lying down, and Georgie says to the patient, "Name?"

"Terrence Weber."

"Your face is dark. I can't see what you're saying."

"Georgie," I said.

"What are you saying, man? I can't see."

Nurse came over, and Georgie said to her, "His face is dark."

She leaned over the patient. "How long ago did this happen, Terry?" she shouted down into his face.

"Just a while ago. My wife did it. I was asleep," the patient said.

"Do you want the police?"

He thought about it and finally said, "Not unless I die."

Nurse went to the wall intercom and buzzed the doctor on duty, the Family Service person. "Got a surprise for you," she said over the intercom. He took his time getting down the hall to her, because he knew she hated Family Service and her happy tone of voice could only mean something beyond his competence and potentially humiliating.

He peeked into the trauma room and saw the situation: the clerk—that is, me—standing next to the orderly, Georgie, both of us on drugs, looking down at a patient with a knife sticking up out of his face.

"What seems to be the trouble?" he said.

The doctor gathered the three of us around him in the office and said, "Here's the situation. We've got to get a team here, an entire team. I want a good eye man. A great eye man. The best eye man. I want a brain surgeon. And I want a really good gas man, get me a genius. I'm not touching that head. I'm just going to watch this one. I know my limits. We'll just get him prepped and sit tight. Orderly!"

"Do you mean me?" Georgie said. "Should I get him prepped?"

"Is this a hospital?" the doctor asked. "Is this the emergency room? Is that a patient? Are you the orderly?"

I dialled the hospital operator and told her to get me the eye man and the brain man and the gas man.

Georgie could be heard across the hall, washing his hands and singing a Neil Young song that went "Hello, cowgirl in the sand. Is this place at your command?"

"That person is not right, not at all, not one bit," the doctor said.

"As long as my instructions are audible to him it doesn't concern me," Nurse insisted, spooning stuff up out of a little Dixie cup. "I've got my own life and the protection of my family to think of."

"Well, okay, okay. Don't chew my head off," the doctor said.

The eye man was on vacation or something. While the hospital's operator called around to find someone else just as good, the other specialists were hurrying through the night to join us. I stood around looking at charts and chewing up more of Georgie's pills. Some of them tasted the way urine smells, some of them burned, some of them tasted like chalk. Various nurses, and two physicians who'd been tending somebody in I.C.U., were hanging out down here with us now.

Everybody had a different idea about exactly how to approach the problem of removing the knife from Terrence Weber's brain. But when Georgie came in from prepping the patient—from shaving the patient's eyebrow and disinfecting the area around the wound, and so on—he seemed to be holding the hunting knife in his left hand.

The talk just dropped off a cliff.

"Where," the doctor asked finally, "did you get that?"

Nobody said one thing more, not for quite a long time.

After a while, one of the I.C.U. nurses said, "Your shoelace is untied." Georgie laid the knife on a chart and bent down to fix his shoe.

There were twenty more minutes left to get through.

"How's the guy doing?" I asked.

"Who?" Georgie said.

It turned out that Terrence Weber still had excellent vision in the one good eye, and acceptable motor and reflex, despite his earlier motor complaint. "His vitals are normal," Nurse said. "There's nothing wrong with the guy. It's one of those things."

After a while you forget it's summer. You don't remember what the morning is. I'd worked two doubles with eight hours off in between, which I'd spent sleeping on a gurney in the nurse's station. Georgie's pills were making me feel like a giant helium-filled balloon, but I was wide awake. Georgie and I went out to the lot, to his orange pickup.

We lay down on a stretch of dusty plywood in the back of the truck with the daylight knocking against our eyelids and the fragrance of alfalfa thickening on our tongues.

"I want to go to church," Georgie said.

"Let's go to the county fair."

"I'd like to worship. I would."

"They have these injured hawks and eagles there. From the Humane Society," I said.

"I need a quiet chapel about now."

Georgie and I had a terrific time driving around. For a while the day was clear and peaceful. It was one of the moments you stay in, to hell with all the troubles of before and after. The sky is blue and the dead are coming back. Later in the afternoon, with sad resignation, the county fair bares its breasts. A champion of the drug LSD, a very famous guru of the love generation, is being interviewed amid a TV crew off to the left of the poultry cages. His eyeballs look like he bought them in a joke shop. It doesn't occur to me, as I pity this extraterrestrial, that in my life I've taken as much as he has.

After that, we got lost. We drove for hours, literally hours, but we couldn't find the road back to town.

Georgie started to complain. "That was the worst fair I've been to. Where were the rides?"

"They had rides," I said.

"I didn't see one ride."

A jackrabbit scurried out in front of us, and we hit it.

"There was a merry-go-round, a Ferris wheel, and a thing called the Hammer that people were bent over vomiting from after they got off," I said. "Are you completely blind?"

"What was that?"

"A rabbit."

"Something thumped."

"You hit him. *He* thumped."

Georgie stood on the brake pedal. "Rabbit stew."

He threw the truck in reverse and zigzagged back toward the rabbit. "Where's my hunting knife?" He almost ran over the poor animal a second time.

"We'll camp in the wilderness," he said. "In the morning we'll breakfast on its haunches." He was waving Terrence Weber's hunting knife around in what I was sure was a dangerous way.

In a minute he was standing at the edge of the fields, cutting the scrawny little thing up, tossing away its organs. "I should have been a doctor," he cried.

A family in a big Dodge, the only car we'd seen for a long time, slowed down and gawked out the windows as they passed by. The father said, "What is it, a snake?"

"No, it's not a snake," Georgie said. "It's a rabbit with babies inside it."

"Babies!" the mother said, and the father sped the car forward, over the protests of several little kids in the back.

Georgie came back to my side of the truck with his shirtfront stretched out in front of him as if he were carrying apples in it, or some such, but they were, in fact, slimy miniature bunnies. "No way I'm eating those things," I told him.

"Take them, take them. I gotta drive, take them," he said, dumping them in my lap and getting in on his side of the truck. He started driving along faster and faster, with a look of glory on his face. "We killed the mother and saved the children," he said.

"It's getting late," I said. "Let's get back to town."

"You bet." Sixty, seventy, eighty-five, just topping ninety.

"These rabbits better be kept warm." One at a time I slid the little things in between my shirt buttons and nestled them against my belly. "They're hardly moving," I told Georgie.

"We'll get some milk and sugar and all that, and we'll raise them up ourselves. They'll get as big as gorillas."

The road we were lost on cut straight through the middle of the world. It was still daytime, but the sun had no more power than an ornament or a sponge. In this light the truck's hood, which had been bright orange, had turned a deep blue.

Georgie let us drift to the shoulder of the road, slowly, slowly, as if he'd fallen asleep or given up trying to find his way.

"What is it?"

"We can't go on. I don't have any headlights," Georgie said.

We parked under a strange sky with a faint image of a quarter-moon superimposed on it.

There was a little woods beside us. This day had been dry and hot, the buck pines and whatall simmering patiently, but as we sat there smoking cigarettes it started to get very cold.

"The summer's over," I said.

That was the year when arctic clouds moved down over the Midwest and we had two weeks of winter in September.

"Do you realize it's going to snow?" Georgie asked me.

He was right, a gun-blue storm was shaping up. We got out and walked around idiotically. The beautiful chill! That sudden crispness, and the tang of evergreen stabbing us!

The gusts of snow twisted themselves around our heads while the night fell. I couldn't find the truck. We just kept getting more and more lost. I kept calling, "Georgie, can you see?" and he kept saying, "See what? See what?"

The only light visible was a streak of sunset flickering below the hem of the clouds. We headed that way.

We bumped softly down a hill toward an open field that seemed to be a military graveyard, filled with rows and rows of austere, identical markers over soldiers' graves. I'd never before come across this cemetery. On the farther side of the field, just beyond the curtains of snow, the sky was torn away and the angels were descending out of a brilliant blue summer, their huge faces streaked with light and full of pity. The sight of them cut through my heart and down the knuckles of my spine, and if there'd been anything in my bowels I would have messed my pants from fear.

Georgie opened his arms and cried out, "It's the drive-in, man!"

"The drive-in . . ." I wasn't sure what these words meant.

"They're showing movies in a fucking blizzard!" Georgie screamed.

"I see. I thought it was something else," I said.

We walked carefully down there and climbed through the busted fence and stood in the very back. The speakers, which I'd mistaken for grave markers, muttered in unison. Then there was tinkly music, of which I could very nearly make out the tune. Famous movie stars rode bicycles beside a river, laughing out of their gigantic, lovely mouths. If anybody had come to see this show, they'd left when the weather started. Not one car remained, not even a broken-down one from last week, or one left here because it was out of gas. In a couple of minutes, in the middle of a whirling square dance, the screen turned black, the cinematic summer ended, the snow went dark, there was nothing but my breath.

"I'm starting to get my eyes back," Georgie said in another minute.

A general grayness was giving birth to various shapes, it was true. "But which ones are close and which ones are far off?" I begged him to tell me.

By trial and error, with a lot of walking back and forth in wet shoes, we found the truck and sat inside it shivering.

"Let's get out of here," I said.

"We can't go anywhere without headlights."

"We've gotta get back. We're a long way from home."

"No, we're not."

"We must have come three hundred miles."

"We're right outside town, Fuckhead. We've just been driving around and around."

"This is no place to camp. I hear the Interstate over there."

"We'll just stay here till it gets late. We can drive home late. We'll be invisible."

We listened to the big rigs going from San Francisco to Pennsylvania along the Interstate, like shudders down a long hacksaw blade, while the snow buried us.

Eventually Georgie said, "We better get some milk for those bunnies."

"We don't have *milk*," I said.

"We'll mix sugar up with it."

"Will you forget about this milk all of a sudden?"

"They're mammals, man."

"Forget about those rabbits."

"Where are they, anyway?"

"You're not listening to me. I said, 'Forget the rabbits.' "

"Where are they?"

The truth was I'd forgotten all about them, and they were dead.

"They slid around behind me and got squashed," I said tearfully.

"They slid around *behind*?"

He watched while I pried them out from behind my back.

I picked them out one at a time and held them in my hands and we looked at them. There were eight. They weren't any bigger than my fingers, but everything was there.

Little feet! Eyelids! Even whiskers! "Deceased," I said.

Georgie asked, "Does everything you touch turn to shit? Does this happen to you every time?"

"No wonder they call me Fuckhead."

"It's a name that's going to stick."

"I realize that."

" 'Fuckhead' is gonna ride you to your grave."

"I just said so. I agreed with you in advance," I said.

Or maybe that wasn't the time it snowed. Maybe it was the time we slept in the truck and I rolled over on the bunnies and flattened them. It doesn't matter. What's important for me to remember now is that early the next morning the snow was melted off the windshield and the daylight woke me up. A mist covered everything and, with the sunshine, was beginning to grow sharp and strange. The bunnies weren't a problem yet, or they'd already been a problem and were already forgotten, and there was nothing on my mind. I felt the beauty of the morning. I could understand how a drowning man might suddenly feel a deep thirst being quenched. Or how the slave might become a friend to his master. Georgie slept with his face right on the steering wheel.

I saw bits of snow resembling an abundance of blossoms on the stems of the drive-in speakers—no, revealing the blossoms that were always there. A bull elk stood still in the pasture beyond the fence, giving off an air of authority and stupidity. And a coyote jogged across the pasture and faded away among the saplings.

That afternoon we got back to work in time to resume everything as if it had never stopped happening and we'd never been anywhere else.

"The Lord," the intercom said, "is my shepherd." It did that each evening because this was a Catholic hospital. "Our Father, who art in Heaven," and so on.

"Yeah, yeah," Nurse said.

The man with the knife in his head, Terrence Weber, was released around suppertime. They'd kept him overnight and given him an eye-patch—all for no reason, really.

He stopped off at E.R. to say goodbye. "Well, those pills they gave me make everything taste terrible," he said.

"It could have been worse," Nurse said.

"Even my tongue."

"It's just a miracle you didn't end up sightless or at least dead," she reminded him.

The patient recognized me. He acknowledged me with a smile. "I was peeping on the lady next door while she was out there sunbathing," he said. "My wife decided to blind me."

He shook Georgie's hand. Georgie didn't know him. "Who are you supposed to be?" he asked Terrence Weber.

Some hours before that, Georgie had said something that had suddenly and completely explained the difference between us. We'd been driving back toward town, along the Old Highway, through the flatness. We picked up a hitchhiker, a boy I knew. We stopped the truck and the boy climbed slowly up out of the fields as out of the mouth of a volcano. His name was Hardee. He looked even worse than we probably did.

"We got messed up and slept in the truck all night," I told Hardee.

"I had a feeling," Hardee said. "Either that or, you know, driving a thousand miles."

"That too," I said.

"Or you're sick or diseased or something."

"Who's this guy?" Georgie asked.

"This is Hardee. He lived with me last summer. I found him on the doorstep. What happened to your dog?" I asked Hardee.

"He's still down there."

"Yeah, I heard you went to Texas."

"I was working on a bee farm," Hardee said.

"Wow. Do those things sting you?"

"Not like you'd think," Hardee said. "You're part of their daily drill. It's all part of a harmony."

Outside, the same identical stretch of grass repeatedly rolled past our faces. The day was cloudless, blinding. But Georgie said, "Look at that," pointing straight ahead of us.

One star was so hot it showed, bright and blue in the empty sky.

"I recognized you right away," I told Hardee. "But what happened to your hair? Who chopped it off?"

"I hate to say."

"Don't tell me."

"They drafted me."

"Oh no."

"Oh yeah. I'm AWOL. I'm bad AWOL. I got to get to Canada."

"Oh, that's terrible," I said to Hardee.

"Don't worry," Georgie said. "We'll get you there."

"How?"

"Somehow. I think I know some people. Don't worry. You're on your way to Canada."

That world! These days it's all been erased and they've rolled it up like a scroll and put it away somewhere. Yes, I can touch it with my fingers. But where is it?

After a while Hardee asked Georgie, "What do you do for a job," and Georgie said, "I save lives."

Killings

Andre Dubus

On the August morning when Matt Fowler buried his youngest son, Frank, who had lived for twenty-one years, eight months, and four days, Matt's older son, Steve, turned to him as the family left the grave and walked between their friends, and said: "I should kill him." He was twenty-eight, his brown hair starting to thin in front where he used to have a cowlick. He bit his lower lip, wiped his eyes, then said it again. Ruth's arm, linked with Matt's, tightened; he looked at her. Beneath her eyes there was swelling from the three days she had suffered. At the limousine Matt stopped and looked back at the grave, the casket, and the Congregationalist minister who he thought had probably had a difficult job with the eulogy though he hadn't seemed to, and the old funeral director who was saying something to the six young pallbearers. The grave was on a hill and overlooked the Merrimack, which he could not see from where he stood; he looked at the opposite bank, at the apple orchard with its symmetrically planted trees going up a hill.

Next day Steve drove with his wife back to Baltimore where he managed the branch office of a bank, and Cathleen, the middle child, drove with her husband back to Syracuse. They had left the grandchildren with friends. A month after the funeral Matt played poker at Willis Trottier's because Ruth, who knew this was the second time he had been invited, told him to go, he couldn't sit home with her for the rest of her life, she was all right. After the game Willis went outside to tell everyone goodnight and, when the others had driven away, he walked with Matt to his car. Willis was a short, silver-haired man who had opened a diner after World War II, his trade then mostly very early breakfast, which he cooked, and then lunch for the men who worked at the leather and shoe factories. He now owned a large restaurant.

"He walks the Goddamn streets," Matt said.

"I know. He was in my place last night, at the bar. With a girl."

"I don't see him. I'm in the store all the time. Ruth sees him. She sees him too much. She was at Sunnyhurst today getting cigarettes and aspirin, and there he was. She can't even go out for cigarettes and aspirin. It's killing her."

"Come back in for a drink."

Matt looked at his watch. Ruth would be asleep. He walked with Willis back into the house, pausing at the steps to look at the starlit sky. It was a cool summer night; he thought vaguely of the Red Sox, did not even know if they were at home tonight; since it happened he had not been able to think about any of the small pleasures he believed he had earned, as he had earned also what was shattered now forever: the quietly harried and quietly pleasurable days of fatherhood. They went inside. Willis's wife, Martha, had gone to bed hours ago, in the rear of the large house which was rigged with burglar and fire alarms. They went downstairs to the game room: the television set suspended from the ceiling, the pool table, the poker table with beer cans, cards, chips, filled ashtrays, and the six chairs where Matt and his friends had sat, the friends picking up the old banter as though he had only been away on vacation; but he could see the affection and courtesy in their eyes. Willis went behind the bar and mixed them each a Scotch and soda; he stayed behind the bar and looked at Matt sitting on the stool.

"How often have you thought about it?" Willis said.

"Every day since he got out. I didn't think about bail. I thought I wouldn't have to worry about him for years. She sees him all the time. It makes her cry."

"He was in my place a long time last night. He'll be back."

"Maybe he won't."

"The band. He likes the band."

"What's he doing now?"

"He's tending bar up to Hampton Beach. For a friend. Ever notice even the worst bastard always has friends? He couldn't get work in town. It's just tourists and kids up to Hampton. Nobody knows him. If they do, they don't care. They drink what he mixes."

"Nobody tells me about him."

"I hate him, Matt. My boys went to school with him. He was the same then. Know what he'll do? Five at the most. Remember that woman about seven years ago? Shot her husband and dropped him off the bridge in the Merrimack with a hundred pound sack of cement and said all the way through it that nobody helped her. Know where she is now? She's in Lawrence now, a secretary. And whoever helped her, where the hell is he?"

"I've got a .38 I've had for years. I take it to the store now. I tell Ruth it's for the night deposits. I tell her things have changed: we got junkies here now too. Lots of people without jobs. She knows though."

"What does she know?"

"She knows I started carrying it after the first time she saw him in town. She knows it's in case I see him, and there's some kind of a situation—"

He stopped, looked at Willis, and finished his drink. Willis mixed him another.

"What kind of a situation?"

"Where he did something to me. Where I could get away with it."

"How does Ruth feel about that?"

"She doesn't know."

"You said she does, she's got it figured out."

He thought of her that afternoon: when she went into Sunnyhurst, Strout was waiting at the counter while the clerk bagged the things he had bought; she turned down an aisle and looked at soup cans until he left.

"Ruth would shoot him herself, if she thought she could hit him."

"You got a permit?"

"No."

"I do. You could get a year for that."

"Maybe I'll get one. Or maybe I won't. Maybe I'll just stop bringing it to the store."

Richard Strout was twenty-six years old, a high school athlete, football scholarship to the University of Massachusetts where he lasted for almost two semesters before quitting in advance of the final grades that would have forced him not to return. People then said: Dickie can do the work; he just doesn't want to. He came home and did construction work for his father but refused his father's offer to learn the business; his two older brothers had learned it, so that Strout and Sons trucks going about town, and signs on construction sites, now slashed wounds into Matt Fowler's life. Then Richard married a young girl and became a bartender, his salary and tips augmented and perhaps sometimes matched by his father, who also posted his bond. So his friends, his enemies (he had those: fist fights or, more often, boys and then young men who had not fought him when they thought they should have), and those who simply knew him by face and name, had a series of images of him which they recalled when they heard of the killing: the high school running back, the young drunk in bars, the oblivious hard-hatted young man eating lunch at a counter, the bartender who could perhaps be called courteous but not more than that: as he tended bar, his dark eyes and dark, wide-jawed face appeared less sullen, near blank.

One night he beat Frank. Frank was living at home and waiting for

September, for graduate school in economics, and working as a lifeguard at Salisbury Beach, where he met Mary Ann Strout, in her first month of separation. She spent most days at the beach with her two sons. Before ten o'clock one night Frank came home; he had driven to the hospital first, and he walked into the living room with stitches over his right eye and both lips bright and swollen.

"I'm all right," he said, when Matt and Ruth stood up, and Matt turned off the television, letting Ruth get to him first: the tall, muscled but slender suntanned boy. Frank tried to smile at them but couldn't because of his lips.

"It was her husband, wasn't it?" Ruth said.

"Ex," Frank said. "He dropped in."

Matt gently held Frank's jaw and turned his face to the light, looked at the stitches, the blood under the white of the eye, the bruised flesh.

"Press charges," Matt said.

"No."

"What's to stop him from doing it again? Did you hit him at all? Enough so he won't want to next time?"

"I don't think I touched him."

"So what are you going to do?"

"Take karate," Frank said, and tried again to smile.

"That's not the problem," Ruth said.

"You know you like her," Frank said.

"I like a lot of people. What about the boys? Did they see it?"

"They were asleep."

"Did you leave her alone with him?"

"He left first. She was yelling at him. I believe she had a skillet in her hand."

"Oh for God's sake," Ruth said.

Matt had been dealing with that too: at the dinner table on evenings when Frank wasn't home, was eating with Mary Ann; or, on the other nights—and Frank was with her every night—he talked with Ruth while they watched television, or lay in bed with the windows open and he smelled the night air and imagined, with both pride and muted sorrow, Frank in Mary Ann's arms. Ruth didn't like it because Mary Ann was in the process of divorce, because she had two children, because she was four years older than Frank, and finally—she told this in bed, where she had during all of their marriage told him of her deepest feelings: of love, of passion, of fears about one of the children, of pain Matt had caused her or she had caused him—she was against it because of what she had heard: that the marriage had gone bad early, and for most of it Richard and Mary Ann had both played around.

"That can't be true," Matt said. "Strout wouldn't have stood for it."

"Maybe he loves her."

"He's too hot-tempered. He couldn't have taken that."

But Matt knew Strout had taken it, for he had heard the stories too. He wondered who had told them to Ruth; and he felt vaguely annoyed and isolated: living with her for thirty-one years and still not knowing what she talked about with her friends. On these summer nights he did not so much argue with her as try to comfort her, but finally there was no difference between the two: she had concrete objections, which he tried to overcome. And in his attempt to do this, he neglected his own objections, which were the same as hers, so that as he spoke to her he felt as disembodied as he sometimes did in the store when he helped a man choose a blouse or dress or piece of costume jewelry for his wife.

"The divorce doesn't mean anything," he said. "She was young and maybe she liked his looks and then after a while she realized she was living with a bastard. I see it as a positive thing."

"She's not divorced yet."

"It's the same thing. Massachusetts has crazy laws, that's all. Her age is no problem. What's it matter when she was born? And that other business: even if it's true, which it probably isn't, it's got nothing to do with Frank, it's in the past. And the kids are no problem. She's been married six years; she ought to have kids. Frank likes them. He plays with them. And he's not going to marry her anyway, so it's not a problem of money."

"Then what's he doing with her?"

"She probably loves him, Ruth. Girls always have. Why can't we just leave it at that?"

"He got home at six o'clock Tuesday morning."

"I didn't know you knew. I've already talked to him about it."

Which he had: since he believed almost nothing he told Ruth, he went to Frank with what he believed. The night before, he had followed Frank to the car after dinner.

"You wouldn't make much of a burglar," he said.

"How's that?"

Matt was looking up at him; Frank was six feet tall, an inch and a half taller than Matt, who had been proud when Frank at seventeen outgrew him; he had only felt uncomfortable when he had to reprimand or caution him. He touched Frank's bicep, thought of the young taut passionate body, believed he could sense the desire, and again he felt the pride and sorrow and envy too, not knowing whether he was envious of Frank or Mary Ann.

"When you came in yesterday morning, I woke up. One of these mornings your mother will. And I'm the one who'll have to talk to her. She won't interfere with you. Okay? I know it means—" But he stopped, thinking: I know it means getting up and leaving that suntanned girl and going sleepy to the car, I know—

"Okay," Frank said, and touched Matt's shoulder and got into the car.

There had been other talks, but the only long one was their first one: a night driving to Fenway Park, Matt having ordered the tickets so they could talk, and knowing when Frank said yes, he would go, that he knew the talk was coming too. It took them forty minutes to get to Boston, and they talked about Mary Ann until they joined the city traffic along the Charles River, blue in the late sun. Frank told him all the things that Matt would later pretend to believe when he told them to Ruth.

"It seems like a lot for a young guy to take on," Matt finally said.

"Sometimes it is. But she's worth it."

"Are you thinking about getting married?"

"We haven't talked about it. She can't for over a year. I've got school."

"I *do* like her," Matt said.

He did. Some evenings, when the long summer sun was still low in the sky, Frank brought her home; they came into the house smelling of suntan lotion and the sea, and Matt gave them gin and tonics and started the charcoal in the backyard, and looked at Mary Ann in the lawn chair: long and very light brown hair (Matt thinking that twenty years ago she would have dyed it blond), and the long brown legs he loved to look at; her face was pretty; she had probably never in her adult life gone unnoticed into a public place. It was in her wide brown eyes that she looked older than Frank; after a few drinks Matt thought what he saw in her eyes was something erotic, testament to the rumors about her; but he knew it wasn't that, or all that: she had, very young, been through a sort of pain that his children, and he and Ruth, had been spared. In the moments of his recognizing that pain, he wanted to tenderly touch her hair, wanted with some gesture to give her solace and hope. And he would glance at Frank, and hope they would love each other, hope Frank would soothe that pain in her heart, take it from her eyes; and her divorce, her age, and her children did not matter at all. On the first two evenings she did not bring her boys, and then Ruth asked her to bring them next time. In bed that night Ruth said, "She hasn't brought them because she's embarrassed. She shouldn't feel embarrassed."

Richard Strout shot Frank in front of the boys. They were sitting on the living room floor watching television, Frank sitting on the couch, and Mary Ann just returning from the kitchen with a tray of sandwiches. Strout came in the front door and shot Frank twice in the chest and once in the face with a 9 mm. automatic. Then he looked at the boys and Mary Ann, and went home to wait for the police.

It seemed to Matt that from the time Mary Ann called weeping to tell him until now, a Saturday night in September, sitting in the car with Willis, parked beside Strout's car, waiting for the bar to close, that he had not so much moved through his life as wandered through it, his spirit like a dazed body bumping into furniture and corners. He had always been a fearful father: when his children were young, at the start of each summer he thought of them drowning in a pond or the sea, and he was relieved when he came home in the evenings and they were there; usually that relief was his only acknowledgment of his fear, which he never spoke of, and which he controlled within his heart. As he had when they were very young and all of them in turn, Cathleen too, were drawn to the high oak in the backyard, and had to climb it. Smiling, he watched them, imagining the fall: and he was poised to catch the small body before it hit the earth. Or his legs were poised; his hands were in his pockets or his arms were folded and, for the child looking down, he appeared relaxed and confident while his heart beat with the two words he wanted to call out but did not: *Don't fall.* In winter he was less afraid: he made sure the ice would hold him before they skated, and he brought or sent them to places where they could sled without ending in the street. So he and his children had survived their childhood, and he only worried about them when he knew they were driving a long distance, and then he lost Frank in a way no father expected to lose his son, and he felt that all the fears he had borne while they were growing up, and all the grief he had been afraid of, had backed up like a huge wave and struck him on the beach and swept him out to sea. Each day he felt the same and when he was able to forget how he felt, when he was able to force himself not to feel that way, the eyes of his clerks and customers defeated him. He wished those eyes were oblivious, even cold; he felt he was withering in their tenderness. And beneath his listless wandering, every day in his soul he shot Richard Strout in the face; while Ruth, going about town on errands, kept seeing him. And at nights in bed she would hold Matt and cry, or sometimes she was silent and Matt would touch her tightening arm, her clenched fist.

As his own right fist was now, squeezing the butt of the revolver, the last of the drinkers having left the bar, talking to each other, going to their separate cars which were in the lot in front of the bar, out of Matt's vision. He heard their voices, their cars, and then the ocean again, across the street. The tide was in and sometimes it smacked the sea wall. Through the windshield he looked at the dark red side wall of the bar, and then to his left, past Willis, at Strout's car, and through its windows he could see the now-emptied parking lot, the road, the sea wall. He could smell the sea.

The front door of the bar opened and closed again and Willis looked at Matt then at the corner of the building; when Strout came around it alone

Matt got out of the car, giving up the hope he had kept all night (and for the past week) that Strout would come out with friends, and Willis would simply drive away; thinking: *All right then. All right;* and he went around the front of Willis's car, and at Strout's he stopped and aimed over the hood at Strout's blue shirt ten feet away. Willis was aiming too, crouched on Matt's left, his elbow resting on the hood.

"Mr. Fowler," Strout said. He looked at each of them, and at the guns. "Mr. Trottier."

Then Matt, watching the parking lot and the road, walked quickly between the car and the building and stood behind Strout. He took one leather glove from his pocket and put it on his left hand.

"Don't talk. Unlock the front and back and get in."

Strout unlocked the front door, reached in and unlocked the back, then got in, and Matt slid into the back seat, closed the door with his gloved hand, and touched Strout's head once with the muzzle.

"It's cocked. Drive to your house."

When Strout looked over his shoulder to back the car, Matt aimed at his temple and did not look at his eyes.

"Drive slowly," he said. "Don't try to get stopped."

They drove across the empty front lot and onto the road, Willis's headlights shining into the car; then back through town, the sea wall on the left hiding the beach, though far out Matt could see the ocean; he uncocked the revolver; on the right were the places, most with their neon signs off, that did so much business in summer: the lounges and cafés and pizza houses, the street itself empty of traffic, the way he and Willis had known it would be when they decided to take Strout at the bar rather than knock on his door at two o'clock one morning and risk that one insomniac neighbor. Matt had not told Willis he was afraid he could not be alone with Strout for very long, smell his smells, feel the presence of his flesh, hear his voice, and then shoot him. They left the beach town and then were on the high bridge over the channel: to the left the smacking curling white at the breakwater and beyond that the dark sea and the full moon, and down to his right the small fishing boats bobbing at anchor in the cove. When they left the bridge, the sea was blocked by abandoned beach cottages, and Matt's left hand was sweating in the glove. Out here in the dark in the car he believed Ruth knew. Willis had come to his house at eleven and asked if he wanted a nightcap; Matt went to the bedroom for his wallet, put the gloves in one trouser pocket and the .38 in the other and went back to the living room, his hand in his pocket covering the bulge of the cool cylinder pressed against his fingers, the butt against his palm. When Ruth said goodnight she looked at his face, and he felt she could see in his eyes the gun, and the night he was going to. But he knew he couldn't trust what he saw. Willis's wife had taken her sleeping pill, which gave her eight hours—the reason, Willis had told Matt, he had the alarms installed, for nights when he was late at the restaurant—and when it was all done and Willis got home he would leave ice and a trace of Scotch and soda in two glasses in the game room and tell Martha in the morning that he had left the restaurant early and brought Matt home for a drink.

"He was making it with my wife." Strout's voice was careful, not pleading.

Matt pressed the muzzle against Strout's head, pressed it harder than he wanted to, feeling through the gun Strout's head flinching and moving forward; then he lowered the gun to his lap.

"Don't talk," he said.

Strout did not speak again. They turned west, drove past the Dairy Queen closed until spring, and the two lobster restaurants that faced each other and were crowded all summer and were now also closed, onto the short bridge crossing the tidal stream, and over the engine Matt could hear through his open window the water rushing inland under the bridge; looking to his left he saw its swift moonlit current going back into the marsh which, leaving the bridge, they entered: the salt marsh stretching out on both sides, the grass tall in patches but mostly low and leaning earthward as though windblown, a large dark rock sitting as though it rested on nothing but itself, and shallow pools reflecting the bright moon.

Beyond the marsh they drove through woods, Matt thinking now of the hole he and Willis had dug last Sunday afternoon after telling their wives they were going to Fenway Park. They listened to the game on a transistor radio, but heard none of it as they dug into the soft earth on the knoll they had chosen because elms and maples sheltered it. Already some leaves had fallen. When the hole was deep enough they covered it and the piled earth with dead branches, then cleaned their shoes and pants and went to a restaurant farther up in New Hampshire where they ate sandwiches and drank beer and watched the rest of the game on television. Looking at the back of Strout's head he thought of Frank's grave; he had not been back to it; but he would go before winter, and its second burial of snow.

He thought of Frank sitting on the couch and perhaps talking to the children as they watched television, imagined him feeling young and strong, still warmed from the sun at the beach, and feeling loved, hearing Mary Ann moving about in the kitchen, hearing her walking into the living room; maybe he looked up at her and maybe she said something, looking at him over the tray of sandwiches, smiling at him, saying something the way women do when they offer food as a gift, then the front door opening and this son of a bitch coming in and Frank seeing that he meant the gun in his hand, this son of a bitch and his gun the last person and thing Frank saw on earth.

When they drove into town the streets were nearly empty: a few slow cars, a policeman walking his beat past the darkened fronts of stores. Strout and Matt both glanced at him as they drove by. They were on the main street, and all the stoplights were blinking yellow. Willis and Matt had talked about that too: the lights changed at midnight, so there would be no place Strout had to stop and where he might try to run. Strout turned down the block where he lived and Willis's headlights were no longer with Matt in the back seat. They had planned that too, had decided it was best for just the one car to go to the house, and again Matt had said nothing about his fear of being alone with Strout, especially in his house: a duplex, dark as all the houses on the street were, the street itself lit at the corner of each block. As Strout turned into the driveway Matt thought of the one insomniac neighbor, thought of some man or woman sitting alone in the dark living room, watching the all-night channel from Boston. When Strout stopped the car near the front of the house, Matt said: "Drive it to the back."

He touched Strout's head with the muzzle.

"You wouldn't have it cocked, would you? For when I put on the brakes."

Matt cocked it, and said: "It is now."

Strout waited a moment; then he eased the car forward, the engine doing little more than idling, and as they approached the garage he gently braked. Matt opened the door, then took off the glove and put it in his pocket. He stepped out and shut the door with his hip and said: "All right."

Strout looked at the gun, then got out, and Matt followed him across the grass, and as Strout unlocked the door Matt looked quickly at the row of small backyards on either side, and scattered tall trees, some evergreens, others not, and he thought of the red and yellow leaves on the trees over the hole, saw them falling soon, probably in two weeks, dropping slowly, covering. Strout stepped into the kitchen.

"Turn on the light."

Strout reached to the wall switch, and in the light Matt looked at his wide back, the dark blue shirt, the white belt, the red plaid pants.

"Where's your suitcase?"

"My suitcase?"

"Where is it?"

"In the bedroom closet."

"That's where we're going then. When we get to a door you stop and turn on the light."

They crossed the kitchen, Matt glancing at the sink and stove and refrigerator: no dishes in the sink or even the dish rack beside it, no grease splashings on the stove, the refrigrator door clean and white. He did not want to look at any more but he looked quickly at all he could see: in the living room magazines and newspapers in a wicker basket, clean ashtrays, a record player, the records shelved next to it, then down the hall where, near the bedroom door, hung a color photograph of Mary Ann and the two boys sitting on a lawn—there was no house in the picture—Mary Ann smiling at the camera or Strout or whoever held the camera, smiling as she had on Matt's lawn this summer while he waited for the charcoal and they all talked and he looked at her brown legs and at Frank touching her arm, her shoulder, her hair; he moved down the hall with her smile in his mind, wondering: was that when they were both playing around and she was smiling like that at him and they were happy, even sometimes, making it worth it? He recalled her eyes, the pain in them, and he was conscious of the circles of love he was touching with the hand that held the revolver so tightly now as Strout stopped at the door at the end of the hall.

"There's no wall switch."

"Where's the light?"

"By the bed."

"Let's go."

Matt stayed a pace behind, then Strout leaned over and the room was lighted: the bed, a double one, was neatly made; the ashtray on the bedside table clean, the bureau top dustless, and no photographs; probably so the girl—who *was* she?—would not have to see Mary Ann in the bedroom she believed was theirs. But because Matt was a father and a husband, though never an ex-husband, he knew (and did not want to know) that this bedroom had never been theirs alone. Strout turned around; Matt looked at his lips, his wide jaw, and thought of Frank's doomed and fearful eyes looking up from the couch.

"Where's Mr. Trottier?"

"He's waiting. Pack clothes for warm weather."

"What's going on?"

"You're jumping bail."

"Mr. Fowler—"

He pointed the cocked revolver at Strout's face. The barrel trembled but not much, not as much as he had expected. Strout went to the closet and got the suitcase from the floor and opened it on the bed. As he went to the bureau, he said: "He was making it with my wife. I'd go pick up my kids and he'd be there. Sometimes he spent the night. My boys told me."

He did not look at Matt as he spoke. He opened the top drawer and Matt stepped closer so he could see Strout's hands: underwear and socks, the socks rolled, the underwear folded and stacked. He took them back to the bed, arranged them neatly in the suitcase, then from the closet he was taking shirts and trousers and a jacket; he laid them on the bed and Matt followed him to the bathroom and watched from the door while he packed his shaving kit; watched in the bedroom as he folded and packed those things a person accumulated and that became part of him so that at times in the store Matt felt he was selling more than clothes.

"I wanted to try to get together with her again." He was bent over the suitcase. "I couldn't even talk to her. He was always with her. I'm going to jail for it; if I ever get out I'll be an old man. Isn't that enough?"

"You're not going to jail."

Strout closed the suitcase and faced Matt, looking at the gun. Matt went to his rear, so Strout was between him and the lighted hall; then using his handkerchief he turned off the lamp and said: "Let's go."

They went down the hall, Matt looking again at the photograph, and through the living room and kitchen, Matt turning off the lights and talking, frightened that he was talking, that he was telling this lie he had not planned: "It's the trial. We can't go through that, my wife and me. So you're leaving. We've got you a ticket, and a job. A friend of Mr. Trottier's. Out west. My wife keeps seeing you. We can't have that anymore."

Matt turned out the kitchen light and put the handkerchief in his pocket, and they went down the two brick steps and across the lawn. Strout put the suitcase on the floor of the back seat, then got into the front seat and Matt got in the back and put on his glove and shut the door.

"They'll catch me. They'll check passenger lists."

"We didn't use your name."

"They'll figure that out too. You think I wouldn't have done it myself if it was that easy?"

He backed into the street, Matt looking down the gun barrel but not at the profiled face beyond it.

"You were alone," Matt said. "We've got it worked out."

"There's no planes this time of night, Mr. Fowler."

"Go back through town. Then north on 125."

They came to the corner and turned, and now Willis's headlights were in the car with Matt.

"Why north, Mr. Fowler?"

"Somebody's going to keep you for a while. They'll take you to the airport." He uncocked the hammer and lowered the revolver to his lap and said wearily: "No more talking."

As they drove back through town, Matt's body sagged, going limp with his spirit and its new and false bond with Strout, the hope his lie had given Strout. He had grown up in this town whose streets had become places of apprehension and pain for Ruth as she drove and walked, doing what she had to do; and for him too, if only in his mind as he worked and chatted six days a week in his store; he wondered now if his lie would have worked, if sending Strout away would have been enough; but then he knew that just thinking of Strout in Montana or whatever place lay at the end of the lie he had told, thinking of him walking the streets there, loving a girl there (who *was* she?) would be enough to slowly rot the rest of his days. And Ruth's. Again he was certain that she knew, that she was waiting for him.

They were in New Hampshire now, on the narrow highway, passing the shopping center at the state line, and then houses and small stores and sandwich shops. There were few cars on the road. After ten minutes he raised his trembling hand, touched Strout's neck with the gun, and said: "Turn in up here. At the dirt road."

Strout flicked on the indicator and slowed.

"Mr. Fowler?"

"They're waiting here."

Strout turned very slowly, easing his neck away from the gun. In the moonlight the road was light brown, lighter and yellowed where the headlights shone; weeds and a few trees grew on either side of it, and ahead of them were the woods.

"There's nothing back here, Mr. Fowler."

"It's for your car. You don't think we'd leave it at the airport, do you?"

He watched Strout's large, big-knuckled hands tighten on the wheel, saw Frank's face that night: not the stitches and bruised eye and swollen lips, but his own hand gently touching Frank's jaw, turning his wounds to the light. They rounded a bend in the road and were out of sight of the highway: tall trees all around them now, hiding the moon. When they reached the abandoned gravel pit on the left, the bare flat earth and steep pale embankment behind it, and the black crowns of trees at its top, Matt said: "Stop here."

Strout stopped but did not turn off the engine. Matt pressed the gun hard against his neck, and he straightened in the seat and looked in the rearview mirror, Matt's eyes meeting his in the glass for an instant before looking at the hair at the end of the gun barrel.

"Turn it off."

Strout did, then held the wheel with two hands, and looked in the mirror.

"I'll do twenty years, Mr. Fowler; at least. I'll be forty-six years old."

"That's nine years younger than I am," Matt said, and got out and took off the glove and kicked the door shut. He aimed at Strout's ear and pulled back the hammer. Willis's headlights were off and Matt heard him walking on the soft thin layer of dust, the hard earth beneath it. Strout opened the door, sat for a moment in the interior light, then stepped out onto the road. Now his face was pleading. Matt did not look at his eyes, but he could see it in the lips.

"Just get the suitcase. They're right up the road."

Willis was beside him now, to his left. Strout looked at both guns. Then he opened the back door, leaned in, and with a jerk brought the suitcase out. He was turning to face them when Matt said: "Just walk up the road. Just ahead."

Strout turned to walk, the suitcase in his right hand, and Matt and Willis followed; as Strout cleared the front of his car he dropped the suitcase and, ducking, took one step that was the beginning of a sprint to his right. The gun kicked in Matt's hand, and the explosion of the shot surrounded him, isolated him in a nimbus of sound that cut him off from all his time, all his history, isolated him standing absolutely still on the dirt road with the gun in his hand, looking down at Richard Strout squirming on his belly, kicking one leg behind him, pushing himself forward, toward the woods. Then Matt went to him and shot him once in the back of the head.

Driving south to Boston, wearing both gloves now, staying in the middle lane and looking often in the rearview mirror at Willis's headlights, he relived the suitcase dropping, the quick dip and turn of Strout's back, and the kick of the gun, the sound of the shot. When he walked to Strout, he still existed within the first shot, still trembled and breathed with it. The second shot and the burial seemed to be happening to someone else, someone he was watching. He and Willis each held an arm and pulled Strout face-down off the road and into the woods, his bouncing sliding belt white under the trees where it was so dark that when they stopped at the top of the knoll, panting and sweating, Matt could not see where Strout's blue shirt ended and the earth began. They pulled off the branches then dragged Strout to the edge of the hole and went behind him and lifted his legs and pushed him in. They stood still for a moment. The woods were quiet save for their breathing, and Matt remembered hearing the movements of birds and small animals after the first shot. Or maybe he had not heard them. Willis went down to the road. Matt could see him clearly out on the tan dirt, could see the glint of Strout's car and, beyond the road, the gravel pit. Willis came back up the knoll with the suitcase. He dropped it in the hole and took off his gloves and they went down to his car for the spades. They worked quietly. Sometimes they paused to listen to the woods. When they were finished Willis turned on his flashlight and they covered the earth with leaves and branches and then went down to the spot in front of the car, and while Matt held the light Willis crouched and sprinkled dust on the blood, backing up till he reached the grass and leaves, then he used leaves until they had worked up to the grave again. They did not stop. They walked around the grave and through the woods, using the light on the ground, looking up through the trees to where they ended at the lake. Neither of them spoke above the sounds of their heavy and clumsy strides through low brush and over fallen branches. Then they reached it: wide and dark, lapping softly at the bank, pine needles smooth under Matt's feet, moonlight on the lake, a small island near its middle, with black, tall evergreens. He took out the gun and threw for the island: taking two steps back on the pine needles, striding with the throw and going to one knee as he followed through, looking up to see the dark shapeless object arcing downward, splashing.

They left Strout's car in Boston, in front of an apartment building on Commonwealth Avenue. When they got back to town Willis drove slowly over the bridge and Matt threw the keys into the Merrimack. The sky was turning light. Willis let him out a block from his house, and walking home he listened for sounds from the houses he passed. They were quiet. A light was on in his living room. He turned it off and undressed in there, and went softly toward the bedroom; in the hall he smelled the smoke, and he stood in the bedroom doorway and looked at the orange of her cigarette in the dark. The curtains were closed. He went to the closet and put his shoes on the floor and felt for a hanger.

"Did you do it?" she said.

He went down the hall to the bathroom and in the dark he washed his hands and face. Then he went to her, lay on his back, and pulled the sheet up to his throat.

"Are you all right?" she said.

"I think so."

Now she touched him, lying on her side, her hand on his belly, his thigh.

"Tell me," she said.

He started from the beginning, in the parking lot at the bar; but soon with his eyes closed and Ruth petting him, he spoke of Strout's house: the order, the woman presence, the picture on the wall.

"The way she was smiling," he said.

"What about it?"

"I don't know. Did you ever see Strout's girl? When you saw him in town?"

"No."

"I wonder who she was."

Then he thought: *not was: is. Sleeping now she is his girl.* He opened his eyes, then closed them again. There was more light beyond the curtains.

With Ruth now he left Strout's house and told again his lie to Strout, gave him again that hope that Strout must have for a while believed, else he would have to believe only the gun pointed at him for the last two hours of his life. And with Ruth he saw again the dropping suitcase, the darting move to the right: and he told of the first shot, feeling her hand on him but his heart isolated still, beating on the road still in that explosion like thunder. He told her the rest, but the words had no images for him, he did not see himself doing what the words said he had done; he only saw himself on that road.

"We can't tell the other kids," she said. "It'll hurt them, thinking he got away. But we mustn't."

"No."

She was holding him, wanting him, and he wished he could make love with her but he could not. He saw Frank and Mary Ann making love in her bed, their eyes closed, their bodies brown and smelling of the sea; the other girl was faceless, bodiless, but he felt her sleeping now; and he saw Frank and Strout, their faces alive; he saw red and yellow leaves falling to the earth, then snow: falling and freezing and falling; and holding Ruth, his cheek touching her breast, he shuddered with a sob that he kept silent in his heart.

ABOUT THE CONTRIBUTORS

Ryunosuke Akutagawa (1892–1927)

Short-story writer, poet, and essayist, Akutagawa was one of the first Japanese modernists translated into English. The 150-plus short stories he completed during his brief career are noted for their macabre subject matter and stylistic precision. Several years after Akutagawa's suicide, his friend Kikuchi Kan established the Akutagawa Prize, generally considered among the most prestigious Japanese literary awards for aspiring writers.

Brian Aldiss (1925–)

By the end of the twentieth century, Aldiss was considered by many to be the elder statesman of British science-fiction writers. He has won science fiction's prestigious Hugo Award twice and at the 1999 Nebula Awards was named a Grand Master.

Sherman Alexie (1966–)

A Spokane/Coeur d'Alene Indian, Alexie grew up on the Spokane Indian Reservation in Wellpinit, Washington, about fifty miles northwest of Spokane. An outspoken activist for Native American rights, he has written poetry, short stories, novels, and screenplays, and he was named one of *Granta*'s Best of Young American Novelists for his first novel, *Reservation Blues.*

Paul Auster (1947–)

Novelist, essayist, translator, poet, and filmmaker, Auster was born in Newark, New Jersey, to working-class parents. He attended Columbia University and traveled back and forth between France and the United States for a number of years. Auster's route to literary fame was both circuitous and unusual, as he chronicled in his memoir, *Hand to Mouth.* Renown came with his series of three experimental detective stories known collectively as *The New York Trilogy.*

Raymond Carver (1938–1988)

Born in Clatskanie, Oregon, Carver was the son of working-class parents. In 1976, his first collection of short stories, *Will You Please Be Quiet, Please?*, was nominated for a National Book Award. Noted for his spare style and blue-collar sensibility, he quickly developed a following. After his death, Carver was acclaimed by many as the greatest influence on the short story since Hemingway.

John Cheever (1912–1982)

The son of a Massachusetts shoe-factory owner, short-story writer and novelist Cheever has been called "the Chekhov of the suburbs." His formal education ended at the age of seventeen when he was expelled from school for smoking. This experience became the fodder for his first short story, and thereafter Cheever was able to support himself as a writer. His 1978 collection, *The Stories of John Cheever*, won the Pulitzer Prize for fiction, the National Book Critics Circle Award, and an American Book Award.

Anton Chekhov (1860–1904)

Considered the father of the modern short story and play, Chekhov was born in the Russian seaport town of Taganrog, near the Black Sea. He began writing short stories while a medical student at the University of Moscow. In 1888, he was awarded the prestigious Pushkin Prize. Suffering from advanced consumption, he died in the German spa town of Badenweiler.

Arthur C. Clarke (1917–)

Sir Arthur Clarke was born in the seaside town of Minehead, Somerset, England. A prolific science-fiction writer and essayist, he is also a Nobel Prize–winning scientist. The recipient of numerous literary awards, Clarke was named a Science Fiction Grand Master in 1985. He has lived in Colombo, Sri Lanka, since 1956.

Daniel Clowes (1961–)

A graduate of New York's Pratt Institute, Clowes was for many years considered a talented underground artist of comic books and graphic novels. With the success of *Ghost World*, the film adaptation of his graphic stories, Clowes garnered mainstream praise. His work has appeared in *Esquire*, *The New Yorker*, and elsewhere.

Richard Connell (1893–1949)

Born in Dutchess County, New York, Connell began covering baseball games for his father's newspaper at age ten and was editing the paper by age sixteen. After serving in World War I, he settled in Beverly Hills, California, where he began writing short stories and screenplays. He is best known for his short story "The Most Dangerous Game."

Julio Cortázar (1914–1984)

Born in Belgium and raised in Argentina, Cortázar was an important Argentine intellectual and author. His short stories and novels are highly experimental and playful; his masterpiece, *Hopscotch*, invites the reader to rearrange the material. In his later years, he became increasingly political, and his literary production diminished. He moved to France in 1951, in opposition to the Perón regime, and lived there until his death from leukemia.

Philip K. Dick (1928–1982)

More popular today than he was when he was alive, Dick has become a cult figure among science-fiction aficionados. Although he won a Hugo Award for best science-fiction novel in 1962 for *The Man in the High Castle*, Dick was destitute most of his life and died just a few months before *Blade Runner*, the film of his novel *Do Androids Dream of Electric Sheep?*, was released. Much of his work has been posthumously optioned for film.

Andre Dubus (1936–1999)

After serving five years in the Marine Corps, where he attained the rank of captain, Dubus became a full-time writer of short stories. Much of his work is set in his adopted home state of Massachusetts. He received numerous literary awards, including the PEN/Malamud Award and the Rea Award for excellence in short fiction.

William Faulkner (1897–1962)

Although he never graduated from high school, he lived in a small town (Oxford, Mississippi) in one of the poorest states in the nation, and he struggled to support a growing family of dependents, Faulkner was able to build a body of work that has earned him acclaim as one of the twentieth century's greatest writers. He received the Nobel Prize for literature in 1949 and two Pulitzer Prizes. He often wrote screenplays and scripts, but he received only six official screen credits, five of which were with director Howard Hawks.

F. Scott Fitzgerald (1896–1940)

Born in St. Paul, Minnesota, Fitzgerald is best known for his novels and short stories chronicling the excesses of America's Jazz Age. He received great praise for his first novel, *This Side of Paradise*, published when he was twenty-four, but by the time he published his masterpiece, *The Great Gatsby*, in 1925, his reputation and career were on the decline. He spent the last three years of his life writing for the movies and died believing himself a failure.

Graham Greene (1904–1991)

Born in Berkhamsted, Hertfordshire, England, Greene was one of the most widely read novelists of the twentieth century. He was also a short-story writer, playwright, screenwriter, and journalist, and served as a movie critic for a number of years. Although several times nominated for the Nobel Prize in literature, he never won.

Ernest Haycox (1899–1950)

Born in Portland, Oregon, Haycox naturally gravitated to writing about the West. Considered one of the all-time best writers of Western fiction, Haycox specialized in historically accurate short stories and novels.

Ernest Hemingway (1899–1961)

Noted for his lean prose style, Hemingway began his career in a newspaper office in Kansas City. During the twenties, he became a member of the group of expatriate Americans in Paris, described in his first notable work, *The Sun Also Rises.* Thought of as one of the great men of American letters, Hemingway received the Nobel Prize in literature in 1954.

Eric Hodgins (1899–1971)

The managing editor of *Fortune* magazine for many years and a regular contributor to *The New Yorker*, Hodgins wrote a number of nonfiction books before his success with the *Mr. Blandings* series. His memoir, *Episode: Report on the Accident Inside My Skull*, received a Blakeslee Award from the American Heart Association.

W. P. Kinsella (1932–   )

Canadian author Kinsella grew up in almost total isolation on a farm in northern Alberta, where he studied at home by correspondence until the fifth grade. In his late thirties he attended the University of Iowa Writers' Workshop, where he fell in love with the Iowa landscape and fused that with his other love: baseball. He received the Houghton Mifflin Literary Fellowship for his novel *Shoeless Joe.*

Denis Johnson (1949–   )

Born in Munich, Germany, and raised in Tokyo, Manila, and Washington, Johnson attended the University of Iowa Writers' Workshop. As a poet, essayist, short-story writer, and novelist, he has received many awards for his work, including a Lannan Fellowship in Fiction and a Whiting Writer's Award.

Dorothy M. Johnson (1905–1984)

Raised in Montana, Johnson moved to New York after receiving a degree in journalism from the University of Montana. There, she worked for a publishing house and began writing short stories with Western themes. Eventually, she returned to Montana, where she lived until her death. In a recent survey by the Western Writers of America, four of the top five stories in the Best Western Short Stories category were written by Johnson.

George Langelaan (1908–1969)

A British journalist and short-story writer, Langelaan published a memoir of his experiences as a British spy, *The Masks of War*, and a collection of stories, *Out of Time.*

H. P. Lovecraft (1890–1937)

Born in Providence, Rhode Island, Lovecraft was deeply tied to New England, where he lived his entire life. Much of his work was fueled by nightmares; as a result, his work blurs the lines between fantasy, horror, and science fiction. He has been highly influential among horror writers and is a cult figure among horror fans.

Jonathan Nolan (1976–   )

Born in London, England, Nolan was raised in the United States and is a graduate of Georgetown University. His first published story, "Memento Mori," was adapted for film by his brother Christopher. He is currently at work on a number of projects, including several screenplays.

Joyce Carol Oates (1938–   )

One of contemporary literature's most prolific writers, Oates has written poetry, short stories, novels, criticism, and essays. She has received the PEN/Malumud Award for excellence in short fiction and the O. Henry Prize for continued achievement in the short story, and she has been nominated twice for the Nobel Prize in literature.

Mary O'Hara (1885–1980)

Born in Cape May Point, New Jersey, O'Hara was the third child of an Episcopal clergyman. In 1905, she married and moved to California, where she was a screenwriter during the silent film era. Her second marriage brought her to Wyoming, where she turned to fiction. O'Hara was also a gifted pianist and composer.

Mary Orr (1918–   )

A short-story writer, playwright, and novelist, Orr started her career as an actress. She began writing while married to director/playwright Reginald Denham, with whom she collaborated on a number of a plays. After the success of her short story "The Wisdom of Eve," she wrote several novels.

Harvey Pekar (1939–   )

A lifelong Cleveland, Ohio, resident, Pekar worked as a file clerk at a V.A. hospital for thirty-five years. His friendship with R. Crumb led to the creation of the comic book series *American Splendor*, which Pekar self-published until the early 1990s, when Dark Horse began to widely distribute the work. He is also a prolific jazz and book critic and an award-winning essayist on the local public-radio station, WKSU. In 1987, he received an American Book Award for *American Splendor*.

Tod Robbins (1888–1949)

Born into a wealthy New York family, Clarence "Tod" Robbins was an accomplished athlete, a society gadabout, and the author of short stories and novels. He specialized in stylish pulp-horror fiction. When mainstream literary success eluded him, he emigrated to the French Riviera. He refused to leave during the Nazi occupation of France and was forced to spend the war in a concentration camp.

Frank Rooney (1913–?)

After spending four years with the U.S. Army in Hawaii during World War II, Rooney toured the country as a member of Maurice Evans's company of *Hamlet*. During that time, he began writing short stories, going on to become a full-time writer and to publish several novels. In 1956, he received a Guggenheim Fellowship as well as a citation from the National Institute of Arts and Letters.

Budd Schulberg (1914–   )

Raised in Hollywood, Schulberg is the son of early film mogul B. P. Schulberg. He is the author of short stories, novels, screenplays, and essays, and he began his screenwriting career in a brief partnership with F. Scott Fitzgerald on the ill-fated *Winter Carnival.* In 1954, he won an Oscar for his *On the Waterfront* screenplay. He was inducted into the International Boxing Hall of Fame in 2001, in recognition of his writing about the sport.

Jean Shepherd (1921–1999)

Raised in Hammond, Indiana, Shepherd worked in local steel mills before entering the arts. In the 1950s, he began a long career as a radio personality, telling stories of his youth, commenting on popular culture, and performing silly songs. He frequently contributed essays to *Playboy* and other magazines and eventually published his popular radio stories in a series of books.

Hagar Wilde (1905–1971)

A successful New York playwright, Wilde also spent time in Hollywood as a screenwriter, where she collaborated with Raymond Chandler and Dudley Nichols, among others. Her story "The Brat," which lampooned Hollywood, won an O. Henry Prize in 1933.

Cornell Woolrich (1903–1968)

Called the father of film noir, Woolrich is a major figure in the noir tradition of crime fiction. His second novel, *Children of the Ritz,* won a contest sponsored by First National Pictures, which filmed an adaptation of the novel in 1929. Woolrich briefly moved to Hollywood and worked as an uncredited screenwriter but soon returned to New York, where he settled back into writing suspense stories and novels. Much of his work has been adapted for film, and he wrote under the pseudonyms William Irish and George Hopley.

CREDITS

Grateful acknowledgment is made for permission to reprint the following works:

"Jerry and Molly and Sam" by Raymond Carver. Reprinted by permission of International Creative Management, Inc. Copyright © 1991 by Tess Gallagher. Reprinted by permission of Tess Gallagher.

"Blow-Up" by Julio Cortázar. From *End of the Game and Other Stories* by Julio Cortázar, translated by Paul Blackburn, copyright © 1963, 1967 by Random House, Inc. Used by permission of Pantheon Books, a division of Random House.

"Your Arkansas Traveler" by Budd Schulberg. Reprinted by permission of the author.

"It Had to Be Murder" by Cornell Woolrich. Copyright © 1941, 1968 by Cornell Woolrich; reprinted by permission of the author's estate through its agent, Barry N. Malzberg.

"The Sentinel" by Arthur C. Clarke. Reprinted by permission of the author and the author's agents, Scovil Chichak Galen Literary Agency, Inc.

"Supertoys Last All Summer Long" by Brian Aldiss. Reprinted by permission of the author and Time Warner Book Group UK.

"The Minority Report" by Philip K. Dick. Reprinted by permission of the author and the author's agents, Scovil Chichak Galen Literary Agency, Inc.

"Herbert West—Reanimator: Six Shots by Moonlight" by H. P. Lovecraft. Reprinted by permission of the Arkham House Publishers, Inc., and Arkham's agents, JABberwocky Literary Agency, P.O. Box 4558, Sunnyside, NY 11104-0558.

"Stage to Lordsburg" by Ernest Haycox. Copyright © 1982 by the estate of Ernest M. Haycox.

"A Man Called Horse" by Dorothy M. Johnson. Reprinted with the permission of McIntosh and Otis, Inc.

"This Is What It Means to Say Phoenix, Arizona" by Sherman Alexie. Copyright © 1993 by Sherman Alexie.

"The Harvey Pekar Name Story" by Harvey Pekar. Reprinted by permission of the author.

"Hubba Hubba" by Daniel Clowes. Reprinted by permission of the author.

"The Wisdom of Eve" by Mary Orr. Reprinted by permission of the author.

"A Reputation" from *Apes and Angels* by Richard Connell. Copyright © 1924 by Richard Connell. Reprinted by permission of Brandt & Hochman Literary Agents, Inc.

"Mr. Blandings Builds His Castle" by Eric Hodgins. Reprinted by permission of Patricia Hodgins.

"Tomorrow," copyright © 1940 and renewed 1968 by Estelle Faulkner and Jill Faulkner Summers. Copyright © 1949 by William Faulkner, from *Knight's Gambit* by William Faulkner. Used by permission of Random House, Inc.

"Babylon, Revisited" by F. Scott Fitzgerald. Reprinted with permission of Scribner, an imprint of Simon & Schuster Adult Publishing Group, from *The Short Stories of F. Scott Fitzgerald*, edited by Matthew J. Bruccoli. Copyright © 1931 by The Curtis Publishing Company. Copyright © renewed 1959 by Frances Scott Fitzgerald Lanahan.

"The Swimmer" by John Cheever. From *The Stories of John Cheever* by John Cheever, copyright © 1978 by John Cheever. Used by permission of Alfred A. Knopf, a division of Random House, Inc.

"The Basement Room," copyright © 1936, renewed 1964 by Graham Greene, from *Collected Stories of Graham Greene* by Graham Greene. Used by permission of Viking Penguin, a division of Penguin Group, Inc.

"The Killers" by Ernest Hemingway. Reprinted with permission of Scribner's, an imprint of Simon & Schuster Adult Publishing Group, from *The Short Stories of Ernest Hemingway*. Copyright © 1927 by Charles Scribner's Sons. Copyright © renewed 1955 by Ernest Hemingway. Copyright outside the United States: © Hemingway Foreign Rights Trust.

"Memento Mori" by Jonathan Nolan. Reprinted by permission of the author.

"My Friend Flicka" by Mary O'Hara. Reprinted by permission of Deirdre Parrot: From *Story*, Jan./Feb. 1941; copyright © 1941 by Mary O'Hara.

"Red Ryder Nails the Hammond Kid" by Jean Shepherd. From *In God We Trust, All Others Pay Cash* by Jean Shepherd, copyright © 1966 by Jean Shepherd. Used by permission of Doubleday, a division of Random House, Inc.

"Shoeless Joe Jackson Comes to Iowa" by W. P. Kinsella. Reprinted by permission of the author.

"In a Grove" by Ryunosuke Akutagawa. Reprinted by permission of the author and Charles E. Tuttle Co. of Boston, Massachusetts, and Tokyo, Japan.

"The Lady with the Pet Dog," translated by Avrahm Yarmolinsky, from *The Portable Chekhov* by Anton Chekhov, edited by Avrahm Yarmolinsky, copyright © 1947, © 1968 by Viking Penguin, Inc., renewed © 1975 by Avrahm Yarmolinsky. Used by permission of Viking Penguin, a division of Penguin Group (USA), Inc.

"Where Are You Going, Where Have You Been?" by Joyce Carol Oates. Copyright © by the Ontario Review, Inc., 1993.

"Auggie Wren's Christmas Story" by Paul Auster. Copyright © 1990 by Paul Auster, originally published by *The New York Times.*

"Emergency" by Denis Johnson. Reprinted by permission of Farrar, Straus and Giroux, LLC: "Emergency" from *Jesus' Son* by Denis Johnson. Copyright © 1992 by Denis Johnson.

"Killings" by Andre Dubus. From *Finding a Girl in America* by Andre Dubus. Reprinted by permission of David R. Godine, Publisher, Inc. Copyright © 1980 by Andre Dubus.